COMEBACK

THE FALL AND RISE
OF THE AMERICAN
AUTOMOBILE INDUSTRY

PAUL INGRASSIA

AND

JOSEPH B. WHITE

A Touchstone Book
Published by SIMON & SCHUSTER
New York   London   Toronto   Sydney   Tokyo   Singapore

TOUCHSTONE
Rockefeller Center
1230 Avenue of the Americas
New York, New York 10020

First Touchstone Edition 1995

TOUCHSTONE and colophon are registered trademarks
of Simon & Schuster Inc.

Designed by Irving Perkins Associates

Manufactured in the United States of America

1   3   5   7   9   10   8   6   4   2

Library of Congress Cataloging-in-Publication Data
Ingrassia, Paul J.
Comeback: the fall and rise of the American automobile industry / Paul J. Ingrassia and
Joseph B. White.
p.   cm.
Includes bibliographical references and index.
1. Automobile industry and trade—United States.   2. Corporate turnarounds—
United States.   I. White, Joseph B.   II. Title.
HD9710.U52I54   1994
338.4′76292′0973—dc20   94-22354
                                                                    CIP
ISBN: 0-671-79214-8
0-684-80437-9 (Pbk.)

PICTURE CREDITS

AP/Wide World Photos: 12
Steve Bera: 2, 4
Chrysler Corporation: 22, 23, 24, 25, 26
Ford Motor Company: 14, 16, 17, 18, 19, 20
General Motors Corporation: 5, 6, 7, 8, 9, 11, 13
Video used by permission of General Motors Corporation;
   still image produced by Luis Blanco, Chelsea Point, NY: 1, 3
Craig T. Mathew, Mathew Photographic Services: 15
Martin J. "Hoot" McInerney: 21
Ykaro/Action Press/SABA: 10
All photographs are used by permission.

To Susie,
Adam, Charles, and Daniel
—PI

To Laurie, Katy, and Annie
—JBW

CONTENTS

CONTENTS

PROLOGUE

THIS IS AN AMERICAN success story, born of a close call with disaster.

It begins on July 24, 1990, at the retirement party of Roger B. Smith, who had spent the previous nine years running General Motors—right into the ground. In 1990, Japanese automakers dominated the world auto industry. Detroit was teetering. The next year, 1991, would bring record operating losses totaling $7.5 billion at the Big Three car companies. One man who saw disaster coming was Chrysler's Lee Iacocca. The biggest booster of American automobiles was so pessimistic about his company's chances for survival that, right at the time of Roger Smith's party, he was secretly trying to sell Chrysler to the Italian automaker, Fiat. The merger failed to occur only because Fiat was even more convinced than Iacocca that Chrysler was headed for extinction.

But just three and a half years later, on January 18, 1994, a day the Motor City recorded a record low temperature of 16 degrees below zero, Chrysler set a record high. The company announced it had earned an unprecedented $777 million in the final three months of 1993. Before taxes, Chrysler had hauled in $1,727 for every car and truck it sold. This time some of the major Japanese automakers, notably Nissan and Mazda, were mired in red ink. Ironically, so was Fiat.

Profit, however, was just half the story. Chrysler was the envy of the auto industry around the world. No company had cars and trucks as stylish and as distinctive. No company seemed to understand so clearly what its customers wanted. Chrysler's new Neon subcompact, launched a few days before the company released its record 1993 results, had shocked the Japanese by offering dual air bags, a sophisticated multivalve engine, and other standard features for a price thousands of dollars below theirs. No longer could Japan lay undisputed claim to leadership in small cars. Robert J. Eaton, who had succeeded Iacocca as chairman of Chrysler, announced that, just as Toyota had been the world's best car company in the late 1980s, Chrysler's goal was to assume that mantle for the late 1990s.

Chrysler was leading the American auto industry's revival, but it wasn't alone. General Motors and Ford, in different ways, were engineering comebacks of their own.

GM, the once all-powerful giant of American industry, had stumbled from blunder to blunder during the eighties. It had squandered billions on factories that wouldn't work while producing luxury cars that looked like economy cars, cars with engines that burst into flames, and cars afflicted with what company engineers glumly called "morning sickness." By January 1992, "the General" stood closer than the world knew to the brink of collapse. Its management had lost touch with its customers and with reality.

GM's directors had watched their company's decline without uttering so much as a peep. They were the laughingstock of corporate America—"pet rocks," in the memorable put-down of former board member Ross Perot, whose self-serving rebellion had led GM to spend $700 million to oust him in 1986.

In 1992, however, GM's directors finally woke up. They engineered a boardroom coup that swept out a generation of leaders wedded to the ways of the past. In the place of these men came a cadre of younger managers who looked outside their company's traditions for the ideas to build a new GM. The revolt at GM set a new pattern for accountability at the top of American corporations.

By the time Chrysler announced its record profits, GM executives had a comeback story of their own to tell. After losing more than $15 billion before taxes in its North American car business in 1991 and 1992, GM's domestic operations would show a pretax profit in 1993 for the first time in three years. As 1994 began, GM still had a long way to go on its road to recovery. But finally the company was moving in the right direction.

At Ford, change came clothed not as revolution, but as rediscovery. Ford had emerged from its brush with near-death in the early 1980s a far better company—certainly the best among the Big Three. It had stood the world on its ear in 1985 with the aerodynamic Taurus family sedan. But in the late 1980s, Ford lost its creative spark and its focus. Its leaders put money into banks and defense companies instead of engines, transmissions, and exciting new designs. By 1989 Ford had become so irresolute that its leaders were willing to let a Japanese company, Mazda, develop a successor to the quintessential American car, the Mustang.

Then a small group of middle managers launched a quest to save the Mustang, urged on by superiors who saw that giving away the creative heart of a company was the ticket to decline. Less than four years later, Ford was fielding a blizzard of orders for the new Mustang, and holding up the team that built it as an example for the rest of the company to follow.

How all this came about is the subject of this book. It covers a dozen years of upheaval and renewal in the American automobile industry. The story of these dozen years is largely of how GM, Ford, and Chrysler, after being humbled, adopted and adapted Japanese methods. It's a story filled with comedy, tragedy, and human foibles. The events span America, Japan, and Europe, while ranging from corporate boardrooms to factory floors. Some of the characters, such as Iacocca and Roger Smith, are well known. Others, such as Frank Faga and Bob Marcell, aren't. But they did things that made a difference.

The watershed event that precipitated Detroit's crisis and ultimately its revival occurred in November 1982. That is when Honda Motor Company started building cars in Marysville, Ohio. Just thirteen months later, Toyota followed by opening its first U.S. assembly plant as a joint venture with General Motors in Fremont, California. It was the Japanese, ironically, who showed that American workers could build quality automobiles, and thus stripped away Detroit's excuses. The Japanese started a new American auto industry. And in the end, Detroit decided to join in.

Along the way, however, came many fits and false starts. Detroit's first challenge was to stop denying that it had fallen behind in the industry that provided nearly 4 million jobs, and separated the world's economic powerhouses from the also-rans.

The early bearers of this message, such as GM vice president Alex Mair, were either derided or ignored. Eventually, though, the message was accepted, because it was delivered by the American people through the cars they chose to purchase.

One of the many ironies of this tale is that, while Detroit decried free trade as a threat to its existence, free trade is what saved Detroit by forcing it to improve. Even Iacocca, America's archprotectionist, admitted as much. "In 1981, the quality of American cars was just plain lousy," he stated in a full-page Chrysler newspaper advertisement that appeared in the spring of 1991. "All of us—Ford, GM, Chrysler—built a lot of lousy cars in the early 1980s. And we paid the price. We lost a lot of our market to the import competition. But that forced us to wake up and start building better cars."

That is another way of saying that America's strength is its openness to things foreign: goods, people, and ideas. Roger Smith, for all his faults, knew when he took over General Motors that the company needed new ideas. His decision to start the joint venture with Toyota gave GM an inside look at the manufacturing and management methods used by the best car company in the world. But Toyota's methods weren't the 21st-century technological extravaganzas that Smith was looking for. He and the men around him utterly failed to understand what Toyota was showing GM. They found it easier to throw money at quality and low productivity than to tackle their root cause. But throwing money at the problems didn't solve them; it only made them more expensive.

Dithering with diversification made matters worse, not only for General Motors, but for Ford and Chrysler as well. They didn't get what they were after: protection from the cyclical swings of the car business and from the inroads of the Japanese. Instead, the Big Three got distracted from the demanding task of developing and producing better automobiles.

Another irony of this story is that, by 1992 and 1993, Japan's car companies had succumbed to the same sins of complacence and arrogance that had almost destroyed Detroit. In part, the Japanese were victims of a double whammy: a deep recession at home and a simultaneous surge in the value of their currency overseas. But the Japanese also contributed to their own comeuppance.

They expanded at home and around the world—with new factories, new models, and new dealer networks—as if there would be no end to their growth. They believed the Japanese economy was recession-proof. And they couldn't imagine that Detroit would narrow the gaps in productivity and quality that had made Japanese cars the most desirable in the world.

The Japanese were caught so unawares that, on October 26, 1992, Mazda took the humiliating step of canceling a planned new luxury-car marque, Amati, even before it was introduced. There was more to come. By 1994 Japan's car companies were closing plants, cutting dividends, and idling assembly lines. All this amounted to a remarkable reversal of roles with Detroit.

Japan's woes, though, did not mean that the battle was over for Chrysler, Ford, and GM. For one thing, the Detroit companies continued to lag behind Toyota and Honda, Japan's best automakers, in quality. More fundamentally, the key to staying ahead in global competition is to understand that the battle is never really over. It is impossible to predict the winners and losers of tomorrow.

In fact, if this story holds any lesson, it is that today's winners tend to become tomorrow's losers, and vice versa. It's harder to stay on top than to get on top.

Susumu Uchikawa, a Toyota production ace and one of the world's foremost manufacturing experts, understood this challenge. In 1984 he was assigned to work with GM managers at the joint venture factory in California. Uchikawa continually preached the gospel of "continuous improvement," that an operation never was good enough because it could always be improved in hundreds of little ways that would add up to a big difference. Problems were opportunities, Uchikawa believed. And to those who acted as if there were no challenges left, he would growl: "No problem is problem!"

It is a fitting moral for this tale.

BOOK I

THE OLD
LIONS

CHAPTER I

DETROIT'S LIONS IN WINTER

THE DETROIT CLUB on the corner of Fort and Cass Streets in the Motor City's downtown is a throwback to a time long ago. The four-story building's exterior is well-worn, rust-red brick. The inside is a gloomy parody of a Victorian men's club. Dark oil paintings mounted in ornate frames loom from the walls. Overstuffed men in overstuffed leather chairs rustle newspapers through the ghostly haze of cigar smoke. In the early 1980s, a local newspaper reporter wandered through the club's reading room while waiting for the businessman who had invited him to lunch, and reacted to the archaic ambience with an act of playful defiance. Striding to the front of the room, he wheeled around and announced at the top of his voice: "Gentlemen, Khartoum has fallen!" With that, he walked out of the club.

This was the perfect place, then, for the officers of General Motors Corporation to throw the traditional "pickle dish party" for their retiring colleagues. The parties got their nickname from the enormous sterling silver platter awarded to each retiree. In the center of this pickle dish is engraved the retiree's name, surrounded by the engraved signatures of his fellow officers. Lest the corporation be accused of squandering shareholder money on frivolity, the officers chipped in $85 apiece to pay for the dish and the dinner that went with it.

The pickle dish party of July 24, 1990, was especially important. The honoree was retiring after forty-one years with General Motors, the last nine of them as chairman of the board. His name was Roger B. Smith.

Before Roger Smith, GM's chairmen were anonymous and faceless men. But Smith changed all that. After he became chairman in 1981, he declared it his mission to make General Motors a "21st-century corporation." To that end he spent billions on splashy, high-tech acquisitions, launched a sweeping reorganization of the entire company, and poured tens of billions of dollars into futuristic factory automation.

But GM's fancy factories built look-alike cars of shoddy quality. The company squandered fully one fourth of its U.S. market share—almost more than Chrysler Corporation across town had to begin with. The factory automation went haywire. In one plant within sight of GM headquarters, robots ran amok and started spray-painting each other instead of the cars.[1] Worse yet, Smith's spending spree so inflated GM's cost structure that the company's core North American auto business was barely breaking even during the late 1980s, the strongest sales years the American auto industry had ever seen. As retirement neared, it was clear that Smith's nine years at the top had been a Reign of Error of historic proportions. Three harshly critical books and a wickedly satirical movie called *Roger and Me* had made Smith the poster boy for American industrial decline.

Yet Smith, at age sixty-five, had plenty of reason to celebrate. On the way out the door he had managed to double his retirement pension, to $1.2 million a year. The neatest trick of all was that he got his board to approve this increase without explaining to the directors what they were really voting on. It happened nine months before Smith's retirement, in November 1989, at GM's monthly board meeting in New York.

Not until April 1990, when a newspaper reporter in Dayton, Ohio, enlisted a local accountant to crunch some numbers in the proxy material that GM had mailed to its shareholders, did the truth finally come out.[2] The GM directors who weren't company employees were as shocked as anyone else, but at that point speaking out in protest would have made them look foolish. So they were trapped. "We were duped by Roger," recalled one director afterward, "and afterward we knew it didn't make us look smart." Smith, for his part, simply hung tough during the storm of criticism, something that experience had taught him how to do. By the time of his pickle dish party the controversy had faded away.

At 6 P.M., when the group gathered for cocktails, Smith was warm and relaxed—totally unlike the driven, dictatorial man who had run GM for almost a decade. "That was a guy wearing a Roger disguise," some of the young officers later joked. "We were waiting for the real Roger to show up."

Like their boss, Smith's fifty-five fellow corporate officers at the party were upbeat. But they had a different reason: Finally Smith was leaving. Most of GM's vice presidents neither liked nor trusted him, but none dared say it. Besides, the primal bonding of the pickle dish tradition was stirring their emotions. The pickle dish party was their own private rite, the closed-door ritual of a secret society. They were like latter-day Knights of the Round Table who would sup together in this gothic, wood-trimmed room with its high vaulted ceiling. A few company PR men came to the cocktail party to make sure things were in order. But when the group sat down to dinner, the PR guys stayed outside. Spouses never, ever attended.

The dining room was decorated with photographic posters of the honoree. At the table, the seating order was strictly prescribed: Chairman-elect Bob Stempel sat in the center, with Smith on his left. Everyone else sat according to rank, with the jittery junior officers attending their first party placed at the far ends. Before dinner, Stempel rose to acknowledge the newcomers, and invited them to say a few words. When dinner was ended, he rose again, and talked about Roger Smith.

He sketched Smith's methodical rise through the ranks, from junior accountant to chairman of the board. He outlined Smith's accomplishments as chairman: the 1984 corporate restructuring, the multibillion-dollar acquisitions, the launching of Saturn Corporation and the dividend hike and stock split of 1989. Stempel never mentioned Smith's epic fight with Texas billionaire Ross Perot, the frightening loss of market share, or the billions of dollars squandered on senseless automation. He simply said that everyone in the room had been through a lot together, that everyone would miss Roger, and that all present would do their best to do him proud by building on his accomplishments. Then he proposed a simple toast: To Roger Smith.

The customary pickle dish slide show followed. This one mixed pictures of Roger at play—hunting and fishing, mostly—with scenes of the chairman on the job. Then Smith rose to speak. He repeated Stempel's recitation of his accomplishments, explaining why they were important for General Motors. The company, he said, was exactly where he had hoped it would be when he became chairman in 1981: well-positioned for the 21st century. When Smith finished, his fellow officers rose to give him a standing ovation. By 8:30 or so, everyone headed home.

This, then, was the dawn of a new decade. It was also the end of an era. A whole generation of Old Lions was walking off the stage in Detroit. These men had started with the automobile industry in the late 1940s and early 1950s, right after World War II. They had climbed the corporate ladder during Detroit's greatest years ever, when America and its automobile industry were the envy of the entire world. Together they had endured some bad times, notably the brutal 1980–1982 industry depression that had almost put Chrysler and even Ford out of business, and had sent tremors through GM. But mostly there had been good times, plenty good enough to make multimillionaires out of men who had known Great Depression boyhoods.

By the latter half of the 1980s the Big Three, especially Chrysler and Ford, were on a roll. The crisis of the early 1980s was only a bad memory, a nightmare that had faded with a new day. Even GM, as inept as it was in the U.S. market, was making tons of money overseas. Those overseas earnings, combined with some slick (though perfectly legal) accounting wizardry engineered by Smith himself, had given General Motors near record profits of $4.22 billion in 1989, Smith's last full year as chairman.

But the profits papered over reality. In October 1990, GM announced an enormous $2.1 billion charge against earnings. The charge covered the cost of closing factories and shedding employees that the company, with its shrunken market share, didn't need anymore. Over the next few months GM would announce a $1.6 billion loss for the fourth quarter, cut in half the dividend that Roger Smith had increased barely two years before, and launch a cost-cutting program in every part of the company.

All that was just a down payment. Still ahead were traumatic decisions to shutter twenty-one more factories and eliminate 74,000 more jobs by the mid-1990s, and the first boardroom revolt at GM since founder William Crapo Durant had been ousted more than seventy years before. It was all stark evidence of how poorly Smith had prepared GM for the 1990s, much less the 21st century. But by the time all this happened Roger Smith was perched comfortably in retirement with his new pension; his last day on the job had been July 31. The Old Lion had an exquisite sense of timing.

•   •   •

SMITH WASN'T THE ONLY chief executive in Detroit to make a well-timed exit. In November 1989, Donald E. Petersen, chairman and chief executive officer of Ford, called a press conference to announce he would step down on March 1, 1990, at the age of sixty-three, two years shy of the normal retirement date. After a decade as president and then chairman of Ford, Petersen said he felt the need to do something else with the rest of his life.

The news shocked Detroit and indeed all of American business. Don Petersen was the most admired chief executive in America, and seemingly for good reason. For three straight years, from 1986 through 1988, Ford had generated higher profits than General Motors, even though Ford was only two thirds the size of its crosstown rival. The Ford Taurus —launched in late 1985, just after Petersen became chairman—had revolutionized automobile styling around the world, even in Germany and Japan. While Japanese car companies were eating GM's lunch, Ford was increasing its U.S. market share year after year. Don Petersen had none of Lee Iacocca's charisma or Roger Smith's notoriety. Despite his anonymity, though, he became a business-school hero, a symbol that American manufacturers could compete and succeed against global competition. This wasn't the stuff of which early retirements were made.

But Petersen had, in fact, made some crucial mistakes. One was getting on the wrong side of the family whose name was on the building. The Ford family had taken a back seat at the company after Henry Ford II's retirement in 1980. But in the wake of the patriarch's death in 1987, the family was starting to reassert itself. Petersen clashed with young scions Edsel B. Ford II and William Clay Ford, Jr., two cousins who were great-grandsons of the company's founder. Both young men were junior executives intent on rising to the top, and they and their relatives controlled 40 percent of Ford's voting stock. They were impatient to get seats on the board of directors and to rise higher in management, but Petersen thought they were pushing too far too fast. He resisted, but they insisted. The Ford boys won, but bitter feelings remained.

Petersen's fight with the Fords was annoying to the company's outside directors, but their problems with the chairman ran far deeper. Petersen might have been a hero to the business world, but the board members were losing confidence in him. They had rebuffed both his plan for management succession, and what they considered his harebrained scheme to buy a major defense contractor. In mid-1989, with the company at the zenith of its prosperity, they decided Ford would be better off without him. So deftly and discreetly, with nary a hint of the public spectacle that had accompanied Henry Ford's firing of Lee Iacocca back in 1978, Ford's directors forced America's most admired CEO to quit. And later, board members shook their heads with amazement when the press and public bought Petersen's explanation that leaving was his own idea.

LEE IACOCCA HAD MANY talents, but knowing when to quit was not one of them. Iacocca turned sixty-five on October 15, 1989. He could have retired then, right on schedule, and gone out a hero, the man who pulled off the Comeback of the Century by saving Chrysler during the early 1980s. But Iacocca loved being chairman of Chrysler. He cherished the perks, the pay, the corporate Gulfstream jet ready to whisk him anywhere from his condo in Boca Raton to his villa in Tuscany to the company's lavish apartment at the Waldorf-Astoria in New York. He craved the constant attention from the press and public. So the last and greatest of Detroit's Old Lions lingered on the stage.

Not only did he stay longer than Smith and Petersen, but his company —always the smallest and most debt-burdened of Detroit's Big Three— fell into the murky soup of recession faster. On the chill-gray winter morning of February 13, 1990, Chrysler summoned reporters to the cramped, dingy pressroom in its aged brick headquarters complex in Highland Park, Michigan, a decaying little town completely surrounded by Detroit's East Side ghetto. The company had chosen this day to disclose its financial results for the previous year. The announcement was due at 9 A.M., but not until ten minutes after 10 did haggard-looking Chrysler PR men walk in carrying copies of the press release in an old cardboard box. They had barely opened the door when the shoving started as the reporters lunged to grab a copy and find a telephone. It was news worth telling.

Chrysler had lost $664 million in the fourth quarter of 1989, more red ink than in any previous quarter of the company's history. Not even during Chrysler's Dark Days of the early 1980s had any individual quarter been this bad. Most of the loss, some $577 million, came from a special charge against earnings to cover the cost of closing two assembly plants.

About an hour later Lee Iacocca strode into the pressroom to hold a news conference. With his company's frightening financial results staring the world in the face, Iacocca launched into his speech and—improbable though it seemed—declared victory. "It's called restructuring to compete," Iacocca declared. "We just got ready for the 1990s to compete in the car and truck business against anybody. We could have muddled through, but we chose not to. We're taking the long view, like the legendary Japanese. That's something we never get credit for doing."

It was vintage salesmanship from the greatest carnival barker Detroit had ever seen. Who else but Iacocca could have parlayed getting sacked by Henry Ford II into a best-selling autobiography that made him the most famous businessman on earth? Who else, after a lifetime of ridiculing car-safety advocates, could have turned on a dime and become the patron saint of air bags? Iacocca brought the same chutzpah to this latest sales job. But in fact Chrysler was retreating, not restructuring. The closing of two assembly plants actually was the closing of *two more* plants. Chrysler had announced another closing about a year earlier. So in the space of just two years the company would be closing one third of its assembly plants. It was as if McDonald's was closing one third of its restaurants, or American Airlines grounding one third of its planes.

But Iacocca wasn't finished talking. He embarked on a six-city, cross-country tour called "Chrysler in the Nineties" to spread the word that Chrysler would, indeed, survive the decade. In April, Iacocca landed his publicity blitz in Chicago. The Chrysler advance team had decked out a ballroom in the venerable Hilton Hotel on South Michigan Avenue with a generous sampling of Chrysler's latest models.

"I'm old enough to remember that the textile industry got wiped out in the 1950s," he declared. "The consumer electronics industry went poof in the sixties. Steel and cars fought for their lives in the seventies. And now Silicon Valley and our jet aircraft industry are right in the cross-hairs of the Japanese. It's amazing to me that, in the last few years, seven Big Three assembly plants have closed, and seven Japanese transplants have opened. You don't have to be a rocket scientist to figure out that there's a correlation between the two."

Even as he bashed the Japanese, though, Iacocca paid them homage. The hottest car on his stage was the Dodge Stealth, which wasn't really a Dodge at all. It was made in Japan by Chrysler's affiliate, Mitsubishi Motors Corporation.

IACOCCA WAS WRONG about the seven plants. In fact, eight Big Three plants had closed. Meanwhile eight Japanese plants had opened, and two more were being built. This buildup had taken less than a decade, because in 1981 there hadn't been a single Japanese car assembly plant in the United States. Most of the new Japanese plants were lined up along the Interstate 75 corridor that connects Michigan with the South. Some of these "transplants," as they were dubbed in Detroit, were joint ventures with the Big Three, and all employed thousands of American workers. But it was the Japanese who ran them. The transplants accounted for more than one of every five cars built in the United States. And still more Japanese factories in the United States turned out car components, ranging from door panels to air-conditioners.

All it took was a day-long drive around Detroit to get a look at this new American automobile industry, springing up right alongside the old one. The place to start was thirty miles northwest of Detroit in the city of Pontiac. Wide Track Drive loops around the center of town and evokes images of the heady 1960s, when John DeLorean's barely civilized hot rod, the Pontiac GTO, delighted teenagers and terrorized adults. GM still operated a truck plant in town, but the company had stopped building Pontiacs in Pontiac in 1988.

From Pontiac, a trek along the local freeways led to the devastated East Side of Detroit. There thousands of homes that once housed auto workers stood abandoned, gutted, and burned out in one of America's worst inner-city ghettos. In 1990, Chrysler's eighty-two-year-old assembly plant on Jefferson Avenue stood abandoned as well. The company had shut it in January, nearly two years before a replacement plant being built nearby was scheduled to open.

Just a few minutes away, on the city's gritty Southwest Side, stood two more shuttered GM plants that had once built Cadillacs, the premier cars from America's No. 1 automaker. In 1985, GM had opened a replacement plant nearby, virtually in the shadow of company headquarters, and had loaded it up with high-tech automation. But the Poletown plant, which took its unofficial name from the Polish enclave that had been bulldozed to make way for the factory, turned out to be a lemon. Much of the machinery wouldn't work; some was downright destructive. Even after months of debugging, the plant stood idle half the time because the cars made there were so ugly that they belly-flopped on the market.

South of the city, however, the picture would change remarkably. In semirural Flat Rock, Michigan, thirty miles southwest of Detroit, Japan's Mazda Motor Company had built a spanking new assembly plant on the site of a former Ford engine-casting factory. The hottest restaurant in

Flat Rock was Sushi-Iwa, a branch of one of Tokyo's largest restaurant chains.

Curving west toward the college town of Ann Arbor, the tour would pass Toyota's technical center in a wooded, campuslike industrial park. There, a growing staff of more than 150 engineers designed and tested parts for the next generation of American Toyotas. And driving back toward Detroit, there would appear Nissan's $80 million technical center in suburban Farmington Hills. The glass-and-steel structure sported a striking front entrance that evoked images of a Japanese folding-paper fan. Its architect was Robert Self, a native Michigander whose father had worked for Oldsmobile for forty-one years. Inside, 500 engineers, mostly Americans and refugees from the Big Three, were developing a new car to be built by Nissan in Tennessee.

In November 1991—just a month before the fiftieth anniversary of Pearl Harbor—Nissan formally dedicated its facility with an elaborate ceremony that was American as apple pie. Some 500 people crowded into the three-story atrium at the center of the building. Aldo Vagnozzi, the white-haired mayor of Farmington Hills, beamed from the dais and praised his community's newest corporate citizen. The two balconies overlooking the atrium were crammed with members of the Farmington Hills High School marching band, arrayed in their full-dress, yellow-and-black uniforms. Suddenly, the atrium shook from tiled floor to glass ceiling with the braying of horns and the booming of drums. The band whomped out a football-field arrangement of "The Star Spangled Banner." When the music ended, band members shouted, "HO!"

Then Yutaka Kume, the balding and bespectacled president of Nissan, moved to the podium. During the next two years, he said, Nissan would increase its purchases of American-made car components by 40 percent. Soon, he reminded his audience, the company would be capable of building 450,000 cars and trucks a year at its expanding manufacturing complex in Tennessee. And right here in the suburbs of Detroit, where just ten years earlier Japanese cars had been banned in some parking lots, Nissan would engineer new models for the United States and Europe. "We're focusing our efforts," he declared as the crowd applauded and cheered, "to make Nissan a truly American company."

THE REACTION OF DETROIT'S Old Lions to what they saw going on right around them was utter, uncomprehending anguish. These men had begun their business lives in the late 1940s and early 1950s, years when

America's hegemony was unquestioned throughout the non-Communist world. Germany and Japan were destroyed. Britain and France were exhausted. Only the United States was still standing. America exported not just money and machinery, but also its ideas and ideals. It was unthinkable that America would ever lose a war. And unthinkable that America would not be No. 1 in anything that really mattered.

At home, the booming postwar economy coupled with the birth of the interstate highway system ushered in a true Golden Age for the American auto industry. America's new prosperity seemed to be built around the car: McDonald's, Holiday Inn, and even television with its vast new potential to tap a mass market of consumers eager to buy the latest that Detroit could produce. Tail fins symbolized the amiable arrogance of the era, but they weren't the weirdest example of America's nouveau-riche kitsch.

In Akron, Ohio, Goodyear Tire and Rubber Company hit upon something even more bizarre: pastel-colored, translucent tires that were lit from within by dozens of tiny electric lights. "It takes little imagination to see it as the tire of the future," Goodyear crowed in a slick marketing brochure.[3] "Will the lady driver want tires to match her car's upholstery —or perhaps a favorite outfit?" Alas, the translucent tires of the future proved to be impractical. The prototypes wore out so quickly that Goodyear's PR men would put regular tires on their cars to drive between cities, and then stop just outside town to change into their hot pink wheels and cruise over to the local auto show. The tires never made it to market.

Such excesses epitomized the sky's-the-limit ethos of the postwar boom. America was so rich, so far ahead of the rest of the world, that there was no need to look anywhere else for useful ideas, and no reason to believe that anything would change. America was alone at the top. And for Detroit, it was a heady time—the era of chrome trim and throbbing V-8 power. These were the years when Lee Iacocca, Donald Petersen, and Roger Smith got their starts in the auto business, and formed their fundamental views of the world.

Iacocca was a young Ford sales rep, futilely trying to sell the safety features engineered into the 1956 Fords against the glitz and power of the '56 Chevrolet. It was a failure that shaped Iacocca's hostile attitude toward safety advances such as air bags for decades to come. Smith, meanwhile, was climbing the twisted ladder of GM's all-powerful financial staff, and soaking up a culture that assumed GM's preeminence in the world auto industry as a matter of divine right.

Petersen, a Minnesotan by birth who grew up on the West Coast, joined Ford in 1949 as a product planner, developing the ideas for new cars. Through the 1950s and 1960s, he worked on a variety of car programs—including those that produced such classics as the Thunderbird and the Mustang.

Despite their different disciplines, all three men, and the other members of their generation, had common ground: the view that life in the 1950s and 1960s was how things were supposed to be. But the 1950s were almost too good for America in the long run. Years later, when the Japanese auto industry raced past Detroit, the men who ran the Big Three simply couldn't believe it. Nothing in their formative years had ever prepared them to believe such a thing was even remotely possible.

How could they believe it? If America in the fifties was the land of endless opportunity, Detroit was the place where dreams came true. It was where long-repressed, poor black men from the South could come and find high-paying jobs whose only requirement was a willingness to work. It was where America's most promising young college men could become big fish in the country's biggest corporate pond. One of those young men was Bennett E. Bidwell.

Bidwell, who eventually would become the No. 2 man at Chrysler, was the funniest man in Detroit. In the twilight of his career, some of his friends took to calling him Two Dog. The nickname came from Bidwell's favorite joke, which went like this:

An Indian brave walks up to the chief who chooses the names for all the newborn babies in the tribe. How do you know, asks the brave, the right name for each child?

"It is easy," says the chief. "When a child is born I just look up, and whatever I see tells me what the name should be. If I see the full moon rising in the sky, the child's name should be Full Moon Rising. If I see a thundering herd of buffalo, the child's name should be Running Buffalo."

Then the chief adds: "But tell me, why do you ask this question, Two Dogs Fucking?"

Bidwell was born on June 22, 1927, raised in Concord, New Hampshire, and went to school at Babson College in Wellesley, Massachusetts, just outside Boston. His career in the auto industry started in 1953, right after he graduated from Babson, when he took a job in Ford's Boston sales office. As he rose through the sales and marketing ranks at Ford, his bawdy sense of humor served him well.

In the early 1970s, for instance, Bidwell was running Ford's Lincoln–Mercury division when the company's finance staff decided to kill the

Mercury Cougar. To Bidwell, this was no small matter. Mercury used a live cougar (named Chauncey) in its television commercials, and the brand's advertising slogan was "The Sign of the Cat." Bidwell wanted to keep the car, but it was hard to fight the finance staff head-on.

So Bidwell carefully chose his battleground, a meeting presided over by Henry Ford II. The chairman asked each man for his opinion, and virtually everyone said the Cougar was too lousy to keep and too costly to replace. Finally Henry Ford said, "We haven't heard from you yet, Bidwell. What do you think?" Bidwell leaned back and said, "I just have one thing to say, Mr. Ford. You can't run a cat house without a cat."

There was a moment of silence, then Henry Ford started to chuckle. After that, everyone else chuckled too. With a well-timed wisecrack, Bidwell had saved his car.

A few years later Bidwell's humor won the day again at a meeting to name a new compact car. Henry Ford liked alliteration—names such as Ford Falcon or Ford Fairlane—and his favorite this time was Ford Phoenix. But GM's Pontiac division, someone noted, already had the name locked up. "Couldn't we call it the Ford Fenix," Henry asked, "and spell it with an F?"

It was such a dumb idea that Bidwell turned to Jim Bakken, a vice president sitting next to him, and whispered: "We could call it the Ford Phuck and spell it with a *Ph*. The ads wouldn't work on radio, but they'd be fine on TV and in print."

Bakken started sputtering like a schoolboy hearing his first dirty joke. Henry Ford noticed the commotion and forced Bakken to regurgitate what he had heard. Henry harrumphed, but the Ford Fenix became the Ford Fairmont.

By 1978 Bidwell had become vice president for North American sales and a protégé of Ford's brash young president, Lee Iacocca. But on July 13 of that year, Henry Ford II called Iacocca into his office and fired him. A few months later Lee landed at Chrysler, bent on revenge, and he invited many of his old cronies from Ford to come along for the ride. Bidwell was one of them. "But I couldn't go over to the enemy camp," Bidwell later recalled. "Most of the guys at Chrysler at the time, the very earliest ones from Ford, were like a bunch of adolescent boys who were going out every night to soap Henry Ford's windows. They wanted to do anything they could to screw Henry, and I didn't want any part of that. So I said no."

Iacocca came knocking again, in early 1981. But by then Chrysler was standing at death's door with seemingly little chance for recovery. So Bidwell again rebuffed his old friend. Instead, after twenty-eight years at Ford, he left to become president and chief operating officer—the second-in-command—at Hertz.

But two years later RCA Corporation, which owned Hertz, put the leasing firm up for sale, and Bidwell's future looked uncertain. Iacocca still wanted him, so on June 2, 1983, Bidwell joined Chrysler as executive vice president, sales and marketing.

Bidwell's quick, acerbic wit was a necessary tool for survival with his Chrysler colleagues. No one-liner was too crude, no opinion was too blunt in the million-dollar locker room they called an executive suite. Bidwell was the company's King of Quips. Not even the Financial Analysts Society of New York, a group whose members could make or break a company's stock with their recommendations, could intimidate him. Once he began a full-dress presentation to the group by announcing that he would unveil demographic data of immense importance to the entire U.S. economy. He displayed charts showing U.S. consumption of rye, barley, and grapes, as well as figures tracking trends in railroad shipments, the birth rate, and housing starts. The punch line: "More people are getting loaded than freight cars," Bidwell said, "and more people are getting laid than cornerstones." The analysts loved it.

No one else could have gotten away with this, but Bidwell was one of a kind. As the Roaring Eighties ended, however, and Chrysler led Detroit into a new crisis, Ben Bidwell lost his sense of humor. On January 8, 1990, he was the keynote speaker at the Automotive News World Congress, an industry conference sponsored by the leading trade journal in the car business. It was evident from the start that Bidwell wouldn't be doing his stand-up comic routine. "These are not funny times we're in today in this business," he told his audience in Detroit's towering Renaissance Center. "They're tough times, and they're probably gonna get tougher for a while."

Thus began a long and bitter lament about Bidwell's vision of an unholy alliance—between American reporters and Japanese car companies—that was poisoning things for Detroit and for America. "The press has given up on America," he declared. "We can't compete. The Japanese are better than everything. It's only a matter of time before they own us lock, stock, and barrel. Is it now a prerequisite, a commandment, to accentuate the negative? Are we dealing with congenital sickos here? Or is it true that good news just won't sell papers? We—the great believers in free enterprise—are having our pants removed, an inch at a time, by a centrally orchestrated, totally committed, economic aggressor. Why can't we grasp the truth of it? Or don't we give a damn anymore?"

The next day reporters showed up wearing yellow T-shirts that said in black letters: "Congenital Sicko." On the back the T-shirts said: "I Survived Ben Bidwell's Media Bash." They gave one to Bidwell as a peace offering.

But Bidwell wasn't a man at peace. He was sixty-two years old, and still a few years short of retirement. But he was suffering from too many cigarettes, too much cholesterol, and too many difficult decisions. Bidwell retired on January 1, 1991, at age sixty-three, another Old Lion stalking off Detroit's stage.

BIDWELL'S BITTER VIEW of Japan's success in the car business was pretty much the standard view in Detroit—at least among people of his age. If Japanese car companies were beating American manufacturers, the game had to be rigged somehow—perhaps by the Japanese, perhaps by the American government, or perhaps by both. The idea that somebody else had to be at fault for their troubles shaped the competitive response of an entire generation of Detroit's Old Lions. It prompted a staggering series of miscalculations.

The first was that Japan's car companies had the unfair advantage of cheap labor in their home country. The Japanese willingness to work for next to nothing wasn't only hurting Detroit, it also was undermining the American standard of living. The men who ran Detroit demanded that the Japanese create a "level playing field" by building factories in the United States. When that happened, they figured, the Japanese advantage would be subverted by the same mulish American workers that they themselves had to put up with.

The Big Three got their wish, all right, beginning with Honda Motor Company's factory in the tiny central-Ohio hamlet of Marysville in 1982. Honda's workers were nonunion, but the company paid them wages equivalent to those earned by the unionized work force at the Big Three. But within a year or so it was evident that Honda was thriving—using American workers to build better cars than Detroit and at a far lower cost. Myth No. 1 was exploded.

Detroit's next scapegoat was robots. If the Japanese were winning, if their factories really did require far fewer workers than comparable Big

Three plants, it had to be because the Japanese had more robots. Detroit's solution was to buy more robots, lots of them, and nobody could buy more than General Motors.

The company would "automate away from those assholes," GM executives said, referring to the disaffected blue-collar masses that they still blamed for their company's woes. GM's plant managers had to provide headquarters with regular reports on how many robots they had on the factory floor. The robot count quickly became the most important manufacturing statistic in the company. Who could be bothered with such minutiae as whether the radios on some cars clicked off when the lights went on?

In just a few years' time GM set out to overhaul its factories and equipment at a cost of $70 billion—an amount of spending unequaled by any corporation, before or since. When the 1980s began, General Motors had the lowest production costs among the Big Three. But by the middle part of the decade, with the spending binge well underway, GM had the highest costs of any major automaker in the world. Myth No. 2 was exploded.

Then came another culprit: the strong dollar. Until 1985 each American dollar was so strong that it would buy, depending on the day, about 240 Japanese yen. This meant that Americans traveling to Japan could find bargains galore, but it also meant that goods manufactured in the United States were expensive in Japan. More important, the reverse also was true. Anything made in Japan—say cars, for instance—could be sold in the United States with an inexpensive price tag. The situation was unfair, Detroit said, and the Reagan administration lent a sympathetic ear.

In 1985 the finance ministers of the world's major industrial nations met in Paris and agreed that their central banks would act in concert to drive down the value of the dollar, and push up the value of the yen. An exultant Lee Iacocca said that if the U.S. currency declined by just 25 percent, so that each dollar would buy only 180 yen, the playing field would finally be level. And he would drive the Japanese automakers back into the sea.

But the dollar didn't drop by 25 percent. Instead, its value dropped a whopping 50 percent, so that by 1988 each dollar would purchase only about 120 yen. With their American profits slashed overnight, Japanese car makers frantically rushed to raise their sticker prices. The trouble was, so did the Big Three. They didn't have the currency-rate problem, so they didn't boost prices as steeply as Honda, Toyota, Nissan, and the others. But instead of holding down their prices and seizing the chance to increase market share, the Big Three used the Japanese price increases as a convenient umbrella. Under it, they could sneak in big price hikes of their own.

The Japanese, meanwhile, adopted far-reaching cost-cutting measures; Honda even ordered the lights turned out in company headquarters during lunch hour. And the Japanese found some silver linings in their cloud: The strong yen made it cheaper for them to buy raw materials from overseas. It also made their U.S. factories, most of which were just coming onstream, far more economical to operate than they would have been had the yen remained weak.

The result: Japan's share of U.S. car sales leveled off during 1987 and 1988, when the Japanese automakers were struggling to absorb the impact of the strong yen. But in 1990 the Japanese share surged to 28 percent, an all-time record. The playing field was level, but the score was still lopsided. Lee Iacocca wasn't driving anybody back into the sea. Detroit's last excuse had vanished. It was time to look in the mirror.

CHAPTER 2

THE NUMMI COMMANDOS

"Bera-san!" the voice on the other end of Steve Bera's office phone line demanded. "We are in need."

In need? In need of what? Steve Bera wondered. What did those guys from Toyota want now?

They had wanted a lot, so far. It was the early spring of 1984, and Steve Bera was working as hard as he ever had in eighteen years at General Motors. For most of that time, Bera had been a very small gear in GM's huge machine. But he was somebody now, one of sixteen young GM managers dedicated to GM's pursuit of The Secret.

The Secret. GM had put its prestige on the line for a glimpse of it. It was flying through storms of legal flak to get at it. Even as Bera sat in his office in the crumbling heart of Detroit, work to build the crucible where The Secret would emerge was cranking up 2,000 miles to the west, in the blue-collar Oakland suburb of Fremont, California.

GM called it New United Motor Manufacturing Inc.—Nummi, pronounced "new-me," for short. Two years earlier, it had been an abandoned GM car factory, a hulking, drab-hued pile with vent stacks rising from the paint shop like the pipes of a huge church organ. For Fremont, the factory was a symbol of failure. But now, something special was happening. GM and Toyota, the giants of the American and the Japa-

nese auto industries, archrivals in the global car wars, were joining forces
at this old plant and building cars together. The stakes were enormous.
Could the Japanese cope with American union labor? Could two fero-
cious antagonists cooperate in such a costly venture? Could GM really
learn The Secret?

The Secret, of course, was how Japanese companies managed to build
cars so well for so little money. Some of the best minds at GM were
stumped. Even Roger Smith, GM's proud chairman and chief strategist,
didn't know for sure. He saw the pieces of the puzzle. But how did they
fit together? *That* was the prize. And Steve Bera was one of sixteen
commandos Roger Smith was counting on to go west, learn the Secret
from Toyota and give it back to the corporation. It was heady stuff for a
forty-one-year-old son of Detroit who saw, dangling before him, a key to
GM's exclusive and highly paid upper executive ranks.

But first, there was this little puzzle to sort out.

"Bera-san!" the Toyota man's voice insisted. "We are in need!"

"What do you mean?" Bera replied.

"Women!" the voice declared.

Women? Bera was stunned. He had worked with this Toyota engineer
and his team for weeks. The Japanese had come to Detroit to visit parts
suppliers and review plans for how parts would get to the Nummi plant.
Bera was their guide through the maze of American parts procurement.
They had worked hard. Now, it seemed, Bera's new colleagues wanted a
little R-and-R. But again, they had a procurement problem. So they
called Bera-san.

Soon, Bera found himself trundling off to a bar in the Detroit suburb
of Troy to chat in the shadows with young women. After he had satisfied
himself there'd be no trouble, Bera would escort the women up to hotel
rooms where his Japanese colleagues waited.

No doubt about it, this was a different world. Bera had grown up in
Detroit, the middle child of three in a family that teetered on the rickety
fence that divided middle class from poor. At age six, the Bera family
had moved to Royal Oak, a suburb just north of the city line. Royal Oak
was a comfortable community, the home of the Shrine of the Little
Flower Catholic Church and the fiery Depression-era radio priest, Father
Charles Coughlin. Not until much later in his life did Bera realize he'd
spent much of his childhood on Royal Oak's poor side.

After graduating from high school in 1961, Bera went to Western
Michigan University in Kalamazoo. That lasted three years. Then his

family ran out of money. It was 1964, and Bera needed a job. Like generations of Detroit men before him, he went into a car factory. Bera started his automotive career not far from the bottom—on the graveyard shift at Chrysler's Mack Avenue stamping plant. There, he pushed a "palm button" that sent the two halves of a big metal press thudding together to turn out another steel piece for a Chrysler car. Bera worked with a team of two other guys. They had a quota of parts to make between 10 P.M. and 6:30 A.M., and Bera's team quickly focused their talents on making the quota in just five hours. They got a system down so that one man could work, while the other two slept. They rotated sleep turns like helmsmen on a ship. Work one hour, sleep two.

Then Bera got a break. In late 1965, a friend told him Chevrolet was hiring people in its production scheduling office. It was white-collar work, a ticket out of the noisy, grimy stamping factory. He applied and got a job.

Now, Bera wore a shirt and tie, and earned $450 a month—decent pay in those days. Instead of the graveyard shift in a noisy factory, Bera worked daytime hours in Chevy's central office across the street from GM headquarters. He had made the grade, Detroit style. The future looked bright.

But in April 1966, four months after starting at Chevy, Bera got a letter from Uncle Sam. Three weeks before Christmas, he found himself aboard a troopship, sailing for Vietnam.

Fortunately, Bera's new job description didn't include getting shot at. Instead, he ran around the Vietnamese countryside fixing communications gear for combat units, and fourteen months after he arrived, he was sent home to resume his old life.

First, however, Bera took a couple of detours. He got married to Sandra Kline, a bookeeper for a Detroit toy store chain whom he met at a party just two weeks after his return to the States. He picked up his old job at GM, but in 1969 he decided to finish college. So Bera reenrolled at Western Michigan, and Sandy got a job as a secretary to support them. At twenty-seven, Bera got to live the life of a college boy again. They didn't have much money, but there was always enough for beer and chips. At night, they'd play cards with friends and shoot the breeze. Bera loved it.

By January 1971, it was time to go back to GM. Bera landed a job as a plant supervisor at AC Spark Plug in Flint, Michigan. His career began to churn. In 1974, he joined the team that moved to Oak Creek, Wisconsin, to set up GM's first catalytic converter factory. A year later, he was back in Flint working at AC Spark Plug. Then, in March 1979, he got an offer to go to GM headquarters and join the corporate production scheduling group.

Bera found himself at one of GM's hottest spots. The Iranian oil crisis had made the business of deciding which GM division got what cars a matter of the highest gravity. GM had built its factories and its marketing franchises on cars powered by muscular, gas-thirsty eight- and six-cylinder engines. But with gasoline lines snaking around every other city block and interest rates at levels previously charged only by loan sharks, anyone willing to buy a car at all wanted a cheap one with an efficient four-cylinder engine. GM didn't have enough to go around. Dealers were panicking. Bera and his group were rationing supplies of four-cylinder cars, and cramming eight-cylinder models down the throats of the marketing divisions to keep the factories running.

For the first time, Bera took notice of the Japanese. They were selling what customers wanted, he realized. GM was not. For thirteen years, he'd staked his future on the proposition that GM was No. 1. Now his faith was shaken.

But it wasn't broken. Not yet. Bera weathered the dismal recession years of 1980–1983 in his staff job. GM lost money in 1980. But in 1981, profits bounced back. Among the Big Three, GM could still build a car for the least money, and it still owned close to half the car market. As the economy rebounded in 1983, GM's dominance seemed assured as profits took off, and the company poured money into new factories and cars.

It was an article of faith at GM that massive investments in sophisticated factory technology, and a top-to-bottom reorganization of the company's North American operations, would vault the No. 1 automaker ahead of Japan, and leave Ford and Chrysler gasping in the dust. But Steve Bera was beginning to see a different side of the Japanese challenge and of GM's responses to it. Because in 1983, Bera began working for an unusual engineer named Leonard Ricard.

Ricard was one of the first GM operatives to have studied Japanese methods in depth. He had begun his research in 1977, after GM shipped him to Japan to help its affiliate, Isuzu, learn more about flexible production systems. But after Isuzu managers began bombarding him with wild tales about a Toyota Production System that had dramatically improved productivity and quality at an Isuzu supplier, Ricard sidetracked his teaching mission and became a student.

Ricard began touring Japanese factories, gathering information and piecing together intelligence. He began warning his bosses in Detroit that the Japanese had a system for building cars that put GM to shame. On July 9, 1978, he found himself back in Detroit as the featured speaker before a group of about 150 executives, including one vice president.

The speech went badly. As Ricard described how Toyota workers could change a massive metal stamping die in just 3.5 minutes—a job GM workers took eight hours to do—one of executives in the audience jerked up his hand. "You've got to be mistaken," the man sputtered. "They may get the die changed in three and a half minutes, but they're not running the press" to make new parts.

"It was three minutes and thirty-one seconds," Ricard replied.

"You're lying," the man retorted.

It was a typical response. Ricard argued that Toyota and Honda accomplished their low-cost, high-quality production with smarter management. His peers in Detroit dismissed him with tirades about the cheap yen and coolie labor. Discouraged, Ricard went back to Japan.

But the shock of the recession and surging sales of Japanese cars gave Ricard a second chance in Detroit. This time, his bosses told him to act as a missionary, preaching Japanese methods to factory managers and suppliers under the aegis of GM's purchasing and shipping office.

Often as not, though, Ricard found that plant managers were indifferent or downright hostile. Why should a plant manager jeopardize his top priority—meeting production quotas—to fool around with proposals from no-rank staffers such as Ricard? Ricard often found himself waved out of a plant manager's office, and sent to talk to underlings who had no more power than himself to make changes.

Ricard had more impact on the young managers assigned to work with him. Bera was one. Ricard became a mentor. And as Bera toured GM factories with Ricard, he began to see things he'd never seen before. One day in the summer of 1983, Bera walked with Ricard through GM's brand new Wentzville, Missouri, assembly plant. Wentzville was one of the crown jewels of GM's factory modernization program. But with Ricard's tutoring, Bera saw it as a monument to waste. The building was huge, far bigger and more expensive than a Japanese factory doing the same work. Parts arrived at the loading dock by the railroad boxcar-load. Along the assembly line, which wound through the factory like a snake, there were enough parts stacked up to supply two or three shifts' worth of production. Big storage bins full of spare parts—and trash—cluttered the floor. Bera was appalled. It was as if GM had withdrawn stacks of $1,000 bills from the bank and strewn them around on the floor.

BERA WASN'T THE ONLY one who had misgivings about GM's system. The chairman of the company wasn't happy, either. Roger Smith was no expert on manufacturing. But he was a whiz with numbers. And the numbers told him that GM, the world's mightiest automaker, didn't know how to build a small car in America that was as good or as inexpensive as a Toyota.

Some of the numbers Smith saw came from James Harbour, an acerbic former Chrysler executive turned consultant. In 1980, he began telling anyone who'd listen that Toyota or Honda could build a car for $1,500 less than GM. Late that year, Harbour traveled to New York to explain his findings to a group of about forty-five GM executives gathered in the boardroom at GM's midtown office tower. Plopping himself in the chair reserved for the chairman of the board, Harbour proceeded to savage GM for building new factories that were twice as big and expensive as they should be, and for designing cars that required gangs of people to build. "You're noncompetitive," he growled. Harbour had delivered similar speeches to executives at Chrysler and Ford and received supportive hearings. The GM executives dismissed him as a loud-mouthed crank. A few months later, Harbour sassed GM's new president, F. James Mc-Donald, in a speech before a large industry conference in Detroit, and was informed he could no longer enter GM property.

But some of GM's own manufacturing experts realized that, if anything, Harbour was too kind. They knew GM's engineers had tried and failed to design a new small car to replace the old Chevette, a dog that contributed more to GM's warranty bill than to its bottom line. The numbers told Smith that the S-car, as the small-car project was known, would be a money loser. Smith killed it.

Abandoning the small-car market, however, was unthinkable. The trauma of the oil shocks was still fresh in the national consciousness, and Washington was pounding on Detroit to replace its gas guzzlers with more fuel-efficient models. More to the point, GM's forecasters believed gasoline prices would keep rising and American consumers would continue to demand small cars. GM had to have a good, small car.

Smith launched a stopgap strategy. He would import small cars from its two Japanese affiliates, Isuzu and Suzuki. But Smith also had higher ambitions. GM should build its own small car, and do it in America. In time, Smith would see to that. But first, he wanted to pick the brains of the masters. Ford had tried and failed to forge an alliance with Toyota in 1981. Now, Smith resolved to give it a try.

So it was that Smith flew to New York on March 1, 1982, for a clandestine meeting with Eiji Toyoda, Toyota's president. The two men hit it off. And soon, their aides began secret negotiations toward an unprecedented alliance: GM, America's preeminent car maker, and Toyota, the GM of Japan, would build cars together in the United States.

It was a bold idea. Making it a reality proved arduous. The negotiators quickly discovered just how different their cultures were. GM's style was to make big splashes. Driven by forecasts of surging demand for small cars, GM declared the new venture should have a factory big enough to build 400,000 cars a year—knockoffs of Toyota's subcompact Corolla—for Chevrolet. Toyota executives dismissed this proposal as absurd. A facility big enough to build 200,000 cars a year would be risky enough, they declared.

The GM team, meanwhile, couldn't believe what its counterparts were proposing to do at the old Fremont plant. The GM negotiators—led by young Jack Smith, a finance whiz who wasn't related to Roger but was one of the chairman's key protégés—asked Toyota how many employees the new venture should have. Toyota's reply was roughly 2,000. "That's just for one shift, right?" one of GM's negotiators declared. "Two shift, two shift," the Japanese insisted. The GM negotiators double-checked. There was no mistake. The GM team was shocked. Toyota had just informed them that it could build a car with about half the labor needed to assemble a GM vehicle.

By early 1983, the deal had come together. Toyota and GM would form a new company, with each parent owning half. Toyota would run the factory. GM would sell the cars through Chevrolet dealers. GM dubbed the car the Nova, reviving a name that had become associated with a clunky rear-drive compact Chevrolet had stopped building several years before.

The strategic heart of the deal was exchange of knowledge. Toyota agreed that GM could send managers to the venture to learn about the Toyota production system. In addition to the sixteen managers who would work at the factory, GM got the right to send employees through the factory on tours. GM also would maintain a Technical Liaison Office just up the road in Fremont to funnel intelligence back to Detroit.

In return, GM would allow Toyota access to its list of preferred U.S. parts makers—a valuable gift for a Japanese company under pressure to build cars in America using American-made parts. Toyota would also get experience dealing with American workers, without the enormous expense of building a new factory from scratch.

In February 1983, Roger Smith and Eiji Toyoda flew to San Francisco, and registered at the Stanford Court Hotel under assumed names. Speculation about a Toyota–GM alliance had been swirling for months. GM's public affairs operatives even had GM's Aviation department file phony flight logs to mislead reporters who were trying to track Smith's movements. Now, Smith and Toyoda were ready to close the deal and lift the veil. They hopped in their limousines and journeyed to the Fremont plant on the east side of San Francisco Bay, south of Oakland. The two men walked together through the ghostly, darkened factory. When they emerged, the venture was born.

Smith was triumphant. At last, GM would be getting firsthand access to the Secret. Nummi was a brilliant, bold stroke. Let Ford and Chrysler whine for protection, GM had cut a deal to see into the enemy's heart.

Others weren't so pleased. Among them was Lee Iacocca. Iacocca, still nursing Chrysler's recovery, was furious that the industry's two behemoths now were proposing to team up. He unleashed a pack of lawyers to snap at GM's heels.

Legal wrangling and an exhaustive Federal Trade Commission investigation ground along through 1983. But GM and Toyota didn't stop work. Confident of victory, the two companies began hammering out details. In that process, Toyota asked for a GM manager to come to Japan to explain how GM went about shipping parts across the vast spaces of North America. The request bounced down the line at GM, and in August 1983 it landed at the feet of Steve Bera.

Bera jumped at the opportunity. That month, he flew to Nagoya for a ten-day quick immersion in the Toyota system. "I'm going to meet the masters," he told himself. He wasn't disappointed. As he toured a Toyota factory, Bera marveled at how fast the workers on the line were moving. He saw the brisk efficiency with which Toyota shuttled the thousands of parts and pieces that went into each car from delivery trucks to the line.

Still, Bera was puzzled. Where were the robots? Where was the high-tech wizardry? The gray factories of Toyota City weren't as technically advanced as the new plants GM was erecting as part of the massive, $70 billion "reindustrialization" program Smith and McDonald were leading. As Bera worked with Toyota's managers, it dawned on him that machinery was only a small part of the Secret. Far more important was the way Toyota managed and orchestrated the work of people. Toyota planned and acted with precision and attention to detail such as Bera had never before seen.

Some of Toyota's tricks were deceptively simple. Instead of using miles of noisy conveyors or $100,000-apiece computer-guided vehicles to ferry parts around a plant, Toyota simply had a worker driving a little tractor, or tugger. The driver circled through the plant like a delivery man dropping off milk. At each stop, he'd pick up a card that told him what parts to bring next. Because the pace of production was predictable and level from day to day, suppliers could precisely time their deliveries to the factory door, and didn't need to finance big inventories. Toyota thus saved millions that otherwise would have gone to conveyors, warehouses, fancy computers, and capital tied up in idle inventory.

Toyota, Bera saw, was substituting discipline for money. The just-in-time parts delivery regime required that Toyota stick close to its assembly schedules. Otherwise, parts might arrive at the plant and sit around. Managers kept track of the number of cars rolling off the line on a lighted board that hung over the line; everyone in the factory, managers and workers alike, could see whether production was falling behind schedule. But if there was a problem—such as a defective part—the Toyota system forced workers and managers to fix it. Toyota workers were trained not to pass mistakes on to the next worker, but rather to stop the line and signal for help to fix the foul-up then and there.

Two months after Bera returned to Detroit, his boss told him GM had a great opportunity for him. The assignment: Join the first team of GM commandos hitting the beach at Nummi.

Bera was reluctant at first. His family roots were all in Michigan, and he wasn't sure going to Nummi would be as good for his career as his bosses seemed to think. His misgivings intensified when he flew to California for an interview with a Toyota manager, during which the Japanese executive sat silent for ten minutes while his eyes traveled slowly back and forth between Bera's face and a piece of paper. But when Bera got back home, he was told the job was his if he wanted it. He said yes.

. . .

IN THE 1950s AND 1960s, the heart of the world's auto industry was a bustling company town in Michigan called Flint. More than 82,000 people worked for General Motors in Flint at the peak in 1955. Through the next decade, GM employed about 70,000 people in Flint—more than in any other single community. Flint's factories churned out Buicks and Chevrolets and much of the hardware that made them run: spark plugs, engines, exhaust pipes, brackets, clamps, and oil filters. Even when Bera had worked there, Flint was, in its grimy way, still a perfect realization of the postwar American dream—a place where men who worked with their hands and backs could expect a job for life, a good paycheck, a new car every couple of years, and a garage to put it in.

By 1984, however, another company town had shouldered Flint aside as a symbol of manufacturing might. It was to this town, Toyota City, Japan, that Steve Bera and a half dozen other GM Nummi commandos flew in February to start boot camp. Toyota City had a lot in common with Flint. It wasn't so much a city as a collection of dozens of gray factories surrounded by the homes of the people who worked in them. From Toyota City's factories poured nearly all the bits and pieces that went into Toyota's cars and trucks. From dawn until late at night, trucks rumbled through the narrow streets, ferrying the bits and pieces to Toyota factories that assembled them all into the Corollas and Celicas that were steadily drawing customers away from the Chevrolets and Buicks of Flint.

Unlike Flint, however, Toyota City was home not just to the factory hands, but to the bosses as well. In a corner of the industrial sprawl stood Toyota's unimposing headquarters building. There the heirs of founder Kiichiro Toyoda had their private offices. For the members of the Toyoda family, and their subordinates, the venture with GM marked a bold step onto the global stage. Memories of Toyota's pathetic first attempts to crack the American market in 1958 still lingered. The Toyota Crowns shipped to California were pathetically underpowered by American standards. They shook and rattled at highway speeds, and boiled over in the deserts of Southern California. In December 1960, Toyota beat a retreat and halted shipments to its eighty-five West Coast dealers.[1] The Toyodas retreated behind the walls of their castle town and resolved to perfect their cars and their manufacturing system. By 1984, their efforts had blossomed into a full-scale revolution of the industry, as the arrival of the GM managers charged with learning the Toyota secret attested.

Bera had agreed to join GM's Nummi squad without knowing exactly what he would do. Most members of the group were in their thirties or early forties—people "who didn't remember Pearl Harbor," one put it later. Most hadn't yet crossed the gulf in GM's hierarchy that separated managers who didn't get bonuses from those who did. None had ever been an assembly plant manager. The highest-ranking man, Robert Hendry, was a member of the financial staff, a bean counter. Bera found himself one of five GM managers assigned to "production control." They would deal with the companies that supplied parts for the Nummi cars and make certain the parts got to the right place in the Nummi factory at the right time.

This wasn't glamorous work. Few people were as anonymous in GM's great bureaucracy as the vice president in charge of purchasing and production control. At Toyota, however, production control was of paramount importance, because precise scheduling of parts shipments was at the very heart of the Toyota system. Thus, Toyota assigned one of its best and brightest managers, Susumu Uchikawa, to be the leader of Bera's group. Bera had encountered Uchikawa before. The first time was during his earlier visit to Japan, when he had sized up Uchikawa as a "fast tracker." The second time was in Fremont. It had been Uchikawa whose silent appraisal in that final interview had so unnerved Bera.

Now, Bera encountered Uchikawa in another role: drill sergeant. "We will teach you the Toyota production system," Uchikawa announced on the first day of class at Toyota City. And with that, a daylong lesson began. In Japanese.

The Americans were aghast. Everything was in Japanese—the handouts, the overhead slides, and the lectures. There were translators. But their English was almost as incomprehensible to the Americans as Japanese. More than once, the GM crew watched in amazement as the Toyota instructors and the translators bickered over the right way to explain a point. It went on like this for a week. Finally, the GM men rebelled. At dinner one night, they found an American whom Toyota had hired to develop training programs in English. Chuck Farley, a burly and ambitious manager who'd been plucked out of GM's Harrison Radiator division, cornered the man: "You've got to do this in English," he demanded. It was easier said than done, however. The Toyota trainers ultimately were reduced to drawing stick figures and simplistic diagrams to elaborate the concepts their broken English couldn't convey. Bera felt like he'd gone back to kindergarten.

BACK IN AMERICA, BERA continued his reeducation. His job, in advance of heading to Fremont, was to accompany the Toyota engineers as they walked through the factories of potential Nummi suppliers. It was eye-opening work. Bera and his Japanese colleagues journeyed one day to a parts shop near Chicago. The plant manager, evidently informed in advance that the Japanese liked things clean, had gone to considerable effort to spiff up his factory. As he escorted his guests around, he pointed to various examples of quality control in action.

At one station, the group came to a halt in front of a woman who was checking parts and throwing rejects into a big bucket. "Tell us about this situation," one of the Toyota engineers said. The plant manager declared that the worker was an inspector, who separated the good parts from the bad ones to "protect our customers."

Bera watched the faces of the Toyota men cloud over. He was still learning, but Bera knew what his Japanese colleagues wanted to hear, and that wasn't it. At Toyota, a machine routinely producing defective pieces would be shut down, and engineers and workers would comb through the line looking for the root cause of the problem that caused the defects. The Toyota drill was to ask "Why?" over and over until the defect was found. Toyota managers even called their problem-solving system the "five whys." Consistently producing reject parts and stationing an inspector at the end of the line to catch them was *muda*, or waste. Toyota managers were trained to abhor *muda*. And *muda* was what this factory was all about.

When the tour ended, the group adjourned to a conference room. The plant manager rattled on about his improvements in housekeeping and quality control, and concluded by asking: "What's your impression?"

One of the Toyota engineers dropped his eyes to the floor. "I have been to many facilities in this country," the Toyota engineer said. "And this is one of the worst I've ever been in."

The plant manager sputtered. Ignoring the man who'd spoken, he turned to Bera. "You guys are only going to be 5 percent of my business," he declared. "The guy down the street is 60 percent of my business, and he is very happy with the way I build my product."

As these confrontations became routine, Bera discovered that the Toyota engineers, polite and awkward in social situations, deployed brutal effectiveness in business transactions. One of GM's parts-making divisions planned to build a small factory in California to make decorative parts for the Nummi cars. Bera brought a group of Toyota production managers to review the plans. After the GM engineers explained their proposal for two hours, the Toyota men took the plans, folded them up, and threw them aside. They proceeded to lecture the GM factory engineers—in English—for another two hours about the wastefulness of their proposal.

IN MAY, BERA MADE the move to California and reported for work. It was an anxious moment. Bera knew a lot about various theories of how to manage the flow of nuts and bolts and steel and glass in a car factory. He'd spent more time than all but a handful of his GM peers learning about Toyota. But Bera had spent most of his GM career in staff jobs. He'd never actually worked in an assembly plant. As he had learned how exacting Toyota managers could be, he wasn't confident he could measure up. To top it off, he would have to march to the orders of the stern taskmaster who'd whipped them through the grueling training sessions in Toyota City.

At forty-six years old, Susumu Uchikawa cut an intimidating figure. Powerfully built, he stood more than six feet tall, unusual for a Japanese. He towered over Bera. More important, Uchikawa was far higher in Toyota's hierarchy than Bera was in GM's. A master of the intricacies of the Toyota production system, Uchikawa had studied at the feet of Taiichi Ohno, the revered pioneer of the Toyota Production System.

In the chain of command among the Japanese at Nummi, Tatsuro Toyoda, brother of Toyota's president, was No. 1, though essentially a figurehead. No. 2 was Kan Higashi, a Toyota director who was the real leader of the venture. Uchikawa was one of Higashi's two top lieutenants.

Although Uchikawa displayed dogged patience in his role as production system professor to Bera and his colleagues, he could be gruff and contentious when underlings questioned him. Higashi, friendly and accommodating by nature, dubbed Uchikawa the "red-necked Japanese." Uchikawa's personal habits did nothing but cement the label. One morning, just before lunch, Bera was sitting at his desk in the open bullpen that served as the Fremont factory's administative office. Suddenly, he became aware of a persistent noise. *Clip. Ching. Clip. Ching.* He looked up, and saw Uchikawa, his shoes and socks off and a big toenail clipper in his hand. He was assaulting his feet, and making the clippings fly. He finished, put his socks and shoes back on, and looked up. "Bera-san," he said. "Want to go to lunch?" Bera waited for him to stop in the men's room to wash up. He didn't.

BERA HAD NEVER ENCOUNTERED a boss like Uchikawa, and he'd never seen a factory run the way Nummi was. In Japan, Toyota managers were every bit as bureaucratic and attentive to hierarchy as their peers at General Motors. Toyota's senior executives worked behind closed doors in wood-paneled suites. They had special places to park their cars. They had hefty expense accounts. Subordinates addressed higher-ups as *kacho*, and *bucho*—the equivalent of an American addressing his boss as "Mr. Manager." But at Nummi, Toyota's managers adapted themselves brilliantly to attack the barriers between labor and management, Japanese and American. At first, those barriers were high.

When GM abandoned the Fremont factory in 1982, it had left behind an embittered workforce and a United Auto Workers local so racked by infighting that UAW headquarters had seized control of its affairs. GM's managers and workers had battled right until the end. They fought over line speedups. They fought over layoffs. They even fought over women's bathrooms. GM had started hiring women at the Fremont plant in the late 1960s, but never got around to installing more than a few women's bathrooms. Women had to walk hundreds of yards—past men's bathrooms—to relieve themselves during breaks.

George Nano had survived some of the worst times as chairman of the Fremont UAW local's bargaining committee in the years just before GM pulled the plug in 1982. Nano hated GM. By August 1984, Nano was working for a union that represented workers at Stanford University when he got a call to come to Fremont for an interview at the plant.

The young GM manager who met Nano presented an unusual proposition. Come back to Fremont, he urged. It's a new management. Things will be different. UAW workers will get a say in quality control and work conditions that they never had under GM. If there was a problem with a supplier's part, for example, the assembly line worker who had to install the piece would go along with engineers to visit the supplier. The production system would reward workers for using their minds, not just their backs. Most important, Nummi wouldn't lay off workers because sales dropped, or because management figured out a way to replace a worker with a machine.

"What do you think?" the enthusiastic manager asked.

"I think it's a lot of bullshit," Nano replied.

But Nano came back, anyway. After all, the wages promised to be as good as the old days at GM. He could pick up where he left off as a UAW leader. Two weeks later, Nano found himself on an airliner bound for Japan.

Despite the happy talk about the new style, Nano hadn't lost his reflexive distrust of management. He spent the entire trip looking over his shoulder, leery that the Toyota managers were watching to see if he drank too much or misbehaved off-duty. He stayed away from after-hours parties. But during work hours, Nano began to appreciate the Toyota system. With twenty years of experience as an inspector in the Fremont factory, Nano had a highly detailed knowledge of manufacturing. He noticed little things, such as the way Toyota used a picture of a snow-man on the big manifest sheet attached to a car so the assembly worker would see immediately that the vehicle was headed for a cold climate. He noticed how Toyota used one conveyor track in the floor to move a car along, instead of two.

Nano got drilled in Toyota's quality philosophy, starting with the concept of *kaizen.* That was the Japanese for the concept of "continuous improvement," or the process of making small changes to make a job easier, or less expensive. Nano recognized the concept immediately. Fremont workers had done this sort of thing on their own to make their lives easier. They'd just never shared their secrets with GM, for fear managers would take advantage of them to speed up the line or eliminate jobs. Nano was still wary, but the more he saw, the more he liked it. The Toyota men came across to him like straight-shooting country boys —which many of them were.

BACK IN FREMONT, the Toyota managers under Kan Higashi were strug-gling to clinch the trust of hundreds of other workers they'd inherited from GM.

A compact, soft-spoken man whose background was mainly in

finance, Higashi was on a hot seat in Fremont. Toyota sold cars around the world, but most of its managers knew next to nothing about how to do business outside Toyota City. Toyota's personnel bureaucracy wanted applicants to Nummi to fill out the same application forms as people in Toyota City. Higashi had squelched that easily, and turned the work of managing personnel and labor relations over to Americans. But he faced far tougher challenges. Toyota's executives needed Americans—both the GM managers and the leaders of the UAW—to act as guides and translators. And Higashi knew the Toyota system wouldn't work in the plant unless he somehow won over the workers, who'd been burned time and again by their former employer.

Higashi's answer was to tear down the GM caste system that separated labor from management. Gone were the executive dining room, the executive parking garage, and nearly all the walls in the administration offices. Gone was the rule that managers wore ties. At Nummi, everyone wore the same blue-and-gray uniform. Higashi told his Japanese subordinates to treat their GM counterparts as equal partners. And he saw to it that hourly workers really did get consulted about how to solve problems. Nano, for instance, got invited along to meetings with Nummi's glass supplier, Libby–Owens–Ford. He went along on a tour of the Libby–Owens–Ford plant in Manteca, California, when a Toyota engineer declared the factory "filthy." In twenty years as a quality inspector with GM, Nano had never done anything like this before.

There was one other thing Toyota did: As the Fremont factory was renovated, all of the bathrooms in the plant got split in half. One side was for men; the other for women.

MEANWHILE, BERA AND THE TEAM assigned to Uchikawa were getting used to the unorthodox methods of their headmaster. After morning stretching exercises, Uchikawa marched his men through endless chalk talks. But his most memorable lessons sprang from his Industrial Zen epigrams. During one meeting, held as the Nummi factory was gearing up for production, Uchikawa assembled his staff and asked for progress reports. Paul Thompson, who was in charge of dealing with Chevrolet on production schedules, spoke first. Then Chuck Farley, who'd been given the unenviable task of whipping the American suppliers into line. Then Ed Muirhead, who dealt with shipments from Japan. Each of them reported some glitch in the start-up routine. Finally, it was Bera's turn to report on his area, which was delivery of supplies workers used in the plant. Bera, in true-blue GM fashion, piped up: "No problems, Uchikawa-san."

"Bera-san," Uchikawa growled. "No problem is problem."

If you say everything is perfect, Uchikawa went on, you won't look for *kaizen*. Bera never forgot it: No problem is problem. Later, when Uchikawa caught Bera slipping into GM-Think, he would grind a knuckle into Bera's skull and chide: "You must use your head!"

Uchikawa walked constantly around the Nummi plant, which sprawled over nearly 70 acres (3 million square feet). The first time they set out to tour the plant together, Bera proposed they ride in a cart—GM style. "The important thing is what you see," Uchikawa chided. "What can you see driving by in this cart?" Besides, Uchikawa said, walking is healthy. Workers can stop you and ask questions or make suggestions for improvement. Managers should walk. And twice a week, that's what Uchikawa, Bera, and their colleagues would do. All around the plant they'd walk. They'd even walk outside, picking up cigarette butts and litter as they went.

Bera and the Americans marveled at the long hours the Japanese managers worked. The GM managers left their Japanese colleagues behind and went home to their families at 7 P.M. As far as Bera could tell, home life didn't mean much to the Japanese. It was a rare night that Bera left after Uchikawa. One evening, the Japanese managers did sneak out early at around 6 P.M. Bera and Farley had stayed in the bullpen, where they were surprised by Higashi. "Where's Uchikawa-san?" Higashi asked, with a concerned look. The next night, Bera left at 7 P.M. A chastened Uchikawa was still there.

NUMMI BEGAN PRODUCING NOVAS in December 1984. The progress was painfully slow at first, as the workers grappled with the new system. But as the cars rolled out at a faster clip, GM's quality checkers made an astounding discovery: The hard-boiled union factory hands Toyota had adopted were turning out some of the best cars GM had ever sold.

Toyota made winners out of GM's rejects with a straightforward bargain: Nummi would give its laborers total job security, train them exhaustively, and involve them in management decisions. In return, workers had to give total commitment to the job. At the most basic level, that meant no radios on the assembly line, no smoking, and little time for lollygagging. Make-work job categories—the kind that in the past meant the operator of a machine couldn't fix the machine if it broke —were eliminated.

When GM ran the plant, Fremont workers had been divided into eighty-two hourly job classifications, each with narrowly and rigidly defined duties. Toyota had just three. Workers spent hours in training classes. A cornerstone of Toyota's system was consistency. There was one way to check a steel fender for dents, one way to attach a nut to a bolt, one way to thread wires through the car. Instructors would drill workers over and over until they learned the Toyota way.

Nummi people worked hard. But Higashi succeeded in convincing hourly workers and union leaders like George Nano that his management was sincere about rewarding the effort. Gradually, workers who'd turned out junk for GM began pouring out cost-saving and quality improvement ideas to Nummi's managers. They also began routinely beating GM factories—by a wide margin—on the company's internal quality scores.

At the time, GM had a scoring system in which 145 was perfect. Most GM factories would celebrate if they hit 120. Nummi quickly began turning out cars that averaged 15 or more points higher. Eventually, Nummi even had some cars hit a perfect 145.

Line workers, who'd never been allowed to make a move without a foreman's approval under GM, now virtually controlled the pace of work on the Nummi shop floor. Toyota demanded that hourly workers participate in "quality circles" and other activities. There was a carrot, however, for the extra effort: bonuses of up to $600 for improving quality and cutting the time to assemble each car.

Toyota's methods also deftly shifted to line workers many of the disciplinary chores that managers had handled under GM. At each work area, Toyota posted a group attendance chart. Members of the work team who missed time got a red mark. Team leaders, recruited from the hourly ranks, were responsible for assuring that each worker signed in and out. The more absences, the more red marks stood out from the chart. Soon, the shirkers got the message to shape up—from their own coworkers. Nummi's absentee rate in 1985 was roughly 2 percent. GM's absentee rate was more than triple that level. Toyota didn't have punch clocks, either. Workers kept their hours.

As time went on, Nummi's system allowed union hands to become part of the factory engineering department. An hourly-wage team leader in the body shop, for example, would sketch out ways to rearrange a circle of welding machines to cut twenty-eight seconds out of the time it took to weld several pieces of steel. At GM, such a task would usually fall to a salaried engineer, with the union protesting the attempt to eliminate jobs.

In the Toyota system, the manager's role was to see that the trust invested in workers to control their own labor didn't lead to mistakes. Foolproofing was a major activity at Nummi. At every step in the assembly process, simple signs, with few words and lots of stick-figure diagrams, explained how parts should look, and how they should fit together. Among the Japanese phrases that began to pepper the speech of Nummi's American workforce was *bakayoke*. In English, that meant idiot-proofing. A machine found to be passing through parts without welding on a critical attachment nut was rewired so the welding gun couldn't fire unless the nut was in its proper place.

Japanese managers and engineers tended to stay in the background in the daily routine of the plant. The front-line bosses and engineers most workers saw were other Americans. The union and Nummi management had disputes over a variety of issues. Eventually, the local would even go through the ritual of calling a strike vote to press for concessions during contract talks. But years after the initial high of the start-up, Nummi's labor relations would still be a model for the industry.

Not so Nummi's relationship with GM.

ONE OF THE LITTLE "continuous improvement" rituals conducted in Bera's group was to compile every Friday a list of Nummi's ten worst North American suppliers. That task fell to Chuck Farley, and virtually every week, nine of the ten losers on Farley's list would be divisions of GM.

Some of the problems were laughable. Early on, Nummi had to shut down the assembly line because GM's Delco Products division had shipped a load of suspension parts so beglobbed with paint that the pieces couldn't be bolted onto the cars. GM divisions were accustomed to shipping parts to assembly plants any day they wanted to in the week before the parts were required. Nummi demanded that shipments arrive at specific times, several times each week. The GM parts factories missed the deadlines time and again, and kept sending planes aloft to carry parts west on time. When the parts arrived, Toyota often found as many as three of every ten were flawed. By contrast, Nummi rejected less than one in 100 of the parts it got from Japan.

The Toyota men didn't give up on GM's parts operations, however. Instead, they tried to reform them. One day, Uchikawa flew to Dayton, Ohio, with Farley to confront a serious problem with GM's Inland division and one of its subcontractors, a small Dayton company called Arkay Industries. Arkay had a contract from Inland to make plastic parts, such as glove boxes and ashtrays, for the Nova. Accustomed to GM standards that allowed 1 percent to 3 percent of any shipment to be defective, Arkay was facing ruin because Nummi was rejecting truckloads of its parts. Arkay had about $2 million in annual sales—but had spent $2 million in a single year of unsuccessful efforts to meet Nummi's quality and on-time delivery demands.

Farley had arranged for Uchikawa to meet Carl Code, an Inland manager, and Art Kuhnash, the owner of Arkay, at Inland's Dayton offices. Code tried to explain that Inland and Arkay had a new plan to make Nummi happy.

Uchikawa cut him off. "Your proposal doesn't make sense," he declared.

Code turned to Farley. "Chuck," he said, "I need your help."

At that, Uchikawa dug his elbow into Farley's ribs. Now, Uchikawa declared, the problem could be solved. He motioned to a young Japanese engineer who had come from Toyota's Detroit office. The man stood and announced that he, Hiroshi Tomomatsu, would now teach Arkay the Toyota system. "My English is very poor," Tomomatsu apologized, "because of my Detroit accent."

Tomomatsu's accent was the least of Kuhnash's concerns. The thought of Japanese engineers snooping around his plant, scooping up information about his costs, and telling him what to do chilled him. "No way," he told himself.

Pride, however, took a back seat to financial reality: Arkay was in trouble. So Kuhnash agreed to spend two months at Nummi with Farley, learning how the Toyota system worked. Gradually, he became a convert. Arkay's plant was one of the worst Farley had ever seen. Within five years, it was transformed into a clean, Toyota-style operation. Art Kuhnash saw his company's sales surge to $35 million a year as Toyota expanded its U.S. operations, and other Japanese companies placed orders on the strength of his success with Toyota. His quality soared to where he could ship millions of defect-free parts, at lower cost than ever before.

THE TOYOTA MAGIC didn't take so easily in Detroit, however. Even the routine business of ordering spare parts flummoxed GM. Confronted with a small car they knew nothing about, forecasters in GM's dealer service operation simply ordered spare parts for Novas on the basis of their experience with the gremlin-infested Chevette. Unlike the Chevette, however, Novas rarely came back to the shop once they left the dealership. It wasn't long before dealers found themselves swamped with spare Nova parts that they didn't need.

Chevrolet, meanwhile, groped for a strategy to sell the Nova to its clientele. Early on, Chevy touted the Nova as an American car with "Japanese quality." But most Japanese car fans opted to buy their Toyotas from Toyota dealers. And many die-hard Chevy buyers were precisely the kind of people who didn't want a Japanese car. Chevy dealers, accustomed to making money on warranty work, began to view the defect-free Nova as a low-profit pain in the neck. That opinion was reinforced by signals from Detroit that top priority was to sell real GM cars, so as to keep real GM factories humming.

As Nummi rolled into its second year of production in 1986, Chevrolet was struggling to sell the 200,000 Novas a year the factory planned to build—a far cry from the earlier declarations that 400,000 Novas wouldn't be enough.

As Nova sales slumped, Chevy and Nummi managers battled over Chevy's refusal to comply with Toyota's precise production planning regime. Chevy would try to slash Nova orders by as much as 40 percent —playing hob with Toyota's effort to keep the pace of production steady, predictable, and profitable. Higashi flew to Detroit twice to complain to Roger Smith in person. Smith was sympathetic, and then delegated the problem to the man in charge of North American auto operations, Lloyd E. Reuss. Reuss did little to help Higashi. Higashi fumed, but could do nothing.

For Bera and the other GM managers at Nummi, GM's sloppiness and ineffectiveness was an embarrassment. "Is there something we can do to help GM sell cars?" Uchikawa would ask.

. . .

As NUMMI CRANKED toward full production, GM began sending hordes of engineers and managers trooping through the factory. Often, they left disappointed that they hadn't found the secret Toyota tools and mystery high-tech processes they thought lay behind Nummi's superior quality scores and productivity.

In addition to the sixteen managers inside the factory, GM had the Technical Liaison Office, which was a combination spy operation and tour arranger for GM managers back in Detroit. But the office's young staffers had neither the knowledge nor the clout to get across to visiting GM executives just what Nummi's secret was. To complicate matters, the head of the liaison office reported to just one of GM's three vehicle-making groups. There was no organizational link between the intelligence analysts and the team inside the factory.

The Toyota executives were puzzled by GM's bungling approach to gathering the intelligence Toyota was offering. Why, they would ask later, hadn't GM sent plant managers to be part of the resident Nummi staff? Why had they sent a corps of junior managers like Bera? How were such men to make an impact on such a huge corporation?

The same question was hitting Bera and his colleagues right between the eyes. By mid-1985, the members of the GM commando squad had begun meeting together after hours once a month, usually taking over the back of a restaurant. The main topic of conversation was "repatriation." That was the word GM was using to describe the process of returning from Nummi, because in a very real way, it was as if the Nummi commandos had been sent off to a foreign land.

This feeling of isolation was intensified by the events back in Detroit. When Bera arrived in Fremont in May 1984, GM had just begun a sweeping reorganization of its North American auto operations. By 1985, it was clear the term "reorganization" didn't adequately describe the corporate cataclysm that was taking place.

The Nummi commandos had missed it all. Now, their old jobs didn't exist. Their mentors had been reassigned. It was as if they had rocketed into space, and the world had disintegrated behind them. The reorganization was supposed to make GM more receptive to new ideas like the low-cost production methods at Nummi. As far as Bera could tell, GM's senior executives hadn't given any sustained thought to deploying the people who happened to know more than anyone else at GM about Toyota's methods.

Even Roger Smith, architect of the Nummi strategy, seemed unsure about what to do. Smith showed up at Nummi in the summer of 1985. Members of the GM squad cornered him in a meeting room and asked what he planned to do with them. "This has to be resolved," Smith agreed. "We have to figure out what's the best way." Then he departed, and nothing happened.

The Nummi commandos resolved to develop a strategy of their own. Over time, they developed not one but a menu of plans. One was to argue that the Nummi group should be shipped en masse to a single factory, and given a free hand to run it the Toyota way. Bera liked this idea, as did many of the others. If they stuck together and took over a high-profile operation, they would have the clout to demonstrate the power of the ideas they'd learned.

Scenario 2 was to split up the group, and assign Nummi alumni to positions of front-line management responsibility. Scenario 3 was to send Nummi alumni in twos and threes to act as advisers to high-level operating managers. But the consensus was that the more the group was fragmented, the less effective it would be.

Bob Hendry, as the highest-ranking GM man at Nummi, fed ideas back to the personnel office in Detroit. The group waited for answers. Still, there was no concrete response.

By late 1985, Bera began to lose hope. Earlier in the year, he had deflected an offer from Uchikawa to leave GM and work at Toyota's new factory in Georgetown, Kentucky, which was scheduled to begin production in 1988. Uchikawa had broached the idea to Bera and Farley over lunch one day. The two Americans were startled by Uchikawa's breach of Nummi's unwritten rule against personnel poaching. But Bera and Farley said they'd consider it. Uchikawa soon left for Japan, and upon his return, he again sought out Bera for lunch.

"Bera-san," he exclaimed. "It is all arranged. You and Georgetown. You will join Toyota."

"Whoa!" Bera replied. "I didn't tell you I'd do it. I said I'd consider it."

"No, it's all arranged," Uchikawa persisted. "You will join Toyota." Bera continued to balk. Not long afterward, Bera learned that Uchikawa got his knuckles rapped for trying to poach talent, and the matter got dropped.

But another alternative began to look better. Lee Sage, a partner with Arthur Young in Detroit, had called Bera that spring to ask if he would be interested in joining him to form a manufacturing consulting practice.

Bera had begged off, figuring it made no sense to walk away from twenty years at GM. Sage kept calling every month, and pitching Bera on the idea of telling the world what he'd learned at the famous Toyota–GM venture.

Finally, in December 1985, Bera gave up. He asked again up the line for some assurance from GM's personnel bureaucracy that he'd be transferred to a meaningful position. He got no reply. Over the Christmas holiday, Bera flew to Columbus, Ohio, to interview with an Arthur Young partner. He got an offer and accepted.

BERA'S DECISION TO QUIT didn't qualify him as a hero. Certainly, not in the eyes of his GM colleagues. They had the same frustrations, but they were sticking it out. To them, Bera was a quitter. Bera, however, did earn some credentials as a prophet. Within a few months of his departure, GM's vice president in charge of personnel and an assistant appeared at Nummi to conduct half-hour interviews with each member of the squad. The result was that GM "repatriated" the Nummi commandos by splitting them up.

Bob Hendry was sent to Europe. Another member of the team went to Saturn as head of the fledgling subsidiary's purchasing operations. In the fall of 1986, four of the remaining managers went to the Chevrolet–Pontiac–Canada group as advisers. Another four wound up at the Buick–Oldsmobile–Cadillac group in advisory jobs. Paul Thompson, who'd worked with Bera under Uchikawa, was sent alone to the Truck and Bus group. He was assigned to a staff job, but refused a promotion to the executive ranks. He couldn't even eat in the same dining room as the executives who ran the show. How could he persuade these men, who'd known years of success and steady bonuses, that everything they were doing was wrong?

Only Chuck Farley was given a factory to run. It was a Harrison Radiator operation in Lockport, New York, that made heat exchangers for air-conditioners. One of Farley's first official acts was to refuse the enclosed office specified for him by GM's handbook. Farley demanded an open office setup similar to the one at Nummi. He got a compromise, an office without a door. Farley tried to clean up the drafty, dirty plant and involve hourly workers in quality control. But Farley quickly found himself isolated and undermined by superiors who had little interest in his ideas. Farley wound up quitting, and taking a job running a Japanese parts-maker's plant in Illinois. Thompson also quit, after he worked for months as part of a high-level effort to replicate the Toyota Production System across GM, only to see the initiative fail.

To Susumu Uchikawa, the scattering of the GM managers he'd taught for so many months seemed a waste. It was a puzzle to the man from Toyota. But Uchikawa would soon see GM make worse mistakes.

CHAPTER 3

THE LIONS ROAR

THERE WAS LITTLE WONDER why Steve Bera and his reform-preaching colleagues at Nummi didn't find many sympathetic ears in Detroit. As Nummi was getting under way, the auto industry was staging a spectacular rebound from the wrenching recession of the early eighties. Between 1980 and 1982 Detroit's Big Three had racked up losses totaling $4.73 billion. But between 1984 and 1988, GM, Ford, and Chrysler together earned a breathtaking $45 billion. The Motor City's tough-town swagger returned with a popular local T-shirt that read: "Detroit. Where the Weak Are Killed and Eaten."

The auto industry's elite, of course, had long since fled the city itself and moved north and west to the suburb of Bloomfield Hills. The Ford family stayed in old-money Grosse Pointe on the east, but that didn't prevent Bloomfield Hills from becoming to Detroit what Beverly Hills is to Los Angeles. Virtually everyone who mattered in the auto industry, and everyone who wanted to matter, lived there, within a mile or two of one another. Lee Iacocca had a sprawling, 1950s-style ranch home on a winding street, and later moved into a luxury condominium just off Woodward Avenue, Bloomfield Hills's main highway. Roger Smith's house backed up to the eighth fairway of the Bloomfield Hills Country Club, the auto industry's most exclusive enclave, where the unassuming white frame exterior of the clubhouse belied the high-level hobnobbing within.

Despite being the bedroom of men who ran the biggest companies in America, companies whose reach spanned the globe, Bloomfield Hills was an inward-looking place. Hondas or Toyotas rarely tread along the rustic dirt roads that fronted the elaborate mansions or the exclusive homes on the area's little lakes. Often, what seemed to matter most was where your house stood in relation to your boss's, as Ben Bidwell had learned one day in 1976. The young Ford vice president was looking for a new home, and one that caught his eye was being sold by John Z. DeLorean, the GM rebel who was quitting to start his own sports-car company. DeLorean took Bidwell on a tour of the house, marched him out to the front yard, and pointed to the bottom of the hill where the president of Ford lived. "What you'll like most about this house, Ben," DeLorean said, "is that you can walk out here to the front yard, and when the wind is *juuust* right, you can piss on Lee Iacocca." Despite misgivings about living so close to the boss, Bidwell bought the house anyway.

A lot had happened since then, both to Bidwell and to Iacocca. They had gone their separate ways for a while—Iacocca to Chrysler and Bidwell to Hertz. Iacocca had had the worst of it. At one point in 1980 Chrysler actually ran out of money, and Iacocca mounted a desperate, but unsuccessful, effort to sell the company to his old foes at Ford. When some Canadian banks balked at joining the bailout effort, R. S. "Steve" Miller, Jr., then Chrysler's treasurer, actually broke down and cried. The nadir came on June 23, 1980, when the company was preparing to convene a cohort of lenders and lawyers in New York to sign the closing papers for the bailout loan. Fire broke out in the building, and the flames raged for hours.[1] At 2 A.M., the Chrysler people had waded in through smoke and water to retrieve thousands of documents. They moved the papers to another building, spent all night sorting them out, and finally signed the closing the next day.

Chrysler made the most of its reprieve. By June 2, 1983, when Bidwell finally caved in to Iacocca's entreaties and joined the company, it was on the cusp of recovery. In fact, on August 12, just two months after Bidwell came aboard, Chrysler staged a celebration in New York. There, in the Jade Room of the Waldorf-Astoria Hotel, Iacocca made the comeback official by handing Edwin "Tony" Hurd, the vice chairman of U.S. Trust Company, a check for $813,487,500. Chrysler paid off the last of its government-guaranteed loans (they had totaled $1.2 billion in all) a full seven years early.

It was a remarkable achievement, considering how close Chrysler had been to collapse three years earlier, and a sweet personal triumph for Iacocca. The master showman wanted to make the most of the occasion with an eye-catching prop: a giant 4-by-8-foot replica of the check that he would hand to Hurd. As Chrysler's PR men planned the ceremony, they talked about placing Iacocca in front of the check "like Patton in front of the flag," just like in the movie with George C. Scott.

There was, however, one glitch. Chrysler wanted the historic check to be signed by Iacocca and his second-in-command, Gerald W. Greenwald. That would seem logical to most laymen, but bankers are different. Despite their rank within the company—or actually, because of it—Iacocca and Greenwald didn't write the checks that paid Chrysler's bills. Lower-level people handled that mundane chore. The signatures of Iacocca and Greenwald weren't on file with Manufacturers Hanover, Chrysler's bank. Manny Hanny would happily honor a check signed by Frederick Zuckerman and Joseph Arpin, the two finance executives who normally paid major bills, but a check signed by Iacocca and Greenwald wasn't worth its weight in sawdust. Zuckerman had to scramble to get Iacocca's and Greenwald's signatures approved so the 8-foot check wouldn't bounce.

"Well, this is the climax of the Chrysler Federal Loan Guarantee drama," a beaming Iacocca announced to the crowd of reporters, lawyers, bankers, and government officials as the ceremony began. "One more time, however, I'd like to say thanks, America, for lending us a hand, not to mention cosigning for a billion bucks, when we really needed it." Then he put in a plug for "our revolutionary new small wagon," soon to be dubbed the minivan, on display in the next room. Finally, after handing Hurd the check, Iacocca quipped: "I'll take a few brief questions and then we're going to celebrate. We're buying you champagne—American-made, of course."

It quickly became clear that Chrysler hadn't been premature in breaking out the bubbly. Just eight months later the company posted $705.8 million in profits for the first quarter of 1984. It was more money than Chrysler ever earned before in an entire year.

. . .

How COULD CHRYSLER have gone from flat broke to record profitability in less than four years? For one thing, it wasn't paying taxes. The huge losses that the company had racked up during its dark days could be carried forward to reduce taxable income, so Chrysler operated tax-free until early 1985. But more fundamental factors were at work.

The trying times of the early 1980s had caused the Big Three to pare costs to the bone. Between 1979 and 1983 Chrysler slashed its white-collar workforce almost in half, to 22,000 from 40,000. Blue collar workers suffered equally. The huge cuts pared the company's cost base dramatically. In 1979 Chrysler had to sell 2.4 million cars and trucks a year just to break even. By 1983 the break-even point was down to just 1.1 million vehicles.

While Iacocca was cutting costs, Americans were starting to buy cars again. The twin terrors of double-digit unemployment and interest rates had sent U.S. car and truck sales skidding to only 10.8 million vehicles in 1981 and 10.6 million in 1982. But the prolonged recession created a huge pent-up demand for new cars that was unleashed with added impetus from the Reagan tax cuts. Americans bought 14.5 million vehicles in 1984, 15.7 million in 1985, and an all-time record 16.3 million in 1986.

All the while, foreign competition was being held in check. In 1981 the Japanese government had agreed to "voluntary" limits on car exports to the United States—1.68 million vehicles a year at first. The quota was conceived of as a "temporary" measure to give Detroit time to shape up. But in 1985 the quota, while being raised to 2.3 million cars, remained in place. One by one, starting with Honda, the Japanese companies began building their own U.S. assembly plants to skirt the quota. At first, though, the Motor City's moguls were too busy ringing their cash registers to fret much.

In 1984 Chrysler, buoyed by the success of its K-car and the new minivan, ran every one of its assembly plants flat-out, on full overtime, all year long. The force of the cyclical rebound was like the tide rushing into the Bay of Fundy. It's the very nature of a business with high fixed costs.

Bringing a new car or truck to market requires an up-front investment of at least a billion dollars. The money pays the "product planners," who determine whether a vehicle will be a family sedan or a sporty coupe, the stylists who shape the car, and the engineers who design the fenders to fit the doors and the engine to mesh with the transmission. All these employees need salaries, benefits, offices, and equipment. Automakers shell out millions more to buy manufacturing tools and machinery, the factories to house them and the raw materials—ranging from steel to plastic to rubber to glass to computer chips—to feed them. And then, as the vehicle's debut nears, the advertising agencies and PR men shell out millions more to hype the new product.

All this happens before a single car is sold. Every new model, then, is a high-stakes gamble. If the car catches on, the payoff is enormous. But if there aren't enough buyers—because the model flops, the car market drops, or both—the losses can be staggering. Which is why the car business is no place for the faint of heart. Instead it attracts men who aren't prone to introspection or to second-guessing themselves. Their outward swagger may mask deep personal insecurities, but when it comes to business, at least, they aren't afraid to roll the dice. "If I had to sum up in one word the qualities that make a good manager," Lee Iacocca would write in his autobiography, "I'd say that it all comes down to decisiveness."[2]

LIDO ANTHONY IACOCCA was typical, in many ways, of the bright college boys who flocked to Detroit right after World War II, when the American automobile industry was becoming an engine of opportunity. The son of immigrant parents in Allentown, Pennsylvania, Iacocca got an engineering degree from Lehigh University and picked up a master's at Princeton before starting at Ford as a trainee in 1946. He promptly discovered he really hated engineering and wanted to get where the "action" was—and finagled his way into sales.

Iacocca made his mark running a Ford sales district in Eastern Pennsylvania. With the 1956 model Fords falling flat, he launched a program that let consumers buy a new car for 20 percent down and payments of $56 a month for three years. He called it "56 for '56," and sales in his district soared. So did Iacocca's career. In 1960, at age thirty-six, he was named vice president and general manager of the Ford division, the company's largest marketing arm. Four years later Iacocca oversaw the development of the Mustang, which landed him on the covers of *Time* and *Newsweek* in the very same week. And on December 10, 1970, Henry Ford II handed him the presidency of Ford.

That made him heir apparent, because Henry didn't have any possible successors from within the family. His two brothers weren't remotely qualified to run Ford, and his only son, Edsel Ford II, was in college at the time. So Iacocca seemed destined to become the first nonfamily chairman of Ford Motor when Henry eventually retired. But on June 13, 1978, just before 3 P.M., Henry Ford called Lee Iacocca into his office and told him, "Sometimes you just don't like somebody."[3]

Underlings of the two men had sensed the tension between them for years. Still, when it happened, Iacocca's firing shocked them. Ben Bidwell had spent the day in his office at Ford's North American Automotive Operations building, less than a mile south of company headquarters. After work he walked to the executive parking garage with Bill Bourke, Ford's executive vice president for North America. Bourke got to his car first, plucked a note that had been placed under the windshield wiper, and then started screaming: "HE FIRED HIM! HE FIRED HIM! I CAN'T BELIEVE IT! HE FIRED HIM!" Bidwell ran over to Bourke and grabbed the note. It was from Henry Ford II, and it said, simply: "Effective tomorrow, you report to Philip Caldwell."

At 10:45 that night, Bidwell got a call at home from Bill Bonds, the tough-talking anchorman for Detroit's *Channel 7 News*. Was it true, Bonds wanted to know, that Iacocca had been fired that day? Bidwell, still shaken, said he didn't really know. Then he said: "Look, something has happened. Please don't use my name, but something really big has happened." Fifteen minutes later, Bidwell turned on the eleven o'clock news to hear Bonds announce that Lee Iacocca had been fired.

It was the best thing that ever happened to Iacocca. If Henry Ford hadn't fired him, he never would have gone to Chrysler, which he regarded as a third-rate outfit that didn't pose a threat to anybody but itself. Iacocca arrived in November 1978 as president and second-in-command to Chairman John Riccardo. He quickly concluded Chrysler was even more poorly managed than he had thought.

GM and Ford built cars to fill dealer orders. If they didn't have enough orders, they would temporarily shut their factories. Chrysler, though, built cars without orders and put them in its "sales bank" so it would always have vehicles ready to ship. It was a gambling tactic that worked well in good times but spelled trouble when the market turned soft. Within months, as the United States plunged into recession, Chrysler found itself with thousands of unsold cars parked in vacant lots around Detroit.

The company needed drastic measures. In September 1979 a despairing Riccardo resigned. Iacocca took the helm and started taking action.

He closed the sales bank for good. He started firing vice presidents, thirty-three of them in just thirty-six months. And he went on television to pitch Chrysler's cars himself.

The commercials were a shot in the dark, really. Shortly after coming to Chrysler, Iacocca had lured away Ford's major advertising agency, Kenyon & Eckhardt. It was a way to thumb his nose at Henry, and also to get agency people he trusted and liked. Notable among them was Ron DeLuca, also a Pennsylvanian of Italian ancestry whose own birthday was just thirteen days after Iacocca's. DeLuca suggested that putting Iacocca on the air would help Chrysler's cause by putting somebody's personal reputation behind the company's products.

Iacocca wasn't wild about the idea. But in the fall of 1979, Chrysler was launching its new subcompacts, the Dodge Omni and its twin, the Plymouth Horizon. At the time Chrysler's credibility was nearly zero. The company's only credible asset was its new chairman from Ford, Lee Iacocca.

His first commercial, on October 22, 1979, was hardly a prizewinner. After an actor extolled the virtues of the new Omni/Horizon subcompacts ("more passenger space than Pinto or Chevette . . ."), the camera cut to Iacocca. "I'm not asking you to buy a car on faith," he intoned. "I'm asking you to compare." His manner was wooden, and his eyes were visibly darting to the teleprompter for reassurance. But sales of Omni and Horizon took off.

So Iacocca stayed on the air, even though the quality of his commercials was spotty at first. The worst was a late 1979 spot portraying Iacocca having a casual chat about Chrysler with his pal Frank Sinatra. "I've been concerned about, uh, the state of business in general in the United States; I'm a man of business myself . . ." Sinatra began, awkwardly and incongruously. Fortunately for Iacocca, Sinatra's opening lines made the singer look so silly that no one remembered his own dismal showing.

But there were high points as well. In one early commercial, Iacocca simply looked the camera in the eye and thanked America for bailing out his company. "The Congress of the United States has passed the Chrysler Loan Guarantee bill," he said. "The New Chrysler Corporation is in business to stay. The jobs of 600,000 workers have been saved. And with that act a special bond has been created with the American people. . . ." His earnest persona gave Chrysler a human face virtually unheard of for a large corporation. Ironically, only Ford, through Henry Ford II, came close. But Henry Ford wasn't an underdog, while Lee

Iacocca clearly was. Americans love underdogs. And Iacocca positioned his company as a scrappy fighter for survival against enormous odds—which indeed it was.

In a late 1981 commercial pitching Chrysler's new LeBaron, Iacocca said: "If you can find a better car, buy it." The line caught on, prompting Chrysler to use it in more commercials. All the while, Iacocca was becoming a familiar face to millions of Americans. This familiarity might have bred contempt if Chrysler had continued to founder, but quite the opposite was happening. On March 21, 1983, Iacocca appeared again on the cover of *Time* under the headline: "Detroit's Comeback Kid." A year later he published his autobiography. It was titled simply *Iacocca.*

The book, like the commercials, wasn't Iacocca's idea. Instead, Bantam Books approached him, figuring that the commercials and Chrysler's comeback had given Iacocca enough name recognition to sell a few copies. Chrysler's PR men were surprised that any publisher might ask their boss to do a book, and still more surprised that Iacocca agreed. Expectations for success were so modest that William Novak, Iacocca's ghostwriter, signed on for a mere $40,000.

But Iacocca's story was more than just a classic Horatio Alger tale. It was a delicious, titillating, dark-side-of-the-moon look at Ford's executive suite, the Ford family, and especially Henry Ford II himself. Iacocca vilified his nemesis as "a real bastard" and "that evil man." He portrayed Henry Ford as a racist, imperious, crude, and cowardly autocrat who fired people on a whim but rarely could bring himself to do the dirty work personally—even sending his PR man to fire Semon E. "Bunkie" Knudson, Iacocca's predecessor as president.

Ford executives officially shunned the book, saying, when asked, that they hadn't read it and didn't care to. Privately, of course, many did read it, or at least started to. One vice president tossed it aside when he got to the part about Ford's executive chef grinding up inch-thick strip steaks to make Henry Ford's hamburgers. He couldn't remember Henry or anybody else having hamburger in the Penthouse, the executive dining room atop Ford world headquarters.

The public, though, loved the book. *Iacocca* hit the best-seller list almost immediately, stayed there for eighty weeks, and sold 2 million copies in its first year alone. A month after it was published, *Parade* magazine erroneously reported that Iacocca was available to make free appearances at "birthday parties, benefits, and bar mitzvahs."[4] The floodgates were open. Letters to Iacocca started pouring into Chrysler's headquarters at the rate of 1,000 a week. He got 553 on one day alone. Chrysler's harried PR staffers first tried to cope by coming in on Saturdays to handle the boss's mail. But they were quickly overwhelmed, and hired a special crew of three people for that task alone.

Iacocca became America's first celebrity CEO. On April 1, 1985, six months after the book was published, *Time* put him on the cover again under the headline: "America Loves Listening to Lee." A few months later he made a cameo guest appearance on *Miami Vice*, portraying a park superintendent who helped the cops snare the bad guys. At Chrysler's assembly plant in the Detroit suburb of Sterling Heights, a worker painted a 20-foot-high "Spirit of '76" wall mural of a colonial fife and drum corps—with Iacocca as lead drummer. "Iacocca for President" buttons started popping up around the country. He never seriously considered running, but it was a delicious thought for a man who had suffered the humiliation of a public firing.

During 1985 and 1986, Iacocca couldn't even make routine business appearances without causing a stir. In February 1986, at the National Automobile Dealers Association's annual convention in New Orleans, Chrysler threw a lavish reception at the Hyatt Regency hotel for thousands of dealers, salesmen, and their spouses. When Iacocca made his entrance, the crowd surged toward him. "I'd rather kiss you than shake your hand," screeched one woman, pressing close to his face as Iacocca instinctively recoiled. People pressed in all around, and cameras flashed in his face like strobe lights on a dance floor. Iacocca was getting so rattled and disoriented that at one point, he introduced himself to one of his own bodyguards. "Hi, nice to meet you," he said, grabbing the man's hand as if he were a guest.

At that point, the bodyguards hustled him out of the room, so he and the crowd could calm down. For all his podium poise and television presence, Iacocca personally was shy, insecure, and deathly afraid of crowds. Before every major speech or appearance he suffered, improbably, from stage fright. Often he would snap at his speechwriters, fling their texts back in their faces, and pace the floor of his office or hotel room like a first-time father outside a hospital delivery room. He wasn't angry, just nervous.

Yet it was typical of this man of contradictions that he loved the limelight. When others threatened to steal it from him, he could get plenty angry. Even if that man was the leader of the Free World.

Iacocca, at President Reagan's request, was head of a national commission to restore the Statue of Liberty and Ellis Island in New York harbor. Iacocca's immigrant roots and public appeal had made him the perfect choice for the job, and he confirmed that by raising an astounding $277 million between 1982 and 1986. By the summer of 1986 the statue's restoration was complete, and the commission was planning a week-long Independence Day gala to celebrate.

Chrysler was planning a celebration of its own. To reward dealers for sticking with the company during its dark days, the company planned a series of lavish parties starting in France and proceeding back across the Atlantic. One third of the dealers would be feted at Louis XIV's palace in Versailles. The next third would board the QE2 in France—Chrysler had booked the entire ship—and sail to Bermuda. The final group would board the QE2 in Bermuda and sail into New York harbor for the Statue of Liberty festivities.

Iacocca took the cruise from France to Bermuda. Then he disembarked with Ben Bidwell and other aides, and flew ahead to New York for a week of nonstop appearances. He was the star of the show, slated to introduce President Reagan at the statue's unveiling on the night of July 3, and at the majestic parade of Tall Ships up New York harbor the next day.

The speculation that Iacocca would run for president as a Democrat in 1988, however, made the White House queasy about his starring role. And Donald Regan, President Reagan's chief of staff, detested Iacocca. Once, in an argument during the loan-guarantee days, Iacocca had called Regan a cocksucker.

So when Iacocca arrived in New York, he was told the White House didn't want him to introduce the President for the Tall Ships ceremony. Instead, that honor would go to "Bus" Mosbacher, a Republican heavyweight and president of the New York Yacht Club, which had helped to organize the parade of ships.

Iacocca went ballistic. Bus Mosbacher, he shouted, never could have raised $277 million. Iacocca went on: He had worked hard to raise the money. He had dedicated his efforts to his immigrant parents. And he wasn't about to be shoved aside. "No fucking way will Mosbacher introduce the President," Iacocca screamed. "Bidwell, you get it handled."

At that point, powerful men started acting like petulant boys. Bidwell told David Wolper, the man in charge of the festivities, that Iacocca wouldn't stand down. A few minutes later, the phone in Bidwell's hotel room rang. The caller, from the White House protocol office, explained that the President really wanted Mosbacher. Bidwell and the protocol man went round and round. Then Bidwell pointedly explained that Iacocca chaired the commission that controlled the ceremonies and the television broadcasts, and that Chrysler was a major sponsor of the events.

"Are you saying, Mr. Bidwell," the White House man thundered into the telephone, "that Lee Iacocca will not accede to the wishes of the President of the United States?"

"That's exactly what I'm saying," Bidwell snapped back. "And if the President doesn't accede to Mr. Iacocca, when the parade of ships begins, the television screens will go blank!"

A half hour later the White House called back, wanting to know whether Iacocca would reconsider. No way, Bidwell replied. Finally, Reagan's men hit on a compromise. Iacocca would introduce Reagan, who would make his remarks and, in turn, introduce Mosbacher to say a few words.

Iacocca was flying as high as Icarus. The man who had been ignominiously fired by Henry Ford II just eight years earlier had become America's folk hero. And become powerful enough to dictate terms to the President of the United States.

"I'D BE VERY SURPRISED if there are any dramatic changes."

That's what Roger B. Smith said when his election as the tenth chairman of General Motors was announced in September 1980. In the annals of forecasts, few, if any, utterances have flown so ludicrously off mark.

Not that it was hard to believe at the time. Anyone outside GM who was looking for a bold, forward-thinking executive would have passed by Roger Smith without a second glance. He was, like many others in GM's elite, a son of the Midwest, born July 12, 1925, in Columbus, Ohio. His father, E. Quimby Smith, had founded a bank in Columbus and was its president when the Depression swept it away. Undaunted, Quimby Smith moved his family to Detroit, where he got a job as controller of the Bundy Tubing Company. Thus, Roger Smith and his three siblings grew up in comfortable middle-class circumstances.

As a teenager, Smith worked a summer in a car factory, but it was merely a way-stop on the road to a professional career. Smith entered the University of Michigan in 1942, a young freshman at seventeen years old, with reddish hair, pasty pale skin, short stature, and a high-pitched voice that made him seem even younger. Among his professors was William A. Paton, who had taught accounting to three men who would precede Smith as chairman of GM.

Two years later, he joined the Navy, riding out the latter months of World War II at the U.S. Naval Research labs in Washington, D.C., and then aboard a cruiser in the South Pacific. By 1946, he was back at the University of Michigan. Three years later, he had earned a bachelor's degree in business administration and an MBA. On the advice of his father, Smith shelved a dream of working in California's burgeoning aerospace industry, and instead signed on at GM as a general accounting clerk in Detroit.

For the next twenty-one years, Smith ground his way up the pyramid in GM's finance staff. He was a consummate workaholic. One day, he returned home to find blood on the seat of his car. He asked his wife, Barbara, what had happened, and learned only then that one of his children had taken a tumble and been rushed to the hospital for stitches.

Smith's penchant for long hours and his waspish manner soured many of his underlings. One would later recall being shooed away from the copy machine in GM's New York office as Smith stormed into the room barking, "Where are my copies? I want them right now!" Smith would work his people on nights and weekends to meet deadlines for presentations to GM's directors, and offer not so much as a thank-you in return.

But Smith's superiors appreciated his tenacity and financial skill. In 1970, Smith won a promotion to treasurer of the corporation, and stepped aboard the express train for the top. He began to whip through high-level posts: vice president of finance in 1971; group executive in charge of nonautomotive operations in 1972; executive vice president for finance and public relations and member of the board of directors in 1974. By then, his eventual election as chairman was a foregone conclusion.

As Smith took the reins at GM on January 1, 1981, he appeared to be just one more in the line of anonymous bureaucrats who had risen to power at GM because of an ability to balance books. Outgoing Chairman Thomas A. Murphy was an avuncular and deeply religious man who attended Mass every morning with his wife, Sis. Smith lacked Murphy's dignified yet grandfatherly personal bearing, but otherwise he seemed cut from the same GM-blue cloth.

Appearances, however, were deceiving.

Smith was, in fact, a highly unconventional thinker by GM standards.

As he had moved closer to the top, Smith had impressed members of the GM board by talking about GM not in terms of the next quarter, but the next century. Smith was fascinated by technology. Long before it was fashionable, he purchased a home computer. He believed GM was moving far too slowly to take advantage of the technological explosion in computers, communications, and manufacturing automation.

Smith had no intention of maintaining the status quo. He wanted to play John F. Kennedy to Murphy's Eisenhower. Just as the youthful Kennedy's election as President promised to "get the country moving again," Smith's accession as GM's chairman held the potential for a new era of progress. Smith was fifty-five years old, young for his office. If his health stood up, Smith would be GM's longest-serving chairman since Alfred P. Sloan, Jr., the man who had created the modern GM in the 1930s and ruled it as chairman for nineteen years. Smith had a special interest in Sloan. During the early 1960s, he had worked with a team of GM aides who helped prepare the great man's landmark memoir, My Years at General Motors. Now, Smith had an opportunity to out-Sloan Sloan.

SMITH DIDN'T GET OFF to a roaring start. In 1980, the combination of recession and Japanese competition that was bludgeoning Ford and Chrysler brought GM its first full-year loss since the 1920s. Its reputation was under siege after a series of blunders, including outfitting Oldsmobiles with Chevrolet engines, and then peddling defect-ridden diesel engines as an answer to the gas crisis. GM earned just $333.1 million in 1981, hardly sufficient considering its $9.7 billion in capital spending that year. Smith ordered massive layoffs and cut white-collar benefits. As the country headed into 1982 with no economic upturn in sight, Smith canceled planned cost-of-living raises for white-collar workers, and declared that he too would share in the sacrifice—by giving up $135 a month out of his $475,000-a-year salary. The anemic gesture was greeted with derisive hoots from UAW officials and GM salaried employees alike.

Smith fared little better when he tried to wangle concessions from the union. In early 1982, UAW president Douglas Fraser struck a deal with Ford under which the union gave up two weeks of vacation and some scheduled pay increases in return for additional layoff benefits. Within weeks, GM got a similar contract from its workers.

But on the very day in April 1982 that GM and the UAW signed the concessionary contract, GM released its proxy statement. That document disclosed a plan to make it easier for GM executives to earn bonuses. Under GM's prior plan, the company would have had to earn well over $1 billion to trigger bonus payments. The new threshold was a flat $1 billion, and a new formula produced bigger bonuses as profits rose from there.

The appearance, of course, was that Smith had been conniving to sweeten the bonus formula for himself and GM's executive corps, even as he pressured the UAW to accept reductions in factory workers' wages. If Smith had set out deliberately to sabotage GM's labor relations, he couldn't have done a better job. Fraser was furious, calling the bonus plan "an absolute outrage." In less than a week, Smith was forced to backtrack, vowing to stick with the old bonus plan for the life of the new UAW pact. But the damage was done.

Smith's relations with shareholders were little better. After enduring brickbats from hecklers and professional gadflies during his first annual meeting as chairman, Smith proposed dividing the 1982 annual meeting at the venerable Fisher Building opposite GM's Detroit headquarters into two parts. The morning session, which he would attend, was to last just an hour with little time for questions. The afternoon session would be moved to GM's Technical Center in suburban Warren, some fifteen miles away. It would be open to questions, but Smith and the directors wouldn't attend. But once again a furor erupted over Smith's plans, forcing the chairman to back down. In all, it was a rough first eighteen months on the job.

But by the first quarter of 1983, demand rebounded enough for GM to boost production by 22 percent. Net income for the quarter soared to $653.1 million—more than half of what GM had earned in all of 1982. GM's top executives cheered the news when it was announced during their triennial conference-cum-party at the Greenbrier resort in White Sulphur Springs, West Virginia. During that same meeting, Smith laid out his vision in a "mission statement" that talked in grand terms of GM's determination to "promote maximum participation" by employees. It also declared that GM "will aggressively seek new opportunities to utilize our resources in business ventures that match our skills and capabilities."

The 1983 mission statement was a prelude to the three great thrusts of Smith's strategy: reorganization, diversification, and "reindustrialization," or automation. GM was celebrating its seventy-fifth anniversary in 1983, and as part of the publicity surrounding the event, Smith issued an essay written from the vantage point of the year 2008—GM's 100th birthday. He wrote of a revolutionary "no-year" car, developed from a "clean sheet of paper" approach to the automobile, that had been a smash hit when launched into a record-setting boom in North American vehicle sales. He wrote of factories that worked "virtually unattended through the night after the second shift has gone home and turned out most of the lights." GM workers would be aided by a "tenfold increase in computer power." And he wrote of "organizational restructuring" that pushed decisions "even lower in the organization."

No one realized it then, but Smith had just tipped his hand to almost everything he was about to do in a two-year frenzy of activity and change. It began in January 1984, with the reorganization of GM's sprawling North American business.

That GM's North American auto operations had failed to respond effectively to Japanese competition was clear to Smith. It was also clear to GM's new president, F. James McDonald. As the resident manufacturing expert in GM's executive suite, McDonald was convinced GM couldn't match Japanese quality, or close the yawning cost advantage enjoyed by Toyota and Honda, without fundamental restructuring. McDonald, was a Saginaw, Michigan, boy-made-good who had been plucked from the obscurity of GM's foundry operations. Compact, balding, and deliberate in manner, McDonald looked and acted every inch the no-nonsense factory boss he was. He was willing to contemplate drastic steps to achieve his goals.

McDonald commandeered the now-empty office on the 14th floor of GM headquarters that he had occupied as executive vice president, and lined the walls with Velcro. There, he began arranging and rearranging boxes that represented hundreds of thousands of people. He was groping for a formula to break down the barriers that separated GM's manufacturing, design, and marketing duchies. Those barriers were high.

Executives at the marketing divisions, for instance, often wanted to produce low-volume variations of a car to hit a certain market niche. But GM's Assembly Division—endowed with a separate budget and separate management—had a rule against building models that would account for less than 5 percent of a car line's total sales. That was good for the manufacturing budget; it wasn't always best for marketing.

Meanwhile, Fisher Body, the big car-engineering operation, had its own rules and procedures that often conflicted with those of the assemblers and the marketers. Ask one of its engineers where he worked and he would say, "Fisher Body," never GM.

But dismantling the old system was no simple task. Each box on McDonald's wall represented an entrenched center of power guaranteed to battle any assault on its prerogatives. As he got deeper into it, McDonald called for help. In 1983, he and Smith signed up the consulting firm of McKinsey & Company. Lower-level managers interviewed by the McKinseyites poured out their frustrations, bemoaning the lack of cooperation among the feuding fiefdoms. The study galvanized Smith and McDonald to action.

In January 1984, they unveiled their plan. In a single blow, Fisher Body and GM Assembly Division were dynamited out of existence. Their pieces were reassembled into hydra-headed entities known as Chevrolet–Pontiac–Canada, or CPC for short, and Buick–Oldsmobile–Cadillac, or BOC.

CPC, Smith said, would focus on small cars. BOC would build large cars. A third group, Truck and Bus, would design and engineer trucks. All three groups would contain engineering, manufacturing, and marketing combined. The idea, eminently sensible on paper, was that making all three functions in each group accountable to one person, the group vice president, would lead to better communication and cooperation among functions, faster product development, and improved quality. No longer could the GM Assembly Division blame quality glitches on shoddy engineering by Fisher Body, or vice versa. "There will be a big change in our systems, a big change in our management philosophy," Smith said. From now on, he declared, decisions will be made by "the guy who is closest to the marketplace."

The response among GM's middle managers ranged from skepticism to outright panic. Quite deliberately, Smith had blown apart the comfortable system that had succored generations of GM bureaucrats. Now, many were wondering whether they still had jobs. The answer, in the case of virtually all of GM's higher-level managers, was yes. That wouldn't be true for many in the lower ranks. And as the new structure unfolded, it became clear that it wasn't as logical as Smith had described. From the start, and ever after, BOC built many of Chevrolet's small cars, while CPC built several of the highest-volume Buick and Oldsmobile models.

The dust hadn't settled from the reorganization bomb blast when Smith lit off another. In June 1984, GM announced that it would buy Electronic Data Systems Corporation of Dallas for $2.55 billion. It was a stunning power play, the first major diversification outside motor vehicles in GM's history. In a single stroke, GM had become one of the world's major data-processing companies. Smith also placed all of GM's computers and computer technicians under EDS's founder—a glib, charismatic billionaire named H. Ross Perot.

To finance the deal, Smith boldly created a new class of GM common stock, tied to the profits from the new subsidiary. Smith did this, in part, to assuage Perot, who wanted EDS to maintain a separate identity in the market. The practical effect, however, was that investors, not GM, put up much of the money for GM's purchase of EDS. Perot took a seat on GM's board, and quickly became a cheerful adjunct to Smith's crusade for change.

With the EDS deal and the alliance with Perot, Smith emerged from anonymity with a bang. The bean counter suddenly became Champion of Industrial America, pouring money and creative firepower into a mighty counterattack against Japan. On April 21, 1985, *The New York Times Magazine* hailed him on its cover as "The Innovator" and gushed over the "mind-boggling" changes he was working upon GM.[5] For the first time in years, people outside the narrow corridors of power in Detroit, Wall Street, and Washington could recognize the name of the chairman of General Motors.

The article's awe-struck tone seemed fully justified. In January 1985, Smith had created a furor by announcing GM's secret Saturn project would become a full-fledged car-making enterprise, and prove that an American company could "leap-frog" Japanese small cars. Saturn would have its own massive high-tech factory and its own dealerships. Governors from seven states went on the *Phil Donahue Show* to make their case to land the factory. The "Saturnalia" madness, as the press dubbed it, didn't subside until July, when GM declared the tiny community of Spring Hill, Tennessee, the winner.

Meanwhile, Smith was teasing Wall Street about a "lulu" of an acquisition tucked up his sleeve. In early 1985, he coyly confirmed an acquisition strategy code-named "Star Trek." Speculation soon focused on Hughes Aircraft Company, the defense electronics giant founded by reclusive billionaire Howard Hughes, as his target. Hughes Aircraft had, upon Hughes's death, become the property of the Howard Hughes Medi-

cal Institute. The institute, devoted to medical research, needed to un-
load the company, both for tax reasons, and to create an endowment
with which to finance its activities.

Smith indeed had decided he wanted Hughes. He saw in the company's 20,000 scientists a brain trust that could propel his dreams of
making GM a "computer integrated industrial enterprise." Moreover,
weapons making was good business, or so it seemed because of the
Reagan Administration's defense buildup. But Smith faced an uphill
battle. The institute had decreed that Hughes Aircraft would be sold to
the highest bidder in a one-bid auction. GM faced two tenacious rivals:
Ford and Boeing Company, the huge aircraft maker.

Smith, though, devised an ingenious strategy. With GM's investment
bankers from Morgan Stanley, he prepared a bid so complex that almost
no one could accurately assess its value. Put simply, GM offered the
Medical Institute about $2.7 billion in cash, and 50 million shares of yet
another new class of GM common stock dubbed GMH. GM declared
these shares would be worth $30 apiece as of December 31, 1989, or
about $3 billion. Otherwise, GM would make up the difference to the
institute.

The real value of GMH stock, however, would depend on the willingness of investors to buy it after GM's price prop expired. The package
was so intricate that the Medical Institute's board had to call GM's
bankers in to explain it. During those meetings, as Smith saw it, the
Morgan Stanley men would unearth valuable clues about the opposing
bids.

It was the key to the whole auction. Ford, the Morgan Stanley men
learned, had weighed in with a huge bid, over $4 billion. So confident
was Ford of victory that, as decision day neared in June 1985, the company dispatched a PR man to Los Angeles to hire a crew of painters.
The minute Ford learned it had won, the paint crew would march into
Hughes's headquarters, adjacent to LA International airport, and paint
Ford's blue oval logo on the roof. After the public announcement, Ford
would fly business reporters to Los Angeles on a company plane—and
swoop low over the Hughes building with the freshly painted Ford oval
adorning the roof.

But the Morgan Stanley bankers set about spoiling Ford's party. As
Smith had envisioned, in the process of "clarifying" GM's bid, they
could adjust its value. By the end, Morgan Stanley had persuaded the
Hughes people to value GM's bid at more than $5 billion. GM won, and

a bushwhacked Ford hastily disbanded the paint crew and recalled its PR man to Detroit.

Smith was ebullient. On June 5, 1985, he called a triumphant press conference in New York. "This is a superhistoric day for us," Smith crowed. "Lulu is home now."[6]

ACTUALLY, THE REAL "LULU" at GM had been right under everyone's nose all along. None of Smith's acquisitions could match the size, scope, and mind-bending expense of his factory modernization program. Between 1980 and 1985, GM spent a staggering $42 billion on new factories, tools, equipment, and products.

GM poured money into three huge new "megafactories," and into gutting and retooling several older facilities. One was an aging complex of factories in Flint, Michigan. In January 1983, GM announced it would build in Flint a superautomated facsimile of Toyota Motor Corporation's Toyota City complex. Dubbed Buick City, it was to be a showcase for GM's new generation of automated assembly technology. GM declared it would use a "sociotechnical systems approach" to marry people and robots in perfect harmony.

Smith's fascination with robots knew few bounds. He had gushed to The New York Times Magazine about the time he saw a robot arm pick up an egg without crushing it. The reality was that Buick City's robots were busily smashing the windshields they were supposed to install. But that didn't dent Smith's enthusiasm. When his staff proposed a factory in Saginaw, Michigan, that would build axles entirely with robots—no people on the shop floor at all—Smith approved the plan even though the axles would cost more than those assembled by UAW hands in an older plant. GM dubbed the so-called lights-out Saginaw plant the Factory of the Future.

Smith's ultimate high-tech bauble, though, was ten minutes east of GM's headquarters in the Polish enclave of Hamtramck. Much of Hamtramck (pronounced ham-TRAM-ick) had been decimated in the 1970s as its white inhabitants fled after Detroit's 1967 riots. When Smith and Detroit Mayor Coleman A. Young allied to bulldoze in one particularly blighted area for a car factory, there was an outcry from the remaining inhabitants. But the neighborhood lost in the scramble for the 6,000 jobs that Smith and Young vowed to create. In the end, all that survived was the district's nickname, Poletown. That was the name Detroiters used for the factory that GM officially called the Detroit–Hamtramck Assembly Center.

Poletown was Roger Smith's thundering reply to the negativists wringing their hands over the decline of American industry. Here, GM would show the world its mastery. Poletown's cars would be a new generation of smaller, more efficient, front-wheel-drive luxury cars—Cadillac Sevilles, Buick Rivieras, and Oldsmobile Toronados. They would be assembled using state-of-the-art technology in a superefficient, sparkling clean factory. Parts would arrive "just in time," and be toted by robot-guided carriers known as AGV's (automated guided vehicles) to the right spot on the line. Engines would be ferried to the car bodies by AGV's, too. Robot arms would do all the painting, and apply all the caulk and sealer to the bodies so they would be perfect every time. Massive welding machines called robo-gates would stitch together car bodies in seconds. Millions of dollars worth of computers would test each car's electrical system for malfunctions. Every day at Hamtramck would be a technological ballet that produced top-quality cars in perfectly executed, tightly timed steps.

Hamtramck plant officials were proud of their facility, and thus were delighted in June 1985 when Susumu Uchikawa, the production expert from Toyota via Nummi, came to visit. Hamtramck's operators had heard plenty about Nummi. They had even adapted some Nummi-style methods for cutting down inventory and involving workers in decisions. But Nummi, the GM managers knew, used old machinery and old technology. It was primitive compared to Poletown.

Uchikawa, however, formed a rather different view. As he walked through GM's showcase, Uchikawa watched the workers fumbling with the AGV's and the other whiz-bang technology. He puzzled over the enormous expenditures for robots and computerized inspection systems that the workers clearly didn't understand. He saw that members of Hamtramck's work teams were spread out across 200 feet of assembly line —and thus couldn't easily talk to each other.

Uchikawa had come to Hamtramck with Paul Thompson, who worked for him at Nummi. At the end of the walk-through, Thompson asked, "Uchikawa-san, what do you think?"

"They have many problems," the Toyota man replied, "that they have not thought of yet."

. . .

DURING ITS DARK DAYS of the early eighties, Chrysler had run out of cash. But after earning $2.38 billion in 1984 and $1.64 billion in 1985, Lee Iacocca and his underlings had so much cash that they didn't know what to do with it all. They needed a plan.

One choice would have been to build new factories and develop new models to expand Chrysler's limited lineup of cars. Every Chrysler product from the LeBaron GTS "touring sedan" to the Dodge 600 to the minivan was derived from the compact K-car, using the same chassis and the same four-cylinder engine. That was great in the early 1980s, when the price and availability of gasoline were dominant issues with car buyers. But by 1985 gasoline was cheap and plentiful again, and Americans wanted bigger cars with bigger engines. Chrysler didn't have them.

But Iacocca saw no reason that the K platform, or chassis, couldn't be adapted to Americans' evolving tastes. Besides, he figured, if a company was going to put all its eggs in one basket, the car business wasn't it. The early 1980s had shown how vulnerable the industry was to recession and high interest rates. Also, the quota on Japanese imports had been eased, and just about every Japanese car company was planning its own assembly plant in the United States. Everybody in the industry was worried about "looming overcapacity," the prospect of too many factories building too many cars for too few buyers. Chrysler had an option to buy a Western Electric factory in Indianapolis and convert it into an assembly plant. But in March 1985 Iacocca let the option lapse. He had other uses for Chrysler's money.

The first was to reward shareholders. In February 1984, Chrysler resumed quarterly cash dividends, at the rate of 15 cents a share, for the first time since 1979. Chrysler hiked the dividend in June and then raised it again in September—to 25 cents a share. Iacocca also earmarked money for Chrysler to buy shares of its own stock. With fewer shares on the market, those that remained in the hands of stockholders were sure to increase in value. In February 1986, when Chrysler announced a three-for-two stock split, the stock price hit $48⅛ a share. Chrysler's shares had soared 1,500 percent since their nadir of $3 back in 1980. "People are making a lot of money on Chrysler stock," sniped a jealous GM executive, "as the company rebounds from disaster to mediocrity."

Iacocca had other plans, too. If Roger Smith could diversify GM, why couldn't he diversify Chrysler? In June 1985, he shelled out $636 million to buy Gulfstream Aerospace Corporation, a maker of executive business jets. The Japanese weren't in the airplane business, at least not yet, and Gulfstream happened to be owned by one of Iacocca's good friends, Allen E. Paulson. The deal paled beside GM's $5.1 billion purchase of Hughes Aircraft two weeks earlier, but it would do nicely for a company of Chrysler's size.

A few months later Iacocca spent another $400 million to buy FinanceAmerica, a subsidiary of Bank of America that lent consumers money to buy anything from washing machines to vacations. Chrysler blended its new catch into Chrysler Financial, the subsidiary that financed cars for both dealers and consumers. Almost overnight, Chrysler Financial became a diversified company, less vulnerable to the cyclical swings in the auto industry. More acquisitions to broaden Chrysler Financial's base of business followed.

Suddenly, like GM, Chrysler wasn't "just" a car company anymore. It was becoming more of a conglomerate, and it needed a new structure to reflect that. On November 7, 1985, Iacocca unveiled it. Henceforth, Chrysler Corporation would become a holding company, with automobiles just one of its several businesses. Its subsidiaries would be Chrysler Motors (cars), Chrysler Aerospace (Gulfstream), Chrysler Financial (lending to consumers and business), and Chrysler Technologies. Iacocca dubbed the latter "the empty box," because he hadn't yet purchased anything to fill it. But he said he would immediately start searching for a high-tech acquisition in the $1 billion range.

While diversifying his company, Iacocca began a program of personal diversification as well. He started writing a syndicated newspaper column. Actually, the column was ghost-written by Mike Morrison, his favorite Chrysler speechwriter. Morrison had achieved the remarkable feat of keeping his job after Iacocca had fired half a dozen other speechwriters between 1982 and 1984.

Iacocca also bought an estate in Italy. It wasn't in the impoverished province of Campania, near Naples, from which his father, Nicola, had emigrated in 1902 at the age of twelve. Instead, Iacocca purchased his villa in the refined Tuscan countryside in north-central Italy near Siena. There he went into the wine business, having grapes grown on the estate pressed into a medium-dry red that he called Villa Nicola, after his father. The label bore a drawing of the Iacocca villa, along with Iacocca's signature, and the corks had "Lee Iacocca" printed on them in block letters to make convenient souvenirs. Chrysler served Villa Nicola, which sold in the United States for about $9 a bottle, at board of directors' dinners and other official functions. The irony, of course, was that Iacocca, whose anti-Japanese fulminations had made him America's greatest import basher, had become an importer himself.

In April 1986, three months before the Statue of Liberty unveiling, Iacocca got married again. His first wife, Mary, had succumbed to diabetes in the spring of 1983, just months before her husband's triumphant early repayment of Chrysler's government-guaranteed loans. And now, three years later, at age sixty-one, he married thirty-five-year-old Peggy Johnson. Iacocca's two daughters—especially Kathi, the eldest—weren't pleased to have Peggy as their stepmother.

The newlyweds, though, brushed this off, and started looking for a new home. Peggy didn't feel comfortable living in the same Bloomfield Hills house that Lee and Mary had called home. She started scouting across town in Grosse Pointe Farms, home to the Ford family. She caused a minor stir by looking at a house once owned by Henry Ford II and just down the block from where he lived at the time.

The Iacoccas, however, ended up not buying a new home, which was just as well. In January 1987, after just eight and a half months of marriage, Iacocca filed for divorce. Publicly, he refused to discuss the matter, although his friends whispered to reporters that Peggy had refused to move to Detroit and insisted on staying in New York. Peggy wasn't saying anything, either. Not until five years later would she go on Geraldo Rivera's television talk show to complain about Lee's decision to have a vasectomy against her wishes, and his insistence on keeping their Bloomfield Hills bedroom looking the way it had when Mary died.[7]

Detroit's newspapers, though, attacked the story like a Hollywood scandal sheet. The Detroit News dispatched a reporter to Miami to interview one of Peggy's former boyfriends. The Free Press countered with an exclusive interview with Peggy's lawyer, under the page-1 banner headline: "Peggy Wants Lee Back—Lawyer Says Iacocca's Divorce Suit Shocked His Wife." The News then sent a team of reporters to New York to stake out Peggy's apartment. Mrs. Iacocca, the paper breathlessly reported, "hasn't been spotted since news of the divorce suit became public. Nor has she been to her favorite nearby Greek restaurant, Enoteca Iperbole, or to Momotaro, her favorite hair salon."[8]

Soon, however, Detroiters tired of the daily divorce diary, and the story faded from the headlines. While the breakup was painful and embarrassing for Iacocca, in the end it barely dented his public image.

Iacocca, like Ronald Reagan, was a Teflon man. Among businessmen he was in a class by himself, writing his own rules, and tackling head-on the sort of potential obstacles that would send other executives ducking for cover.

In April 1987, four months after the divorce filing, Chrysler disclosed that Iacocca had been paid a whopping $20.6 million for the previous year. Some of the money was a payback, because Iacocca had worked for just $1 a year in 1980 to set the tone for sacrifice that had saved Chrysler. Still, $20.6 million was breathtaking, even by the standards of the "greed is good" 1980s. Worse yet, three years earlier Iacocca had publicly criticized GM and Ford for "overpaying" their CEOs salaries less than one tenth that amount. "You reach a point of asking how high is up," Iacocca had sniped. "We as an industry had better start acting responsibly."[9]

But now Iacocca was unabashed about his own haul. "That's the American way," he told reporters. "If little kids don't aspire to make money like I did, what the hell good is this country? You gotta give 'em a role model, right?"[10] The public loved it.

Two months later, a real crisis struck. Chrysler was indicted by a federal grand jury in St. Louis for disconnecting the odometers on cars driven by its executives, and then selling the cars to the public as new. Paying big bonuses to the boss was one thing, but defrauding the public quite another. Almost as bad as the federal case was the public ridicule. "Hey, Fred! Did you buy a new car?" asked a character in a cartoon that ran in the Detroit *News*. "I'm not sure," replied the other character, standing next to his car. "It's a Chrysler."[11]

With criminal charges pending, the advice Iacocca got from his lawyers was clear and unequivocal: Say nothing. Anything Iacocca said, the lawyers feared, might later be used in court against Chrysler. Iacocca heard the advice, but then brushed it aside. The real question, he sensed, was how Chrysler would fare in the court of public opinion, not in the court of law. A week after the indictment, he called a press conference. "Did we screw up? You bet we did," he declared in his best let's-talk-straight mode. "I'm damned sorry it happened, and you can bet it won't happen again. That's a promise." Chrysler's actions, he confessed, "went beyond dumb and reached all the way out to stupid."[12]

No other CEO in America would have dared say those things. Chrysler's lawyers were aghast, but the public cheered. Instead of mealy-mouthing, Iacocca had 'fessed up and promised to compensate buyers who had been cheated. Within days the issue was defused.

•   •   •

IACOCCA WASN'T CHRYSLER'S only colorful character. His supporting cast
was filled with strong personalities and enormous egos. The strongest,
physically and otherwise, was Richard E. Dauch.

Dick Dauch grew up milking cows on a farm in northern Ohio, where
his athletic prowess earned him a football scholarship to Purdue University in Indiana. In 1960, playing linebacker and fullback, he was captain
and most valuable player of Purdue's freshman squad. But then knee
injuries took their toll. Dauch was able to earn two varsity letters, but
he needed a profession other than football. He got his management
degree in 1964, spent twelve years at General Motors, and then jumped
to Volkswagen in 1976 to help start the company's factory in Pennsylvania, the first foreign assembly plant on U.S. soil. In 1980 Iacocca
brought him to Chrysler as vice president for manufacturing.

With his craggy good looks, football-player physique, and locker-room
manner, Dauch was just the man to whip Chrysler's ailing factories into
shape. He attacked the job like a Purdue fullback hitting the Ohio State
line. "TMT, TME," he would shout at his troops, meaning: "Tell me
truth, tell me early." He sat in meetings squeezing a wrist-grip exerciser,
prompting finance staffers to mimic him by squeezing collapsible paper
clips. His presentations to Chrysler's directors were veritable halftime
talks that prompted standing ovations in the boardroom.

But Dauch terrorized as well as inspired. His staff meetings were
known as huddles, and staff members were called killer gophers. Their
job was to run Dauch's errands, but they were powerful and mean enough
to kill careers. New killer gophers had to endure a session in which
Dauch peppered them with questions: What's the launch date for the
LH project? When do we get P-zero prototypes of the C-bodies? Recite
the key dates on the P-car launch curve. Then Dauch would tell the
rattled newcomer: "Now you know what you don't know. Go find out."

Dauch's language was as crude as his methods. Once he commandeered an executive conference room to chew out his staff, deriding the
men as "cocksuckers, mother-fuckers and just a bunch of swinging
dicks." His voice thundered into the next-door office of Steve Miller,
the finance vice president and genteel scion of a wealthy Oregon family,
whose sister was visiting him that day. The next day Miller had warning
signs posted in the conference room: "Caution! Conversations in This
Room May Be Overheard."

Frederick Zuckerman, Chrysler's treasurer under Miller, was a character of a different sort. He had a fetish for grocery-store coupons. Each Friday night, when he flew from Detroit back to his home in New York, Zuckerman carried with him a bag of doggie biscuits. A puzzled aide finally asked why he didn't just buy his pet's biscuits in New York, and Zuckerman explained: "They don't allow double coupons in New York."

Freddy, as colleagues called him, also was a ladies' man who boasted that, between marriages, he "never dated anybody over thirty." Chrysler's drivers loved to tell how Zuckerman's toupee once slipped off while he was making out in the back seat of a company limousine in New York.

Then there was Bob Lutz. A Swiss-born, former Marine Corps fighter pilot fond of fast cars and big cigars, Lutz was an executive vice president of Ford and member of the board of directors when he fell from favor in 1986. So at age fifty-four, with his huge ambition and granite-jawed good looks both intact, he accepted Iacocca's invitation to defect to Chrysler.

Within a year of his arrival, Chrysler purchased Lamborghini. And Lutz, a rebellious sort who eschewed Bloomfield Hills to live among the intellectuals out in Ann Arbor, started driving a Lamborghini Countach to and from work. He would blast home along Interstate 94 at 140 miles an hour, grinning as he glanced in the rearview mirror to see headlights evaporating like fireflies behind him. "You only risk getting caught between seventy-five and ninety-five miles an hour," Lutz would brag. "After that, you're safe."

Chrysler did have some tamer sorts—notably Jerry Greenwald, Iacocca's No. 2. A dapper man with suave good looks, Greenwald was one of the few Jews to make it big at one of the Big Three. He grew up near St. Louis, the son of a poultry distributor, became an Eagle scout, and got a scholarship to Princeton. Then he joined Ford's finance staff, earning a reputation as a details man and a boss pleaser.

In the late 1970s, when Greenwald was running Ford of Venezuela, he got word that Henry Ford II was coming for a visit. Greenwald sent underlings to Miami to gather the proper amenities, including any type of liquor that the hard-drinking Henry might desire. But Henry had just gone on the wagon, and upon arrival asked for ginger ale—about the only liquid that Greenwald's task force hadn't obtained. The boss had to settle for 7-Up instead. Greenwald remembered the incident for decades.

Greenwald's own protégé, Steve Miller, had an impish, dry wit that served him well in Chrysler's wacky world. During the bailout negotiations of 1980, he began one crucial meeting by telling the bankers that Chrysler was filing for bankruptcy. As his listeners sat in stunned silence, Miller added: "Gentlemen, I would like to remind you that today's date is April 1."

Miller's alter ego was his wife, Maggie, the resident wild woman in Detroit's sea of subdued corporate wives. An entire room of the Millers' Bloomfield Hills home was devoted to an elaborate gingerbread village that Maggie had baked from scratch. But to view it, one had to walk through a hall lined with Maggie's collection of medieval prints depicting scenes from Hell. The Hell hallway became an unforgettable experience for any visitor to the Millers' home.

Maggie didn't reserve her uninhibited behavior for the house. Once Miller invited Maggie to join him at a dinner meeting of Chrysler managers, where he was the featured speaker. After his speech Miller invited questions from the floor, and the first hand to shoot up was Maggie's. "How would you be running Chrysler differently, Steve," she asked, "if you were chairman instead of Lee Iacocca?"

The group was startled to see Miller being put on the spot by his own wife. But he quickly recovered. "My first move," he replied, "would be to ban spouses from attending corporate meetings." The Chrysler men howled with laughter.

Among all these men, the closest to Iacocca was Bidwell. It was he who could stand up to Iacocca, and who could defuse tension at the office with timely humor—intended or otherwise.

One unintended joke began one evening, when Bidwell went fishing at a lake near his home, and hooked himself in the back of the head. He had to drive to a hospital emergency room to get the hook out. A few weeks later, he returned from a trip to Australia, where he had purchased an authentic aboriginal boomerang. Anxious to try it, he trotted out to the fairways at the Bloomfield Hills Country Club, and let it fly. The boomerang worked perfectly, flying right back to Bidwell and striking him squarely in the nose. Back in the emergency room, he got the same nurse, who asked him: "Aren't you the same guy who was in here with a fish hook in his head?"

It was, all told, a swashbuckling crew at Chrysler. Every man except Dauch had come from Ford, prompting them to call themselves the "Gang of Ford." In 1986 and 1987 they were on top of the world, and bought a string of companies that included Lamborghini and Electrospace Systems, a Dallas defense contractor. The biggest prize was American Motors Corporation, maker of Jeep.

AMC, as Detroiters called it, had long been a basket case. It was on the verge of failure in 1978 when Renault, France's state-owned automaker, bought a 46 percent stake in the company—only to shell out millions to subsidize AMC's losses. AMC's cars had included the plug-ugly Pacer, the long-nosed Gremlin, and the boxy Renault Alliance, all of which performed even worse than they had looked. But Jeep was a jewel.

Chrysler's executive suite, though, was sharply divided on whether to buy AMC. The most vocal opponent was Hal Sperlich, the intense and talented product planner who had been fired from Ford even before Iacocca, and had led Chrysler in developing the minivan. But in the end only one vote mattered: Iacocca's. In March 1987, Chrysler persuaded Renault to sell its stake, and a few months later it bought the rest of AMC for $1.1 billion in cash and Chrysler stock. Overnight, Chrysler's size increased by 20 percent.

But in October 1987, just two months after Chrysler closed the deal, the stock market crashed. Chrysler had to idle factories for the first time in four years because of slow sales. A worried Iacocca launched a cost-cutting program that included dismissing 3,600 white-collar workers, nearly 10 percent of Chrysler's total including AMC. And he abruptly halted Chrysler's corporate shopping spree.

Chrysler's free-wheeling executives, though, knew that after surviving the early eighties, they could handle anything. "The management of this company has zero doubt about staying profitable in the next recession," Greenwald told the *Wall Street Journal* at year's end. "What do you want from me? To wish the next recession would hurry up so I can prove myself?"[13]

CHAPTER 4

THE GENERAL LOSES COMMAND

SATELLITES. MISSILES. COMPUTERS. Software. Workerless "lights out" factories. Smart robots. Computer-controlled cars. Fighter jet instrument displays on the dashboard. To hear Roger Smith talk about General Motors at the peak of the 1980s boom, in the full flush of his victory in snaring Hughes Aircraft, it was hard to think of GM as the world's largest maker of connecting rods.

Connecting rods are to cars what offensive linemen are to football. They do their jobs in total anonymity, but if they fail, there's no forward motion. Just as few athletes start their careers aiming to be an offensive tackle, so few young GMers start their climbs up the great pyramid hoping some day to be responsible for connecting rods—8-inch-long pieces of iron that attach pistons to the crankshaft of a motor. Connecting rods weren't where the glory was at GM. Selling cars and counting the money—those were the pathways to the top. Making connecting rods? That was boring, boring, boring.

Not, however, to Alex Mair. Mair was different. He looked every inch the consummate General Motors vice president, with his silver hair, his rugged good looks and his blue suits. He even had a solid-blue

GM pedigree. His father was a Scot who had come to America in 1912, and wound up as a tool and die maker at GM. Alex attended the General Motors Institute, GM's West Point for aspiring managers, and signed up with the General in October 1939 as a draftsman in the engineering department. World War II intervened. He fought in the Pacific, and witnessed firsthand the subjugation of Japan. In November 1945, he even visited the starkest symbol of Japan's defeat, the atom-blasted city of Hiroshima. Four months later, he was back home, ready to restart his career at General Motors. It would prove to be a successful one. Mair rose steadily in the engineering ranks, serving as chief engineer at Chevrolet in the late 1960s.

In 1972, Mair made vice president and was assigned to run the GMC Truck division. Then in 1977, he moved into a more prestigious post as general manager of the Pontiac division. Pontiac's sales were taking off, thanks to the enthusiastic response to a new line of "downsized" rear-drive cars brought out in response to the first fuel crunch. Mair, by that time, had become more sensitive than many of his peers to the issue of quality. Every morning, he would walk into the Pontiac factory and check 100 cars for defects. He pointed out flaws to managers in the plant. But they brushed his criticism aside. Their only worry was that they couldn't ship cars fast enough.

Mair was transferred out of Pontiac in 1978, and named vice president in charge of GM's technical staffs, the army of engineers headquartered at GM's huge Technical Center in suburban Warren, Michigan. He had actually done well for a man of his unusual temperament. Real GM vice presidents spent their days in meetings. Mair skipped many of the ones to which he was invited. Real GM vice presidents generated dozens of memos to their staffs. Mair rarely wrote anything down. While his peers lugged thick reports to strategy meetings, Mair would arrive with just a candy bar in his briefcase. In a company that glorified slick marketing, bold promises, and financial derring-do, Mair dedicated himself to burrowing into the mechanical innards of cars.

Mair's studies of GM's cars had prompted him to adopt some unorthodox opinions about America's No. 1 automaker and its position in the global car wars of the 1980s. In August 1981, he had made an impassioned speech to the executive committee, including Roger Smith, warning that GM's preeminence was threatened. Using hand-lettered signs and poster-sized flip charts, Mair declared that GM had to change the way it designed vehicles, and take drastic action to improve quality.

GM, Mair added, should put a squad of people to work studying how the Japanese had gotten ahead in cost and quality. "Time has run out," Mair declared, flipping to a sign bearing those words in thick, bold letters.

Mair got a budget to launch the Vehicle Assessment Center, soon nicknamed the Mona Lisa room. In this top-secret hideaway, Mair and his staff dismantled Japanese, German, and American-made vehicles. Mair's engineers weighed, photographed, measured, and analyzed parts from dozens of Toyotas, Hondas, BMWs, and Fords, as well as Chevrolets, Pontiacs, and Cadillacs. Mair even had a special room full of high-performance German and Japanese motorcycles—which he admired because of their precisely crafted engines. Mair's crew of engineers captured the sounds of various engines and transmissions on tape. They measured friction, efficiency, and transmission smoothness. They charted how long it took the car bodies to rust. They toured Japanese factories, noting every detail of how GM's rivals put cars together. Mair's investigators used reverse engineering to deduce how much rival companies spent to build their vehicles.

No one, Mair would say, knew more about the relative competitive positions of the world's automakers than GM. In five years, Mair's Mona Lisa operation had become the industrial equivalent of the Smithsonian Institution. Mair was its proud curator. How he loved to take initiates on tours to show off what he had learned. His eyes twinkled. A smile played across his mouth. He'd rub his hands together, and gush over the sculpted beauty of a Honda motorcycle's cylinder head.

Mair was gifted with a soothing baritone voice, a facility for simple, declarative sentences, and a personal manner that was a disarming blend of the awkward and the avuncular. In his talks, he came across like television's Mr. Wizard explaining to the kiddies how water boils. It was this role—the friendly, unthreatening Mr. Wizard—that Alex Mair adopted one day in 1986 to explain his findings to the engineers developing Smith's ultimate weapon against Japan, the new Saturn car.

Striding to a table, Mair picked up two connecting rods.[1] He explained that one came from a 1.8-liter GM engine that was used in the Chevrolet Cavalier, and the other came from a similar engine made by Honda. Even a nonengineer could see a big difference. The Honda connecting rod appeared smoother, lighter, and cleaner. Why was that? Well, Mr. Wizard explained, "The most significant difference, other than size, is that the Chevrolet, or GM rod, has weight pads. At the bottom and on the top."

Mair elaborated: It's crucial that the four rods in each engine all have the same weight at the top and the bottom, so the engine will run smoothly. At GM, rods are forged by the thousands and shipped off in big bins to assembly plants. But in those bins, rods forged from new dies would weigh less than those forged from older, worn dies. To get four rods of the same weight from a random shipment, GM had developed machines that weighed each rod, then ground metal off the rectangular weight pads at the ends until the rod balanced properly.

Mair pointed to the end of the Honda part. It was smooth and round. There was no rectangular weight pad. Honda, Mair explained, made rods four at a time, and kept them together until they reached an engine. That way, Honda eliminated the weighing and grinding GM used to adjust for the variation in the weight of each rod.

Mair anticipated the reaction from GM managers: So what? He had the answer. He put down the two connecting rods, and picked up the pistons that went with each one. "Now remember," he said. "The top of this rod has a weight on it. There will be an average height for that weight. . . . That generates a greater distance between the piston pin and the top of the piston than is required for a rod that doesn't have the weight. So it makes the piston higher."

Mair held the pistons together, and sure enough, the GM piston was about a quarter inch taller than the Honda one. Not only that, the GM piston had three rings around it to protect against friction damage. The Honda piston had just two. Honda thus spent a third less money every year on piston rings, and on the labor it took to attach them in the engine factory. Honda also saved the cost of the machines that weighed and ground the rods, and the cost of pouring and shipping iron that was destined to become scrap when it was shaved off the finished part.

Mair delivered his verdict: "Not only is the [GM] piston higher. But the block, and the engine, have to be that much higher. There's the extra material, the extra weight, the extra height of the hood. All those things have a domino effect on the vehicle."

A domino effect, he explained, that made the GM car heavier, less responsive, slower-accelerating, and less efficient than the Honda. When customers complained, as they often did, that the Chevy Cavalier couldn't seem to get out of its own way, this was at the root of the problem. Everything about the Cavalier was heavier and clumsier—the flywheel, the clutch, the action of the gearshift lever, the tires, etc. Quality suffered, too. The Cavalier's clunky clutches generated three to four times the number of complaints as Honda's lighter, smoother mechanisms.

Mair's logic, boiled down, was no more sophisticated than the nursery tale that begins, "For want of a nail," and ends, "the kingdom was lost." But it was compelling. Mair estimated that GM added about $145 per car to its costs because of decisions traceable to the sloppy way it manufactured one unglamorous piece of iron. Considering that GM built 4.7 million cars a year, this amounted to $681 million worth of waste.

This wasn't news to GM's top brass. The wrenching changes Smith had forced GM through in 1984 were aimed at curing the institutional inertia that fostered such waste. But here it was, 1986, and nothing had really changed. And Mair had lots more. After observing that GM had invented the modern automatic transmission in the 1930s, he would have an assistant play tapes of a GM Hydramatic transmission and a Toyota Camry gearbox. The Hydramatic rumbled and roared like a jet taking off. The Toyota purred like a Siamese cat.

Mair coyly observed that colleagues sometimes objected to this comparison, and to an accompanying chart that ranked Cadillac as having the noisiest transmissions of any GM had tested. "People say, 'I don't believe that. I just drove in a Cadillac and it was very quiet,' " Mair would say. "That's true. Because we spend a lot of money and a lot of engineering talent to mask that noise"—by packing insulation under the hood.

Mair didn't worry that he infuriated his peers. He saw that GM was using Band-Aids to treat cancer. All around the Mona Lisa room, Mair had dozens of charts that reduced the results of his staff's tests to graphs. In each graph, red bars showed the scores for Japanese manufacturers, green bars represented Europeans, and yellow bars represented GM and other U.S. manufacturers. On virtually every chart, the yellow bars representing GM's products and factories were at the bottom; red bars clustered at the top. The message was clear: GM had a bad system that produced bad products. Reorganization, reindustrialization, and diversification hadn't changed that.

Bulky connecting rods and noisy transmissions were but two of hundreds of problems Roger Smith's GM ignored in its headlong rush into automation and diversification. Some of the problems were obvious to anyone. For an August 1983 cover story in *Fortune* magazine, GM opened the doors to some of its newest plants to tout what executives declared was a dramatic makeover.[2] GM executives rattled on about how they were developing new cars in teams, like the Japanese. They showed off changes designed to cut down on wasteful stockpiles of parts in the factories, just like the Japanese. They boasted about innovative new models in the works.

Fortune delivered its verdict in a striking cover photograph. It showed four maroon GM sedans lined up door to door. These were the Chevrolet Celebrity, Pontiac 6000, Oldsmobile Cutlass Ciera and Buick Century —GM's new entries in the midsized family car market. In keeping with the ancient wisdom of Alfred Sloan, the Buick cost more than the Chevrolet. But all four cars looked virtually identical.

THE LOOK-ALIKE CARS, the forty-year-old engine technology under their hoods, the whiny transmissions—Alex Mair warned Smith about all of this, and more.

GM was reorganized, diversified, roboticized, and computerized. But as the look-alike Buicks and Oldsmobiles dramatized, America's preeminent manufacturer had purchased the industrial equivalent of the Emperor's new clothes. Where was the great improvement? There was almost none. GM was spending $2 billion a year on warranty claims, or roughly $300 for every car and truck. On the three measures of success that mattered—quality, manufacturing efficiency, and new product design—GM by 1985 was dead last in the industry.

Even so, it took more courage than most GM executives had to argue in 1985 that GM could be hurt by gnats like Honda or Chrysler, or even by more substantial rivals like Ford or Toyota. After all, GM was still the world's largest and richest manufacturer. The company had earned record profits of $4.5 billion in 1984, and owned 44 percent of the U.S. car market. GM had always crushed the competition in the past. What could possibly prevent it from triumphing now? With revenues approaching $100 billion a year, GM was more a nation than a business enterprise. Some 565,000 people worked for GM in the United States and Canada alone. Another 250,000 people labored for GM in Europe, Africa, the Middle East, and Asia. More than 16,000 dealerships worldwide sold GM cars and trucks. GM wasn't just the world's biggest car maker. It was the world's largest data processing company, thanks to its acquisition of Electronic Data Systems Corporation. It was, with its purchase of Hughes Aircraft, the world's largest defense electronics concern. General Motors Acceptance Corporation was one of the world's largest consumer lending operations, a bank in everything but name. GM factories in Chicago built about half the railway locomotives sold in America. GM was a leading manufacturer of gas turbine engines used in tanks and big diesel engines for heavy trucks and mining equipment.

But there was more. GM owned a vast archipelago of divisions that made almost every kind of widget used in a car. GM's parts operations were like nothing else in American industry. Indeed, they were most analagous to the Japanese *keiretsu*, the families of companies bound by interlocking stock ownership that were a favorite bogeyman of the Motor City's Japan bashers.

These divisions, such as AC Delco, which made spark plugs, and Delco Products, which made shock absorbers, operated as virtually separate companies. Many of them once had been independent companies before GM swallowed them up in the early 1900s. But in heartland milltowns like Dayton, Ohio, Flint, Michigan, Kokomo, Indiana, and Lockport, New York, many people thought of themselves as employees not of General Motors, but of Delco, AC Spark Plug, or Harrison Radiator. GM's assembly divisions bought parts from these divisions as if they were separate companies. The catch was that the assembly operations had little freedom to reject Delco's price for fuel injectors and award the business to an independent contractor, even if the independent was offering better quality and lower prices.

This didn't mean that GM kept all its money in-house. Thousands of companies that spun carpet, banged out brackets, machined screws, fabricated computer chips, formulated paint, designed machine tools, programmed robots, or processed rubber, glass, or plastic all depended on GM for business. GM's factories bought some $60 billion a year worth of goods and services from suppliers around the world—some owned by GM, but many not. Most of that money was spent in the United States. Cash from GM cascaded through every level of the American economy, from massive steel mills and tire factories to hundreds of small manufacturers that supplied valves and springs and sprockets to GM's parts operations. GM money was everywhere—from the neighborhood bar that poured beer for off-duty GM factory hands, to Madison Avenue, where GM spent nearly $1 billion a year for advertising, to the booming Sunbelt areas of Florida and Arizona where GM retirees flocked with their pension checks. When Charles E. "Engine Charlie" Wilson, GM's president during the 1940s and early 1950s told Congress, "What's good for General Motors is good for America," he was merely telling the truth.

Next to the federal government, there was no other single institution with as much power to affect the American economy.

But as 1985 dawned, this huge institution was in trouble. For more than thirty years after the end of World War II, GM had reigned supreme over an unprecedented boom in the world's largest car market. In 1946, Americans bought just 2.4 million new cars and trucks. By 1978, sales of new cars and trucks had grown nearly sixfold to 12.4 million.[3] And nearly half of those cars and trucks had rolled off a GM assembly line. Those years had taught a generation of GM executives, including Roger Smith, that the world was predictable: That the market always grew over the long term, that the competition was always weaker, that sales lost in a bad year could always be reclaimed, and that GM could control styling and pricing standards for the industry because it was bigger and more efficient than any rival. When GM got ready to launch a new car, its planners confidently projected sales on the basis of how the previous model had done. Likewise, as the U.S. economy began recovering in the early 1980s, GM's economic forecasters declared that sales of cars and trucks in the United States would continue to grow until they peaked at about 17 million vehicles a year. A similar straight-line projection justified the forecasts that GM would continue to control some 45 percent of the market, just as it had in the past.

By 1985, however, GM's backward-looking culture was badly out of step with the reality of the new American auto industry. The stable oligopoly that had nurtured Roger Smith's career was shattered. Detroit's four automakers—GM, Ford, Chrysler, and American Motors Corporation—were no longer the only major manufacturers building cars on American soil. Volkswagen had led the foreign invasion when it opened its car factory in western Pennsylvania in 1978. But the real invasion had begun in 1982, when Honda began building Accord sedans in Marysville, Ohio. Nissan quickly followed, opening its Tennessee plant in 1983. By 1985, Nissan was churning out 150,000 Sentras and pickup trucks a year. With Nummi as a springboard, Toyota was scouting for a place to put its own American factory. The assumption—which proved correct—was that other Japanese car makers like Mazda, Mitsubishi, and Subaru would come tumbling after.

All these Japanese factories in America's heartland portended the biggest shakeup in the supply-and-demand equation of the U.S. car industry since the Great Depression. Imports could be blocked with tariffs and quotas. But stopping the flow of cars from plants that employed Americans was another matter entirely. Depending on who did the guessing, there promised to be capacity to build 1 million to 2 million more vehicles in North America than customers would buy. Not only that, but Japanese parts-fabricators were setting up hundreds of plants in the United States to serve their allied automakers, and to grab some Big Three business besides. These posed a clear threat to GM's parts factories. As the GM managers assigned to Nummi had discovered, many of GM's parts divisions had become grossly inefficient and slipshod.

Sorting out which factories would live and die in the 1980s promised a return to the kind of Industrial Darwinism GM hadn't experienced since its early days. Survival of the fittest, however, was a game Roger Smith's GM was ill-equipped to play in 1985.

How could this have happened?

Part of the answer was that GM's very size turned against it. The parts plants, for example, which had been an advantage in the 1950s and 1960s, became huge liabilities. Manufacturers in Europe, Mexico, and Asia gained the capability of matching the products of GM's operations at a fraction of UAW wage rates.

But GM had problems much closer to home. Front-line managers in GM's plants and in its design and engineering offices were virtually paralyzed by the chaos that followed the 1984 reorganization. GM's old Fisher Body Division had been hostile to new ideas. But it did exercise a kind of rough discipline that prevented GM's marketing divisions from running wild in their efforts to customize cars with special door handles or shift levers that inflated costs without giving customers anything of value. Likewise, GM's Assembly Division had a production control manual that spelled out how a factory was supposed to work. It might have been a starting point for emulating the Toyota system. But it was junked when GMAD was dissolved. Smith's eagerness to erase the vestiges of the past swept away not just the scale model of the carriage that sat in the Fisher Body building's lobby, but much of GM's vital institutional memory as well.

Thus, by 1985, the reorganization was achieving an almost miraculous result. It was proving that there was something worse than the old GM. Too late, Smith and McDonald would realize they had pushed their massive organization into a corporate nervous breakdown. They had lashed their underlings to transform GM's cars from the familiar rear-drive technology to new front-drive architecture. They had ordered factory managers to install hundreds of robots, and adopt bits and pieces of a Japanese operating system that even top managers barely understood. Then Smith and McDonald had ripped away the last vestiges of stability that had been provided by GM's old hierarchy. Disoriented and fearful for their jobs, many lower-level managers simply ducked. They waited to be told what to do, bucked critical decisions up the line, and suppressed problems in numbing rounds of interdivisional meetings. The reorganization hadn't changed the company's bedrock culture. The executives running North American operations were the same. They just had different jobs. GM's bureaucratic structure had changed, for the worse. Smith had hoped the reorganization would allow for shrinking GM's army of paper-pushers. Instead, the bureaucracy got more complex. Instead of one vice president in charge of manufacturing, GM now had five.[4]

DESPITE THE ORGANIZATIONAL CHAOS, Smith drove ahead with his technology binge. GM had to keep "biting into the future," he'd say. The biggest danger, he would say, would be in spending too little.

But GM had fallen into a trap. In his Mona Lisa room, Mair had cardboard scale models of GM's new assembly factory in Orion Township, Michigan, GM's new plant in Zaragoza, Spain, the renovated Buick City factory in Flint, and a Suzuki plant in Japan. The models showed how much floor space each factory required to produce seventy-five cars per hour. The Orion model was roughly half again as large as the Suzuki factory. In other words, GM had bought roughly 50 percent more concrete and steel to produce the same number of vehicles as Suzuki. The Orion plant's bigness inflated all sorts of other costs—for heating, lighting, conveyors, asphalt for the parking lot. And did all that expense buy GM efficiency? Mair's technicians had the answer: A chart of overall manufacturing efficiency showed the low-tech Nummi factory was nearly four times more productive than the roboticized Orion behemoth.

In the 1950s, 1960s, and even the 1970s GM executives could count on one thing for sure. They had the money to spend competitors into the ground and still have plenty to spare. Staggering torrents of cash flowed through GM's accounts. But by 1985, GM had begun spending more than it took in. GM ended 1984 with $8.6 billion in cash. But that hoard began melting away as Smith shoveled money into the Hughes acquisition and the factory automation crusade. GM's break-even point in North America—the number of vehicles it had to sell to cover fixed

costs—had surged from 4.3 million cars and trucks in 1983 to 5.6 million
in 1984. Profit margins were melting. Japanese automakers were earning
5 cents more operating profit on every dollar of revenue than GM. Even
more embarrassing, Ford and Chrysler were earning about 3 cents more
operating profit per dollar.

It didn't take a sophisticated financial analyst, however, to smell that
GM was heading for a fall. GM's customers knew full well that something
was rotten. Despite all of Jim McDonald's earnest exhortations to improve quality, the reorganized, technologized GM was producing some
of America's worst cars.

There were, for example, the 1986 and 1987 model Buicks and Oldsmobiles equipped with 3.8 liter fuel-injected V-6 engines that stalled
seemingly at random—at highway speeds, in straightaways, and during
turns. Most of the cars were equipped with power steering and brakes, so
when the engine quit, the steering and the stopping mechanisms quit,
too. One owner of a 1986 Buick Park Avenue, who happened to be in
charge of leasing vehicles for his company, complained to GM that when
his car stalled out at 55 miles per hour he veered off the road to avoid
another vehicle and found himself and his frightened family flying over
a set of railroad tracks.[5]

GM engineers knew this was no joke. As early as January 1986 they
had formed a Stalling Task Group to study the problem. One July 1986
memo issued by the task force was copied to twenty-four different people
involved in the search for a solution. At various times, managers from
the Buick, Oldsmobile, and Pontiac marketing divisions, the Buick–
Oldsmobile–Cadillac group, the Flint Automotive manufacturing division, the Buick–Olds–Cadillac Powertrain division, the AC Spark Plug
Division, the Rochester Products division, and the GM Service Parts
Operations all joined the fray. One early response was a mass mailing to
dealers of 12,000 "drivability kits" that contained parts to replace nearly
all the critical components of a fuel injection system. The cost was put
at $303 a car. But GM couldn't keep up with the demand.

Dealers received notices from GM that the stalling was the result of
defective parts. Most customers, however, were kept in the dark. GM
would pay for repairs for some customers whose cars were damaged in
stalling accidents, but only after the victims agreed to sign forms that
released GM from legal liability. Eventually, GM would process a staggering 2.7 million warranty claims for stalling problems between late
1985 and 1991. Some 45,000 people would complain to GM or to federal

regulators about stalling in 1986 and 1987 GM cars. At least two people would die and thirty-two others would be injured in 429 accidents attributed to sudden stalling. But not until federal safety investigators demanded a recall in 1991 did GM finally agree to acknowledge the defect to customers.

Stalling was just one problem. There were many others. Complaints poured in to GM, and to various consumer watchdog agencies, about blown transmissions, engines that leaked oil, and power-steering mechanisms that seemed to freeze up on cold mornings. The latter problem was so widespread that GM engineers even gave it a nickname: "morning sickness."

Most of the trouble-plagued cars GM built in the mid-1980s were forgettable mediocrities. One, however, became an infamous symbol of GM's corporate disease.

Its name was Fiero.

THE PONTIAC FIERO was a rare thing for GM. It was a unique, idiosyncratic creation that burst from GM's galaxy of bland, interchangeable automobiles. It was a car that left an indelible mark on GM's corporate psyche. For the Fiero project embodied what many of GM's young lions wanted a New GM to be. But when their ambitious experiment collided head-on with the Old GM, it crashed and, literally, burned.

The Old GM had never liked the idea of a sporty, two-seater Pontiac from the moment it began knocking around among Pontiac engineers in the late 1960s. A sporty Pontiac roadster would steal sales from Chevrolet's sporty two-seater, the Corvette, the brass declared. No dice.

But Pontiac's engineers didn't give up. John DeLorean, the renegade vice president who fathered the GTO and its muscle-car progeny, had taught a generation of Pontiac engineers that sporty sold—just like sex. They were loath to give up that winning formula, even after the oil crises of the 1970s forced DeLorean's muscle cars off the road. It wasn't until 1978, however, that some young Pontiac planners hit on a strategy for bootlegging the dream car past the corporate guard dogs. Instead of a muscle car, the Pontiac Kids proposed a fuel-efficient, four-cylinder "commuter car" that just happened to have two seats. The corporate brass was intrigued. And when Pontiac engineers brought back a running prototype in less than six months, they bought it.

There was, however, a major condition. The whole project—from design to tooling up the plant—had to be finished for just $400 million. That was a fraction of what GM spent to bring a typical car to production. The challenge demanded a bold new approach. Pontiac handed the job to a bold man: Hulki Aldikacti.

Aldikacti was a Turkish emigré who had gotten a master's degree in mechanical engineering from the University of Michigan in 1955. The next year, he signed up with GM. Aldikacti was no kid—he had punched in twenty-two years by the time the "commuter car" challenge landed in his lap. He had worked under DeLorean in the GTO days, and jumped at the chance to make one of his dream cars come to life.

With his bare-bones budget in hand, Aldikacti began to assemble a team to bring the car to production. It was an operation such as GM's old guard had never seen.

Most of GM's engineers fell into two camps: car engineers and manufacturing engineers. In 1980, these two camps were as separate as church and state. Car engineers created blueprints for vehicles. After they were done, factory engineers were supposed to figure out how the pieces sketched on the blueprints could be fabricated and assembled. A frequent response of the manufacturing engineers, however, was to dismiss the car engineers' plans as "no-builds." That meant, "There is no way to build such a design in the real world." Back and forth the plans would go, as the car engineers and factory engineers fought, and money and time went down the drain.

Aldikacti had no patience for this, and no money, either. By coincidence, GM was shutting a body-making operation in Pontiac, and had manufacturing engineers looking for jobs. Aldikacti snared some for his team and sat them down next to his car engineers. For the first time anyone could remember, a GM car project leader had both product-development and production people working for him. That this was how Japanese automakers were developing new cars faster than Detroit was almost beside the point. Aldikacti's concern was that everyone would now be "partners to the crime." There'd be no way for manufacturing engineers to say "no build" after his design was done. Aldikacti's response to engineers who tried to shirk tough calls was to growl: "I'll make an arbitrary decision."

Aldikacti made plenty of those, anyway. One was to make the new car's skin out of plastic. Aldikacti had been intrigued by the possibilities of plastic body panels for years. Now, he had a reason to try them: The dies to make plastic fenders and doors cost a small fraction of what it cost GM to make dies for metal body pieces. At first, GM's engineers couldn't figure out how to build a steel undercarriage that didn't warp out of shape. Warped frames meant the plastic exterior panels didn't fit together right. Aldikacti solved that problem after a late-night brainstorming session with one of his manufacturing engineers. The solution: Assemble the frame with little metal pads—just like the ones on Alex Mair's connecting rods—and then use a special machine to drill bolt holes exactly where they had to be to hold the panels on straight. The idea worked, and won Aldikacti GM's prestigious Boss Kettering Award (named for the pioneer who had developed the first electric car starter) for engineering innovation.

Aldikacti's unorthodox methods and his brusque manner made him unpopular with many in GM's bureaucracy. Three times he was informed by counterparts at other GM divisions that his car had been killed by the corporate bean counters. Each time, however, the death notice proved premature. "It's like a weed," Aldikacti would say of his car.

In fact, the car's survival depended on a phalanx of high-ranking defenders. Chief among them was William Hoglund, the vice president who'd taken over Pontiac in 1980. Pontiac was Hoglund's first high-profile executive post after years bouncing around in the finance ranks. Tall, friendly, and blunt-spoken, Hoglund cherished his Swedish heritage (he was born in Sweden and spent much of his youth in Europe) and his status as a member of GM's nobility—both Hoglund's father and his brother were GM vice presidents.

This blue-blood pedigree notwithstanding, Hoglund had a reputation as a maverick among his peers in GM's finance ranks. For one thing, his subordinates loved him. As comptroller of Pontiac during the early 1970s, Hoglund eagerly solicited the ideas of junior staffers, and conducted free-wheeling meetings in the Pontiac cafeteria that underlings dubbed "love-ins." As general manager of Pontiac, Hoglund would throw parties at his Birmingham home for the automotive press where he and his wife would dance and party into the wee hours of the morning.

Hoglund took over Pontiac as the division was lurching into a trough. Stripped of its hot rods, Pontiac had stumbled badly in the late 1970s. Its cars were bland, its customers old, and its future bleak. Hoglund quickly made it known he wanted dramatic action to revitalize the division's image. In 1982, Hoglund took his top three dozen staffers to a hotel in Ann Arbor for a two-day "image conference" that dwelt extensively on how wonderful and exciting Pontiac had been under DeLorean.

When the dust settled, Hoglund declared that "excitement" would be Pontiac's new watchword. The division would rebuild itself with cars that were "exciting" and "different."

"Exciting" and "different" described only one car in Pontiac's future product lineup at the time: Aldikacti's commuter car. It was a low-priced two-seater, something the American market hadn't seen in years. It had an engine in the middle driving the rear wheels—a striking departure from the flood of front-engine, front-drive cars hitting the market from Japan. As the prototypes took shape, the exterior lines took on a decidedly un-GM look, evocative of Ferrari and Porsche.

Under the stylish skin, however, Aldikacti's tight budget was taking its toll. Aldikacti reluctantly cannibalized GM's corporate parts bin for key components, such as the suspension. Aldikacti dreamed of a light, punchy aluminum block V-6 for his car. But developing a new engine would have cost more than Aldikacti had to produce his whole car. So instead, he had to make do with an antiquated four-cylinder engine GM already manufactured for Pontiac. That motor was best known by its colorful nickname, the "Iron Duke," so-named for its heavy iron block. The Iron Duke, however, was too bulky to fit into Aldikacti's tiny car. The solution: Equip the engine with a new, smaller oil pan. The engine fit, but it would always run a quart low.

These compromises, however, didn't dampen Pontiac's enthusiasm for Aldikacti's car. To the contrary, the commuter car was the catalyst for a burst of innovation under Hoglund.

To build the 100,000 cars a year his marketing team had been committed to sell, Hoglund negotiated a deal to reopen a shuttered factory on the far side of GM's sprawling manufacturing complex in Pontiac. There Hoglund and his staff launched a crusade to prove that cooperation between management and labor would resolve the quality problems that GM's top executives wanted to solve with robots.

To that end, Hoglund brought in W. Edwards Deming, a crusty, idiosyncratic management consultant who had become a virtual deity in Japan. During the 1950s, Deming taught Japanese manufacturers his unique system for controlling and improving quality, and earned Japan's gratitude for helping to transform "Made in Japan" from a synonym for shoddy to an icon for quality. Deming's system mixed rigorous measuring and statistical analysis—designed to spot defective goods before they were shipped to customers—with a management philosophy that stressed giving more power and responsibility to workers. The Japanese government even established a prize in Deming's name awarded to companies displaying the greatest commitment to quality. American manufacturers largely ignored Deming during the 1960s and 1970s. But Japan's success during the early 1980s sent hundreds of American executives scrambling to Deming's door. The gruff, balding, octogenarian, who worked out of his Washington, D.C., home, was particularly sought after in Detroit, where he worked with both Ford and some units of GM.

At Pontiac, Deming gave Hoglund's troops the same messages he'd given the Japanese decades before. With managers, Deming was often coarse. "You guys don't even know what questions to ask," he'd declare. With hourly workers, however, Deming was solicitous and sympathetic. He'd comment frequently that most quality problems were the fault of bad management. Deming quickly became a hero on the shop floor.

To run the new car plant, Hoglund in 1982 brought in a thirty-seven-year-old manager named Ernie Schaefer, who along with his top lieutenant, Dennis Pawley, began leading the cheers for teamwork. Schaefer had come to the new car venture after a stint running a new Pontiac engine plant. There, Schaefer had encouraged efforts by his staff to get blue-collar workers involved in laying out the engine assembly line. Now, Schaefer got a mandate from Hoglund to go even further.

The new car plant didn't have an official UAW local. But Schaefer asked union officials to appoint a provisional local chairman to sit in on planning sessions for the factory. This was putting the cart ahead of the horse before there was even a cart. But the union, encouraged by the success of the efforts in the engine plant, went along and appointed a man named Jerry Lewis to lead the as yet nonexistent local. Schaefer and Lewis and their aides began brainstorming. The more they talked, the more rules they agreed to break.

Early on, Lewis declared that if Schaefer was serious about having GM managers and UAW laborers work as teammates instead of blood enemies, he'd have to include a UAW official on the plant's management staff. This was an unheard-of breach of the Berlin Wall between labor and management. But Schaefer agreed. Next to go were some of the most potent symbols of the caste system that separated "white collar" from "blue collar" at GM. There would be no special executive parking garage at the new plant, and managers agreed not to wear neckties. Schaefer was amazed by the vehemence of the union men's feelings about ties. To him, it was just part of the uniform. But to Jerry Lewis's troops, the salaried men's ties were like neon signs that blared: "I'm better than you are."

Other, more substantive, departures from tradition evolved as the new factory took shape. In early 1983, fifteen members of the union-management group journeyed to Japan for a two-week tour of plants run by Toyota, Nissan, Isuzu, and Suzuki. There they saw Japanese laborers working in small teams that would meet regularly to discuss problems in their work area. They also saw that in some plants, hourly workers could pull cords or push buttons to stop the assembly line when they saw a defective car rolling by.

At GM, controlling the assembly line's speed was a fundamental privilege of management. Many of the fights between management and labor at GM revolved around management efforts to speed up the assembly line—the better to produce more cars and make more money. Old-line GM plant managers would sooner pass out hand grenades at the plant gate than allow a laborer to slow down the line. But the men from Pontiac returned from Japan convinced it was time to try a new way. Every Wednesday morning, the assembly line would stop for thirty minutes while teams held meetings in special alcoves equipped with picnic tables and blackboards. And at regular intervals along the new line, Pontiac engineers installed buttons that allowed workers to stop production. A ghost of the old GM remained. To keep the line stopped, a worker had to keep holding the button down until a foreman arrived. Only managers had the keys that could shut down the line for an extended period.

Still, by GM standards, the new Pontiac plant was a workers' paradise. As icing on the cake, Hoglund even allowed hourly workers to come up with a name for Aldikacti's car. The name they picked was Fiero.

The Fiero hit the market in late 1983, just as the country was shaking off the chills of recession. Most of Detroit's other cars reflected the glum zeitgeist of the Carter years, with their boxy, "sensible" designs and earth-toned color schemes. The little red Fieros arrived like the first robins of spring. Young women, especially, loved the car's perky looks. Everybody loved the prices, which started at less than $10,000. Such a low-priced sporty car hadn't been seen in the United States for years. It was a smash hit.

Pontiac's marketing staff had promised their corporate overseers they could move 100,000 Fieros a year to justify the cost of the factory and engineering investment. It was an estimate some in the division thought imprudent. But Pontiac sold 101,000 vehicles in the first model year. As an added bonus, the Fiero streaked past the other low-priced two-seater that hit the market that year, Honda's CRX.

Pontiac staffers were giddy with delight. With fuel economy fading fast as a concern for American car buyers, Pontiac revived Aldikacti's dreams of making the Fiero the springboard for a triumphant leap back into the performance game. To be sure the automotive press got the message, the division's public relations staff held early previews for the Fiero at race tracks.

Indeed, Pontiac was working on plans to enter the Fiero in racing competition long before the car hit showrooms. Eventually, the division would budget some $10 million to the Fiero racing program. In May 1984, Pontiac got the Fiero selected to be the pace car for the Indianapolis 500. Engineers started work to shoehorn a V-6 engine into the car to broaden its appeal to the hot-rod set. Pontiac's rivals scrambled to catch up. In late 1984, Toyota launched an angular, midengined two-seater called the MR-2 that seemed a direct steal of the Fiero idea. Flat-footed Ford executives were reduced to parading a prototype, Italian-designed two-seater called Barchetta at auto shows, and hinting that it might be available late in the decade.

Meanwhile, the labor relations experiments at the Fiero factory were attracting attention from the very top of the corporation. Teams of managers from other divisions began visiting the plant. Roger Smith himself took a tour—and even shucked his tie for the occasion. The Fiero became a celebrated example of the advantages of teamwork and innovative thinking. Deming himself used the plant as a case study, as did other management gurus.

The only problem was that the Fiero was doomed.

Some of Pontiac's engineers knew almost from the start of production that the Fiero had a disquieting tendency to become, quite literally, a hot rod. On October 6, 1983, less than three months after production began at the Pontiac plant, a Pontiac engineer wrote an "urgent" memo to report that two Fieros had suddenly caught fire during test drives. The engineer blamed the fires on antifreeze leaking out of badly installed hoses onto hot exhaust pipes. Aldikacti himself saw a Fiero catch fire at GM's test track.

But Fieros flamed out more than one way. Pontiac engineers fought an eighteen-month long battle to get GM's Saginaw foundry division to stop shipping batches of defective connecting rods for Fiero engines. The foundry managers, who got paid on the basis of tons of iron shipped out the door, had little financial incentive to spend money to fix Pontiac's warranty problems. After one meeting, a Saginaw foundry manager wrote that ". . . 60 percent to 90 percent of the rods produced do not exhibit" defects. Of course, this meant that from one to four of every ten rods were defective. Pontiac was still complaining in December 1984 —more than a year after Fiero's launch—that "no permanent solution has been found" to the problem of hairline cracks in connecting rods for the Iron Duke. Sure enough, Fieros began suffering breakdowns caused by broken rods.

A connecting rod that breaks at high speed is like a shrapnel grenade detonating inside the motor. In Fieros, chunks of broken metal flew with such force that they ripped through the engine block. Oil would spill onto the hot exhaust pipes, and often ignite. The Iron Duke engines used in early Fieros also suffered from a defect in the way their blocks were cast that, in some cases, caused the engines to leak oil or lose coolant. Since the Iron Dukes in Fieros ran a quart low to begin with because of the customized oil pan, losing more oil quickly created big trouble.

GM engineers and Fiero plant workers knew of these problems, and many more. They discovered that some of the engine cooling fans on early Fieros were wired backward. That meant the fans sucked hot air back into the engine. Engineers rewired the fans. Pontiac engineers fired off bulletins to dealers warning about other problems—poorly installed radiator hoses, leaky gaskets, and bad wiring.

"If you wouldn't want your family riding in it, recall it," Jim McDonald would say when asked about GM's policy toward recalling cars. In practice, however, GM operatives were reluctant to push for an expensive recall of a popular new model. When a Fiero burned, GM often handled the loss as a warranty claim, and paid for repairs as each case came in. Sometimes, GM and its insurance company quietly worked out deals to pay off victims of Fiero fires.[6] GM continued this approach even as complaints about the Fiero's defects began pouring in to Pontiac and to regulators at the National Highway Traffic Safety Administration in Washington. By the end of 1985, GM had reports of 112 Fieros that had caught fire—one for every 1,700 sold at the time. By August 1986, the pace of fire reports had quickened sharply, and Washington's safety enforcers, the bureaucrats at the traffic safety administration, began to stir.

"This . . . appears to be a serious problem," Philip W. Davis, NHTSA's top defect detective, wrote to GM in a letter demanding information on the Fiero's problems.

This epistle confronted GM with two unpleasant choices. Recall the Fieros to fix the fire hazard—and endure a damaging public relations blow. Or circle the wagons. GM decided to circle the wagons. Two months after NHTSA's letter went out, GM's C. Thomas Terry, whose job it was to deal with the feds, wrote to pooh-pooh the concerns. "Any time an individual experiences a vehicle fire, it can be a very traumatic experience," Terry wrote. "In the case of the [Fiero] engine compartment fires, the evidence indicates the actual risk to motor vehicle safety is minimal."

This serene view of what it was like to have a car engine burst into flame a foot from one's backside wasn't shared by the rapidly growing number of Fiero owners who had experienced the phenomenon.

By the middle of 1987, the fire count for 1984 Fieros hit a rate of about twenty blazes a month. Fieros were blowing up at a rate of one for every 508 cars sold. No other mass market car had ever come close to this rate of fires—at least, as far as the federal safety watchdogs knew.[7] If the Fiero fire rate was applied to all the cars on the New Jersey Turnpike at rush hour, there would be burning hulks every quarter mile and hundreds of people running around in panic.

As it was, victims of Fiero fires told hair-raising tales in their complaints to GM and the government. One twenty-two-year-old woman reported that her Fiero caught fire while she was driving with a male friend at 4:30 A.M. on the Southern State Parkway on Long Island. The couple wound up at the emergency room where the man got treated for burns on his hands. A Fiero owner in Missouri complained that she'd taken her car in to the dealer nine times because of electrical problems that caused her dashboard lights to blink and the engine to sputter when she turned the headlights on. Finally, her Fiero quit running on a back road, and when she pulled over she discovered the car was on fire. She tried to extinguish the blaze with a pair of blue jeans, but to no avail. The car burned to the ground. This was no exaggeration. A Fiero in flames was an amazing sight. When the plastic skin ignited, the result was a brilliant bonfire no steel-bodied car could match.

Back at Pontiac, however, the fires were overshadowed by a more pressing concern. The Fiero was becoming a money loser.

Hoglund had shielded the Fiero plant from the wrath of the bean counters when the plant fell short of its production goals in 1984, just as he had silenced critics within Pontiac who didn't think managers should go around without neckties. This had been easy to do, because the Fiero was a certifiable hit. By 1987, however, things had changed. Sales had plunged from the heady peaks of the first two years. In the 1986 model year, Fiero sales dropped to 71,283 cars, down 21 percent from the year before.[8] Production for the year was 21 percent below the budget forecast. Sales in 1987 were slumping even further behind both the budget and the previous year.

Hoglund, the Fiero's champion, had been promoted to a new job. In his place GM had assigned J. Michael Losh, an ambitious thirty-eight-year-old finance staffer who became GM's youngest vice president when he took over Pontiac from Hoglund in July 1984. Losh's boyishly casual public manner belied a tough way with a buck. And the Fiero was losing more bucks than it was taking in.

The Fiero's troubles became obvious in January 1987, when GM laid off 1,200 workers on the Fiero plant's night shift. The layoff, a response to the sales slump, battered the trust Hoglund and his staff had nurtured among union leaders. Worse was to come. Federal safety regulators had backed GM into a corner on the issue of Fiero fires and were demanding action. In September, GM agreed to recall all the 1984 Fieros and make repairs aimed at reducing the fire hazard. One was installing an oil filter that gave the engine capacity for the full four quarts of oil. Another, however, was a sticker that Fiero owners were instructed to place on the little door that hid the cap to the gas tank. "Check engine oil at every fuel fill," the sticker read. It was a lawyer's repair, somewhat akin to the warning labels on the sides of cigarette packs. The sticker effectively transferred responsibility for the Fiero's oil leaks to the owner. GM staunchly refused to admit there was anything inherently wrong with the Fiero's design.

GM's public relations operatives knew the recall would batter the company's reputation, and the Fiero's market appeal. In a clumsy attempt to limit the damage, GM delayed announcing the recall until 4:31 P.M., November 25, 1987. This just happened to be the night before Thanksgiving, a time when most auto reporters would be more interested in roasting their own turkeys instead of GM's. The stunt didn't work. The Fiero recall generated torrents of bad press and blighted sales. All that was left was to arrange the funeral.

In late 1987, Losh responded to pressure from his superiors and commissioned a top-to-bottom review of the Fiero's finances and its sales prospects. The result wasn't a pretty picture. The cheapest 1988 model Fiero had a sticker price of less than $10,000. But the car cost more than $12,000 to build. Among the bigger budget items, after materials, was

$431 a car in warranty costs. Even backing out the arbitrary charges for corporate overhead, the cheapest Fieros cost more to make than their starting sticker price. More expensive versions of the car did carry some profit, but not much.

In addition, GM by now knew how many labor hours it took the workers at Nummi to assemble a small car designed by Toyota. The Fiero factory was putting nearly twice as much labor into its small cars—and that was when the robots in the body shop worked properly and the paint ovens weren't causing acnelike blisters in the plastic body panels.

The great Fiero experiment was now caught in a vicious downward spiral. The more GM raised its price to cover the bloated costs, the fewer people wanted to buy the car, particularly in the wake of the recall.

The Fiero plant's union leaders fought to save the car. In early 1988, a few weeks after the recall, a delegation from the Pontiac local tracked Losh down in a room at the Waldorf-Astoria in New York. For more than half an hour, the union men begged Losh to save the car. They talked up plans to build a hot-looking Fiero convertible. Losh promised to think about it. In reality, there was only one thing left to say.

Shortly after that, Donald Ephlin, the UAW's top negotiator at GM, walked into a lunch meeting with the labor relations staff at the Chevrolet–Pontiac–Canada Group headquarters in Warren, Michigan. Sitting beside the labor staffers were Robert Schultz, the vice president in charge of the group, and David Campbell, the group's manufacturing boss. The two men hadn't been expected. Their presence spelled trouble. Just hours before, Ephlin had been warned that the Fiero was in jeopardy. Now, Schultz and Campbell delivered the blow: The Fiero would die at the end of the model year in the fall.

"Boy," Ephlin snapped. "It went downhill fast. It was sick this morning, and now it's dead."

"When should we tell the employees?" one of the CPC men asked. "It's too late," Ephlin said. "You should have told them long ago."

For Ephlin, this was a tragedy. For four years, he had held the Fiero up as a model of what cooperative labor relations could achieve. He had staked his reputation and his union career on labor-management partnership, which he referred to as "jointness." Now, GM was knifing jointness in the back. But Ephlin was powerless to stop it. On March 1, David Campbell marched onto a podium in the Fiero factory and delivered the plant's death sentence in a terse announcement. A murmur of shock rippled through the crowd. A solitary voice boomed: "Boo!"[9]

Then, the workers turned and walked back to their stations.

That wasn't the last word on the Fiero, however. Not by a long shot. In December 1989, GM recalled every one of the 244,000 four-cylinder Fieros it had built to fix problems that caused fires. Four months later, GM recalled every single Fiero—six cylinder and four cylinder—to make more repairs.

Inside GM, the Fiero had been a bright symbol of GM's new wave. Aldikacti's product team and the people at the Fiero factory had, indeed, been years ahead of their time. But the failure of their car to survive the compromises demanded by the GM system turned their success into just another Detroit flop.

The crowning indignity came in 1989, when tiny Mazda Motor Corporation launched a little two-seat roadster called the Miata.

The day the Fiero's death was announced, Mike Losh had insisted that the Fiero failed not because of quality problems, but because Americans had lost interest in two-seater cars. Mazda made a mockery of Losh's excuse. With its simple technology and exterior lines that echoed the British Triumph and MG roadsters of the 1960s, the Miata became an instant smash hit. At the peak of the Miata frenzy, buyers were offering to pay $4,000 or more over sticker to get one of the retromobiles. Sighed one gloomy Pontiac official: "The Fiero could have been a Miata."

THE FIERO WAS A tragic failure. But it was far from the biggest mistake GM made in the first six years of Roger Smith's chairmanship. A far more dangerous miscalculation became evident in the fall of 1985 as the superautomated Hamtramck factory in Detroit began to churn into action.

Roger Smith called Hamtramck "the most modern auto plant in the world today." A GM brochure hailed it as "the passage to the future." Hamtramck was, indeed, the realization of Roger Smith's and Jim McDonald's ambitious strategy for making GM a 21st-century car company. GM's public relations operatives spewed out Texas-style statistics to dramatize the bigness of the thing—"21 miles" of conveyors, "27,200 tons of structural steel" in the walls, nearly 8 miles of wire buried in the floor as pathways for the automatic guided vehicles that replaced human forklift drivers, 113,000 cubic yards of earth bulldozed during plant construction, and so on.

But as soon as it opened, GM's industrial showcase turned into a basket case.

Susumu Uchikawa, the man from Toyota, had warned that GM was courting disaster by packing so much exotic technology into a brand new plant with a new workforce building a new car. Toyota would never juggle that many variables at once—that was why Nummi had started with old technology and an old car. Now, Uchikawa's prophesy began to unfold. As Hamtramck's assembly line tried to gain speed, the computer-guided dolly wandered off course. The spray-painting robots began spraying each other instead of the cars, causing GM to truck the cars across town to a fifty-seven-year-old Cadillac plant for repainting. And robots installed Buick Riviera bumpers on Cadillac Sevilles. The robots, it seemed, couldn't tell the cars apart. Customers would later make the same observation.[10]

GM's factory hands were stymied by the confusing array of robots and software. When a massive computer-controlled "robogate" welding machine smashed a car body, or a welding machine stopped dead, the entire Hamtramck line would stop. Workers could do nothing but stand around and wait while managers called in the robot contractor's technicians.

Hamtramck was supposed to erase the nearly $2,000 a car cost advantage Toyota enjoyed. Instead, it turned into a Waterloo for Smith and his automation campaign. Hamtramck was a fantastically expensive and inefficient parody of Toyota's system. The plant had hundreds of robots, but it also had 5,000 workers on the payroll, just like an old-style GM factory. To see how uncompetitive that was, GM executives didn't have to fly to Toyota City. They could drive to the next county and look at Ford's luxury car factory in the Detroit exurb of Wixom. Wixom had fewer robots and only about 3,700 workers. But it was outproducing Hamtramck by a wide margin.

Too late, GM executives realized their mistakes. GM hadn't reorganized work so that fewer people could do it, using the lessons of Nummi. They had simply grafted robots onto the old, inefficient system. Moreover, instead of easing robots onto the line a few at a time, providing for inevitable debugging problems with redundant equipment, GM bet the entire Hamtramck production system on the proposition that leading-edge automation would work instantaneously. When, instead, automated guided vehicles used to deliver parts broke down, or robotic paint systems fouled, the whole plant ground to a halt.

Compounding the technical problems with Hamtramck's robots was the complex design of GM's cars. Hamtramck's cars were overloaded with electronic gadgetry and hard to build. The front and rear bumper of a Cadillac Seville had more than 460 parts, and took thirty-three minutes of labor to put together. Two years after it opened, Hamtramck put a stunning 100 hours of labor—five times as much as Toyota—into building each car. In 1985, the year the plant started production, GM's spending on "maintenance and repairs" jumped by 18 percent to $5.4 billion from $4.6 billion the year before.[11]

GM's customers, of course, cared nothing for labor costs and balky automatons. They were simply aghast at the squat, cramped vehicles GM was trying to pass off as high-priced luxury cars. The Cadillac Sevilles and Eldorados, Buick Rivieras, and Oldsmobile Toronados that Hamtramck produced looked for all the world like the Pontiac Grand Am and Buick Skylark compact cars GM had launched a year earlier. This wasn't a fluke. A group of top executives from Buick had viewed the Riviera and the Skylark side by side prior to their launches, and had been unable to tell them apart without looking at the logos on the wheel covers. The horrified brass had delayed the luxury cars by a year, and ordered engineers to make the Seville, Eldorado, and Riviera several inches wider than originally planned. The cobbled-up results looked like cinderblocks on wheels.

GM executives would later argue, with some justification, that the Hamtramck cars would have seemed to be master strokes had gas prices gone to $3 a gallon—the price predicted during the time that the cars were designed. But the rationalizations didn't matter. Hamtramck wound up working at less than half speed, producing many of its Cadillacs for decidedly undistinguished service in rental car fleets. Hamtramck was a financial and strategic debacle that was the beginning of the end for Roger Smith's bold 21st-century vision and his aura as Detroit's great innovator.

Wall Street and the public got their first inkling that something was amiss with Smith's reorganized, reindustrialized, technojuggernaut when they studied GM's earnings statement for the third quarter of 1985. Buried under a blizzard of big numbers was a stunning surprise: GM had an operating loss of $20.9 million. More trouble showed up in the financial reports for the end of 1985, which disclosed that GM's cash reserves had shrunk by 40 percent in one year.

For public consumption, Smith painted blue skies. "GM has made real progress toward its long term goal of becoming a 21st-century corporation," he declared in May 1986 at the annual stockholders meeting in the cavernous Fisher Auditorium across Grand Boulevard from GM headquarters. GM had "an outstanding year" in 1985, Smith said. "We're taking risks. We're growing and prospering." Certainly, Smith and GM's other executives were. The 1985 executive bonus pot was $218 million. Smith raked in a total of $1.9 million in salary and bonuses for the year.[12]

Smith continued to defend his ambitious capital spending plans. "The gamble is if you don't spend," Smith said. "And that's a gamble I'm not willing to take."[13]

But Smith had quite a different message for his top subordinates. And as GM's fortunes continued to sag in 1986, he took dramatic steps to drive it home.

In early April 1986, GM managers received orders to cut spending for travel and meetings. As a warning shot, it was a popgun blast. But it was soon followed by a signal everyone could understand. The Japanese yen was surging in value, erasing the price advantage Japanese car makers had enjoyed during the first half of the decade. In March, Smith gloated: "Our prices are going down, their prices are going up." But a month later, GM abruptly raised prices on most of its cars. GM needed cash, and the Japanese price increases offered an opportunity to grab some. Smith seized it.

GM had scheduled another of its triennial management conferences at the high-priced Greenbrier golf resort in White Sulphur Springs, West Virginia. GM executives loved the Greenbriers. "Listen to speeches for four hours, play golf for four hours, drink for twelve hours and sleep for two," was the Greenbrier drill, as Bill Hoglund once described it. The conference was a party to celebrate achievements, and reward success. But Smith ordered the 1986 Greenbrier party canceled. Instead, GM's top 500 North American Operations managers were ordered to attend a meeting on June 23 in the spartan surroundings of the old Fisher Body conference hall on the grounds of the Warren Technical Center. Wags dubbed the conference TechBrier.

TechBrier was a remarkable event. GM's buttoned-down leaders addressed their troops in a state of controlled panic. Though cloaked in fighting rhetoric, the speeches by senior executives were confessions of strategic failure and financial weakness on a scale that would have stunned the shareholders who had heard Smith's glowing forecast just a month before.

GM's top finance man, F. Alan Smith (no relation to the chairman), delivered a dour report that crystallized GM's dilemma. GM had increased its sales $21 billion between 1983 and 1985—just as if it had bought a company the size of Chrysler, Alan Smith said, scowling down from the podium. But GM was earning virtually no profit on the extra business. Operating income was on a track to fall $5 billion below the levels projected in the corporation's plans. Ford could now build a mid-sized car with twenty-five hours of labor in a plant staffed with 3,200 people. GM took sixteen hours longer to build a similar car in a plant staffed with 5,000 people. Ford had achieved these levels of efficiency without coming close to GM's capital spending.

GM planned to spend another $35 billion on its auto business between 1986 and 1989. "For the same amount of money, we could buy Toyota and Nissan," Alan Smith said. "This would almost double our worldwide market share. Can we expect to double our worldwide share with our spending program?" The answer, unsaid, was painfully obvious.

Roger Smith weighed in. With his squeaky voice and fidgety mannerisms, Smith was a poor public speaker, and this day was no exception. Smith read his speech in a singsong cadence, his eyes obscured by the glare of lights off his glasses. GM executives had to "inspire" GM's middle management to "let go of the rock of stability and swim with us across the river of change," said Smith. He delivered the line as if he were calling on everyone to eat more oatmeal. Then, Smith got to his real point.

"The hard truth is, our results aren't good," he declared. "We talk so much about the 21st century, I'm afraid we've lost sight of today. Our head count is going up, our costs are going up, our capital spending is going up, and our profits are going down. We need results. Right now. Not in five years. Not in the 21st century. But today."

It was an incredible performance. Who, after all, was the "we" Roger Smith was talking about? The GM executive who talked incessantly about the 21st century was Roger Smith. The man who approved hyper-ambitious product programs was Roger Smith. The man who had signed off on billions of dollars of robots that didn't work was Smith.

Jim McDonald, of course, had plenty of responsibility, too. But with fifteen months to go before retirement, a weary McDonald was free to give voice to the great fear that engulfed the people in the TechBrier meeting, most of whom were operating managers like McDonald. "We're going to improve ourselves right out of the ballgame," McDonald said.

Appearing to fight back tears, McDonald told the audience how he had first started attending GM's triennial executive conferences more than thirty years earlier, when he was a young foundry manager in Defiance, Ohio. At the end of each session, McDonald said, a senior executive would always say: "You're a helluva group. You've worked hard. And I'm proud of you."

"Well," McDonald continued, "I can say you're a helluva group. I know you've worked hard. But I can't say I'm proud of you. Because we haven't accomplished what we set out to do."

It was a stinging blow, and McDonald tried to soften it. He urged his underlings to dig in, turn GM's slide around and make him proud again. But he refused to close on an upbeat note. Instead, the old warrior issued a prophecy: "GM is now at a critical point in its long history. The next few years will determine whether GM remains a world leader, or quietly slides into second-class status."

FOR AMERICA, 1986 was a golden year. The economic recovery ignited by Ronald Reagan's tax cuts and the plunge in oil prices was kicking in the afterburners. It wasn't morning in America, as Reagan's famous campaign slogan had it. It was high, blazing noon. On the coasts, soaring property values made middle-class homeowners rich. Credit was easy. Paychecks were fat. On Wall Street, fortunes were being made—a few illegally, as it turned out. The buoyant stock and real estate markets had economists rhapsodizing about the "wealth effect" felt by people who owned rapidly appreciating assets. Ford sold Tauruses and Lincolns like hotcakes. Chrysler had a smash hit with its minivans, and piled up cash after years in the desert.

GM was missing the party.

The gloomy TechBrier flogging session demoralized GM executives. Little of what followed improved their moods. Smith and McDonald jammed on the brakes. They canceled $88 million in orders for new robots from a factory automation venture Smith had formed with a Japanese company. The massive GM-10 project for a new family of midsized cars to fight the Taurus was cut back to four factories from seven. Smith also took aim against GM's "frozen middle" management. GM built twelve cars per worker in North America compared to Ford's eighteen. In August, Smith launched a drive to cut 25 percent of the 132,000 jobs in its North American managerial ranks.[14] The mechanism for prying bureaucrats from their desks was so-called voluntary early retirements. It quickly became clear that managers asked to leave had little choice.

Smith even signed off on halving the budget for his beloved Saturn project. Saturn's managers were buckling under the strain of trying to launch an all-new division, with all-new computer and manufacturing technology, and an all-new factory big enough to build 500,000 cars and engines a year. McDonald had concluded it simply couldn't be done. Better to drop some of the technology experiments, such as the dream of a "paperless" office, and cut the size of the factory in half with the understanding that a "second module" might be built someday.

There was no way, however, to get back the money GM had already spent on Taj Mahal factories like Hamtramck, and Smith's "lulus," Hughes Aircraft and EDS. GM's fixed costs were gobbling up profits. The slumping demand for GM's cars was choking the flow of cash that GM needed to finance its huge capital-spending program. By midsummer, GM's market share had slid to about 40 percent. Smith's price increase and the poor quality of GM's cars were driving away customers in droves. GM tried desperate measures to jump-start its stalled engine. In late August 1986, the General stunned its rivals by declaring it would finance new cars at an annual interest rate of just 2.9 percent. "The Big One," GM called its sale. And a Big One it was. Customers stormed dealerships as Ford and Chrysler followed the Big One's lead. Sales soared, and kept on flying. When the dust settled, 1986 went down in history as the all-time record sales year for the American auto industry. A stunning 16.3 million new cars and trucks rolled onto the road.

GM, however, paid dearly. In the third quarter of 1986, GM reported another operating loss—this one of $338.5 million, or more than ten times the deficit that had alarmed the corporation a year before. GM's cash reserves were so depleted that Smith arranged for GMAC, the finance arm that lent money to car buyers, to make a $5.2 billion "loan" to GM itself to replace the money bled out of the auto operations.[15] But the faster Smith scrambled, the worse things got. After GM raised prices for 1987 models by 5 percent or more in the fall of 1986, showroom traffic evaporated.

Roger Smith, onetime industry hero, needed a savior. He got Ross Perot instead.

H. Ross Perot had been one of Roger Smith's proudest acquisitions when he joined GM's board of directors in 1984. In a single stroke, GM had made the Texas billionaire its largest individual shareholder with the acquisition of his interest in EDS. Smith had seen Perot as a perfect foil for his effort to shake up GM. If Smith's troops wouldn't listen to his fresh ideas, maybe they'd follow the example offered by the stunningly successful entrepreneur from Texarkana. Long before he ran for President, Perot was a business legend. He had championed the cause of prisoners of war in Vietnam, dramatizing their plight by hiring a plane to fly Christmas gifts to North Vietnam in 1969. The plane never landed, but Perot became a star. A decade later, he formed a private army to snatch captive EDS employees out of Iran. That exploit yielded a best-selling book (produced under his close supervision) and a television miniseries that portrayed him as a sort of corporate Rambo. Smith wanted the iconoclastic Perot to sprinkle some of this swashbuckling magic on GM's risk-averse time-servers.

Smith and Perot's corporate Mutt and Jeff act didn't last long, however. The more Perot learned about GM, the more appalled he became. Accustomed to operating in a company whose employees sprang to action at the sound of his voice, Perot was baffled by GM's ponderous bureaucracy. Inspired when UAW leader Don Ephlin urged GM's board to pay more attention to labor management relations, Perot began delivering sermons to Smith and GM's directors about how the company should "feed the troops" before it feeds the generals. Perot's suggestion that executives should suffer along with hourly workers got a chilly reception.

But Perot didn't back off. Instead, he challenged Smith head-on.

One of the first big clashes between the two came over Smith's proposal to buy Hughes Aircraft in 1985. Perot began to pump lower-level operatives for nuts-and-bolts information about the deal, and soon concluded that Hughes was a dog. The company, he would say, earned 65 percent of its profits from less than 1 percent of its contracts. Smith disputed this. Perot retorted that the chairman was feeding him bad numbers.

The spat came to a head when Perot stood up in a board meeting and delivered a lengthy speech in opposition to Smith's "lulu." The speculative bubble in the defense industry was at its peak and bound to burst, Perot argued. GM was foolish to buy at the top. In hindsight, this was a prescient analysis. At the time, however, Perot got nowhere. He cast a lone vote against the deal, refusing to go along with the board's custom of giving the CEO unanimous support.

Perot had tried to upstage Smith in front of his directors, a provocative act by any measure. But he was about to do far worse.[16]

Perot had sold EDS to GM, lock, stock, and floppy disk. Few of EDS's top executives in Dallas, including Perot, liked to admit it. They talked about the "alliance" or the "merger," as if EDS had bought the auto giant, and not the other way around. EDS had its own class of stock and its own bonus system. And as far as Perot was concerned, GM's finance staff wasn't supposed to snoop in EDS's affairs.

GM executives couldn't comprehend this. GM had advanced its subsidiary nearly $1 billion in interest-free loans, and was shoveling more than $2 billion a year into EDS's coffers directly from its auto operations. GM's auditors had a clear obligation on behalf of GM shareholders to account for the billions paid to EDS and its shareholders. But Perot refused to allow GM's audit staff to look at EDS's books.

By the spring of 1986, the fight for control of EDS began to boil over. Ross Perot's folksy Texarkana twang and country boy mannerisms— he would wear both belt and suspenders—belied a vicious competitive instinct. Perot spent an inordinate amount of time, for a famous billionaire, chatting with reporters. That was because Perot understood the power of the media in a way that Roger Smith did not. And by early 1986, Perot was ready to employ his media savvy to flay Smith.

First, Perot sent Smith several not-so-subtle private warnings that he intended to attack him in public if he couldn't get satisfaction in the dispute over control of EDS's affairs. Then, Perot started giving "off the record" interviews to reporters, laying the groundwork for what would come. Perot painted a portrait of GM and its leader that was anything but flattering.

"Roger Smith works on everything in the world but GM business," Perot said in a six-hour tirade to two *Wall Street Journal* reporters in May 1986.[17] "He would rather deal with South Africa than make cars. He is the basic problem here; you're looking at the cancer.

"Roger started screwing around with the EDS compensation system. I said to him, 'You come down here and explain this to our people.' He did that, and found himself in a meeting with real people, who told him just what they thought. He lost control, just totally lost control. His lips were quivering, he was turning blue, and he said, 'How dare you talk that way to the chairman of GM!' At that point, he lost me forever.

"I have told Roger, you and I have two choices: You're going to do the right thing, or we're going to fight in public. It's sicker than hell. Roger creeps around, and tries to get me thrown off the board. I called him and said, 'I know you are trying to get me thrown off the board, but don't even think about it. Don't even try. You tell those old farts [on the board] that if they love pain forever, try it. If you ever decide to fire me, it's nuclear war.

"I wrote Roger a letter last fall, and told him he was a bully. He called me back, and butter wouldn't melt in his mouth fast enough. Roger— how shall I say it?—Roger seems to enjoy harsh treatment. When I've had my hard conversations with him is when he's been the nicest. If I had had any idea he was this way, I wouldn't have sold EDS." To make the point that he wouldn't back away from a fight, Perot crafted an unforgettable line: "Roger has touched the tar baby."

In June, Perot began putting his gripes on the record. He railed against GM in volleys of quotable barbs. "It takes five years to develop a new car in this country," he said. "Heck, we won World War II in four years." Of GM's stuffy culture, he quipped to *Business Week:* "The first EDSer to see a snake kills it. At GM, first thing you do is organize a committee on snakes. Then you bring in a consultant who knows a lot about snakes. Third thing you do is talk about it for a year."[18]

The press devoured it all. Perot's comments gave witty, authoritative voice to the doubts about Smith and GM that were flourishing already among members of the business press, not to mention thousands of unhappy GM customers and GM employees. Here was a member of GM's board, who was also the company's largest individual stockholder, saying in outrageously forthright terms that GM really was a disaster.

Smith was stunned. "We get along fine," he said in a lame reply to one of Perot's early broadsides. The obvious fiction made the chairman look foolish. Perot kept talking circles around him. An exasperated Smith finally retorted that Perot's critique of GM's executive privileges sounded odd coming from a man whose own plush Dallas aerie was a veritable museum of Frederic Remington sculptures, rare books, and a copy of the Magna Carta. But it was too late.

Perot's attacks had their intended effect. The members of GM's executive committee found their regular luncheon discussions in the executive dining room turning repeatedly to the nasty Texan. Some among GM's brass even worried that Perot would try to make GM the target of the world's biggest corporate takeover. Perot kept it up. He insisted that his only motive in going public with criticism of GM management was to help GM improve. This was far from the whole story, however.

What Perot and his closest colleagues among EDS's top management really wanted was out of GM, one way or another. Perot had put this plainly in a May 1986 letter to Smith. Perot enumerated his grievances, then proposed a list of possible solutions. One was that GM should sell EDS. Another was that GM should buy his stock.[19]

By September 1986, Smith was ready to accommodate Perot. Morton Myerson, the former president of EDS and Perot's right-hand man, broached to Smith the idea of selling a chunk of EDS to AT&T, the telephone giant, and to EDS shareholders. Smith deputized several of his underlings to negotiate a deal. But after an initial burst of excitement, the talks went nowhere.[20]

In early November, as the AT&T negotiations were winding down, Thomas Luce, a Dallas lawyer who had represented both Perot and EDS for years, met GM's top lawyer, Elmer Johnson, for lunch in New York. Luce told Johnson the time had come for GM to consider simply buying out Perot's stock. Luce observed that pending changes in the tax laws made it imperative that any deal be closed before the end of the year. Johnson and Luce began exchanging drafts of an agreement.

Almost simultaneously, Smith dropped a bombshell. On November 6, GM announced that as part of its "turnaround," it would close nine factories and parts of two others, eliminating nearly 30,000 jobs. Smith insisted the shutdowns had been in the works for years as part of GM's reorganization and plant modernization. GM had built new factories; some old ones had to go, he reasoned. This was true, for the most part. UAW leaders had seen the closings coming. What shocked UAW leaders was Smith's decision to bundle all the plant shutdowns together and portray them to Wall Street as aggressive cost cutting. The announcement was a public-relations disaster that teed up GM for the real detonation just three weeks later.

At noon on December 1, GM announced officially what America had learned from the front page of the *Wall Street Journal* early that morning.[21] GM would pay Ross Perot $700 million to surrender his stock and leave GM's board. It was a stunning sum. Also stunning was the bizarre fine print of the divorce settlement. To get his money, Perot had agreed to stop criticizing GM management, or forfeit up to $7.5 million. And for five years, Perot was forbidden to buy GM stock or act in any way to "control or influence the management" of the company. The latter clause was striking confirmation that Smith and GM's directors actually feared Perot might try to lead a takeover of the world's largest corporation.

Wall Street didn't need to see the fine print to decide that the buyout was a bad deal. GM's stock plunged $1.375, while GM's Class E shares, which were tied to EDS's performance, lost $4.50, or about 14 percent of their value. Perot, meanwhile, insisted on having the last word. The billionaire called a press conference in Dallas and berated GM's board for giving him enough money to buy "a brand spanking new car plant and the jobs that go with it" just to shut him up. Perot declared he would deposit the money in an "escrow account" to give GM's board time to reconsider.

It was all public relations posturing; no escrow account ever existed.[22] But Perot was a folk hero, and nobody bothered to check.

The firestorm over the Perot buyout blackened GM's reputation, and singed the reputations of GM board members, too. There was no way to quiet the outrage caused by the juxtaposition of the Perot buyout and the announcement that GM planned to throw nearly 30,000 people out of their jobs. Perot had outflanked his nemesis, taken GM's money, and left the directors to endure the scorching outrage of the shareholders and the car-buying public. For GM and Roger Smith, the Perot buyout was a disaster. And worse was yet to come.

CHAPTER 5

FORD'S UNLIKELY HERO

In late November 1984, Ford Motor Company's top 400 executives from around the world gathered at the posh, pink-walled Beach Club in Boca Raton, Florida. It was the triennial gathering of senior management, when the company's top brass would lay out its vision for Ford's future. Henry Ford II was on hand, even though he had retired from active management four years earlier. The grandson of the first Henry Ford, Henry II had seized control of the company in 1945, after his father's untimely death and his grandfather's senility had plunged Ford Motor into chaos and crisis. Henry II had ruled Ford Motor with an autocrat's iron hand for the next thirty-five years, disposing of a succession of presidents—Lee Iacocca was just the most famous—who had displeased or disappointed him.

Now cast as the aging patriarch, Henry II, at age sixty-seven, was visibly fragile. He stood shakily behind the podium and gave a moving speech that, ironically, endorsed a more open and participative style of management than he himself ever had seen fit to practice. His successor, Philip Caldwell, whose own retirement as chairman and chief executive officer was less than three months away, delivered a farewell address. "It is abundantly clear from nature and from history that only the fittest survive," he declared, "and it is no different in the world automobile industry: the fittest will survive, and we must be the fittest."

But the most intriguing presentation, notable in later years for its irony, came from a man named Will Caldwell (no relation to Philip), the company's chief financial officer. Will Caldwell praised the company's comeback from the depths of the auto industry's depression. Back in 1982, he noted, Ford's total net worth amounted to merely $6.1 billion. Now, it stood at $22.5 billion. After losing an unprecedented $3.3 billion between 1980 and 1982, Ford had posted record earnings of $1.9 billion in 1983 and was headed for another record, $2.9 billion, in 1984. Debt was down, and U.S. market share was rising. In short, Caldwell said, Ford had come through the wilderness.

But the company wasn't entirely out of the woods, he warned. For one thing, the Japanese car companies held a huge advantage. Thanks to lower wages and higher productivity, their costs were a whopping $2,600 per car less than Ford's. General Motors, the industry giant, had a lesser but still significant cost advantage over Ford of $500 to $800 a car. GM's huge size provided economies of scale that Ford couldn't match. GM also had more vertical integration, or in-house production of parts that Ford had to buy from outsider suppliers. And now, GM was launching a frightening investment binge.

Historically, GM had outspent Ford 2–1 on new plants, new equipment product development. That made sense; GM was about twice as big as Ford. But in recent years, Caldwell told his listeners, GM's capital spending had been *three times* the level of Ford. GM was plunging heavily into industrial automation: robots, electronic quality-control equipment, high-tech spray-painting systems and the like, all in a concerted effort to leap-frog the Japanese. The key question: Would GM, by investing so heavily, simply spend Ford and Chrysler into oblivion?

Ford certainly couldn't match GM's spending surge. Ford's record profits were just beginning to rebuild a balance sheet that had been battered by the recession. And in late 1984, Ford was entering the final stages of the most expensive new-car program in its history: a $3 billion outlay to develop a new midsized car. The project was a huge roll of the dice, almost a bet-the-company proposition, and not just because of the money involved. The car would be, far and away, the most radical expression yet of the aerodynamic styling—derided by competitors as "the jellybean look"—that Ford had introduced on the 1983 Thunderbird. One of the chief engineers on the project was a man with the all-too-appropriate name of John Risk. He got the car's code name from his wife's horoscope sign: Taurus.

The Taurus's styling was so avant-garde that Ford decided to show the car to the press and public months ahead of its launch date. That way, the company figured, prospective buyers wouldn't be too shocked when they saw the shape in a showroom. Ford's PR and marketing staffers wanted to unveil the car at the Chicago Auto Show in February 1985. But there was one problem: The show was a few days after Philip Caldwell would step down as chairman.

This was no small matter, especially in Caldwell's mind. Ever since Henry Ford II had tapped him to run the company after firing Iacocca in 1978, Caldwell felt he had never gotten the public credit he deserved for saving Ford Motor. In large measure he was right. Caldwell, who had served on Admiral Chester Nimitz's staff during World War II, was remarkably cool and resolute in a crisis. During Ford's darkest hours in the early 1980s, he made the life-or-death decision to plunge Ford Motor deeply into debt so it could afford to develop the Taurus. But Caldwell was confident the risk was worth it. He had enormous analytical skills, and the determination to examine any problem from every conceivable angle.

His eagerness to do that, however, often drove subordinates crazy. The deliberate Caldwell was derided by underlings as a "pluperfect Wasp" for his stiff personality. He was infamous for holding "iron kidney meetings" that sometimes lasted from 8 A.M. until 10:30 at night, with hardly any bathroom breaks. That wasn't a particular problem for Caldwell because he didn't drink coffee or tea. A graduate of Muskingum College, a tiny, church-affiliated school in east-central Ohio, Caldwell also didn't drink alcohol, didn't smoke, and didn't cuss, all of which prompted the hard-living Henry Ford once to ask him, "Phil, just what do you do?"

One thing Caldwell did, sometimes, was get angry at answers he didn't like. Once, when he ran Ford's overseas operations, a promising junior executive named Alexander Trotman turned down a chance to be Caldwell's chief of staff. Caldwell called young Trotman into his office and pulled a pointed scissors out of a leather scabbard. Then he preceeded to repeatedly stab the blotter on top of his desk while telling Trotman his career at Ford was all but finished. Caldwell couldn't have been more wrong; Trotman's future at Ford would prove brighter than either man imagined.

One man Caldwell particularly disliked was Donald E. Petersen. Henry Ford had installed Petersen as Ford's president while Caldwell was chairman, and recently—over Caldwell's objections—had designated Petersen to succeed Caldwell at Ford's helm. Aides surmised that the friction between the two was partly Napoleonic; Caldwell stood just 5-feet-6, while Petersen towered above him at 6-feet-2. But whatever the reason, Caldwell couldn't stomach the thought of Petersen getting credit for the Taurus, a car developed mostly on Caldwell's watch.

So Caldwell decided Ford would unveil the Taurus to the automotive press in late January, just before Petersen became chairman on February 1. Ford's public-relations department took the hint that the unveiling party should serve double duty as a farewell salute to Caldwell. So David Scott, the company's top PR man, hired Robert Janni, the showman who had choreographed the opening and closing ceremonies for the 1984 Summer Olympics in Los Angeles. Janni went to Hollywood to rent the MGM sound stage, the place where *Gone With the Wind*, *Wizard of Oz*, and *Mutiny on the Bounty* all had been filmed. His plan was to throw a gala bash that would attract hundreds of Hollywood stars and dazzle automotive reporters with glitter and glamour.

The preview began the morning of January 29 with a press conference that attracted 412 journalists from around the world—a record for any new car. Caldwell conducted a press conference in the morning, after which Ford presented an afternoon of "technical seminars" about the car. At dinnertime, reporters and guests were bused over to MGM, where Janni, in keeping with Taurus's futuristic styling, had outfitted the stage like a spaceship, with "computer banks" serving as the bars. R2D2 robots wheeled about serving drinks to the 1,200 guests, who included Danny Thomas, Ethel Merman, George Kennedy, Linda Carter, and Tony Danza. On stage, two enormous white columns of gossamer concealed the cars, waiting to be unveiled at just the right moment.

At the last minute, forty-eight Los Angeles Ford dealers showed up uninvited, creating a musical-chairs scramble for seats—among celebrities and commoners alike—as dinner began. When the crowd finally settled down, custom-made candelabra with lights arranged like swirling galaxies descended from the ceiling to hover above each of the 120 tables. The lights were dimmed just as the waiters (outfitted in space suits) began serving flaming baked Alaska for dessert. And when Dave Scott walked up to the podium to introduce Caldwell, the lights inside the gossamer columns began to glow.

Scott's introduction was brief and simple, but what happened next was stupefying. The formal, staid Caldwell, electrified by the atmosphere, literally ran up to the podium. He grabbed Scott's hand, pumped it like a man possessed, seized the microphone, and shouted to the guests: "THIS IS THE GREATEST NIGHT OF MY LIFE!" As the crowd hollered and clapped, Caldwell waved his arms, tossed his note cards over his head and shouted again. "I'M GOING TO THROW AWAY MY SPEECH. COME UP AND SEE THE CARS!" The guests leaped from their seats in unison and surged to the stage as the gossamer columns were lifted to reveal the Taurus. The evening was a smashing success.

But not to everyone. Later, as the crowd milled about, Scott was relaxing with a drink when Don Petersen approached him. His taut, thin lips parted just enough for him to spit out his disgust. "This is the worst fucking display of tackiness and excess," Petersen said, "that I've ever seen in my life."

DONALD EUGENE PETERSEN was born on September 4, 1926, on a farm in Pipestone, Minnesota, to Danish–Norwegian parents, the third of three boys. He grew up poor. His father, Bill, and one of his brothers suffered from asthma, so when Don was two, the family moved to the West Coast. The Petersens lived in Long Beach, California, for eight years, part of the time in a mostly Mexican neighborhood. Then they moved up the coast to Portland, Oregon, where Bill Petersen sold gas station equipment, and his wife, Mae, worked as a seamstress and house-keeper to help pay the bills.

In high school one of Don's closest friends was Isakau Hiramura, a bright and engaging Japanese-American boy. But in 1942, when the boys were juniors, the Hiramura family and all the other Japanese-Americans in Portland were rounded up and sent to a detention center in Hunt, Idaho. For young Don Petersen this was an end of innocence, the intrusion of a distant war into an American childhood. He was bewildered and angry at the loss of his friend. Don and Isakau faithfully wrote each other for nearly two years. Then they simply lost touch.

After college at the University of Washington (magna cum laude, 1946) and a stint in the Marine Corps, Petersen earned his M.B.A. from Stanford in 1949, and then joined Ford. He spent most of the 1950s moving up the ranks of Ford's product planners, the men who coordi-nated the activities of engineers, designers, parts purchasers, and others to develop new cars. By 1957, at the age of thirty, Petersen was head of product planning for Lincoln, Ford's luxury nameplate.

His timing was terrible. A year later the United States dipped into recession, and Ford suffered a spectacular failure with the Edsel. And Petersen got a new boss named Jim Nance, an abusive autocrat with a penchant for profanity and a habit of humiliating subordinates in open meetings. So Petersen, who had considered quitting Ford several times during the decade, finally did it.

But the night he resigned, he got a call at home from Bob McNamara. McNamara, a brilliant technocrat who would later become John Kennedy's Secretary of Defense, was then running the flagship Ford division, and clearly was headed for the presidency of the company. He asked Petersen to come in the next day and talk, and Petersen reluctantly agreed. McNamara's offer was simple. He wanted Petersen to rescind his resignation and accept an immediate transfer out of Lincoln and into the Ford division. His job would be vaguely defined at first, but something would work out in time. The Petersens had recently adopted their first child and were looking to adopt another, so Don agreed to stay.

In the 1960s, Petersen worked for Lee Iacocca, playing a key role on the team that developed the Mustang. But he wasn't a rising star; instead he rattled around through a series of middle-management jobs. Then he got lucky. In September 1969, Henry Ford suddenly sacked Semon E. "Bunkie" Knudsen, whom he had lured from General Motors just nineteen months earlier to become Ford's president. Lee Iacocca moved into the president's office. And in the fallout from the shakeup, Petersen, who had just turned forty-three, became a corporate officer—vice president for car planning and research.

He was almost a manic perfectionist, obsessed with the details of a car's overall look and supremely confident—usually with reason—of his own good taste. He hated garish ornaments like wire wheel covers and vinyl roofs. Later, as chairman, Petersen would ban vinyl roofs from Ford cars until dealers persuaded him that, because some customers were willing to pay for them, the edict should be lifted.

Petersen would pore over the details of selecting his own P car, as the personal cars provided to executives were called, making sure the carpet matched the interior trim, the seat belts complemented the upholstery, and so on. Then he would assign an aide to shepherd his car through the factory, making sure it got built with appropriate care. Doing it could be a thankless task.

One year, after learning that some executives were ordering custom colors on their P cars, Henry Ford angrily ordered the plants to stop doing such special work. Petersen, though, wanted his new car with a brown interior and beige seat belts, a color combination that wasn't standard. When an aide objected, citing Mr. Ford's order, Petersen threw a fit. Apparently oblivious to the irony that he was behaving like the abhorred Nance, he ordered the young man out of his office to get the job done.

The terrified aide phoned the manager of the plant that built the model Petersen had ordered, and pleaded for a special favor. No way, said the manager, he wasn't willing to defy Henry Ford and put his own job on the line to please Don Petersen. But Petersen's aide saw his own job at risk, and pleaded again. The plant manager offered a solution. He would build a standard car, but throw a set of beige seat belts in the trunk, and ship the car to a Ford engineering facility in Dearborn known as Building No. 3. There, Ford mechanics could switch the seat belts, and present the car to Petersen. And that's just what was done.

Such behavior didn't escape the notice of Henry Ford. One day Petersen summoned a promising young aide, Jim Capolongo, and said, "I've got a problem with Henry Ford. Every time I open my mouth in Product Planning Committee meetings, he shoots me down. I can't talk in the meetings anymore." Instead, Petersen said, he would tell Capolongo exactly what to say, and let Capolongo do the talking. The scheme worked. Petersen stayed out of Henry Ford's cross-hairs, and his product ideas moved forward.

In 1971 Petersen took charge of Ford's truck operations. He spent four years there without getting raises or stock options; he even went without a bonus in some years. He figured he had peaked at Ford, and decided to look around. A long-time friend of his was part of a family that owned a chain of hardware and garden stores near San Francisco, and wanted Petersen to join the company to oversee a major expansion. Petersen agreed. At the last minute, though, the family split over the expansion issue and decided to sell the company. Petersen stayed at Ford.

But just a year later, in 1975, he broke out of his holding pattern. A man named Bob Hampson had taken charge of Ford's sprawling North American Auto Operations, and liked what Petersen was doing in trucks. So when Ford needed a new executive vice president for Diversified Products Operations—a grab bag that included Ford's steel mill, its paint business, and a host of other items—the nod went to Petersen.

DPO was far removed from the glamour of the car business. But suddenly, and unexpectedly, Petersen had broken into the rarefied ranks of
senior management.

In 1977 Henry Ford invited Petersen to have lunch with him in the
penthouse atop the Glass House, the nickname for Ford's glass-and-steel
headquarters in the Detroit suburb of Dearborn. It was the first time
Petersen had dined with Henry Ford alone, and the aging monarch was
gracious and cordial.

He told Petersen he was going to form an Office of the Chief Executive, with Philip Caldwell joining Henry and Iacocca in Ford's ruling
triumvirate. It was a barely veiled hint that Lee Iacocca's days at the
company were numbered, and Petersen got the point. Henry also asked
Petersen to leave DPO and become executive vice president for international operations, one of Ford's most crucial jobs. However Henry had
felt about Petersen in prior years, one thing was clear: In the turmoil
that was sure to accompany Iacocca's ouster, Henry needed experienced
executives.

The international job meant a lot of travel, so Petersen got in-depth
exposure to European design. Petersen also got firsthand exposure to
something far more important: Henry Ford. As Mr. Ford (nobody in the
company dared call him Henry) was winding down toward retirement,
he wanted to visit Ford factories and offices around the world one last
time. He and his then-mistress (and eventual third wife), Kathy DuRoss,
did a lot of traveling with Petersen and his wife, Jody. Jody was a kind
and gracious woman who accepted Kathy instead of snubbing her, as
other Ford corporate wives had done. Henry Ford started getting increasingly comfortable with Don Petersen.

On March 13, 1980, Ford Motor announced that Philip Caldwell
would succeed Henry Ford as chairman. That didn't surprise anybody,
but the next part of the announcement was a shocker. Bill Bourke, who
had run Ford's North American Operations and was the odds-on favorite
to succeed Caldwell as president, would be leaving the company. And
Donald Petersen would be promoted to president. Again, Petersen had
emerged seemingly from nowhere, and now he was the No. 2 man in the
world's second-largest car company.

But there wasn't much time to savor this triumph. While the international operations that Petersen had overseen were doing well, Ford
North America was a mess. The Iranian oil crisis had hit Americans
with astounding force. In the spring of 1979, the Ford plant in Los

Angeles that built the Thunderbird—a boxy V-8 behemoth at the time —had been working two shifts a day and full overtime. Boats carrying unsold Japanese cars, with their tiny, four-cylinder engines, were stacked up in Long Beach harbor. But six months later, after the crisis struck, the Japanese were selling every car they could ship, and Thunderbird sales had plunged so low that the Ford factory went on furlough. In February 1980, Ford closed its L.A. plant for good; a dozen other Ford factories met the same fate.

In the desperate days of April 1980, Petersen paid a visit to Ford's styling studios, about a mile from the Glass House. He hadn't been part of North American car operations for nearly a decade, and didn't know what he would find. It was depressing. Ford's cars of the future looked like the boxy and boring cars of the present. Ford's focus group sessions —in-depth interviews with panels of consumers—were turning up dozens of young people who had never driven a Ford, lately or otherwise, and wouldn't even consider one. To them, Fords were irrelevant.

Petersen buttonholed Jack Telnack, the company's brightest young designer, and pointed to a prototype of the 1983 Thunderbird. "Is that the kind of car you'd really like to drive yourself?" he asked. "Would you like to see it parked in your driveway?" No way, Telnack replied. Well, Petersen suggested, why not try something different, something you really like? There was little to lose.

Petersen wasn't the only Ford executive urging the designers to take a new tack, but it sure didn't hurt to have the president do some prodding. When the aerodynamic 1983 Thunderbird debuted, Lee Iacocca derided it as a "flying potato." But soon, customers who had crossed Ford off their shopping lists were coming back into the showrooms. A year later, Ford continued the aerodynamic styling theme with two new compacts, the Ford Tempo and Mercury Topaz. Quality was improving also. By 1984 the company's recovery was well underway, and the big issue at Ford was who would succeed Philip Caldwell as chairman.

Petersen, as president, clearly was the leading candidate, but his promotion wasn't a sure thing. Caldwell preferred Harold A. "Red" Poling, the executive vice president who ran Ford's North American business. Poling, like Caldwell a financial man, clearly had a lot to offer. It was he who had made the tough decisions to close factories and dismiss employees that had returned Ford to financial health. Thanks to him, Ford wasn't stuck with the enormous cost of unneeded plants and people. And just a few years earlier, Poling had turned around Ford's operations in Europe—providing the life jacket of overseas profitability that allowed Ford to survive its frightening losses in North America in the early 1980s.

Petersen was prepared to quit the company if he didn't become chairman. But with his product-development background, he was getting deserved credit for improving Ford's cars and trucks. And he had Henry Ford on his side. On October 29, 1984, Ford announced that Petersen and Poling each would move up one notch—Petersen to chairman and chief executive officer, Poling to president and chief operating officer. "Ford has astonished everybody by making an orderly transition," said David Healy, the veteran automotive analyst at Drexel Burnham Lambert. Indeed, it was the first such transition in Ford's eighty-two-year history.

Things sure had changed around Ford. For years the company had been run by Henry Ford II and Lee Iacocca, two of the best-known businessmen on earth. Petersen and Poling, in contrast, were unknown outside Detroit. Petersen had an enormous intellect that qualified him for membership in Mensa, a society for high IQ types. He also had an ego to match; when he had learned as a young man that he might be eligible for Mensa, he promptly wrote the Marine Corps to get access to his intelligence tests, and then mailed in the results along with his application for membership. But decades of working under Henry Ford and the ever-jealous Caldwell had taught Petersen to keep his ego under tight control.

Which was just as well. Between 1983 and 1985, Chrysler and GM emerged from the recession like bullets from the barrel of a gun. Iacocca was becoming an American icon, and Roger Smith was being hailed as an industrial visionary. Ford wasn't doing badly, but it had none of the pizzazz of its crosstown rivals. Petersen's low profile was sparking serious worry in the Ford public relations department.

So in the summer of 1985 the PR men arranged for "Pete," as the new chairman was nicknamed, to appear on NBC's *Today Show* and to address the Midwest Governor's Conference on Michigan's Mackinac Island. He delivered a reasoned discourse on Ford's efforts to "integrate new manufacturing technology with the capabilities of people."

But the miniblitz by the PR department didn't work. In August 1986, *The Economist,* the respected British news magazine, ran a lengthy article about Detroit's Big Three.[1] It included a photograph of each company's chairman—Lee Iacocca of Chrysler, Roger Smith of General Motors, and Philip Caldwell of Ford. The fact that Caldwell had retired eighteen months earlier said it all. Despite his climb to the summit, hardly anybody knew who Don Petersen was.

THE LAUNCH OF THE CAR that revived Ford Motor Company would have made a Lawrence Welk edition of the Edsel look promising. In late 1984, a year before the Taurus's debut, Ford executives were fighting over the look of the car's front end. The conservatives wanted a traditional grille. The radicals favored a stark, striking look with the Ford oval logo set in the middle of a grilleless front. The research showed consumers preferred the grille, but in the end Caldwell and Petersen decided to gamble on the "floating oval."

As the launch date approached, things got worse. Red Poling, by now ensconced as Ford's president, worried that the Taurus's sleek, curvy lines might be too radical after all. Two factories, one in Atlanta and the other in Chicago, were supposed to build the Taurus. But Poling told the Chicago plant to delay switching over to the new car, and to keep building the boxy Ford LTD and Mercury Marquis models for a while. That way, Poling figured, Ford would hedge its bets in case the Taurus flopped.

All during this time, a series of quality glitches delayed the car's debut date repeatedly, from midsummer until fall until finally December 26, 1985. But when the Taurus arrived, it turned out the defects hadn't been solved. Within a week, Ford recalled 4,500 Taurus and Mercury Sable models to replace defective ignition switches. Two months later the company issued another recall notice, to replace window glass that didn't meet government safety standards. Most embarrassing, the cars' pollution-control devices emitted a distinct and powerful rotten-egg odor. When a new owner's neighbors would walk over to admire the first Taurus on the block, the car would smell like a giant that had broken wind in the driveway. Ford took five months to fix the problem.

By any objective measure of defects—or "things gone wrong" in automotive jargon—Taurus sales should have been stalled like commuters on rush-hour freeways. Instead, the Taurus and its Mercury Sable twin flew off dealer lots. With its sleek, rounded lines, the Taurus showed that, after years of losing ground to cleverly designed imports, an American company could build a car with a European flair. Ford's well-traveled executives (most of them had served a stint in Europe) saw the popularity of Braun coffee makers, Dansk furniture, and almost everything sold at

Crate & Barrel. The Ford people were thinking like yuppies, while the GM guys—with their bland, cookie-cutter sedans—were thinking like, well, GM guys. For decades, Chevy built it, people bought it, and that settled it. But Taurus changed that. And because the Japanese were still selling just small cars, the Taurus quickly became the sedan of choice for the smart, upper-middle-class American family.

Within three months, Ford's top brass knew the Taurus and Sable were a huge hit in a segment of the market—midsized family sedans— that had been owned by General Motors for decades. Poling hurriedly ordered the Chicago plant to drop the LTD and switch to Taurus. And Ford's marketing mavens, relieved to learn that buyers would forgive a few defects on a car with plenty of pleasing attributes, invented the term "things gone right" to explain their success.

The Taurus wasn't, however, the engine that powered Ford's explosion in earnings. The car had cost too much to develop. The real money came from a gaggle of aging behemoths: the Ford Crown Victoria, Mercury Grand Marquis, and the Lincoln Continental, Town Car, and Mark VII. Called the Panther cars because of the code-name for their chassis, all were relics of the era of rear-wheel-drive land barges. In the energy crisis of the early 1980s, General Motors had poured billions of dollars into down-sizing its big, luxury models because it expected gas prices would continue to soar. Ford, and especially Don Petersen, wanted to follow GM's lead. But the company simply didn't have the money to develop new luxury cars and the Taurus at the same time. Ford hung on to its old geezers.

Then gas prices started falling, many Americans started looking for big cars again, and Ford's were virtually the only ones in sight. Because the factory tooling for the Panther cars had long been paid for, the extra mileage that Ford was getting from them was pretty much pure gravy. Almost by default, Ford had a huge advantage in the most profitable segment of the car market. And Ford's marketing men were looking for a way to drive the point home.

No man was looking harder than Thomas J. Wagner, a roly-poly native of Peoria, Illinois, who ran the company's Lincoln–Mercury division, home to most of the company's big cars. Wagner had joined Ford's sales operations in 1963, and by 1985 had endured more than two decades of getting whipped by GM. But now GM was saddled with a stable of Cadillacs, Buicks, Oldsmobiles, Pontiacs, and Chevrolets that looked unappealingly alike. Tom Wagner saw his chance, and he took it.

He called in Lincoln–Mercury's ad agency, Young & Rubicam, and said he was tired of the same old commercials that showed cars cruising along winding roads to the tune of upbeat Muzak. He wanted something hard-hitting and different, something to exploit Lincoln–Mercury's advantage over GM. The agency responded with a commercial titled "The Valet."

It showed a tuxedo-clad man and his well-dressed wife walking out of their club and asking the valet to pull up their black Cadillac. But as the couple climbed into the car, another man sheepishly interrupted and said, "Excuse me, I believe that's my Buick." The hapless couple found another car and the husband asked the valet, "Is this my Cadillac?" The valet responded: "No, it's an Oldsmobile, I think." Soon the whole parking lot was erupting into pandemonium with club members trying to sort out whose cars were whose.

Just then, a relaxed and dapper gentleman strolled up to the valet and said, "My Lincoln Town Car, please." He promptly got his car, without hassle or humiliation, while the narrator intoned: "There's nothing like a Lincoln."

"The Valet" didn't sit well with Don Petersen. He deemed it too snotty and thought it might rile GM into similar negative advertising attacking Ford. But the commercial had strong backing from Wagner's second-in-command at Lincoln–Mercury, thirty-six-year-old Edsel B. Ford II. Edsel Ford was a great-grandson of the company's founder, the only son of Henry Ford II, and—with his family controlling 40 percent of Ford's voting stock—clearly destined for a greater role in company affairs. Even as chairman, Don Petersen couldn't entirely ignore Edsel's wishes.

So "The Valet" went on the air in the fall of 1985, and the impact was immediate. Ford and Lincoln–Mercury dealers simply couldn't keep enough Panther cars in stock. Cadillac dealers started flooding GM headquarters with complaints that the Ford commercial was making their cars look ridiculous. Losing sales was aggravating, being laughed at unbearable. GM's look-alike car problem had been embarrassingly obvious already, but "The Valet" commercial punched the point home into America's living rooms with savagely effective ridicule. For GM executives, however, the worst was yet to come.

One night that fall, nearly 200 people gathered at suburban Detroit's Oakland University for the annual black-tie dinner of the President's Club, a fund-raising arm of the school. The well-heeled crowd was liberally studded with senior executives from GM, Ford, and Chrysler. At the end of the evening, as the crowd began to disperse, a driving rain started to pelt the unpaved driveway outside. School officials quickly rounded up students to retrieve cars for their guests. None of the cars had claim tickets, so the students would simply drive up and call out a description.

"A BLACK CADILLAC!" shouted one of the impromptu valets. But then an anonymous voice shouted back from the crowd: "No, IT'S A BUICK!" As everybody started to titter, someone else yelled, "No, IT'S AN OLDS-MOBILE!" Then another voice called out that it was a Chevy instead. By this time the crowd was roaring with laughter, and new shouts of ridicule rang out every time a GM car pulled up. The scene was just like the television commercial—life imitating art, as it were.

The GM men on the scene—including Lloyd Reuss, the executive vice president running the North American car business—kept brave smiles pasted to their faces. But there was no escaping the fact that, here they were, being publicly humiliated, right in their own backyard. Now things had really gotten out of hand. Spitball fights and name-calling were fun in the sixth grade, but everybody was grown up now, weren't they? Something had to be done.

Thus it was that Don Petersen got a phone call from another man who occupied a corner office in Detroit. It was Roger Smith, the chairman of GM. Like his predecessors at The General, Smith was used to talking down to his counterparts at GM's smaller crosstown rivals. But now Smith was pleading. Was there anything Don could do, please, to get those damned "Valet" commercials off the air? Let's both say positive things about our own products, implored Smith, resorting to the states-manship that befit his position, instead of saying negative things about each other.

Shortly afterward Roger Smith received a letter of reply from Don Petersen. Ford, Petersen said, would back off. After the current round of air time was used up, Ford would discard "The Valet." The Young Turks at Ford, including Edsel Ford, would be disappointed, but they just didn't understand. At its very heart, at the pinnacle of executive power, De-troit was an exclusive men's club with its own unwritten code of conduct. Members, after all, had to follow the rules.

THE TAURUS'S TAKEOFF and the resurgence of the Panther cars were merely a prelude for Ford. On February 17, 1987, the company reported that its net profits for the prior year had surged to $3.3 billion. It was an all-time Ford record, and, incredibly, it handily exceeded the $2.9 billion profit that General Motors had announced less than two weeks earlier. Even more startling was Ford's margin in pretax profits, the truest test of how companies compare. Ford's $5.1 billion was nearly double what GM had earned before taxes, and more than the pretax profits of GM and Chrysler combined! And this from a company that was 40 percent smaller than GM alone. Suddenly, Ford started stealing headlines from Chrysler and GM.

The Ford people had to pinch themselves to prove they weren't dreaming. Ford had not outearned General Motors for sixty-two years—since 1924. That was before the days when GM's Alfred P. Sloan had invented modern marketing ("a car for every purse and purpose") and roared right by Henry Ford, who insisted consumers could have any color they wanted as long as it was black.

Before Sloan, Ford Motor was the world's biggest car company; it even had 75 percent of the market in Japan. But ever since the 1930s GM had so dominated the auto industry that the GM divisions—Chevy, Pontiac, Olds, Buick, and Cadillac—saw their main competition as each other, certainly not Ford. Every time Ford came up with a hit—like the Falcon, the Mustang, or the Maverick—it would simply suck sales away from other Ford models, leaving GM's market share unscathed. GM had, far and away, the best dealers, the most affluent customers, and the strongest financial condition. Less than three years earlier, down at Boca Raton, Will Caldwell had sounded the alarm about how GM's spending blitz might wreak havoc on Ford. But now Ford was doing damage to GM; it had pulled off the biggest upset since Joe Namath and the New York Jets won Super Bowl III.

Ford's incredible earnings feat of 1986 was just the beginning. For three straight years Ford racked up record upon record upon record, hauling in so much money that the company's senior executives simply couldn't believe it, and in fact didn't really know what to do with it all. In 1987 Ford's net income, after taxes and everything else, hit an amazing $4.6 billion. That was a record not only for Ford, but for any auto company in history, topping the $4.5 billion that GM had earned in 1984.

The very next year Ford beat its own record again, earning an astounding $5.3 billion. It was an all-time record for any manufacturing company in any business, and well over half of Ford's overall earnings

during the entire decade of the seventies. On July 19, 1988, Standard &
Poor's Corporation, one of the two major concerns that rates the credit-
worthiness of American companies, boosted Ford's rating to "double A,"
higher than the rating for General Motors—once the bluest of blue chips
—for the very first time.

Ford shareholders were richly rewarded. In the depths of the recession,
between 1981 and 1983, Ford had suspended payments of quarterly cash
dividends to shareholders, a move that, among other things, crimped
the lavish lifestyles of members of the Ford family. But over the next five
and a half years, beginning in July 1983, Ford boosted the dividend
eleven times, while declaring a 2 for 1 stock split along the way. As a
result, a Ford share that paid no dividend at all in June of 1983 paid a
whopping $6 a share per year (adjusted for the split) in June of 1989.

On top of all this, Ford committed more than $2.5 billion of corporate
funds to buying back shares of its own stock. That was enough to acquire
nearly one fourth of all the shares outstanding, a move that had the most
welcome effect of pushing up the price of the remaining shares. Ford's
stock had touched bottom at $3½ a share in the gloomy days of 1981.
But by 1989 it hit an all-time high of $56⅝, capping a decade-long surge
of more than 1,500 percent. The contrast between Ford's resurgence and
GM's nosedive was so marked that Ford's total market value on the New
York Stock Exchange actually exceeded that of General Motors. The
elation in Dearborn was matched only by the frustration inside GM's
fortresslike headquarters on West Grand Boulevard in Detroit.

The causes of Ford's financial explosion were as simple as they were
profound. The company was making Detroit's best cars at a time when
America's longest postwar economic expansion was sending industrywide
sales soaring to unprecedented levels. Fords sported distinctive aerodynamic styling and set quality standards that, while not up to Japanese
levels, stood out as the best among the Big Three. And while GM had
been carrying costly excess manufacturing capacity, Ford had tailored its
shoes to fit the size of its feet.

The company had closed thirteen factories between 1979 and 1983 in
the process of slashing its hourly work force from 191,000 people to just
101,000. It was a drastic downsizing that could have wreaked havoc with
labor relations, except that Ford used the crisis creatively. In 1979, it
had launched Employee Involvement, a program to solicit suggestions
from workers on how to improve quality and productivity. GM had a
similar program, but only on paper. Ford really meant it. It hired a new

head of labor relations, Peter Pestillo, from outside the auto industry, and he marshaled senior management to work with union officials to achieve results.

An early test had come in 1980, when Ford told the union it would close its woefully uncompetitive metal-stamping plant near Cleveland. When the union begged for a reprieve, Ford flew Joseph D'Amico, the factory's firebrand UAW leader, to Japan, to tour factories there and gauge the competitive challenge firsthand. For D'Amico, it was like Paul's trip to Damascus. The union developed a plan for saving $15 million a year at the Cleveland plant by eliminating such nonsensical rules as one that required millwrights to walk alongside forklift drivers whenever the drivers were moving machinery.[2]

In 1984 Ford entered a stretch of nearly six straight years in which it didn't take a single day of factory "down time" to reduce inventories of unsold cars. In 1988 the company sold nearly as many vehicles in North America as it had a decade earlier, but with only about half as many hourly workers. Many factories were working maximum overtime schedules—two ten-hour shifts a day instead of the standard eight-hour schedules. In a volume-driven business such as automobiles, this was a recipe for minting money.

Most notable was the assembly plant in Wixom, Michigan, twenty-five miles northwest of Detroit. Wixom, which in contrast to the new General Motors high-tech plants was more than twenty-five years old, was home to Ford's luxury cars, the Lincoln Town Car, Continental, and Mark VII. In 1987 the company launched a radically new Continental, switching the car from rear-drive to a front-wheel drive chassis based on the Ford Taurus. The new Continental embraced the European concept of understated "functional luxury," as opposed to the vinyl-roof and velour-seat garishness so often promoted by Detroit. The car became an overnight success, and the factory was straining to keep up with the demand for Lincolns.

In 1988 Wixom alone posted profits of around $1.5 billion, making it the single most profitable car plant in the world. Suddenly, Cadillac wasn't the Cadillac of the industry anymore. That mantle had passed to Lincoln.

The good times were rolling right into the paychecks passed out at the Glass House. In 1987 Ford's top forty-four executives earned bonuses (in addition to their regular salaries) that averaged nearly $1 million apiece. The riches trickled down to the factory floor, too, albeit on a more modest scale. In 1982 Ford had signed the auto industry's first profit-sharing agreement with the United Auto Workers union. The union had hesitated to embrace profit sharing because Ford wasn't making any profits at the time, and no one knew when it would.

But now, the union's gamble was paying off big, at least at Ford. In 1987 Ford paid its workers an average of $2,100 apiece in profit sharing, in addition to their regular wages. Then in 1988 profit-sharing checks averaged a whopping $3,700—about 10 percent of the typical worker's annual wages—and some skilled tradesmen raked in nearly $7,000. In both those years GM workers got nothing at all in profit sharing, because the company's North American car operations had virtually no profits. Ford's executives piously said that they didn't intend to gloat at the contrast—but then summoned Detroit's television stations to shoot footage of smiling Ford workers gleefully getting their checks. GM was handed yet another humiliation.

By now, this striking contrast between Ford and GM was taking a personal turn. In December 1987, President Reagan held a state dinner at the White House to honor Mikhail Gorbachev, the Soviet leader then at the height of his power at home and at the pinnacle of adulation in the West. His visit was the social event of the year at the White House. The press zeroed in on how Nancy Reagan and Raisa Gorbachev were doing their best to upstage each other even as their husbands were hitting it off famously. Less noticed was how the gala dinner reflected the pecking order among the chairmen of Detroit's Big Three.

Lee Iacocca, the most famous of the three chairmen, wasn't even invited; he had been persona non grata at the Reagan White House for years. GM's Roger Smith, a loyal Republican, did get invited. He was seated at a table with "a Marshal Androkrofus or something," as he recounted afterward on a Detroit radio talk show, apparently referring to Sergei Akhromeyev, deputy minister of defense. But Don Petersen didn't have to struggle to remember whom he sat with. He dined at the head table, with Reagan and Gorbachev. No matter that he was the least known of Detroit's chief executives among the general public. Don Petersen was quickly becoming the most admired among the people who really mattered.

It wasn't just because Ford was running roughshod over its biggest domestic rival. Petersen was emerging as a corporate philosopher, an enlightened businessman whose thoughtful, people-oriented ideas carried relevance to all those who cared about America's fate in the rowdy new world of global competition. He was the first high-level American auto executive to embrace the ideas that W. Edwards Deming had preached with such effectiveness in Japan.

In 1980 Petersen, while at home in Detroit, had watched an NBC television white paper on Deming, and later had arranged for him to be hired as a consultant to Ford. Deming had come into the company and preached his message: Big corporations should scrap ruinous competition among individual employees. Instead, they should teach people to work together, learn to trust their employees, and concentrate on small but continuous improvements that will produce big results over time. Petersen boiled all this down into one word, "teamwork," and he repeated it over and over again, like a mantra.

On Christmas of 1986, when Ford was on the verge of outearning GM for the first time, Petersen had the windows of the Glass House lit up at night to spell a special message: "Thank You, Team." In 1987, when the Ford Thunderbird Turbo Coupe won *Motor Trend* magazine's Car of the Year award, Petersen accepted on behalf of "the entire team." He insisted that the award ceremony be attended by a half a dozen Ford employees—including a factory worker and a marketing man and an engineer—to represent those who had worked on the car. After the ceremony he took the employees and their spouses to dinner at the Whitney, a century-old, downtown-Detroit home of a Michigan lumber baron that had been converted into one of the city's most elegant restaurants. And he proposed a toast to the team, saying: "Where I grew up out West we have a saying. If you see a turtle sitting on top of a fencepost, you know he didn't get there by himself."

Petersen spearheaded the formation of a statement of "Mission, Values, and Guiding Principles" for Ford. MVGP, as it was called for short, was a sort of corporate Ten Commandments that dedicated the company to "People, Products, and Profits," in that order. The statement declared: "Employee involvement is our way of life. We are a team. We must treat each other with trust and respect." Petersen had the statement printed on hundreds of thousands of laminated three-by-five cards, and passed out to every Ford employee in the world. And when underlings brought him new proposals he asked, "How does this square with MVGP?"

Petersen also started an Executive Development Center to provide special training to Ford's top 2,000 officials from around the world.

Groups of fifty or so would spent a week in a conference center near company headquarters, hearing presentations about Ford's strategy and applying what they learned in case-study sessions built around small teams. The weeklong sessions gave participants a chance to learn about the company, but more important, a chance to get to learn about each other and about working together. And at the end of each week, on Friday afternoon, each group would have an informal meeting with one of Ford's most senior officers, often Petersen himself.

At one of the early sessions, in 1986, the Ford men were told to dress informally—just as they had done all week—for the Friday afternoon chat with the chairman. But cultural change didn't come easily at a formal, rank-conscious place like Ford. After all, Ford was a place where vice presidents were entitled to send their memos on special blue paper, and the chief executive's office used "pumpkin-colored" stock, while mere plebeians had to make do with ordinary white. So despite the instructions to dress casually, several attendees darted back to their rooms after lunch to change into their suits before Petersen arrived.

After they returned, the people who hadn't changed clothes started teasing them, when suddenly Petersen pulled up out front. He climbed out of his car wearing his suit and tie, and those who had changed clothes exchanged knowing smiles at having the last laugh. But then, to their horror, Petersen opened the back door of his car, took off his coat and tie, and threw them onto the back seat. The group broke into laughter as those who had changed clothes scurried back to their rooms to change again.

Petersen's push for a new corporate culture was embraced by many people at Ford. Joseph Kordick, a devoutly religious man who ran the company's parts and service division, told underlings at meetings that he wanted Ford to be the "most loving, caring" company on the face of the earth. At one managerial meeting in New Orleans he asked everyone to stand up and hug the person next to them—and everybody, albeit awkwardly, complied.

But not everybody was so enthused about Petersen's program. One particular skeptic was the brilliant but brash Bob Lutz. In May 1986, Lutz, then executive vice president for truck operations, sent his troops a biting memo that brutally satirized the new Ford culture. "Ford terminology in memos, meetings, and reports is changing at an accelerating rate," Lutz wrote. "New words are emerging almost daily as yet another group strives for supremacy in communicative obfuscation."

With that, he offered a guide to the "new Ford-speak," consisting of three columns of words. By choosing one word at random from each column, any corporate troglodyte who was having cultural adjustment problems could start spouting phrases like "interactive postadversarial consensus" or "team-oriented transformational buy-in." And for the hard cases who needed even more help, Lutz offered a glossary of new Ford terms alongside their outmoded counterparts. The new term for committee was "interactive synergistic substructure." A bigger committee was now an "enhanced synergistic substructure."

The memo was widely copied and passed around the company, and it made Lutz a folk hero among many managers. But in career terms, it made him a dead man. Within weeks of the memo's appearance, Lutz jumped ship to Chrysler, becoming the latest member of Lee Iacocca's Gang of Ford.

None of this internal dissent reached the public. What did was a growing chorus of public praise for Don Petersen. The *Wall Street Journal* touted Ford's cultural revolution under his aegis. In 1987 *Motor Trend* named him its Man of the Year, and the *Gallagher Report*, a business newsletter, gave him its Best Executive Award. In 1988 *Fortune* magazine put Petersen on the cover and reported that his peers rated him as America's most effective executive, ahead of John Welch of General Electric, John Akers of IBM, and even Lee Iacocca. In 1989 the National Management Association named Petersen its American Manager of the Year. *Chief Executive* magazine named him its Chief Executive of the Year. And the Detroit *News* named Petersen the Michigan CEO of the Decade.

On October 2, 1989, Ford's corporate philosopher delivered a moving summary of the thinking that had brought him such acclaim. There were no PR men at his side or reporters in the audience; this wasn't the place for that. The setting was Christ Church Cranbrook in the elite Detroit suburb of Bloomfield Hills, where Petersen's fellow members had invited him to talk about how his personal values affected his business decisions.

"When people are treated with decency and respect, confidence and trust, and empowered in the business of the company, they perform better, and they learn more," he said. "And that's the wellspring of continuous improvement, which is one of Ford's formal Guiding Principles. . . .

"Does God live in quality, teamwork or involvement? I sense that some people believe business, by its very nature, is out of sync with Judeo–Christian values. That, somehow, there is an automatic contradiction between making sound business decisions and doing the right thing—as we understand it from the teachings of Christianity.

"That interpretation is without foundation. . . . In fact, it seems to me that fundamentally sound beliefs and principles are an absolute requirement for progress, whether in the specifics of an individual life or enterprise, or the totality of human relations in our society. Remember the words of Psalm 127: 'Unless the Lord builds the house, they labor in vain who build it; unless the Lord guards the city, the watchman stays awake in vain.' "

CHAPTER 6

DEAD IN THE WATER

Ross Perot had at least one thing right about Roger Smith: GM's chairman fretted constantly about his public image. That was why one of his confidantes was Jack McNulty, GM's vice president for public relations. McNulty was Smith's personal image consultant. A craggy-faced, heavy-smoking, hard-drinking Irish pol, McNulty had worked as an aide to John D. Rockefeller III and Lyndon Johnson before joining GM. He prided himself on having a broader world view than fellow vice presidents who'd spent their entire careers on the GM payroll. But for all his savvy, McNulty had trouble keeping up with his restless boss. McNulty knew he'd fallen behind the curve whenever Smith called him into his office and declared: "Jack, we're dead in the water." It was a phrase McNulty came to dread. Early 1987 was one of those "dead in the water" times. In the wake of the Perot disaster, GM wasn't just dead in the water, it was on the rocks.

Roger Smith, the great "innovator" of 1985, was now the archvillain of American industry—the man who doled out megabucks to billionaires and pink slips to factory workers. Smith launched a series of visits to GM plants, ostensibly to boost morale. But the visits turned ugly, as workers jeered and hooted at the grim-faced chairman. The loathing for Smith among GM employees was matched by the public's disgust with the company's bland, defect-ridden, underpowered cars. During the summer 1986 war with Perot, GM's market share had arced into a nosedive. Smith had started the year with 42.5 percent of the U.S. car market. In December 1986, GM captured just 34 percent. Put another way, some 850,000 buyers had walked away from GM, taking with them some $10 billion in revenue. As the full extent of the damage from the Perot fiasco became clear, Smith launched a dogged crusade to convince skeptics that GM was bouncing back.

GM's campaign was heralded in a four-page "Dear Fellow Stockholder" letter sent on February 10 over Smith's signature. "I can report to you that, at General Motors today, better trained employees are using the most advanced and sophisticated technology to build lower cost, higher quality automobiles," the letter declared. It went on to list "strategic goals" GM would pursue: Building cars that set "industry standards" for quality; replacing older "less efficient" factories with new ones; pursuing a "major cost reduction" program; and "strengthening GM's partnership with EDS and Hughes Aircraft."

In sum, Smith declared, GM would produce a 15 percent after-tax return on shareholders' equity by 1990, compared with 9.6 percent in 1986, and cut annual costs by $10 billion as of the same year.

Fred Astaire couldn't have danced any better. GM's "lower cost, higher quality" automobiles were actually higher cost and lower quality, on average, than any other vehicles on the market—GM's own internal studies said so. And so did most outside surveys, notably those performed by the Bible of the informed car buyer, *Consumer Reports*. GM's older factories were "less efficient" than those operated by Ford or the Japanese. Some of GM's new factories, however, were even worse. Hamtramck was only the most egregious example.

As for the strategic goals, only one was new: The cost-cutting plan. And the details of that purge offered more insight to GM's troubles than to its supposed strengths. Capital spending would be cut immediately. In other words, the technology binge begun in the late 1970s and pursued by Smith for six years was over. GM was selling its heavy truck operations, its bus business, and its heavy diesel engine operations. GM couldn't figure out how to make money in these businesses. GM would dump 25,000 white collar workers in 1987, and another 15,000 in 1988. Put another way, GM was extravagantly overstaffed. GM, Smith said in his letter, would "review" its parts operations and "eliminate uncompetitive component manufacturing operations" to save $500 million annually. That, of course, conceded that a substantial number of uncompetitive operations existed.

Just one week after Smith's letter went out, Ford announced that, in 1986, it had outearned its colossal rival for the first time since the Great Depression.

FORD'S COUP SHOOK the denizens of GM's 14th-floor executive suites. Smith and his subordinates struggled to rationalize their failure. But they quickly lapsed into incoherence. Explaining away GM's skidding market share caused the most trouble. In January 1987, Smith declared that GM's 1986 market share of 41 percent was "abnormally low." Jim Mc-Donald put it more bluntly. "The guy who says we're going to be at 38 percent is smoking opium," GM's president growled. The new head of North American car operations, Lloyd Reuss, declared: "Our penetration is down, and it's my job to get it back up." It could have been the punchline to a joke in *Playboy*, but the straitlaced Reuss didn't get the double entendre.

Then, in February, Smith wavered. GM's new goal, he declared, was to "maximize profits . . . not maximize market share." Pressed on this, Smith eventually insisted that GM's official goal was to recapture 40 percent of the market. This figure would take on considerable significance in the years ahead.

Meanwhile, Smith began a frantic effort to buy back Wall Street's affection. He froze salaries for GM's middle managers, then declared GM would spend a staggering $5.2 billion to buy back common shares.[1] It was, in effect, a bribe to persuade Wall Street's traders to bid up GM stock. The fewer GM shares around, the higher the value of the remaining shares would be, at least in theory. The buybacks would be certain to further drain GM's cash reserves, which had already fallen by $4.5 billion during the previous two years. The money Smith was proposing to dump into shareholders' pockets was enough to fund the development of two or even three new lines of cars, or several new engines or transmissions, all badly needed.

Smith touted his program tirelessly, even appearing on *Wall $treet Week* with Louis Rukeyser. Smith adopted a mantra to brush off critics: "I'm not as good as they said I was," he said. "And I'm not as bad as they say I am."

. . .

THAT JAUNTY QUIP didn't change the fact that Roger Smith's industrial powerhouse was sputtering. A chorus of GM bashing was rising from Wall Street and the press. Perot wasn't the issue anymore. It was Smith's leadership. In early October 1987, Smith flew to New York for a board meeting, and spent an evening commiserating with friends over dinner about the unfair treatment GM was getting. The next day, Smith cornered his image master, McNulty.

"I've got an idea," the Chairman said. "We'll have a new kind of Motorama."

McNulty was taken aback. "That's a throwback to the 1950s," he blurted.

Indeed, it was. GM's Motoramas had been a pure expression of Eisenhower-era marketing glitz. The company would hire the grand ballroom at the Waldorf-Astoria Hotel, and put on a combination automotive circus and Las Vegas revue.[2] Troops of well-scrubbed young men and women would sing and dance in celebration of the latest fantasy creations from the fertile minds in GM's design studios—torpedo-nosed sports cars, sleek roadsters with glass bubble tops, a Pontiac Club de Mer that looked like a cross between a fighter jet and a mako shark. Some years, the Waldorf show would hit the road, touring the major cities around the country to whoop up interest in GM's new models. For their day, the Motoramas were highly effective. From 1949 to 1961, the Motoramas drew some 10 million people, by GM's count. But as television became a fixture in every American home, GM abandoned the Motoramas and turned its attention to the new medium, which could reach more people in a single minute than the Motoramas touched in over a decade.

As McNulty struggled to grasp what his boss had in mind, Smith pressed on. "We'll do it in New York," Smith said. McNulty still didn't get it. He began ticking off a list of possible venues, including the Coliseum exhibition hall.

"No," Smith said. "I want to do it in the Waldorf."

IT WOULD BE JUST LIKE the glory days, when Smith was a young GM recruit, America was No. 1, and GM was King of the Road. The Waldorf show would feature gleaming new cars, a glamorous, admiring crowd, and a big black tie dinner in the hotel's Starlight Terrace.

Putting together the pieces of the Waldorf show, officially titled "Teamwork and Technology for Today and Tomorrow," became GM's obsession for the final eighty-eight days of 1987. GM's marketing and public relations minions worked through the Christmas holidays to produce a stunning realization of the chairman's vision. Design studios were commandeered. Engineers scurried to bolt together prototypes of cars that weren't due to hit the market for months, if ever. One of GM's advertising agencies fired up a massive new campaign, complete with an eight-page magazine insert and a new wave of television commercials. The show's $20 million budget, and the distraction it created, had beleaguered GM managers grinding their teeth. Disaffected staffers quickly coined a new name for the Teamwork and Technology show: "Rogerama."[3]

OF ALL THE SPECIAL EFFECTS conjured up for Smith's spectacle, none was more ambitious than the video wall. This was a technological marvel on a par with any of GM's cars. The idea was to produce a video extolling GM's unique marriage of "teamwork and technology" that would play across a giant wall built with 240 individual television screens. Behind the wall, a sophisticated computer system would slice images up so that each screen carried the right piece of a picture. The screens also could create montages of images.

Armed with a $3 million budget, GM hired a Hollywood producer named Bob Rogers to create the video, produce original background music, and execute the complicated technological tricks required to make it play across the screens. Rogers, whose company created such multimedia displays as the MGM Studio tour at Walt Disney World in Florida, usually took two years to assemble such a display. GM gave Rogers just seventy days. No one had ever before created a display of this type on such a gigantic scale in such a short time.

At times, the video wall threatened to become the GM public relations staff's answer to Hamtramck. To produce their video portrait of the world's largest corporation, Rogers and his crew decided to film a series of stream-of-consciousness interviews with GM employees. The workers were candid about the corporation's woes, but leavened their criticism with optimism that GM could change for the better. Rogers found the realism of GM's rank-and-file employees exhilarating.

Smith got his first look at the video wall display in December at a cavernous, unheated warehouse that belonged to a design shop near GM's Warren, Michigan, Technical Center. McNulty invited Smith and Robert Stempel, who had succeeded McDonald as GM's president that summer, to screen the video at 6:30 A.M. Stempel arrived first. Confronting the massive display, he blurted out: "What hath God wrought?" When Smith arrived, he rubbed his eyebrows and declared: "Wow." Smith sat down, and the screens flickered to life.

But instead of a paean to the technological prowess of the world's largest corporation, Smith saw an earnest GM employee talking about the corporation's mistakes.

"Jack!" Smith snapped. "What the hell is this?" McNulty reassured him that the total effect was positive, which it was. But Bob Rogers' mild-mannered effort at cinéma vérité had unnerved his high-powered clients. GM had never allowed low-ranking employees to speak in such a public forum without scripts. It was unheard of! Rogers found the ruckus puzzling. The GM employees he'd filmed struck him as terrific ambassadors for the company. "I feel like I've got a big secret," one young engineer had said. "The fun is back," declared another employee. "The communication . . . it's great," bubbled a third man. Why, it was downright remarkable that people could say such things after all GM had been through.

Rogers' video was saved, in the end, by Smith's insane deadline. Rogers told McNulty there simply was no time to redo the video. After minor tinkering, the final film reflected Rogers' original vision.

The video wall saga didn't end there. Rogers and his crew of German technicians began setting the video wall up in the Waldorf's ballroom as soon as Guy Lombardo's orchestra began clearing out after New Year's Eve. On January 4, 1988, the night before Teamwork and Technology opened, Smith swirled into the ballroom with his wife, Barbara, and Walter Fallon, former chairman of Eastman Kodak Company and a member of GM's board of directors at the time. They settled into chairs in front of the 240 screens that made up the huge display, and McNulty called for the technicians to roll the tape. The massive array of screens flickered briefly, then froze in a scramble of fractured images.

"Gosh," Smith said. "Is that the way it's supposed to look?"

The answer, of course, was no. The German technicians jumped into action, reverting to their native tongue as they barked and cursed over their headsets. Rogers, listening in on his own headsets, thought he was inside a U-boat that had just been hit by a depth charge. Out front, McNulty nervously informed the chairman that it was only a minor glitch. But almost as soon as the tape began to roll again, it froze.

Fortunately for McNulty, the technicians discovered the problem: A powerful electrical surge had stormed through midtown Manhattan and fried the delicate computer equipment that controlled the video wall. By the next morning, the equipment was repaired, and a huge surge protector installed to prevent another meltdown. At 7 A.M. the opening morning of the show, Smith appeared for a final test. The video wall performed perfectly. Smith, however, didn't.

THE OPENING DAY of the Teamwork and Technology show was January 5, 1988, and the scene was everything Smith had imagined. The Waldorf's main ballroom was transformed into an industrial wonderland. There were gleaming, futuristic "concept" cars like the scoop-nosed Pontiac Banshee and the V-12-powered Cadillac Voyage, computer systems from EDS, and even a few real models such as the new, front-drive Cutlass Supreme. The thousands of shareholders, GM employees, and Wall Street professionals who'd received invitations to the show wandered through the displays, marveling at such sights as the minidesign studio, complete with a clay model of a car, and a Hughes communications satellite. GM's barkers didn't discourage anyone who thought that the pretend cars, such as the Voyage and the swoopy Buick Lucerne, were prototypes of cars Cadillac or Buick intended to sell. Elsewhere in the hall, displays and videos trumpeted GM's newfound "teamwork" with the UAW.

Smith, meanwhile, sought to reclaim his image as a prophet of change. "The old ways we used to do business, when too often we used to work against each other, I can tell you right now they are gone forever," he declared. "It's part of a dark history." Defending the enormous cost of his technology and diversification campaigns, Smith said, "We planned for the long term . . . our vision is starting to pay off."

But Smith couldn't carry through on this rhetoric. He read nearly all of his remarks, including those made in private conversations with groups of invited guests, from prepared scripts. When he did talk off the cuff, he got in trouble.

Right after his opening speech on the first day of the Waldorf show, Smith took questions from a gaggle of 300 reporters. John White, the crusty, middle-aged automotive writer from the Boston *Globe,* demanded to know what GM offered to compete with the $6,995 Dodge Aries and Plymouth Reliant sedans Chrysler was touting as the best bargain in the family car market.

"You have to look at value," Smith said. "I think our best competition in General Motors against that car right now happens to be a two-year-old Buick, that you can go down to your dealer and get, and you can get better value for that than you will the new Chrysler at that price. There's no question in my mind."

White was aghast. "A used car, sir?" he asked. "Yes," Smith insisted.

Another man might have played the line as a joke at Chrysler's expense. Smith, however, made it sound as if people with only $6,995 to spend simply weren't good enough to buy a new GM car. The GM executives standing nearby gritted their teeth, realizing Smith's remark would get played as fresh evidence of his hopeless arrogance toward GM's customers.

The good news, for GM, was that the cynicism of the business press was largely drowned out by the boom and clang of the $20 million GM publicity machine. Smith and Stempel found a far friendlier audience among the guests and dignitaries, and on television. The two executives did a grueling fifty-three interviews for television stations around the country, and the major networks. Stockholders oohed and aahed at the sleek cars, although some were simply nonplussed. One elderly woman in a black mink poked her head into the Oldsmobile Aerotech, a single-seat racing car that had no relationship at all to the staid sedans Olds actually sold. "This car will go 250 miles an hour," a GM staffer declared proudly. "Not with me in it," replied the puzzled shareholder.

GM also pulled out the stops to court big investors and business leaders, even sending jets from its corporate fleet to fetch some VIPs to the party. That night, Smith and some 250 of the highest rollers in American finance and industry gathered for a sumptuous black tie dinner in the Starlight Terrace. Lesser lights gathered in two other rooms in the hotel, and Smith and his executive corps circulated among the guests.

Amid the whirl, one GM executive did stand out, and it wasn't the chairman. Instead it was Bob Stempel. He had won the race to succeed Jim McDonald as president in the spring of 1987, in what many inside GM saw as a come-from-behind victory over Lloyd Reuss, the flashy executive who ran the North American car business. Stempel struck some of GM's board members as a bit of a plodder. In the end, however, Stempel's track record simply stacked up better than Reuss's. Stempel had initiated a much-needed overhaul of the truck business, selling off unprofitable heavy truck and bus operations. Overseas operations, meanwhile, were showing signs of returning to profitability after years in the red. Precisely who was responsible for that would become a point of contention. But in early 1987, Stempel got a lot of the credit. Reuss (pronounced Royce), meanwhile, had disillusioned some key members of GM's board of directors with his failure to improve profits or sales in GM's domestic car business.

Stempel certainly had been a popular choice among GM's rank and file. The new president's booming voice and hearty, frank manner contrasted sharply with Smith's bullying and wheedling. The same day as Smith's used-Buick faux pas, Stempel gave interviews in which he said GM had a "reasonable chance" at rebuilding its market share to 38 percent from 36 percent. By GM standards, this was a blast of candor. Stempel also could make speeches and social conversation without a script. In short, he came across as a GM executive with a human touch.

As the Teamwork and Technology show journeyed from New York to Dallas to Los Angeles to Chicago, Stempel's enthusiastic speeches won warm applause, even from workers who had little chance of remaining on GM's payroll long enough to take part in the glorious 21st Century Smith envisioned.

THE TEAMWORK AND TECHNOLOGY show revealed a lot about GM, but not in the way Smith had intended. The hyperbole of the extravaganza —the show cars, the video wall, and Smith's speeches—put a spotlight on how far from this idealized vision GM really was.

GM's "teamwork" with the UAW was like a bad marriage held together for the sake of the kids. UAW vice president Don Ephlin lent his prestige to the show, giving a talk about the importance of joint labor and management efforts to improve quality. But most rank-and-file GM workers cared more that, for two years in a row, GM doled out big bonuses to Smith and other executives while workers got layoff threats instead of profit-sharing checks. GM brought in hundreds of workers from plants in Tarrytown, New York, and Linden, New Jersey, to mingle with the crowds of shareholders and money managers at the invitation-only Waldorf show. The workers had plenty of time to spare, since GM had furloughed their factories because the cars and trucks they built weren't selling.

As for technology, GM was hard-pressed to show anything it had in production that broke new ground. GM trotted out its new four cylinder engine, called the Quad 4, which had four valves per cylinder instead of the two per cylinder standard in other GM engines. The extra pair of valves helped the Quad 4 burn fuel more efficiently, and crank out more horsepower from a smaller block than the old Iron Duke that powered most of GM's small cars. But modern four-valve-per-cylinder engines were news only to people who'd never purchased a Toyota or a Honda. And as GM customers would discover, the Quad 4 was a rough, noisy beast compared to its Japanese competition.

Financially, GM was still deteriorating. In early January, shortly after the Waldorf show, Alan Smith, the top finance man, delivered another grim appraisal of GM's North American operations. Ford was earning $800 a car more than GM in North America, more than double the margin of the year before. Costs were spiraling higher. Market share was tumbling to new lows. Chevrolet–Pontiac–Canada, the larger of the two huge engineering-manufacturing-and-marketing operations created in 1984, was so inefficient that its factories would have to build 171 percent of their expected production quota just to break even. In other words, Chevrolet–Pontiac–Canada's chances of just breaking even depended on Ford, Honda, or Toyota going out of business.

Even Roger Smith began to realize it was time to try something new.

THE TEAMWORK AND TECHNOLOGY show was still rumbling around the country on April 22, 1988, when GM's top executives trooped to New York for a meeting with securities analysts. That very day, GM had reported that profits for the first quarter of 1988 rose 18 percent from the year before. But things weren't as rosy as they seemed.[4]

Upon closer inspection, it turned out that all of the improvements and then some stemmed from a new way of booking manufacturing costs. The accounting shuffle, perfectly legal but a marked departure from GM's traditional, conservative standards, improved first quarter profits by a whopping $224.2 million.

But after more than two years of watching GM fail to deliver on its glowing promises, restless investors weren't impressed. GM's financial statements obscured the performance of the company's North American operations, but it was obvious from GM's sales reports that its domestic car business was still deteriorating. Teamwork and Technology had boosted GM's stock in January. By April, though, Wall Street's bears were growling again.

The key to understanding the rot at GM's core lay in the decades-old wisdom of Alfred P. Sloan, who made GM a great power in the 1930s, 1940s, and 1950s. Sloan's most famous contribution to American business was his realization that cars could be sold as expressions of a buyer's personality and social status, not just as appliances. The "car for every purse and purpose" strategy that dethroned Henry Ford as the king of the American auto industry sprang from this insight. Chevrolet aimed at young and budget-conscious buyers, Pontiac, Oldsmobile, and Buick at middle- and upper-middle-class customers, and Cadillac appealed to people who had enough money to drive the very best, and highest-priced, luxury automobiles.

But Sloan's real triumph was lassoing the chaotic collection of companies assembled by financier Billy Durant and turning them into an industrial powerhouse. Sloan accomplished this with a system that decentralized authority for daily operations and product design, but imposed a puritanical financial discipline from the top. In a lengthy 1924 essay, Donaldson Brown, then GM's vice president for finance, summarized how GM really worked.

Under Sloan and Brown, GM's policy was to earn 20 percent return on equity even if the plants ran at only 80 percent of capacity. This "standard volume" approach controlled critical decisions about capital investment, pricing, the size of the labor force, and sales forecasts. This last was of critical importance.

"Forecasts," Brown wrote, "provide the basis for financial control."[5] If the corporation's sales and share forecasts were inflated, it would lead to unrealistic pricing, excess capacity, increased costs, and depressed profits. Inflated sales forecasts encouraged large capital investments that couldn't be repaid and still provide the required 20 percent return on equity.

Sloan forced GM to adhere to this discipline even during the boom years of the 1950s. GM became a money machine so powerful that its executives fretted as much about capturing too much market share, and risking federal antitrust action, as they did about losing money in a cyclical slump.

When Roger Smith took over, GM could still make money running its plants at about 65 percent of capacity. But Sloan, who'd kept watch over his successors even after his retirement in 1956, was dead. The old discipline was fading. A "good news culture" took hold of the company and stifled frank discussion of the mounting challenges to GM's dominance.

The roots of GM's self-delusion ran deep. For decades, Smith and the other members of GM's finance staff rose through the ranks convinced that the company's operating men were not to be trusted. GM's finance men were an elite corps. They had the best block of company seats in Tiger Stadium—right behind the first-base dugout. And it was their job to impose cost discipline on the impulsive—and usually lower-paid— minions in marketing, manufacturing, and engineering who were incapable of any self-restraint. The finance men were the source of The Numbers. They controlled the information about profit and loss, which in turn controlled what executives got paid. And the finance staffers were reluctant to share their powerful secrets with rivals on the operating side.

The operating men resented their second-class status, of course. Their reaction, perversely enough, often was to conform to the wastrel role that finance slotted for them by demanding more money to build sexier cars or shinier factories. During the 1970s, the damage from this internal warfare was contained. That was partly because Tom Murphy, the finance-man chairman, and Elliott M. "Pete" Estes, his operating-man president, both were affable types who liked each other and maintained vestiges of the old restraint. But GM was also able to shrug off mistakes, notably the declining quality of its cars, because its rivals were too weak to capitalize on them.

But in the 1980s, GM's dysfunction turned disastrous.

Jim McDonald, who succeeded Estes as GM's president and top operating man, kept sales and production forecasts consistently high, on the theory that this was the only way to force his sales staff to hustle. And he systematically excluded finance staffers, the self-appointed sources of discipline, from the forecasting process because he didn't want them meddling in his turf. Roger Smith, meanwhile, took a largely hands-off attitude toward McDonald. The two men didn't really get along, and Smith was too busy planning the 21st-century corporation to get involved in operating details. Besides, it was easy for Smith to rationalize his No. 2 man's optimism.

After all, Smith would say, Chrysler was begging for handouts in Washington, Ford had one foot in the grave, and Japanese companies were just dipping into the least profitable market segment. What share the Japanese got seemed to come from Ford and Chrysler. Against that backdrop, Smith didn't believe dissidents who warned that GM could have less than 40 percent of the car market by the end of the decade.

That was unthinkable, like the notion that the United States could be the world's biggest debtor nation, or that the Soviet Union could collapse.

The result was a historic blunder. Nothing panned out the way GM expected. Instead of dying, Ford rode the Taurus, the Lincoln Town Car, and its newly efficient factories to record profits. Chrysler not only lived, it prospered. The Japanese defied expectations, too. They were supposed to fall back after the orchestrated doubling in the value of the yen during the mid-1980s, which drove up the cost of Japanese cars in the United States. But instead of boarding boats back to Tokyo, the three big Japanese manufacturers—Toyota, Nissan, and Honda—moved rapidly to expand their American factories, design studios, and supplier networks. They also began selling more expensive cars, partly to offset the strong yen's impact on small-car profit margins, and partly because their customers wanted them.

By the mid-1980s, Toyota, Honda, and Nissan were invading the midpriced and even the luxury car markets—Honda's Acura Legend had proved in 1986 that "Japanese luxury car" wasn't an oxymoron. Toyota's stunningly successful Lexus LS 400 would follow three years later and revolutionize the luxury market that once had been the preserve of Cadillac, Lincoln, and a few German manufacturers. But the big market share gains came from cars such as the Honda Accord and Toyota Corolla, which were made in America and aimed right at the heart of Detroit's market. In all this, the Japanese got unwitting help from Detroit's Big Three. GM, in particular, raised prices almost as fast as the Japanese during 1986 and 1987. Confronted with the choice between a high-quality Toyota or Honda, and a Chevrolet that cost only a few hundred dollars less, an increasing number of Americans opted for the Japanese model.

By the spring of 1988, it was clear that the eleven factories Smith had ordered closed sixteen months earlier wouldn't be enough. As Stempel surveyed the situation in early 1988, he was torn. He was no Jim McDonald. He understood that GM had too many factories and too many employees. He knew the red ink in GM's North American car operations would make it hard to hit the goal of showing at least $8 a share in profits for 1988. "We need a magic wand," Stempel complained at one staff meeting in advance of the conference with stock analysts. "We need $4 a share from someplace."

But Stempel was reluctant to force the most obvious solutions to the cost problem, namely plant closings and layoffs. Moreover, his friend Lloyd Reuss, then the head of North American car operations, was arguing against retreat.

Stempel liked Reuss. The two engineers spoke the same language. "That's an exciting set of curves," Stempel once gushed when Reuss showed him a chart of the torque and horsepower ratings of a GM engine. Reuss was a bold, dominating personality who declared with no hesitation that GM could recapture a 40 percent share of the U.S. car market by 1992. Reuss based his optimism on a fleet of new vehicles then taking shape under his supervision in GM's design studios. The cars would hit the market in late 1990 and 1991.

Stempel decided to go with a compromise. He would tell the world that GM planned to operate at 100 percent of capacity by 1992 and "get its capacity in line with demand." But the company would be vague about how this would be accomplished. Stempel would have to shut more plants and ease thousands more employees off the payroll eventually. But the process could be dragged out for years, giving Reuss time to reclaim more sales.

To sell this to Wall Street, Stempel talked tough. No longer, Stempel said at the April 1988 meeting with securities analysts, would GM chase sales at the expense of profits. Instead, GM would match its North American capacity to its sales. Wall Street cheered the news. GM's stock soared $1.25 a share as word of the strategic reversal crossed the Dow Jones wires.[6]

ROGER SMITH, THOUGH, still couldn't put the issue squarely. GM's massive investments in "flexible technology," allowed the company to "reach higher" for market share using fewer factories, Smith said. Grabbing a pen and paper, Smith would sketch out how GM would reduce the number of different car chassis it used to produce its more than 100 car models. GM's three compact car families, he said, would wind up as one. GM's large front-drive models would be built on a single chassis, instead of two.

Smith was sketching the blueprint for a far smaller operation. Each of the boxes on Smith's little diagram actually represented hundreds of engineers, and thousands of factory workers in parts and assembly plants. Eliminate a chassis—a "platform" in Detroit lingo—and you could eliminate thousands of jobs that existed only because a Pontiac Sunbird was

1.6 inches shorter than a Pontiac Grand Am—and thus used different sheet metal dies, underbody parts, exterior moldings, rear windows, shock absorbers, and so on. Smith wanted GM factories to deal with only a few thousand different combinations of engines, transmissions, and body decorations, not with trillions as they had in the past.

It made perfect sense. But Smith simply denied the implications of what he was saying. "It really isn't a retreat," he insisted. "We're not setting 37 percent as a cap. We'll still be able to reach market shares of 44 percent or 45 percent. We're not giving up market share potential. . . . It's a realignment of capacity."

Of course, one man's realignment of capacity was another man's pink slip. In Chicago for a stop on the Teamwork and Technology tour, Smith spoke to an audience that included a group of GM workers bused in from a nearby metal stamping factory. GM had launched "one of the most far reaching industrial transformations in history," Smith said. As part of that transformation, however, GM had earlier announced that the Chicago stamping plant would close. In the face of this bitter irony, Stempel dutifully sounded the company line: "We are not a shrinking corporation."

But GM was a shrinking corporation. And it was about to shrink some more.

The new Pontiac Grand Prix coupe shown off at the Waldorf, along with its Car of the Year trophy from *Motor Trend* magazine, represented one of the first fruits of the biggest new-car program GM had ever attempted. GM had plowed $7 billion into the so-called GM-10 program. With four assembly plants and four new model lines, GM-10 was bigger than Saturn, bigger than the EDS acquisition, and even bigger than the Hughes Aircraft deal. GM had once dominated the midsized family car market, reaping rich profits and breeding generations of loyal middle-class buyers. The Ford Taurus had derailed this profit machine. Now, after six years in the making, the GM-10 cars—the Grand Prix, the Chevrolet Lumina, the Oldsmobile Cutlass Supreme, and the Buick Regal—would be the engines driving GM's comeback.

In the fall of 1987, nearly two years after the Taurus's launch, the first Buick Regals rolled into showrooms. They were followed in early 1988 by the Grand Prix, then the Cutlass Supreme—bearer of the name that had adorned the best-selling car in America in 1986. The Lumina would round out the GM-10 lineup a year later.

GM cranked up its public relations apparatus to build the appropriate excitement. Executives declared the new cars to be the highest quality midsized vehicles in GM's history. They vowed the modern styling of the new cars would put to bed the carping about look-alike GM models. Ford's Taurus and Sable—which Stempel called the "bulls and fuzzy animals"—would be put back in their place. As the first of the cars rolled out, Reuss assured GM's board everything was "great."

Charged up by the brass, GM dealers waited for the throngs of buyers to materialize.

And waited.

By June 1988, it was clear: The new cars were duds.[7] Worst of all was the Cutlass Supreme. Reuss had been so smitten by the Supreme's lines that he declared the car should be priced *higher* than a comparable Taurus. He'd even ordered a second set of production tools made to equip a second assembly plant to build the cars. Reuss had miscalculated badly. By June, GM had enough of the new Oldsmobiles on hand to last until the end of the model year on September 30. The extra production tools would never be needed.

Reuss offered excuses. He argued that in the highly competitive market of the 1980s, companies couldn't expect to hit huge home runs as in the past. The simple truth was the GM-10 program was a disaster.

One of the biggest mistakes was obvious to the most undiscerning shoppers. GM's new midsized "family" cars had just two doors. This made them useless to the largest group of customers in the segment, namely members of the postwar Baby Boom generation, who were then entering their prime child-rearing years. These people wanted cars with four doors. That way, the kids could get in and out of the back seat without a struggle. But GM had scheduled the coupes to come first, on the basis of past sales, and Smith rejected proposals to speed up the sedans. In so doing, he missed the biggest demographic trend in a generation.

IN THE END, however, it didn't matter how many doors the GM-10 cars had. Even after the sedans appeared, sales of the GM-10 models languished. The cars were everything a major new model shouldn't be—overweight, overpriced, and underwhelming.

The bland styling of the GM-10 cars turned out to be the least of the problems. As GM engineers tore apart Tauruses and gathered intelligence about the factories in Atlanta and Chicago where they were built, they realized their crosstown rival had designed cars that not only were better looking but also a lot cheaper to build. Building a Grand Prix was like assembling a jigsaw puzzle. It required some thirty-five hours of assembly labor. Building a Taurus took about twenty hours of assembly labor. In 1988, this translated to a roughly $300 per car advantage to Ford—on assembly labor alone.[8]

Ford's advantage was all the more stunning because GM had spent billions to outfit the GM-10 plants with the latest automation. The result was four more Hamtramcks. Just programming and running the robots in the Doraville, Georgia, plant that built the Cutlass Supreme cost $860 a car in payments to EDS, according to one internal GM cost study. Within a few years, plant managers would scrap many of the robots and put in lower-tech equipment that cost less to operate.

Overall, the new Cutlass Supreme lagged a whopping $700 a car behind the profitability of the old rear-drive Cutlass Supreme that had propelled Oldsmobile sales over 1 million cars in 1986, according to a GM internal study. The GM-10 cars also cost $470 more each to build than the cars they were designed to replace, the aging front-drive A-body sedans featured on the *Fortune* cover. These numbers assumed GM would hit all its optimistic targets for parts cost and actual sales prices. GM ultimately didn't come close to its rosy scenarios.

Quality completed the nightmare. GM conducted nine recalls of GM-10 cars built between June 1987 and December 1988, covering problems that could cause wheels to come off, hoods to fly open, and brakes to fail. One defect, covering more than 112,000 early Pontiac Grand Prix GM-10 models, involved a defective switch that not only prevented the brake lights from flashing, but also caused the cruise control to reengage *after* the brakes were applied. "In either case," federal regulators noted dryly, "it could result in a crash without prior warning."

The General now was in full retreat. By 1988, GM had enough factories in North America to build about 7.6 million vehicles a year. But the company only managed to sell about 5.5 million cars and trucks. Many of GM's most expensive, modern factories—including the ones building the GM-10 cars—were running at a fraction of profitable speed because sales were falling so far short of management's outsized forecasts. As a result, Smith's juggernaut was falling further and further behind its smaller rival, Ford, in profits per vehicle sold. It was precisely the kind of situation that Alfred Sloan and Donaldson Brown never would have tolerated. But Smith, Stempel, and Reuss seemed paralyzed. Eventually,

GM would lose as much as $1,800 on every GM-10 car it sold—and GM's leaders simply plugged the losses into their budgets. For Don Ephlin, the UAW leader at GM, the GM-10 disaster demolished any hope of salvaging thousands of union jobs GM's blunders had put in jeopardy. Ephlin could only shake his head and ruefully say: "The Taurus was the car that turned Ford around. The GM-10s were the cars that turned GM around."

CHAPTER 7

PEOPLE POWER

As GM STUMBLED from debacle to debacle, the men around Roger Smith began to focus on the future. As a group, the half-dozen executives who made up Smith's inner circle had several things in common. Nearly all of them realized that GM needed to change. But they were struggling with two fundamental questions: Could Smith be part of the solution? And dare they risk their careers by pushing him too far?

The top contender to take Smith's place was the star of Teamwork and Technology: Bob Stempel. Stempel was the consummate "car guy," and the popular favorite among GM's engineers and salespeople. The son of a banker, Stempel had started his automotive career fixing cars in his hometown of Bloomfield, New Jersey. Armed with a degree in mechanical engineering from Worcester Polytechnic Institute in Massachusetts and two years with the Army Corps of Engineers, Stempel landed a job as a junior engineer designing wheels and other hardware at Oldsmobile in 1958. His first big break came when he got assigned to the team of engineers working on the 1966 Oldsmobile Toronado. The Toronado was the first mass-market front-wheel-drive car GM had ever attempted, and there was considerable apprehension up and down the corporate ladder about the car.

Stempel emerged as a leader among young Oldsmobile engineers who solved the riddle of how to fit the new front-drive transmission *and* a monstrous 407-cubic-inch engine under the Toronado's rakish hood. More importantly, Stempel impressed GM's president, Edward Cole, during presentations on the project with his command of the details of the design. Stempel's star began to rise.

Stempel's second big break came in 1973, after Congress demanded that automakers act quickly to reduce the soot and fumes spewing from automobile tailpipes. GM had researched the potential of various devices that could filter exhaust. But now GM had to get a working system from lab bench to full production in less than two years. In 1973, Cole called on Stempel to lead a massive effort to put the filter devices, called catalytic converters, on every 1975 model GM car.

The catalytic converter project was an unprecedented undertaking. GM almost never launched new technology on all its cars at once, let alone a device that had the potential for fouling up the operation of the engine. Stempel threw himself into the task, lassoing together engineers from eleven GM divisions. He immersed himself in the project. People working on the project got used to seeing Stempel, tall and big-boned, loping through the lab with his diminutive boss, Cole, bustling along at his side.

Stempel came through in the clutch again. GM's across-the-board launch of the catalytic converter was a coup that left Ford and Chrysler gasping in the dust. For Stempel, the catalytic converter was the rocket that launched him onto the fast track. In November 1978, Stempel was named vice president in charge of Pontiac. At age forty-five, Stempel began a job-hopping whirlwind that took him through six posts in less than nine years. Stempel's tenure at Pontiac lasted just long enough for him to champion approval of the Fiero project. In September 1980, he was transferred to GM's money-losing Adam Opel AG subsidiary in Germany. There, he launched a revitalization of Opel's sorry cars, and pushed construction of GM's first major assembly plant in Spain as a lower-cost alternative to Opel's German factories. Years later, the manager of GM's Spanish plant outside the northern city of Zaragoza would remember fondly how Stempel backed his requests for a big budget to train the newly hired workers. At the time, instructing workers in the nuances of new manufacturing technology was an afterthought in most GM operations. At Zaragoza, the extra training helped the plant become one of GM's highest-quality operations.

But just two years after going to Germany, Stempel was called back to

Detroit again to run Chevrolet. Opel continued to lose money, but that didn't slow Stempel's advance to the top. International operations, after all, weren't very important to GM. Chevrolet, the world's largest automotive brand, was.

At Chevy, Stempel became swept up in Jim McDonald's planning for the earth-shaking 1984 reorganization. McDonald included Stempel in a small group of executives who holed up for days at a time in a motel near the Detroit Metro airport debating how GM would look when its huge central engineering and manufacturing organization was smashed to pieces. When the reorganization was rolled out, Stempel emerged as head of the sprawling Buick–Oldsmobile–Cadillac group, while Lloyd Reuss, another McDonald protégé, took charge of the even larger Chevrolet–Pontiac–GM of Canada conglomerate. Both groups would have been solidly in the top tier of the Fortune 500 if they'd been spun off as separate car companies. Reuss's CPC operation alone was roughly the size of Ford's domestic operations.

As Stempel and Reuss headed into a neck-and-neck race to succeed Jim McDonald as president, Stempel's partisans shaped an appealing image for their man: Bob, the Humane Reformer.

"Bob Stempel," one of his long-time aides often said with an admiring smile, "is just a big, good old shit." And so he was. Bob Stempel was by far the nicest guy in GM's upper ranks—even his rivals at Ford and Chrysler thought so. In contrast to Chairman Smith, Stempel had a genuine interest in the well-being of his underlings, and took the trouble to hail by name employees far beneath him in rank. GM's engineers worshipped Stempel. Once, GM's design staff showed Stempel a prototype of a fuel-conscious Chevrolet Corvette that had a six-cylinder engine where the standard V-8 was supposed to be. "Where's its balls?" Stempel growled. Die-hard Corvette engineers were jubilant.

Stempel's Car Guy Reformer image was nurtured carefully by his friends, and by his wife, Pat. No retiring corporate spouse was she. Pat Stempel was a smart woman with strong opinions, which she didn't hesitate to express to Bob's peers or, just as important, to their wives. Pat Stempel's penchant for eccentric outfits, like the backless black sweater and leather miniskirt she sported to the opening night of the 1988 Detroit Auto Show, was one of many little gestures of rebellion against GM's stuffy culture. Bob, for his part, would occasionally sport huge cuff links in the shape of a crab, representing his astrological sign, Cancer. Stempel also resisted joining the Bloomfield Hills Country Club, as every blue-blooded GM vice president was supposed to do. But when he won the presidency in 1987, he joined the club—in more ways than one.

People who'd worked with Stempel over the years knew that the bold reformer image was an exaggeration. The real Bob Stempel was often cautious to a fault and doggedly loyal to his "team," even when some of its members weren't serving him well. These doubts soon resolved themselves around Stempel's attachment to another fast-track engineer: Lloyd Reuss.

Reuss was the Spirit of the Old GM given flesh and form in a custom-tailored three-piece suit. A spindly, quick-talking native of Belleville, Illinois, Reuss radiated energy and optimism. Reuss's corn-country accent, which tortured "Chevy" into "Chivvy," and his relentlessly sunny outlook made him easy for outsiders to underestimate. But inside GM's power circles, Reuss wielded enormous power. With Stempel's imprimatur, Reuss controlled billions in future product spending, and held the careers of hundreds of GM's most ambitious executives in his hands. GM was a global company. But no one had risen to its top ranks from overseas operations. The domestic auto business was still the launching pad to the top, and Reuss was poised to be Stempel's No. 2 man all the way through the 1990s.

Reuss's rise at GM was remarkable, considering that during his thirty-four-year career he had walked away unscathed from the scene of disasters that would have destroyed his career at almost any other company. In January 1970, Reuss, then just thirty-three years old, was named project engineer for the Chevrolet Vega. That car, which GM trumpeted as its sally against imported small cars, turned into a nightmare. In 1972, GM issued three mass recalls, the largest covering 500,000 Vegas, to fix defective axles, balky throttles and problems that caused fires. The Vega's aluminum engine was notorious for buckling and leaking. Reuss spent months at GM's big engine plant outside Buffalo, New York, sometimes working seven-day weeks, trying to get the problems fixed. He failed, and the Vega ultimately succumbed to the engine design flaws. Still, Reuss impressed his bosses as a can-do guy, and kept moving up.

Jim McDonald, particularly, liked Reuss's upbeat attitude, snappy attire and eagerness to forge ahead without being deterred by naysayers from finance. McDonald championed Reuss's career at Chevrolet and later. Reuss's first big, high-visibility job came when he took over as vice president in charge of the Buick division in 1980 and led the transformation of Buick's sprawling Flint factory into an automated showcase. Just as at Hamtramck, however, Buick City's robots went haywire when the factory started up in 1985. It took a full-scale rescue mission by Reuss's successors to salvage the plant. But Reuss had already moved on—and up. In 1986 he became head of all GM's North American car operations, reporting to McDonald. Stempel, at the same time, was put in charge of trucks and international operations. Both got the title of executive vice president, but Reuss appeared to have moved a half step ahead of Stempel in the race for GM's presidency.

Like his superiors, McDonald and Roger Smith, Reuss was enthusiastic about taking risks with expensive technology to attack GM's quality and efficiency problems. He backed an ambitious plan advanced by his Chevrolet–Pontiac–Canada managers to buy some $2.5 billion worth of high-speed metal stamping presses to improve the productivity of GM's metal-fabricating operations. GM virtually cornered the worldwide market for stamping presses as the premier Japanese press makers scrambled to meet its demands.

But trouble started almost as soon as the new presses arrived at GM's plants. To begin with, the Japanese transfer presses—when they were running properly—could churn through about twice as much metal as Reuss's manufacturing experts had expected. That, coupled with the steep decline in sales, meant GM needed only about half as many of the presses as it had ordered.

Often as not, however, the new press systems weren't running properly. GM's stamping plant managers and workers, after all, had never seen presses as complicated as these. One day in 1986, a young GM manufacturing manager arrived to check out GM's showcase automated stamping plant in Mansfield, Ohio, in advance of a tour by the board of directors. He discovered that all five of the new press lines were stopped dead by a maintenance snafu that resulted in the huge presses splitting steel sheets like stale graham crackers. By the time Reuss's operatives figured out that they'd gone too far, it was too late to cancel orders for many of the presses. GM was stuck with expensive Japanese presses that would never run efficiently enough to earn back the money sunk into them.

Reuss's record of costly blunders didn't stop there. He signed off during the gestation of the GM-10 cars on a plan to depart from GM's traditional practice of equipping each assembly plant to build more than one model. GM liked to make factories "flexible" in this way so that if the

Buick version of a car didn't sell, the factory could build more Oldsmobile and Pontiac models. But as the GM-10 cars neared production,
Reuss and others in his camp argued that to achieve high quality—the
No. 1 goal of the GM-10 program—GM should dedicate three of the
four GM-10 factories to building just one model each. One model, fewer
variations, fewer chances for the assembly workers to screw up, the
argument went. Thus, the GM-10 factory in Doraville, Georgia, got the
Cutlass Supreme, the new plant in Fairfax, Kansas, got the Pontiac
Grand Prix, and the Oshawa, Ontario, No. 1 got the Chevrolet Lumina.
It was another gigantic error. Within two years of the GM-10 cars'
botched launch, it was clear that one plant would have sufficed for the
Cutlass Supreme and Grand Prix. But because of the way Reuss's operatives had outfitted the Doraville and Fairfax plants, it was virtually impossible to change course without spending hundreds of millions of
dollars to shut down and retool.

At Ford, an executive who made such a mistake would have lost his
job. But at GM, the penalty was rather less severe. Although Reuss lost
the race for president to Stempel in 1987, his authority was expanded to
include all GM's North American auto operations—trucks as well as
cars. Reuss viewed that as an endorsement. As the race to succeed Smith
shaped up, Reuss still considered himself a solid contender to make
president in the post-Smith era.

Behind Stempel and Reuss, the field was difficult to handicap. F. Alan
Smith should have been a contender. Like the chairman, Alan Smith
had ascended through the ranks of GM's powerful financial staff to become chief financial officer. A colorless character, F.—for Farquhar—
Alan Smith seemed born to the bean counter's role. Smith had established himself as GM's official party-pooper with his glowering performance at the 1986 TechBrier management meeting, and his periodic
warnings in the two years after that gathering that GM's financial
strength was imperiled by the bungling in North America. These sermons, however, grated on the chairman. Finally, one day, Roger
snapped, "Alan, I'm getting tired of hearing this shit." Thus in June
1988, Alan Smith found himself among the corpses of those who had
dared to speak their mind to the chairman. F. Alan was pushed out of
the chief financial officer's job into a secondary role as executive vice
president for the corporate support staffs—excluding finance.

The man who took Alan Smith's place as Roger Smith's top numbers
man was Robert T. O'Connell. The second of five sons of a New Haven,

Connecticut, police officer, O'Connell was a mountainous man with an acid wit, an intimidating manner, and prodigious appetites for work and food that worried friends and inspired enemies to cruel behind-the-back barbs. One of the milder ones was the nickname "Roto," a play on his initials, and on the notion that he was as relentless as a Roto-Rooter sewer-cleaning machine. O'Connell's favorite breakfast before a full day of bureaucratic warfare was a stack of pancakes with two jugs of syrup, sausage, bacon, a pot of coffee, and half a pack of cigarettes.

One thing everyone agreed on was that O'Connell had a remarkable facility in his chosen field. At Roger Smith's behest, O'Connell was generating with liberal accounting—always approved by the auditors— the profits that GM's hapless domestic operating executives seemed unable to produce by building and selling cars. Some of the accounting maneuvers were easy to spot—such as a $1.24 billion reduction in depreciation charges engineered in the third quarter of 1987 by refiguring the estimated useful lives of GM's plants and tools, and the big gain from shifting the method of booking manufacturing costs in early 1988.[1] Some, however, were all but invisible to investors. GM, for instance, began cutting back on the amounts it deducted from net income to provide for warranty claims, citing improved quality. GM quality, however, didn't improve as dramatically as the company assumed. In another move, Smith would authorize a sweeping liberalization of pension accounting practices that pumped up GM's bottom line in 1990. While no one questioned the legality of this, it ran against GM's conservative, old-time religion.

O'Connell also unnerved some of his colleagues with the gallows humor that attended his execution of what he wryly called his "marching orders." Asked one day what earnings for the coming quarter might be, O'Connell replied with the punch line from a hoary joke about accountants: "Whatever you want me to make them."

Then, there were the dark horses. Chief among them was Bill Hoglund, the champion of the Fiero and the union-management teamwork experiments at Pontiac. Hoglund had continued along his nonconformist track as head of the Saturn small-car subsidiary and later as the vice president in charge of the Buick–Oldsmobile–Cadillac group. At Saturn, he nurtured a revival of the old Fiero team spirit, sowing the seeds of a democratic, ties-off relationship with the UAW. At BOC, Hoglund closed down executive dining rooms, and delivered frank assessments of GM's shortcomings both internally and in the press. Hoglund's enemies whispered that he was a better talker than a worker, and his outspokenness secured him a permanent place in Roger Smith's doghouse. But Hoglund was a popular figure among GM's rank-and-file and among dealers.

Another dark horse was Jack Smith, the young executive vice president who'd almost overnight in 1987 steered GM's European operations to profitability. Jack Smith—no relation to either Roger or Alan—had pushed GM Europe into the black by yoking together a seasoned group of frustrated German managers from Opel and a small crew of aggressive young executives who had worked for him on GM's finance staff. But Smith had never run any of GM's major U.S. marketing or manufacturing operations. His experiences outside the United States appeared to qualify him to stay where he was, running GM's international businesses.

The most intriguing choice to replace Roger Smith would have been none of the above, however. That would have been Elmer Johnson.

Among the group of career GM managers surrounding Smith, Johnson stood out because he was a genuine outsider. Johnson had come to GM in 1983 from a secure and lucrative position as the managing partner at the Chicago law firm of Kirkland & Ellis. Smith had wooed the erudite lawyer relentlessly, for many of the same reasons he had been attracted to Ross Perot. Like Perot, Johnson was an antibureaucrat. Unlike Perot, Johnson was willing to work within the GM system to change it. Smith landed Johnson by promising him a portfolio as a sort of roving provocateur. Johnson accepted because he harbored ambitions of succeeding Roger Smith and becoming GM's Revolutionary in Chief.

Johnson cultivated an offbeat, almost bohemian image. He had spent seven years getting up in the wee hours of the morning to plow through a reading list of 150 "great books"—including Plato's *Republic* and D. H. Lawrence's *Lady Chatterley's Lover*—that most people gave up on in college.[2] He approached corporate management as a philosophical exercise, and even joined a University of Chicago professor in coauthoring a treatise on morality in management. To top it off, Johnson was an amateur musician. A picture of Johnson playing his trumpet on the cover of the Detroit *Free Press* Sunday magazine in August 1987[3] crystallized his image as a corporate eccentric—and prompted plenty of snickering among his detractors at GM. There was Elmer, they said, literally blowing his own horn.

But behind the soft-spoken, philosophy-major facade, Elmer Johnson was a rugged corporate street fighter whom rivals misjudged at their peril.

The U.S. government's safety bureaucracy had learned that the hard way, in the celebrated X-car case. In 1983, the National Highway Traffic Safety Administration demanded that GM recall the X-cars, its first generation of mass-market front-wheel-drive models, charging the cars had a dangerous defect in their brakes. Moreover, the regulators ordered GM to pay a $4 million fine for trying to cover up the problem. Johnson declared "nuclear war." He refused to back down, and tumbled the case into federal court in Washington, D.C. There, Johnson's crack team of product liability lawyers proceeded to devastate the government's case. The X-car died in 1985, a victim of bad publicity and poor quality. The government ultimately tallied 4,282 complaints of brake failures, 1,417 accidents, and eighteen deaths. But GM won the legal battle by arguing that X-cars were no more likely to skid out of control during braking than other cars of its class. U.S. Judge Thomas Jackson ruled in April 1987 that federal regulators hadn't proved that GM's cars presented an "unreasonable risk" of skidding. GM won the subsequent appeals, as well, and avoided a costly recall.

Johnson also had done more than talk about corporate revolution. In his career as a corporate lawyer, he'd been a key player in high-level boardroom coups that had toppled the chief executive officers at International Harvester, Firestone Tire and Rubber, and Westinghouse Electric. Indeed, Johnson once boasted to his staff about his experiences counseling "once-great organizations that lacked power of institutional self-renewal at critical junctures."[4] And it was no secret to Johnson's confidantes that he saw GM as another "once-great" organization in need of a major overhaul from bottom to top. A Yale graduate with a law degree from the University of Chicago, Johnson was appalled by the legions of GM managers and engineers who got by with only undergraduate degrees from Midwestern football schools or, worse yet, the General Motors Institute. Johnson was equally disturbed by GM's unwillingness to confront the United Auto Workers union to reduce its bloated labor costs.

Johnson's calls to arms attracted a following among a group of young GM executives who shared his frustration with the company's ossified culture. When Roger Smith elevated Johnson to the board of directors in early 1987, speculation swirled around the company that Johnson might actually succeed Smith and start putting his radical ideas into practice.

But soon after his promotion, Johnson began wearing out his patron's welcome.

The more Johnson learned about the way Smith and GM's other top executives operated, the more dismayed he became. Johnson kept trying to argue that GM was in trouble and needed to take radical action. Johnson even decided to buck Smith over the chairman's No. 1 pet project: Saturn.

Saturn had grown like topsy in the five years since Roger Smith broached it amid the furor over the Nummi venture with Toyota. In 1985, Smith had stunned the industry—and his subordinates—by declaring that Saturn would become a stand-alone subsidiary of GM with a mandate to take a "clean sheet of paper" approach to cracking the Japanese hold on the small-car market. It was a bold declaration for a subsidiary that consisted of little more than a handful of young vice presidents, a cadre of UAW idealists, and a prototype "little red car" that had none of the attributes of a commercially viable vehicle.

By late 1987, however, Saturn had become a true company within a company. Armed with a $3.5 billion budget, Saturn engineers, many of them refugees from the Pontiac Fiero project, were designing a real car and a brand new engine to go with it. Construction would soon start on a massive new factory in Spring Hill, Tennessee, south of Nashville. Smith was touting the project relentlessly as the key to the future of GM.

But behind the glass doors that sealed off the executive offices on the 14th floor of GM's Detroit headquarters, Saturn was looking more and more like Roger's Folly. Johnson became convinced that GM couldn't afford Saturn at a time when it was closing plants, slashing budgets, and straining to hide from investors the true severity of the collapse in North American profitability. Finally, during October and November 1987, Johnson decided to challenge Saturn head-on. In the wake of the October 19 stock market crash, Johnson argued that GM should use the cover of the market panic to cancel the Saturn plant. Carefully, Johnson tried to assemble a coalition of his peers, including Stempel and Alan Smith, to force the chairman to back down.

But Johnson misjudged his man. Smith made support for Saturn a test of loyalty for the men who hoped to replace him. One by one, they backed down. The coup de grâce came at a meeting of the GM board's finance committee on Pearl Harbor Day 1987. Johnson gave an impassioned speech against Saturn. GM is "lying wounded on the battlefield" and should focus its efforts on fixing the operations it had, not building new ones, he argued. But Smith portrayed Saturn as a patriotic mission.

GM could cancel the venture and save money, Smith said. But who then would prove that an American company could compete in the small-car market against Japan? John Smale, the chairman of Procter & Gamble Company and a leader among GM's outside directors, sided with Smith and Saturn. "If GM doesn't take this bold step, nobody else will," Smale said. Saturn got its money. Johnson realized he was finished at GM.

Johnson decided to go out with a bang. On January 21, 1988, he delivered a lengthy memorandum to Smith and the executive committee. The document, titled "Strengthening GM's Organizational Capability," was a smoldering manifesto for revolution. With a skill honed by years of practice at the bar, Johnson presented a blistering indictment of Roger Smith's reign.

"Two weeks ago," Johnson began, "we presented an inspiring and exhilarating exhibit on Teamwork and Technology. Then, last Friday, we were presented with Alan Smith's materials on the stark realities of GM's current cost problems."

In just two sentences, Johnson laid bare the deception at the heart of Smith's leadership. It was just the start. "We have relied almost exclusively on 'clean slate' strategies that ignore the internal obstacles and end up trying to circumvent rather than transform GM's organization and culture," Johnson wrote, throwing Smith's "clean slate" phrase back in his face. GM's culture, he continued, "is based on a twofold vision of reality . . . that became dominant in GM by the late 1950s: First, that we live in a very stable, reasonably predictable world; and second, that GM's overwhelming competitive advantage lies to a large degree in its ability to achieve monumental economies of scale." Both assumptions, he argued, were no longer valid. But most of GM's top managers had failed to grasp that. Instead, they had continued to shuttle from job to job every two years, isolated from real responsibility for the success or failure of a given product or program.

Johnson prescribed harsh medicine. GM should demote or dump many of the top 500 managers, make it harder for the senior 4,000 executives to earn bonuses, form product teams with engineering and manufacturing under one management, dump money-losing parts operations, and slash the number of committees at the top. To be as efficient as Ford, Johnson continued, GM would have to cut 80,000 people out of its hourly workforce, then numbering 360,000 people.

Smith's initial response was stunned silence. Johnson's proposal to hold an executive committee meeting to discuss his memo died without result. Johnson soon began to negotiate the terms of his departure. By summer, he was back in Chicago, commuting to work by foot from his high-rise apartment on Michigan Avenue to his old offices at Kirkland & Ellis.

WITH JOHNSON'S EXIT, Roger Smith was alone at the top. But nothing seemed to be going his way. Smith literally wore the strain of holding GM together on his face. His cheeks and nose were red and blotchy with a rash that Smith's underlings ascribed to stress. He appeared preoccupied and detached, rambling in speeches, and making loopy gaffes in his off-the-cuff remarks. During a March 1988 interview with a Detroit television station, Smith said, "Both Mother and Dad were unfortunately killed in an automobile accident. It was very sad."[5] In fact, his father had survived the 1970 crash that killed his mother, and didn't die until nine years later. GM's public relations operatives pleaded with the station to excise the quote from the piece, but it refused. In April, Smith was hounded during a trip through Sweden for telling a Swedish business magazine that he "felt sorry" for Swedish automakers Volvo and Saab. The Swedes bristled at the patronizing comment, and Smith was at pains to explain that what he was "trying to say" was that all foreign automakers faced a tough time in the United States as the dollar weakened. Smith's detractors wondered aloud whether he would finish his term or retire under the cover of "health problems."

Once again, GM was dead in the water. Smith needed a new plan. And so it was that he stumbled at last into what may have been his most poignant hour as GM's chairman.

Smith remained fascinated by outsiders who challenged GM's cultural shibboleths, despite his failed relationships with Ross Perot and Elmer Johnson and despite his inability to alter his own dictatorial style. And so he began acquiring new gurus, among them a young consultant named Mark Sarkady. Sarkady's message, put simply, was that GM's senior management needed to stop telling underlings to change, and start changing themselves so that others would follow their example. Sarkady was a decidedly un-GM type. He would fly in from his home in the suburbs of Boston and lead his buttoned-down clients through sessions that had more in common with encounter-group therapy than business meetings. One of Sarkady's favorite "team-building" exercises involved having two executives pull a rubber band.[6] Each had to trust that the other wouldn't let the rubber band snap back. In Sarkady's meetings, participants didn't simply say things. They "shared."

As goofy as it seemed, this kind of approach resonated with many of GM's younger managers. The Baby Boomers in the generation represented by Steve Bera and the team sent to Nummi weren't flower children. Most spent the late 1960s in business school, or the military, or working up the ladder at GM, not marching against the Vietnam War. Still, these young managers held decidedly different views about authority than those who'd joined GM in the Organization Man days of the 1950s. These younger GM managers devoured texts by Tom Peters, W. Edwards Deming, and others who preached the gospel of transferring decision-making power from senior executives to middle managers and factory hands. "Teamwork" and "empowerment" were the buzzwords of this new generation.

Saturn was furthest out of all. There, managers and union workers intent on escaping the old adversarial roles formed teams to navigate an outdoor obstacle course set up near Saturn's Tennessee factory. To get through the course, team members had to help each other scale a 40-foot wall while roped together, and pass each other through a net. The climax of the obstacle course was the "trust fall." That called for team members to throw themselves backward off an elevated platform into the waiting arms of colleagues. Saturn had hourly workers involved in virtually every management decision, including such minutiae as the style of uniforms and whether to pave the parking lot at the factory. Saturn's organizational chart was a series of interlocking circles, not the classic GM pyramid of boxes and lines. Saturn people had an almost religious fervor. But they weren't alone. Encouraged by Saturn's example, hundreds of other GM workers were escaping their cubicles to navigate rope obstacle courses, shinny up flagpoles, and even meditate in management retreats.

The "people power" frenzy came to a climax in October 1988, when more than 900 GM managers gathered at the luxurious Grand Traverse Resort outside the Northern Michigan town of Traverse City.[7] A five-hour drive north of Detroit, Traverse City nestles at the base of the aptly named Grand Traverse Bay on Lake Michigan. The rolling hills overlooking the cold blue waters are dotted with cherry orchards, vineyards, and pastures. The Grand Traverse resort improved on this serenity with one of the Midwest's most challenging golf courses.

But this meeting would be a stunning departure both from the boozy Greenbrier routs, and from the surly TechBrier whipping session two years before. To begin with, GM managers were informed before they headed north that this wasn't a "management" conference, it was a "leadership" conference. Suits and ties could stay home. Proper attire would be shirt sleeves, sports jackets, and sweaters.

As the conference got rolling, the departures from the past became more dramatic. GM's top eighteen executives, known as the Group of Eighteen, dropped their formal titles and reemerged as "champions" of various initiatives. F. Alan Smith threw off his finance-man facade and was reborn as the Champion of the People, articulating the new GM People Philosophy of trust, honesty, truth, teamwork, customer satisfaction, and continuous improvement. To signal the new attitude, Smith even dropped the initial F. from his name.

Bob O'Connell, the new finance chief, became the Champion of Strategic Business Management. Lloyd Reuss, dressed in a gray sport coat with a red sweater vest, unveiled a Framework for Greatness, an immodest label coined by one of Reuss's speechwriters for the effort to make GM first in "high quality, low cost, speed to market, and customer satisfaction." But the most stunning convert of all, it seemed, was the chairman himself.

Roger Smith knew that many of the people in the huge meeting room regarded him as an ogre. He had only to read the hostile—albeit anonymous—comments from GM managers that salted nearly every major story about the company in the press. Smith's temper was a legend among his subordinates. Presented once with a plan to redesign a line of Buick and Oldsmobile sedans in a way that promised a savings on warranty costs, Smith had snapped: "Never try to sell me a program by giving me bullshit about future warranty costs."

But in the months before the Traverse City conference, Smith had shown signs he was trying to change. At a gathering of the Group of Eighteen in March 1988, Smith launched an attack on one of his senior subordinates when Sarkady cut him off. "How would you feel, Roger, if somebody asked you a question like that?" the consultant said. Smith stopped. "You're right," he said. The chairman then declared he was sorry, and asked the question more politely. For Smith's colleagues, who'd learned the hard way that correcting the chairman in a meeting was a ticket to purgatory, it was a miraculous moment.

Now, with 900 GM executives looking on, Smith tried to prove he'd "bought in" to the new approach. Dressed in an open collared shirt, Smith kicked off the conference by declaring he wanted to be more "participative." He stumbled over the word, but carried on: "We are working to change the culture of General Motors, to make it more participative and trusting," Smith said. The chairman admitted he hadn't been in the vanguard on this. But now, he vowed, "I'm in."

Smith's most memorable demonstration of zeal for the new way didn't come in a speech, however. During a session devoted to reports from various discussion groups, David Hansen, Pontiac's young chief engineer, decided to begin his presentation from the group at Table 37 by complaining about the chill in the drafty ballroom.

"We'd like to lick the temperature problem in this corner of the room," Hansen said.

"I put a sweater on," retorted Smith. "We need fifteen-cent solutions to million-dollar problems." It was an old response, pure Roger Smith. But Hansen, one of GM's forty-something generation, was swept up in the spirit of people power. "Can I borrow your sweater, sir?" Hansen shot back. Everyone in the room braced for a tirade—Hansen had obviously gotten carried away, sassing the boss that way. But instead, Smith wheeled from the podium and began striding toward Hansen's table. With a gleeful grin on his face, the chairman began pulling off his brown cardigan sweater. The two men met, and Smith presented the sweater to his young underling. The room burst into applause.

It was magic. GM's young lions lit up. At last, it seemed, the Boss was ready to change for real. Finally, the right message was coming from the top. "We're building a team. It's like spring training, and we're going to the championship," gushed one young manager during a break. Many of the Young Turks donned blue buttons with the declaration of solidarity Smith had used: "I'm in."

Smith tried to capitalize on the buoyant mood with a hopeful valedictory that offered a sharp contrast to the bitter admonition Jim McDonald had delivered two years before. "A corporation, like any living thing, must change to survive. . . . We, you and I, have the courage to change," Smith declared. "Let's keep GM where, in our memories, it always has been: Number One. Number One in everything and every way we do things."

· · ·

But Roger Smith's efforts at self-reform were running afoul of his even stronger desire to convince the world that his bold moves had led GM to the edge of the promised land. More and more, his administration became hostage to the Big Fib.

The Big Fib was that GM had turned the corner and begun a fundamental turnaround in its North American car business. In the third quarter of 1988, GM had surprised Wall Street by reporting $859.2 million, or $2.46 a share, in profit—as much as $1 share higher than some analysts had expected. "We had the turnaround some time ago, but it didn't always come through to the bottom line," an exultant Smith declared.[8]

But when he got back behind the locked doors on the 14th floor, Smith was less sanguine. "What are we going to do about CPC?" he demanded at one meeting, referring to the huge and grossly unprofitable Chevrolet–Pontiac–Canada operation.

The room went silent. Neither Stempel, nor Reuss, who had been responsible for CPC one way or another for six years, said a word. Smith was incredulous. "What?" he asked. "CPC is losing $3 billion a year and no one has any ideas?" Finally, Bill Hoglund, who'd been exiled to the task of turning around GM's unglamorous and unprofitable parts operations, spoke up. "Well," he offered, "one problem is that we replaced Celebrity, which is a low cost car, with the Lumina, which is a high cost car. Now we're losing $1,800 a car."

It was as if he'd belched. Nobody responded. The Lumina sedan was a product of the disastrous GM-10 program. Hoglund's succinct summary of that program's failure was a direct challenge to Reuss and every other executive in the room to face the reality of that debacle. But nobody wanted to discuss it. Later the same day, Hoglund raised the same issue again in a different meeting without Smith. Reuss turned on him. "What are you trying to do to me today, Bill?" Reuss snapped. "Kill me?"

The message was clear. The only appropriate news was good news. This was especially so when it came to the board of directors. Smith took a strict view of GM's tradition, which was that management ran the company, and the board kept its distance. To this end, Smith skillfully managed the flow of information to board members.

Just before the regular meetings on the first Monday of each month, for example, members of the board's powerful finance committee would get thick stacks of briefing papers known as the redbooks. In these piles of single-spaced documents would be data about every aspect of GM's business. The trouble was that board members had no time to read and digest it all before Smith had the books snatched away at the end of each meeting.

Not only that. In meetings, the management members of the board, the so-called inside directors, would sit on the opposite side of the table from the nonexecutive, or outside directors. Inside directors also got different versions of the redbook than their counterparts across the table. In the management redbooks were papers marked "backup" that contained details about GM's performance that the outside directors weren't supposed to see.

What the outside directors did see, more often than they cared to, were stultifying slide shows that accompanied upbeat presentations by management. The boardroom would darken, and a projector would begin clicking through dozens of slides, called blue burn-ins, each meticulously made with white lettering on a GM-blue background. To assure that board members didn't miss anything, the executive giving the presentation would read every word on the slides. In the darkened boardroom, the droning repetition induced an effect like two shots of Novocain to the jaw.

Smith dealt harshly with anyone he suspected of trying to puncture this cocoon. Once, he flew into a rage upon learning that Ira Millstein, the lawyer who had advised the board in the Perot fiasco, was talking to the directors outside board meetings. He stormed up to Millstein's office on the 32nd floor of the GM building in New York, and barged in to berate the lawyer for his meddling. "Sharing" was fine for management meetings, but Smith drew the line at surrendering control of what was shared with his bosses.

SMITH HAD GOOD REASON to suspect that Millstein was stirring up the board. Shortly after Elmer Johnson's departure, GM's outside directors had refused Smith's request to put three more GM officers—O'Connell, Hoglund, and Jack Smith—on the board. Smith's proposal was a bald push to stack the board with people beholden to him, but he was still surprised when the outsiders stood up to him. The episode had leaked out to the press, raising doubts about Smith's hold on power. For the rest of his term, Smith wanted no more trouble from his directors—or Wall Street. In his determination to go out a winner, Smith took a series of actions designed to silence the carping about his leadership.

In December 1988, Smith gave an interview to the *Wall Street Journal* in which he broadly hinted that he would urge GM's board of directors to raise the common stock dividend. The payout to shareholders should rise if earnings hit $14 a share, Smith declared, "because we can't invest that much money back in the business."[9]

This was a stunning statement, although not for the reasons Smith intended. GM, having wasted billions, still had lots of ways it could usefully spend money, starting with developing replacements for its mainstream engines, which were twenty or more years behind the latest Japanese technology. The handicaps Alex Mair had identified so dramatically still hadn't been fixed. Not only that, many of GM's highest volume cars were far behind the competition in design and technology. GM's top-selling small car, the Chevrolet Cavalier, was nearly eight years old. But no replacement was in sight. Because of dated designs and poor quality, GM was forced to shell out $700 in retail discounts for every vehicle it sold in North America—a 40 percent increase from the year before. Given sharply increasing production from Japanese-run factories in the U.S. heartland, there was no reason to think this $3.6 billion annual cash drain would ease.

But GM's directors went along. On February 6, 1989, they approved a $300 million bonanza for shareholders. For the first time in thirty-four years, GM split its common stock, two for one. The board raised the quarterly dividend, too, by 20 percent to 75 cents a share, or $3 a share on an annual basis. Smith crowed in triumph. "This sends a message to our stockholders that we've got a fundamental improvement in our earning power," he declared. Later that month, GM announced "record" profits of $4.86 billion, or $7.17 a share.

This "record," however, had several asterisks. More than half the total had come from GM's European and overseas operations, which had pulled in a staggering $2.71 billion. All of GM's domestic operations, with $117 billion in sales, had managed just $2.15 billion in profits. And much of that came from nonautomotive activities: EDS, Hughes Aircraft, and General Motors Acceptance Corporation, the huge financing arm. Even including profits from financing, GM's North American operations earned just $338 on every vehicle sold—only one-fourth the profit per vehicle earned overseas. GM's U.S. market share had slid to 36.1 percent, the lowest level since before the Great Depression.

More important, Ford once again earned more than GM. Despite having only about two thirds the revenue, Ford racked up a staggering

$5.3 billion in profit for 1988. If GM had matched Ford's profit margins, it would have earned not $4.86 billion, but $6.6 billion. Ford earned $1,014 in operating profit for every vehicle it sold—46 percent more than GM ($693 per vehicle).

Undaunted, Smith's Good News Crusade surged on into 1989. In August, GM gathered securities analysts for another meeting, this time at GM's Milford, Michigan, test track. This was an annual summer event. As in the past, the analysts were treated to test drives in GM's hottest new cars. This year, the highlight was the fire-belching ZR-1 Corvette, a 375-horsepower brute GM intended to sell for nearly $60,000. But there was more than the usual interest in what GM's top brass would say after play time. Roger Smith had less than a year to go as chairman. The men directly under him were jockeying for position in the succession race. Stempel clearly had the inside track to the top, but there were spoils aplenty to be divided among those right behind him. Roger Smith would have a lot to say about who got what in the coming administration. Not surprisingly, Smith's "team" set about polishing the chairman's legacy even as they sought to prove that a "new GM" was emerging from the trials of the previous three years.

Each member of the executive committee was assigned a role. Bob Stempel played tough cop. GM would close more factories to eliminate the drain of paying for unneeded capacity, he vowed. He just didn't say when. Lloyd Reuss was product champion, dazzling the analysts with visions of a wave of new cars that would bury the upstarts. Alan Smith, born again as a prophet of cultural change, stripped off his jacket, dumped his script and waded into his audience like a daytime television talk show host. GM, he said, would follow "the North Star of caring for the customer." Analysts who remembered the straitlaced finance man of old could barely contain their amazement.

But the keystone of the day was a lecture from Roger Smith's finance wizard, Bob O'Connell. "Our great leader," as O'Connell hailed his chairman, had so skillfully diversified GM that it now could earn $6 a share, or nearly $3.5 billion, before a penny of profit from U.S. vehicle sales was counted. Even if car sales in America tanked in a recession, O'Connell declared, GM would earn money, and have more than enough cash to cover a fat dividend. O'Connell's message was aimed squarely at a small group of naysayers who were warning investors that GM's profits could fall to $2 a share in 1990.

It was a masterful assault. One of a stock analyst's greatest fears is being wrong, especially about a stock that outperforms the market in a recession. O'Connell was warning the bears they were going to be embarrassed at how wrong they were about GM. It worked. GM stock jumped $1.63 a share the day after the meeting as most analysts declared that they too were "in."

As far as most people inside GM were concerned, the Roger Smith era couldn't end soon enough. As 1989 drew to a close, GM's fortunes turned for the worse again. The company's share of the car market collapsed to a new post-Depression low. One customer survey found that GM's cars got fewer recommendations, on average, than any brand except the Yugo, a comical subcompact from Yugoslavia that had become the industry's benchmark for bad quality. Smith, himself, had become a laughingstock, thanks in part to a satiric movie titled Roger and Me that used the GM chairman as a villainous foil in a portrait of the decline of Flint, Michigan.

So it was with a collective sigh of relief that GMers began getting the news on the night of April 2, 1990, that the succession race was over.

The next morning, Smith delivered the news at a press conference in the ground floor car showroom at GM's Detroit headquarters: Bob Stempel, fifty-six years old, would be the next chairman of General Motors. GM's new president would be Lloyd Reuss. For the first time, GM's two top officers would be engineers—"car guys," not "bean counters." Jack Smith would become vice chairman in charge of international operations, keeping his previous duties but with a new title. Robert Schultz, who had been executive vice president in charge of EDS, Hughes, and technology, would stay in that role but also become a vice chairman, too. In effect, Jack Smith and Schultz had received consolation prizes. Schultz, at fifty-nine, clearly was out of contention for the top. Jack Smith, fifty-one years old, still had a shot at being GM's chief executive. But by the time Stempel retired, Jack Smith would be sixty, and have relatively little time to make a mark.

The real losers in the race didn't even show up for the press conference. Bob O'Connell was on vacation, Roger Smith said. Alan Smith was at his desk. Bill Hoglund was on a business trip in Texas. Hoglund had suffered the most humiliating defeat. As head of GM's parts operations, he would be the only member of the management committee who didn't report to the new chairman. Instead, Hoglund would answer to Reuss, a man he considered to be fundamentally incompetent.

The only cloud visible on the horizon was the odd matter of Reuss's

title. Most previous GM presidents had also carried the title of chief
operating officer. But not Reuss. He would simply be "president." GM's
kremlinologists didn't take long to deduce that this slight represented a
no-confidence vote from GM's board. In fact, Stempel had gone to the
mat with the outside directors to make Reuss his No. 2 man. The board's
choice would have been Jack Smith.

Stempel, however, wanted a "product man" at his side, not a finance
guy. No matter that Jack Smith had done something neither Stempel
nor Reuss had accomplished during the previous six years: He had led a
major money-losing GM operation out of the red. Stempel, however,
didn't see Jack Smith as the linchpin of that achievement. The European
turnaround, he often said, had taken years of effort by many people, not
least among them himself. Stempel preferred Reuss, who believed, as did
Stempel, that new cars would save GM.

Reuss was unfazed by the withholding of the chief operating officer's
title. He was the president of General Motors. He would get paid more
than Jack Smith or anyone other than Stempel. That's how real car guys
kept score. Besides, Reuss didn't like to dwell on the negatives. When
the formal press conference was done, he dived into a crowd of reporters
and unabashedly summarized his game plan: "Our long-term interest is
to make 40 percent market share in passenger cars, and 35 percent in
trucks."

THE APRIL ANNOUNCEMENT of the new top management lineup began a
queasy four-month interregnum. In May, GM reported first quarter
profits fell 54 percent from the year before, largely because of a dramatic
22.5 percent slump in North American sales. Second quarter profits fell
38 percent. It became an open secret that shortly after Smith retired,
GM would announce more plant shutdowns. The embarrassing controversy over Roger Smith's $1.2 million annual pension merely intensified
the yearning among his underlings for the day when he would finally go.
In July, Smith accomplished his dream of driving the first Saturn car off
the assembly line. But Saturn executives barred reporters from the factory in a clumsy effort to keep their distance from the tarnished image of
GM and its boss.

Finally, on August 1, 1990, Bob Stempel took control, and led GM's
new management team into its first press conference. GM's leaders were
now a "team," he said. Stempel used the word "team" a total of twenty-

seven times to drive home the point. In an effort to signal a break with his predecessor, Stempel declared he wanted the focus of attention at GM to be its cars, not its chairman.

"We've been through enough mergers, diversifications, and acquisitions for a while," Stempel said. "I look for this team to focus on cars and trucks." Reuss took up that banner, trundling out a graphic illustration of his "Framework for Greatness" that looked like a pie plate balancing on an arrow. The bean counters took back seats, literally. O'Connell and Alan Smith were placed farthest away from Stempel on the dais.

On his first day in GM's driver's seat, Stempel was as buoyant as a freshman who'd just made it to the varsity squad.

"I feel terrific this morning." He grinned. "Someone on the radio said, 'Guess who's got a new job today?' And they mentioned my name."

The next day, August 2, 1990, Iraq invaded Kuwait. Americans recoiled from the sudden threat of war in the oil fields. Car sales evaporated. And the world's largest corporation watched the earth open under its wheels.

CHAPTER 8

CHRYSLERCRASHES

On a warm June night in 1987, Jerry Greenwald, the No. 2 man at Chrysler and heir apparent to Lee Iacocca, took his wife, Glenda, to dinner at Detroit's most venerable old-line eaterie, the downtown London Chop House. He was driving Chrysler's newest product, a Lamborghini Countach. Chrysler had acquired the Italian car maker some two months earlier at the behest of Greenwald himself, who had serendipitously learned that Lamborghini's Swiss owners wanted to sell the company.

Lamborghini made only about 400 cars a year, less than a Chrysler assembly plant produced on a single eight-hour shift. But Greenwald simply couldn't resist the thought of owning the company, and neither could Iacocca. Buying Italy's most prestigious automotive marque represented a triumphant homecoming, of sorts, for a man whose father had fled his homeland in poverty more than eight decades before.

The Countach, bristling with a 420-horsepower engine and a $127,000 price tag, was the very antithesis of the boxy, practical K-cars that Chrysler was peddling to a buyer base weighted toward blue-collar workers and elderly people—"grandads and Joe Six-packs," in the words of Ben Bidwell. Lamborghini's cars were ostentatious and outrageous. After hearing Bob Lutz boast about driving a Countach home from work at warp speed, Greenwald wanted to try it himself.

After dinner, he and Glenda headed north on Interstate 75 toward their home in Bloomfield Hills. Greenwald hit the accelerator, and the car responded like a horse straining at its bit. Not until the speedometer needle passed 125 mph did the Countach stop lurching forward and enter a smooth, cruising mode. Greenwald was having the time of his life—until he heard a siren wailing and saw lights flashing in the rearview mirror. "I could lose this guy if I wanted" was his first thought. But his second thought was how the headlines would look if he got caught. Greenwald pulled over.

The wide-eyed state trooper admired the Countach, and asked Greenwald how fast he was going. "I don't exactly know," Greenwald replied, more or less honestly. After a bit of banter about the car, the state trooper wrote Greenwald a ticket for going 70 in a 55 mph zone. Greenwald was perversely proud of it, like the proverbial schoolboy Goody Two-Shoes who gets his first detention and proves, thereby, that he really isn't a complete nerd after all. Greenwald later bragged to his Chrysler colleagues that he was insulted for getting ticketed for going a mere 70—because he couldn't hold the Countach's speed *down* that low.

Chrysler kept the incident quiet (Greenwald's pride in his escapade had limits), but years later it would seem an ill omen. For four straight years, from mid-1983 through mid-1987, Chrysler had done everything right. American consumers snapped up the company's faceless, mechanically identical K-car derivatives—the Dodge 600, Chrysler LeBaron GTS, Plymouth Caravelle, Dodge Lancer, and the rest—as fast as Chrysler could build them. Lee Iacocca became a hero. But suddenly, Chrysler seemed snake-bitten.

Some blunders started out innocently. In 1984, Iaccocca had struck a deal with Allesandro de Tomaso, an Argentinian former race-car driver and an old friend from his Ford days. De Tomaso had gained control of Maserati, the legendary Italian sports car company, and convinced Iacocca that Chrysler and Maserati could do business together. Chrysler would finance Maserati's development of a luxury two-seat coupe, and Chrysler would sell the car in its own dealerships.

Iacocca loved the idea. He thought Chrysler could sell between 5,000 and 8,000 of the new coupes a year, just for starters. Those weren't big numbers, but with a price tag of $35,000 or so, the profit per car promised to be huge. The luxury coupes would provide a "halo effect" to help move Chrysler's product line and customer base upscale. Chrysler's marketing men mused aloud about calling the car the Lido, after their leader. They dropped that idea, but the project went forward. In December 1986, Iacocca predicted that the Maserati coupe and a new "stretch" version of the minivan would help Chrysler average $1 billion a year in profits for the rest of the decade. Greenwald was skeptical about Maserati, but his worst-case scenario had Chrysler losing $10 million on the project.

It quickly became apparent that this coupe was no coup. Iacocca and De Tomaso agreed to mate a Maserati body with a Chrysler engine, which was taking the worst from each partner. Chrysler's engines were reliable but pedestrian. Maserati's engines, meanwhile, packed a lot of punch, but building bodies with "fit and finish" was a skill the Italians couldn't grasp.

As a result, the car was woefully underpowered. The gaps between the fenders and the doors were as big as canyons. The chrome trim around the wheel wells kept falling off. The power windows worked sporadically at best. The convertible top wouldn't snap into place properly, and the removable hard top wouldn't fit, either. The car leaked so badly that workers virtually needed raincoats to drive through the spray booth that tested each car for water tightness.

Chrysler moved its chief engineer on the car, Bob Davis, to Milan, to help out. But the comedy of errors continued. Davis's son, upon turning eighteen, got drafted into the Italian army. The boy escaped induction, but not without a hassle.

Meanwhile, the Chrysler and Maserati people fought over everything. The Italians wanted natural wood for the car's steering wheel, while the Americans wanted fake wood grain. They compromised on leather. As the project dragged on, de Tomaso kept asking Iacocca for more money. The Chrysler people, he complained in his heavily accented English, were causing the problems. "I am treated worse zan ze sheet in ze meedle of ze road," he would tell Iacocca. "At least you step over ze sheet. But your people, zey are stepping right on top of me."

Iacocca berated his underlings and kept shipping money to Milan. To solve the power problem Chrysler and Maserati gave the car a six-cylinder engine from Mitsubishi, but that added cost and complexity. Undeterred, Chrysler bragged about the car in its 1985 annual stockholders' report, and put a "sneak preview" picture in the 1986 annual report. Iacocca unveiled prototypes of the car, to be called the Chrysler TC (for

Touring Coupe) by Maserati, in 1986 and again in 1987. It was "the most introduced car in history," moaned Steve Miller, Chrysler's chief financial officer, as deadlines passed with no TC in sight.

Finally, in the spring of 1988, Iacocca turned in desperation to Dick Dauch, his vice president for manufacturing. Dauch dispatched a SWAT team to Milan. When the killer gophers arrived, in July, they found 200 cars in varying degrees of disrepair parked near the assembly line in the Maserati factory. They scrapped more than 100 that were beyond hope, and declared that another sixty were fit only for test drives. Only thirty-five of the first 200 cars could be salvaged for public sale.

By the time the car arrived in Chrysler's showrooms, two years of promotional hype had given way to boredom. Worse, dealers were horrified to see that the $35,000 luxury coupe looked almost identical to the Chrysler LeBaron coupe that cost less than half that price. "We never intended to sell the Maserati," Ben Bidwell explained sarcastically. "The idea is to put the cars side by side, so people will buy the LeBaron." The joke was too painful to be funny. In desperation, Bidwell slapped a whopping $7,000 rebate on the TC.

In the end, Greenwald gladly would have settled for losing $10 million on the TC, or even twenty times that. The money Chrysler invested to bring the car to market—buying the necessary machine tools, devoting engineering and marketing talent to the project, buying hundreds of plane tickets between Detroit and Milan—totaled more than $400 million. In November 1989, after just 7,300 cars were built, Chrysler announced it would kill the TC. Virtually all the investment was lost.

BIDWELL'S CRACK ABOUT BUILDING the TC to help sell the LeBaron coupe was appropriate, because the LeBaron wasn't selling, either. Its rounded, eggshell styling was the best to come out of Chrysler in years. But the LeBaron coupe's beauty was only skin deep. Under the hood, it carried the same four-cylinder, 2.2-liter engine that had powered Chrysler cars since 1980. The engine was reliable. But by 1986 gasoline was cheap and plentiful again, and Americans wanted bigger cars with bigger engines. Chrysler didn't have them. The LeBaron coupe was an underpowered car with a wallowing suspension and wobbly steering. The car, in short, was like a grandmother in a miniskirt. It epitomized Iacocca's strategy of dressing up the K-car in different outfits to save money.

He and Greenwald believed the K-car's underpinnings—the chassis, suspension, and basic engineering—would carry Chrysler through the early to mid-1990s, thus sparing them the burden of spending billions to develop totally new cars. If Americans wanted more luxurious cars, Iacocca would adorn his K-cars with vinyl roofs, wood-grain side panels, leather seats, wire wheel covers, and fancy grilles. The LeBaron Sedan, yet another K-car spinoff launched in 1989, combined an assortment of Iacocca's favorite ornaments with a tufted burgundy interior so gauche that sitting inside, as one automotive magazine opined, was like "being inside a trombone case."

As for bigger cars, Iacocca's recipe was to "stretch" the K-cars like a piece of taffy. The K-cars got longer and longer, but they couldn't get proportionately wider. Widening a chassis requires reengineering the axles, the engine compartment, and the basic underframe, which amounts to developing a brand new vehicle. That's what Iacocca didn't want to do.

Thus the new line of cars the company launched in 1987—the Dodge Dynasty, Chrysler New Yorker, Chrysler Fifth Avenue, and Chrysler Imperial—were simply long, longer, longer-still, and longest-ever versions of the K-car. The Imperial was so long and thin that it looked like a giant Virginia Slims cigarette on wheels. Steve Miller found it so disgusting that he refused to show slides of the Imperial in his presentations to automotive analysts. Worse yet, all four cars, code-named the C bodies, carried boxy styling personally decreed by Iacocca himself. Chrysler's designers had recommended rounded styling patterned after the Ford Taurus, but Iacocca would have none of it.

Chrysler's cars were a generation gap on wheels. The tastes of affluent young Americans—those with the most money to spend on new cars— were evolving in ways that Iacocca simply didn't understand. The Baby Boomers' definition of luxury didn't include useless, ostentatious ornaments. Vinyl roofs were about as relevant to them as Glenn Miller music.

Young Americans didn't have the instinctive dislike of Japanese cars that people of Iacocca's generation, especially men who had fought in World War II, bore in their bones. They admired "functional luxury," cars with punchy multivalve engines that provided a high-revving feel of excitement behind the wheel. Increasingly, they wanted "driver's cars" with taut steering, road-hugging suspension, and sophisticated cassette radios and CD players. Chrysler wasn't providing any. Bob Lutz, who knew better, publicly decried the notion that Chrysler's cars were "yestertech." But in doing so, he coined a term that stuck to the cars like hot tar from a newly paved road.

Chrysler's dearth of new cars didn't faze Iacocca, though, until October 19, 1987, the day the stock market crashed. The sickening slide on Wall Street—the Dow Jones Industrial Average plunged a record 508 points that day—exposed Chrysler's weaknesses. The company was overburdened with debt. Buying American Motors had cost only $200 million in cash, but it also required Chrysler to take on some $700 million of debt and $300 million of unfunded pension liabilities. Because it was spending so much on acquisitions, Chrysler made minimal payments to its pension funds in 1987, leaving them with a $2.7 billion shortfall at year-end. The debt was only one part of a cost structure that was spinning out of control.

In the early 1980s, Chrysler had slashed its break-even point, the number of cars the company had to sell before turning a profit, in half, to 1.1 million vehicles a year. By 1987, though, the company's break-even point had bounced back to more than 1.9 million vehicles. Even with the purchase of American Motors, Chrysler should have had a break-even point of no more than 1.5 million cars and trucks a year. But the holding-company structure Iacocca had established to diversify the company added costs. The parent company and the subsidiaries had parallel PR departments, legal staffs, accounting departments and so on. Bringing the American Motors people on board added to the duplication. And as Chrysler's costs were soaring, its sales were sliding because its cars were so dowdy.

In late October of 1987, just after the market's crash, Chrysler idled one of its two assembly plants in St. Louis for two weeks. It was the first time in four years that the company had furloughed a factory because of slow sales. At the same time, orders for the original K-cars, the Dodge Aries and Plymouth Reliant that had debuted in 1980, were plunging. Chrysler had added three assembly plants when it bought American Motors. All of a sudden, it didn't need them.

The logical move was to close the aging Detroit factory where the K-cars were built. But the facility was Chrysler's only assembly plant in the city of Detroit, and Mayor Coleman Young had worked hard in 1979 to help the Chrysler bailout effort. Union politics were important, too. The Detroit factory stood on Jefferson Avenue, just four miles due east of Solidarity House, the UAW's headquarters. It was in one of the city's worst neighborhoods, where jobs were virtually nonexistent. Closing

Jefferson Avenue, as the plant was called after the street that it straddled, would have touched off a powderkeg.

So when 1988 began, Iacocca and Greenwald opted, instead, to close the ancient factory in Kenosha, Wisconsin, that had belonged to American Motors. No matter that Kenosha had just been retooled, at a cost of $200 million, to build the Dodge Omni and Plymouth Horizon, which Chrysler had moved out of a plant in Illinois. Or that Chrysler would have to spend another $200 million to move the tooling again to Jefferson Avenue. Or that Iacocca had promised Kenosha workers, as well as the state of Wisconsin, to keep Kenosha open for five years. On January 27, Chrysler announced the decision.

The result was a firestorm of criticism. Iacocca had postured his company as a corporate savior that would rejuvenate American Motors, quite the opposite of the corporate raiders who had dominated Wall Street. He had raised Kenosha's hopes high, and he was dashing those hopes after just five months.

Rudy Kuzel, the firebrand chairman of UAW Local 72 in Kenosha, sprang into action. He dispatched Kenosha workers to picket Iacocca in New York, and another crew to demonstrate during Chrysler's news conference at the Chicago Auto Show. "Iacocca Lied," their placards read.

Then Chrysler played right into Kuzel's hands. On April 19, one day after opening contract negotiations with the UAW, it disclosed that Iacocca's pay had totaled a whopping $17.9 million the previous year. A week later Chrysler compounded the error by announcing it would continue to build the K-car, but in Mexico instead of Detroit. "Maybe we'll call it the 'Chrysler Ole!'" quipped one Chrysler PR man, who had despaired of explaining his company's latest faux pas.

His grim humor was well founded. Moving the K-car to Mexico made a mockery of Iacocca's buy-American posturing and anti-import blustering. Rudy Kuzel, whose plant was the odd man out in the shuffling, snarled: "Lee Iacocca represents what's wrong with corporate America. He doesn't care any more about America than Joe Stalin did."[1]

The episode, together with the Maserati mess, showed the dark side of Chrysler's free-wheeling corporate culture. The towel-snapping, locker-room informality of Chrysler's executive suite could produce great creativity—but also incredible chaos. Too many decisions were made at Chrysler because they seemed like a good idea at the time. The Maserati project was launched on Iacocca's whim. The confusion over Kenosha, the K-car, and the Omni/Horizon stemmed from the failure of anybody to think more than one step ahead. Shoot first, aim later was how many decisions got made.

Eventually, the Kenosha uproar forced Iacocca to back down, at least a little. On April 27, 1988, Chrysler announced that, although it wouldn't cancel its controversial production moves, it would delay them. For a few more months, the Omni and Horizon would still be built at Kenosha, and K-car production would continue at Jefferson Avenue in Detroit. In September the company pledged $250 million as a peace offering to retrain Kenosha's workers for other jobs. For Chrysler and Lee Iacocca, the worst seemed to be over. Instead, it was still to come.

WHILE THE KENOSHA AFFAIR was a fiasco, Chrysler at least could hope for better results from American Motors' other two plants. The Toledo factory was nearly as old as Kenosha, but its product—the four-door Jeep Cherokee—was selling well. Before long, Toledo's union leaders agreed to work-rule changes that allowed Chrysler to boost Cherokee production substantially.

American Motors' third plant, meanwhile, was a modern facility in Bramalea, Ontario, that was the company's crown jewel. Completed in 1987, just as Chrysler was buying American Motors, the factory was earmarked to produce a new sedan that Renault had developed for AMC. Having borne the expense of developing the new car, Renault wanted to recoup its investment. So in selling its controlling stake in AMC to Chrysler, Renault insisted on a contract requiring Chrysler to sell at least 300,000 of the new sedans, or else pay penalties.

Chrysler was happy to oblige. The car was styled by Giugiaro, the renowned Italian designer, and it came with a peppy V-6 engine that Renault had developed with help from Volvo. Designed in Italy, engineered in France and Sweden, and to be assembled and sold in North America, the new car epitomized the new global auto industry. Chrysler's plan was to make it the centerpiece of a new marque, Eagle, aimed at the Yuppies flocking to AMC dealers to buy Jeeps. AMC dealers would henceforth be called Jeep/Eagle dealers, and the new car would be christened the Eagle Premier. In the TV commercials, Iacocca pointed to a new Premier standing beside a Jeep and said: "If you're going to put a new car alongside a legend, you'd better do it right."

And then, nothing happened. American car buyers responded as if they had never heard of the new car, which indeed most of them hadn't. Chrysler now had six different brands (Chrysler, Plymouth, Dodge, Eagle, Jeep, and Dodge Truck), just one less than GM, which was four times as big as Chrysler. The company couldn't afford enough advertising to promote all six. Besides, French cars had a long legacy of failure in the United States that the Premier, despite its new Chrysler brand name, couldn't overcome.

In June 1988, just six months after the car went on sale, Chrysler shut the Bramalea plant for two weeks because unsold Premiers were stacking up on dealer lots. The plant was closed for six of the first sixteen weeks of 1989. By that fall it was working the equivalent of just one day in five. Chrysler couldn't sell nearly enough cars to meet its contract with Renault. Iacocca found himself building a car he couldn't sell, and then having to pay penalties for not selling it. The penalties topped $200 million—on top of the huge cost of carrying a plant that was mostly idle.

As CHRYSLER'S MISTAKES MOUNTED in number, they climbed in cost as well. The tab for the Maserati mess exceeded $400 million. The cost of moving the Omni and Horizon twice (from Belvidere to Kenosha, and from Kenosha to Detroit) was another $400 million. The Premier disaster cost $200 million. Iacocca spent $2 billion on acquisitions, and another $1.85 billion on a massive stock buyback program. The total: $4.85 billion. It was money that Chrysler could have spent to develop new cars and new engines—things the company, conspicuously, didn't have.

But the cost of Chrysler's escapades couldn't be measured in dollars alone. There was also the drain on management's time and attention, which was no small matter. The executive committee spent endless hours exploring and debating possible acquisitions instead of discussing how to improve Chrysler's cars. The diversification effort was so overriding that Chrysler even briefly considered changing its name; one corporate identity consultant suggested Chryco.[2] The Maserati project and the Kenosha mess kept everyone at the top preoccupied. But the most distracted man of all was Iacocca himself.

He had much besides Chrysler to occupy his thoughts: the book, the Statue of Liberty, the newspaper column, the wine and olive oil businesses, the divorce, the Iacocca Foundation (to support research in diabetes, which had killed his first wife, Mary) and the Iacocca Center for Productivity at Lehigh University (his alma mater). The newspaper orgy that had followed the breakup of his brief second marriage illustrated the burden of fame that, increasingly, preoccupied and afflicted Iacocca. There were other incidents, too, some of them bizarre.

In September 1987, when Henry Ford II lay hospitalized in Detroit with a pneumonia that would prove fatal, Iacocca's daughter Lia got married at St. Hugo's Church in Bloomfield Hills. Shortly before the ceremony, a Chrysler PR man, on hand to handle the local society reporters, got a call from the Associated Press. A priest at the Iacocca wedding, the reporter said, had dropped into Henry Ford's hospital room. "Was he carrying a secret message from Iacocca?" the reporter asked.

The Chrysler PR man, John Guiniven, scoffed at the question. No priest from the Iacocca wedding had dropped in on Henry Ford, he said, and none had reason to. But just to be sure, Guiniven checked with St. Hugo's priests. Everyone said no, until Guiniven put the question to a priest from out of town. Father John Mericantante, from Hialeah, Florida, was a casual friend of Iacocca's children. On the way to the church, Father Mericantante happily explained, he had stopped at Henry Ford Hospital (named for the first Henry Ford) and walked into the room of Henry Ford II. Mr. Ford looked awful, Father Mericantante told Guiniven, so he had given the sick man the last rites of the Catholic Church.

Guiniven was stunned. Anyone who wasn't from Mars knew about the blood feud between Lee Iacocca and Henry Ford. It was outrageous for a priest who was a friend of Iacocca's family to waltz into Henry Ford's hospital room—uninvited—and administer the last rites. All Guiniven could say was "But, Father, Mr. Ford isn't even Catholic." To which Father Mericantante replied: "One of his ex-wives was Catholic. That's good enough for me."

It was Keystone Kops time. Guiniven ran to tell Iacocca on the front steps of the church, and Iacocca was visibly startled. "What the hell?" he exclaimed, as he was swept away to line up for the wedding pictures. Guiniven called the AP back to confirm that the visit had occurred, and to explain that Iacocca had had nothing to do with it. Nonetheless, by the time the ceremony ended, the steps of St. Hugo's were filled with reporters asking questions. Was the priest on a peacemaking mission from Iacocca? Or had he carried a curse from Iacocca to Henry Ford?

Did he bring any dead fish into the hospital room—just like in *The Godfather?*

Guiniven wanted to scream at that last question, but he stifled himself. He tried to shoo the reporters away, but then Father Mericantante walked out and started holding forth. The priest told the reporters he was shocked to find Henry Ford looking far worse than the hospital had disclosed.

With that, Guiniven tried to pull the priest back inside the church, but Father Mericantante would have none of it. When Guiniven's voice got testy, Father Mericantante asked: "Sir, are you Catholic?" Guiniven snapped back: "I was, until today."

When Guiniven finally cornered Iacocca to describe what had happened, Iacocca was furious. He made a phone call of apology to the fuming Ford family, but the damage was done. The next day's Detroit newspapers were full of reports about the incident. The usual society wedding stories got short shrift. Iacocca had always wanted to be a celebrity, just like Henry Ford, but now he was learning that it wasn't always fun.

Amid all this, the car business was moving more quickly than ever before during Iacocca's forty-year career, but Iacocca wasn't moving with it. His biggest product successes, the Ford Mustang and the Chrysler minivans, had been brilliant packaging innovations that had disguised mediocre mechanical underpinnings. The ill-fated TC had sprung from the same formula.

But the pace of product innovation was accelerating in the auto industry, just as it was in computers and in consumer electronics. The Japanese were leading the way in deploying (though not necessarily developing) high-revving multivalve engines, electronic engine controls, four-speed automatic transmissions, antilock brakes, traction control, and more. A man more focused on his job might have moved with the market.

But Iacocca, instead, was juggling his job with the obligations and opportunities of his own fame. It was no easy task. The huge success of his first book led him, inevitably, to write a second one. *Talking Straight,* published in 1988, was a compendium of Iacocca clichés that was no more entertaining, or successful, than the typical Hollywood sequel. But writing it simply came with the territory of *being* Lee Iacocca. He was becoming a prisoner of his persona.

In October 1989 Iacocca traveled to China, for a look at the company's joint ventures to build Jeeps in Beijing and engines in Manchuria. He was received with fanfare, and stayed in a house reserved for visiting heads of state. His schedule included a quiet sightseeing visit to the Great Wall.

Shortly after Iacocca arrived at the Wall, however, a young Chinese guard recognized him, and approached him. "Mr. Iacocca, I read your book," he said in broken English (apparently referring to the first one). Others overheard, and Iacocca was mobbed, not only by the Chinese but also by Japanese tourists. The ruckus forced him to flee and retreat to Beijing.

When he came home from the Far East, he found Chrysler on the cusp of crisis. On October 26, 1989, the company reported that its earnings from operations for the third quarter had plunged 80 percent to $22 million, or just 10 cents a share—its worst quarterly performance in seven years. A one-time gain from the sale of stock in Mitsubishi Motors had bolstered the bottom line, but the company's business was rapidly deteriorating.

For the rest of 1989, bad news kept popping out of Chrysler, staccato style. On November 5 the company said it would close its assembly plant on Jefferson Avenue in Detroit, two years before a replacement factory was scheduled to open. The Omni and Horizon subcompacts, after making the expensive factory-hopping trek from Illinois to Wisconsin to Michigan, had run out of gas. The very next day Chrysler announced that, to cut costs, it was scrapping the holding-company structure it had established four years earlier to accommodate its diversification effort. And on December 6, Chrysler announced it would try to sell Gulfstream and Electrospace Systems, marking a humiliating end to the company's drive to diversify. The stage was set for 1990, Lee Iacocca's *annus horribilis*.

"WHAT MOST OF YOU have been reporting as a series of bad news items and crisis items, that's all part of our plan. That helter-skelter, up and down, back and forth Chrysler actually has a plan, and a damned good one, I might add."

It was a profoundly incongruous statement, and not the only one that Lee Iacocca made on the morning of February 13, 1990. An hour before Iacocca's press conference began, Chrysler had announced it was closing not only the Jefferson Avenue plant in Detroit, but also one of its two assembly plants in St. Louis. That meant the company would be closing a total of three assembly plants (including Kenosha) in fifteen months, thus forfeiting the capacity to build 675,000 cars a year. Chrysler said the plant closings had caused it to lose $664 million for the fourth quarter of 1989, the largest quarterly deficit in its history.

"I know the word for financial results like these is 'disappointing,' " he scolded reporters. "I suspect I'll see it in about half of your headlines tomorrow. But please, don't put that word in my mouth. I'm proud, damned proud, about what the people at Chrysler were able to do in 1989. Think about it, only an $87 million operating loss in the last quarter."

At most companies, that wouldn't be anything to boast about. And while Chrysler had eked out earnings of $359 million for the entire year, in the auto industry that was pocket change.

By 1990, making cars had become a high-stakes global poker game. Companies had to ante up huge sums to develop cars and trucks that were fresh—in technology as well as in styling—in an increasingly crowded market. Chrysler wasn't producing anything fresh. The only way to move Chrysler's aging cars was to cut prices. The company shelled out record rebates of more than $1,200 per vehicle in the fourth quarter of 1989, three times what it paid two years earlier. "Things are tough right now," Iacocca said at his press conference, "but I'm sort of enjoying it." By that standard, the fun was just beginning.

MARKET SHARE WASN'T the only thing Iacocca's company was losing. It was losing people as well, including members of the team that had steered Chrysler through its dance with death in the early 1980s. Some losses were inevitable, of course, from an executive suite filled with aggressive personalities and enormous egos. Chrysler had gotten a taste of this as early as 1988 when Hal Sperlich, one of Iacocca's long-time loyalists and friends, had bailed out, with a nudge from Iacocca himself.

Sperlich had been fired by Henry Ford II in 1977, and thus had landed at Chrysler a year before Iacocca did. He played a key role in developing the K-car, and then used the chassis as the basis for Chrysler's minivan. It was one of Sperlich's ideas Henry Ford had rejected, but went on to become Detroit's most successful vehicle of the eighties. Sperlich's reward was being named president of Chrysler by Iacocca in 1984.

But Sperlich could be as combative as he was brilliant. He was so assertive and abrasive that Bidwell had refused to report to him. "I know every one of Hal's speeches," he would snap. "He knows every one of mine, which are shorter." Sperlich, in turn, would barely talk to Dauch. Thus the people who engineered Chrysler's cars wouldn't talk to the men who built them.

Clashing with Bidwell and Dauch was one thing, but opposing Iacocca quite another. Sperlich argued vehemently against Chrysler's stock buy-back program, the purchase of Lamborghini, and—most of all—the acquisition of American Motors.

Thus in January 1988, Iacocca decided to move Sperlich out of product development and put him in charge of Chrysler Technologies, the "empty box" of the diversification drive that Sperlich had vigorously opposed. Sperlich, who at fifty-eight years old was well shy of normal retirement age, got the hint, and said he wanted to quit. Neither Iacocca nor anyone else tried to change his mind. "It's a grind," Sperlich explained to the press. "I decided I wanted a little more freedom."[3]

Sperlich's departure set in motion continuous shuffling and reshuffling of the executive suite. To replace Sperlich as president of Chrysler Motors, Iacocca chose both Bidwell and Lutz. Bidwell became president (Product and Marketing) while Lutz got to be president (Operations). When a reporter asked why Chrysler Motors needed two presidents, Bidwell reminded her that the company had four different models named LeBaron (the LeBaron coupe, convertible, sedan, and GTS). Then he quipped: "For any company crazy enough to have four LeBarons, two presidents certainly aren't out of line."

The idea of copresidents was quickly deemed unworkable, so Iacocca made Bidwell chairman of Chrysler Motors and Lutz president. During a five-year time span Bidwell held five different jobs: executive vice president of Chrysler Corporation, vice chairman of Chrysler Corporation, vice chairman of Chrysler Motors, copresident of Chrysler Motors, and chairman of Chrysler Motors. During the same period Greenwald held three different posts: vice chairman of Chrysler Corporation, chairman of Chrysler Motors, and then vice chairman of Chrysler Corporation again.

Steve Miller, meanwhile, went from vice chairman of Chrysler Corporation to executive vice president and then back to vice chairman again. Along with those titles, he either was or wasn't, depending on the year, chairman of Chrysler Financial Corporation (the money-lending subsidiary) or chief financial officer of the parent company. "Lee's rearranging the furniture again," the Chrysler men would say as each new set of titles was announced.

Each reshuffling contained clues to who was hot and who was not in Iacocca's mind. As Chrysler's fortunes sank, it became increasingly clear that the company's coupon-clipping treasurer, Freddy Zuckerman, was on the "not" list.

In May 1988, Zuckerman had completely upstaged Iacocca at Chrysler's annual shareholders meeting. After Iacocca had disclosed that Chrysler's profits would fall short of Wall Street's forecasts, Zuckerman pulled reporters aside and described the company's problems in painstaking detail: Rebates were soaring, the AMC acquisition had added excess plant capacity, and Chrysler was finally starting to realize the need to spend more money on developing new cars. It was all true, but it wasn't exactly what Chrysler wanted the press to dwell on. And when the next day's newspaper reports mentioned Zuckerman's name more times than Iacocca's, Iacocca hit the roof.

By 1990 Zuckerman had opened his mouth too many times, so Iacocca told Steve Miller to get rid of him. In May, word leaked to the press that Zuckerman was being pushed out.

When the story broke, the next big-name departure from Chrysler was well in the works, although Iacocca didn't know it. Just as Iacocca had grown tired of Sperlich and Zuckerman, so now Jerry Greenwald, his second-in-command, was getting tired of him.

Without Iacocca, Greenwald never would have made it out of middle management at Ford. He had made a fortune at Chrysler, thanks to the low-priced stock options he had accumulated during the company's dark days. At Chrysler he had become Iacocca's right-hand man and heir apparent. But Greenwald was more apparent than heir. The more he waited, the more he wanted to run Chrysler himself.

Iacocca kept dangling the carrot in front of him. "Get ready, next year's the time," he had told Greenwald in 1983. But next year came and went, and Iacocca stayed in place. Twice more, over the next few years, Greenwald had gotten the same promise from Iacocca, but nothing ever happened. Iacocca clearly liked being chairman of Chrysler, and Greenwald believed nothing short of death would change that. By 1990 he was fifty-four years old, but wasn't sure when he would get his chance at the top. Iacocca had turned sixty-five in October 1989, and still hadn't set a firm date for retirement. But then, for Greenwald, opportunity knocked.

The employee unions at United Airlines wanted to pool their resources to buy the airline for more than $4 billion, and run it as an employee-owned corporation. Doing that, though, would require borrowing huge sums of money, which in turn would require a CEO with a solid reputation with Wall Street and the banks. Spencer Stuart, an executive head-hunting firm hired by the unions, decided to approach Greenwald.

The unions offered Greenwald a compelling deal. He would finally be CEO of a major company. United would become the largest employee-owned company ever, so Greenwald, as its leader, would get a chance to make business history. As well as a chance to make another fortune. To lure Greenwald, United's unions offered to pay him a $5 million signing bonus, and an additional $4 million if their ambitious project couldn't be completed. The $9 million safety net proved irresistible.

In late May 1990, just after the Zuckerman story broke, word started to leak out of Wall Street that Greenwald was headed for United. Greenwald panicked. He hadn't yet told Iacocca, and he didn't want his boss to read about his move in the newspapers. He told Chrysler's PR men to flatly deny the rumor, and then said he was taking off for a few days to visit his sister on the West Coast. Instead he flew to Italy, to meet Iacocca at Iacocca's Tuscan estate.

Iacocca was livid. Greenwald, he said, was disloyal, like a soldier deserting his commander in a time of need. He urged Greenwald to stay, and promised him the chairman's job by the end of the year. But Greenwald had heard the same promise too many times. It was a game, he figured, like Lucy in the Peanuts comic strip swearing that, this time for sure, she would let Charlie Brown kick the football instead of jerking it away at the last moment. Besides, $9 million was hard to turn down. Greenwald told Iacocca his mind was made up. After a day and a half of berating and cajoling, Iacocca gave up.

Iacocca decided to return to Detroit immediately to announce the news, and the two men boarded a Chrysler corporate jet. When they walked into Chrysler's headquarters, Bidwell saw Greenwald—whose dress and grooming were always impeccable—in a rumpled shirt and suit and a day-old stubble of beard. "Are you in or out?" Bidwell asked, even though Greenwald's appearance had already answered his question. "I'm out of here," Greenwald replied.

. . .

IACOCCA FELT ANGRY and betrayed by Greenwald's departure, but Bidwell was jealous. He had been trying to negotiate his own departure from Chrysler for nearly a year. The pace of his work and the constant setbacks of recent years were slowly killing him. The business had stopped being fun, and Bidwell had stopped being funny. His doctor ordered him to cut down on cholesterol, smoking, and stress. His low-cholesterol diet was working, but he was batting only one for three. Every time he told Iacocca he wanted to leave, though, Iacocca would talk him into staying.

In the summer of 1989, Bidwell had walked into Iacocca's office, chest X-rays in hand, to present pictorial proof that he had to retire early. Iacocca recoiled in fright. "Oh God, no, don't show me the pictures," Iacocca had said. "I had to look at Mary's X-rays when she was sick, and I just can't take it." So Bidwell dispensed with the show and tell, and instead made an impassioned verbal plea. He walked out with a compromise: He would cut his hours to 60 percent of normal and take a 40 percent pay cut, about $200,000 a year.

But after a few months, Bidwell realized that working for Iacocca part-time meant sixty hours a week instead of eighty. His health was getting worse instead of better; so was his attitude.

When 1990 began, Bidwell was seething at the daily pounding that Chrysler was taking in the press. He decided to lash out in return, and picked his keynote address to *Automotive News* magazine's World Congress of industry leaders as his platform. He drafted the speech himself, filling it with the venom of his indignation, and scaring his public relations underlings half out of their wits. They prevailed upon him to sanitize the speech, although he insisted on retaining his reference to reporters as "congenital sickos." He got in a few other zingers as well.

"Hunting season on GM started a few years ago and lasted for an especially long time," he declared. "I guess it's now hunting season on Chrysler. I had to laugh out loud when in the same week, the *Wall Street Journal* headlined a story on Chrysler, 'Bumpy Road.' And *Fortune* magazine headlined a feature article, 'Bumps Ahead at Ford.' Ten days later, the Detroit *News* editorialized: 'Detroit could be facing a very bumpy ride.' Not much product differentiation there, right? A little like stretching and bending the K-car."

Bidwell's bitterness wasn't reserved for the press alone. Increasingly, he was turning his frustration on his colleagues inside Chrysler. He was tired of hearing them demand that he sweeten rebates to boost sales, and then complain when higher rebates caused profit margins to shrink. "What do you want this time?" he would ask sarcastically during meetings. "Tastes Great or Less Filling? You can't have it both ways."

Finally, Iacocca gave in. He asked Bidwell, who was sixty-two, to stay at Chrysler through the end of 1990 to avoid the appearance of mass desertion in the wake of Greenwald's and Zuckerman's departures. But word leaked anyway, and Bidwell, despite his anger at the press, had no stomach for lying. On June 11, 1990, he issued a statement that confirmed both his impending retirement and his weary anger at the world. "It's time to put all this speculation to rest," he declared, "and let the media go back to covering some of the other important stories of our day —such as perestroika, democracy in Eastern Europe, and the search for a cure to AIDS."

A few months later, with his departure nigh, Bidwell presided over the annual press conference—called the "short lead," in Detroit parlance— to tout Chrysler's lineup for the coming model year. "This is my last short lead press conference," he declared in Nixonesque fashion. "You won't have Ben Bidwell to kick around anymore."

BY THE SUMMER OF 1990, Lee Iacocca was a shaken and lonely man. The departures of Sperlich and Zuckerman had been Iacocca's doing, but he had never imagined that Greenwald and Bidwell would desert him. They weren't the only ones. Chrysler was losing other people, including key executives just below the rank of vice president. In July, to stem the exodus, Iacocca gave the company's top 1,800 people special grants of Chrysler stock if they would stay on the job until January. The departures slowed, but they didn't cease.

Nor did the flow of plagues afflicting Chrysler. In the spring of 1990 Ford launched the Explorer, ending the Jeep Cherokee's status as the only four-door "sport-utility" vehicle on the market. The Explorer combined a roomy interior with such carlike comforts as cupholders and a split, fold-down rear seat. Not only did Ford trump the Cherokee, it underpriced it as well. By September, Explorer sales were racing ahead, while Cherokee sales plunged 22 percent from the prior year.

Even worse, Chrysler's one true technological innovation was going haywire. In the 1989 model year, Chrysler introduced a new, electronic four-speed transmission, the Ultradrive. Four-speed transmissions employ a wider range of gear ratios than a three-speed, thus providing faster acceleration in low gear and better fuel economy on the highway. Chrysler boasted that the Ultradrive's sophisticated electronics made it the first transmission ever to adjust to each driver's individual habits. It would provide a rapid shift in gears, for example, for drivers who liked to roar away from stoplights. The Society of Automotive Engineers gave Chrysler an award for innovation.

Consumers were less impressed. Many found their Ultradrives stuck in what the company euphemistically called "limp mode." That meant the transmission wouldn't shift beyond second gear, so drivers had to limp to the nearest dealer at around thirty miles an hour. Some owners had their transmissions repaired or replaced two or three times, only to limp in again for more surgery.

As the problem spread, it showed up in the owner surveys conducted by *Consumer Reports* magazine. In its February 1991 issue, CR reported that fully 20 percent of Chrysler's 1989 model minivans equipped with the Ultradrive had experienced transmission problems. For 1990 models, the trouble rate was a still-outrageous 10 percent. "It's a lemon—steer clear," the magazine advised its readers.

It was panic time at Chrysler. By 1990, profits from the minivan were all that was keeping the company alive. Company officials had traced the problems to a faulty seal that had let fluid leak into the wrong cavities, causing the transmission to engage two gears at once and thus burn out the clutch. To counter the *Consumer Reports* article, Chrysler launched a concerted—and expensive—effort to contact 1.1 million minivan owners by phone. The crisis passed, but only after Chrysler paid millions to appease irate customers.

Until this point in his incredible career, Lee Iacocca had shown precious few signs of being a man given to second-guessing himself. His firing from Ford, he firmly believed, wasn't his fault, but that of an evil Henry Ford. But in 1990, alone and beleaguered, Iacocca began an uncharacteristic bout of soul-searching. He was still blaming the Japanese—it was as natural as putting on his pants in the morning—but it began to occur to him that he might have played a role in Chrysler's woes. No other company in Detroit—indeed, few anywhere—was so closely identified with a single man who wasn't even its founder. Having led Chrysler back from the brink of extinction to the greatest corporate comeback in American history, Iacocca himself had put his company on the brink of being on the brink again.

On a sticky, steamy day in late August, with his sixty-sixth birthday just two months away, Iacocca summoned two reporters from the *Wall Street Journal* to his office. It was filled with mementos of his forty-four-year career in Detroit: replicas of the checks with which Chrysler had repaid its bailout loans, a stuffed-toy Lee Iacocca driving a car while puffing on his trademark cigar, and framed copies of *Time* and *Newsweek* covers bearing Iacocca's beaming face. The interview was supposed to last only forty minutes, but Iacocca took that long just to warm up. Sitting on his couch, talking in a virtual stream-of-consciousness monologue, he talked about how he had made a mess of things, and how, in the twilight of his career, he was trying to forge Comeback II. "I'm confessing my sins here," he said.

His biggest sin, he explained, was trying to diversify. He saw GM and Ford moving into defense, aerospace, and financial services, and figured that was the wave of the future. "If I made a mistake, it was following those other companies, and maybe those were grandiose schemes. We didn't need a holding company. That's what made us top-heavy. If we went astray—you know, people do go astray now and then in many areas —man, we got focused in a hurry. I've been through crises, and I know them. And I'm not afraid of them.

"Jesus Christ, I want to be sincere with you guys. I never worked harder in my life than in the last couple years. What happened in '85 or '86? Well, then you had a bit of sloughing off; maybe in the whole organization. I might have been so tired that I laid back on the oars a little bit. But, boy, it's full hands on the tiller now. Hey, the bullets are real.

"If you ever pick a distraction, pick the right one. We shouldn't have had forays in the defense business. But don't blame it on the Statue of Liberty or on writing a book. I mean, Jesus, that's like saying, 'What do you do with your nights?' Well, none of your business. I don't go out to the bars. I don't go on long vacations. My work is my life. Why should I apologize for writing a book that sold seven million copies? I still get flooded every night with letters from kids saying it changed their lives."

"The fact that you lose some good guys isn't all bad, but Jerry [Greenwald] was a jolt. Jesus, I had no rumor. I never heard a word. He called me—I'll never forget—I was in Monte Carlo, of all places. I'd stopped there to see the Grand Prix. Lamborghini was fielding its first team, and the phone rang, and he said, 'I'd like to come see you right away.' I said, 'See me where? Christ, I'm in France.' He said, 'I gotta come. It's that important. It's personal.' I said, 'Oh, wait a minute. Don't give me that crap. What do you mean you want to come over? What's on your mind?' He said, 'Well, I'm thinking of leaving.' That was the first time I'd heard even a whimper. In Detroit, usually you hear rumors if somebody talks to someone. I was stunned. It just blew me away."[4]

And so it went, for two and a half hours, the confessions of an anguished soul. Three years earlier Iacocca had mesmerized America. Pundits predicted he would run for President. Now he was alone, nearly deserted, and scrambling to save his company again. He did, however, have one ace up his sleeve.

In the summer of 1989 he had stopped in Rome to have lunch with Giovanni Agnelli, the chairman of Fiat. In 1983 Fiat had pulled out of the U.S. market—where its shoddy quality spawned the joke that the company's name stood for "Fix It Again, Tony"—but Agnelli was a formidable force. Fiat had revived itself in the mid-1980s to become one of Europe's hottest car companies.

Iacocca and Agnelli talked about potential cooperative ventures, such as joint development of a vehicle, but it quickly became clear that the possibilities went far beyond such limited measures. They decided the only deal that really made sense would be a BIG deal, meaning a full merger of their companies. They ordered their underlings to begin negotiations. In late 1989 and the first half of 1990, the talks had turned serious.

On the surface, the companies seemed a good fit. Fiat had no operations in North America, while Chrysler had none in Europe. A merger would give both companies instant geographic diversification that would help them weather the inevitable periodic slumps in their respective home markets. In 1985 Fiat had come within an inch of merging with Ford of Europe, but the talks ultimately collapsed over the issue of who would control the merged organization. But that wasn't a problem this time. Iacocca was willing, even eager, to let Fiat take control. For him, a megamerger would be a spectacular way to end a legendary career. And a Fiat–Chrysler combination would have the right chemistry because both Iacocca and Agnelli were Italian.

Trouble was, though, they weren't the same *kind* of Italian. Agnelli's family controlled Italy's largest industrial empire, and both Agnelli and Fiat were symbols of the nation itself. What's more, Agnelli was a patrician, a blue-blood through and through. His last public appearance in

Detroit, in October 1985, had been at the side of Henry Ford II, his good friend and, like Agnelli himself, a world-renowned inheritor of a family business empire. Both men had an imperial manner and a jet-setting lifestyle that appealed enormously to Iacocca. "Lee loves rich people," Jerry Greenwald had liked to say.

Agnelli, though, felt far more comfortable with a fellow aristocrat like Henry Ford than he did with Iacocca, an upstart who lacked the breeding and manners to which Agnelli was accustomed.

Moreover, as the discussions between Chrysler and Fiat unfolded, more substantive complications surfaced. In September 1989, when the talks began, Chrysler's stock was selling for $27 a share, and Iacocca was hoping to get Agnelli to bite on a price of $35. But in the ensuing months Chrysler's fortunes plunged, and so did the price of its stock. By September 1990, Chrysler shares were hovering just above $9. Iacocca didn't want to sell for that price, but Agnelli didn't want to pay much more.

In fact, Agnelli was becoming wary of buying Chrysler at any price. Chrysler's deterioration was alarming, and the Italians worried that they might buy a company on the verge of collapse. Besides, the collapse of communism had convinced Agnelli that Eastern Europe was more promising for Fiat than the hypercompetitive U.S. market. It would have been nice to expand in both places, but Fiat didn't have enough money.

On November 2, 1990, Iacocca and Steve Miller met Agnelli and Fiat's president, Cesare Romiti, in New York. By this time, the idea of a merger had been abandoned, and the discussions had turned mundane: Would Fiat like to distribute Chrysler minivans in Europe? Would Chrysler like to buy components from Fiat? But during the meeting Agnelli explained that, to his mind, it was all or nothing between the two companies, and since a merger wasn't desirable to Fiat, it would have to be nothing. "The best deal was going to be a huge deal," he said. "Anything smaller would be a distraction."[5]

That evening Agnelli called a press conference to announce that Chrysler and Fiat had broken off their negotiations. A reporter asked whether the companies might try again in the future, and Agnelli responded with a simile worthy of an Italian nobleman. "These things usually don't happen again," he explained. "It's like being in love. After you break up, it is unlikely that you go back to court the same woman again."[6]

. . .

AFTER THE FIAT TALKS COLLAPSED, Iacocca tried the longest of long shots: peddling Chrysler to Ford. He had tried the same ploy, in much the same dire circumstances for Chrysler, back in 1982—only to have Henry Ford II reject the idea. But now, in late 1990, his archnemesis was dead, and Iacocca thought a last, desperate lurch, outlandish though it seemed, was worth a try.

The Ford people were wary. Just a year earlier their company had shelled out $2.5 billion to buy another troubled car company, Britain's Jaguar, only to see Jaguar's sales nosedive right after the deal was closed. Ironically, Ford could have bought Chrysler for not much more than it had paid for Jaguar—even though, in any given year, Chrysler sold some thirty-five times more cars than Jaguar did. But the Ford family wasn't eager to make another high-risk acquisition, especially not one involving Lee Iacocca. In early 1991, after nearly three months of talks, Ford said no. Chrysler would have to go it alone, or not at all.

Meanwhile, Iacocca had less cosmic issues to deal with, and one of them was Dick Dauch. In years past Iacocca could have left the Dauch patrol to Greenwald, who had a way of putting up with Chrysler's manufacturing chief at times when others threw up their hands. One day, for instance, Dauch had marched into Bob Lutz's office and demanded to see him, only to be told by Lutz's secretary that her boss was unavailable. "I've been here since 6:30 this morning waiting to see him," Dauch shouted, and then emitted an obscenity.

With that Dauch stomped away, Lutz's secretary burst into tears, and another Keystone Kops episode began. A fuming Lutz made a beeline to Greenwald to demand that "something be done" about Dauch. Greenwald, in turn, managed to soothe Lutz's nerves, and then the two men together trooped over to see Iacocca. Eventually Chrysler hired an industrial psychologist to "try to calm Dauch down," as Greenwald put it.

But by 1991 Greenwald was gone. Lutz, whose power had grown steadily, was Chrysler's president, and he hated Dauch. The two men almost came to blows one day when Lutz was walking out of a meeting and an angry Dauch deliberately blocked his way. "Don't you ever try to take me on physically," Lutz snapped. "You may be a former football player. But I'm a former Marine, and I'm trained to kill."

Not long after that, Lutz called Dauch into his office and told him he was fired. Dauch went straight to Iacocca to appeal, but Iacocca confirmed the verdict. On April 11, "Coach" Dauch announced his retirement from Chrysler. He was forty-eight years old.

Dauch's departure, on top of all the others, left Chrysler with an executive suite far different from the one of just two years before. Chrysler had had thirty corporate officers in the spring of 1989. By the spring of 1991, eleven of those, more than one third of the total, had departed, voluntarily or otherwise.

Iacocca had turned Greenwald's departure the year before into a financial windfall for himself. When Greenwald left in May of 1990, the Chrysler board panicked. Frightened by the thought that the sixty-five-year-old Iacocca might leave without an obvious successor in place, the board decided to line his pockets so he would do what he wanted to do anyway—stay on indefinitely. Iacocca played right along.

For starters, the board gave Iacocca a 15 percent salary hike for 1990, to $4.6 million. Then the directors offered him a big carrot—123,750 shares of Chrysler stock—to stay on the job until December 8, 1991. They also dangled a bigger carrot for Iacocca to stay even longer: 62,500 Chrysler shares for each quarter that he remained as chairman after December 31, 1991. The shares were in addition to Iacocca's salary, stock options, and other pay. The board even agreed to have Chrysler buy Iacocca's two residences—one in Bloomfield Hills and the other in Boca Raton—for $1.7 million, to spare Iacocca the "distraction" of having to sell them himself. In April 1991, when all this was disclosed in the fine print of Chrysler's proxy statement, Chrysler employees were shocked and outraged.

Lee Iacocca, in employees' eyes, once had been a gutsy and inspiring leader, the CEO for the common man. He had worked for a salary of just $1 during the crisis of 1980, inspiring his troops to a spirit of "shared sacrifice" that saved the company. Never mind that back then, in lieu of salary, Iacocca had received armfuls of low-priced stock options that later rewarded him spectacularly. He had earned that money by saving the company and boosting the value of the shares.

A decade later, Iacocca again was calling for sacrifice from Chrysler employees. He had launched a draconian cost-cutting campaign with a steadily rising target—first $1 billion, then $2.5 billion, then $3 billion—that included eliminating 11,000 white-collar workers, more than 30 percent of Chrysler's total. Those who dodged the ax had to pinch pennies. They were ordered to cancel company-paid subscriptions to newspapers, magazines, and technical journals. They had to sit in economy class instead of business class on long international flights.

By April 1991, Chrysler's cash and securities—its corporate bank account—had plunged to $2 billion, down from $4.32 billion just nine months earlier. In October 1991, Chrysler had to bolster its battered balance sheet by selling new stock at a paltry $10.25 a share. That was less than half the average price of $21.13 a share that Chrysler had paid, on Iacocca's orders, to repurchase shares of its own stock over the prior six years. Chrysler had bought high and was selling low.

In the midst of all this, though, Iacocca was living high. Chrysler's purchase of his two homes, though it cost the company less than $50,000 after the houses were resold, became a symbol of his imperial lifestyle. There were other symbols, too.

Chrysler's fleet of corporate aircraft had just one top-of-the-line Gulfstream G4, and it was reserved for Iacocca almost exclusively. The in-flight service was thoughtful in ways that passengers on regular commercial flights couldn't imagine. Oreo cookies, the chairman's favorite snack, always were available. And once, when Iacocca's third wife, Darrien, brought her pet poodle along when she and Lee were visiting Chrysler's factories in Mexico, Chrysler's air-travel department arranged for the dog's landing papers—the canine version of a visa.

Wherever the G4 took Iacocca, a convoy of limousines was waiting. One was for Iacocca and whomever he chose to ride with. A second limo carried the ever-present entourage of bodyguards and aides. Sometimes a third carried the luggage.

Nothing on Iacocca's itinerary would be left to chance. Before his arrival, staffers from Chrysler's local sales-zone office would drive the convoy's route at the precise time of day that Iacocca would take it—to check out traffic conditions, the likely travel time, and anything else that might affect the boss's comfort. And when Iacocca went to New York, Chrysler's luxury suite in the Waldorf Towers was always ready.

The suite, number 38M, was supposedly available to any company official who had business in New York. In reality, it was almost exclusively Iacocca's.

The nine-room apartment was renovated—at a cost of about $2 million—right in the middle of Iacocca's cost-cutting campaign. What Chrysler got for its money was a marble-floored kitchen complete with Sub-Zero refrigerator and a Jenn-Air microwave oven and stove. The suite's expansive sun room featured a raised, angled ceiling, a fully stocked wet bar (with plenty of Dewar's, Iacocca's favorite scotch) and a television console with a 34-inch screen. The TV was a top-of-the-line Mitsubishi, imported from Japan.

Just off the sun room was an outside patio with a northward view up Park Avenue. The living room furnishings included another Mitsubishi TV, a cherry-wood desk, and built-in bookshelves. Iacocca's master bed-room suite had a king-sized bed, valet cabinet with a TV (Mitsubishi again), a sitting room with its own desk, phone, and full-length wall mirror, and a marble-floored bathroom with another phone next to the toilet. All the faucets—in the kitchen, powder room, and both bath-rooms—were plated with gold.

The boss's perks and pay wouldn't have dented morale had Chrysler been riding high. Back in 1985 and 1986, Chrysler employees had glowed over their boss's celebrity status and lifestyle, just as the moon reflects light from the sun. But in 1991, Chrysler was cruising toward a $795 million loss. The company was going to be passed in U.S. car sales by both Honda and Toyota. Although Chrysler's sales of Jeeps, mini-vans, and pickup trucks put it ahead of the two Japanese companies in sales of cars and trucks combined, it was humiliating to be outsold in cars alone by not one, but two, Japanese companies. Chrysler's debt ratings plunged to junk-bond status.

Every time that Iacocca announced a new and higher cost-cutting target—"we're tightening the tourniquet," he would say—his troops felt they were being sentenced to another winter at Valley Forge. But Iacocca didn't know the feeling. He was unabashed in his embrace of what his underlings quietly derided as "The Four P's: power, podium, perks, and pay."

Iacocca, despite his success in life, could never get enough of the Four P's. A man of contradictions, he was an immigrant's son who had never outgrown the sense of being an outsider, despite rising to the pinnacle of American business. And despite his enormous wealth, well over $50 million by 1990, Iacocca was basically a cheapskate.

Once, he and Darrien asked her three children to attend a dinner in his honor. They accepted, and called Chrysler's travel department to charge their plane tickets to Iacocca's personal American Express card, figuring Iacocca wanted to pay their way. But when Iacocca saw the bill for $2,000—mere pocket change for him—he placed an angry call to the travel department and chewed out the staff.

On another occasion, he and Darrien invited another couple to dinner at their condominium in Bloomfield Hills. Darrien prepared the meal herself instead of having it catered, and the guests complimented her for taking the time and trouble.

"In some ways my life isn't too different from an ordinary housewife's," Darrien replied. "Just today I ran out to the drugstore to buy lightbulbs."

"Why the hell did you do that?" Iacocca snapped.

"Well, Lee, a couple of bulbs were burned out around here," said Darrien, somewhat surprised at his outburst.

"Next time tell me about it," Iacocca ordered. "I'll bring lightbulbs home from the office."

Iacocca wasn't nearly as stingy with the company's money. His underlings figured that his worst nightmare would be taking a commercial flight instead of the company jet. And in December 1991, they got a vivid illustration of how right they were.

One day, shortly before Christmas, Steve Miller met with an official of the Detroit Symphony Orchestra to discuss the orchestra's fund-raising campaign. The meeting lasted ninety minutes, partly because it was interrupted three times by an irate Iacocca. Chrysler was near its nadir in those days, with its market share sagging even as its losses and debt load were soaring. Iacocca, though, wasn't screaming about any of those problems. Something truly scary was sparking this explosion.

Chrysler was having trouble getting clearance to land his personal plane—the G4—at Tokyo's Narita Airport, where Iacocca was going in January with the entourage of American CEOs accompanying President Bush on a trade mission to Japan. Iacocca was facing the prospect of flying commercial, just as the chairmen of Ford and GM were planning to do.

Northwest Airlines was so thrilled at the prospect of having Lee Iacocca in its first-class cabin that it offered to keep the seat next to him vacant to assure his privacy. But that wasn't good enough. "Northwest may have first class," one Chrysler man quipped, "but it doesn't have God class."

After Iacocca's third (and mercifully last) intrusion on the orchestra meeting, Miller stopped trying to hide his embarrassment. He looked at his guest, smiled wanly, and said: "After a few more months, that man won't be my boss anymore."

CHAPTER 9

FORD FALTERS

Aɴᴛʜᴏɴʏ S. "Tᴏɴʏ" Kᴜᴄʜᴛᴀ lived Detroit's version of the American Dream. After growing up in Belleville, Michigan, a small town near Ann Arbor, he quit college after one year to become a draftsman in a Detroit "job shop"—one of the many that handled overflow engineering projects for the car companies. There he toiled for seven years, drawing blueprints of everything from fenders to piston rods, before starting in Ford's drafting room in 1957. By 1965 Kuchta was thirty-four years old, the father of six children (eventually there would be eight), and had earned an engineering degree in night school. And his ascent through Ford's engineering and product-development ranks was underway.

At first Kuchta worked on components: fuel systems, wheels, and exhaust systems, to name a few. In the midsixties he led the Ford team that developed a "collapsible" steering column that wouldn't spear drivers during head-on collisions. By the early 1970s, he had reached Ford's grade level 13, which was something very special. Tony Kuchta had the right number.

Ford people habitually refer to each other by their grade-level number. In most of America, to say "she's a ten" means a woman is oozing with sex appeal. At Ford, though, it means she—or he—is a member of middle management, eligible for a company-subsidized lease car, though not for a bonus. It isn't until level 13 that people begin to get important. Being a 13 puts you on what Ford's personnel department calls the "PSR," or private salary roll. It's a supervisory position with a bonus, prestige, and perks. Among the latter are the symbolic "rug and a jug," a carpet in your office and a chrome water pitcher on your desk. Some 13s, especially the new ones, flaunt their status by having their secretaries march down the hallway every morning to fill the pitcher with water —even though they never drink from it during the day. Thirteens also get the treasured right to have a company-subsidized lease car even after retirement. Lots of 12s hang around Ford for years hoping to become a 13 before they retire. But Tony Kuchta was headed higher.

By 1976 he had reached grade level 16, which wasn't quite the stratosphere of being a corporate officer, but it was close. As a 16, Kuchta became a member of the "E-roll," or executive salary roll. He got a free new car every year and the right to park it in the executive parking garage—where it would be filled with gas daily and washed three times a week, all at Ford's expense. Besides that, he could lease two cars at subsidized rates that included low-cost insurance, a handy extra when you have eight kids.

E-roll status made Kuchta one of the top 500 or so people in Ford, and put him on a first-name basis with most of the company's top people. One of them was Don Petersen. "Pete's class," Kuchta would say. "He acts like a vice president. On trips he stays in the best hotel room, or a suite if possible. At dinner he orders the right wine. If I ever get to be a VP, I want to be like Pete."

In 1986 Ford put Kuchta in charge of the MN-12, the company's code name for the new Thunderbird and its automotive sibling, the Mercury Cougar. Back in 1983, the Bird, as it was known inside Ford, had been the first Ford car to get the daring new aerodynamic look, and thus had paved the way for the stunning success of the Taurus. Kuchta's job would be not only to improve the looks of both the Bird and the Cougar, but also to make them performance cars: "BMW fighters," as his bosses put it.

So instead of getting only a "face-lift," or new exterior styling, the new cars would get far more: a brand new platform, or chassis, so Kuchta would have complete freedom to make engineering and styling improvements. The cars would be, in Detroit's idiom, "all new from the ground up." By December 1988, Kuchta's cars were ready to hit the market to a chorus of carefully orchestrated fanfare.

Ford's PR department trooped in automotive writers to conduct interviews with Kuchta, a blunt man who hid neither his derision for the competition nor his pride in his own product. He dispensed with the rules of gentlemanly competition that normally prevailed in Detroit, and openly sneered at the competing GM-10 coupes—Pontiac Grand Prix, Olds Cutlass Supreme, and Buick Regal—being sold by General Motors. "Those are nothing cars," Kuchta told one interviewer. "They're losers because they aren't giving the customer what he wants." The GM cars were small and underpowered, he explained, with none of the muscle, heft, and refinement that coupe buyers really wanted.

The Cougar and the Bird were 5 inches longer than the GM coupes, and 375 pounds heavier. Their engine was far bigger—3.8 liters versus 2.8 on the GM cars—and thus packed more horsepower.[1] Instead of opting for front-wheel-drive, as had General Motors, the new Ford coupes retained a rear-drive format, just like a BMW or Mercedes-Benz or any other great European road car. True driving enthusiasts, everyone knew, preferred the handling, acceleration, and "road feel" of rear-wheel-drive.

To make sure the handling was truly responsive, Kuchta gave his cars independent rear suspension instead of the solid rear axle that was on previous Thunderbirds and Cougars. That too was just like a BMW or a Mercedes. Other innovations included Ford's first high-tech gas tank. It was molded in one piece from space-age plastics instead of stamped from pieces of steel that had to be welded together. "We're putting a lot of engineering into these cars," Kuchta would declare.

Underneath their skins the Cougar and Thunderbird were mechanically identical, but they did get different exterior styling. The Thunderbird was aggressively sleek, intended mainly to appeal to men. The Cougar got a more formal roofline, targeted at women. Ford's marketing strategy was to put the initial emphasis on the Thunderbird. As its launch date neared, Ford rented catering halls in twenty-nine cities around the country to throw splashy parties for local notables.

The 15,000 guests were entertained by the world's oldest teenager, Dick Clark, on a private, live broadcast beamed to each party by satellite. Partygoers got a tape of sixties songs that included "Fun, Fun, Fun" by the Beach Boys, with its refrain: "She'll have fun, fun, fun till her daddy takes the T-bird away." *Popular Mechanics* magazine named the Thunderbird the "best of the best" among new products for 1989. And the Thunderbird SuperCoupe, the version of the car that packed the most horsepower and the highest price tag, quickly copped *Motor Trend* magazine's coveted Car of the Year award. It was the third time in four years that a Ford product had been so honored.

To celebrate each previous victory, Ford's senior executives had treated the engineers, stylists, and others on the product-development team, along with their wives, to a lavish dinner. The site was always the Whitney, the one-time mansion transformed into a restaurant. The MN-12 team members were laying the plans for their fete when, on January 17, 1989, they prepared to receive a more formal pat on the back. Kuchta convened seventy-five or so team members in the lobby conference room of Building No. 3 in Ford's engineering complex to hear from the top three people in the company: Chairman Don Petersen, President Harold "Red" Poling, and Executive Vice President Phil Benton. When the mandarins arrived, Kuchta made some brief introductory remarks, after which Petersen turned to Poling and said, "Red, why don't you start?"

And then the MN-12 team got an icy cold shower.

"I would have hoped to come here to convey a more positive message," Poling began. "But unfortunately, I can't." He said he didn't give a damn about the Car of the Year award, or any other honors the new Thunderbird had won. Nor did he care much that the MN-12 team had launched the Thunderbird on schedule, something that even the much-heralded Taurus team hadn't managed to do. What he did care about were the targets that the MN-12 team had set for the weight and the cost of the new car. And the team had missed both those targets by a mile.

The Thunderbird and Cougar had come in nearly $900 per car over their budgeted cost, enough to slash Ford's profit margin on each Bird and Cougar it sold by more than 30 percent. As for weight, the new models ran more than 250 pounds per car over target. This was no small matter. A bloated Bird and Cougar would consume more gasoline than they should have, and thus make it more difficult for Ford to meet the federal government's stringent fuel-economy standards.

Ironically, much of the reason for the cost and weight overruns were the very engineering features that Kuchta had been touting to the press. Independent rear suspension, for example, provided far better driving performance than a solid rear axle. But it also sharply increased the cost of engineering and assembling the car, and added extra weight as well.

"You signed up for a set of numbers," Poling said, "but you didn't deliver. You made a commitment, but you didn't keep it." Again and again he hammered home the importance of meeting targets, and expressed his extreme disappointment with the MN-12 team. When Poling finally finished, Petersen spoke up briefly to echo those sentiments. Then the executives took their leave.

The team members sat through it all in stunned silence. They had expected to be praised and thanked, but instead they had received a painful and humiliating dressing down. Most of them were lower- to midlevel managers—9s, 10s, 11s, and 12s—and the big decisions on cost and weight control were made at levels well above theirs. They were more bewildered than angry—except, that is, for Kuchta. He was furious that his underlings should be subjected to a tongue-lashing when the responsibility for crucial decisions had been his.

After the big shots departed, he rose to speak. "You guys did a great job," he said. "We didn't meet all our objectives, but we do have a plan to get the excess cost and weight out of the car." Shortly thereafter, the meeting broke up. And the dinner at the Whitney got canceled.

WITHIN HOURS, WORD OF the tongue-lashing spread throughout Ford. Suddenly, Don Petersen's high-toned rhetoric about participative management, mutual respect, and empowering employees rang hollow. Holding people accountable for falling short of their assigned goals was appropriate and necessary. But if Petersen really meant what he said, how could he have allowed Red Poling to upbraid a loyal, long-time Ford executive right in front of the man's underlings?

Kuchta wasn't an engineer run amok, bent on loading his new cars with gadgetry despite the cost. Early in the game, in fact, the MN-12 team had examined the feasibility of outfitting the new Thunderbird and Cougar with all-wheel drive—a four-wheel drive variant that operates without the driver shifting in or out. Ford paid Porsche, the legendary German sports-car maker, to study the idea. But Kuchta then rejected all-wheel drive as too expensive and not necessary.

In the end, the trouble with the MN-12 was that Kuchta had been handed an impossible task: to build a BMW at the cost of a Ford. When the car's cost—inevitably—started climbing way beyond the target, Kuchta recovered from his initial shock and faced a simple choice. He could delay the project, go back to the drawing board to redesign key components and eliminate some features to make the car cheaper to produce. Or he could forge ahead to launch the Bird on time, and then double back to whack off cost and weight over the next year or two.

To Kuchta, the choice was unfortunate but obvious—mainly because Ford had to sell more cars with "passive restraints" such as the automatic seat belts in the Cougar and Bird to meet federal safety standards. Kuchta opted to launch the cars on time, and that's what he told his bosses. Anybody who didn't get the message wasn't paying attention.

That's what the real problem was at Ford: People weren't paying attention. In running Ford during the bleak early 1980s, Philip Caldwell had benefited from the luxury of adversity—though it had hardly seemed to be a luxury at the time. By the late 1980s, however, with the company enjoying the greatest prosperity in its history, too many people weren't watching the nuts and bolts of the business. "Moses never got in trouble till he crossed the Red Sea," Caldwell used to say. His point: It was human nature to go astray when times got good. But the people at the top were responsible for keeping the company on course during good times as well as bad. And the man at the very top was Don Petersen.

Intellectually, Petersen understood the often-underestimated challenge of running a company during periods of prosperity. In late 1985, when Ford was just beginning its surge, Petersen publicly promised that the company would cut its white-collar work force by 20 percent by 1990. There would be no need for mass firings, he explained, but the company wouldn't replace many of the people who would retire or quit. That would make Ford more efficient.

But after making his promise, Petersen seemed to forget it. In 1990, Ford had only 4 percent fewer white-collar workers than it had back in 1985.[2] Petersen had made a commitment but hadn't kept it—just like Tony Kuchta.

There was one big difference between the two men, though. Kuchta knew that his failure in the eyes of his bosses meant his career at Ford was finished. The point was driven home during his next annual performance review, when he was told that his bonus for 1988 would be less than half of what he had expected before Poling's tongue-lashing. Kuchta got the message. In March 1989 he asked for "executive separation," which was Ford-speak for early retirement.

For the next two months, while his retirement package was being prepared, Kuchta felt like a leper. None of Ford's senior executives, with whom he had worked for more than three decades, called to wish him well. He didn't get the good-bye letter from the chairman that was customary for someone of his rank. He didn't know whether his bosses were holding on to their anger or just too embarrassed at their own behavior to contact him.

But Kuchta's retirement party, held in the ballroom of the Fairlane Club just a mile from Ford's headquarters, was a sellout, despite the absence of the higher-ups. Among the 230 people who attended were more than a dozen who drove up from the Ford factory in Lorain, Ohio —where the Thunderbird and Cougar were built. Kuchta was overwhelmed. He might have been a nonperson to the big shots, but his colleagues had reached out in friendship and support. In May 1989, at age fifty-eight and grade level 17, Tony Kuchta closed the door on his thirty-two-year career at Ford. By that time, Don Petersen's job was in jeopardy, too.

As 1988 BEGAN, Ford's new corporate wealth was becoming an alluring distraction to Petersen, and not without reason. The company had to deploy the $10 billion in cash it had accumulated even after all the dividend increases and stock repurchases. Petersen's solution was the same one reached by Roger Smith and Lee Iacocca: diversification. But Ford had far more money to play with than GM and Chrysler. Investment bankers were descending on Dearborn with proposals for Ford to buy everything from brokerage houses to meat packers. The meetings of senior executives to discuss diversification seemed endless.

Eventually, Petersen and his top underlings decided Ford should have three lines of business. Cars, of course, was one. The second was financial services. Ford was already in that business through its Ford Motor Credit subsidiary, which lent money to dealers to finance their inventories, and to consumers to buy Ford cars. To expand this business, Ford went on a buying binge. It bought a California savings and loan, a consumer-lending company in Philadelphia and then another (much larger) one in Dallas. All were part of the whopping $6 billion Ford spent on acquisitions, on top of shelling out $4.2 billion to buy back its own stock, between 1985 and the summer of 1989.

But the $6 billion didn't sate Petersen's appetite. He announced Ford wanted to buy a high-tech company as its third line of business. Having lost Hughes Aircraft to GM back in 1985, Petersen was on the prowl to land Ford an aerospace giant of its own.

His rationale was that Ford had to boost the price/earnings ratio of its stock. Even as its earnings hit record after record, investors would pay no more than five or six times the company's annual earnings-per-share for Ford stock. Companies in different businesses with far more mediocre records were commanding "p/e ratios," in Wall Street jargon, of 10 or 15 for their shares, and high-tech companies were accorded p/e's of more than 20. If Ford could do half as well, the price of its stock would nearly double—even on top of the gains of the last few years. But first, Ford had to convince Wall Street it could stay profitable during the next recession. Petersen knew his promises weren't enough. Diversification, he decided, was the key.

But as Ford focused on diversifying, it started to coast in the car business. The failure to follow through on the promised white-collar staff cuts was but one indication of complacence. Another was Ford's laxity in controlling costs, as the Thunderbird and Cougar amply illustrated. In addition, the quality and reliability of Ford cars, which had improved steadily throughout the 1980s, suddenly plateaued in 1988 and 1989. And most surprising, Ford lost its taste for innovation in styling—the very thing that had marked the company as daring and innovative during the mid-1980s. The new Escort due to debut in the spring of 1990 looked remarkably like the old model. And so did the new Taurus that Ford was developing for introduction in the fall of 1991.

On the plus side, in 1988 Petersen hammered out a plan for Ford to modernize its engines and transmissions. But that plan, which was far more important to Ford's future than diversification, had been long overdue. The four-cylinder engine in the Ford Tempo and Mercury Topaz, for example, was a sawed-off version of the six-cylinder engine that had powered the Ford Falcon back in the early 1960s.

At least the continuing blundering of General Motors was forgiving Ford's lapses in the United States. There was no such luck in Europe. After losing a startling $2.21 billion between 1980 and 1986, GM Europe launched a series of successful new models that left Ford in the dust. The profits from Ford of Europe had literally kept the entire company afloat during the deep U.S. recession of the early 1980s. But suddenly, Ford of Europe couldn't seem to do anything right.

While GM consolidated its European product-development engineers in one place—the German town of Rüsselsheim, just outside Frankfurt—Ford split its engineers between Germany and England. Even when the two groups managed to agree, they had to waste endless hours flying back and forth to coordinate their efforts.

As a result, the new European Escort (a different car from the Ford Escort sold in the United States, despite its similar styling) launched in

1990 was a spectacular flop. It tended to roll and sway so much on the highway that Ford eventually had to add a stabilizing bar to the chassis. Worse yet, the European Escort had an old engine so rough and noisy that even Ford conceded it had a "stumble problem" while warming up. And the car's interior was so plastic-tacky that one British automotive magazine likened it to "a refugee camp."[3]

Being distracted by diversification while the car business stumbled was bad enough, but Petersen's other problem was worse. He had fallen into the trap of believing his own public relations. Ford's stunning financial success in 1986, 1987, and 1988 had made Petersen a business hero, and he eagerly threw on the mantle of corporate philosopher. Time and again, Petersen would tell interviewers and audiences that he didn't want Ford employees to be subjected to the same abusive treatment that he himself had encountered during his climb up the corporate ladder. Instead, he said, employees at all levels should be treated with dignity and be trusted to do their jobs. He took his cue from management guru W. Edwards Deming, who preached that executives should "drive out fear" from their organizations. As Petersen himself put it, "When people are treated with decency and respect, confidence and trust, and empowered in the business of the company, they perform better and they learn more."[4]

The trouble was, though, Petersen had trouble practicing what he preached.

Behind his controlled persona and gracious manner in public, Petersen had a fiercely explosive temper. The onset of his anger was signaled by distinct physical characteristics: His lips tightened, his eyes darted back and forth, and his right hand turned to fiddling with his watch band. Sometimes he would yank the watch off his wrist and fling it across the room, letting loose a verbal tirade at the same time. Once his underlings grimly joked among themselves: "Let's buy Pete a basket of Timexes, so he doesn't have to risk breaking his Rolex when he gets pissed off."

Petersen's explosions could leave victims with painfully vivid memories of the incidents, years and even decades later. In the summer of 1968, for example, Ford's market researchers discovered a big hole in their plan for the new Torino model that was just over a year away from launch date. The product plan didn't provide for a fastback version of the car, and suddenly fastbacks were hot. If the Torino was to have a fastback, Ford would have to move quickly to develop the design and

order the factory tooling. But Petersen, then the head of product planning, was on vacation, and so were most of his immediate underlings.

It fell, then, to a junior staffer named Jerry York to put together the
plan for the fastback. Young York worked eighteen-hour days for two
weeks, and then holed up in his office for a last-minute, around-the-
clock spurt on the weekend before Petersen was due back from vacation.
That Monday morning the plan finally was ready, and the exhausted
York took it to his boss, a middle manager named Bill Brown, for review.
Brown thought the plan looked good, and decided Petersen should see it
right away. With his young underling in tow, Brown walked over to
Petersen's office.

Petersen reviewed the papers for a few minutes, and then shouted a
merciless tirade of criticism that left young York, who had put forth a
superhuman effort while Petersen was on vacation, stunned and devastated. Intimidating York was quite a feat, because the Ford fledgling was
a West Point graduate who had successfully endured the cruel hazing of
the plebe system at the military academy. Jerry York was used to getting
yelled at long before he came to Ford.

When York and Brown walked out of Petersen's office, York, by then
shaking, turned to Brown and said: "My God, that was a terrible meeting." But Brown nonchalantly turned to him and responded, "No, it
wasn't so bad. Not for a meeting with Don Petersen."

In the pressure-cooker atmosphere of Ford's North American operations, Petersen was tightly wound. He suffered from severe headaches,
and when he ran car planning and research, he would lie down on a
couch in his office during the afternoon to cope with the pain. Even
while lying down, though, he would often summon an underling and
deliver a scathing critique of the man's work. One man who had received
this treatment for days on end went home one night and said to his wife,
more out of sympathy than anger, "Don Petersen is filled with devils."

In the late 1970s and early 1980s, however, Petersen seemed to gain
better control over his temper. His outbursts abated, in both frequency
and intensity. Men who had known Petersen for years figured he was
mellowing with age. They also surmised that Petersen—knowing that
Philip Caldwell didn't like him, but knowing also that the departures of
Iacocca and others gave him a real shot at becoming chairman—was
putting forth a superhuman effort to rein in his emotions.

His intelligence and his talent were undeniable, and they shone
brightly during these crucial years. Petersen helped push Ford to the fore

in styling and product development, and won the company's top job as
his reward.

By 1988, though, the checks on Petersen's behavior had disappeared.
Philip Caldwell was retired. Henry Ford Ii was dead. And the adulation
that Petersen was receiving in the business press was more than enough
to go to any man's head. The old Don Petersen, who had never entirely
disappeared, returned.

In January 1989, he led a Ford entourage to Washington to attend the
Bush inauguration. When the group checked into the Park–Hyatt Hotel,
a Ford security man named Marty Stacey suggested putting a "block"
on phone calls to Petersen's suite. That way, the calls could first be directed to, and screened by, the security center that Ford had set up in
the hotel. Petersen, though, replied that blocking his calls wouldn't be
necessary.

That evening, Petersen got an irate call from the owner of a Lincoln
Continental who had somehow learned that the chairman of Ford was
staying at the Park–Hyatt. After he managed to get rid of the caller,
Petersen picked up the phone, called the Ford security suite, and started
screaming at Stacey. Why, he demanded to know, had this man been
allowed to call his suite directly? He launched a vicious tirade so long
and loud that other Ford men in the security suite could hear the chairman's voice, coming through the phone, all the way across the room.

The next morning, Stacey, still rattled, was getting on the hotel
elevator when the doors opened and there, riding down alone, was
Petersen himself. It was a truly frightening moment. But Petersen was
cordial and pleasant, behaving as if nothing untoward had happened the
day before. Petersen could separate his outbursts of temper from his
preaching about teamwork and dignity in the workplace. Others, however, could not.*

.   .   .

* In an interview in his office in Birmingham, Michigan, on January 10, 1994, Mr. Petersen
said: "You can live with a tendency to anger, and at the same time have a real caring about people.
The two are not incompatible." The next day, Petersen called one of the authors to say: "I believe
I was the principal advocate [of cultural change at Ford]. I took the initiative to make it all happen."
He added, "No one can live like a saint every day of their lives."

While acknowledging, in these interviews, occasional outbursts of temper, Mr. Petersen said he
did not recall any of the specific incidents described in this chapter. The descriptions are based on
interviews with current and former Ford employees and executives, more than a dozen of whom
confirmed either the specific episodes or the general pattern of behavior.

PETERSEN'S BEHAVIOR TOWARD UNDERLINGS, bad as it was at times, wasn't enough to topple the chairman of one of the nation's largest and most successful companies. Nor had Ford lost enough momentum to stir the board of directors to revolt. But together, the two problems left Ford's chairman without a strong base of support within his own company at a time when he was alienating both the board and the Ford family itself.

When Henry Ford II was alive, he had handled company affairs for the family with complete confidence in the finality of his word. But his death on September 29, 1987, had left enormous uncertainty in the company-family relationship. Henry's youngest brother, sixty-two-year-old William Clay Ford, Sr., the last surviving grandson of Henry Ford I, became the family patriarch. He was also vice chairman of Ford Motor, although for decades he had left company affairs mostly to Henry while he himself focused on his professional football team, the Detroit Lions.

Among the next generation of Fords, the great-grandchildren of Henry I, only two held positions of prominence in the company. One was Edsel B. Ford II. The youngest child and only son of Henry II, Edsel was thirty-eight when his father died, and general sales manager of Ford's Lincoln–Mercury division. Growing up in the shadow of his strong-willed and flamboyant father had left Edsel somewhat stiff and reserved, and always conscious of his special place in the Ford family dynasty. But he had a gift for self-deprecating humor. Once, he complained to a colleague at work that his wife had run up an outrageous MasterCharge bill during the past month. "What's the big deal, Edsel?" the colleague said. "You can afford it." Edsel replied: "I know. But this bill was twenty-six pages long!"

His cousin, William Clay Ford, Jr., was eight years younger. William Jr. had been spared most of the pressures with which Edsel grew up, because William Clay Sr. had largely avoided the public eye. "Billy," as he was called, had an athletic frame that contrasted with Edsel's stout build. He was also more outgoing and brighter than his cousin. Whereas Edsel took five and a half years to get through Babson College,[5] Billy graduated from Princeton and then earned a master's degree in management from MIT's prestigous Sloan School of Business. His position, when Henry II died, was managing director of Ford of Switzerland.

Both young Fords harbored aspirations to run the company themselves one day. That didn't sit well with Petersen. He regarded both as light-weights, and abhorred the thought that, unlike himself, Edsel and Bill

Jr. might rise to the top of Ford Motor because of their name instead of their talent.

Others inside Ford Motor, including many in the executive ranks, thought Petersen was being obtuse. Edsel and Billy were enormously wealthy young men who didn't have to work a day in their lives. These people admired the fact that two heirs who could have chosen a life of idle leisure were willing, indeed eager, to come to work in the company. Edsel and Billy weren't morons. And even if they weren't the most talented young men in the company, their family standing, their very Fordness, should count for something. If that made Ford Motor something less than a pure meritocracy, well, everyone who invested in or worked for the company knew that beforehand.

Whichever view one took, this much was clear: The Ford family controlled Ford Motor. Only family members were eligible to own Class B stock, which was given superweighted voting power when the company went public in 1956. Thus while family members owned only about 10 percent of the equity in Ford Motor, their shares were worth 40 percent of the votes. After Henry II died, the family held a meeting and decided to vote its shares as a bloc. The family also set up a special fund to purchase Class B shares from any individual member who wanted to sell them. That way, the Class B stock would remain in existence for decades to come instead of being sold outside the family and, thus, converted into ordinary shares—diluting the family's control. Don Petersen knew all this. But he still did things that made the Fords furious.

For years, Ford Motor directors and officers had been allowed to charter company aircraft for personal use when the planes weren't being used for business. This privilege was available to dozens of people, but in practice—with a rare exception or two—only members of the Ford family used it. Before he became a company director, Edsel took ski trips to Idaho and other sojourns on Ford planes chartered for him by his father. Four months after his father died, Edsel became a director, and thus able to charter planes himself. He liked the comfort, convenience, and security of a private plane. And after all, Edsel did have the money. He always paid the bill.

But in early 1988, within weeks of Edsel's and Bill Jr.'s election to the board, Petersen had the rules rewritten, eliminating the right to charter company planes for private use. Edsel was furious. He saw the change as a direct and personal slap at himself, which indeed it was. He complained to the executive in charge of the Ford fleet, asking whether the new rule had come directly from Petersen. The executive, feeling trapped, replied, "It's just the new policy. That's the way it is." Edsel backed off, but he wasn't happy. *

The airplane flap was a petty slight, but Petersen's decision to keep Edsel and Billy off committees of the board of directors was more substantive. Each of Ford's nineteen other directors was assigned to a committee, and virtually all the discussions that shaped key decisions were conducted at the committee level. By keeping the young heirs off board committees, Petersen effectively excluded them from meaningful deliberations. Neither Edsel nor Billy uttered a single word during the first nine board meetings that they attended.

The two chafed under the arrangement. They knew they had less experience than the other Ford directors. But unlike the other directors, the major share of their personal wealth, and that of their family, was invested in Ford Motor. That gave them an enormous stake in company affairs, one that nonfamily directors couldn't match.

By late 1988, Edsel was fed up with his treatment by Petersen. Firing Petersen was out of the question. At that point, not even Edsel Ford had enough clout to dump the most celebrated corporate executive in America. So Edsel did what frustrated dissidents in many organizations do. He went public.

Just after Christmas of 1988, *Fortune* magazine hit the newsstands with a cover story headlined: "The Young Fords: Struggling for Control of the Family Company." Written by veteran automotive reporter Alex Taylor III, the article included some pungent quotes from Edsel. "I've made it clear on one or two occasions to Mr. Petersen," Edsel said, "that it does seem a bit odd to me that there are three classes of directors: inside, outside, and Billy and me." He added that he and Billy weren't much more than guests at board meetings: "Typically, we walk in, shake a few hands, and leave after the meeting."[6]

The article created an instant stir. The feud between the young Fords and the chairman of Ford Motor became front-page news. Just ten years earlier, Henry Ford II had fired Lee Iacocca in part because he feared Iacocca would try to muscle the family out of company affairs if he became chairman. Now Henry's worst scenario appeared to be coming true, at the hands of Don Petersen.

---

*Mr. Petersen, in an interview on January 10, 1994, denied ordering the change in the chartering policy.

On January 4, 1989, just a week after the *Fortune* article appeared, Edsel and Petersen appeared together at the Ford exhibit at the soon-to-open Detroit Auto Show. Reporters and photographers turned out in droves, hoping for a public bloodletting. Instead, each man said kind words about the other. And after Petersen turned to leave he wheeled around suddenly, as if forgetting something, and walked over to shake hands with Edsel. Dozens of cameras clicked and whirred in cadence.[7]

The public smiles and handshakes, though, meant nothing. Before the day was out, Edsel acknowledged to reporters that the *Fortune* article was substantially correct. Petersen, like Lee Iacocca before him, was fighting a battle he couldn't win. In May 1989, just over five months after the *Fortune* article appeared, Edsel and Billy were made members of Ford's executive and finance committees—the two most important committees of the board. But that wasn't the end of Petersen's problems.

FOR FORD'S OUTSIDE DIRECTORS, mediating between the Ford family and Petersen was annoying. But other issues were downright disturbing. In February 1989, Ford shut its plant in Hermosillo, Mexico, for two weeks because the car made there, the Mercury Tracer, wasn't selling well. It was Ford's first temporary factory furlough in more than five years. The economic boom of the eighties was ending.

This wasn't the time, then, for Petersen to push for a major acquisition outside the auto industry. But at Ford's board meeting on March 9, Petersen presented the directors with a diversification strategy. They said no, just as they earlier had axed his ambitious plan to acquire Lockheed, the big Los Angeles aerospace and defense company, for a price of some $3.5 billion. Board members were aghast.

The Cold War—and with it the outlook for defense contractors—clearly was winding down. By 1987, Ford's directors fully realized they had gotten lucky a couple years earlier, when the company had "lost" the bidding for Hughes Aircraft to GM. Petersen, nonetheless, had made an earnest presentation about the supposed high-tech synergies between automobiles and aerospace.

Most CEOs avoid confrontations with their boards by discreetly sounding out key directors before they bring major matters into the boardroom. But Petersen, flush with his executive-of-the-year accolades, hadn't bothered doing that. Several directors expressed opposition to the Lockheed plan, and it quickly became clear that the board didn't like the idea at all. Then Petersen compounded his error. Instead of retreating as gracefully as possible under the circumstances, he whined. "I have worked so terribly hard to bring this proposal before you today," he declared, his voice rising with emotion. "I would have expected, and certainly hoped, for more support. I'm sorry you didn't see fit to provide it." The directors were moved, but not in the way that Petersen wanted. Afterward, one outside director—himself a CEO—took Ford's chairman aside and said, "I would have been ashamed to bring that presentation before my board."

Increasingly, in matters great and small, the tone of the dialogue between Petersen and his directors was getting terse. At one meeting, when a director raised a point that Petersen didn't like, the chairman snapped: "I don't agree with you. And I resent you bringing that up." The director soon forgot about the point in question, but he didn't forget how Petersen had reacted.

Petersen, who was headed toward his sixty-third birthday on September 4, 1989, was especially unpolitic in handling the sensitive matter of management succession. He intended to retire on schedule, at age sixty-five, in the fall of 1991, a year after the retirement of his second-in-command, Red Poling. The man to succeed him as chairman, he told the board, was Allan D. Gilmour.

Gilmour, fifty-four years old in the spring of 1989, had a lot going for him. After joining Ford in 1960, he became the prize protégé of J. Edward Lundy. Lundy was the legendary chief financial officer who had trained a whole generation of Ford "high pots," as those with high potential were called, to put together elaborate reports to senior management with meticulous attention to detail—making sure the tabs in the black binders were the right color and were properly aligned. Unlike the reclusive Lundy, Gilmour was an erudite and witty man who was comfortable on a public platform. When a reporter once asked him whether the recession of 1991 would ever end, Gilmour quipped, "If it doesn't, you'll have a lot bigger story than interviewing me."[8]

In other ways, though, Gilmour had much in common with his mentor. Like Lundy, he was a lifelong bachelor. And also like Lundy, he had spent his entire Ford career in finance—always evaluating the work of others, but never running anything himself. His complete lack of operating experience said more about Ford's haphazard approach to grooming future leaders than it did about Gilmour himself. But the gap on his résumé made the Ford board, and the Ford family, uncomfortable. The directors asked Petersen for some other options to consider, and Petersen said he had none. He made it clear that if the directors didn't like his succession plan, they should come up with their own.

THE LATE SUMMER AND fall of 1989 was an extraordinarily intense time for Ford's board of directors. As the board wrestled with the Petersen problem, it also entertained another proposal from Petersen for a blockbuster acquisition. This time he wanted to stick close to Ford's core business and buy the legendary British maker of luxury cars: Jaguar PLC.

At the beginning of the 1980s, Jaguar had looked certain to be extinct by the middle of the decade. After being nationalized by the British government in 1967, and then folded into British Leyland, Jaguar had proceeded to become a bloated, civil-service-style bureaucracy turning out some of the shoddiest cars on the planet. The company's venerable Brown's Lane flagship factory in Coventry, smack in the midst of Britain's decaying Midlands, was a dank and gloomy edifice where too many workers turned out too few cars. There seemed to be virtually no hope in sight for the car that had once been the fondest dream of millions of British and American schoolboys. Then John Egan arrived on the scene.

Egan was a feisty, ruddy-faced Irishman who took the helm at Jaguar in 1980. His job, he said, was like the old American television series, *Mission: Impossible*. Jaguar was losing an astounding £50 million a year on annual sales of just £150 million. But change was in the air. Margaret Thatcher's fledgling government, determined to denationalize its decrepit industrial dinosaurs, was encouraging managers to stand up to militant unions. Egan quickly declared that Jaguar had to boost productivity and quality to stay alive. He slashed 3,500 workers, some 30 percent of the total, off the payroll. And he ordered his managers to list the 150 most common defects on the cars (they had no trouble finding that many) and solve them.

In 1984, Egan took Jaguar public. It was a hard sell, and the shares fetched just £1.75 each. But at least the company was alive and standing on its own feet. And Jaguar cars were starting to sell again. Egan's quality improvements helped. So did the Reagan stock market boom in the United States, which ushered in a conspicuous consumption era in which luxury cars roared back into style. Jaguar was well positioned.

The classic muscularity of its styling, and its luxurious interiors of leather and burled walnut, exuded a snob appeal perfect for the boom years. Jaguars evoked the image of British aristocrats motoring off to their country estates in cars that were gentlemen's drawing rooms on wheels. And the combination of a weak pound sterling and a strong American dollar made its cars both affordable and profitable in the United States. In 1986, Jaguar sold 25,000 cars in the United States, up from just 3,000 cars five years earlier. Egan was knighted by the Queen, and the British press dubbed him "England's Lee Iacocca."

The good times, though, didn't last. Jaguar's U.S. sales dropped in 1987 and again in 1988, as sterling strengthened and the dollar declined in value. The XJ6, launched in 1986 as Jaguar's first new model in eleven years, suffered from a rash of defects, and thus resurrected the old bugaboo about Jaguar quality. Egan, or Sir John, as he was now known, figured Jaguar lacked the financial strength and the product-development capability to survive over the long haul. In 1987, he tried to talk Toyota into buying a substantial stake in Jaguar. But Japan's premier car company was in the midst of developing its own luxury marque, Lexus, and politely declined. A year later, Ford came along.

In late 1988, Don Petersen invited Sir John to meet with him at Ford's stately townhouse on Grafton Street in London. Jaguar, Petersen explained, needed a deep-pockets parent like Ford. And Ford, in turn, needed a marque higher in luxury and prestige than Lincoln, which was still second to Cadillac in the United States and completely unknown in Europe. Petersen proposed that Ford acquire Jaguar for between £4 and £5 a share.

Now it was Sir John's turn to decline. He found Petersen polite, if somewhat stiff, but he didn't like the American's proposal. For one thing, he thought a price of £8 to £10 a share was more appropriate. On a more fundamental basis, he doubted that Jaguar could thrive as a wholly owned subsidiary of Ford. Ford would be tempted to integrate Jaguar into its own operations, he figured, and thus rob Jaguar of the distinct snob appeal that was its most precious asset. "When an elephant gets in bed with a mouse," Sir John said to Petersen, "two things happen. The elephant doesn't have much fun. And the mouse gets killed." The meeting ended.

By then, though, Egan knew Jaguar was in play. During the next six to eight months he contacted some other car companies that might opt for less stifling terms. The two top General Motors executives in Europe, Jack Smith and Bob Eaton, came up with an idea Sir John liked.

GM, they said, would buy a 30 percent stake in Jaguar. It would let

Jaguar purchase components through Adam Opel, its European subsidiary, thus giving Jaguar huge economies of scale that it couldn't afford on its own. GM also would help Jaguar design a new "near luxury" car that would broaden's Jaguar's market. The car would be built on an Opel frame and use mostly Opel components, including a new V-6 engine far more modern than anything Jaguar had. But Jaguar would handle all the styling, inside and out.

Sir John loved the idea. In secret meetings on the weekend of September 16 and 17, 1989, he and the GM men hammered out the specifics. The only hitch, he told Smith and Eaton, would be if word of the deal leaked out, and caused the price of Jaguar's shares to rise far above what GM wanted to pay. To make the plan work, he explained, he would need two things: secrecy and speed. He got neither.

The weekend had hardly ended when word of the Jaguar–GM deal started to leak, and Ford sprang into action. It issued a terse press release, saying it wanted to "lay the foundation for a long-term asociation between Ford and Jaguar." Sir John announced that he didn't welcome Ford's approach, but nonetheless, Jaguar shares started to surge. Between September 18 and 22, they jumped from around £4 a share to nearly £6 —an increase of almost 50 percent. By October 6, the price topped £7 a share.

Stock-market speculators were betting that a full-scale bidding war between Ford and General Motors was about to begin. In truth, GM was rapidly losing interest, because its financial staff had calculated that Jaguar's stock already had climbed too high. During the next three weeks, though, Sir John kept the talks with GM alive. The British government, he hoped, might not allow a complete takeover of Jaguar by Ford or any other foreign company. And even if the government gave Ford a green light, the prospect of another bidder in the wings would force Ford to pay Jaguar shareholders a premium for their stock. GM willingly played along.

On October 31, the British government announced it wouldn't block a takeover of Jaguar. The next morning, at 9 A.M., Ford delivered a letter to Sir John, offering £8 a share if Jaguar would drop its opposition and call a special shareholders meeting to approve the bid. Then followed eighteen hours of intense negotiations, as Sir John insisted on £9 a share. In the end, the two companies split the difference. Ford would pay £8.5 a share for Jaguar, making the total price £1.6 billion, or nearly $2.5 billion.

It was a breathtaking sum for a company that had lost nearly $2 million in the first half of the year, and was about to face a fearsome onslaught from Lexus and Infiniti, the new luxury brands being launched by Toyota and Nissan. "Ford's victory may be Pyrrhic, leaving GM with the last laugh," the *Wall Street Journal* declared the next day.[9] GM executives, in fact, already were laughing in public. They issued a statement saying their own valuation of Jaguar was "significantly below what Ford offered." GM's judgment was quickly borne out when Ford killed a new sports car Jaguar was developing, because the vehicle was hopelessly overweight and inadequate.

Not long after the takeover, Sir John got a visit from Ford Vice Chairman Red Poling. Poling remarked that the £1.6 billion that Ford was paying far exceeded the value of Jaguar's tangible assets, which were just £300 million. Sir John acknowledged that, and related a little parable about buying a sausage from a street vendor. "When you buy sausage, you buy the meat and you buy the sizzle," he explained. "You have just paid £300 million for the meat, and £1.3 billion for the sizzle." Poling didn't laugh.

THE PURSUIT AND PURCHASE of Jaguar was one of the few things that united Ford during 1989. The Ford family, the board, Petersen and the rest of senior management all favored the deal, disastrous though it was. But even as the fight for Jaguar was unfolding, Ford's board was wrestling behind the scenes with what to do about Petersen.

Ford's most influential directors, including Bill Ford Sr., had become disenchanted with their chairman. It was a lot of things: the fighting with the Fords, the ill-timed proposal to buy Lockheed, and the mishandling of the management-succession issue. Directors were put off by Petersen's testiness during board meetings, and worried about the company's direction in the car business. They conferred among themselves in late spring and into the summer, and right after Labor Day they made their move.

The board sent one of its own as an emissary to Petersen to ask him to retire early. The man chosen for the task was Clifton Wharton, Jr., a distinguished academic—he had been president of Michigan State University and later chancellor of the State University of New York—whose sixteen years on the board made him the dean of the outside directors. His words, the other directors felt sure, would carry lots of weight with Petersen.

And they might have, if Wharton had been direct. Instead, he chose
to be oblique. It was sometimes good for a man, he told Petersen, to
retire with his health intact and with plenty of active years left in his
life. It was something Petersen should consider, Wharton suggested,
adding that no man should be stuck with the burdens of leadership for
too long a time. Petersen didn't get the hint.

Nor did he a few weeks later, in late September, when Bill Ford,
Sr. talked with him along similar lines. Bill Sr. was a mild-mannered
nonassertive, man—"He couldn't say shit if he had a mouthful of it," a
Ford director once said of him—and firing people just wasn't in his
blood. He had, after all, put up with thirty years of mediocrity from his
football team. After dropping his broad, gentle hints to Petersen, Bill
Sr. quickly realized that he wasn't getting through, and decided that
someone willing to be blunt was needed. He got on the phone to another
Ford director and said, "Don doesn't understand we want to fire him. I
can't tell him. Will you do it?" The man at the other end of the line was
Drew Lewis.

Lewis had been on the Ford board only three years, but he had no
problem saying exactly what was on his mind. At age fifty-seven he was
a short man, physically robust, with shiny gray hair and piercing blue
eyes. Between 1981 and 1983 he had been Ronald Reagan's secretary of
transportation—where he had espoused free trade, to the consternation
of Detroit, but had eased up on some of the regulations he believed were
killing the auto industry. Now he was chairman of Union Pacific, one of
the nation's venerable railroad companies. After taking the helm there
in 1987, Lewis had wasted little time whipping the company into shape.
He moved the corporate headquarters out of New York City to Bethlehem, Pennsylvania, chopping hundreds of staff jobs and slashing the cost
of office space in the process. He was engaging and assertive, and never
one to mince words. He assured Bill Ford he would get the message to
Petersen.

On the afternoon of Wednesday, October 11, 1989, Lewis walked
into the chairman's spacious corner office on the 12th floor of the Glass
House. The regular monthly meeting of Ford's board was scheduled for
the next day, and the battle for Jaguar was in full swing. But Lewis had
called Petersen's secretary in advance to set up a private appointment
with him. After Petersen greeted him, Lewis quickly got down to business.

"Don," he said, "nobody else is going to tell it to you straight, but I
will. You've got to leave. The board wants you out. We want Red

as chairman." Lewis didn't dredge up all the details of the directors' dissatisfaction. Instead he focused on the succession issue. The board had reservations about Gilmour, he said, and wanted some time to develop some other options. Poling could delay his retirement for a few years, Lewis explained, to make the plan work. But there was no getting around the fact that Petersen had to go.

The man who had flown off the handle at a thousand little things during his career kept his composure. He was controlled and subdued, as if he was too stunned to react. After recovering from the initial jolt, he told Lewis he would expect a generous severance package if he agreed to go without a fuss. Lewis said he could work that out with the rest of the board. Then he left.

The next day, at the formal board meeting, Petersen was unusually quiet. He didn't say anything about the conversation he had had with Lewis the previous day, and neither did Lewis. The board meeting proceeded routinely, dominated by a discussion about the Jaguar situation. It was like a family gathering where everybody knows about the dirty linen, but nobody wants to talk about it. Petersen, though, knew his time was up. A few days later he started calling Lewis about the severance agreement. Petersen wanted, among other things, a car, a company-paid office, and a pay package that would make him whole, virtually as if he had stayed as chairman until his sixty-fifth birthday. His total package topped $10 million. Lewis agreed.

On November 9, at the next board meeting, the drama played out precisely according to the script. Petersen formally announced to the directors that he would "resign." The board accepted his resignation, and elected Poling to succeed him. Petersen would stay on as chairman and CEO until the end of February. The matter was settled quickly and cleanly, without argument. Petersen left right after the meeting for Washington, to attend a White House state dinner for President Corazon Aquino of the Philippines. He returned the next morning, Friday, for a press conference to announce his departure.

"I am here today to announce that I have advised the board of directors that I have decided to retire from the company effective March 1," Petersen began, "and that my partner and friend Red Poling has been elected chairman and chief executive officer to succeed me on that date. I have been chief operating officer or chief executive officer for ten years, and I think it is time for me to make a change in my life."

Petersen's declaration that he had decided, as he put it, to "repot myself" struck many in his audience as odd. Senior auto executives rarely quit to smell the flowers unless forced. Still, next day the press played the story of Petersen's departure the way he presented it. Back in Bethlehem, Drew Lewis looked at the glowing articles about Petersen's early retirement with delighted disbelief. He turned to an aide and said: "We sure covered that one up good." *

---

* Mr. Petersen has consistently said that he left Ford voluntarily. In interviews in his office on August 18, 1992, and on January 10, 1994, he said he retired early to avoid a coincidence in which the company's top three executives would retire at roughly the same time. The version of his departure in this book is based on the accounts of current and former executives, officials, and directors of Ford Motor.

CHAPTER 10

THE JAPANESE JUGGERNAUT

Even as Japan's automakers surged to worldwide prominence and then to dominance in the 1980s, the biennial Tokyo Motor Show remained a backwater. Japanese cars had become marvels of quality and efficiency. But they remained, for the most part, bland and boring econoboxes virtually devoid of personality—the way most Westerners viewed the Japanese people themselves. What's more, the Tokyo Show lacked a proper display site. The cars were scattered among a series of drab gray buildings that typified Japanese cities, despite the country's newfound wealth.

But by October 1989, with the decade nearing an end and Detroit nearing another recession, all this had changed. In 1986 Honda had launched Acura, a luxury-car division that proved the Japanese could succeed in the segment of the market with the most prestige and the fattest profits. Toyota and Nissan quickly followed with their Lexus and Infiniti marques. Honda was developing a new Acura model, the NSX, a high-tech, all-aluminum sports car with a 270-horsepower engine and a $70,000 price tag. Japanese cars had become anything but boring.

At the same time, the Japanese government had just finished building a new, world-class exhibition center in Makuhari, on the eastern fringe of Tokyo. At Makuhari the products of Japan's nine car companies could be effectively displayed in one place. And while Makuhari was a half hour by train from central Tokyo, it stood in the midst of a newly booming area not far from Tokyo Disneyland. It was appropriate, then, that the 1989 Tokyo Motor Show was a display of power, imagination, and whimsy so spectacular that it was hard to tell where Disneyland ended and the Motor Show began.

Suzuki showed the cute and curvy Cappucino, a futuristic minicar, and the Escudome, a sporty van with a popout rear tent for camping—and a sign that invited owners (in near-English) to "go back to the nature." Honda unveiled a min-motorcycle called the Monkey and a somewhat larger cousin, the Gorilla.

The Nissan S-cargo was a tiny delivery truck designed to look like a snail, not to be confused with a competing vehicle from Mitsubishi, the Guppy. Daihatsu, Japan's smallest car company, displayed a bubblelike micro-car called the Sneaker (it could seat just one person in front, and hold a bag of groceries and a small child in the rear), and an assortment of other oddities called the Fellow 90, the Leeza Spider, and the Hijet Dumbo.

The Nissan Boga was a "keyless" car whose doors unlocked by reading and recognizing the owner's fingerprints. Not to be outdone, Mazda unveiled a "fragrance control system," a gadget that pumped scents of lavender, jasmine, mint, or perfume through a car's air-conditioning system at the push of a button.

The goofy gadgets and playfully named "concept cars" cost millions of dollars to produce, but that was no matter. The Japanese car companies were raking in record amounts of money, thanks to their rapid expansion overseas and the boom in car sales at home. Their exhibits were meant to impress and delight Japanese car buyers—as well as visitors from around the world. The dozens of Detroiters on hand included Chuck Jordan, the elegant and arrogant vice president for design at GM. Jordan's son, Mark, had followed in his father's footsteps as an automotive designer. But Mark had spurned the Big Three to join Mazda, where he had styled the stunningly successful Miata, a two-seat convertible whose lines evoked the classic British roadsters of the fifties and sixties.

Besides the fantasymobiles, the visitors also saw the latest in automotive technology. Toyota mounted a Celica coupe on a tilted, revolving stand that repeatedly split apart to reveal the car's inner workings. An air bag deployed over and over again, bursting out of the Celica's steering wheel and then being sucked back in. The scene looked like a giant blowing bubble gum. Other displays included lightweight engines made entirely of ceramics, "active" suspension systems that provided bursts of power to the shock absorbers to counter bumps on the road, and "continuously variable" automatic transmissions that boosted gas mileage by operating without individual gears.

Alongside all this, the displays of the U.S. and European automakers were weak tea. The dowdy Russian exhibit featured the latest version of the infamously inept Lada, and a dark blue prototype model called the Kompakt. The General Motors exhibit, the company's first at the Tokyo show in ten years, displayed a boxy Buick station wagon with fake wood-grain side panels—long since out of style in America and conspicuously out of place in Japan. Even Chuck Jordan was momentarily humbled. "We've got to get out of the Detroit mentality," he dourly declared while viewing the scene, "and become part of the world mentality."

THE 1989 TOKYO SHOW delivered yet another stunning wake-up call to Detroit's Old Guard. Japan was on a roll. In 1989, the Honda Accord outran the Ford Taurus to become the best-selling car in America—the first time a foreign nameplate had ever accomplished that feat. But the Accord wasn't an anomaly. Nearly all the major Japanese car makers were making big gains. As a group, Japanese manufacturers grabbed 25.4 percent of all U.S. car sales in 1989, up from 22.8 percent the year before.[1]

Much of Japan's success was made in America. The vast majority of Honda Accords were built in Ohio, by American workers assembling parts that increasingly were produced in the United States. Even Detroit's establishment couldn't ignore Honda's feat. In October 1989, shortly before the Tokyo Motor Show, Soichiro Honda, Honda's eighty-two-year-old founder, rolled up in an Ohio-made Accord to the Henry Ford museum in Dearborn, Michigan. The diminutive former mechanic's genius for engineering had propelled Honda from a small-time scooter maker to the only successful auto company founded after World War II. Now, he had come to America to see the first Accord ever assembled in Marysville enshrined in a display of landmark American cars. In Japanese, Honda paid humble homage to Henry Ford, recalling how as a young boy he'd knelt to smell the oil that dripped from a Model T that drove through his town. But this was Honda's moment of triumph. He had lived to hear himself hailed as Henry Ford's equal on the very ground that his boyhood idol had once trod.

Conservative Toyota, Japan's car-making colossus, had lagged behind Honda in establishing a strong manufacturing base in the United States. But by early 1990, more than 870 Camry sedans were rolling off the assembly line every day at Toyota's spotless new plant in Georgetown, Kentucky, just outside Lexington.

That wasn't all for Toyota. In a gleaming white building in Newport Beach, California, the company's American designers were squishing plaster in balloons, dreaming up fluid shapes for a new luxury coupe. In Ann Arbor, Michigan, Toyota was hiring more engineers and laying plans to expand a technical operation that would help American suppliers understand Toyota's engineering specifications, and thus produce parts for Toyota cars. Plans were taking shape for a test track and research facility in the deserts of Arizona. Toyota's ambition, financed by its huge U.S. profits, was to create a new American auto company.

It all added up to a stunning invasion of the Big Three's home ground. By early 1990, Toyota, Nissan, Honda, Mazda, Mitsubishi, Isuzu, and Subaru all were building cars in America. At varying speeds and varying levels of investment, the Japanese companies were moving to root themselves deeply in the American industrial heartland—just as GM and Ford had rooted themselves in Europe, seventy years earlier. Indeed, the Japanese in 1989 crossed a significant symbolic threshold when their factories combined to produce more than 1 million vehicles in the United States.

For Detroit, it was frightening. The new American auto industry seemed to have everything going for it: younger, largely nonunion workers, more efficient factories, higher quality cars, and the good will of the smartest, richest, and youngest American car buyers.

The Japanese companies hadn't done this on their own. Behind their success in America stood an unlikely crew of refugees and castaways from Detroit. These refugees could be found everywhere—from the factory floor at Toyota's Georgetown plant, to Nissan's engineering offices in suburban Detroit, to the sun-bleached Los Angeles basin, where the U.S. headquarters of Toyota, Honda, and Nissan formed a Motor City West south of downtown's skyscrapers. These Americans were harnessing their understanding of American culture—how cars were sold, what kinds of cars Americans wanted, what features Americans liked—to the manufacturing and managerial advantages their Japanese employers had over Detroit. By 1990, the dean of Japan's cadre of Detroit refugees was a pugnacious man called "Captain Crunch." His real name was Bob McCurry.

. . .

IN FEBRUARY 1990, with memories of the 1989 Tokyo Motor Show still fresh, the auto industry's top guns converged in Chicago for that city's big annual show. Roger Smith, six months from retirement, used GM's annual Chicago Auto Show press luncheon to deliver his valedictory, declaring GM strong and fit for the 21st Century. Bob McCurry, the top American in Toyota's U.S. sales operations, was on hand too. He had been a heavy hitter at Chrysler until twelve years earlier, when his bosses dumped him overboard. Now McCurry wanted revenge, and he looked to have a good chance of getting it.

Toyota's sales were booming, led by the stunning success of the new Lexus LS 400 luxury sedan. The LS 400, launched in August 1989, had changed everything for Toyota. Indeed, it had changed everything for Cadillac, Lincoln, BMW, Mercedes-Benz, Jaguar, and any other company that claimed to offer the finest car in the world. With the LS 400, Toyota had created a car that was more powerful than all but the highest-priced Mercedes models, quieter than a Cadillac, and of such high quality that it became the gold standard of the industry. But the most amazing achievement was the LS 400's price: just $35,000.

Mercedes and BMW executives sniffed that a "mass marketer" like Toyota couldn't compete in the same circles as a true "luxury" car. America's well-heeled car buffs, however, paid no heed. The LS 400 achieved for Toyota precisely what company patriarch Eiji Toyoda had intended. No longer was Toyota viewed as the stolid purveyor of dull econoboxes—cars that seemed like offspring of the looms and sewing machines that had been Toyota's first products, before it started building automobiles.

Nothing Detroit offered could compare with the LS 400 for technical mastery. Under the hood was a 32-valve V-8 engine that revved up to 250 horsepower, yet was so smooth that a person could balance a pyramid of full champagne glasses on the hood, then wind out the engine to full throttle without spilling a drop. Lexus staged this eye-popping trick at the car's sumptuous coming-out party at Pebble Beach, and used it again in television advertising. Detroit had no reply.

The Lexus wasn't all. The new Celica sported a swoopy shape designed not in Japan, but at Toyota's studios in California. The California designers also had produced the stunning Previa, a new minivan with a forward-reaching design and a futuristic interior that made Chrysler's minivans look like delivery trucks.

As executive vice president at Toyota Motor Sales U.S., Bob McCurry played impresario for it all. Now, Toyota had the hardware to make a serious run at blowing past Chrysler to become the third largest seller of passenger cars in the United States. Never mind that Toyota's archrival, Honda, was positioned to do the same. Back in Detroit, Honda was respected and admired. But Toyota, with nearly $10 billion in its corporate coffers, the world's most efficient factories, and now supercars like the LS 400, was FEARED.

Nothing could have made McCurry happier, except a fresh chance to brag about this success. The 1990 Chicago Show afforded him a forum: Toyota's annual late-night "Afterglow" party for the motoring press. Toyota rented the Presidential Suite of Chicago's posh Nikko Hotel, brought in carts full of fancy desserts and expensive booze, and served it all up until well after midnight.

The star attraction was McCurry himself. McCurry rolled into the Nikko bash pumped up after a celebratory dinner with some dealer friends. Waving a wineglass, he expounded on the superiority of Toyota's new vehicles, the ambitious plans he had to add more dealers and more models, and the stupidity of his adversaries in Detroit. As his public relations deputies cringed, McCurry threw aside the diplomatic straitjacket that Toyota executives religiously wore when talking about Detroit. "We'll KILL 'em," McCurry growled with a gleam in his eye. "We'll KILL 'em."

ROBERT B. McCURRY was born on July 10, 1923, in Burnham, Pennsylvania, a small town dominated by a big steel mill. His mother was a teacher, his father a salesman for Prudential Life Insurance. As a boy, McCurry would ride around the central Pennsylvania farm country with his father as he sought out new clients and collected payments. It was a hands-on approach to selling that McCurry would emulate later in life.

During World War II, McCurry trained as a turret gunner on B-17, and later B-29, bombers. But he never served overseas. Instead, newly married and eager to avoid combat missions over Japan, he tried out for the Second Air Force's football team in Colorado Springs, Colorado. Years later, McCurry would still heave a sigh of relief that he made the team. In 1946, McCurry enrolled at Michigan State University, and became a college football star. Three years in a row, McCurry's teammates voted him captain. It was an unprecedented streak. Even more remarkable, McCurry didn't play a glamour position like quarterback or linebacker. He was the center.

McCurry stopped playing football in 1948. But the formula of team spirit and bare-knuckled aggressiveness that got him through all those autumn Saturdays served him well in his new career: selling Chryslers. For more than twenty years, McCurry ground out the yardage, starting as a district sales manager in Chicago. After a stint as manager of the Los Angeles zone in the late 1950s, McCurry became convinced that Chrysler should pay more attention to the popular culture trends welling up among the youth of Southern California. McCurry bought a wooden skateboard as a memento of his time in L.A., and went back often to keep his finger on the pulse of the city—despite constant razzing from peers that his only real interest was golf.

McCurry truly did love golf. As his status grew at Chrysler, one of his favorite perks was playing with the famous pros under contract as Dodge pitchmen. But McCurry loved cars and winning even more. In the late 1960s, he decided Dodge had to become a serious contender in stock car racing. He ordered the Dodge racing team to start making movies of pit stops to analyze why it was slower than the competition. "In football," he explained, "you make movies of the game, and you study the movies."

Then, he commandeered a small team of engineers to put together a new car. The result, partly cobbled together in McCurry's garage, was a souped-up version of the 1969 Dodge Charger Daytona with a three-foot tall spoiler wing bolted to the trunk. It was, quite simply, the most outrageous car on the road. Dodge sold just enough of them to qualify the car as a "street" model for NASCAR racing rules. The company lost $5,000 on every one—a jaw-dropping sum considering that some new cars didn't cost that much in those days. But Dodge became a winner on the NASCAR circuit. And when McCurry got assigned to pump up Chrysler's Marine division in the early 1970s, he took the same flamboyant style out on the waves, commissioning a series of souped-up racing boats. It was during this seafaring sojourn that McCurry got the Captain Crunch nickname, an allusion to the popular cereal and to his sales techniques.

By the late 1970s, McCurry was back onshore as group vice president in charge of Chrysler's sales and marketing. He had developed a loyal following among Chrysler dealers, but was becoming increasingly unpopular at company headquarters. McCurry had a take-no-prisoners style that inspired either admiration or fury, but rarely indifference. One of his favorite tricks when checking up on a dealer was to sneak around to the back and walk in through the service department. By the time the dealer discovered he was on the premises, McCurry had eyeballed the operation and was ready to administer a dressing-down. He minced few words with dealers he suspected weren't pulling their weight.

One Christmas season, a Louisiana Dodge dealer named Arthur Tait called McCurry to wish him a happy holiday. Tait was an ex-football player, too. In fact, in 1947 his Mississipi State team had played McCurry's Michigan State squad in East Lansing and lost 7–0 in one of the year's big upsets. McCurry would often tease Tait that he'd rushed too many yards without his helmet.

But this Christmas, McCurry wasn't in a jovial mood. At the time, Chrysler was pushing to clear its infamous "sales bank." This was a euphemism for the vast collection of unsold cars that Chrysler built to keep its factories running—even though no dealer had ordered them. As the parking lots where these cars were stored filled up toward the end of the year, it became the duty of every sales executive to force every Chrysler dealer to buy truckloads of cars from the sales bank.

Tait, however, was staging a little rebellion. He refused to order his share of sales bank cars for the logical reason that he didn't need them. But no sooner had Tait delivered his Christmas best wishes than McCurry barked at him over the phone. "You haven't taken one damn car," he declared.

"Don't get mad," Tait replied.

"I don't get mad," McCurry snarled. "I get even." Tait hung up the phone. Then he picked it up again, dialed Chrysler's local zone manager and ordered the cars.

McCurry's magic was that he could do this, and Tait still loved him. Because, in the end, McCurry saw to it that Tait made lots of money. All over America, there were former poor boys who had been put on the road to millionairehood by Bob McCurry.

McCurry also punched a ticket that few of his peers had in the 1970s: He had dealt extensively with a Japanese car company. In 1969 and 1970, McCurry, as head of Dodge, was assigned to work with a Chrysler team negotiating a partnership with Mitsubishi Motors. At the time, Mitsubishi was a pipsqueak assembling barely 100,000 vehicles a year, or roughly half the annual output of a single Chrysler plant. Chrysler wanted a cheap little car to sell through Dodge dealerships. McCurry was amused by how little his Japanese counterparts seemed to know about product design. But he also learned that to do business with his new partners, he had to pull in his sharp elbows and be patient.

McCurry remembered a moment during a break in the talks, when a Mitsubishi executive ushered him to the top of the company's Tokyo office tower. Stretched before him was a view of the Tokyo harbor, bustling with boat traffic. "Many ships every day," the Mitsubishi man said. "And they must go out full."

Eight years later, ships full of cars from Japan were putting Chrysler against the ropes. Once renowned for its engineering, Chrysler had fallen behind the technological curve as tougher antipollution laws forced automakers to redesign their engines, and shift toward lighter cars. Customers began turning their backs on Chrysler's balky boats. To cover the problem, Chrysler's management just pumped up the sales bank.

McCurry, meanwhile, fumed at his "bean counter" bosses. He had long fought them over quality, styling, and sales strategy, and had lost most of the battles. McCurry was angry about being forced to sell cars he knew were junk. His own wife, Jane, had almost driven her Plymouth Volare into Lake St. Clair in Grosse Pointe because the brakes had failed. And he was tired of bullying friends like Arthur Tait into buying cars that nobody wanted from the sales bank.

In July 1978, McCurry pulled the plug. He confronted his boss with an ultimatum to fix the quality problems and stop the sales bank madness. "I can't sell this," he declared. Within days, McCurry was out. At fifty-five years old, he headed off to his vacation home in Rehoboth Beach, Delaware, to retire.

McCURRY'S RETIREMENT, though, didn't last. Bored with what he called "honey-do" jobs around the house, McCurry started listening to the offers friends were throwing his way. In December 1979, McCurry agreed to take over as manager of the Toyota distributorship in the Mid-Atlantic region.

Captain Crunch was back at the helm. The first day on the job, he fired an underling who showed up late for a meeting. He told another subordinate, "If you want to work here, get rid of the beard." He began visiting all the dealers, and pushing them to spiff up their Toyota stores. At the same time, Toyota sales began to catch fire as Americans— rattled by the oil embargo, rising interest rates and impending recession

—began to look for alternatives to Detroit's expensive gas guzzlers. Toyota sales in the Mid-Atlantic region jumped more than 40 percent on McCurry's watch.

The performance got McCurry noticed at Toyota's U.S. headquarters in the Los Angeles suburb of Torrance. By 1982, he was running the Los Angeles sales region. There, he cultivated dealers like Dominic Longo, who had bought Toyota franchises almost as afterthoughts. McCurry demanded that Longo drive a Toyota to company sales meetings, instead of his customary Rolls Royce. Every week, McCurry would go to Longo's office and listen to his complaints and his stories. Finally, Longo invited McCurry and his wife to dinner at his home in Beverly Hills. Turning to Jane McCurry, Longo said: "Your husband's come to see me for six months, and all he does is nod his head and say yes. I LIKE him." More important, Longo began to like selling Toyotas. Soon, Longo Toyota was the biggest Toyota dealership in America.

Still, McCurry resisted the repeated advances from Toyota to take a bigger role at the U.S. sales headquarters. That is, until Yukiyasu Togo arrived in 1984.

Togo was quite unlike the executives Toyota had sent from Japan in the past. Togo had gotten his start with Toyota not as a pencil-pushing salaryman, but as a race driver. His road-rally career was cut short by a crash that left him with a pronounced limp. In 1961, he was reassigned to push sales of a "sky-parking" system that he had invented. The machine hoisted cars up and placed them in above-ground parking structures; it became Toyota's answer to the problem of parking in Japan's cramped cities.[2]

During the 1970s and early 1980s, Togo helped to blaze trails for Toyota overseas. In the mid-1970s he ran Toyota's operations in Thailand. To get in tune with the local culture, he shaved his head and spent six weeks in the habit of a Buddhist monk begging with a bowl for rice. During the early 1980s, Togo ran Toyota's Canadian sales arm, a small tail wagged by the huge American dog.

In September 1983, Toyota put Togo in charge of its U.S. sales operations. He had finally arrived in the big leagues, only to face a big-league problem. Toyota, Japan's automotive giant, was getting its pants taken off in the world's largest car market by Honda, a relative pipsqueak. Togo's job was clear: Blow away Honda, and anyone else who got in the way of Toyota's ambition to own 10 percent of the U.S. vehicle market. This goal was critical to Toyota's great ambition, which came to be known as Global 10, to take over 10 percent of vehicle sales worldwide, and thus become one of the most powerful manufacturers on the planet.

As he surveyed his turf, Yuki Togo saw Bob McCurry was just the American he needed to accomplish his goals. Togo wooed McCurry, finally going to his house for dinner to convince Jane that her husband should take the job. In late 1984, he did.

McCurry and Togo seemed born to be a team. McCurry had spent a lifetime perfecting his role as a relentless head knocker. Togo, in contrast, played the role of "good cop." Togo relished disarming mannerisms. His business cards were round, with a line-drawing of his smiling face. He was an audio freak, with a superb high-end audio system and a bulging collection of music. Togo saw to it that Toyota became a prized patron of the Los Angeles Philharmonic Orchestra.

But Togo's real passion was flying. Unfazed by his youthful misadventures in race cars, Togo became an avid student pilot. He started with airplanes, but got really excited by helicopters. Togo had a helipad installed at Toyota's office campus in Torrance, and often would take a break during the day to climb in the 'copter and buzz the building. His subordinates dreaded his enthusiastic invitations to go for a ride.

Like his American partner, Togo also enjoyed rolling around the country to visit dealers in their offices, soaking up the vibrations of the market. "You can't make good strategy sitting in an ivory tower," he would say. Unlike many of his Japanese counterparts, Togo liked keeping a high profile with his employees. When Toyota sold 1 million cars and trucks in the United States in 1986, Togo ordered in champagne and called a meeting of all the sales staffers in the atrium of the Torrance headquarters. There, he passed out $50 bonuses that quickly became known as "Togo bucks."

McCurry, however, didn't bother softening his image. Instead, he'd wake up at the crack of dawn on Monday morning, scan the weekend sales reports that had come in on a machine installed in his Palm Springs weekend home, and steam west toward Torrance with a car phone glued to his ear. The first calls would go out to Toyota dealers on the East Coast. Then, McCurry's calls would hopscotch west. His message never varied: Sell! Sell! Sell! Employees got the same treatment. The least desirable seat on a Toyota plane heading across country was the one next to McCurry. Its occupant usually got a four-hour performance review.

McCurry's tactics, however, represented precisely what Togo and Toyota needed to realize their potential. Toyota had everything a successful car company required—well-designed, reliable vehicles; a superior, low-cost manufacturing method; and access to loads of cheap capital, thanks to the booming Japanese economy. What Toyota lacked was the know-how to capitalize fully on these strengths in the United States. Toyota needed American managers to lead its manufacturing executives at Nummi—the California joint venture with GM—through the maze of American parts suppliers. And so also, Togo needed McCurry to teach him how to punch the buttons that turned on American car dealers and buyers.

McCurry was eager to make the match. Toyota had cars McCurry didn't feel ashamed to sell. The trick was convincing the Japanese bosses back in Toyota City, mainly conservative finance men and cautious engineers, to loosen up a bit. Soon, Captain Crunch would get his chance.

DURING THE EARLY and middle 1980s, Toyota had rarely encountered the problem of having too many cars and not enough buyers. The quotas that capped shipments of Japanese-made cars to the United States so limited the supply of most Toyotas that dealers typically complained of having not enough cars to sell. In fact, they often used this artificial shortage to tack a surcharge on the sticker price, and pad their profits. But in 1988 and 1989, things started to change.

The Nummi plant in California was churning out Corollas, and the new Kentucky factory, which built Camrys, was expanding its production monthly. Toyota's exports of cars from Japan, while reduced, remained substantial. Thus the company found itself stuck with a large and growing supply of cars. And McCurry found himself forced to rent land to store the cars. The only two options were to cut factory production or slap rebates on the cars to boost sales. Togo, however, seemed reluctant to make either move. McCurry, the scarred veteran of Chrysler's sales bank, took him aside.

"Togo-san," McCurry told his boss. "Let me explain my philosophy of 'the first loss is the cheapest.' " The Camrys, McCurry argued, weren't getting any more desirable baking in the parking lots. Dealers thought it would take discounts of $2,000 a car to move the merchandise. That was expensive, but three months later, the sacrifice would be even worse. McCurry had seen this hoary car-salesman's maxim proved time and again in his career at Chrysler. Togo, however, had never really faced such a situation. "If we don't move these cars in sixty days," McCurry insisted, "it'll cost us more and more." Togo mulled it over. "Bob-san," he replied, "we do."

McCurry sounded the charge. In August 1989, Toyota launched a nationwide sales blitz. When the dust cleared, Toyota had posted its best sales month ever in the United States. "August was a 'Shake, Rattle 'n' Roll' month," McCurry declared in a chest-thumping press release. The only problem was that it also was a "Bust the Budget" month. The huge discounts had put Toyota Motor Sales USA $40 million over its budget for the year.

This was a serious matter, and Togo knew he had some explaining to do. There was only one man for the job. Shortly after the sales blitz, McCurry was in Japan when he got a call from Togo. "Bob-san," Togo said. "You will explain your philosophy of 'first loss is cheapest.' " And explain it in person, he added, to Shoichiro Toyoda, nephew of Chairman Eiji Toyoda, and the company's president and chief executive officer.

Togo, conveniently, was in Los Angeles, so McCurry had to handle the task on his own. McCurry got an audience with Toyoda—who was reverentially referred to inside the company as "Dr. Toyoda" because of his Ph.D. in engineering. McCurry explained his Motor City marketing wisdom to Japan's mightiest industrial shogun, while a translator struggled to render his car-guy slang into Japanese. Toyoda pondered it all, then delivered his judgment: "Bob-san. I understand. It's okay."

Consummate salesman that he was, McCurry had talked his way out of a jam. It was far from the only time McCurry got his way with Dr. Toyoda. McCurry's ability to line up pros like Chi Chi Rodriguez or Lee Trevino as golf partners when Toyoda visited America didn't hurt. But it was clear to those around McCurry and Togo that Toyoda was impressed by the success of his two brash subordinates as they rode America's economic boom in the late 1980s. Toyota's sales in the U.S. grew from about 727,000 cars and trucks in 1983 to more than 945,000 in 1989, an increase of some 30 percent. Toyota Motor Sales USA had become a $20 billion operation—equivalent to No. 22 on the *Fortune* 500 list.

McCurry made no secret that he wanted Toyota's American operations to function more like an independent car company. He wanted Toyota City to give Americans more say in product design. McCurry admired Toyota's quality. But he detested the angular styling and pedestrian colors favored by Toyota City. McCurry dismissed Toyota's designs as "Origami cars," a snide reference to the Japanese art of folding paper into crisp, sharply angled shapes. It was McCurry's opinion that Toyota wouldn't realize its potential with American car buyers until it started producing vehicles with fluid, rounded exteriors and smooth, well-appointed interiors. He wanted Toyota to follow the stylish example of the Ford Taurus instead of catering to Tokyo taxi drivers.

Toyota had established a small design studio in California in 1973. Initially, however, the American studio got its way only with the Celica, a sporty but relatively low-volume number aimed at the American youth market. McCurry began fighting to change this. He enlisted Togo to champion the California studio's avant-garde concept for a new minivan to replace the boxy, Tokyo delivery van that Toyota had offered during the late 1980s. And with Togo's help, he took on Toyota City over the design of the car Toyota was counting on to whip Honda, the 1992 Camry.

All through the 1980s, the Camry had trailed the Honda Accord in the United States. The cars were roughly the same size and price, and aimed at the same audience: Young, middle-class families disenchanted with Detroit. It was the biggest single segment of the market—not including pickups and minivans. But ever since Accords started rolling out of Honda's Marysville, Ohio, factory in November 1982, Honda had run circles around Toyota.

By 1988, however, Toyota was moving in the heavy artillery. Most important was the new assembly plant in Kentucky, which by 1991 would be ready for full speed production of the new Camry then taking shape in the engineering labs and design studios of Toyota City. This Camry would be nearly as big as a Taurus. It would have a muscular V-6 engine available as an option. Its body would contain some of the same high-technology steel used in the Lexus LS 400 to deaden unpleasant road noise and vibration. It would, in short, be the car to put Honda back in its place and put Toyota squarely in the mainstream of the American market.

So it was with considerable anticipation that McCurry and Togo arrived in Toyota City in early 1989 for their first look at the new Camry's styling. Ushered into the design studio, the two men stared at the car for several moments.

"What do you think?" Togo asked.

"No way!" McCurry snapped. "That's a Japanese Camry, not an American Camry. We can't stand that type of styling."

McCurry quickly made his specific objections crystal clear. The car was "stiff, totally stiff." It was another origami car. "Look at the doors," he said. "The lines are rigid and straight." McCurry complained to one of the senior executives on the project, a leader of the team that had designed the Lexus LS 400. "We can't sell this type of car in America," McCurry insisted. The Japanese engineer heard McCurry out, then observed that changing the shape of the car's doors was very expensive.

Indeed, it was. Few single aspects of a car's architecture are as critical as the doors. Change the size and shape of the doors and you start a chain reaction: The roof, the fenders fore and aft, the side frames, the glass, and hundreds of other pieces of hardware and decorative trim all have to be altered as well. McCurry understood this. But he refused to back down. Togo backed him up. And the two men decided to take a big chance. By coincidence, Togo and McCurry had an audience scheduled with Dr. Toyoda at the time. The Camry wasn't on the agenda. McCurry and Togo resolved to bring it up. Fortunately, Dr. Toyoda made it easy for them. "How do you like the Camry?" he asked.

"We don't," came the reply.

"What's wrong?" Toyoda asked, speaking in Japanese. McCurry and Togo unloaded. The doors were too angular. The styling was flat. The car wasn't wide enough. There wasn't enough space for passengers inside. Americans wouldn't like it.

Toyoda listened sympathetically, and to McCurry's surprise and delight, he threw his weight on the side of his U.S. salesmen. Later, McCurry learned that Toyoda called in Shiro Sasaki, the executive vice president in charge of engineering, and ordered the American Camry redesigned.

Thirty days later, McCurry and Togo were summoned back to Japan. Once again, they were ushered into a design studio. There, in clay, was the car they wanted. It was smooth, fluid, and muscular-looking—a little like a scaled-down version of the Lexus LS 400. For Bob McCurry, it looked like the foundation for another winning season.

It was with this triumph in hand, and the prospect of more to come, that Bob McCurry swaggered into Chicago's Nikko Hotel in February 1990. Back in Toyota City, engineers were working on prototypes for another one of his favorite projects: a truck that could take a bite out of Detroit's monopoly among farmers, contractors, and ranchers who would drive nothing but a big, tall, full-size pickup. Toyota's California styling studio was about to get a big expansion, in recognition of its streak of winning designs. McCurry even put Toyota's ambitions on the line in public. The company, he said, wanted to sell 1.5 million cars and trucks a year in the United States by the mid-1990s—a 50 percent increase from the 1989 levels. Honda, which didn't even make trucks, could never match that.

Whether Bob McCurry, by now sixty-six-years old, would be co-captain of the team when it crossed the goal line seemed unlikely. But Captain Crunch showed no signs of slowing down. And despite periodic blasts of anti-Japanese rhetoric from Detroit and Washington, Toyota seemed to be pursuing a McCurry-style game plan to blow past Honda and push further and further into Detroit's end of the field.

The fact that Japanese companies now had assembly plants in Ohio, Michigan, Indiana, Illinois, Kentucky, and Tennessee was helping their cars win greater acceptance in the one place where they still weren't entirely welcome—the Midwestern heartland. In fact, Toyota and the other Japanese companies were making unprecedented inroads in the Big Three's very bastion, Detroit itself. Proof positive came in a phone call that McCurry had gotten just a few months before his Nikko Hotel manifesto from an old friend who was, perhaps, the most prominent and successful car dealer in Detroit. His name was Martin J. McInerney, Jr.

RATHMOR ROAD IS the most exclusive street in Bloomfield Hills, Michigan. It backs up to the eighth fairway of the Bloomfield Hills Country Club, and over the years it has boasted the homes of some of the heaviest hitters in Detroit. Among them: both George Romneys (senior and junior); Roger Smith of General Motors; Bill Hoglund, the GM executive vice president; Dan Kelly, vice chairman of the big accounting firm Deloitte & Touche; and Robert Vlasic, heir to a pickle fortune and chairman of Campbell Soup. But the biggest house on the block belongs to none of the above. Instead, it belongs to a car dealer named Hoot.

Martin J. McInerney, Jr., aka Hoot, started building his 25,000-square-foot brick mansion in 1989, after tearing down the handsome home that previously occupied the lot. His children were all grown, but Hoot wanted something bigger for himself and his wife. For starters, there were ten bedroom suites, each complete with its private bathroom, fireplace, wet and dry sauna, and remote-control TV that, at the flick of a button, rose up out of the sculpted-carpet floor. The bathtub in the master bedroom suite was set atop a marble pedestal, three steps high. The house had two three-car garages, a cherrywood-paneled elevator, and a domed ceiling in the entrance hall that stood 22 feet high. Inside, the house was cooled by ten jumbo heating and air-conditioning units. Outside, it was hard to tell the swimming pool from the oversized fountain, with its remote-control switch that adjusted the height of the spray.

The neighbors regarded the new house with equal amounts of awe and envy, which was just fine with Hoot. He loved to show visitors the high-tech, silent-flush toilets in each of the bedroom suites—except for the servants' quarters, where a regular toilet sufficed. And he loved to boast: "My house is bigger than the clubhouse" of the Bloomfield Hills club, which lay just a chip shot across the fairway. "I don't think they like that too well." Hoot was exaggerating a bit, but he was, after all, a car dealer.

The house and the neighborhood were a long way from Hoot McInerney's roots. He was born on January 23, 1929, on the East Side of Detroit, in a neighborhood that by the 1980s had become one of the city's worst ghettos. After he got rich, Hoot and his older brother, Tom, once revisited the house of their birth, and paid the people who lived there $100 to show them through it. Their friends told them they were lucky to get out alive.

As a young man, Hoot served in the Marine Corps, and then dropped out of Detroit's Wayne State University because he was bored. In late 1951 he landed a job with a Ford dealership in Grosse Pointe. He stayed for a decade—running the parts department, service, sales, and eventually becoming general manager. He learned the business from the ground up, and by 1962 he wanted his own dealership. Too many others were ahead of him at Ford, so Hoot tried Chrysler. That's when he met Bob McCurry.

Chrysler, at the time, was in one of its periodic crises. Dealers in cities around the country had gone out of business, but Chrysler wanted to keep the stores open under new ownership. McCurry took a liking to Hoot because he displayed the same street smarts that McCurry prided himself in having. Some of this savvy showed through in Hoot's jokes, which often doubled as proverbs. "In the Mafia," he would say, "one and one isn't two. It's eleven. If two people know something, eleven people know it."

So McCurry signed up Hoot to run Northland Chrysler–Plymouth, then on Seven Mile Road in Detroit, as a company-owned store, and Hoot obliged by doubling Northland's sales in his first year. That persuaded McCurry to sell him the store, so Hoot took the biggest gamble of his life. At age thirty-three, with a wife and five children, he sold his home, moved the family into a rented house, and used the $5,000 proceeds to borrow $250,000 in working capital. His timing was perfect, because the economic boom of the 1960s produced a bonanza for car companies and their dealers. Within a year, Hoot paid off the loan and bought a new home.

Hoot's methods were simple. To keep expenses low he kept his building clean but plain. He targeted specific groups of buyers, notably Chrysler factory workers, who got a company discount known as the A plan. And so they would buy from him, as opposed to other Chrysler dealers, he paid $25 to every worker who sent in a coworker who bought a car. He called the men who made the referrals "bird dogs," and he treated their friends well. Being Irish and Catholic, he also targeted priests and cops, and pretty soon FBI agents from around the Midwest were buying their cars from Hoot McInerney. He hired Alex Karras, the All-Pro football lineman for the Detroit Lions, to sell cars for him in the off-season. The two men became fast friends, and Karras drew in yet another special class of customers—Detroit's professional athletes.

In 1966 Hoot moved Northland one mile north to be near Detroit's first suburban shopping center, and started raking in profits he had never dreamed of. So in 1969 he bought another Chrysler–Plymouth dealership, his second, in Sarasota, Florida, and was off and running. Then followed a Lincoln–Mercury in suburban Detroit; a Ford dealership in Port Huron, Michigan; another Lincoln–Mercury outlet in Maumee, Ohio; a Cadillac dealership near Detroit; and then a store that sold all three Ford brands—Fords, Lincolns, and Mercurys—in Maui, Hawaii. His trips to Hawaii, where he had a condominium, became tax deductible.

At one point Hoot's empire included eighteen different dealerships, including three in Hawaii and others in Michigan, Ohio, and Florida. Many were once-troubled franchises that he bought at bargain prices, turned around, and sold for a handsome profit—so the number of stores he owned varied from year to year. Hoot earned $10 million in his best year, $5 million-plus in an average year, and stayed in the black even during recessions.

Amid all this, however, Hoot McInerney's business methods remained staunchly conservative. "You always had better look at the downside," he liked to say, "because it's there." Thus he never pledged the assets of one of his dealerships to finance the acquisition of another. Unlike most dealers, he never even borrowed money from "the factory," as dealers called the car companies, to finance his inventory of cars and parts. His office at Star Lincoln–Mercury—at the corner of Telegraph and Twelve Mile Roads in suburban Southfield, Michigan—was outfitted with cheap wood-grain paneling and industrial-grade furniture.

But when the tacky plastic phone rang on Hoot's desk, the caller was likely to be a customer who was rich, famous, or both: Sparky Anderson, manager of the Detroit Tigers; Lou Holtz or Bo Schembechler, the football coaches at Notre Dame and Michigan; or Tom Monaghan, founder and owner of Domino's Pizza. And Hoot's clout and connections were amply evident from the photographs on the wall: Hoot with actor Dennis Weaver, Hoot with Edmund Cardinal Szoka (the Catholic archbishop of Detroit), Hoot with Governor Jim Blanchard of Michigan, Hoot with House Speaker Tip O'Neill, and Hoot with President George Bush. "Bush is the kind of guy you'd like to have marry your daughter," Hoot would say, "but you wouldn't let him in the family business."

In 1982, when he bought a Cadillac store near Detroit, Hoot scored an automotive hat trick, having at least one franchise from each of the Big Three. Besides Cadillacs he sold Chryslers, Plymouths, Dodges, Fords, Lincolns, and Mercurys. But one thing he didn't have, deliberately, was an import franchise. As the eighties unfolded and the Japanese juggernaut continued, some other prominent Detroit dealers bought import stores to build their business and protect themselves in case the Big Three kept losing market share. But not Hoot. He thought Americans should buy American cars. The fact that, year by year, more and more Japanese cars were built in America didn't make any difference. Auto workers in Detroit were still losing their jobs, and to Hoot that was the end of the debate. At least until he took a closer look at what was happening around him.

Chrysler, the company that sold him his first store, owned nearly 25 percent of Mitsubishi Motors. By the late 1980s, when Lee Iacocca was bashing the Japanese at every turn, most of Chrysler's best products—the Dodge Stealth, Plymouth Laser, and Dodge Colt—were actually made by Mitsubishi. Ford, likewise, owned 25 percent of Mazda, and sold the Mazda-made Ford Probe as if it were a real Ford. General Motors owned 38 percent of Isuzu, and had built joint-venture factories in the United States and Canada with Toyota and Suzuki. The Big Three, in other words, were brazenly sleeping with the enemy. Hoot McInerney, meanwhile, was in danger of getting left behind. And what if another energy crisis hit, and the rush to Japanese cars accelerated even in Detroit? A prudent businessman—and Hoot was that above all else—had to hedge his bets, even if just a little.

Which is why, in late 1989, Hoot called his old friend Bob McCurry with an idea. He wanted to open a Toyota store adjacent to his Cadillac dealership in Mount Clemens, Michigan, a suburb twenty-five miles northeast of Detroit. Mount Clemens was an unlikely place to put up a Toyota sign. The town was in Macomb County, a stronghold of the United Auto Workers union. Macomb County's towns were to UAW members what Bloomfield Hills was to Detroit's executive class—the bedroom location of choice. It was the home of Reagan Democrats, blue-collar workers whose disgust with the wimpish liberalism of the Democratic Party had produced landslides for Ronald Reagan in 1980 and 1984. But while President Reagan was a free trader, the Reagan Democrats of Macomb County weren't. Three different dealers had tried to open a Toyota store in Mount Clemens over the years, and all three had gone out of business.

Hoot, though, had a plan, which he outlined to McCurry. By opening the Toyota store right next to his Cadillac franchise, he could keep his investment and expenses to a minimum. He wouldn't need an office manager, a parts manager, a switchboard operator, or a body-shop manager. His employees at the Cadillac store could handle those duties for the Toyota dealership as well. Hoot figured he could open for business by investing just $200,000, instead of the minimum of $1.5 million it took to open a typical new dealership. That meant he wouldn't have to sell many cars to make the store profitable. McCurry liked what he heard, and approved his old friend's dealership application on the spot. In June 1990, McInerney Toyota opened its doors.

The store made money from the start, partly because of the McCurry-inspired 1992 Camry. It hit the market fifteen months after McInerney Toyota opened, and proved a huge success for Hoot and for Toyota dealers around the country. Camry sales, while remaining behind Accord, surged 8.7 percent in 1992, a year when Accord sales dipped 1.4 percent.[3] Captain Crunch had posted a sweet victory.

In the process of selling Toyotas, Hoot McInerney became a confirmed believer in Japanese quality. In his other dealerships, warranty repairs provided an important part of cash flow. And when customers brought their cars in for warranty work, they often would have routine maintenance work done at the dealership as well.

But the Toyotas he was selling didn't need many warranty repairs. In 1992 Hoot submitted so few warranty claims to Toyota that his dealership started offering customers free oil changes, so they would bring their cars in for maintenance. None of his other dealerships had to do that. Star Lincoln–Mercury's warranty claims were running over $2 million a year, which meant customers were coming back in all the time. "So what the hell is this stuff about quality being Job One?" Hoot growled, in reference to Ford's advertising slogan.

Hoot's long-time friends at Chrysler, Ford, and GM didn't like his decision to sell Toyotas. But they didn't hold it against him, either. Business was business, after all, and Big Three executives understood that. And they understood that Hoot's ties to Bob McCurry ran deep—all the way down to the roots of the McInerney fortune.

So it was that, on May 5, 1992, Big Three managers turned out for the Hoot McInerney Charity Roast and Auction. Alex Karras flew in from Hollywood to be one of the roasters. The others included Detroit radio personality J. P. McCarthy, who doubled as emcee, and Ben Bidwell, seventeen months into retirement.

"What an intimidating program to be in, surrounded by stars of screen and airwaves," Bidwell began. "This is like the spot on the old Ed Sullivan show before Elvis Presley sings, where they want to kill some time and they bring on the dog that farts the Star Spangled Banner." The crowd laughed.

"I came to talk about obscene executive bonuses," Bidwell said. "Do you know what the captains of industry are doing with their ill-gotten loot? Buying and building obscene temples."

With that, a slide projector flashed a picture of Roger Smith's house onto a screen. "That house was bought with all the money the GM shareholders paid Roger Smith," Bidwell said. The projector clicked again, past pictures of the Bloomfield Hills dwellings of Lee Iacocca, Red Poling, and Don Petersen.

He continued: "Well, the jig is up on self-gratification. It's time to get back to good, old American values, the kind that built this house." A picture of Hoot's new home—far bigger and more ostentatious than the others—popped onto the screen, and the crowd exploded into a roar.

"This isn't the house of some corporate fat cat. It was built by the sale of an occasional car and truck to members of the clergy, teachers, widows, FBI agents, and members of the Lions. It was built the American way, the humanitarian way, one sucker at a time. Chrysler, Plymouth,

Lincoln, and Cadillac built it—all American cars. The only thing Toyotas paid for was the doorbell. It plays, 'Old McCurry had a farm, Tora, Tora O.' "

The crowd's laughter was unrestrained, and Bidwell delivered his punch line. "This picture says why I want to be Hoot McInerney! I want to be Hoot McInerney! Unfortunately, the position is still occupied."

The crowd leaped to its feet. Hoot rose and embraced Bidwell. J. P. McCarthy leaned toward the microphone and said in his rich radio voice, "Thank you, Two Dog."

CHAPTER 11

LEE LEAVES

Arthur C. "Bud" Liebler was used to being late. It went with the territory of being Lee Iacocca's PR man. As vice president of public relations for Chrysler, Liebler was always lingering late in the office listening to an Iacocca monologue or figuring out to how to put the best spin on the next Chrysler announcement. And the announcement Chrysler was preparing to make on Monday morning—March 16, 1992 —was a blockbuster. Robert J. Eaton, the president of General Motors Europe, would jump to Chrysler as designated heir to Lee Iacocca.

It was as if the mayor of, say, Houston had managed to get elected President of the United States. Eaton would be leapfrogging a handful of far more prominent, and more likely, candidates. The news surely would create shock waves both inside and outside Chrysler. All of which was why Liebler had spent most of Saturday, March 14, in his office. And why he was late to meet his wife, Nancy, for dinner at the Birmingham Country Club in suburban Detroit.

At 8:30 P.M. Liebler finally arrived, apologized to Nancy, and tried to unwind during dinner. But it didn't help when he ran into a Chrysler colleague, Fred Hubacker.

Hubacker, a finance man, wasn't a corporate officer. He was a group controller, an upper-middle manager whose job wasn't big enough to place him among Chrysler's elite. When Liebler said hello to Hubacker, he was careful not to mention Eaton.

"I couldn't say a word," Liebler told Nancy on the way home, "because Fred is completely in the dark. Come Monday morning, he and a lot of other guys are in for a big shock."

Maybe a lot of other guys, but not Fred Hubacker. He was the man who had made it all happen.

BOB EATON AND FRED HUBACKER were born nearly 1,000 miles apart, but they had a lot in common. Both grew up in small towns in the Midwest. Eaton's home was Arkansas City, Kansas, a hamlet on the Arkansas River just north of the Kansas–Oklahoma line. Hubacker lived in Cheboygan, Michigan, a picturesque place on Lake Huron, enduring several surgeries for a club-foot that left him with a pronounced limp. For college, both chose a big state university. Eaton majored in mechanical engineering at the University of Kansas, while Hubacker got a marketing degree from Michigan State. And both men began their careers in Detroit right out of school.

GM, where Eaton started as an engineering trainee in the Chevrolet division in 1963, swaggered in those years. It held about 65 percent of the U.S. market, and regarded Chrysler and Ford as competitors barely worthy of that name. The Japanese weren't even on the map.

Chrysler was an altogether different place. It was a boom-bust outfit, prospering during good times but barely creaking through recessions. Hubacker started in August 1966 on the finance staff.

Because they worked for different companies, Hubacker and Eaton weren't likely ever to meet each other, much less become friends. As fate would have it, though, Connie Eaton and Margie Hubacker taught at the same grammar school in Warren, a suburb just north of Detroit. One night the teachers threw a party, and Bob and Fred got roped into going.

Before long, the Hubackers and the Eatons were doing a lot of things together—going to movies, out to dinner, playing golf, and even riding dirt bikes, something both men did for kicks. Both couples had two sons, and each set of boys was only a year apart. Every year the two families vacationed together. In the early years, when neither couple had much money, they would rent a two-bedroom cottage on northern Michigan's Higgins Lake, and spread sleeping bags on the living room floor for the boys. Later, as they grew more prosperous, the Eatons and Hubackers bought vacation condominiums virtually next to each other on a more upscale northern Michigan playground, Walloon Lake.

The two families remained extraordinarily close, even after Bob's career zoomed ahead while Fred's more or less meandered. Eaton scaled GM's product engineering ranks, becoming an executive engineer in 1973 and assistant chief engineer at Oldsmobile in 1979. In 1982 he was elected a GM vice president, in charge of the advanced engineering staff.

Hubacker, meanwhile, spent the seventies wandering in and out of middle-level Chrysler finance jobs. In 1979 and 1980, when Chrysler was careening toward the brink of bankruptcy, he hung on, even as Chrysler's new chairman, Lee Iacocca, fired hundreds of company veterans and replaced them with other refugees from Ford. The Ford guys got virtually all the top jobs, but Hubacker, fortunately, got along well with them. As Chrysler forged its comeback by launching the K-cars and the minivans, his career moved ahead in steady, though unspectacular, fashion. Eaton, meanwhile, climbed even higher in the GM hierarchy, becoming a group vice president in 1986 and president of GM Europe in 1988.

The Eatons' move to Zurich, home of GM Europe, proved difficult for both families. The Eatons weren't gone more than a few weeks before Margie hopped on a plane to visit Connie. A few months later, for the Eatons' first Christmas in Europe, the boys skied together in the Alps.

The Eaton-Hubacker story might have ended here, a warm and enduring friendship of the sort that's all too rare in modern America, important to their families but of little note to the rest of the world. Then in 1991, with Chrysler struggling for survival for the second time in a decade, the company's directors started to wrestle with finding a successor to Iacocca.

BOB LUTZ HAD AN IDEA about who ought to succeed Lee Iacocca: him. On January 14, 1991, one month shy of his fifty-ninth birthday, Lutz was named president of Chrysler. The job made him second-in-command, right behind Iacocca and ahead of Vice Chairman Steve Miller, who was ten years Lutz's junior and the only holdover (besides Iacocca) from the crew that had saved Chrysler in the early eighties.

GM Vice President Alex Mair comparing GM and Honda connecting rods in 1986. Throughout the 1980s, Mair warned GM that it was falling behind Japenese manufacturers.

GM Manager Steve Bera at work at New United Motor Manufacturing Inc. The joint venture between GM and Toyota that saved GM's old Fremont, California, car factory gave GM a close-up look at how Toyota was beating Detroit. But GM's bureaucracy resisted the lessons Bera and other GM managers learned from Toyota.

GM Chairman Roger Smith at the Traverse City, Michigan, "people power" management conference in October 1988. "We need fifteen-cent solutions to million-dollar problems," he said.

GM Chairman Roger Smith at the 1988 Traverse City, Michigan, "people power" management conference, handing his sweater to a subordinate after the younger manager had complained that the room was too cold. The moment galvanized young GM executives hoping for cultural reform.

GM Chairman Robert Stempel and his "team" before the fall. Clockwise from left: Executive Vice President William E. Hoglund, Vice Chairman Robert Schultz, Vice Chairman Jack Smith, Chief Financial Officer Robert T. O'Connell, Executive Vice President Alan Smith, President Lloyd E. Reuss (seated, at right) and Stempel (seated, at left).

GM Chairman Roger Smith at GM's Saturn factory in Spring Hill, Tennessee, after driving the first Saturn car off the assembly line in July 1990. Smith pumped more than $3.5 billion into Saturn, saying it would revolution-ize the U.S. auto industry. But production problems pushed Saturn nearly $1 billion into the red in 1991.

7

GM Chairman Roger Smith announces that Bob Stempel will succeed him. "Our objective isn't to shrink the business at General Motors," Stempel declared.

General Motors Robert C. Stempel at the February 24, 1992, news conference during which he announced GM lost a record $4.45 billion in 1991.

John G. Smale. The former Procter & Gamble chairman was the reluctant leader of GM's boardroom revolt.

Ira M. Millstein. The affable Weil, Gotshal & Manges partner was the catalyst for the boardroom coup that toppled GM Chairman Robert Stempel, telling wavering GM directors in 1992 that they had to take dramatic action to save America's largest company.

10

GM President John F. Smith, Jr., at the dedication of Opel's innovative new factory in Eisenach, formerly in East Germany. Just five weeks later, Smith would become GM's chief executive as GM's outside directors ousted Bob Stempel.

11

Louis Hughes at the September 23, 1992, dedication of the Opel-Eisenach factory. Hughes, who would become one of GM's top five executives in November 1992, wanted Eisenach's lean manufacturing system to be an inspiration for change throughout General Motors.

12

José Ignacio López de Arriortúa relaxes on vacation in 1993. The flamboyant cost-cutter's defection from General Motors to Volkswagen in March 1993 ignited a bitter war between the two auto giants over charges of industrial espionage.

13

Ford Motor Chairman Philip Caldwell unveils the Taurus in January 1985. The Taurus, which revolutionized American car design, launched Ford's resurgence and devastated General Motors.

Ford Motor Chairman Donald E. Petersen, who led Ford's turnaround in the late 1980s by advocating a culture of respect and empowerment for employees. But his struggle to live up to his own standards eventually alienated the Ford family and his board of directors.

Ford's heirs apparent, Edsel B. Ford II (standing, left), and William Clay Ford, Jr., great-grandsons of Henry Ford, with William Clay Ford, Sr., as they celebrate Ford Motor Company's ninetieth anniversary, in front of a replica of the first Ford assembly plant.

Henry Ford II
("Hank the Deuce").

17

18

Will Boddie, the
leader of the team of
Ford engineers that
developed the 1994
Mustang.

19 John Coletti, leader of the original Ford "skunk works" team assigned to devise a plan to save the Mustang, and the car that resulted.

As head of Ford's North American Operations, Alex Trotman (left) championed the team that saved the Mustang. On October 4, 1993, Ford Chairman Harold A. "Red" Poling (right) announced during ceremonies to launch the car that Trotman would succeed him.

20

Super dealer Martin J. "Hoot" McInerney. Hoot got rich selling Chryslers in Detroit, but after years of refusing to sell Japanese cars, Hoot finally got a Toyota franchise from his old friend and former Chrysler executive Bob "Captain Crunch" McCurry.

Bennett E. Bidwell, one of Lee Iacocca's top lieutenants at Chrysler. Nicknamed "Two Dog," Detroit's funniest executive became embittered as Chrysler slid back into trouble during the early 1990s.

Gerald Greenwald. Chrysler's vice chairman and Lee Iacocca's heir apparent quit the company in 1990 in frustration over Iacocca's refusal to set a retirement date.

Fred L. Hubacker. The Chrysler middle manager was the match-maker between Chrysler's board and Iacocca's eventual successor, GM Europe head Robert Eaton.

Lee Iacocca introduces his successor, Robert Eaton (center), as Chrysler President Robert Lutz maintains a stoic pose.

Bob Marcell, leader of the Chrysler team that produced the Neon.

Chrysler's executive-suite exodus—specifically the departures of Sper-lich, Greenwald, and Bidwell—had put Lutz in pole position.

Born in Zurich, the son of a prominent Swiss banker, Lutz was edu-cated at Berkeley and was fluent in English, French, German, and Ital-ian. He flew jet fighters for the U.S. Marine Corps in the late 1950s before finishing college and joining GM in Europe. There he advanced steadily before switching to BMW, where he rose to become vice presi-dent of sales and a member of the board. In 1974 he jumped ship again, this time to Ford. In twelve years he climbed to executive vice president for international operations and won a seat on the board of directors, only to fall out of favor when Ford's European business started to stumble. In 1986 Iacocca lured him to Chrysler as an executive vice president.

Once there he increased his influence over product development—even though his taste and vision were the polar opposite of Iacocca's. Iacocca's ideal car was the 1982 Frank Sinatra edition of the Chrysler Imperial. It had a vinyl roof, wire wheel covers, pillowed velour seats, the initials FS on the front fender and came in just one color—baby blue—to match its namesake's eyes. To Bob Lutz, the car was a bad joke.

He thought cars should be precision driving machines with tight steering, firm suspension, and seats that held occupants in place in-stead of cushioning their behinds. It was a European view, but Lutz thought that Americans, especially well-educated young people with high incomes, were ready for it. He was appalled to learn that the engineers on one new project wanted to mount the engine transversely under the hood, or "east–west" in Detroit parlance, instead of length-wise to enhance handling and performance. He ordered the engine's direction switched, explaining: "God intended engines to run north–south."

The flippant remark said a lot about Bob Lutz. His huge talent and vision (his engine decision ultimately was vindicated) were matched by his enormous ego and his big mouth. He couldn't keep either under control.

When his name appeared below Steve Miller's in Chrysler's 1990 annual report, Lutz went nuts. He demanded that the order be changed for next year. It was. Likewise, Chrysler staffers quickly learned that, on memos intended for both Miller and Lutz, it was always politic to list Lutz first.

In 1991, as Lutz's second marriage fell apart, he seemed compelled to describe the details of their breakup at every possible chance. He regaled reporters with stories about his wife's demands for money and for their vacation home in Wyoming. He sent a memo to Chrysler's directors, informing them he shouldn't be held responsible for her bills. Once, in a speech to thousands of automotive engineers, he departed from his text to complain that his divorce was costing him $20,000 a month in lawyer bills alone.

Lutz also contradicted Iacocca in public, routinely and repeatedly. When Iacocca declared that Chrysler needed an overseas partner to develop a new small car, Lutz told reporters Chrysler could do a better job by itself. Lutz argued against the Fiat merger talks, and when the negotiations collapsed he didn't bother to conceal his delight.

But worst of all, Bob Lutz contemptuously derided Iacocca time and again. "Could you believe what that doddering old fart just said in there?" he would whisper to Bidwell after Iacocca's staff meetings, even though he knew Bidwell would report straight back to Iacocca. And Iacocca heard other reports that, in one meeting, Lutz had referred to him as "the guinea who runs this place." Iacocca never asked Lutz whether this was true, but he was more than willing to believe it.*

Lutz also would sneer at Iacocca's preoccupation with his perks. "Every day, that man gets more and more like Henry Ford," he would say. "He thinks, 'It's my company, it's my airplane.' It's disgraceful."

Lutz's many loyalists inside Chrysler tried to persuade him to shut up. But Lutz seemed to have a death wish. Just as Iacocca, as the No. 2 man at Ford, had self-destructed with Henry Ford II, Lutz, as No. 2 at Chrysler, was destroying himself with Iacocca. History was repeating itself.

Iacocca didn't want to fire Lutz, but he desperately wanted to stop him from becoming chairman. To help build his case, Iacocca consulted with Lutz's former bosses at Ford, Don Petersen and Red Poling. Iacocca also enlisted help from Bidwell, who even in retirement remained his closest confidant, as well as a Chrysler consultant. It was all part of a campaign Iacocca dubbed ABL: Anybody But Lutz.

* * *

---

* Lutz did, on occasion, use ethnic epithets in his speech, say people who worked with and for him. He denies, however, referring to Iacocca in this way.

BEN BIDWELL DIDN'T LIKE Bob Lutz much more than Iacocca did. If Lutz ran Chrysler, Bidwell figured, the name might as well be changed to Lutz Motor Company. It had already been Iacocca Motor Company, in essence, for fourteen years. Now, despite his friendship with Iacocca, Bidwell believed the company needed a new style. He wanted a strong leader, but one more willing to delegate than either Iacocca or Lutz. Someone, in short, like Roger Penske.

Penske, who was nearing his fifty-fourth birthday in early 1991, was a former champion race-car driver. He had bought a Chevrolet dealership in Philadelphia after retiring from the sport in 1964 and parlayed it into a business empire with annual sales of $2.6 billion. His various car and truck dealerships sold 40,000 vehicles a year. His private holding company, Penske Corporation, formed a joint venture with General Electric's finance arm to lease a fleet of 56,000 trucks to the public.[1]

In 1988, Penske bought control of a company called Detroit Diesel, a maker of engines for heavy trucks and army tanks, from General Motors. Under GM, Detroit Diesel was a dog. Between 1982 and 1987, it had racked up $600 million in losses. By 1987, the company's share of the heavy-truck engine market had plunged to just 3.2 percent, down from 29 percent in 1979.[2]

Penske waded into this mess with both sticks and carrots. Six days after taking control of the company he fired 440 salaried employees, nearly a quarter of the white-collar work force. Next, he convened a mass meeting of the hourly workers and laid down the law: Clean up the clutter on the factory floor and get the girlie calendars off the walls. But he also told the workers he wanted to save their jobs.

When Detroit Diesel's plant manager asked for $500,000 to renovate the dingy cafeteria for hourly workers, Penske toured the cafeteria and told him to boost his budget. Two months and $800,000 later, Detroit Diesel opened a gleaming new lunchroom where managers and hourly workers ate side by side. Later, Penske installed a $5 million training and physical fitness center built jointly with the United Auto Workers union.[3]

All the while, Penske pushed hard to launch a new heavy-truck engine, the Series 60. It was the first heavy diesel with the kind of sophisticated electronic fuel system used to bolster mileage and cut pollution in cars. The Series 60 proved a runaway success. By the spring of 1991, the company's market share had roared back to 25 percent.[4]

Penske had accomplished this stunning turnaround with the same top management and hourly work force that couldn't shoot straight under GM.

Detroit Diesel alone would have made Penske attractive to Ben Bidwell and Chrysler's directors, but there was more. Penske Corporation owned Team Penske racing, the hottest outfit on America's Indy Car circuit. Selling cars, leasing trucks, and making diesel engines had made Roger Penske rich, but Team Penske made him famous—and provided a marvelous marketing tool. Team Penske's Indy cars sported the Detroit Diesel name. And Penske would haul his top Indy drivers, including Rick Mears and Emerson Fittipaldi, to the factories of big truck makers like Navistar Corporation, a major Detroit Diesel customer, to sign autographs and hobnob with workers.

Bidwell started to recruit Penske, at Iacocca's behest, in March and early April of 1991. Their talks quickly got serious enough that, on April 11, Bidwell met with five of Chrysler's outside directors to discuss Penske.

Penske, meanwhile, started delving into a review of Chrysler's operations. On May 16, he and Bidwell boarded a Chrysler jet and flew to Tulsa, where Chrysler's car-rental operations were headquartered, to take a firsthand look.

Then on Sunday, May 26, Rick Mears of Team Penske won the Indy 500 for the fourth time. Penske called Iacocca after the race, flush with the excitement of victory, and arranged to meet with him that week to seal his agreement to come to Chrysler. Penske called Bidwell as well, and told him he would bring Mears and Fittipaldi to speak at Chrysler's national dealer meeting that summer. It would be a spectacular extension of Penske's practice of wooing key customers at trackside.

Three days later, on the evening of Wednesday, May 29, Iacocca had his driver take him over to Penske's home in Bloomfield Hills. But as the two men began talking, a snag surfaced. In Penske's mind, Iacocca would retire soon after he came to Chrysler—if not immediately, then certainly within a few months. Iacocca, though, wanted to stay on for another couple of years, continuing to run Chrysler and evaluating Penske in the meantime.

There was no middle ground. Iacocca wasn't ready to walk away from the Four P's just yet. Penske, who was his own boss, wanted no part of being watched by Iacocca. When their meeting ended, he wanted no part of coming to Chrysler, either.

Bidwell, who was in New York, was furious at the news. The next day he flew back to Detroit, and marched in to see Iacocca.

"How could you do this?" Bidwell demanded. "You were supposed to leave. That was the deal. Everything was set."

Iacocca replied that, after he had left Ford in 1978, he jumped to Chrysler as second-in-command with no assurance of when, or even whether, he would succeed the company's chairman, John Riccardo. "Why couldn't Penske do the same?" he asked.

"There's one big difference," growled Bidwell, the only man who could talk to Iacocca like this. "Henry Ford had fired you. When you came to Chrysler you were unemployed. Roger Penske is employed! He runs his own company! That's the difference!"

Bidwell despaired that the ABL campaign was dead. He didn't know Fred Hubacker was about to go to work.

IN LATE 1991, Hubacker had heard scuttlebutt that the search for a new CEO wasn't going well. So in November he skipped through Chrysler's chain of command and, without telling his bosses, wrote a private letter to Iacocca.

He suggested that, as Iacocca scouted for potential successors, he consider Bob Eaton, the president of GM Europe. Hubacker quickly stated that he didn't mean to diminish any in-house candidates, such as Bob Lutz or Steve Miller. He also acknowledged that he and Eaton were close friends. But Eaton, Hubacker noted, had led GM Europe's ascendance as the most profitable car company in the world, despite the parent company's woeful performance in North America. His skills as a team builder, Hubacker added, were first-rate.

Iacocca was shocked Hubacker had signed the letter. Should Lutz or Miller find out, they surely would be angry, and might retaliate. "Here's a guy with balls!" Iacocca thought.

He didn't know the half of it. Hubacker had written his letter without checking with Eaton first. His only suggestion that Eaton consider coming to Chrysler had occurred that previous summer. The two men were sharing martinis and cigars at Hubacker's home in Birmingham, the Detroit suburb for Bloomfield Hills wannabes. Eaton confided that he was worried about GM, and Hubacker replied: "Lee won't be around forever. You ought to come over here." It was just a joke. But later, as Hubacker thought about what he had said, it seemed to make sense.

A few weeks after getting Hubacker's letter, Iacocca summoned him to his office. They talked for an hour. At the end Iacocca said, "I want to meet Bob. Can you arrange it?"

HUBACKER WAS THE PERFECT go-between. If Lee Iacocca had called Bob Eaton's office at GM Europe, alarm bells would have started ringing instantly back in Detroit. But Fred Hubacker was Eaton's best friend, and his calls didn't raise eyebrows.

So he called Eaton and asked him, "Would you be willing to meet with Lee Iacocca?" When Hubacker explained what he had done, Eaton nearly fell off his chair. If his bosses at GM discovered he was even considering jumping to Chrysler, he might as well jump out a window.

But Eaton, fifty-one years old and a twenty-nine-year-veteran of GM, had become disillusioned with his company. He also knew that, no matter what happened, he would never run GM. He was less than two years younger than his boss, Jack Smith, GM's vice chairman for international operations. Sooner or later, Smith was certain to succeed Bob Stempel. The best Eaton ever could hope for at GM was No. 2. Being No. 1 was better. He agreed to see Iacocca.

The Eatons were returning to Detroit in mid-December for the holidays, which provided the perfect cover for a meeting. Bob came a few days before Connie, and on December 17 he drove over to Iacocca's condominium in Bloomfield Hills. Iacocca ushered him into his study, poured him a drink, and the two men proceeded to talk for the next ninety minutes. The meeting went well, but when Eaton left he wasn't sure what, if anything, would happen next.

The next night, with Connie still in Europe, Eaton met the Hubackers for dinner at the Bloomfield Hills Country Club. "Well, Bob," Margie teased, "did you screw it up?"

BOB EATON DIDN'T KNOW how strong his position was. Iacocca had turned sixty-seven two months earlier, and Chrysler still didn't have a succession plan. That didn't bother Iacocca—he wanted to stay forever —but Chrysler's outside directors were feeling the heat from Wall Street and the press.

The directors had been jolted and embarrassed by the strident criticism of the goodies they had lavished on Iacocca—the huge stock grants, the fat raise, the purchase of his houses—in the wake of Greenwald's departure. The rest of the world regarded the board members as Lee Iacocca's lapdogs.

The directors, for their part, were stuck with an aging chairman who didn't want to step down, and couldn't easily be pushed because he was a living legend. They had no clear successor in sight because Iacocca and Lutz hated each other. The chances of an orderly transition seemed about as good as making a car that could run on water.

The outside directors recognized they were in a mess, and had to do something. In late 1991 they started meeting among themselves, without Iacocca, for the first time. And they started a campaign of delicate diplomacy.

One night, board member Joe Antonini, the chairman and CEO of K-Mart, met Iacocca for dinner at Ristorante di Modesta in suburban Detroit. Over wine and pasta they talked—man to man, chairman to chairman, paesano to paesano. Let the succession process flow, Antonini urged. Keep it moving, one step at a time, and bring the board the best candidate you can find. Don't risk being shut out of the process by dragging your feet.

It was a tactful but firm message. And to back it up, the directors told Iacocca they wanted to meet in small groups, without him, to sound out Chrysler's senior executives about succession. The board was taking control of the process.

The meetings with Lutz produced no surprises. He told the board members he had earned the chance to run Chrysler by completely overhauling product development and engineering. The first new cars to be developed under his direction hadn't yet hit the market, but they promised to be successful.

The other top internal candidate, Steve Miller, took an entirely different tack. The board's top priority, he said, should be keeping Bob Lutz at Chrysler. Lackluster cars had almost killed Chrysler in the late 1980s, Miller said, and Lutz had the product vision that the company badly needed. Miller said he was willing to be part of any Lutz/Miller arrangement, even if it meant him serving under Lutz as No. 2.

It was a statesmanlike approach that Miller could well afford to take. At age fifty he was ten years younger than Lutz and could wait for his turn at the top. But Miller didn't stop there. He gave each director a memo stating that Chrysler needed a less imperious style of leadership.

The memo warned, diplomatically but clearly, that even in retirement Iacocca would try to pull the strings at Chrysler, and that the board would have to stand up to him.

Miller's memo found its way to Iacocca, who was livid at the act of disloyalty.

Miller knew he was finished at Chrysler. On February 24, 1992, he resigned. The last member of Iacocca's comeback team from the early eighties was gone.

IACOCCA HAD LIKED EATON at their first meeting, deeming him confident without being cocky. In January, Iacocca spoke with Eaton several times by phone, always after Hubacker had run interference to make sure it was safe.

Eaton was returning to the United States in early February to visit Stanford University, where he was on the engineering school's advisory board. Stanford was just a hop down the coast from Seattle, home of Malcolm Stamper, chairman of the Chrysler board's nominating committee. The energetic Stamper, a Detroit native, had begun his career as a GM engineer before leaving after fourteen years to join Boeing. There he oversaw development of the 747, the world's first commercial jumbo jet, and rose to president and later vice chairman before retiring in 1990.

A Chrysler director since 1984, Stamper had taken to calling Iacocca "Bigfoot," in reference to the huge tracks of his presence, and Iacocca got a kick out of it. Stamper wanted Bigfoot to make a graceful exit, but wasn't sure it would happen.

On February 7, 1992, Eaton, Stamper, and Iacocca—who had been in Mexico—converged on the San Francisco Airport and met in a private room at the American Airlines Admirals Club. Chrysler was selling a private placement of preferred stock that day, and Iacocca kept getting called away to the phone. Stamper and Eaton talked for two hours, much of the time alone.

Stamper's first question was why Eaton would want to leave GM to come to Chrysler.

Eaton replied that he wanted to run his own show. He had gotten a taste of that being president of GM Europe, which was far removed from corporate headquarters in Detroit. Now he didn't want to be transferred back as "just another guy on the boulevard," referring to GM's West Grand Boulevard address.

Stamper liked the answer. He also liked it when Eaton flatly declared, "I'm no Lee Iacocca," and would never to try to imitate Iacocca's public persona. That would suit the directors just fine. Eaton also explained that companies should organize themselves around teams that focused on a single project or product, to produce faster decisions. Stamper was delighted. That's how he had developed the Boeing 747, and that was the structure Chrysler was adopting as well.

At one point, when Iacocca was in the room, Stamper turned to Eaton and asked, "Now, Bob, I assume you're interested in coming to Chrysler only if the job is CEO, right?"

"That's right," replied Eaton.

Stamper's message was clear. He didn't want a rerun of the Penske fiasco. Iacocca, sensing this, turned to Eaton and chimed in: "I don't want you unless you want to be CEO."

MEANWHILE, ANOTHER MAN was entering—or actually reentering—the Chrysler succession race: Jerry Greenwald. Iacocca's onetime heir apparent had angered his former mentor by leaving to lead the United Air Lines employee buyout in the spring of 1990. But later that year, in December, the Greenwalds threw a party at their place in Aspen, and Iacocca showed up. Midway through the evening Iacocca strode to the front of the room and called for Greenwald to join him.

"Hey, Jerry, you don't have to do what he says anymore," someone shouted, and everyone laughed. But Greenwald went anyway. Iacocca shook his hand and told the group what a great guy Jerry was. Greenwald knew then that he was forgiven.

Greenwald had collected his $9 million contingency fee after the UAL buyout had fallen through, so he was plenty rich. He also was plenty bored. He had tried to make a new career in investment banking in New York, but it didn't suit him.

So not long after his fifty-sixth birthday, in September 1991, Greenwald launched his campaign to return to Chrysler as chairman. He enlisted Bidwell to lobby director Robert Lanigan, retired chairman of Owens–Illinois, a packaging and container company based in Toledo. He phoned Joe Antonini and said: "I cannot be any more emphatic in telling you how much I want that job." In one way or another, Greenwald contacted almost every one of Chrysler's outside directors.

But Greenwald was bearing heavy baggage. No one blamed him for jumping after the big money in the UAL deal, but bringing him back certainly would spark resentment in the ranks. Bob Lutz, who had gotten wind of Greenwald's overtures, made it clear that if Greenwald returned, he would walk.

It was a classic stalemate. Iacocca vetoed Lutz. Lutz vetoed Greenwald. Bob Eaton, in contrast, had no enemies.

AFTER THE SAN FRANCISCO rendezvous Eaton went to visit GM headquarters in Detroit, and then flew down to Cincinnati. There he met with John Smale, the retired chairman of Procter & Gamble and an outside director of GM. Smale, at the behest of GM's other outside directors, was conducting detailed private interviews with twenty or so high-level executives about how to reverse the company's shocking decline.

Eaton candidly told Smale that GM wouldn't pull out of its tailspin without making major changes at the top. But he didn't mention his talks with Iacocca or Stamper. He didn't have a job offer and wasn't sure he'd get one, so it was far too early to say anything. Eaton then flew on to New York, where he climbed aboard the Concorde to return to Europe.

A few days later, Hubacker called again. Stamper had given Eaton rave reviews. Now Stamper wanted to bring the two other members of Chrysler's nominating committee—Lanigan and Jean de Grandpré, the retired chairman of Bell Canada—to meet him. They set the meeting for March 2 in Zurich.

On March 1, a Chrysler jet fetched Stamper in Seattle, and then flew to Florida to pick up Lanigan and de Grandpré before crossing the Atlantic. The directors landed the next morning, and by the time they arrived at the Dolder Grand Hotel they barely had time to wash up before meeting Eaton. The four men talked for more than three hours over lunch in a private room.

Eaton declared that the only job that could attract him was chairman and CEO. He also told the directors that, from what he knew, there was no need to clean out Chrysler's entire executive suite and bring in a whole new management team. In any event, Eaton added, that wasn't his style.

Then Eaton dropped a minibombshell. GM's outside directors, he said, were on the verge of making major management changes. He wasn't sure just how the changes would affect him. But he knew that, if he stayed with General Motors, he would soon be heading back to the United States in a senior position.

The directors didn't think he was bluffing. Eaton seemed far too straight for that. Now they knew that, if they wanted to hire Eaton, they would have to step lively.

That night, Eaton flew down to Geneva for dinner with Bob Stempel, who was in town for the city's annual auto show. Stamper, de Grandpré, and Lanigan stayed in Zurich and returned to the United States the next day—convinced that Eaton was their man.

CHRYSLER'S DIRECTORS DECIDED to hold a special board meeting in New York on the night of Saturday, March 14. It wasn't anyone's idea of a fun weekend, but it had to be done. They would bring Eaton over from Europe so the entire board could meet him, and decide then and there whether to hire him.

So far, the three months of secret meetings and phone calls between Eaton and Chrysler had remained a tight secret. It was too good to last. And it didn't.

Word that Eaton was in the running leaked to New York Times reporter Doron Levin, who put the question to Eaton. Eaton tried to sidestep the issue, but in the end, not wanting to lie, acknowledged he had talked to Iacocca. The Times ran with the story on Thursday, March 12.[5]

With the word out, Eaton called his boss, Jack Smith, in Detroit. Smith was gracious. "Hey, Bob, I see you made the papers," he laughed. Later, Eaton talked to Stempel, who wasn't so laid back. He said he wanted to know by Sunday night whether Eaton was staying or going. No extensions and no excuses.

On Friday Eaton flew to Hungary, for the opening of a GM factory there. Reporters shouted questions to him about Chrysler, but Eaton just smiled and turned away. Late that night he returned to Zurich, packed, and grabbed the first flight to London on Saturday morning. There he boarded the Concorde for New York under the code name "Mr. White."

In the morning he arrived at Kennedy Airport, where a Chrysler driver met him and whisked him off to the Waldorf. There he was met by the real Mr. White—Glenn White, Chrysler's vice president of personnel—who briefed him on the drill for the day. Then Eaton went to his room to wash up.

White, meanwhile, set about putting the necessary paperwork in place. He asked Hubacker to write a personal letter of recommendation for Eaton, vouching for his character, and to fax it to the Waldorf. Hubacker, in a tizzy, wrote that Eaton was a great person with a wonderful family, and a man of "unprincipled integrity." That prompted another phone call from White.

"Hey, Fred," he said, "I can't give this letter to the board." When Hubacker reread the letter, he realized his mistake. Sheepishly, he wrote another letter, this time calling Eaton a man of "uncompromised integrity."

Around 4 P.M. Eaton was summoned to meet the board. At first Iacocca was there, but then he left, and Eaton met with the outside directors alone. They questioned him about management philosophy, quality control, shareholder value, product development, and more. It was grueling for Eaton, whose day was now more than twenty hours long because of the time change. The meeting lasted through dinner, and about 8:30 P.M. one of the board members said: "You can go back to your room now, Bob. We might want to talk to you again later."

Eaton replied: "I might not be coherent later."

AFTER EATON LEFT, Iacocca came back. It was clear the directors wanted to bring Eaton in as vice chairman and announce immediately that he would succeed Iacocca as chairman and CEO nine months later, on January 1, 1993. It wasn't exactly what Iacocca had in mind.

He was willing to let Eaton become CEO, as he had told Eaton at the Admirals Club. But Iacocca wanted to stay as chairman himself for two years after retiring, until the end of 1994. He made a last-ditch effort to hang on, and the discussion turned testy. A couple of board members told Iacocca that, if he stayed as chairman, he would constantly interfere with Eaton. "Bullshit," Iacocca replied. The board stood its ground, though, and Iacocca had to settle for being chairman of the executive committee.

Around 10:30 P.M., the directors summoned Eaton back into the room. When he entered, everyone stood up and applauded, and Eaton felt a tingle in his bones. The job was his.

Eaton's longest day, however, wasn't quite finished. He placed a phone call to Connie, back in Zurich, to tell her the news. Then he called the Birmingham Country Club in suburban Detroit and asked to talk to Fred Hubacker. At the club, sitting a couple of tables away from Hubacker, was Bud Liebler, the PR chief. He didn't notice when Hubacker was summoned to the phone. Nor did he notice that as Fred was walking back into the dining room after talking to Eaton, he flashed his wife a thumbs-up sign. She let out a shriek.

Back in New York, with his phone calls finished, Eaton pored over his new employment contract himself. Lawyers didn't make house calls at midnight, not even in New York. The only change that Eaton requested was to strengthen the language that specified when he would take over as chairman and CEO. The Chrysler directors readily agreed.

At 2:30 A.M., Bob Eaton, who had begun the day in Zurich as a vice president of General Motors and ended it twenty-seven hours later in New York as chairman-to-be of Chrysler, fell asleep.

THE NEXT MORNING, Sunday, Iacocca called Greenwald to tell his former protégé what had happened. Greenwald was shattered. Both men knew Greenwald had been Iacocca's first choice. Now they had a brief but emotional conversation. "It was like two old soldiers, trying to be brave in defeat," Greenwald would later recall.[6]

Eaton, meanwhile, flew to Detroit, and went to Iacocca's Bloomfield Hills condo to meet Chrysler's senior executives. He talked to Lutz one-on-one, and asked him to stay on as president. Lutz was sixty years old, reeling from a bitter and expensive divorce and had nowhere else to go. He said he would stay.

After Eaton and Iacocca called Bob Stempel with the news, Eaton went to the Hubackers' for dinner with Fred and Margie. It was as joyful a reunion as the three friends had ever had. As they sat and talked, Bud Liebler dropped by.

Liebler had been asked to take Eaton a draft of the press release that Chrysler would issue the next morning. He was puzzled at being told that Eaton was at Hubacker's house. Maybe Hubacker had known last night at the country club what was going on, Liebler thought, and maybe there was a lot about Fred Hubacker he didn't know.

Around 9 P.M. Hubacker figured the reporters staking out Eaton's house would have given up, so he drove Eaton home. The Eatons had kept their house in Bloomfield Hills, figuring to return there when GM transferred Bob back from Europe. But Eaton, despite his new stature, didn't have a car at the house. He didn't have any food there either.

So at 7 A.M. the next day—Monday, March 16, 1992—Hubacker drove up in a Mitsubishi-made Dodge Stealth to take Bob Eaton to work. He brought along a banana to fortify Eaton before the press conference and the hullabaloo to follow.

JUST BECAUSE THE SUCCESSION issue was settled didn't mean Iacocca was ready to retire. He had broken into senior management at Ford nearly forty years earlier, and since then he hadn't had to buy his own gas, carry his own bags or—as his wife now knew—buy his own light bulbs. A small army of spear carriers had handled those jobs and a thousand others. He couldn't imagine all this being yanked away in nine months.

Iacocca was a walking dichotomy. He was a superb public speaker who suffered from severe stage fright until the moment he went on. He loved hobnobbing with the rich and famous, yet was a hero to the man in the street. He could get viciously angry with his critics, yet could disarmingly confess his own mistakes. He donated $14 million of profits from his autobiography to diabetes research, but he often was unabashedly greedy.

In his final months as chairman, Iacocca devoted himself to walking out with as much as he could get. He complained that, because he had been at Chrysler just fourteen years, his pension would be only half the amount of Roger Smith's and Don Petersen's. So he wanted a fatter pension. For staying as chairman of the executive committee, Iacocca wanted—besides salary and perks—generous stock options: 375,000 shares a year for two years. He also wanted continued access to the corporate jet.

Iacocca was emotional about the options and the jet. In his mind Chrysler wouldn't exist without him, so the stock he already had received wasn't enough. As for the corporate jet, Iacocca could hardly remember life without one. Because his celebrity status had helped save Chrysler, he figured, the company owed him security. Like a child afraid of the dark, Iacocca was paranoid about venturing out in public to fly commercial. "Everybody is pawing at you and pushing at you," he would complain to Stamper. "You don't know what it's like, Mal."

Iacocca was only half right. Stamper knew nothing about being a celebrity, but he knew plenty about flying commercial. His former company, Boeing, didn't have any executive jets, even though it was the biggest aircraft maker in the world. The Chrysler board had taken enough grief for buying Iacocca's two houses and for lavishing stock grants on him in the wake of Greenwald's departure. Nobody wanted to endure a similar outcry over airplanes or more stock.

The directors, in fact, were flabbergasted at Iacocca's attitude. Over the years Iacocca had received, either in grants or options, nearly 2.9 million shares of Chrysler stock. Within nine months after his retirement the stock would top $55 a share, a fivefold increase from 1991, making Iacocca's shares worth nearly $160 million. His salary and bonuses were just gravy.

As his negotiations with the directors dragged on, Iacocca started stamping his feet. He mused aloud about suing the board. And he threatened to disclose how much Chrysler had paid over the years to director Joseph Califano's law firm, Dewey Ballantine of New York. But it was all just bluster. Iacocca knew he would look absurd trying to tell a jury Chrysler had cheated him. And Chrysler's legal fees to Dewey Ballantine had been approved by Iacocca himself.[7]

In the end the directors added $95,000 a year to Iacocca's pension. Instead of additional stock grants or options, he got a two-year consulting contract at $500,000 a year. He was allowed to charter Chrysler planes for personal use at his own expense for a year after his retirement. Later, after lobbying the board, he got that extended to two years.[8]

The bickering and bitterness lasted for months. "They said they'd take care of me," Iacocca grumbled. "But they didn't take care of me to my satisfaction."[9] By the late summer of 1992, however, Iacocca was distracted. His final months at Chrysler's helm were a series of farewell fetes, a flag-waving finale to a legendary forty-six-year career.

In August, Chrysler rented the University of Nevada—Las Vegas arena, and flew in dealers for a good-bye party. Vic Damone, Wayne Newton, and Rich Little performed. Actor Ricardo Montalban mouthed one more time the words he had immortalized in Chrysler commercials: "Rich Coreeenthian leather."

Tip O'Neill, the retired speaker of the House, showed up to recite nostalgic recollections of how Iacocca had wooed Congress to get the 1980 government loan guarantee. And then Frank Sinatra strode on stage to sing "I Did It My Way," as a film recapping Iacocca's life and career played on a giant video screen behind him.

Next came the Paris Auto Show, where Iacocca hosted 400 guests at the Ritz under a custom-built tent that enclosed the hotel's largest garden. Chrysler commissioned the tent to match precisely the baby-blue color of its trademark.[10]

In October, the Society of Automotive Engineers feted Iacocca and his family at the Greenbrier resort in White Sulphur Springs, West Virginia. Dinner was served on the hotel's gold setting: bone china covered with 22-carat vermeil, and gold-rimmed crystal goblets. Chrysler ordered gold-lamé napkins for this affair. Guests got crystal paperweights in the shape of Chrysler's pentastar, and engraved with Iacocca's autograph.[11]

By early December, Iacocca was worn out from all the partying. Chrysler threw a reception for him in Washington but he didn't show up —because, the guests were told, he had the flu. In reality it was a bad hangover. The night before, the Chrysler board had thrown a black-tie party for him at 21 in New York, and Iacocca didn't get to bed until 2 A.M.

Nonetheless, later that month, just a couple weeks before passing the baton to Eaton, Iacocca and his wife hosted yet another dinner. It was at the Ritz-Carlton in Dearborn, Michigan—right across a freeway from Ford headquarters, where Henry Ford had fired him fourteen years before. There were just four guests: Bob and Connie Eaton, and Fred and Margie Hubacker. The three couples laughed about Hubacker's cloak-and-dagger dealings that had brought Eaton and Iacocca together. "You ought to build a goddam shrine in your house to Hubacker," Iacocca told Eaton, "because without him you wouldn't be here."

For the Hubackers it was a memorable evening that underscored the utter improbability of what Fred had done. He had been with Chrysler nearly twenty-nine years. But this was the first time that Margie had met the chairman of the board.

DURING 1992 CHRYSLER'S BOARD accomplished what had seemed impossible. It had found a successor to Iacocca without sparking civil war at the company. It had resisted Iacocca's insatiable demands without fomenting a public feud. And amazingly, amid all the backbiting, infighting, and plotting in the executive suite, Chrysler was starting to put some pretty good cars on the road. By December, the company was in the budding stages of a comeback. Its new midsized sedans launched three months earlier had buyers pouring into Chrysler showrooms. Iacocca was going out on a high note. But the succession saga had one act left.

In March 1993, just after Iacocca retired, Chrysler agreed to sell its automotive plastics operations to Textron, a Rhode Island-based conglomerate. And Fred Hubacker, out of the blue, got an offer to run that and other businesses for Textron as a group vice president.

Hubacker was just forty-seven years old, and his career at Chrysler looked brighter than ever. Thanks to his own efforts, after all, his best friend had become chairman of the company.

But that was just the trouble. Hardly anyone at Chrysler knew about Hubacker's role in bringing Eaton to the company, but word was spreading on the grapevine that Eaton and Hubacker were friends. "Better be nice to Fred now," Chrysler staffers would say to each other. To Hubacker, this meant any promotion or accomplishment would be attributed to his friendship with Eaton. That wouldn't be good for either man. The dilemma was the latest ironic twist in this most remarkable of friendships.

For advice, Hubacker turned to his best friend, Bob Eaton. Eaton was struck by the eerie parallels to the decision he himself had faced a year earlier. A compelling job offer had dropped right into Fred's lap, and now Fred had to decide whether to leave the company where he had spent his entire career.

Eaton told Hubacker he would be sorry to see him leave Chrysler. But he acknowledged that working in the same company might prove awkward for both of them. The bottom line, Eaton said, was this: "It is one hell of an opportunity, Fred. They don't come along often." On May 1, Hubacker resigned.

"Two years ago, you couldn't get a million to one odds that I would be at Chrysler and Fred would be somewhere else," Eaton would say later. "But it happened. It's funny, sometimes, how life works out." [12]

LEE IACOCCA DIDN'T waste any time cashing in on Chrysler's second comeback. In August 1993 he declared his intention to sell 1.2 million Chrysler shares—worth just $12 million two years earlier—for a cool $53.3 million. Less than a month later, on September 2, he resigned from Chrysler's board. The move gave him greater leeway to sell more Chrysler stock, thus locking in his wealth. Besides, Iacocca didn't like being part of something when he wasn't in charge.

The ex-emperor was learning that life without a court could be fun, and even funny. He moved to Palm Desert, California, where one day, like a latter-day Rip Van Winkle, he drove into a self-service gas station, something that didn't exist when he had last bought his own gas in the early 1960s.

"Fill her up, buddy," Iacocca said, after he pulled his car to a stop. The attendant gave Iacocca an unknowing look and replied, "Pump it yourself, Mac."

CHAPTER 12

GM: THE APRIL COUP

Detroit in winter isn't the destination of choice for high-powered New York lawyers with vacation homes in Palm Beach. But now, on a snowy January 15, 1992, Ira Millstein found himself headed there for his second visit in less than two weeks. The first had occurred ten days earlier, when the General Motors board of directors met in Detroit. Millstein, who served as legal counsel to the independent directors, had attended, as usual. One man who did not attend, however, was Board Chairman Bob Stempel. He was in Japan, accompanying President Bush on a trade mission. The most memorable moment occurred when Bush vomited into the lap of Japan's Prime Minister during a state dinner, and had to be hauled off to a hospital. As Stempel had feared from the start, the trip proved pointless.

GM's independent directors, though, had found Stempel's absence convenient. They used the company's monthly board meeting to talk privately among themselves, without the chairman or any other member of management present. They had been doing this, off and on, since the waning months of Roger Smith's regime in the spring of 1990, but the latest discussion had a particularly sharp focus. GM had lost a mind-numbing $12.5 billion in 1991 in its North American automotive business.[1] In terms of straight cash flow, as opposed to earnings, GM was bleeding at the rate of more than $1 billion per quarter—$462,000 every hour of every day. The company's share of U.S. car sales had plunged to just over 35 percent from nearly 45 percent just seven years earlier, and it was still sliding.

After years of complacence followed by an aimless, uncoordinated restlessness, the independent directors realized the truth: GM was dying. Someone had to act. During their private powwow, GM's directors finally had made a decision. Now it was Millstein's chore to inform Stempel.

When Millstein had called Stempel's office to arrange the meeting, the chairman's secretary had tried to put him off, citing her boss's busy schedule. Millstein then told her he was calling at the request of the board, and begged her to consult with Stempel. After she did, a meeting was set up posthaste, and Millstein promptly made arrangements to fly out from New York. When he landed at Detroit Metropolitan Airport, Millstein didn't even have to ride into town. Stempel and Harry Pearce, GM's vice president and general counsel, were waiting for him in GM's private terminal. The three men adjourned to a conference room to talk.

Millstein began explaining to Stempel that the independent directors were worried. Ten days earlier, he added, on the night before the January board meeting, they decided they needed to know a lot more about what was going on at GM. So they had asked John Smale, the retired chairman of Procter & Gamble and a GM director since 1982, to launch a fact-finding mission. Smale would ask for detailed data about GM's sales, costs, and quality levels compared with competitors. He also wanted to meet, alone, with a dozen or two of the top GM officers under Stempel, to ask their candid assessment of the company's condition.

Smale wasn't trying to undermine Stempel, Millstein added. But directors of troubled companies—and GM certainly qualified—had a clear legal obligation to step up their oversight, and he had advised GM's board members to do just that. Millstein showed Stempel the board's resolution asking Smale to report back on his findings, and also a memo for Stempel to circulate among GM's senior officers, asking their cooperation.

Stempel listened attentively and politely, and then started asking questions. He wanted Millstein's personal opinion of what the independent directors were "really seeking."

"Really seeking?" Millstein was stunned at the question. Concealing his chagrin, he tried delivering his message again.

The directors, he said, wanted a radical shakeup at General Motors. The company had to change, fundamentally and immediately. The directors were worried, Millstein said, that the company didn't have the right people in the right jobs. He didn't add the obvious: that Stempel's management team was essentially the same group of men who had led GM from disaster to disaster in the late 1980s.

Stempel didn't argue or protest. After ninety minutes he said a cordial thank-you. The lawyer then hopped back on the GM jet, returned to New York, and started calling the directors to report Stempel's strangely placid reaction. "What is Bob going to do?" Smale asked. Millstein replied: "I don't know."

IT WASN'T THE FIRST time the GM board didn't know what to expect from Bob Stempel. The first time occurred back in April of 1990, when the board elected him to succeed Roger Smith as chairman. Stempel had played the loyal lieutenant to Smith, causing several directors to harbor reservations about him. But they were hoping that, after Stempel officially took over on August 1, 1990, he would repudiate Smith's legacy and bloom as his own man.

At first, Stempel seemed to do just that. Early on, he scrapped the rigid seating chart at management committee meetings—long a symbol of GM's frozen upper-level hierarchy. He moved the meetings to a round table in his office side room, and let everyone choose his own seat. In September, Stempel negotiated a new UAW contract that pledged $3.35 billion to provide steady incomes for hourly workers laid off as GM retrenched. In return, he extracted commitments from union leaders to cooperate in making GM's factories more efficient.

In November, Stempel bit the bullet that Roger Smith had ducked. He ordered a $2.1 billion write-off, the largest in GM's history, to cover the costs of closing seven of the auto giant's thirty-eight domestic assembly plants, and a handful of components factories, too. GM was tailoring its shoes to fit a smaller pair of feet, just as Ford had done with remarkable success a decade earlier. The massive write-off "covers all foreseeable circumstances," declared Bob O'Connell, the finance chief.

In February 1991, with the Persian Gulf War underway and auto sales tilting into their worst slump since 1982, Stempel bit down harder. He announced a 47 percent cut in GM's common stock dividend. Ford and Chrysler later would make similar moves to conserve cash, but Stempel had acted first. He also slashed executive bonuses and outlined plans to cut 15,000 people from GM's salaried staff by 1993. At last, it seemed, GM had a leader strong enough to administer the bitter medicine necessary to reverse its organizational sclerosis.

But Bob the Bold had turned out to be a fleeting persona. As 1991 wore on and GM dived deeper into the red, Stempel's response was to counsel patience. The company was in fundamentally good shape, he told the board, and what it mainly needed was an end to the recession. It became increasingly clear that GM's losses were mounting faster than Stempel's appetite for dealing with them.

While the seating charts at management committee meetings changed, the meetings themselves remained as vacuous as before. They bogged down in the minutiae contained in countless gray-covered reports —items such as whether the New Departure Hyatt division, GM's internal maker of ball bearings, should change its benefits plan. The real issue should have been whether GM should even *have* its own ball-bearing division, given that the division was too inefficient to compete against Japanese rivals.

That wasn't the only fundamental issue that never got addressed. GM's North American operations had twenty-seven different departments that purchased parts, materials, and supplies. The system was grossly inefficient, and suppliers played it for profit. Cadillac, for instance, paid $1.12 each for a plastic part that covered the shock absorbers on cars. The purchasing agents at the division that built Buicks, however, had gotten a similar part for just 48 cents apiece. Chrysler's components subsidiary at one point was selling the same electronic part to three different GM divisions, at three different prices.

Mindless duplication permeated GM's product development and manufacturing. GM, for example, had four different platforms for its compact sedans—sold as Saturn, the Chevrolet Cavalier, the Pontiac Grand Am, and the Chevrolet Corsica. Customers considered these cars interchangeable. But GM had armies of engineers, purchasing agents, and accountants devoted to nurturing the trivial distinctions in size and weight among them. GM executives had discussed consolidating these overlapping platforms since Stempel was named president in 1987. They had made little progress. What was duplication to one man was a job to another. Likewise, Stempel and President Lloyd Reuss had done little to reckon with GM's enormous disadvantage in productivity. GM staffers would routinely confront Reuss with numbers that showed Ford with a 25 percent to 30 percent advantage in labor costs per vehicle.

Reuss and his underlings would ignore the data or declare that it was wrong.

BOB STEMPEL HAD SPENT decades in the GM system. He was loath to launch an all-out attack on the stultifying status quo, because it would have required another wrenching overhaul of GM's entire North American organization. Stempel didn't want this. He believed, with good reason, that Roger Smith's sweeping 1984 corporate reorganization had been a first-class fiasco. "I don't like to shoot first and aim later," he would say. Bob Stempel wasn't about to lob a hand grenade into the middle of his organization, as his predecessor had done. No way.

Instead, Stempel wanted to solve GM's problems step-by-step over a period of years: evolution, not revolution. GM's success in Europe, he believed, was proof positive that the gradual approach could work. After losing more than $2 billion between 1980 and 1986, GM Europe had made a remarkable about-face—earning an average $1.8 billion a year over the next four years. In Stempel's mind, this turnaround had begun between 1980 and 1982, when he himself had run Opel.

Others at GM knew better: Europe's financial turnaround didn't start until much later. They also realized that GM's European experience couldn't justify a go-slow approach in the face of North America's collapse. GM could afford to carry European losses for years, because Europe was a small part of the company's total business. North America, though, was GM's heart. The huge losses there couldn't be sustained. And in North America, unlike Europe, GM faced the full fury of Japan's onslaught.

But Stempel wouldn't budge. He had a deep belief in continuity and loyalty. As the months of his chairmanship unfolded, it was increasingly clear that he was especially loyal to one man: Lloyd Reuss.

Reuss's ties to Stempel, three years his senior, ran broad and deep. The two men belonged to the same fraternity of engineers—"car guys." When Stempel was chief engineer at Chevrolet in the mid-1970s, Reuss, then chief engineer at Buick, would call him up for advice on technical problems. Reuss and Stempel saw each other as trustworthy colleagues in an organization where the insufferably arrogant bean counters had long lorded it over the car guys.

Stempel and Reuss, as chairman and president, pushed the finance men to the back benches. "Bob and Lloyd," said one GM consultant

who worked with both men, "were the revenge of the operating guys."
Reuss, indeed, had a way of managing his billion-dollar budgets that
made the bean counters grind their teeth. Say a modest restyling of a
vehicle was projected to cost $600 million. The engineers in charge
would estimate the cost to be, say, $650 million. If they later did the job
for $600 million, or perhaps a little more, they would look like heroes.
The key was inflating your cost estimates from the start.

Reuss knew the game because he had played it dozens of times himself
on his way up the corporate ladder. So he approved product programs
with wild abandon, confident that he could beat tens of millions of
dollars, and even more, out of each project's estimated cost.

Trouble was, the savings often didn't materialize. Instead, by the end
of each budget year, Reuss and his underlings would have to scramble to
reconcile their overambitious product spending plans to GM's diminish-
ing supply of cash. New models that had soaked up money and engineering talent suddenly would get shelved—their designs doomed to get
staler and staler, just as had happened with the GM-10 cars.

Reuss wasn't alone. From vice presidents to plant managers, GM executives lived in a financial fantasy land. Their primary mission was to hit
a target called OP, or operating profit. But operating profit was a slippery
number. If a plant manager's OP looked bad, he, or occasionally she,
could simply charge off expenses to "central office," or to another division.

In 1990 and 1991, a favorite gambit was to push the cost of paying
laid-off UAW workers into the ether of central office, thus dressing up
the OP at the plants. GM thus found itself in the absurd position of
having plenty of "profitable" factories even though the corporation as a
whole was losing billions.

The biggest charade of all, though, was the strategy of supporting
market share with sales to rental car fleets. In the late 1980s, each of the
Big Three had bought hefty stakes in the major rental-car companies:
Ford invested in Hertz, GM invested in Avis and purchased majority
control of National Car Rental, and Chrysler acquired Thrifty, Dollar,
and Snappy. At first, the idea was to get control of some important
customers by giving them much-needed infusions of capital. But the
strategy turned into a trap. When sales to real people slumped in 1990,
Detroit began pouring more and more cars into the rental fleets. Instead
of shipping new vehicles to the rental fleets once or twice a year, the Big
Three started sending shipments three or four times a year. To sweeten
the deal for the rental car companies, the automakers agreed to re-

purchase the cars at a guaranteed price. Then they would auction the repurchased cars to dealers for resale as used cars, often with as little as 6,000 or 7,000 miles on them.

Each of the Big Three played this game, but no one played it like Reuss. GM had far more excess production capacity than anyone, and thus far more cars to dump into the rental fleets. All told, GM sold more than 800,000 cars to rental fleets in 1991—roughly a quarter of its total car sales.[2] When the deep discounts, the rebates, and the losses on resale of repurchased rent-a-cars were factored together, GM often wound up losing more than $1,000 on every rental car it sold.

Reuss, however, saw fleet sales as a way to keep the factories running. Never mind that the subsidies were a disaster for profits and cash flow. GM executives, especially operating guys like Reuss, didn't generally worry about cash flow, because the company had never needed to conserve cash. Besides, Reuss was confident that the new cars he was preparing to launch in late 1991 and early 1992 would vault GM back to 40 percent market share, and solve the cash flow problem at the same time. On this point, Reuss was adamant.

Some forecasters inside GM projected that the company would have only a 34 percent market share by 1994. These numbers bolstered the negativists who argued for permanently closing more plants. But by the time Reuss's management reviews were completed, the company's official internal forecast was boosted to nearly 37 percent.

It didn't take long in this atmosphere until numbers meant nothing. General Motors, under Alfred P. Sloan, had invented modern corporate financial control. Spending and investment were based on the discipline of realistic, conservative sales forecasts. But by the middle of 1991, GM couldn't even tell its outside directors how much money it was making or losing (losing, in reality) on individual car lines. The control system was shattered.

Reuss did have a vision for reforming GM, and he expressed it in a diagram. It was a pyramid filled with jibberish and jargon under the headings Vision, Mission, Values, Objective, Strategies, Initiatives, and Goals. The Strategies section alone had seven subsections titled Quality, People, Cost, Fast, Great, Marketing, and Materials Management. And under these seven subsections there were twenty-six different strategies. It was more than anyone could keep track of or focus on—much less actually implement—even if there were "only" nine "capital S Strategies," as Reuss called them.

The rest of GM's management committee, and most other senior executives, despaired of Reuss. They deemed Stempel's loyalty to him the auto industry's version of fatal attraction. They couldn't understand how Stempel—or GM's board—could stand by while Reuss led GM's U.S. vehicle operations to pretax losses totaling nearly $22 billion in 1990 and 1991.³ Something had to give. And as 1991 drew to a close, it did.

On November 7, 1991, Standard & Poor's Corporation—the 500-pound gorilla of the credit-rating industry—announced it was considering snatching away the top-drawer, A-1 rating for commercial paper issued by General Motors Acceptance Corporation. The significance of the warning was largely lost on the general public.⁴ But inside GM, it set off alarm bells.

Commercial paper is a short-term corporate IOU. GMAC, the financing arm of General Motors, had long been able to sell billions in commercial paper at rock-bottom interest rates, thus raising cheap capital. GMAC then lent out this money at much higher rates to GM dealers and to people who bought GM cars. It was a banker's version of buy-low, sell-high, and in 1991 it had allowed GMAC to contribute more than $1 billion to GM's suffering bottom line.

Now S&P was threatening to eviscerate this crucial operation. The big money-market funds that bought large amounts of commercial paper would be reluctant to lend to a second-rate credit risk. And if other debt-rating agencies followed S&P's lead, money-market funds would be obligated by federal regulation to dump most of their GMAC paper.

GM's financial foundations, once solid as the Pyramids, were wobbling dangerously. Stempel had presented the board with a plan to shore up the foundations by selling billions of dollars of new common and preferred stock—the latter being securities that carried fixed dividends and were little different, in essence, from a loan. But S&P's action threatened to derail the stock offerings. So on December 9, when GM's board convened at the EDS offices in suburban Washington for its regular monthly meeting, many directors were expecting Stempel to present a plan for addressing the challenge.

But the board's hopes that Stempel would put forth a crisis plan were quickly deflated. The more the chairman talked, the less he seemed to say. The best course for now, he explained, was to get the product lineup ready to take advantage of the eventual economic upturn. In the meantime, the board would do best to be patient.

Some board members, out of frustration, tried to rally support for more radical ideas. They even broached the possible sale of EDS. That was quickly ruled out. In the end, GM's directors did nothing.

Wall Street's response was harsh. As it became clear that GM wouldn't make the anticipated cost-cutting announcement, analysts and investors concluded GM really had no clue how to save itself. That afternoon, GM's stock plunged to a new four-year low—down by 1⅜ to 27⅝. The sell-off wiped out $825 million in shareholder value.

FINALLY, WALL STREET had Bob Stempel's attention. The plunge in GM's common stock came as the company was preparing to sell $1.5 billion of new preference shares. Now the Street was signaling that investors might simply refuse to buy them, denying GM a badly needed financial transfusion. Stempel had to act, and quickly.

And so at 2 P.M. on December 18, 1991, a haggard-looking Stempel strode before a phalanx of cameras in the fifth-floor press room at GM headquarters. The first thing he did was extend a vote of confidence to Lloyd Reuss. Rumors that Reuss might be ousted were starting to pop up in the press, but Stempel said, "One thing I want to emphasize as I start: Contrary to many published reports, the management committee and the roles of its members remain unchanged."

Then Stempel outlined the things that would change, and they were enormous. GM would close twenty-one more North American factories within three years. Some 74,000 jobs would vanish from the company by 1995. Of that total, 24,000 jobs would be eliminated in 1992 alone. GM would cut capital spending. It would sell several large nonautomotive operations, such as its railway locomotive business. By 1995, Stempel said, GM's domestic auto operations would employ roughly 321,000 people—half the total employed in 1985.

"GM," Stempel intoned, "will become a much different corporation." It was a stunning declaration of retreat.

Stempel didn't name the doomed factories, saying he would need another couple of months to decide. It would also take that long, he added, to calculate the size of the write-off. But he did say that the hit list would include one of the two big assembly plants building the large, rear-drive Chevrolet Caprice.

It had been evident for months that GM didn't need two plants to build the Caprice and its hulking sister cars, the Buick Roadmaster and Oldsmobile Custom Cruiser. In the string of flops conceived under

Reuss's regime, the redesigned 1991 Caprice was one of the most spectacular. The car's predecessor—a big, boxy, V-8 sedan designed in the
1970s—had been a sturdy favorite of cab drivers and cops. But the new
one was a flawed attempt at aerodynamic styling that looked like the
mutant offspring of a jelly bean and an armored car. The car's design
had flopped in consumer tests before its launch. Reuss had ignored the
warnings. Now, Stempel was admitting that GM's management had
miscalculated. But the penalty would be paid by workers at one of the
two Caprice plants—the Willow Run factory near Detroit or GM's assembly plant in Arlington, Texas.

Setting up a fight-to-the-death between Arlington and Willow Run
proved to be a blunder of the first order. Within hours of the Stempel's
press conference, workers at both plants became stars in a real-life television news drama about America's industrial decline.

The next day, December 19, Stempel flew to Washington to brief
Bush administration officials on GM's plans. Back in Detroit, Stempel's
underlings gathered in the headquarters executive dining room for the
traditional officers' Christmas reception. With Stempel in Washington,
Reuss played host. He read a telegram from Stempel, apologizing for
missing the gathering, and wishing everyone and their families health
and happiness for the holidays. Then Reuss, never a man to let his hair
down, gave his underlings a rare glimpse of his feelings.

The difference between success and failure, he said, comes down to
finding strength within yourself. The unthinkable alternative is to decide
that the challenges at hand are too difficult, and to accept failure. In
these trying times, Reuss went on, every GM officer had to look within
himself. Christmas was a sign that they should have faith—faith that
everyone in the room would find the strength to succeed.

As the reception wound down one of the younger officers, himself a
Reuss skeptic, pulled Reuss aside and, in a very un-GM gesture, hugged
him. "It must really be rough," the young man said to the president of
GM.

"You don't know how rough," Reuss replied.

ON THE SURFACE, Bob Stempel's December 18 announcement was just
the sort of bold, tough move that the GM board wanted. In truth, the
directors were far from pleased. The whole sequence of events that led
up to Stempel's announcement was baffling.

At the December board meeting, Stempel had shown little inclination to move. Two days later, he rushed out a statement to say that big cutbacks were coming—in the process forcing the delay of the previously scheduled sale of preference stock. Then, he announced the cutbacks, only to say that he would put off disclosing specifics until February. Worse, from the directors' standpoint, Stempel had waited until the night before the December 18 press conference to inform them of the outlines of his plan. It was typical of how Bob Stempel dealt with his board. He took copious notes during board meetings, but he wouldn't follow up with written replies to questions that directors raised. In fact, he didn't even answer their letters. GM's directors had finally had enough.

In 1991, GM's independent board members fell roughly into four camps: business leaders, "Washington types," academics, and a lone religious leader. They were men and women of sober judgment who, by and large, knew little about the car business.

The most prominent and respected business leader was John G. Smale. At age sixty-three, the Canadian-born Smale could look back on a career that was legendary in American marketing circles.

He first rose to prominence at Procter & Gamble in the mid-1950s, when he was brand manager for the company's Crest toothpaste. Crest was the first fluoride toothpaste, but sales were languishing because Americans didn't know fluoride from fibrosis. So Smale, using P&G's extensive clinical tests of Crest, lobbied the American Dental Association to endorse the company's product. When the ADA said yes, Smale printed the endorsement on every tube of Crest. And he hammered the point home in slice-of-life television commercials, in which the punch line invariably was, "Look, Ma, no cavities." Crest soon became America's best-selling toothpaste, and John Smale's career took off as well.

A direct, no-nonsense man, Smale thrived in P&G's Calvinist culture, which banned short-sleeved shirts, drinking at lunch, and leaving any scrap of paper on one's desk overnight. P&G's products included some of the best-known brands in America—Ivory soap, Tide detergent, Comet cleanser, and Charmin toilet paper. But the company was so publicity-shy that its corporate name never appeared in any advertising. This suited Smale as well; he would sooner brush with Colgate than grant an interview or give a speech. "I'm basically a dull guy," he once said, which was as close to a boast as he could muster.

In January 1981, when Smale became chief executive officer, P&G was suffering from the onset of corporate sclerosis. Smaller, faster competitors were outflanking P&G with such innovations as liquid soap, gel toothpaste, and herbal shampoos. But Smale sped the pace of product development by shortening P&G's exhaustive test marketing procedures. And he made major acquisitions, something P&G had long shunned, to push the company into the fast-growing business of over-the-counter pharmaceuticals. By the time Smale retired as chairman and CEO in January 1990, P&G was larger and more profitable than at any time in its history.

Smale kept a low profile on GM's board, never publicly breaking ranks. But by 1988, he had begun making waves with his increasingly persistent and skeptical questioning of Roger Smith's policies. He would pointedly ask during board meetings why GM was falling so far behind Ford in quality and profitability. At one point, convinced that Smith was hiding information from the board, Smale quietly sounded out some of his board colleagues about the possibility of ousting Smith. He got nowhere. And he stayed quiet.

Like Smale, GM's other directors also were vigorous leaders in their chosen fields. But together, in GM's boardroom, Smale and the other directors had behaved like bewildered sheep as GM declined during the 1980s. By late 1991, however, Smith had retired, and the directors had finally concluded that Bob Stempel wasn't going to lead a bold move for change, after all. Every director knew the stakes at GM were enormous: jobs, families, communities, and a goodly portion of the industrial might of the nation. As the magnitude of GM's troubles became clear, the directors also began to fear being tarnished with complicity in history's largest corporate crack-up.

Amazingly, though, these high-powered members of America's elite didn't know what to do next. They had never taken an active role in company affairs. Now, they saw they had to, and fast. Common sense told them this. So did their lawyer, Ira Millstein.

IRA MILLSTEIN WAS a senior partner in the prestigious New York firm of Weil, Gotshal & Manges—located, by coincidence, in the General Motors Building on Fifth Avenue at 59th Street in New York. In addition to his busy legal practice, Millstein had begun to establish credentials as a corporate-governance guru in a 1981 book, *The Limits of Corporate Power*.

Millstein had begun working regularly with GM's board in 1985, handling a relatively mundane matter. GM was in the process of issuing a new class of common stock in connection with its $5 billion purchase of Hughes Aircraft. The new common shares, called GMH, represented a dividend interest in the earnings of the GM subsidiary that included Hughes. The GMH shares thus were similar to the GME shares that General Motors had issued to finance the purchase of EDS in 1984.

These so-called alphabet stocks essentially allowed Roger Smith to generate new money from investors to finance acquisitions. But GM directors worried that holders of GM's regular common stock —nicknamed "GM Classic" on Wall Street—could attack the company for slighting them in favor of the new shareholders. GM's general counsel at the time, Elmer Johnson, told the board it needed independent advice. And at his suggestion, the board hired Millstein.

Millstein's introduction to the GM board came just as the company's fortunes were teetering. In the aftermath of the December 1, 1986, Perot buyout, the directors knew they were likely to face lawsuits from angry shareholders. Again at Johnson's suggestion, they turned to Millstein. In the months of litigation that did, indeed, follow the Perot fiasco, Millstein developed close relationships with board members. He also became fast friends with Johnson's protégé and successor as GM's general counsel, Harry J. Pearce.

Powerful people found it easy to like Ira Millstein. Though he celebrated his sixtieth birthday in 1987, his close-cropped white hair, raspy-voiced New York accent, and exuberant personality gave him an oddly boyish demeanor. While forceful, and even passionate, in pressing his views, he could counsel business bigwigs on the intricacies of corporate law without seeming to lecture them.

During the late 1980s, Millstein delved deeply into the rarefied field of corporate governance.[5] He helped establish the Institutional Investor Project at Columbia University, a think tank for the role of big pension funds in corporate affairs. He wrote books and academic papers, and cultivated a network of activist pension fund managers, including Dale Hanson, the head of the $41 billion California Public Employee Retirement System, or Calpers. Big pension funds such as Calpers were emerging as the primary owners of corporate America. They bought massive blocks of stock in major companies, and tended to hold their stocks for years rather than flip them for quick profits. Best of all, in the view of Fortune 500 executives, the big institutions were reliably passive supporters of management. Millstein, however, exhorted them to assume a new role.

Big funds, Millstein said, were silly to nitpick corporate chiefs over such issues as antitakeover defenses and proxy voting rules. If chronic underperformance caused a company's stock to sag, he said, big investors should go after the board of directors. Directors, after all, are supposed to represent shareholders.

The most celebrated 1980s solution to corporate lethargy, of course, was the hostile takeover. Poor performance would depress the price of a company's stock, making it attractive to corporate raiders. They would buy out existing holders and recoup their investment by cutting costs, breaking up the company, and selling it in pieces.

Millstein, however, argued that this was too destructive. The lives and livelihoods of thousands of people were disrupted as companies were bought, sold, divided, and bought again. And the system gave rise to spectacular insider-trading scandals, sending Dennis Levine, Ivan Boesky, and later the biggest kingpin of them all, Michael Milken, to jail. The better solution, Millstein believed, was for big institutional shareholders to act like "responsible owners," and put the heat on the boards of underperforming companies. Corporate directors, in turn, had to become bolder. Millstein even declared that independent directors shouldn't hesitate to dismiss a chief executive who didn't perform.[6]

All of this was incomprehensible avant-gardism to GM's officers. GM's board hadn't dumped a chief executive officer since Billy Durant, the financial swashbuckler who founded GM, was ousted by the DuPonts and the Morgan Bank in 1920. True, GM had once separated the board chairman's duties from those of the chief executive officer. But since the ascension of Frederic Donner in 1958, the two posts had been combined. It seemed more likely that Elvis would be found alive than that GM's board would stage a revolt against management.

But behind the scenes, members of GM's board were listening to Ira Millstein's earnest voice. Millstein was coming at GM's directors from two sides. As their lawyer, he advised them to act more independently. At the same time, in his role as corporate governance activist, Millstein was telling big GM shareholders like Calpers' Hanson who sought his advice to put pressure on boards from outside. Millstein sometimes took impish delight in being a protagonist in what he saw as a good cause. By December 1991, Millstein's carefully orchestrated advocacy had convinced a core group of GM directors that something had to be done.

Among the most eager for action was Tom Wyman, the former chairman of CBS. For years he had been privately disgusted with, and ashamed of, the performance of the GM board and the company alike. Now Wyman was determined to act. As GM's disastrous December of 1991 unfolded, Wyman joined Millstein in pressing John Smale to undertake a special fact-finding mission for the GM board. Smale was the best candidate for the task because he had the stature and, thanks to his retirement, the time.

Smale was anything but eager. He declared that he wouldn't volunteer for the job. "I'll have to be drafted three times before I do it," Smale said. "And if there's a single outside director against this, I won't do it." In the days between Christmas and New Year's, Wyman and Millstein worked the phones, pushing GM's other directors toward the unanimity Smale demanded.

GM's DIRECTORS hold most of their monthly meetings in New York, in the board room on the 25th floor of the GM building. It's a reverential setting; the meeting table is as big as a small pond, the name of each director is engraved on a brass plaque affixed to his or her chair, and the stony faces of former GM chairmen stare down from the heavy-toned oil paintings on the wall. But the first board meeting of 1992 was scheduled to begin in Detroit on Sunday night, January 5. There would be the customary dinner, followed on Monday by a tour of the Detroit Auto Show. In other words, business as usual.

Instead, Sunday became a turning point.

Most of the directors were still at home that Sunday morning when, at 9 A.M., Millstein assembled seven or eight of them on the telephone for a conference call. It was Wyman's idea, so he spoke first. He laid out his concern that the board didn't have a grip on what was happening at GM, and proposed that Smale be formally deputized as fact finder for the outside directors. Then he asked Millstein for his advice.

By now Millstein had delivered the same spiel so often that he dubbed it his "red flag speech." Directors of troubled companies have "heightened duties of oversight," the lawyer explained. GM's directors already had peppered management with letters, phone calls, and questions. But now they could and should do more—including meeting alone to assess management's performance candidly, and asking Smale to take the role that Wyman had suggested. Smale chimed in to lay out his conditions,

and the group agreed to convene a private meeting of all the outside
directors that night.

Stempel had made other plans for his directors that evening. Although
he was in Japan with President Bush, he had arranged for the board to
get after-dinner presentations from Reuss; finance chief Bob O'Connell;
Jack Smith, the vice chairman for international operations; and Bob
Schultz, the head of GM's technology businesses. As scheduled, the
directors gathered in a private dining room at the Ritz-Carlton hotel in
Dearborn. But when dinner was done, Stempel's emissaries were asked
to cut their presentations short. At around 8:30, Reuss, O'Connell, and
the other executives left the room, along with former chairman Roger
Smith, who still sat on the board. The doors closed with Millstein still
inside.

A couple of hours later, the group had hashed out a resolution. It
read:

> John Smale is designated by the independent directors, acting unani-
> mously, to be their representative, to act on their behalf with management,
> and to develop such information as may be necessary and desirable to
> further enable these directors to fulfill their responsibilities diligently and
> prudently during this period of difficulty for the corporation. . . . Mr.
> Smale is requested to report to the outside directors as he deems desirable.

Smale insisted on adding: "Mr. Smale will also report on his activities
to the Chairman of the Board."

Ten days later, on January 15, with Smale heading off on a previously
planned vacation, Millstein arrived in the GM terminal at Detroit Metropolitan Airport to brief Stempel on what had transpired.

ON FEBRUARY 24, 1992, a day GMers would later dub Black Monday,
Bob Stempel summoned reporters to GM's fifth-floor press room for his
second blockbuster news conference in two months. The purpose this
time was to name most of the twenty-one factories that GM would
shutter over the next three-and-a-half years, and also announce GM's
financial results for 1991.

The financial numbers were horrific: a record $4.45 billion after-tax
loss for the year, including a $2.82 billion charge for plant-closing and
restructuring costs. Stempel tried to downplay the damage, explaining
that without the restructuring charge, GM had shaved its fourth-quarter

loss to $520 million from more than $1.5 billion a year earlier. "What that says is we're getting our hands around this kamikaze that was going down like a rock," he declared, in a memorable mixing of metaphors.

Stempel then ended the Arlington-versus-Willow Run battle. The ax fell on Willow Run, whose 4,000 employees would lose their jobs in the summer of 1993. Also on the hit list was the plant in North Tarrytown, New York, that built GM's pointy-nosed APV minivans. The 3,500 workers there would suffer the consequences of another Reuss-sponsored product disaster. GM had once billed these plastic-bodied vehicles as an innovation. But the APVs carried less cargo than a Dodge Caravan, their plastic bodies didn't save weight or cost, and their rakishly sloped noses made it impossible for a driver to see the front end while parking. Sales never reached GM's forecasts.

Stempel went on to disclose a major corporate restructuring, something he had long tried to avoid, to eliminate GM's duplicate engineering organizations. The top-heavy Buick–Olds–Cadillac and Chevy–Pontiac–Canada groups created by Roger Smith would disappear, merging into a single North American Operations. But Stempel couldn't bring himself to say, publicly and clearly, when this would happen, or acknowledge that he was undoing his predecessor's 1984 corporate reorganization.

Indeed, Stempel's most definitive statement came when a reporter asked about the rumors that Reuss's job was in jeopardy. Stempel looked straight ahead and declared: "Lloyd's my man."

But LLOYD REUSS wasn't anybody else's man at General Motors. John Smale was finding this out firsthand. By the time of Stempel's press conference, Smale had spent a month delving deeply into the condition of the world's largest manufacturer, and had another month to go. He was poring over internal reports and outside data on GM's quality, productivity, finances, and costs—and how they compared with other car companies. He was holding private conversations lasting two to three hours with about twenty senior GM officials.

Some of the officers poured out their complaints as if they had been dying to be asked. Others demanded to know why the board had stayed asleep for so long. Smale maintained his usual poker-faced manner during the interviews, but he was startled by what he was finding. By March 22, he was ready to report.

It was a Sunday, the second day of spring, but three inches of snow fell in New York. Shortly before 9 A.M., the independent directors slipped into the white marble GM building at the southeast corner of Central Park. Instead of heading to GM's offices, though, they convened in Weil Gotshal's conference room on the 30th floor—five stories directly above the GM boardroom. It was a fitting location; this meeting was straight from the Millstein handbook.

Smale started by methodically listing his findings, one by one. First, a yawning quality gap remained between GM and its competitors, despite management's repeated assurances to the contrary. Second, by any measure—hours per car, workers per factory, dollars per car—GM was far and away the most inefficient company in the auto industry, despite its massive investments in technology and automation during the 1980s. GM used thirty to thirty-five hours of labor, on average, to assemble each car. Ford needed just twenty to twenty-five.

Third, GM's projected sales fell way short of its manufacturing capacity, and it wasn't at all clear that Bob Stempel's proposed cutbacks would close the gap. Fourth, GM was far slower than other automakers in developing new products and bringing them to market. And fifth, most GM executives wanted sweeping changes in the company's organization and structure, beyond what Stempel was proposing.

Of course, all this was exactly what the nation's business press, and most of Wall Street's auto analysts, had been saying for years. Stempel and Reuss, like Roger Smith before them, had pooh-poohed the criticisms, ascribing them to negativists who didn't understand what GM was doing. Now Smale was telling his fellow directors that the critics had been right all along.

But the most jarring items in Smale's report were the responses to the two questions he had asked at the end of each interview. First he had asked each executive to rank his level of confidence in Bob Stempel's game plan on a scale from 1 to 10—with 1 being high and 10 being low. Most of the answers had been between 6 and 8. The only person confident of the plan was Reuss.

The second question: On the same 1-to-10 scale, what are the chances that GM can avoid a financial crisis in the next six months to a year? Smale had expected answers of 2 or 3, indicating that a crisis was unlikely. Instead, he had gotten lots of 6s and 7s. It was jolting.

GM was a company careening out of control, and not just in its automotive operations. In late 1991, the company's internal auditors had discovered that a Long Island Chevy dealer had swindled GMAC out of some $437 million. The dealer, Edward McNamara, had borrowed billions of dollars over several years to finance the purchase of thousands of vans that he said he was exporting overseas. The trouble was, the vans had never existed. But McNamara had kept his scam going by using each new GMAC loan to pay off his old loan, minus a cut for himself.

Incredibly, more than a dozen different checkpoints that GMAC had built into its lending procedures had failed to detect the fraud. The computer program that GMAC used to flag large loan balances proved to be a joke. When a dealer's loan balance hit $99 million, the program would simply cycle back to zero and start counting again instead of sending the signal to begin additional loan-verification checks.

Then there was the departure of Bob Eaton to Chrysler just a week earlier. When Eaton was weighing Chrysler's offer, Stempel had declined to talk with him about his future at GM until he decided whether to stay. Several directors saw Stempel's response as one of pure GM arrogance, and didn't like it one bit.

Clearly, the time had come for a housecleaning. But after years of having done nothing, the only thing the eleven directors could agree to do was move step-by-step. And the next step was shaking up the men just under Stempel, to give both him and General Motors a fresh start.

Now somebody had to bell the cat.

ON MARCH 25, three days after his Sunday report to the board, Smale summoned Stempel to Cincinnati. Despite his retirement, Smale remained chairman of P&G's executive committee, and kept an office at company headquarters. When Stempel arrived, Smale quickly came to the point.

"As you know, Bob, I was asked in January by the other outside directors to evaluate your plan for recovery," he told Stempel. "We've concluded it won't work."

Then Smale gave Stempel the same report he had delivered to the outside directors the previous Sunday. The upshot, he said, was that management changes were necessary. At the very least, Lloyd Reuss had to go. The outside directors wanted to meet privately with Stempel on the coming Saturday in Chicago.

"The Saturday meeting will be tough, Bob, very tough," Smale said. "We've been trying to send you messages all along. We know you don't agree with a lot of what we've concluded. But on Saturday, you have to tell us, as convincingly as you can, how you are going to fix this company.

"Don't get hung up on the details." Smale added, "We're going to ask you whether you can really be the change maker at GM."

THE MEETING on Saturday was as advertised—tough. The directors gathered at the Marriott Suites hotel near Chicago's O'Hare Airport. (With Marriott CEO Bill Marriott on the board, it was always politic to meet at one of the chain's hotels.) This time, with Stempel, Millstein, and the outside directors all on hand, Smale gave his report again, for the third time in a week.

Then it was Stempel's turn to respond.

The plans that would revive General Motors, the chairman told his board, were already in place. He reminded the board that there was a recession on, and chided the directors for seeming to lose sight of that fact. "You've got to have the patience," Stempel said, "to stick with me."

After Stempel finished, the group recessed for coffee and muffins, which were waiting in an adjoining room. As they filled their cups, some of the directors rolled their eyes at each other in silent mockery of what they had just heard. Even board member Leon Sullivan, a Philadelphia minister and still a Stempel supporter by and large, leaned over to a colleague and whispered, "Maybe this is more serious than I thought. You folks might have a point here."

The meeting resumed, and the directors delivered their verdict. Stempel would have to shake up his executive suite. That meant promptly getting rid of Lloyd Reuss and replacing him as president with Jack Smith. As head of GM's prosperous international operations, Jack Smith somehow had learned a skill that Reuss never had seemed to master— making money. The directors also told Stempel they had serious qualms about the performances of three other men: Bob O'Connell, Bob Schultz, and Alan Smith, the executive vice president for corporate staffs. Finally, the directors wanted to institutionalize Smale's role by having him replace Stempel as chairman of GM's executive committee. In essence, Smale would be GM's "lead director," as described in Millstein's writings. The directors asked Millstein to draft changes in GM's corporate bylaws to make it happen.

A shaken Stempel flew back to Detroit to deliver the bad news.

WHEN STEMPEL PROMOTED somebody to become an officer of GM, he would often shake the man's hand and say, "Welcome to the club!" To him, GM's executive ranks were just that. Stempel simply didn't have the heart to boot Reuss out of the club, despite the board's demands.

On Sunday, the day after the Chicago showdown, he met with Reuss to break the news: Jack Smith, who had worked for Reuss for nearly two years in the mid-1980s, would take over as GM's president. The news hit Reuss like a hard kick in the stomach.[7] Despite GM's huge losses, the speculation in the press, and the board's obvious unrest, he had never believed his job was on the line. Stempel's strong public support had affirmed his belief. So how could this be happening? Reuss was just fifty-five, with a lot of good years left in him. His first thought was of quitting to look for work elsewhere. That's exactly what GM's directors were assuming Reuss would do.

But Stempel continued talking. He wanted his friend to stay. Reuss could take charge of two key GM operations: Saturn and the electric-car project. And Stempel would keep Reuss on GM's management committee.

Lloyd Reuss was a stubborn man. He had grown up in the GM family. His son Mark, just twenty-nine years old, was a GM engineer. Reuss wasn't one to turn tail and run, after thirty-six years with GM. In his mind, he hadn't failed, but was only being used as a scapegoat to shock the GM organization. He knew how to swallow his pride, and the perks and pay in the GM executive suite were pretty good. Reuss decided he would stay on in the reduced role Stempel offered.

The next day, Monday, Stempel convened the management committee—Reuss, O'Connell, Jack Smith, Alan Smith, Bob Schultz, and Bill Hoglund, the components chief—to tell everyone that changes were afoot. "The board is at the end of its rope," Stempel said. "I'm enormously frustrated, not with any of you but with them. They've panicked. They're being totally unreasonable."

In the days that followed, Stempel continued to behave like a man fighting a rear-guard action instead of leading a charge for change. GM's directors had expected the dressing-down in Chicago to produce results. Instead, Stempel was dithering. A few days after the Chicago meeting, he called Smale with what the P&G man considered a monumentally dumb idea: keeping Reuss as an executive vice president of General Motors.

On Sunday afternoon, April 5, GM jets brought the directors to Dallas. It was the home of EDS, and the meeting had been scheduled there months earlier as a corporate field trip, to let board members see the latest technology from their computer-services subsidiary. The GM people—directors, officers, and supporting cast—started checking into the Marriott Quorum Hotel near EDS headquarters. So did Millstein.

After dinner that night, Stempel sat down with his board and pleaded for Lloyd Reuss's career. Reuss was still valuable, Stempel said. He should stay as an executive vice president. As for O'Connell, Stempel wanted to keep him as executive vice president and chief financial officer. If the board insisted on a new CFO, they could have Hoglund, who had started his career in finance. In that case, Stempel suggested, O'Connell should stay as an executive vice president and become chairman of GMAC, to clean up the mess there.

After hearing Stempel out, the directors asked Stempel to leave, so they could meet alone with their lawyer.

Late that night, Stempel was summoned back. This time only four people were in the room: Smale, Millstein, and directors Ed Pratt, former chairman of Pfizer, and Dennis Weatherstone, the chairman of J. P. Morgan, the investment bank. As a concession to Stempel, Smale said, Reuss would be allowed to stay, although the directors wanted both him and Alan Smith off the board. Besides becoming president, Jack Smith would get the title of chief operating officer, which the board had withheld from Reuss two years earlier. As for O'Connell, the directors were uncomfortable with him remaining as CFO. But they would resume that discussion in the morning.

Stempel returned to his suite, and summoned Alan Smith. "The board is undermining me," he said, his voice quavering with emotion and fatigue. Then he described the changes.

Alan Smith, who had been a GM director for eleven years and had been the favorite to succeed Roger Smith as chairman at one time, didn't like leaving the board. But his own career clearly was in eclipse, and he felt losing his seat was a small price to pay for some long overdue changes. "Jack will be a great improvement over Lloyd as president," he told Stempel.

Stempel also talked to O'Connell, who still couldn't believe what he was hearing. At 12:38 A.M., Detroit time, he called his wife, Kathy, who was at their Bloomfield Hills house. "Something bad is going to happen to me tomorrow," he said. "I'm not sure just what." He asked her to call their son, Jason, a football player at Vanderbilt University, to warn him as well.

When Jason came to the phone, Kathy O'Connell struggled through her tears to explain what was going on. When Jason finally understood, he said: "It's just like Kennedy, Mom. Dad got shot in Dallas."

THE NEXT MORNING—Monday, April 6—Ira Millstein caught an early flight back to New York. His work in Dallas was done. Now, he could savor a moment of triumph. Few philosophers in any arena, let alone one as specialized as corporate governance, see their theories enacted. Millstein had just watched his ideas change history at the largest industrial company on earth. GM's directors didn't need him to finish the job.

At 10 A.M., the board's finance committee convened in a plain conference room at EDS headquarters. Two minutes beforehand, Stempel pulled Hoglund aside and told him, "You're going to be CFO, replacing O'Connell." But it wasn't until shortly before 2 P.M., just as the full board was about to meet, that Stempel grabbed O'Connell. "I can't save you," he said. Finally, O'Connell realized he would lose his CFO job, his executive vice president rank, and his seat on the management committee. He suddenly felt nauseated.

At 4:43 P.M., Dallas time, GM sent a press release over the nation's news wires under the bland headline: "GM Management Changes." It began:

> The appointment of John F. Smith, Jr., as president and chief operating officer of General Motors Corporation, effectively immediately, was announced today by Chairman Robert C. Stempel. In his new position, Mr. Smith will be in charge of all North American vehicle and component operations as well as GM's international operations.
>
> This appointment and others described below were unanimously approved by the Board of Directors, upon recommendation by the chairman. . . .

It was a lie.

Two days after that momentous April 6 announcement, with the press speculating that John Smale, as the new chairman of the board's executive committee, had supplanted Stempel as the real boss at GM, Smale issued a second statement. "Contrary to recent media reports, neither I nor any of the other outside members of the General Motors Board of Directors intend to involve ourselves in the day-to-day business of GM," the statement said. "That job is the responsibility of Bob Stempel, who has the board's full support and confidence. . . ."

That was a lie, too.

CHAPTER 13

GM: THE OCTOBER REVOLUTION

BOB STEMPEL, far from enjoying his board's full confidence, was on probation. On April 8, 1992, two days after the GM board's uprising, Director Ann McLaughlin talked to a longtime friend on the phone. "This isn't a one-two punch," she confided. "The idea isn't to demote Reuss and O'Connell one day, and then fire Stempel next. But we made it quite clear to Stempel that he will have to perform. If he turns himself around and reforms everything, maybe he can stay."

The spring of 1992 brought a brief period of hope for Stempel. On April 29, GM announced it earned $179 million in the first quarter, its first profitable quarter since 1990. The black ink, coupled with the board's obvious sense of urgency, buoyed Wall Street's confidence in the company. Thus, a month later, GM was able to replenish its corporate coffers by selling $2.9 billion of new common stock. It was the first time GM had sold new common shares since 1955, and constituted one of the largest common-stock offerings in history.

Jack Smith, meanwhile, was moving with surprising speed. The day after he became president, Smith started grilling executives in North American Operations to learn what Reuss had left behind. He discovered that some of Reuss's planners had outlined a shock therapy program, dubbed the Plan to Win, to reverse North America's losses. It didn't go far enough, but Smith decided it would do as a start. Within days, he convened the North American Operations strategy board, consisting of the executives who ran car and truck manufacturing, marketing, parts, finance, purchasing, and other disciplines. The strategy board, established in the waning weeks of Reuss's regime, was patterned after the board Smith had used at GM Europe to make decisions quickly. Reuss, however, had devoted strategy board meetings to ethereal discussions of "teamwork." Smith made it plain his board would be different.

From now on, Smith declared, the strategy board would be a "fully functioning decision-making body" that would take action. Soon, the strategy board was meeting as often as four days a week, beginning at 7:30 A.M. and often running until 6 P.M. The canned speeches of the old GM committee meetings gave way to free-flowing, and often contentious, debates. And in contrast to Stempel's committee meetings, the strategy board debates yielded decisions.

One of the first came on April 24, when GM announced that the Chevy–Pontiac–Canada and Buick–Olds–Cadillac car-engineering groups would be merged. Gone in a flash were the duplicative and competing organizations Roger Smith had created in 1984. Jack Smith had taken just three weeks to do what Stempel and Reuss had said would take a year or more.

Next, Smith's strategy board attacked GM's central office bureaucracy, derided within GM as "the checkers who check the checkers." GM had 13,000 central office functionaries. Smith slashed that army to just 2,000 people. Next came a quick curtailment of the cash-draining rental-car deals Reuss had sanctioned. Propping up market share at any cost was out. Instead, Smith issued a new directive: "Stop the bleeding."

Smith and his inner circle of aides had another watchword: urgency. On May 5, Smith gave plant managers and division heads just three weeks to submit new budgets with detailed plans for cutting waste. He directed aides to beat the bushes for money-saving ideas. One manager in GM's spare parts operation pointed out that GM produced and stocked two shock absorbers that were identical, except that one was blue and the other black. Eliminating one color would save $1 million a year in production and inventory expenses. Smith told his aides to approve such changes on the spot.

Smith's most radical move was bringing in an import from GM Europe:

a hard-driving Spanish purchasing executive named José Ignacio López de Arriortúa. GM's Detroit bureaucracy had never seen anything like López. One of his first acts was handing out to his troops a dietary and philosophical epistle called "Feeding the Warrior Spirit," written in his own distinctive English.

"Sometimes with your bad habit of feeding you are killing yourself," the document began. It banned sandwiches, sugar, and french fries, and advised instead: "Drink the fresh juice of fruits and vegetables mixed with your saliva, step by step," because they are "ideal for interior body cleaning."

López then began administering an interior body cleaning to GM's parts suppliers. GM, he was convinced, would be saved only if he led a crusade to slash $4 billion or more from its purchasing costs immediately. López started ripping up GM's components contracts, and demanding new bids, with price cuts of 10 percent or more. Suppliers howled, but Smith and López refused to back down. GM needed cash to survive. The fastest way to get it was López's way.

Smith was moving so fast that even his own organization had trouble keeping up. Weeks after he restructured the engineering ranks, the old BOC Flint Automotive Division was still sending reports to BOC headquarters—even though BOC didn't exist. Memos to Smith would arrive at the president's office on the 14th floor of GM headquarters, only to have to be rerouted. To get closer to the action, Smith spent most of his time at the new North American headquarters at the GM Technical Center in Warren. It wasn't long before the 14th floor became almost deserted.

One man who remained there, however, was Bob Stempel.

INSTEAD OF BEING jolted into action by the board's uprising, Stempel seemed shocked into paralysis. He went to one or two meetings of the NAO strategy board, but then stopped coming. He ignored the board's direction to replace Alan Smith and Bob Schultz, two holdovers from the old regime. When Smale pressed him on the matter, Stempel replied that the demotions of Reuss and O'Connell had put GM through enough trauma for the time being. He seemed oblivious to Smale's prodding.

Smale was digging into his new role as head of GM's executive committee—which now consisted of six independent directors plus Stempel. Smale was setting the agendas for the meetings of his committee and of the entire board, just as Millstein's theories prescribed. He gave Stempel specific formats for submitting regular progress reports to the board about quality, finances, and other topics. He wanted Stempel to be management's liaison to the board. But Stempel wasn't responding.

On June 28, Smale gave the independent directors on the executive committee a progress report of his own. He was delighted, he said, with Jack Smith. In contrast, Smale said, Stempel was sulking—convinced that he was getting a bad rap, and that the board was treating him unfairly.

"Unfortunately," Smale said, "Bob Stempel doesn't show any signs of being a change maker."

IN EARLY JULY, Smale gave Stempel a list of problems that the executive committee wanted to discuss. Among them: how to fix Saturn.

Saturn had become an excruciating dilemma for GM. It was launched in 1990 as a "different kind of car company" dedicated to worker-management teamwork and to treating customers like kings. Saturn's Spring Hill, Tennessee, factory became a mecca for Washington types and academics who wanted a firsthand look at the "partnership" GM executives declared would rejuvenate American manufacturing.

Saturn scored with consumers, who raved about the car's value and the service at Saturn dealerships. Saturn had granted its initial dealers —dubbed "retail partners" in its New Age corporate jargon—huge sales territories in return for their commitments to sell cars in a civilized manner. It was a genuine innovation, because Saturn dealers didn't have to fight each other for customers. Saturn also priced its cars roughly $1,000 below rival Japanese models while still allowing dealers a profit of more than $1,000 a car. Dealers could thus offer a bargain, and still make plenty of money.

The trouble was, Saturn was a financial black hole. Eighteen months after building its first salable car, the $1.8 billion Saturn factory still was limping along at about 75 percent of its capacity. Months after launch, the Saturn paint shop held bins full of marred plastic hoods and fenders, a testimonial to a plague of glitches. Saturn, cast as a "revolutionary" auto plant, had missed the most important revolution of all: Toyota-style "lean" production. Building Saturns required as many workers, or more, as in a traditional GM plant. Toyota could build a Corolla with just twenty hours of assembly-plant labor. Saturn required more than thirty hours of labor to build its Corolla fighters. Saturn lost nearly $1 billion in 1991. Some inside GM joked that the company would lose less money if it simply gave a Chevrolet—free—to anyone who asked for a Saturn.

Of all people to deal with this disaster, Lloyd Reuss would have been last on almost anyone's list. But Stempel had insisted on putting Reuss in charge of Saturn. Stempel assured Smale that Reuss was "working very hard." But Smale was far from satisfied.

Smale had lots of other concerns. He wanted Stempel to outline a "vision of the future" for GM. He wanted Stempel to finish overhauling the executive suite. And he wanted Stempel to articulate a long-term plan for reshaping GM's relationship with the United Auto Workers union.

As if on cue, GM's labor relations exploded.

Bob Stempel had tried to buy cooperation from the UAW in 1990 by agreeing to pay laid off workers up to $3.35 billion over three years, even if they did nothing but sit at home. But any goodwill evaporated after Stempel's December 1991 declaration that more than 50,000 UAW members would lose their jobs. By the summer of 1992, the relationship between Stempel and Stephen Yokich, the UAW vice president assigned to GM, had broken down. The volatile Yokich was furious with the way the GM chairman had handled the Willow Run–Arlington face-off. Yokich also maintained that Stempel had broken a promise to keep production of the Camaro and Firebird in the United States. Instead, GM moved the cars to a plant in Quebec represented by the separate Canadian Auto Workers union. Yokich considered this an unforgivable breach of trust.

The UAW's anger came to a head at a stamping factory in Lordstown, Ohio. There, GM wanted to shut a 240-person shop that made stamping dies and other production tools. Local union officials cried foul. On August 27, Yokich let them walk out. Within hours, GM had to shut assembly plants that relied on stamped parts from Lordstown. The massive Saturn complex was one of the first factories forced down.

The beleaguered Stempel spent the Labor Day weekend at his vacation home on the Jersey shore, keeping up with negotiations to settle the dispute. By the time the strike ended nine days later, GM had lost some $70 million worth of production. The settlement allowed GM to close the die shop, albeit a year later than planned. The company also agreed to shift more production of Chevrolet Cavalier and Pontiac Sunbird compact cars into the adjacent Lordstown assembly plant from a factory in Mexico. That represented a major win for the UAW.

GM executives argued they had preserved a key principle by establishing the right to shut the tool room. But that wasn't the real issue. The Lordstown strike dramatized the UAW's unwillingness to cooperate in cutting costs. Yokich threatened to strike one key plant after another in what another union leader called "Apache raids" to protest GM's cutbacks.

The union's guerrilla war underscored GM's staggering competitive disadvantage. By GM's calculations, the company spent nearly $2,000 more on labor than Ford for every vehicle it built. Long-term, such a huge cost gap pointed in only one direction: extinction.

But Stempel's efforts to whittle this gap were being overwhelmed by the costs of the 1990 labor contract. GM could shut every factory it had in the United States, and most of its wage costs would roll on. Stempel had made labor at GM a fixed cost—pegged at the highest levels in the industry. The only way out was to allow death and attrition to take their toll, and periodically offer costly early-retirement deals. When Stempel signed the contract in 1990, he never envisioned paying out the full $3.35 billion fund allocated to "income security." But the recession blew that plan. By mid-1992, GM was on track to shell out nearly every penny by the time the contract expired in September 1993.

The huge payments to idled workers accelerated GM's financial deterioration. GM's overall operating loss for the 1992 second quarter came in at $1.58 billion, even worse than the year before. At the rate GM was burning cash, it would take less than a year for the company to run through the $4.7 billion it had raised through its various stock offerings over the prior year.

Again, Wall Street smelled trouble. By September, GM's stock was trading as low as $30.75, far below the $39 a share at which the huge $2.9 billion stock offering had been sold that spring. Going back to the money well would cost GM dearly.

For the second time in less than a year, the credit-rating agencies stepped in. In late September 1992, Moody's Investors Services issued a grim statement signaling its intention to downgrade GM's debt and pull its top-tier commercial paper rating. Standard & Poor's was sure to follow.

The wolf was at the door again.

. . .

On Sunday evening, October 4, Smale convened the executive committee at GM's offices in New York. In his hand, Smale had a four-page report on the major issues facing the company.

"We've got a problem, and it's serious," Smale began. "We've got to get our hands around how bad things might get."

GM's North American Operations, Smale continued, were worse off than he and Jack Smith had first thought. It would be four years before GM had new midsize sedans to replace the high-cost, poor-quality GM-10 models. Until then, GM would have to struggle with outdated products in the heart of the market. The same was true in minivans, where a successor to the failed APV vans wasn't scheduled to hit the market until 1996. Meanwhile, cash flow was still negative. And looming ahead were two bombshells that could turn GM's balance sheet into a smoking crater.

A new accounting rule was about to force companies to recognize their liabilities for the future costs of medical care for retirees. While the figures weren't final, it was evident that GM faced a staggering charge against net income of $20 billion or more.

At the same time, Smale reported, finance staffers were surfacing some truly ugly numbers from GM's pension funds. Roger Smith had decided in 1990 to assume that retirees would die two years sooner than before, and also that the funds would earn 10 percent more per year than before. This, along with some earlier pension accounting changes, had boosted GM's earnings, just as Smith had intended.[1] It helped GM to justify contributing no extra cash to its retirement funds during 1989, 1990, and 1991. But since then, neither interest rates nor GM's retirees had cooperated. The former had plunged, while the latter remained stubbornly robust.

GM's pension assets, fully adequate just a few years before, now fell $11 billion short of liabilities. Because of the shortfall, GM would have to reduce shareholder equity by an extra $1.9 billion—and start diverting into the pension funds cash that might otherwise have paid for new products.

Smale went on. National Car Rental, GM's small rental car agency affiliate, quietly had become an enormous cash drain. Processing National's requests for fresh capital to replace money lost on operations had become an annual ritual for GM's finance bureaucracy. At Smale's insistence, GM had ended this game, and taken a $300 million write-off to reflect losses at National. But as Smale dug further into the issue, he discovered that the real losses at National were closer to $1 billion.

Smale's colleagues on the executive committee were beside themselves. Back in June they had already approved a $749 million write-off
at Hughes Aircraft, once the pride of Roger Smith's diversification drive.
GM had become the Surprise of the Month club. Taken individually,
any of the items on Smale's list of horrors was cause for alarm. Together,
they created the picture of a company in a death spiral. It didn't seem
possible that GM could go bankrupt. But the directors just didn't
know.

Until now, Stempel hadn't been part of the meeting. Methodical and
meticulous, Smale wanted the independent directors to hear his report
and discuss it before bringing in Stempel. Beforehand, however, he had
asked Harry Pearce, GM's general counsel, to fully brief Stempel on the
contents of his report, so Stempel would be ready to reply. Now Smale
summoned Stempel into the room, went through his report again, and
then put direct questions to Stempel. "What will you do about all this?"
he asked. "Do you have a worst-case scenario?"

To Stempel, the questions didn't make sense. He believed he already had a plan for fixing GM, which he'd articulated in February.
He was now managing for the long term, moving step-by-step to close
plants and develop new models. GM's directors were panicking, in
Stempel's view, while he was trying to provide a steady hand at the
helm. Stempel replied that he didn't have a worst-case scenario, because it wouldn't be realistic. In that moment, Bob Stempel sealed his
fate.

The next day, Smale asked Dennis Weatherstone, chief executive
of the J. P. Morgan bank, Tom Wyman, and another director, Anne
Armstrong, to oversee a detailed investigation of GM's financial condi-
tion that would determine whether a crisis indeed was imminent.
Weatherstone offered to send in a team of crack financial analysts from
Morgan to do the job.

Weatherstone soft-pedaled the move, equating it to getting a second
opinion from a doctor when facing a major medical decision. In reality,
bringing in the Morgan SWAT team was tantamount to a no-confidence
vote on Stempel's leadership. Later, Wyman complimented Weatherstone on his courage. GM was a big Morgan client, and offending
GM's chairman wasn't a good customer-relations move.

"Please, Tom," the banker replied dryly, "don't attribute any altruistic
notions to me. I just want to make sure that GM can stay around to give
us more business."

· · ·

IN THE DAYS FOLLOWING the disastrous October 4 meeting, Ira Millstein's office became a nexus of revolution. The lawyer was coordinating the contacts among the outside directors and helping cajole the stragglers. Also, at Smale's request, Millstein's partner, Robert Messineo, drafted changes to GM's corporate bylaws. These would permit an outside director to become chairman of the board, without also serving as chief executive officer. Millstein had advocated just such a split for years.

Stempel remained oblivious. In August and September he had sensed that several directors were turning against him, but he didn't see that his job was in immediate danger. He went on working, as if nothing had changed.

On Monday, October 12, Stempel and Reuss convened a high-level meeting to review GM's electric car, a pet project of Roger Smith's. Smith had gone to Washington in April 1990, a few days after naming Stempel as his successor, to declare that GM would be "the first company since the early days of the auto industry to mass-produce an electric car." By the mid-1990s, Smith promised, GM would be selling the Impact, a super-sleek, electric-powered car whose prototype GM had already unveiled in California.

It was an impulsive decision, like the one that had given birth to Teamwork and Technology in 1988. GM didn't have the know-how to build a battery-powered mass-market automobile that was affordable to the average consumer. But the Impact, unlike T-and-T, wasn't a $20 million PR stunt. It was, potentially, a $1 billion undertaking. GM had little hope of recovering that kind of investment in the Impact, let alone making a profit. But here were Stempel and Reuss, who had presided over rivers of red ink, deliberating a plan to send still more down the hole on another mistargeted car—just as if GM had all the money in the world.

Jack Smith, who had been invited to the meeting, was sitting close to the door, with an empty chair between himself and Stempel. He said nothing, even as the meeting dragged on for nearly two hours. Finally, at about 4 P.M., Stempel turned to Smith to ask him what he thought.

"Bob, you can't afford it," Smith replied tersely. "Now if you'll excuse me, I've got another meeting to attend." And with that, he walked out of the room.

The managers of the electric car knew that their program was finished. What they didn't know was that Bob Stempel was, too.

By now, Wall Street was starting to sense that the ground was shaking under Stempel. On October 12, the same day as the electric-car meeting, the *Wall Street Journal* ran a "Heard on the Street" column that began: "General Motors Corp.'s outside directors are once again escalating their role in running the struggling automaker."[2] The next day, Tuesday, October 13, The Washington *Post* went a big step further. It carried a front-page piece by reporters Warren Brown and Frank Swoboda, declaring that the outside directors had told Stempel to get tough with the UAW, or risk losing his job by the end of the year.[3]

By chance, that morning found Stempel in Washington. His first meeting was with William Reilly, the head of the Environmental Protection Agency. Around noon, he arrived at the Willard Hotel for a meeting with Dr. Leon Martell of the Conference Board, the business forecasting group of which he was a director. But as the discussion got going, Stempel began to feel ill. He felt queasy and couldn't catch his breath. He excused himself, went to the bathroom, and returned to announce he needed a doctor.

Within minutes, GM's chairman was in the back of an ambulance, heading to George Washington University Hospital. By 12:30 P.M., he was in a hospital bed, listed in serious condition. He was alert, however, and called an aide back at headquarters to assure him there was no reason to get excited.

Instead of excitement, there was pandemonium. Frantic staffers scrambled to track down Stempel's wife, Pat, who was riding at a Detroit area hunt club. The aides offered to commandeer a GM plane to fly her down to Washington, but Stempel talked to her by phone and prevailed on her to stay home. Meanwhile, as doctors began a battery of tests to diagnose the cause of Stempel's trouble, GM's PR staffers launched into crisis mode—a pattern they knew all too well—and wrestled with how to break the news. The last thing they wanted was a speculative orgy from the press and Wall Street suggesting that bad health would force the embattled chairman from power. Their solution: a brief, low-key press release issued late in the afternoon, saying Stempel was "resting comfortably" and was "anxious to return to work."

A day and a half later, on October 15, Stempel left the hospital and returned to Detroit. GM didn't disclose a diagnosis, but said only that the chairman would be back on the job the next day. Stempel did return to work, but he retreated into the sanctum of his 14th floor corner office, venturing forth so rarely that the people around him began to worry. Alan Smith dropped in a couple of times, ostensibly to ask about business matters but really to check on how Stempel was doing.

"Are you OK, Bob?" Smith would ask. "What's this stuff I'm reading about in the papers?"

"Certain people on the board have some tough attitudes." Stempel shrugged, making it clear that he didn't want to elaborate.

James Crellin, one of Stempel's aides, decided to bring his boss a candid assessment of the dangers he faced. Crellin, a former Detroit newsman who ran GM's corporate PR staff, sent Stempel a memo. The title: "Saving General Motors."

"The media is working itself into a frenzy of speculation," Crellin wrote, "questioning the future of General Motors and your authority and tenure as chairman. The only way to control this ongoing criticism of GM is to have Mr. Smale issue a statement that expresses confidence in GM's management.

"We are getting beyond a debate about whether Bob Stempel or Jack Smith is running the corporation. The question is becoming, 'Is anyone in charge?'"

During the weekend of October 17 and 18, Stempel mulled over Crellin's memo and the idea of seeking a statement of support from Smale. On Monday and Tuesday, in between meetings and yet another quick trip to Washington and back, Stempel and Crellin talked it over. Then events spun out of control.

On Wednesday, October 21, the Washington *Post* carried yet another front-page article by Swoboda and Brown. "The outsiders who control the General Motors Corp. board of directors want Chairman Robert C. Stempel to step down within the next month," it began, "but they are still debating who will succeed him, board and management sources said yesterday."[4]

For the second time in a week, GM's PR machine lurched into crisis mode. "The Washington *Post* story is based on rumors, speculation, and anonymous sources," Bruce MacDonald, GM's vice president for PR, declared in a statement that GM distributed nationwide. "There is absolutely no substance to reports that Bob Stempel will be asked to step down as chairman."

MacDonald's statement, however, couldn't squelch the story. Stempel now knew he needed what Crellin had suggested, a statement of support from Smale. That afternoon, he authorized Crellin to draft one.

On Thursday morning, October 22, Stempel headed over to the design dome at the GM Tech Center in Warren. The analysts from Moody's were coming in for a meeting, and Stempel wanted to make a strong pitch for keeping a top-tier commercial-paper rating. Showing the Moody's people GM's newest hardware was sure to help.

In midmorning, Crellin left his office at GM headquarters and drove out to meet Stempel, carrying the statement of support that Stempel had asked him to draft. He wanted to show it to Stempel, and fax it to Smale's office in Cincinnati, so Smale could issue the statement forthwith.

Just as Crellin arrived at the design dome, his car phone rang. It was his secretary, calling to say that Harry Pearce, GM's general counsel, had called with a message: John Smale had just issued a statement of his own.

Crellin rushed into the building, and found a downcast Stempel sitting in an empty office.

"Well, Bob, I guess it's too late," Crellin said. "I just got a call, and Smale has put out a statement."

"Yeah, I know," Stempel replied, his voice strained with fatigue and sorrow.

"The GM Board of Directors has taken no action regarding any management changes at GM," Smale's statement said. "However, the question of executive leadership is a primary concern to the Board of Directors of any company, and GM is no exception. The GM Board of Dire.ors continues to carefully reflect upon the wisest course for assuring the most effective leadership for the Corporation."

Stempel was stunned. "I'm not an English major," he thought to himself, "but you could be a second grader and read that one." Smale's statement, drafted with Millstein's help, all but confirmed the "rumors" that Bruce MacDonald had vigorously denied a day earlier.

Stempel returned to his office. He spent the rest of Thursday and part of Friday calling some directors to see what support, if any, he might have on the board. He found sympathy, but no support. On Friday afternoon, Crellin, sitting in his office, got a call from Stempel's secretary. She was crying.

Stempel had just faxed to Smale a proposed letter of resignation. By late afternoon, Smale and most of the independent directors had discussed the letter in a conference call, and agreed to accept it. Bob Stempel became the first GM chief executive to be ousted since the board dumped company founder William Crapo Durant, seventy-two years earlier.

It was a historic moment, but the world would wait three days to know. Because the stock market had closed for the week by the time the deed was done, Millstein and Smale decided GM could wait until Monday morning to announce the news. Bob Stempel went home for the longest weekend of his life.

BOB STEMPEL LOVED being chairman of General Motors. He was fifty-nine years old, and had started at the company thirty-five years before, at a time when a nonfinance chairman was about as likely as a non-Italian pope. But he had bucked the odds and made it to the top.

GM had been his life. He loved cars and being known as a "car guy." He had a good marriage but no really close friends, even within the company, and no abiding outside interests. He didn't play golf or tennis, or hunt, fish, or ski. It seemed to Stempel so unfair, so terribly wrong, that he should be forced to leave GM in disgrace after so many years of such loyal and productive service. What did the outside directors know about making cars? Nothing. They knew about placating Wall Street and saving their own hides, but nothing about what it was like to tell a working man that his plant was closed, and that he wouldn't have a job to support his family. The chairman of GM, as Stempel saw it, had to weigh competing interests and considerations that outsiders could never begin to understand.

That Sunday morning he phoned his colleagues at their homes, to tell them the next day's news.

"Alan, you've been good enough to support me and to care about me," he said to Alan Smith, "and to ask me how I'm feeling and how I'm doing. Well, this has gone on long enough. I can't stand the stories, the speculation, the leaks, and the lack of support. I'm resigning."

"I'm sorry, Bob," Smith replied. "I'm real sorry that it didn't work out."

. . .

Stempel's letter of resignation was released to the world at 9 a.m., Monday, October 26. "Today, I informed the General Motors board of directors that I was resigning as chairman and chief executive officer, effective immediately, and that I would serve at the pleasure of the board until a successor could be named," it said. "I could not in good conscience continue to watch the effects of rumors and speculation that have undermined and slowed the efforts of General Motors people to make this a stronger, more efficient, effective organization."

That same morning, Stempel checked into Beaumont Hospital in suburban Detroit under an assumed name for an examination, via catheter, of the interior of his heart. It took all day, and confirmed what the doctors at George Washington University had believed: He had a faulty heart valve. Within two weeks, he would undergo surgery to correct the problem.

GM's directors hadn't known during the tumultuous days of late October that Stempel was so gravely ill. He could have legitimately used his health problem to make a face-saving exit. But Stempel, iron-willed and stubborn to the last, would have none of it.

The same day Stempel's resignation became public, Jack Smith, Harry Pearce, and John Smale flew to New York, to meet with Millstein and piece together a new top management for GM. The new team—to be announced a week later, at the November 2 board meeting—wouldn't include Lloyd Reuss, Alan Smith, or Bob Schultz. When Jack Smith returned from New York, he told each of the three men the news.

"It doesn't look good, Alan," he said to Alan Smith. "They're cleaning the place out."

"Does that include me?" Smith asked.

"Yes, it does," Smith replied to the man who had once been one of his mentors. "It isn't the way I want it, but it's the way it has to be."

On November 2, a week after Stempel's resignation was announced, the board gathered at the GM Building in New York for its regular monthly meeting. But there was nothing regular about it. The directors elected John Smale as GM's first nonexecutive chairman since 1937, the year before Jack Smith was born. Smith was elected CEO in addition to president. At age fifty-four, he was GM's youngest chief executive since Alfred P. Sloan got the job in 1923, when he was just forty-eight.

The board also bypassed an entire generation of GM executives—men who had climbed the corporate ladder for decades and had stood within a rung or two of the top—to install just under Smith a trio of Baby Boomers, whose average age was just forty-four. The youngest was G. Richard Wagoner, thirty-nine, the new executive vice president and chief financial officer. The day before, Wagoner had been running GM of Brazil, a post for young executives starting to learn the ropes of running an operating division. Now, he was one of the five senior officers of the company.

Also promoted to executive vice president was Louis R. Hughes, who was forty-three. Jack Smith's longtime ally and the head of GM Europe, Hughes got control over all GM's international operations. The third new executive vice president was Harry Pearce, the company's top lawyer, who got purview over EDS and GM Hughes Electronics. At age fifty, Pearce wasn't a true Baby Boomer, but in many ways his was the most unorthodox appointment of all.

Wagoner and Hughes, despite their youth, were GM veterans. But Pearce had joined GM just seven years and one month earlier, after being lured away from his law practice in Fargo, North Dakota, by Elmer Johnson. He remained close to Johnson, who had left GM in 1988 after despairing that the company would ever change. In 1990, when Stempel became chairman, Pearce had taken it upon himself to interview senior company officers privately and compile a list of recommendations that became known as the Black Book. Only a relative newcomer would have tried something so risky. His report concluded that GM had to overhaul its culture and business methods, immediately and radically, but like so many other GM reports it had simply gathered dust.

Pearce had spent most of 1992 relaying warnings to Stempel from Millstein and the board, to no avail. Now, in his new job, the GM lawyer would have the chance to implement his own advice from the Black Book, starting immediately.

The final member of GM's ruling quintet was Bill Hoglund. At fifty-eight, the former Young Turk who had revived Pontiac in the mid-1980s and later launched Saturn now was the old man of the group. He had spent most of the Stempel era in exile, until becoming chief financial officer in April. Now he shifted again into a broader role as Smith's guide in navigating the swamp of GM's North American operations.

For all five men, it was a heady but frightening moment. Hughes, punchy after a long flight from Zurich, summed up the improbability of it all. Ushered into the board room, he blurted out to the directors: "I hope you all know what you're doing."

IN TRUTH, the GM directors didn't begin to understand the full implications of what they were doing.

"This isn't an exercise in corporate governance," Smale said after the board meeting broke up. He was speaking to a small group of reporters who were pulled away from the dozens milling about the lobby and ushered upstairs for a "deep background" briefing.

"We will do everything we can to convince our employees and the world that management is running the business, and we're not," Smale added. "There's no attempt to suggest that what we've done ought to be the model for any other company."

There Smale turned out to be wrong. In the months to come, boards would rise up at the bluest of America's blue-chip corporations: American Express, Westinghouse, Kodak, and even IBM. None of these boards would follow the GM model by separating the job of chairman from that of CEO. But they would hold the chairman accountable for his performance and dismiss him for falling short. Accountability was a notion increasingly familiar to middle managers all across America in the new era of global business competition. But CEOs had remained above it all.

Until, that is, the GM directors—awkwardly and belatedly—rose in revolt. Their actions seemed to give other boards an implied permission to cast aside their own rubber-stamp roles and become active, functioning bodies. If even the GM board could do it, other boards could, too. It was, a Kodak executive would say months later, the "post-Stempel world."[5]

THE NOVEMBER 2 MEETING found Jack Smith in a place where he was distinctly uncomfortable: facing television cameras. The first time was in the morning, when GM wheeled its cameras into the boardroom so Smith could announce the management changes to GM employees around the world on closed-circuit TV.

"The Mark of Excellence has faded in recent years," Smith declared, referring to the GM trademark. "It will be coming back strong, and you will be proud to be part of that comeback.

"Our board of directors has acted because GM was incurring losses so large that even GM couldn't continue to sustain them. But we have acted in time. And we do have a plan. . . . This is clearly the beginning of a new era at General Motors. It will not be an easy process."

Later, in the afternoon, after GM announced the board had slashed the quarterly dividend in half to 20 cents a share, Smith went downstairs to hold a press conference. The lobby was filled with reporters who had been waiting all day long.

"Is GM on the verge of entering Chapter 11 bankruptcy proceedings?" one wanted to know.

"No, we're nowhere near Chapter 11," Smith wearily replied. "We're a very strong company from an asset point of view." A few minutes later another reporter asked virtually the same question, and Smith, normally unflappable, got testy. "I don't understand this conversation about Chapter 11," he snapped. "It's ridiculous."

The questions were clumsy, but they weren't ridiculous. The GM directors, after all, had been asking the same thing. The questions reflected the reality of how far GM had fallen, and how far it had to go to recover.

THE SURGEONS AT Beaumont Hospital fixed Stempel's heart, but they couldn't heal his heartache.

Right after the New Year, Stempel, 30 pounds lighter, showed up at a Chevrolet press conference at the Detroit Auto Show. He stood in the back, and when reporters noticed, they immediately abandoned the speaker and rushed to talk to him. He had little to say, except that he was doing well. Later, he wandered into a restricted area in a Chrysler exhibit, and a security guard—not knowing who he was—shooed him out. A Chrysler executive across the room watched the scene in horror, but couldn't get there in time to stop the unintended insult.

Officially a consultant to GM, Stempel came and went from his office regularly during January and February, as if he were still chairman. The GM officers who saw him smiled and offered pleasantries; they didn't know what else to say. His continued presence on the 14th floor was awkward in the extreme, but Stempel couldn't let go. Not until March 1, 1993—four months after his resignation—did Stempel finally pack his belongings and move out of the GM Building.

• • •

WITH THEIR COUP complete, GM's directors set about tying up the loose ends. One of those was Roger Smith. He had dominated and deceived them during his nine-year term at GM's helm, and now they wanted him off the board altogether.

Smith, however, wasn't one to be pushed around. Six months before Stempel's ouster, the board had sent Smith a message by lopping 15 percent off his $1.2-million-a-year pension. It was a partial atonement for unwittingly adopting rules that doubled Smith's pension on the very eve of his retirement in 1990. Smith was still getting just over $1 million a year. Then, the night before the November 2 board meeting, Smale sent an emissary to Smith with the message that he should resign along with Stempel and the rest. Smith sent word back that he wanted his full pension back before he agreed to go.

Smale turned up the pressure.

On January 12, 1993, Smale convened the board to hear the J. P. Morgan SWAT team's analysis of GM's financial management. "GM and GMAC are not facing liquidity crises," the report began, largely because Jack Smith's cost-cutting was starting to reverse the cash drain in North America. That was reassuring, but the report went on to indict Roger Smith's leadership and legacy.

GM should make its accounting for pensions, warranty costs, and other items "at least as conservative as its competitors," the Morgan team said. If GM had used more conservative accounting in 1991, the Morgan people said, the company's cash drain that year would have been closer to $7.5 billion instead of the $3 billion indicated in its financial statements. Morgan recommended that GM consider selling the crown jewels of Smith's diversification crusade, EDS and Hughes Aircraft, as well as several GM parts operations. And finally, Morgan said, GM should stop obfuscating the disaster in its core business and start releasing clear profit-and-loss numbers for North American Operations every quarter, something Roger Smith had refused to do.

When the Morgan team was done, Smale turned to Rick Wagoner, the new chief financial officer. Smale ticked off the proposals one at a time, and asked, "I'd like your thoughts." On each point, Wagoner replied, "We wholeheartedly agree."

Roger Smith sat through it all in silence, with the pained look of a man who had just gulped down a goldfish. He was isolated, discredited, and clearly not wanted. A few days later Smale told him, matter-of-factly, that his pension wouldn't be increased, and that he wouldn't be renominated as a director in the spring.

Smith bristled, snapping at Smale that the board seemed determined to destroy his reputation. But two weeks later he backed down, and announced he would step down from the board effective April 1. He showed up for his last board meeting in March, smiling and shaking hands, as if nothing untoward had happened. *

ON FEBRUARY 18, 1993, with the memories of the October coup still fresh and the wounds still raw, some forty officers of General Motors gathered once again at the Detroit Club for a pickle dish party. This one was to bid farewell to Lloyd Reuss, Bob Schultz, and Alan Smith. Bob Stempel was supposed to be honored, too, but he had refused to come. He had resigned, he said, not retired. Everyone understood. Stempel was far too hurt to attend.

As the officers gathered at the Detroit Club, a few of their wives— just six or eight—met uptown at the Whitney for their own little farewell dinner. The idea of separate retirement dinners for officers and wives could only make sense at a company that still regarded chrome-bedecked Cadillacs as the most desirable cars on earth. Despite the boardroom revolution, some things would never change.

The wives at the Whitney watched the same films—reviewing the life and career of each retiree—that the officers saw. And afterward, the retirees' wives were invited to say a few words, just as their men were doing across town. It was painful, especially for Maurcine Reuss, who had cried through much of dinner. "It's hard to leave General Motors at any time," she said through her sobs. "But it's especially hard to leave this way. It really, really hurts."

Back at the Detroit Club, her husband was faring better. It had been obvious from the start of the party that nobody knew quite what to say to Reuss, Schultz, or Alan Smith, because nobody had ever attended a pickle dish party where the three honorees had been dumped. The cocktail conversation was stilted and awkward, and it didn't improve over dinner.

When it came time to speak, however, Reuss was firmly in control of his emotions. "I'd rather be staying than going," he said. "But I'm going. There is life after GM."

---

* Roger Smith, in an interview at GM headquarters on November 11, 1993, said he did not seek the restoration of his pension in return for leaving the board. Three persons close to the situation maintain that he did.

With that, Reuss described, in disciplined detail, how he would organize his new life, just as if he were making a presentation to the management committee. Indeed, he had spent hours preparing his parting
remarks.

"I have spent thirty-six years at GM shaping steel," Reuss told the
group. "Now I'll spend some time shaping lives." He would work with
Focus HOPE, an organization founded by a Detroit Catholic priest to
provide education and job training to inner city children and adults. He
would devote time to a new group of religious schools in Detroit, and to
Vision 2000, whose goal was getting children in the fifth through seventh grades interested in science and technology. He would do more
work with his church, and more traveling with his wife.

"It is neither wealth nor splendor, but friends and occupation that
give happiness," Reuss said, quoting Thomas Jefferson. "During thirty-
six years at General Motors, I've made a lot of friends, had a great
occupation, and found a lot of happiness." It was a warm speech, devoid
of bitterness or anger. Outwardly, at least, Reuss was upbeat, confident,
and optimistic—as always.

Schultz, like Reuss, was completely in character. His speech was much
shorter and more relaxed. He had enjoyed working with everyone, he
said, and had many fine memories of the good times they had shared.
Now he was looking forward to doing a lot of fishing in Colorado, where
the streams were clear and cold, and the trout were big. He wished
everyone well.

Then Alan Smith rose to speak.

"I have a high level of confidence in Jack and his new team," Smith
declared. "They are functioning in a way that I have never seen General
Motors function before." He went on to describe how, as a youngster on
the GM finance staff in the 1960s, he was told that manufacturing people
and sales people could not be trusted. He was sure, he continued, that
the manufacturing and sales people likewise were told by their bosses
that they couldn't trust the finance staff. None of this, he now knew,
was true.

Then Smith recalled his days in New York, in the GM treasurer's
office. He and his fellow staffers used to prepare elaborate answers to
questions that might be asked at the annual stockholders meetings. To
questions about management salaries there always was a pat answer:
Nothing is more expensive than poor management. "Now I've learned
firsthand here at GM," he said, "that this was really true."

At this there was some uncomfortable squirming in the audience, but Smith went on: "What happened at this company can't ever be allowed to happen here again. This loss of trust with the board. This loss of contact, of communication, with the board over us and with the organization below us. Our group, the Class of '92, had the intelligence and the know-how and the energy to make changes. But the chemistry and the culture didn't work. Now you who remain have to communicate with each other and with the board, openly and honestly.

"A lot of us, and a lot of you, were involved in doing things that didn't work. I've been gone three or four months now, and I'm out of the loop. But you who remain are in the loop. You might not feel like it on some days, but think of all the people who are working for you. They can really feel out of the loop. So you've got to take the time to talk to them. And to listen to them. And to make them understand that if we don't take care of the customer, we are dead. That is why we at GM lost our market."

Then Smith sat down, and silence filled the room. This wasn't what people had expected from Alan Smith, the seemingly stiff and stone-faced finance man whom they had known for decades, but never really known at all. Finally, someone had said out loud what this pickle dish evening was really all about. A collective catharsis took hold.

GM's new CEO rushed to seize the moment. "This will never happen again," Jack Smith declared, his voice rising. "And We Will Win!"

BOOK II

THE YOUNG
LIONS

CHAPTER 14

THE BUBBLE BURSTS

Among the Japanese auto executives who gained power and prominence during the 1980s, Shoichiro Irimajiri stood out as the quintessential Honda man. Irimajiri (pronounced EAR-ee-muh-JEER-ee) not only had an unusual name, he was as quirky, daring, and unconventional as his company. He hailed from the rural island of Shikoku, the Japanese equivalent of Nebraska, which is separated from the main island of Honshu by Japan's Inland Sea. Irimajiri was born in 1940 and grew up in a postwar Japan that was fascinated with two things: America and technology. One of his clearest childhood memories was finding a book on airplanes that contained an article, "Wonder of Aeronautics," written by the famed American test pilot Chuck Yeager. From that day on, Irimajiri wanted to be an aeronautical engineer.[1]

He majored in that subject at Tokyo University, where he was a pretty fair pitcher in intramural baseball. While in college, Irimajiri worked for a month as an intern at Mitsubishi Heavy Industries, the company that had produced the famed Zero fighter during the war. But in the postwar world, Mitsubishi's mission was to repair American-built aircraft. Irimajiri was bored.[2]

Which is why, as he neared graduation in 1963, Irimajiri broke with convention. As a fresh graduate of Japan's most prestigious university, he was expected to join Mitsubishi or one of Japan's other established, blue-chip companies. But instead, Irimajiri shocked his parents and professors by opting for a fifteen-year-old company that made motorcycles: Honda Motor.

It was the beginning of a career that surged rapidly upward in tandem with Japan's postwar prosperity. In 1982, at age forty-two, Irimajiri was named a managing director of Honda, the youngest ever. Two years later he was dispatched from Japan to Ohio, to take the helm at Honda's fledgling manufacturing complex there. And in 1988, after four hugely successful years in the United States, Irimajiri was promoted back to Japan as the odds-on favorite to become the president of Honda one day.

But on March 18, 1992, Shoichiro Irimajiri made a surprise announcement. It provided a metaphor for what was happening to Honda and to the rest of the Japanese auto industry as well.

HONDA MOTOR's free-spirited, unorthodox culture stemmed directly from the personality of the company's founder, Soichiro Honda. He was born in 1906, the son of a blacksmith in the village of Komyo, 160 miles southwest of Tokyo. Decades later he would recall being so intoxicated with the sight of his first car, a Ford, that he smeared his face and hands with the oil that had dripped out from underneath. Honda would imbue the company that bore his name with the same reverence for hands-on engineering.[3]

Honda Motor, like many of its future customers, was born after World War II. Between 1948 and 1963, Honda built a reputation as a premier maker of small motorcycles.[4] Then in 1963, just as the American Baby Boom generation was reaching driving age, Honda made its breakthrough in America with an advertising campaign built around the motto: "You meet the nicest people on a Honda."

Until then, motorcycles meant Hell's Angels. But Honda's marketing made motorcycles appealing to ordinary, middle-class Americans.[5] It even spawned a 1964 Beach Boys song, "Little Honda," that went: "It's not a big motorcycle, just a groovy little motor bike." Honda started to become a household word.

Two other things happened at Honda in 1963. The company built its first automobiles—a minitruck with a 30-horsepower engine and a prototype sports car called the S-500. And Shoichiro Irimajiri signed on.

Irimajiri's early years at Honda were less than promising. Assigned to Honda's fledgling Formula One racing team in 1964, Irimajiri quickly learned about failure as Honda's cars became the joke of the European-dominated circuit. One day in August 1965, after a particularly disappointing breakdown in the British Grand Prix, Irimajiri got a humiliating dressing-down from Mr. Honda himself. Irimajiri had designed a piston for the Honda race car that failed because of a flaw that any one of the team mechanics—men with less schooling than Irimajiri but more real-life experience—could have spotted. "I hate college graduates!" Honda ranted. "A company does not need people like you who use only their heads."[6]

Irimajiri survived, and a few years later found himself getting a second chance as a key player on a far more important project. Pressed by pending U.S. clean-air regulations, a crack team of Honda engineers had been assigned to develop an engine that could satisfy the new law. The result was the CVCC, for Compound Vortex Controlled Combustion. Not only was the CVCC powerful for its size, but it was the world's only engine that could meet the U.S. clean-air standards without a catalytic converter attached. In 1974, with the United States reeling from the Arab oil embargo, Honda introduced the Civic CVCC. It was a smashing success. The eight men on the All or Nothing Team that developed the engine jumped on the fast track. The lead engineer, Tadashi Kume, became president and CEO of Honda Motor in 1983. One of Kume's key underlings on the CVCC project, Irimajiri, rose with him.

HONDA'S DECISION to build cars in the United States—making it the first Japanese company to do so—eventually would be portrayed in business schools as a bold and brilliant gamble. The men who made the decision, though, were following what they deemed to be a conservative game plan.

Honda wanted to expand, but the obstacles in Japan seemed insurmountable. Toyota and Nissan dominated the market, accounting for half of Japanese vehicle sales. That left the other half for nine other Japanese manufacturers, including Honda. America, however, had just four automakers—the Big Three plus tiny American Motors. All of them were plagued with inefficiency and shoddy quality. The Civic CVCC had shown that Americans were receptive to Honda products as alternatives to Detroit's clunkers.

The big unknown to Honda was American workers, who were widely portrayed as lazy, oafish, and spoiled. The Honda men figured that, even if this were correct, it was probably a management problem instead of a labor problem. But they weren't sure. To hedge their bet, they decided to start by building motorcycles, which would require far fewer workers than building cars. They chose bucolic Marysville, Ohio—thirty miles northwest of Columbus—because it was south of the United Auto Workers' heartland, but still fairly close to parts suppliers. The site and all the early employees were carefully selected by Shige Yoshida, a gentle man with flawless English—and vivid boyhood memories of American planes bombing his home town of Yokohama during the war.

The motorcycle plant opened in late 1979, and clicked so quickly that within a year, Honda announced it would build an auto-assembly plant at Marysville as well. The car factory opened with production of the Accord in late 1982.

In the same year, Irimajiri was promoted to a managing director of Honda, the equivalent of a corporate vice president in the United States. He moved into manufacturing as manager of Honda's sprawling assembly plant at Suzuka, southwest of Tokyo. In June 1984, Kume tapped Irimajiri to become president of Honda of America Manufacturing.

To spare the Americans from fumbling with his tongue-twister name, Irimajiri asked to be called Iri-san, Mr. Iri, or simply Iri. He was short but powerfully built. His eyes were bright and riveting—and so nearly Western in appearance that when fatigue made his eyelids droop, the Americans would say to him, "Mr. Iri, today your eyes look Japanese!" Irimajiri said he had two goals for Marysville: to produce cars of world-class quality, and to be the best place to work in the U.S. auto industry. He set another goal for himself: adapting to America.

He stopped smoking, took up golf, and started jogging five miles every morning. He mastered English so well that he conducted news interviews without a translator. And the frequent presence of empty hamburger wrappers in his car testified to his new affinity for McDonald's.

An early test of Irimajiri's efforts came when Marysville's quality auditors kept finding squeaks and rattles in the Accord dashboards. Honda couldn't afford the perception that its American-made cars were inferior to those built in Japan. Irimajiri asked that the quality data be fed back to the assembly line, so workers could trace the trouble to its roots and develop "counter measures," Honda-speak for solutions. That was how Honda had always solved production problems in Japan.

But not in Ohio, it soon became clear. The squeaks and rattles persisted, prompting a puzzled Irimajiri to call a meeting of the plant's top managers, both Japanese and Americans. In Japan, he explained, teams of workers would devise their own counter measures in a process that worked much like baseball. If a batter hits a fly ball behind third base, any one of three players can catch it: the third baseman, shortstop, or left fielder. No one has to be told in advance who should catch the ball. The players decide on their own.

That was fine for baseball, the Americans replied, but naive for an assembly line. They insisted the best analogy for factory work was football. Each player is assigned a specific function—to block an opponent or to run a certain pass pattern. The players work together by performing their individual tasks.

The analogies persuaded Irimajiri to change the production system. He had workers—or "associates" in Honda parlance—put their employee ID numbers on every dashboard they installed. Before long, the rattles virtually disappeared.

Irimajiri was surprised and delighted. It was clear to him now that Americans had far different expectations of factory work from Japanese. In Japan, while the line between managers and workers was clear, workers were used to taking responsibility for improving a factory's operations. Americans wanted more specific orders. They were willing to use their brains as well as their bodies, but it didn't come naturally yet. They would need more structure and more individual recognition.

Honda's Japanese factories used "quality circles," small discussion groups in which workers offered suggestions for improving everything from quality to productivity to safety. Irimajiri Americanized this process at Marysville. Workers who made suggestions were asked to implement the ideas themselves. The only requirement, the workers were told, was to use their KKD, a Japanese acronym for words that, in English, meant Experience, Intuition, and Guts.

Irimajiri would frequently stroll through the factory floor—a hostile place for managers in many Big Three factories—to ask workers individually about their ideas. And every two months, he hosted little awards ceremonies to present certificates to people who made successful suggestions. The top 100 contributors got their names posted in the plant. Honda also built an employee sports center complete with swimming pool, gym, and fitness room adjacent to the factory.

All these moves were remarkably simple. But by late 1985, Marysville's quality and productivity levels had become the envy of Detroit. And the plant had evolved from an oddity to a manufacturing mecca, where executives from the Big Three and even from outside the auto industry would come to watch what Honda was doing. Often, they were amazed.

On September 19, as the last 1985-model Accord was rolling off the end of the plant's assembly line, workers began building the completely redesigned 1986 model at the beginning of the same line. At Big Three factories, similar major model changes took two or three months, during which the plants were idled at enormous cost for the installation of new tooling and machines. But Honda, thanks to eighteen months of careful and clever planning, had done it in less than a day.

Two months after this feat, the Harvard Business School invited Irimajiri to speak at its Corporate Leadership Forum. He didn't talk about corporate strategy or management methods or quality control. Instead he chose a sports analogy, not football or baseball, but auto racing. "We often think about racing activities as being important to research and marketing," Irimajiri said. "But the real importance of racing is in the development of the racing spirit."[7]

With that, he launched into an explanation of racing as the model for Honda's overall corporate quest. "Despite the preparation, despite the practice and teamwork, everything is unpredictable in racing," he said. "When a problem arises, you have to find the solution now. . . . The same is true in the manufacturing plant.

"Throughout the plant, we operate with minimal inventories. Partly, it is a method by which we maintain quality and avoid large batches of scrap parts. But more importantly, if a problem develops, a solution must be found immediately or the entire plant will be stopped. This technique requires that we pay constant attention to what we are doing—that we maintain an atmosphere in which quick response to problems is the norm."[8]

In a nutshell, Irimajiri had described the essence of Japan's manufacturing advantage. It wasn't singing the company song or doing calisthenics before work in the morning—as comically portrayed in *Gung Ho*, a popular movie of the day. Nor was it workers who slept by their machines at night and worked themselves to death during the day. Instead, it was creating a system in which problems had to be solved promptly, because the consequence of ignoring them was too severe. And as Honda had proved in Marysville, it was a system that could work in America.

Irimajiri finished his speech with a pointed summation of Honda's values and his own: "We believe the winner takes all. In our racing activities throughout the world, second place is seldom remembered and never honored. For us, winning the race is the final goal—nothing else."[9]

To the largely American audience, this sounded like Vince Lombardi. For a Japanese, Irimajiri seemed very American indeed.

IRIMAJIRI HAD CHOSEN an auspicious time to talk about racing. In 1983 Honda had reentered Formula One racing after a thirteen-year absence, and by late 1985 it was clear the company was a comer. When the 1986 season began, Honda-powered cars started winning race after race. And in September of that year, Honda cars won their first Constructors' Championship, the international Formula One title. It wouldn't be Honda's last.

Irimajiri seized the chance to inspire his troops. Every July he brought the Honda drivers and their cars to Marysville. The private road on the company's complex was turned into a minitrack for the drivers to zip around on before signing autographs. Irimajiri himself usually took a few laps. He became a fast friend of Ayrton Senna, the world champion from Brazil, who drove Honda engines to victory after victory.

Honda was racing ahead on other fronts as well. In March of 1986, the United Auto Workers union suspended what once had seemed a determined organizing drive at Marysville. The union concluded that its support among the workers was so slim that the UAW gave up without a vote.

A month later, Honda opened a second assembly line at Marysville, making it one of the largest assembly plants in the United States. The expansion provided another test of Irimajiri's mettle. When the second line started up, nearly all the workers on the first line's night shift wanted to transfer to work days on the second line. That left the second shift with all the newly hired workers, and the number of defects soared. Problems like this didn't exist in Japan, where workers even at established plants routinely alternated their shifts, working days one week and nights the next. But when Irimajiri set up the same schedule at Marysville, he was inundated with complaints.

To Irimajiri this was just like racing—an unanticipated problem that required a quick solution. He offered experienced workers premium pay to work night duty for several months, so the new employees could learn from them. The workers agreed. After the initial hiccups, the second shift came smoothly on line.

Such events prompted the American managers at Marysville to develop a parable. There was a pesky fly buzzing around the office, the story went, and each of them was asked to get rid of it. Scott Whitlock, the blunt-talking Columbus attorney who had switched careers to become Marysville's plant manager, would wait until the fly landed on a wall. Then he would bulldoze the wall. Ed Buker, a lanky young man who had joined Honda a month before Irimajiri arrived at Marysville and quickly became his protégé, would take aim with a shotgun and blast the fly out of existence. Southern-born Al Kinzer, the first American hired at Marysville, would sing a country song in his off-key drawl, causing the fly to flee.

But Irimajiri, in contrast, would sit down with the fly. He would listen to the fly, talk to it, and persuade the creature to change into something more useful—perhaps a honeybee that would pollinate the flowers around the plant.

Everyone laughed at the story, because it captured the men's personalities so well. For Irimajiri, motivating workers on an assembly line—where jobs were physical, repetitive, and boring—was just the sort of challenge he loved. And every day, Honda had more and more American workers to motivate.

In September 1986, Honda opened an engine and components plant in Anna, Ohio, a hamlet fifty miles southwest of Marysville. The move, yet another first among Japanese automakers, made Honda's American manufacturing operations more than just an assembler of imported parts. Instead, the company was rapidly becoming an integrated manufacturer in North America. Two months after the Anna plant opened, Honda began building Accords at a new assembly plant in Alliston, Ontario, northwest of Toronto.

Honda was setting sales precedents as well. In the spring of 1986 it launched a new division, Acura, to sell what a few years earlier would have been a contradiction in terms: Japanese luxury cars. On the surface, like everything else Honda did, it was a bold and risky move. But the company carefully hedged its bets by developing the two Acura models, the Legend and Integra, off its existing platforms for the Accord and Civic. Honda was betting that American Baby Boomers —who had come of age driving its cars and now were coming into affluence—would want upscale alternatives to the snobby, overpriced European marques and to the creaky, oversized land barges from Detroit.

The bet paid off spectacularly. Acura sold nearly 53,000 cars during its first nine months, helping Honda's U.S. car sales surpass Toyota's and Nissan's in 1986 for the first time ever. Honda's surge was also helped by the announcement in August 1986 that its cars had topped the customer satisfaction survey compiled by J. D. Power & Associates, an influential California consulting firm. In 1987, Acura's first full year in existence, its U.S. sales more than doubled to nearly 110,000 cars, more than Mercedes, BMW, or Volvo. Also that year, Acura and Honda swept the top two spots on the Power satisfaction survey. And *Time* magazine put the company on its cover with a fawning article headlined "The Honda Way."[10]

Honda's amazing success was punctuated in September 1987, when President Kume traveled from Tokyo to Columbus to unveil a new strategic vision. With Irimajiri and other company officials at his side, Kume announced that Honda intended to make its U.S. operations a completely self-reliant car company, capable of designing and engineering cars, making components and assembling automobiles all by itself. Honda, he said, would build a second U.S. assembly plant in Ohio's East Liberty township, just a few miles from Marysville. It would expand its engineering and product-development operations, as well as the Anna engine plant. And Honda would export cars from North America to Europe, the Far East, and even to Japan itself.

The announcement stunned the moguls in Motown. They had been shrinking their companies because, they complained, American workers weren't productive and Japanese competitors were unfair. Now here was Honda proclaiming an enormous expansion in America, and thus giving the lie to all of Detroit's excuses. As if to rub it in, within weeks after the announcement Honda sent the first car it built in America—an Accord sedan with license plate USA 001—to Detroit's Henry Ford Museum, to go on permanent display. A few months later, on March 7,

1988, Honda started translating Kume's words into action by exporting U.S.-built Accords to Japan.

Honda was a full-fledged phenomenon. Other car companies rushed headlong into joint ventures and partnerships, but Honda remained stubbornly independent and true to its motto: "Carry Your Own Torch." Chrysler soon launched an in-house study to find out why Honda was succeeding where it was failing. Teams of M.B.A. students around America did much the same. What the Americans discovered was totally beyond their experience.

In contrast to the palatial private offices occupied by the big shots in Detroit and throughout corporate America, Honda's executive suite in Japan was a large, open room. The thirty or so occupants had only a desk and a phone to call their own. They spent most of the day sitting around conference tables or milling about, and talking in a process the company termed *waigaya*, loosely translated as "shooting the breeze." This open, free-flowing exchange of ideas, Honda men explained, was essential to creativity. And *waigaya* was a key element of the company's *kyowa sei*, or "republican system," in which Honda's president was merely the first among equals, and decision-making was spread among the senior executives.[11] Corporate personality cults, à la Iacocca, were nowhere to be found.

It was to this unconventional executive suite that Irimajiri was summoned in 1988. On June 30, he was promoted to headquarters as managing director for Honda manufacturing worldwide. When he had arrived in Ohio, Honda had 2,000 manufacturing employees in America. Now that he was leaving, there were 6,400. It was only a matter of time, Honda watchers figured, until he became president of the company.

Just before he left, Honda threw an emotional farewell fling in Ohio for a man who had arrived as a boss and was leaving as a friend. The party was held on a Saturday afternoon, when the factories weren't running, and employees and their families could relax. To symbolize the changing of the guard, Irimajiri threw a ceremonial "last pitch" to Hiroyuki Yoshino, his successor. Yoshino had been Irimajiri's college roommate, and also his catcher on their baseball team during their days together at Tokyo University. It was a fitting ceremony in any language.

. . .

By the time Irimajiri left Ohio, Honda had become the Pied Piper for other Japanese car companies in America. Toyota, Nissan, Mitsubishi, Mazda, Subaru, Isuzu, and Suzuki joined Honda in building assembly plants in the United States, Canada, or both. Toyota and Nissan geared up to launch their own luxury divisions—Lexus and Infiniti—to capitalize on the runaway success of Acura.

By the end of the eighties, the convergence of Japanese and American cultures that had begun in Marysville started to take root even in Detroit. The Japanese had things that Detroit's automakers desperately wanted: high-quality, low-cost components as well as an abundance of manufacturing expertise. The number of Japanese companies with branches in Detroit surged from fifty in 1982 to nearly 300 by 1990. Most were related to the auto industry.

One of the most successful belonged to one of Japan's Big Five trading companies, Mitsui, which set up shop in suburban Southfield to sell Japanese steel. Mitsui's biggest customer, Lee Iacocca notwithstanding, was Chrysler, which bought Japanese steel for the same reason Americans were snapping up Japanese cars: good prices and high quality. Iacocca's Japan bashing sometimes strained the relationship, but what really rankled the Mitsui staffers was having to drive Chrysler cars.

The Japanese companies flocking to Detroit to tap a new market themselves became a market for local entrepreneurs of all sorts. Raymond & Dillon, a small Detroit-area law firm, hired an English-speaking woman from Japan as its marketing director and signed up nearly seventy Japanese corporate clients, comprising some 20 percent of its overall business. One of the city's biggest law firms—Dickinson, Wright, Moon, Van Dusen & Freeman—hired two Japanese lawyers and a Japanese paralegal, and started conducting seminars and publishing a little newsletter for its Japanese clients, all in Japanese.[12]

The local accountants weren't far behind. Virtually every one of the Big Six accounting firms hired Japanese staffers in Detroit to serve this growing segment of the area's otherwise stagnant business base. Deloitte & Touche, which audited the books of General Motors and Chrysler, put five Japanese accountants on its Detroit staff to lure new business. Coopers & Lybrand, Ford's auditor, hired six.[13]

The Sheraton Oaks Hotel in the suburb of Novi, northwest of the city, hired a local Japanese woman as "director of Japan marketing." Not to be outdone, the Hyatt Regency Hotel in Dearborn, a stone's throw from Ford headquarters, opened a sushi restaurant that was a branch of a well-known Tokyo chain.

Suburban Detroit hospitals also avidly pursued Japanese customers. One put bilingual forms in its emergency room. Another started offering birthing classes in Japanese.

By 1990 the Detroit area had 3,500 Japanese expatriates, who were forming a little infrastructure of their own. A Japanese school offered Saturday language and culture classes to children in three separate locations. Ayako Kinoshita, the wife of a Coopers & Lybrand partner, published a local Japanese newsletter with such practical advice as what questions to avoid asking Americans (How old are you? How much money do you make?). The Kinoshitas were invited to join the Indianwood Country Club, not as exclusive as Bloomfield Hills but still a prestigious club that signaled their participation in the American good life. [14]

Anti-Japanese hostility, to be sure, remained just below the surface in Detroit, and reared its head at unexpected moments. Once, when Mrs. Kinoshita called a house painter, he recognized her Japanese accent and snapped: "Why did you people bomb Pearl Harbor?" Startled, she replied that she was terribly sorry the attack had occurred—and then hung up the phone and called another painter. [15]

But more typical were efforts by Japanese and Detroiters to embrace each other's cultures, sometimes with comic results. One such episode occurred to a man named Martin Rowell.

Rowell was British by birth. But he had become an American citizen and gone to work for a leading components company, Allied Signal Automotive. He lived in suburban Bloomfield Township, twenty-five miles northwest of Detroit.

In the fall of 1990, the Rowells got new neighbors, the Takai family. Mr. Takai was in his midforties and worked for a small Japanese parts supplier. He was thrilled to be living in America, and eager to sample American customs. His English was halting and his wife's nonexistent, so the Takais did most of their communicating with neighbors through their sixteen-year-old daughter. One day, right around Christmas, Mr. Takai and his daughter knocked on the Rowells' door to ask for advice. They had no experience in mowing lawns, they earnestly explained, because there weren't many lawns in Japan. But they were eager to try, and wanted to know what lawnmower to buy. Would a "sit-on" mower be best?

Their lawn was too small for that, Rowell replied. He suggested buying a power mower from Sears, after it went on sale. The Takais didn't understand what a sale was, so Rowell explained.

In mid-March of 1991, Mr. Takai dutifully went to Sears and purchased a self-propelled power mower, on sale. He asked Rowell to help him assemble the machine, and Rowell happily assisted. After the mower was assembled, Mr. Takai couldn't get it to start. Rowell trooped back over to the Takai garage to demonstrate how to operate the manual choke. When the mower revved up, Mr. Takai smiled with the excitement of a man irresistibly drawn to a chore that most Americans detested.

For the next three weeks, Mr. Takai repeatedly knocked on Rowell's door, anxiously asking whether the grass was ready to be mowed. Finally Rowell said yes, and Mr. Takai asked him for tips on technique. Should one start in the middle of the lawn, or on the edge? Was it best to mow along one edge, or on all sides?

After Mr. Takai finally started mowing, culminating months of eager anticipation, Rowell stuck his head out the door to see how his neighbor was doing. Mr. Takai was zipping right along, smiling and waving enthusiastically as he went. Across the lawn, his daughter was hard at work, too. She was wielding the family's camcorder, videotaping her father proudly mowing a lawn for the first time in his life.

IN OCTOBER 1989, Soichiro Honda, nearing his eighty-third birthday and in fragile health, took a triumphant tour of Honda's factories in Ohio. He was the auto industry's last living entrepreneur, the founder of the world's only successful car company started after World War II. For Honda's workers in Ohio, his appearance was like Henry Ford I returning to life.

Workers scrambled to pose for pictures alongside their visitor. They cheered, applauded, and pushed their company caps in his face for him to autograph. Mr. Honda loved it all. He stood in an electric cart and rode along the Marysville assembly line, which was stopped for the occasion, with his wife pulling on the tails of his jacket to keep him from bolting away. Finally, he burst free and plunged into the crowd, flashing a thumbs-up sign and saying, *"Arigato domo, domo,"* Japanese for thank-you very much.

At the engine plant in Anna he planted a tree, after fighting off an aide who wanted to spare him the trouble of lifting the shovel. The old man's spirit, if not his body, was still intact. From Ohio he went to Midland, Michigan, to become the first Japanese inducted into the Automotive Hall of Fame. Honda Motor was at its height.

Shoichiro Irimajiri, meanwhile, was readjusting to life in Japan, though not always easily. When he had first returned from Ohio, he had tried commuting to work on a Honda motorcycle, before eventually surrendering to Tokyo's traffic and switching to the train. The commute and his heavy work load left little time for golf or jogging, but there were other satisfactions.

In late 1989, Honda won its fourth consecutive Formula One racing title. The company launched its fourth-generation Accord, the first version of the model to leap from compact status squarely into the midsize class. The Accord now was competing directly against the Ford Taurus, the Pontiac Grand Prix, and other family sedans, and it was beating their wheels off. On January 4, 1990, came the stunning news that, during the prior year, the Accord had been the best-selling car in America, the first time ever for a foreign nameplate.

Even without Acura, Honda had outsold Oldsmobile in 1989 with only one third as many dealers. In all, Honda had sold a record 783,000 cars in the United States that year, and its goal was 1 million a year by the mid-nineties. Meanwhile, Honda was building its first assembly plant in England, a major extension of the manufacturing network that Irimajiri was running around the globe. The future seemed bright, for both Irimajiri and Honda.

Then the unexpected happened.

On May 10, Honda announced President Kume would retire and be succeeded by a veteran company engineer. His name was not Irimajiri, however, but Nobuhiko Kawamoto. In the race for the presidency of Honda, Irimajiri had finished in the place without honor—second.

Honda watchers around the world, from Detroit to BMW headquarters in Munich, were surprised and puzzled. Honda was the most international of all Japanese car companies, the only one, in fact, to sell more cars in America than it did in its home market. And Irimajiri, having built Honda's North American manufacturing operations into the wonder of the automotive world, had far more U.S. experience than Kawamoto.

Not that Kawamoto was a slouch. Behind his boyish, friendly face was the mind of a brilliant automotive engineer. Like Irimajiri, he had worked under Kume on the team that had developed the CVCC. Unlike Irimajiri, though, he hadn't veered into manufacturing, but instead had stayed at Honda R&D Company, the subsidiary responsible for developing new cars. He rose through R&D's ranks to become the subsidiary's president in 1986.

Kawamoto's career path, in fact, had closely paralleled the one followed by Kume himself. Honda R&D was an elite organization within the company, holding the same power, mystique, and exalted status that the finance staff had enjoyed at General Motors for five decades. While Irimajiri had been off on his foreign adventure, Kawamoto had kept close to the center of power in Japan. In many ways, he was the safer, more conventional choice for president.

And playing it safe seemed to be increasingly in vogue at Honda, despite the company's long record of innovation. The 1990 Accord moved Honda into the midsize market, but beyond that there was little to distinguish it. Its styling was handsome, but not eye-grabbing. Instead of air bags—which Chrysler, of all companies, was moving fastest to make standard in its cars—Honda had stuck with awkward motorized seat belts. And the other hot safety option, antilock brakes, wasn't offered, either. The Accord was beating the competition largely because the competition was weak.

A reader of *Car and Driver*, in a letter to the editor of the magazine, put it succinctly. "Hondas are unquestionably competent," he wrote, "but dull."[16]

WHILE IRIMAJIRI hadn't won Honda's presidency, his consolation prize was a job that most men would kill for. He was named executive vice president for research and development as well as worldwide production. He wasn't in charge of sales or finance, but he was Kawamoto's strong right arm, running the entire operating side of Honda's business. And at just fifty years of age he was four years younger than Kawamoto. There was still an outside chance he would become president of Honda one day.

He threw himself into his new job with the same intense energy that had made him successful all his life. Honda's new assembly plant in Ohio was accelerating its production rate. The new English factory was preparing for startup. And the company was adding a third assembly line at the Suzuka factory in Japan, where Irimajiri himself had once been plant manager. Honda wanted the extra capacity in Japan because its factories there were producing flat-out.

Japan was enjoying the effects of a remarkable "Bubble Economy." The Tokyo stock market hit unprecedented heights, and land prices soared so much that the value of the Imperial Palace grounds in central Tokyo exceeded the value of all the land in the state of California. Japanese people felt rich, and they were buying record numbers of cars. Car sales in Japan soared 13.5 percent in 1988, another 18.5 percent in 1989, and then another 16 percent in 1990. Three straight years of double-digit increases were unprecedented. [17]

Like Honda, all Japanese manufacturers saw no end in sight. Toyota and Nissan started building new, highly automated assembly plants on the southern island of Kyushu, about the only place in the country without an acute shortage of labor. In Aichi Prefecture, home of Toyota City, workers were so scarce that Toyota loaded a new assembly line at its Tahara factory with enough automation to build luxury cars with just fifteen and a half hours of labor per vehicle—compared with thirty-four hours per vehicle in the average GM plant. Mazda's domestic sales surged 67 percent between 1987 and 1990, as the company launched a program to double its dealerships and the number of models it made. The company also started an internal study aimed at launching its own luxury brand—Amati—to compete with Lexus, Infiniti, and Acura.

In the United States, meanwhile, the Honda Accord topped the sales charts in 1990 for the second straight year. As 1991 began, the U.S. economy was reeling from the Persian Gulf War and the onset of recession. But the Japanese auto industry had its throttle wide open, thanks to the booming home market and to continued gains in the United States. The Japanese, as always, seemed immune from the economic swings that buffeted the rest of the world.

But they weren't. Changes were afoot that most Americans, who had been cowed by the Japanese for fifteen years, could scarcely begin to imagine. Nor did the Japanese see what was happening—even after, ever so lightly, they tapped on their brakes.

IN EARLY FEBRUARY 1991, Honda quietly decided to cut 25,000 cars out of its first-quarter production schedule for the U.S. market. Most of the reduction, some 20,000 cars, would be accomplished by shipping fewer cars from Japan. But the company's plants in Ohio would build 5,000 fewer cars than they had previously planned.

Cutting 25,000 cars was a baby step by the standards of Detroit, which during the Gulf War was slashing hundreds of thousands of cars from its factory schedules and shutting plants for weeks at a time. GM's first-quarter production plans, in fact, were the company's lowest in thirty-six years. But for Honda, even a tiny cutback was unprecedented. Only once since 1970 had Honda's U.S. sales declined from the prior year, and that was only because of government import quotas. Throughout the 1980s, while Big Three factories ran up and down like roller-coasters, Honda's production plans had pointed in just one direction—up. Now Honda was discovering there was another direction as well.

Later in the month, Honda discovered its cuts weren't enough. The company rented a former U.S. Army depot in central Ohio to store an additional 2,000 cars that the factories had built, but that dealers hadn't ordered. In Lafayette, Indiana, meanwhile, the Subaru–Isuzu factory was storing 7,000 unsold cars and trucks. And in Georgetown, Kentucky, Toyota rented an overflow storage lot adjacent to its existing property—just in case.

During the early and mid-1980s, even in recession years, Japanese cars were in such short supply that dealers could pack hundreds or even thousands of extra dollars onto the sticker price. They even took to calling it "the pack." Now, though, the Japanese actually had plenty of cars, and their dealers were learning a new word: discount. For the first time in twenty years the Japanese didn't seem to be walking on water anymore. Back in Tokyo, at Honda headquarters in the chic district of Aoyama, Nobuhiko Kawamoto surveyed his new global empire and reached a startling conclusion.

The collegial, unstructured management scheme that had made Honda the world's fastest-growing and most admired car company, he decided, had outlived its usefulness in a rapidly changing world. The "republican system" that made everybody responsible for decisions meant that nobody was responsible. Cost overruns were common. The atmosphere in the one-room executive suite was so distracting that, whenever Kawamoto wanted to work undisturbed, he stayed at home. Americans remained ardent admirers of Honda's free-form style, but Kawamoto found it burdensome. Honda wasn't a little company anymore. The company needed a top-down management structure, just like any other large organization.

On February 20, Kawamoto climbed into a black Acura Legend limousine and headed across Tokyo to the office of Mr. Honda. The company's aging founder wasn't a major shareholder anymore, so Kawamoto didn't need his permission for anything. But the old man was deserving of respect.

Kawamoto bowed to Mr. Honda, sat down, and told him, "Not everything you taught is right for the future. From here on, I will do things that may not be agreeable to you. Please allow me." Mr. Honda nodded, and soon afterward Kawamoto left.[18]

Soon, Honda Motor started giving its U.S. dealers unprecedented discounts of $900 a car to spur sales of the Accord. More significantly, Kawamoto announced Honda would break with its past by adopting a more traditional hierarchy—complete with individual responsibilities, and even private offices, for executives.

Mr. Honda wouldn't be able to judge the results for himself. On August 5, 1991, six months after Kawamoto had come calling, the legendary patriarch died. He was eighty-four years old.

IRIMAJIRI HAD JUST one problem with his company's new top-down structure—that he himself wasn't on top. In principle, he agreed with what Kawamoto was doing, and urged him to move even faster. Irimajiri started to see a future for the company that looked starkly different from the past.

For two decades, the Japanese auto industry—and especially Honda —had enjoyed nearly nonstop growth. This had continued even in the mid-1980s, when the world's major industrial governments pushed up the value of the yen and made the price of all Japanese products, including cars, more expensive overseas. The Japanese had shrugged off this challenge because they had a big advantage in factory efficiency, and because the Big Three stupidly helped by slapping on big price increases of their own.

In 1990 and 1991 the yen continued to rise, and finally pushed Japanese car prices higher than those of competing models from Detroit. But the Japanese could command premium prices, because their cars were better in terms of quality, technology, and overall distinctiveness. By late 1991, however, those advantages were disappearing.

Even as they railed against the Japanese during the eighties, the Big Three had been working hard behind the scenes to become more like their archfoes. Free trade, though Detroit despised it, had forced the American car companies to improve every aspect of their operations. They were catching up in plant productivity, engine technology, and quality. Detroit had even passed the Japanese in installing safety features, such as antilock brakes and air bags, in midpriced cars.

As Irimajiri saw it, cars were becoming more like commodities. A Taurus and an Accord weren't much more different to many Americans than wheat from Kansas and wheat from Nebraska. Honda no longer could count on either continual sales growth or the ability to charge premium prices.

"Not only Honda, but all the Japanese car companies will slow down," Irimajiri told visitors to the 1991 Tokyo Motor Show, which was far more subdued than the extravaganza of two years before. "Adjusting to slower growth is the biggest issue for the Japanese auto industry in the 1990s. Until last year, our industry was built on the concept of rapid growth. Most senior managers believed we could expand our operations on a global basis forever. But the reality is far different."[19]

And far less pleasant as well. Irimajiri looked tired and haggard. The energetic and upbeat man who had once given Japan's automotive juggernaut a human face and an attractive personality was losing his verve. Now the fun was fading. Even in Marysville, workers who suggested new ideas had to justify them with paperwork and analysis, not just KKD. And in Tokyo, Kawamoto was saying publicly that Honda might pull out of Formula One racing, even though the company's engines were racking up a remarkable sixth consecutive championship.

To Irimajiri, Formula One was close to sacred. Honda was shelling out nearly $100 million a year on Formula One, but Irimajiri counted it money well spent. He reiterated to reporters what he had told the Harvard Business School: that racing was essential to Honda's special spirit and morale, and he couldn't imagine withdrawing, whatever the cost. His disagreement with Kawamoto provided a rare public glimpse of discord at the top of a major Japanese corporation. But Irimajiri couldn't expect to win. In top-down management the boss got his way.

As Honda ended 1991, its luster had faded. The Accord retained its status as the top-selling car in America for the third straight year. But the Acura marque, after leading the J. D. Power satisfaction survey for four years in a row, tumbled to fourth place, behind Lexus, Infiniti, and Mercedes-Benz. Honda's overall U.S. sales dropped 6 percent—

although because competitors dropped further, the company's market share rose.

There was no such consolation for Honda in Japan. There, the bursting of the bubble economy sent car sales into their steepest drop in a dozen years. Honda fared worse than average. It lost third place in the sales race to Mitsubishi, and was in danger of dropping behind Mazda as well. Kawamoto declared that he, Irimajiri, and Yoshihide Munekuni, the third member of the company's ruling troika, would take personal charge of Honda's auto business in Japan.

To adjust to the new austerity, Honda cut hiring in Japan to only 130 college graduates in the spring of 1992—far below the 500-plus hired the previous year. As profits plunged, the company also slashed its capital spending around the world. For the first time in more than a decade, new construction in Ohio came to a stop. The company would finish the assembly plant it was building in England, because it needed a European production base to head off the threat of protectionism there. But after that, a dozen years of nonstop construction around the globe would halt.

As Irimajiri looked into the future, he didn't like what he saw, either for Honda or for himself. He was throwing himself at the company's problems, working marathon days without break, but he couldn't seem to make a dent in the work. In his Ohio years there had always been someone to take some of the pressure off him and help put things in perspective. But he didn't seem to have such a confidant in Tokyo. In career terms, his chances of becoming president were uncertain at best. And even if Irimajiri eventually got the job, would he want it? Honda remained a great company in many ways. But the spirit and the excitement of the growth years were gone, perhaps forever.

On March 18, 1992, Honda issued a terse release that caught the automotive world by surprise. Executive Vice President Shoichiro Irimajiri had resigned, effective immediately, the company said, because of ill health. He had a heart disorder brought on by excessive stress, a company spokesman explained, and had been admitted to a hospital.

A month later, Susan Insley, a Honda executive from Ohio who had been especially close to Irimajiri and his wife, happened to be in Japan. The night she arrived, the phone in her hotel room rang, and she heard a voice that sounded both strange and familiar. "Susan," said the voice, "this is Iri."

They met a few days later, and Irimajiri looked terrible: thin, tired, pale, and gaunt. He had lost the youthful and growing Honda that he loved, and now Honda had lost him. His eyes looked very Japanese indeed.

IRIMAJIRI GOT OUT just in time. Four months after he resigned, Honda disclosed a second, and far bigger, U.S. production cut: 12 percent, or 28,000 cars. In the fall of 1992 came more bad news. Honda disclosed that its pretax profits for the fiscal year ending in March 1993 would plunge 24 percent, far more than previously expected.

When 1992 ended, the Accord was dethroned by the Ford Taurus after a three-year reign as America's top-selling car. Ford had needed huge discounts and heavy sales to rental fleets to win, but there was no denying its victory. And no denying either that, for the first time in seven years, Honda had fallen behind Toyota in U.S. car sales. The goal of selling 1 million cars a year in America by the mid-1990s was long gone.

The gap with Toyota was far larger counting the various forms of trucks—pickups, minivans, and Jeep knockoffs—that Honda didn't even make. These vehicles, not traditional sedans and coupes, were the fastest-growing segment of the American market. Honda, once so tuned in to America's Baby Boomers, now didn't have the vehicles they most wanted. In December 1992, the company moved, belatedly, to fill the gaping hole in its lineup by agreeing to buy off-road vehicles from Isuzu, and sell them under the Honda name. This was a far cry from "Carry Your Own Torch." But years of complacency and dithering in product development had left Honda with little choice.

Isuzu, in return, would get Honda cars that it could market as Isuzu products. Isuzu's car sales had fallen so far that the company had decided —with a push from GM, which owned 37 percent of Isuzu's stock—to abandon sedans and coupes altogether. Instead it would concentrate on trucks, its traditional strength, and would enter joint ventures to get cars from other companies.

The Honda–Isuzu marriage of convenience was a graphic sign of Japan's automotive retreat, and far from the only one in 1992. Daihatsu declared it would abandon the U.S. market altogether, the first time a Japanese company had done so since Toyota withdrew temporarily more than thirty years earlier. Mazda killed the Amati line before it even hit the market, even though the company had already built a new plant in

Japan to make the cars and signed up sixty-seven U.S. dealers to sell them. The Subaru–Isuzu factory in Indiana was running far below the break-even level.

Even mighty Toyota suffered. Its superautomated assembly line at the Tahara factory was running on just one shift because the cars were wanting for buyers. Toyota men were fretting that they had poured too much money into sophisticated robotics there. Car sales in Japan plunged more than 8 percent in 1992 on top of their 4.6 percent decline the prior year—marking the first time since World War II that Japanese sales dropped for two years in a row.[20]

On February 23, 1993, Nissan did the once-unthinkable: It ordered the permanent closing of one of its Japanese factories, the aging Zama plant on the outskirts of Tokyo. It would be the first factory closing in Japanese automotive history.

Nissan said it would maintain Japan's lifetime employment tradition by offering Zama's 5,000 workers jobs in other Nissan factories, but that move was just a fig leaf. Some of those factories were so far away that many older workers would take early retirement instead, in effect laying themselves off. Two years earlier Japan's auto executives had fretted about their country's labor shortage, but those days suddenly seemed distant.

As the year continued, the bad news mounted. Perversely, even though Japan's worst postwar recession deepened, the yen surged even higher in value, as Washington talked down the dollar to help American manufacturers. During the summer, the U.S. dollar declined to 101 yen, meaning the Japanese currency had more than doubled in value since the mid-1980s. The dollar bounced back a bit to between ¥107 and ¥110 the rest of the year, but that didn't help the Japanese much. During 1993 alone the yen surged some 20 percent, making Japan a highly expensive place to build cars despite the legendary efficiency of its factories. A Toyota Corolla, once the quintessential economy car, now sold for $17,000 in the United States. Americans who didn't understand the arcane world of foreign exchange did understand that this was too much to pay for a subcompact car. For the Japanese, it was a real-life nightmare.

Japan's car companies never had envisioned a domestic recession so deep or a currency so strong—much less both problems hitting at the same time. They had expanded flat-out during the 1980s, and now they were stuck with costly factories they didn't need and cars they couldn't sell. Complacence and arrogance, it turned out, weren't made only in America.

In 1993, Japan's automobile industry received its reckoning. Two of the Big Five car companies, Nissan and Mazda, plunged into the red. Mazda and Subaru laid off some of their American staffers. Nissan and Mazda fired the heads of their U.S. marketing operations. Honda fared better than most. The company remained barely profitable, although it idled two of its ten assembly lines in Japan indefinitely, and put a third line on inactive status in the spring of 1994. Because of the strong yen, Honda said it would phase out exports of Accords and Civics from Japan to the United States by the mid-1990s. After that, all Civics and Accords sold in North America would be built there.

Two years earlier, Irimajiri had predicted a new era of slow growth for Honda and the other Japanese car companies. Now, things had gotten far worse far faster than he had believed possible. In the spring of 1993, as a consultant to Honda, he toured North America and Europe to assess the state of the industry. What he saw surprised him.

In Bramalea, Ontario, Irimajiri saw an assembly plant where Chrysler was building a new line of midsized sedans with just over twenty hours of labor per car. It was about as good as any plant anywhere except Tahara, but Bramalea didn't have Tahara's huge automation costs. With his penchant for detail, Irimajiri homed in on the car's exhaust system. It had been developed with an outside supplier, and could be attached to the car in one piece with an ease and efficiency that boosted productivity and quality at the same time. Close relationships with suppliers, components that clicked into place, and world-class efficiency—these were pages right out of Japan's textbook. But this wasn't Japan.

Irimajiri also visited factories in Europe. In France he saw a factory supplying wiring assemblies to Renault with a just-in-time delivery system as good as anything in Japan. Four years earlier, Chrysler and Renault had been the worst car companies on their respective continents. Now they were arguably the best, or close to it. The two companies closest to death, thought Irimajiri, had made the most radical reforms to stay alive.[21]

What he saw amounted to an impressive comeback in the making. The Americans and Europeans were taking enormous strides toward the productivity and quality-control techniques that had been pioneered by the Japanese. Some companies were leaders, and others—notably GM in North America and Volkswagen in Europe—were laggards. But the overall trend was unmistakably clear.

In Europe, Irimajiri saw one plant that particularly amazed him. It was in a place where, just three years before, the issues hadn't been productivity or quality or cost control. Instead, the issues had been far more fundamental: communism versus capitalism, and dictatorship versus freedom. Now this factory, though brand new, was nearly as good as anything in Japan. It was in a German town that was just a tiny dot on Europe's newly changing map: Eisenach.

CHAPTER 15

TOMMY LASORDA'S TEAM

THE AUTOBAHN THAT LEADS northeast from the German financial capital of Frankfurt sweeps through a pastoral landscape of rolling hills and broad valleys checkered with farms, small towns, and woodlots. A few kilometers east of the big American military base at Bad Hersfeld the highway crosses a deep valley. Through this gash in Germany's center ran the fences and the deadly minefields that for four decades separated West from East, democracy from communism, and one of Europe's most prosperous economies from the sooty deprivation of socialism. Had the Western Allies held this valley and the ground just four kilometers further east at the end of World War II, the historic city of Eisenach might have been one of West Germany's more prosperous small cities. It has a first-rate tourist attraction—the 900-year-old Wartburg castle, where Martin Luther, and later the poet Johann Wolfgang von Goethe, took refuge. It is the birthplace of Johann Sebastian Bach. Sightseers would have flocked to see the city's elegant central square. Eisenach might also have proclaimed itself a mecca for car enthusiasts. The German automaker BMW's first car factory was in the city. If the Western Allies had kept Eisenach, BMW might have stayed.

But when Germany was cut in two, the Russians got Eisenach. Instead of tourism and prosperity, Eisenach got checkpoints and barbed wire. Its historic buildings and medieval monuments moldered in dingy smog until they had the musty hue of a cheap cigar. The Soviets took over BMW's plant,[1] and eventually the East German communists used it to build their idea of a luxury car: the Wartburg.

The Wartburg did have a certain panache, at least compared to its infamous East German rival, the Trabant. The Wartburg had a steel body, instead of a flimsy plastic exoskeleton like the Trabi. Its sooty engine cranked out 55 horsepower, enough to make it a hot rod by Eastern Bloc standards. East Germans waited years to get their hands on a Wartburg. By the late 1980s, the managers of state-owned Automobilwerk Eisenach wanted to expand their production in a new plant just outside town, and develop a new model to take the place of their twenty-five-year-old vehicle. AWE, as it was called, had partly finished its new plant in November 1989 when the first sledgehammers hit the Berlin Wall, and the German Democratic Republic began to vanish like a bad dream.

The Wartburg soon vanished as well. But Eisenach would remain a center for automobile production, thanks to a group of young upstarts from the United States, Canada, and Western Germany. These newcomers had trained at GM's various joint ventures with the Japanese: Nummi in California, a similar joint venture with Suzuki in Ontario, and at a third one with Isuzu in England. They would get the opportunity that Steve Bera and the original group of Nummi commandos had been denied at General Motors six years earlier: to go into a factory together, take charge, and prove that GM could run a Japanese-style "lean" production plant. Their special challenge, though, would be to employ newly liberated East German workers, who had spent decades toiling in a system that made even GM's traditional factories look like models of efficiency.

THE COLLAPSE OF EAST GERMANY was more than a victory for political freedom. It was an economic independence day for 17 million people. East Germans were ravenous for Western consumer goods, and tops on most East German shopping lists were cars—real cars. Cars provided mobility, and in a state that had imprisoned its people for four decades, mobility was the purest expression of freedom. The only question was who would sell the East Germans the cars they wanted.

Volkswagen took the first leap in December 1989, when Chairman

Carl Hahn made an emotional pilgrimage to his native town of Chemnitz in the east. There, the head of West Germany's largest automaker declared his company would rescue the faltering East German auto industry. A few days later, just before Christmas, Volkswagen announced an agreement with the East German government to develop a replacement for the pathetic Trabant, manufactured near Chemnitz (which the Communists had renamed Karl-Marx-Stadt). Volkswagen agreed to put as much as 6 billion deutsche marks into the effort, and East German officials suggested that Volkswagen eventually would take a hand in rejuvenating AWE as well.[2]

Volkswagen's coup alarmed Lou Hughes, the forty-one-year-old American who ran GM's big German subsidiary, Adam Opel AG. He had no time for the usual months-long process that preceded billion-dollar gambles at GM. Opel had to take a plunge on gut instinct and faith, or risk sitting on the sidelines as East Germany's economy made its historic turn.

And so, on a steel-gray winter's day in early January 1990, Hughes climbed into a car and turned onto the autobahn. A couple of hours later, he was bumping across a desolate back road through the no-man's-land of barbed wire and land mines that led to an East German border crossing.[3] A sign at the border declared, *"Herzlich Wilkommen"*—hearty welcome—belying the distinctly inhospitable signals sent by the prison-style watchtowers and fences all around. As Hughes rolled through the East German countryside toward Eisenach, he saw West German flags flying from the houses. At the AWE factory itself, there were more West German flags. And on one of the tall brick smokestacks, there was painted in large white letters the word: *Frieden*—Peace.

Hughes toured the factory and was aghast. The air was foul with the soot of the dirty coal the East Germans burned for heat. The factory made GM's trouble-plagued American plants look like the best Toyota City had to show. It took AWE nearly 10,000 people to turn out a mere 70,000 cars a year, or just seven cars per worker annually. Opel's huge Rüsselsheim complex turned out eighteen cars per worker in a year. Rüsselsheim, Hughes knew, was no match for Toyota, which had a fully integrated manufacturing complex in Japan that cranked out 370,000 cars and trucks a year with 7,000 people—an amazing average of nearly fifty-three per employee.

Still, Hughes was determined that Opel should grab Eisenach before VW did. On March 11, 1990, just three months after Hughes's first visit, Opel and the AWE management signed a joint-venture agreement calling for AWE workers to put the finishing touches on a few thousand Opel Vectra bodies shipped in from the West. For Hughes, however, this was only the beginning. For in the disillusionment and despair of AWE's managers and workers, Hughes sensed a far greater opportunity.

HUGHES'S JOURNEY TO EISENACH had come even as he was beginning a personal odyssey that would lead him to a fundamental rethinking of his approach to business and to the world. Running Opel was a big job for a man of his relative youth. In the fall of 1990, a few months after he sealed the deal to put Opel in control of the old AWE and its Eisenach operations, Hughes spent a week working on an Opel assembly line under the tutelage of lean-production apostles from the Kaizen Institute of Europe. The institute, founded in Japan, is dedicated to spreading the Japanese practice of *kaizen*, or continuous improvement, through hands-on teaching. Hughes spent most of the week installing wiring in Opel Vectras, while the Kaizen Institute's teachers coached him in how to make changes to eliminate *muda*, or waste, in the process.

Hughes had a managerial version of a religious awakening. All the disconnected nuggets of information about the Toyota "lean" production system that he had come across while helping to negotiate the deal that established Nummi, and all the books, speeches, and competitive-analysis reports he had read since then, suddenly made sense. Hughes finished his week convinced that Opel, indeed all of GM Europe, had to make adopting lean production their top priority. Hughes raved about his experience to his boss, Robert Eaton, then president of GM Europe. Later, Eaton led another group of senior GM Europe executives in another week-long lean-production workshop. He returned a convert, too.

But now that GM Europe's top executives had gotten fired up about Toyota-style lean manufacturing, they confronted the same problem as their counterparts back in Detroit. Few of the managers and workers who spent every day building cars understood the Japanese methods, or had much enthusiasm for trying them. At Opel, Lou Hughes faced IG Metall, a union that made the United Auto Workers union look like pussycats. IG Metall represented Germany's auto, chemical, *and* steel workers. Its powerful leaders had little use for Japanese ideas that would cut jobs. Hughes was convinced that Opel had to embrace lean production to avoid the disastrous mistakes GM was making in America. The men who ran GM in North America had dispatched the lessons of Nummi to committees that turned the crisp, common-sense Toyota system into a porridge of "synchronous strategies" spewed out in dozens of manuals that few plant managers bothered to read.

Hughes was enough of a finance man and was close enough to Jack Smith to know just how perilous GM's condition was becoming as its financial losses in North America mounted in 1991. He also saw that GM Europe had little room to gloat. True, GM Europe was racking up more profit on every vehicle sold than any other car maker on the continent. But the game was rigged. Europe's car-producing countries had erected stout barriers to any substantial sales of Japanese cars. GM Europe thus could charge hundreds or even thousands of dollars more for its vehicles than GM could have demanded for the same cars in the United States. It was a dirty little secret within GM that GM Europe would lose money, too, if it had to sell cars at North American prices. Hughes wanted to change that.

THE MYSTERY OF HOW TO produce dramatic change, either in a company or an individual, fascinated Hughes. He had worked on himself for years, trying to moderate and rechannel the aggressiveness that earned him the nickname "Mad Dog" during his younger years in GM's Treasurer's Office. In Europe, Hughes had discovered a perfect therapy: glacier climbing in the Alps. In the company of a trained guide and a small group of climbers, Hughes saw the workaday concerns receding to a pinpoint dot in the sweeping panorama of rocks and snow. What argument over Opel's profit margins could be more important than making sure you didn't trip while edging across an ice ridge that straddled a 1,500-foot-deep ravine?

Hughes found the threat of sudden, violent death accelerated a marvelous adjustment of personal perspective. Life, he found himself thinking, was full of icy ridges. One misstep, and you'd be history. But the payoff for taking risks was exhilarating, like the day Hughes came down from the icy flanks of Piz Bernina and confronted a group of English tourists trundling off a gondola in their Bermuda shorts. Hughes saw the pasty, winded tourists as "before" pictures of himself. But he had pushed on. He could make it to the summit on his own.

Mountain climbing, though, was one thing. Forcing people to break out of daily work habits established over decades clearly was another.

Here, Hughes discovered the analogy wasn't mountain climbing. It was weight loss. It was the seemingly endless, often disappointing slog of transforming an obese couch potato into a trim, health-conscious jogger. GM Europe had to work a transformation just that difficult in its factories.

Mass production, after all, was a very comfortable system for those who had mastered it. A mass-production factory was full of safety nets for managers whose prime task was to make the daily production quota. The nets included back-up tools, huge warehouses full of spare parts, and plenty of spare people. And the lines of authority were nice and clean. Management gave orders. Hourly laborers did what they were told. By contrast, lean-production factories had no extra machines, no extra people, no warehouses of spare parts for use "just in case." All that was regarded as waste. The slightest mistake at any station on the assembly line could bring the whole plant to a halt, because a lean-production system was designed that way. That's how managers and workers, together, identified and eliminated problems.

Hughes saw that Japanese methods had turned Germany's mass production industries into dinosaurs. The Tyrannosaurus Rex of the German auto industry was Volkswagen's huge complex in Wolfsburg, where 60,000 people bolted together Golfs and Jettas for sale throughout Europe and overseas. Opel's own home factory at Rüsselsheim, just outside Frankfurt in the Main River valley, was a close cousin.

At Rüsselsheim, some 17,000 workers toiled away at some of the highest wage rates on the Continent. They didn't just assemble cars. They bent exhaust pipes, screwed together engine parts, and even boiled laundry. The main Rüsselsheim assembly plant, erected on the rubble of Opel's pre-World War II operations, was once a potent symbol of West Germany's postwar miracle. Three stories tall and nearly two miles long, Rüsselsheim was Opel's answer to Toyota City and Flint, Michigan.

But by the early 1990s, Rüsselsheim was a mess. In the dimly lit assembly halls, workers from fifty nations—speaking some twenty different languages—groped through tubs and boxes scattered along the line to find parts that matched the cars at their work stations. On the factory's third floor was a relic of GM's automation binge. Instead of using a simple circle of hangers to carry dashboards past workers who would put them together, Rüsselsheim had dozens of expensive automatic guided vehicles—or AGVs—each toting a single dashboard along a tortuous track up and down a football-field-sized hall.

While Opel's factory struggled with an excess of modern technology, its corporate culture was stuck in the Middle Ages. Cafeterias for lower-ranking employees didn't have silverware, evidently on the grounds that hourly laborers couldn't be trusted not to steal company-owned forks and knives. Workers brought their own utensils from home. Executives, of course, got silverware in their separate dining rooms, as well as table service. This rigid hierarchical separation made it unlikely that any ideas workers had about improving operations would ever reach management.

The more Hughes learned, the more he worried that Opel was heading for a fall. By 1990, the dike Europe had built around its auto industry was starting to spring big holes. Toyota, Nissan, and Honda were building new factories in Britain, inside the protective walls of Europe's tariff fortress. They planned to do in Europe what they had done nearly a decade earlier in the United States. By 1993, all three would be ramping up these factories and launching thousands of cars into the European market—cars Hughes estimated would cost $1,000 per vehicle less than his Opels. There was no time to waste. Opel's system had to change.

Hughes had started attacking the Old Opel within weeks of his arrival as chairman in April 1989. One of his first moves was to close Opel's executive dining room, and order that rank-and-file employees be given silverware, at last, in the company commissaries. He sliced out some of the layers of hierarchy that encrusted Opel's main offices and factories. And he began hammering Opel's smugly successful managers and union leaders with the message that Japan was leaving Opel behind.

Preaching, however, wouldn't transform a company as rich as Opel was in 1990 and 1991. Hughes concluded he had to do something more dramatic. That was where Eisenach came in.

Eisenach offered the perfect place to demonstrate that the "lean" way could work in Germany. The East German workers had just scrapped their entire social system. They were desperate to learn new ways of working as well as living. The question was, Who would teach them? Hughes sought out his mentor, Jack Smith, then GM's vice chairman for international operations. Smith had a suggestion: Talk to Tommy LaSorda.

TOMMY LaSORDA, in the minds of most people, was the manager of baseball's Los Angeles Dodgers. His only connection to getting "lean" was the TV commercials he made for the Ultra Slim-Fast diet drink.

Smith, however, had in mind another Tom LaSorda. This LaSorda wasn't related to the baseball figure, nor was he famous, although his family was well-known in Canadian auto-industry circles. In the early 1980s, LaSorda's father, Frank, had been president of the union local that represented Chrysler's factories in Windsor, Ontario, right across the river from Detroit. His grandfather, Harry Rooney, had gone to jail in the 1930s while fighting to organize the original United Auto Workers union chapter at Chrysler's Canadian operations.

Young Tom, however, wanted to be on "the other side" of the labor-management divide. In 1977, at age twenty-three, he took a job as a labor relations staffer at GM's sprawling factory in the Toronto suburb of Oshawa. Later, he moved out to the plant floor as a foreman. By 1987, the thirty-three-year-old LaSorda had reached the bonus ranks as direc-tor of service engineering for the Buick Division in Flint. He seemed well-positioned for a solid career in GM's middle ranks. But LaSorda was restless. When a call went out in 1987 for volunteers to join GM's new Canadian joint-venture factory with Suzuki Motors—called Canadian Auto Manufacturing Inc., or Cami (pronounced CA-mee) for short—LaSorda volunteered, looking for a new challenge.

He wasn't disappointed. After a month of intensive training in Japan, he became director of production for Cami. Suzuki was no match for Toyota in many respects. But the Cami plant was a model of lean effi-ciency compared to the GM Oshawa factory where LaSorda had gotten his start. The more LaSorda learned from living in the Suzuki version of lean production, the more solid became his conversion to what he called "the lean-production religion."

By December 1990, LaSorda had become vice president of production at Cami. He was thirty-five years old, with blond, boyish looks that belied his growing stature within General Motors. With the end of his fourth year at the joint venture coming up in April 1991, LaSorda was a candidate for transfer back to the "real" GM. But he worried that he was heading for the same fate as his counterparts from Nummi. He knew many of the Nummi alumni. He had watched them return to the parent company with the fervor to change things, only to get swallowed up by the beast. LaSorda wanted to do better. Ideally, he wanted to run a plant himself, and have under him a team of other lean-production converts who could help him succeed where the Nummi alumni had failed. It was a godsend, then, when he got a call from Lou Hughes inviting him to visit Eisenach.

In December 1990, LaSorda flew to Frankfurt, and then toured the tiny "kit" operation Opel had set up in Eisenach to finish partially assembled cars. He saw Opel's mother plant in Rüsselsheim. Then he met Hughes for dinner at the Nassauer Hof, an elegant hotel near the old gambling casino in the Frankfurt suburb of Wiesbaden. Hughes, an intense and voluble man, had a terrible cold and was losing his voice. Nevertheless, for the next two and a half hours, he croaked out his bold vision for Eisenach.

In February 1991, Hughes said, Opel would begin building a real assembly plant there. Hughes wanted it to become Opel's showcase for lean production efficiency and quality—Europe's answer to Nummi. The parallels were striking. Nummi, in the beginning, was a GM factory in Fremont, California, that had closed, the victim of a failed system of management. Likewise, Eisenach's workers had seen their old system fail. Like Fremont, Eisenach could get a fresh start. There was no old factory to keep running, no old products to ship to dealers. Like Fremont, Eisenach was far enough from headquarters to maintain independence, but close enough to serve as a living role model for the new way.

LaSorda was intrigued. And as Hughes's voice gave out, LaSorda took the opportunity to spell out his own vision. He was very interested in the Eisenach job, but only if he got to bring along a team of people who knew how lean production worked and could help him train the other managers and workers in the system. "One person can't do it," he told Hughes. At Cami, Suzuki had 100 Japanese managers as resident "advisers" to keep the lean production process on track. Cami had even built a dormitory for these trainers. LaSorda knew he couldn't get that many people, even if GM had them. But he reminded Hughes about the frustrations and failures that the Nummi alumni encountered after they had been split up, and Hughes readily understood. Within a few weeks, Hughes called LaSorda at Cami to offer the job on LaSorda's terms. LaSorda set about picking his team.

TOM LaSORDA SHARED the name of a famous baseball manager, but Frank Faga's name could have fit perfectly into the pantheon of alliterative names—Dizzy Dean, Mickey Mantle, Brett Butler—fate seems to assign to baseball stars. Frank Faga (pronounced FAY-guh), however, didn't get past Little League. He was born in Flint, Michigan, on April 10, 1958—during the boomtown days for the city that also had given birth to General Motors—and grew up a GM brat. His father, also named Frank but with a different middle name, was a manufacturing man who eventually ran some of GM's biggest assembly plants.

Young Frank, however, didn't want to follow in his father's footsteps. Instead, he enrolled at Michigan State University, and graduated in 1980 with a degree in anthropology. He believed his education "taught me to stand outside your own culture and look back inside." It would prove remarkably practical training, though Faga wouldn't see that for many years. After getting his degree, Faga worked at temporary jobs for a couple of years, hoping to save enough money to continue his anthropology studies in graduate school. Along the way he submitted a job application at GM without much intention of working there. But in 1982, he got a call from a GM manager named Denny Pawley, who was stationed at a plant in Pontiac, Michigan. Faga liked Pawley, and decided to take the job he offered: a low-level supervisor on the Pontiac Fiero assembly line.

Faga—a short, slight man with dark hair and skin and a neatly trimmed beard—looked too bookish to be a factory boss. But Faga's literate, inquisitive approach to life soon served him well when he was assigned to work in the section of the plant that made the Fiero's doors.

One of the many glitches that bedeviled the Fiero was that the doors often didn't fit properly. It would be a problem with any car, but it was especially critical with the Fiero. The Fiero's body consisted of plastic panels bolted onto a steel underframe. If the doors didn't fit properly, the huge mill-and-drill machine that bored holes in the frame to allow attachment of the panels wouldn't work.

When the mill-and-drill rejected a door, it usually meant there was something wrong with most of the 500 or so other doors that were already built and stacked on racks, waiting to be attached to cars. The door-molding machines could be adjusted fairly quickly to produce good doors. But meantime, before those could be used, the 500 already-built doors had to be put on cars—after being hand-pounded into shape with rubber hammers. It was an expensive way to make cockeyed cars.

Faga realized the smart thing would be to eliminate the 500-door backlog by not making doors until just before they were ready to be used. To do that, the plant would have to stop its practice of making doors only on the day shift, and building up a backlog to be used at night and part of the next morning as well. Also the machines on the subassembly line that made the doors would have to be clustered close together instead of strung out, so racks of partially produced doors wouldn't have to be shuttled from one machine to the next. Faga sketched out his plans for one of his bosses. "Have you ever heard of the Toyota Production System?" the man asked. "This is it."

Before long, Pawley and the other bosses had accepted his ideas for revamping the door-production line. The experiment was a success: door quality improved dramatically, and the number of workers needed in door production dropped from twenty-two to twelve, a near doubling of productivity.

Faga became a hero, even though he thought he was just using common sense. To him, it was only natural to arrange welding tools in U-shaped groups, or "cells," instead of in a traditional straight assembly line. "Think of how you make breakfast," Faga would say. "When you make eggs and toast, you put the toast in. Then you crack the eggs. The toast pops. You butter it. You flip the eggs. You work many machines at once. That's why kitchens are U-shaped. My grandma knew this!"

In May 1987, as the Fiero was starting its death spiral, Tom LaSorda called Faga. General Motors, LaSorda explained, was setting up a new joint venture with Suzuki in Canada, similar to the one it had with Toyota in California. LaSorda would be the top GM manufacturing man at the new plant, and wanted Faga to come work for him as manager of the body shop, the area where the vehicle bodies were welded together. Faga jumped at the chance. It would be a chance to get out from under the shadow of his father, because GM's Canadian operations were largely separate, at least at the middle-manager level, from those in the United States. More important, Faga had heard about the wonders occurring at Nummi, and wanted to join a Japanese joint-venture plant himself.

In October, Faga, along with LaSorda and the other Canadians and Americans who would help manage the new plant, went to Japan. There they received a month of training—the first two weeks in a classroom, and the second two at the Suzuki assembly plant in Hamamatsu, about 120 miles from Tokyo. His Suzuki adviser, Shigeo Makino, explained that his company had studied the Toyota Production System, then adapted it to Suzuki's own needs. If you saw a friend wearing a nice suit, Makino explained, you might buy the same suit for yourself, but in your own size, not your friend's size. Suzuki called its adaptation the Nagare Production System, using the Japanese word that meant "flow like a river."

When Makino and the other Suzuki men arrived in Canada to prepare to open Cami, Faga and his colleagues took them to visit some GM factories. At one stop, the group saw workers sitting around and reading newspapers after their assembly line had broken down. "Faga-san, your workers are studying very hard," said one of the Japanese, using a euphemism to express his surprise at the scene. Other times, the Japanese were less polite. Once the group saw automated guided vehicles transporting steel sheets hundreds of yards across the factory floor to a worker who fed the sheets into a press. Using expensive AGVs was the very antithesis of lean production, under which the metal sheets would have been stored right next to the press. The worker proudly showed off the system. Afterward, however, Faga heard the Japanese laughing uproariously among themselves. The term he heard the loudest through their chortles was "AGV."

But some encounters were more rewarding. In February 1988, Faga took Makino and the others to visit the plant his father managed, in Lake Orion, Michigan, some forty miles north of Detroit. As his father led the group through the factory, he often stopped to greet workers by name and chat about their work. The elder Faga even stooped to pick up pieces of trash or debris he saw along the route. "Faga-san," one of the Japanese said later, "your father is a Japanese manager." It was the highest compliment the man could bestow.

Faga spent just over three years at Cami, and thoroughly immersed himself in Japanese production techniques used to manufacture a small, Jeeplike vehicle sold by Suzuki as the Sidekick and by GM as the Geo Tracker. In February 1991, GM transferred him again, to its sprawling, multiplant assembly operations in Lansing, Michigan. It was an operation that could have swallowed Faga whole. But just a month after his arrival, he got another call from LaSorda. LaSorda had used Lou Hughes's clout to get permission to approach Faga despite his recent transfer, and ask him to come to Eisenach. Faga would be part of the elite team that would start from scratch to make Eisenach a lean production model for GM operations in Europe and around the world. Faga had just begun building a new house in a Lansing suburb, and his wife was pregnant with their second child. He told LaSorda yes.

LASORDA WASN'T GOING to get many more quick yeses as he moved to get his project underway. In March 1991, he and Hughes took a two-week trip to Cami and Nummi. As the two men toured the two joint venture plants, slowly working through each department, LaSorda convinced Hughes that Eisenach wouldn't work, at least not the way Opel's manufacturing engineers had designed the plant. The engineers had laid out Eisenach's machinery in long lines—not the kitchen-style, U-shaped cells that allowed one worker to perform three or four jobs.

Eisenach was to be strictly an assembly plant instead of a fully integrated manufacturing complex like Rüsselsheim, which produced everything from engines to fenders. LaSorda wanted the new plant to build 150,000 cars a year with just 1,850 employees divided among three eight-hour shifts—a productivity level comparable to Nummi and double that of other Opel factories similar in scope. But the Opel layout would require a work force 30 percent larger than what LaSorda wanted. He stunned his Opel counterparts when he declared at their first meeting that Eisenach, as they had planned it, was overstaffed by some 600 employees and wouldn't be competitive.

Hughes was discouraged, too. "We were at zero," he recalled later. His staffers at Opel liked to talk about lean production, but many had no idea what it was. LaSorda brought the matter to a head. He and his team told Hughes they wanted the authority to tear up Opel's design, and lay out the factory their way. They got it.

As construction on the new Eisenach plant rolled along during 1991, the Opel executives in charge of building it butted heads with LaSorda's team time and again. The two sides argued over the placement of machinery. They argued over the location of the plant administration offices. They even struggled over where to locate the cafeteria. It became clear that many Opel managers didn't accept LaSorda, Faga, and their fellow "advisers." Opel was a very German, very proud organization. LaSorda and his ragtag bunch of young outsiders weren't scoring points by constantly declaring that everything Opel knew about building and running a factory was wrong.

The philosophical clash extended to even seemingly minor details, such as how machinery would be anchored. Opel engineers typically specified that machines be anchored to the floor on solid concrete foundations, for safety's sake. But at Cami, LaSorda learned it was better to leave most machinery free-standing, or held in place with only a few light bolts. That way, machines could be skidded quickly into new positions to allow for fast model changes, or improved efficiency.

Hughes wound up driving out to Eisenach once or twice a month to smooth ruffled feathers. He was constantly having heart-to-hearts with

LaSorda—who wasn't always a diplomat—or soothing Opel egos. But he backed up LaSorda and his team in the battles with the traditionalists in Opel's hierarchy.

In one case, LaSorda demanded that Eisenach have authority to run production scheduling and manage delivery of parts according to its own rules. LaSorda wanted what the Japanese called "level scheduling" of production. Regular GM or Opel factories might equip 80 percent of the cars built on a Monday with air conditioning, then install half that number of air-conditioners the next day, depending on the orders that got processed that day. Such variation was frowned upon by the Japanese. The more unpredictability thrown into a system, they reasoned, the greater the chance for mistakes. LaSorda took his problem to Hughes, and Hughes ordered the Opel marketing and material management organizations to give LaSorda what he wanted. In another case, LaSorda asked for a team to help set up a just-in-time *kanban* system for controlling the flow of parts inside the factory. Within ten days, Hughes got LaSorda the people he had asked for.

Despite all the trials, by June of 1992 construction of the plant was nearly complete, the first 500 workers had been hired, and training was well under way. One of the key training exercises, developed by Frank Faga, was playing with Legos.

Legos, of course, were the snap-together, plastic, building-block toys that kids used to build castles, airplanes, bridges, or almost anything else they could think of. Faga used Lego blocks to build cars, in a little assembly-line game that he developed to illustrate the Toyota Production System.

He had developed the game back in 1986 and 1987, when he was teaching himself the Toyota system at the Fiero plant in Pontiac. Only then he wasn't using Legos, but little pieces of paper that he would have the game's participants fold and staple into various shapes. During his years at Cami, he decided to use Legos because they were easier and more fun to manipulate.

To start the exercise, Faga would seat four people in a row at a long table to form a miniature assembly line. Each person represented a different department in an assembly plant: stamping, body welding, paint, and final assembly. In a real plant, bottlenecks develop between paint and assembly, because those are the most complicated tasks. So in the Lego game, the paint and assembly people would be assigned to attach two or three blocks to the body of the "car" being built, instead of just one. The Lego cars would have to be built in a specified color sequence: red, blue, green, yellow, and back to red again. After every player was instructed in just what to do, the game would begin.

The first two people on the Lego line, representing stamping and body welding, would snap their blocks together with ease and efficiency, and pass them down the line. At first, the paint and assembly people could keep up. But inevitably, that quickly changed. Before long they would be swamped, and partially built Lego cars would be backing up behind them. As the paint and assembly players struggled to keep pace they would make more and more mistakes—buildings cars of the wrong color, or attaching some of the blocks in the wrong places. All the while, the stamping and welding players would be pushing more and more cars down the line, until eventually they would sit idle while waiting for the other players to catch up. The scene reminded Faga of an old "I Love Lucy" episode in which Lucy and Ethel got a job decorating cakes in a bakery, and scrambled to keep up while unfinished cakes dropped off the end of the conveyor belt and plopped onto the floor. More to the point, it was a scene common in a typical GM assembly plant built around a mass production system.

With everything going haywire, Faga would stop the game and change the rules. Under the new system, the paint and assembly people at the end of the line controlled the pace, so cars would be pulled through the system instead of pushed through. The assembly and paint workers would finish a car, then signal for a new car to be passed along from welding. Now, they had no trouble keeping up, and their errors disappeared. So did the growing "inventory" of half-built cars waiting to get into the paint station. It quickly became clear that the stamping and welding jobs at the beginning of the line could be consolidated into one, thus reducing manpower. Every time a group played the game, productivity, quality, and inventory control improved under the "pull" system.

Some of the German managers at Eisenach deemed the Lego game childish, and discouraged Faga from using it with the workers. Then, during one of his frequent visits to Eisenach, Lou Hughes played the game. In late 1991, Hughes had spent three days at the Eisenach plant, going through a production training orientation alongside real workers. For him, Faga's Lego game crystallized everything he was trying to communicate about the advantages of lean production. He started insisting that visitors to the Eisenach plant—ranging from managers at other Opel factories to roving reporters—play the Lego game. When Robert

M. Kimmitt, the American ambassador to Germany, visited the Eisenach plant in April 1992, several months before the start of production,
Hughes made sure he played the Lego game, too.

After that, Faga took his Lego show on the road, again at the behest
of Hughes. In May he performed at Frankfurt, at the annual Opel management conference. And in June, Faga went to the new European
Disneyland near Paris to play with Lego blocks at a meeting of the top
180 executives in all of GM Europe. To punch home the point, Hughes
handed each attendee a fake American $1,000 bill encased in lucite. It
represented the cost gap on each car between Opel and the Japanese.

The Lego game, for all its value, didn't erase all the tension in the
summer of 1992 as the Eisenach plant careened toward the start of
production. "Playing with Legos is easy," Tom LaSorda would say. "Im-
plementing the system in a plant takes guts." Especially because the
newly hired eastern Germans, while learning the efficiencies of lean
production, found themselves grappling with enormous adjustments in
all phases of their lives. The concepts of individual initiative, merit, and
achievement were utterly foreign, and often viewed with suspicion. Each
worker at Cami had put forth an average of ten suggestions per month
for improving the plant's operations. The Eisenach monthly average was
just two suggestions per worker.

"In today's society, everyone just thinks of themselves," Steffen
Glandien explained to a visitor one day. "The old East Germany was a
place where people stuck close together. We had to." The twenty-one-
year-old Glandien had just finished a two-year training program at the
old AWE factory in 1990 when East Germany and the Wartburg disappeared, rendering his newly acquired skills useless. So he quickly lined
up for a job at Opel, and was one of the first people hired at the new
Eisenach plant. To celebrate his good fortune he decided to sell his
Soviet-made Lada, which had been a prestigious car in East Germany,
and buy a new Opel Astra, a subcompact model that had succeeded the
venerable Opel Kadett. Buying the Astra was no problem, but Glandien
quickly found that nobody wanted to buy Russian cars anymore. He
wound up giving the Lada to a friend.

At the Eisenach plant, Glandien learned how to install dashboards,
which involved unlearning everything he once knew. In the old Wartburg factory, a couple dozen people built dashboards piece by piece into

the cars as they rumbled down the assembly line. At Eisenach, a single worker did the same job in a fraction of the time, slapping dashboards into the cars in a single piece before fixing them in place with plugs and washers. Glandien marveled at the difference.

The methods LaSorda, Faga, and the other GM advisers touted required far more initiative than the jobs at AWE—or even the jobs in traditional Opel factories. In the section of the plant where engines were prepared for installation into the cars, there would be just eight workers. At one station, one man would have to perform twenty-one different operations to assemble the mechanism that connected the gear-shift lever to the transmission, and then install that component on the transmission housing. At a regular Opel plant, this would have been a job for at least two people—one to bolt and rivet together the gear-shift connector, and another to install the mechanism. Moreover, the gearshift installer at Eisenach was expected to build the fixtures that held the parts in place while he riveted them together.

Leaders of the Eisenach local of IG Metall, Germany's powerful industrial union, reacted warily to LaSorda's pitch for initiative and teamwork. The union insisted that every aspect of the new system—including the style of the gray uniforms that laborers and managers would share, and the six-level wage system (compared to the ten levels at Rüsselsheim)—had to be written into a contract. Eventually, there were more than a dozen side agreements. Harald Lieske, an AWE survivor who won election as head of the Eisenach union local, would complain to LaSorda that many of the middle managers sent to Eisenach from Opel didn't live the teamwork philosophy LaSorda preached. "They say they want to coach," Lieske said. "But the area leaders order people too much."

Eisenach struggled to balance its ideals of flexibility and creativity with the rigid discipline that LaSorda insisted on. But that's how it had to be, LaSorda knew, in a plant that lacked expensive safety nets. A worker who left a box of parts outside one of the yellow-tape squares on the floor risked an immediate reprimand. Managers making their rounds bobbed up and down in midsentence to snatch scraps of paper from the spotless concrete floor. "You can't pass by," Rudiger Gundacker, a manager in the final assembly area, explained to one visitor. "People watch you."

This obsessiveness had a payoff. At Eisenach, workers had little trouble finding the parts they needed to do their jobs. If the right box wasn't in the yellow square, they hit a button that signaled a delivery worker to forward another box. Work areas were brightly lit—in one section of the plant there was even a skylight to let in the sun. The clean, white plant fixtures provided a hospitallike atmosphere that was a far cry from the sooty gloom of the old AWE plant, and from the dim halls of Rüsselsheim. Eisenach's body shop had almost no overhead conveyors. At Rüsselsheim, the clanking din of conveyor chains carrying half-finished bodies hundreds of feet between machines forced all conversations to take place at a shout. Eisenach's workers had to make many of their own tools. But that meant they didn't have to put up with fixtures designed by engineers at Opel's Technical Development Center who had never worked on an assembly line.

Eisenach's wary workers didn't jump to offer labor-saving suggestions to their new bosses. But enough offered ideas to dispel the notion that the East Germans would forever cling to the dilatory habits of Communism. One man used a piece of string to solve the problem of how to keep parts handy while he put the finishing touches on the dashboard of a car moving down the line. He arranged the plugs and washers required for the job in a small tray that hung from an overhead track. When a car moved into his station, he looped the string from the rack to the door hinge of the car. Then, as he sat in the car putting the finishing touches on the interior, the tray followed alongside like a puppy on a leash. Over a year, the string saved miles of walking and hours of wasted time.

The former AWE workers weren't complete strangers to working like this. They had helped each other and shared ideas under the old AWE management. But they had done so for survival in a warped system. Slowly, the former AWE workers came to believe that LaSorda and his team were different. A transformation began similar to the one Toyota had launched nearly a decade earlier among the battle-hardened veterans of GM's plant in Fremont, California. "It's not that hard for a young person to get used to the new production system," young Glandien concluded. And even Harald Lieske finally decided to share a fax machine with LaSorda as a symbol of labor-management cooperation. "If we are to become competitive," the union leader said, "we must go this way."

WHILE EISENACH WAS TAKING its baby steps in early 1992, Opel was surging through another succesful year, piling up huge profits. But

Hughes was more convinced than ever that Opel was too complacent about the coming competitive threat from the Japanese. He tried to attack Opel's smugness head-on. He convened mass meetings of thousands of Opel workers at Rüsselsheim and at a sister operation in Bockum to dramatize the need for change. At one meeting, he spoke for forty-five minutes, in German, pounding home the message that Opel's costs were too high and its quality too low. Nissan, Hughes noted, could sell its British-made Primera for far less than Opel charged for a similar car.

Egged on by their union leaders, some workers hooted, whistled, and jeered as Hughes insisted, "We're going to get lean." Not without reason, the Opel union feared losing thousands of jobs in the shakeout that loomed over the horizon. Every time the hecklers reached a new crescendo, Hughes would brush them off, shouting: *"Vielen Dank, vielen Dank"*—thanks very much. The experience, however, was proof positive of the need for Eisenach as a catalyst for change. The biggest impediment to reform and renewal at Opel was the complacency of success. Rüsselsheim and Bockum were full of it. Eisenach, arising out of the ashes of Communism, didn't bear that burden.

On September 23, 1992, work stopped at Eisenach, and LaSorda, Faga, and the plant's workers gathered to celebrate the official opening of the plant. An area of the plant was cleared, and a stage erected. Leading the pack of dignitaries on hand was Helmut Kohl, the chancellor of the newly unified Germany, for whom Eisenach was a symbol of his ambition to rebuild the East. Also there was Jack Smith, who by now was the president of General Motors and was just six weeks away from replacing Bob Stempel as CEO.

Lou Hughes was there, too, ebullient at the realization of his dream. For him, Eisenach pointed the way to a better, more secure future for both Germany and GM. Such a future was far from assured. Plenty of hard work lay ahead. But here, in a place that had been enemy territory less than three years earlier, Canadians, Americans, Germans, and other Europeans had established a true lean-production factory. It wasn't the best plant in the world, at least not yet. But it could compete effectively with the Japanese. That was solid ground for hope. Eisenach had been home to Luther, Bach, and Goethe. Hughes wanted the factory to take a place in history alongside these giants. He wanted this plant to produce not just cars, but inspiration.

So it was that on that dedication day, Hughes declared, in a passionate speech he delivered in German, that Opel would build a monument at the factory that would remind all who came there of what East Germany and Eisenach had overcome. In the audience, Frank Faga felt tears coming to his eyes as Hughes described the memorial: a piece of the old Berlin Wall that had divided Germany, and which had seen the deaths of hundreds who had tried to breach it in the search for freedom, would be installed at the plant. On the piece of the Wall, there would be a plaque, engraved with a quotation from Goethe:

> *Der Mensch hat die Kraft, das Gutes zu wollen und zu vollbringen. Wer was Gutes beginnt, soll niemals weilen.*

"Mankind has the power to do good," Goethe wrote some 200 years earlier. "He who would begin something good should never hesitate."

It was a fitting motto, and not just for Germany. Back home in Detroit, too, the time for hesitation had ended.

CHAPTER 16

THE MUSTANG

In April 1964, a fast-rising young Ford executive found his face on the cover of both *Time* and *Newsweek* magazines next to a picture of a snappy-looking two-door car. The executive was Lee A. Iacocca. The car was the Mustang.

Like Iacocca, the immigrant's son made good, the Mustang was a unique product of the American dream. The first children of the postwar Baby Boom were turning eighteen. They wanted to cruise down beachfront boulevards by day, and neck under the stars by night—all to the subversive beat of rock and roll. The Mustang—a light-footed, inexpensive car in an age of ponderous leviathans—was rebellion, rock, hormones, and hot sunshine in a nifty $2,368 package. Ford unveiled the car on April 17, 1964, at the New York World's Fair, and overnight it joined the Beatles and the Hula-Hoop in the long line of consumer culture explosions launched by the exuberance of the Baby Boomers. In 1966, two years after the car's debut, Ford sold 600,000 Mustangs, making it one of the most successful new cars in Detroit's post-Model T history. The Mustang was the All-American car.

Just as the Mustang epitomized Detroit's postwar zenith, later it reflected the industry's post-Arab oil shock decline. Iacocca's perky little coupe first grew fat and heavy in the late 1960s. Then after the first oil embargo in 1973, Ford transformed it into a pathetically underpowered compact called the Mustang II. In 1979, the Mustang was redesigned and regained a small measure of sportiness. Ford offered a version with a brawny 5.0 liter V-8 engine that was popular with die-hard American muscle car fans who didn't care for the heavier Chevrolet Camaro. But the 5.0 liter Mustang was expensive, and the standard Mustang with its four-cylinder engine was a dumpy rattlebox.

Like it or not, the old Mustang was on its last legs. The 1979 car was a quality nightmare and sadly inferior to faster, better-designed Japanese rivals such as the Toyota Celica or the Mitsubishi Eclipse. The Mustang magic began to fizzle. After hitting a post-1982 peak of 172,602 in 1987, Mustang sales by 1989 had fallen to 161,000 cars a year. That wasn't enough business to support a big new engineering program, or carry the costs of the ancient Dearborn assembly plant where the car was built. Viewed strictly as a business proposition—and not an exercise in nostalgia—the Mustang was a loser.

That was why, in the late 1980s, Ford almost killed the All-American Mustang. Company planners wanted to put the Mustang name on a car built by Ford's Japanese partner, Mazda, at its factory in Flat Rock, Michigan. Ford even prepared mock-ups of a bumper cover for the car, eventually called the Probe, with the Mustang logo embossed on it.

When this plan leaked out, with the help of outraged Ford staffers, Mustang fans, many of them members of organized Mustang clubs, bombarded Ford executives and automotive magazines, notably *Car and Driver*, with angry calls and letters. They denounced the proposed "Mazdectomy" of their beloved car, and vilified Ford for even thinking of offering a "Maztang" as a substitute for the real thing.

The Save the Mustang crusade coincided with some deep soul-searching at Ford headquarters. The daring design of the Taurus had earned Ford a reputation as one of America's model corporations during the 1980s. Ford's quality had surged past its Detroit rivals, and its productivity was fast approaching Japanese levels. Ford built as many vehicles in 1988 as it had in 1978—but with only half as many workers. The idea that a company with such strengths couldn't save the Mustang seemed unthinkable to some people at Ford.

One of those people was Alexander Trotman, the man in charge of Ford's North American Operations. Trotman realized there was something way out of whack with a system that consumed more than $1 billion and four years to design and engineer a new car. An Englishman who was schooled in Scotland and had worked for Ford in Australia and Europe before coming to Dearborn, Trotman knew that Mazda had designed its popular Miata convertible for about $280 million. That was dirt cheap by any standard. But as of 1990 Ford hadn't found the formula for even coming close to that level of efficiency in product development. Indeed, Ford seemed to be heading in the opposite direction, with a massive program to produce a new compact car for the European and U.S. markets by 1993. The program, code-named CDW27, had a budget of $6 billion, including the costs for the new car, new engines and transmissions, and retooled factories on two continents. Even if the car (eventually dubbed the Mondeo in Europe and the Contour in the United States) was a smash hit, it would take years to recover such a gargantuan investment. In the dog days of summer 1989, Trotman badgered his underlings to come up with better ideas for cutting product engineering costs.

"If the Japanese can do it," Trotman would ask, "why can't we?"

That challenge launched a crusade to save the Mustang from the glue pot. It was begun by an unlikely crew of middle managers who called themselves skunks.

O. J. "JOHN" COLETTI loved cars. He'd loved them as a child, almost from the time when he was just four years old and his family moved to Detroit from Newark, New Jersey, in 1953. By the time he was a senior in high school, Coletti was as car crazy as any Motor City native. He devoured hot-rodding magazines, spent days under the hood, and nights tearing up and down muscle car cruising strips like Gratiot Avenue. Confronted at the end of high school with the possibility of dodging bullets in Vietnam, Coletti enrolled at Wayne State University in Detroit to study engineering. He kept his gearhead credentials in good order, though, moonlighting as an engine mechanic for his street-racer pals and tooling around Detroit in a customized 1968 AMX, essentially a shortened-up AMC Javelin. Beefed up à la Coletti, the car could pop its front wheels off the ground from a standing start.

Coletti became a professional car guy in January 1972, when at age twenty-two he joined Ford as a product design engineer. His real job was following A. J. Foyt around as a "bagman" on the Ford Autolite Spark Plug Racing team. Less than a year later, in 1973, the first oil crisis shattered Coletti's hot-rod heaven. Ford canceled its racing program, and Coletti wound up getting a real job in the company's engine operations. It was a grim time for Ford, especially for someone like Coletti who loved speed and power. But things began to look up. Coletti got himself assigned as the ignition system engineer to develop a turbocharged four-cylinder engine for the redesigned 1979 Mustang. Then in 1983, Ford brought back the Mustang convertible. Coletti celebrated by beginning a personal ritual. Every year, he'd roll down to a Ford dealership and buy a brand new, bright red, V-8-powered Mustang convertible with a white leather interior and a stick shift. Coletti would pamper and baby the car until it was time for a new one.

Coletti's chance to make more of his love affair with the Mustang came out of the blue in September 1989, about three months after he'd been promoted to design engineering manager for small cars. Coletti's boss called him into his office, and declared that Alex Trotman wanted to try to save the Mustang and the Dearborn factory that assembled it. Would Coletti tackle the job of leading a small "skunk works"[1] team to study the problem? Coletti was struck speechless for a moment. Finally, he got the words out: "I'd be honored."

Coletti meant it. This was a dream assignment. He'd gotten good and sick of people blabbering about how the Japanese could do this and the Japanese can do that. "They're not superhumans," Coletti would say. But the Japanese did know something about designing cars on the cheap that Ford didn't know. Now it was Coletti's job to figure out what that was.

Coletti was like a sergeant drafted to lead a secret foray behind enemy lines. Officially, Ford hadn't budgeted money to develop a new Mustang. That meant Coletti had to operate on a shoestring, outside the mainstream of the Ford bureaucracy. He quickly rallied seven other managers, and they began holding regular meetings every Thursday at 4 P.M. Among the group's members were a person from Ford's planning staff, an executive from design staff, a marketing manager, and someone from the engine operations. The group's members spanned Ford's class structure from grade 8 to grade 15. Coletti, a grade 13, was the leader even though another member outranked him because Coletti represented the car program office, the pros at pulling together various departments to get new vehicles done. But Coletti was relieved that everyone quickly dispensed with protocol and got down to business.

During the winter of 1989 and early 1990, Coletti and several other team members launched a global brainstorming effort. Coletti flew to Europe to pick the brains of experts at German and Italian engineering and toolmaking companies. A man named Dia Hothi, whose regular job was assistant manager of the Dearborn assembly plant that built the Mustang, led trips to Australia and Japan.

The more the skunks learned about how other companies designed new cars, the less impressive Ford's system appeared. Traditionally, designing a new Ford meant coordinating the efforts of hundreds of engineers scattered all over Dearborn and some adjoining communities as well. The people who did blueprints for chassis parts worked on a different floor from the engineers who tested the parts. And the engineers who designed the air-conditioner compressor worked in an entirely different building and in an entirely different department from the people who designed the dashboards behind which the air-conditioners had to fit. Managers in the dashboard department couldn't tell engineers in the air-conditioner department what to do. They had to play memo and telephone tag with the air-conditioner engineers' supervisors to get their approval. The all-too-common result was that few of the parts for a new car fit properly the first time they came together in a prototype, or even the second time.

Ford senior executives, meanwhile, were famous for declaring at the eleventh hour that they didn't like the way a fender curved and that it should be changed—"tweaked" in Detroit's argot. Tweaking cost Ford millions every year in last-minute tool and die changes. And even if top managers bit their tongues, the engineers inevitably had to order late changes to fix misaligned parts. Usually, it took three prototypes before everything matched well enough to start production. Even then, plenty of fixes didn't get made until after the first cars were shipped to showrooms.

Coletti's group realized that saving the Mustang would require a radical departure. That, in turn, would mean stepping on the toes of important people in Ford's chain of command. But Coletti had a trump card.

One evening early in 1990, Coletti was relaxing at the Fairlane Club, a Ford management hangout not far from company headquarters. A trim man with a neatly clipped mustache and a Scots brogue approached him.

"Hello," the man said. "I'm Alex Trotman."

"I know who you are," Coletti replied. Trotman made himself

comfortable, and began talking about the Mustang project. He came to the point with a simple question: "Why should we do this?"

Coletti couldn't contain himself. "I can't imagine Ford without a Mustang," he said. "Alex, if you go to a man in the deepest part of Tennessee, and ask him what a Jaguar is, he might tell you it's a cat. But if you ask him what a Mustang is, he'll tell you it's a Ford."

Coletti's barely veiled barb about Ford's disastrous $2.5 billion Jaguar investment was impolitic. But Trotman was unfazed. Instead, he offered Coletti encouragement and asked: "When will I see you again?"

Coletti assured him it would be soon.[2]

SOON CAME SOONER than expected. Coletti's skunks had realized by the beginning of 1990 that a serious deadline was bearing down on them. Federal safety regulators had decreed that all cars sold after September 1, 1993, had to have "passive restraints." In plain English, that meant air bags. Putting air bags in a car wasn't a small matter. It required overhauling the car's dashboard, steering column, and wiring—all expensive undertakings. Ford's bean counters wouldn't go along with outfitting the old Mustang with air bags. Either the Skunk Works team figured out how to deliver a new car, with air bags, by the fall of 1993, or else the old Mustang would die without being replaced.

This situation gave new urgency to the team's efforts. In January 1990, Coletti and two other members of the team went to Europe to gather more information from engineers and toolmakers in Italy and Germany. On the flight back to Detroit, Coletti and one of his colleagues began hashing over what they'd learned. A plan began to gel. The cornerstone was the deadline for starting production of a new car: October 1993. The two worked backward from there. They knew how long toolmakers needed to produce dies and welding equipment once they had final design blueprints—roughly a year. That meant the clay model of the exterior of the car had to be "frozen," or approved with no further major changes, by August or September 1990.

The reaction to this proposal among some Ford higher-ups was sheer disbelief. It was hard enough to imagine meeting Trotman's original goal of developing the new Mustang for about the same cost as the Miata. Ford engineers had been struggling with a program called Concept to Customer that was supposed to bring a car to life in forty-eight months. These efforts had failed. Now, the ragtag Mustang group was proposing to shave four months or more off a timetable no other Ford program had met.

Trotman, however, had a different reaction when the Skunk Works team discussed its plan with him in February 1990. Coletti arranged to have a classic white 1964 Mustang positioned alongside a clay model of the new car sculpted by Skunk Works designers. Side by side, it was clear the Skunk Works group envisioned a new car that evoked memories of the original. Trotman was impressed and enthusiastic. "There's going to be a Mustang," he declared. Within three months, Coletti and his team had boiled their plan down to five clear elements. Of those, only one presented a problem: the cost. The team had wanted a new Mustang for only about $300 million, or 70 percent less money than a typical Ford project.

"We cannot meet our investment objective," Coletti conceded. "The best we can do is $565 million." Trotman replied: "I'll take it."

"I'LL TAKE IT" didn't mean the Mustang team had a blank check. Among other things, they still had to convince Trotman's boss, Chairman Harold "Red" Poling, the same man whose iron-fisted management had salvaged Ford in the early 1980s, and later had been the undoing of the ill-fated Thunderbird team. Poling wouldn't accept an emotional appeal. The team would need a detailed timetable for engineering and building the car, a realistic budget, and styling guaranteed to deliver a home run on the cheap. As of May 1990, the skunks didn't have any of these.

The look for the new Mustang had taken shape during early 1990 among a small group of stylists in Dearborn. The stylists had started by pondering images that had no obvious connection to cars. In one exercise, the designers plastered a wall in their office with pictures of Harley-Davidson motorcyles. The Mustang designers agreed that a Mustang lover would probably be the kind of person who appreciated the Harley mystique—muscular, All-American, rebellious.

Far more influential in guiding the stylists' hands was the classic look of the original Mustang. Three design elements, or "cues," from the original had to be incorporated into the new car: the scoop that graced the sides, a taillight segmented into three bars, and a chrome pony running across an open grille. The last feature, the most recognizable signature of the original Mustang, had been dropped during the 1980s as a concession to Ford's aero styling trend.

The trick would be to reconcile the opposing forces of nostalgia and modernity. One of the styling group's first efforts was a clay model that came to be known as Bruce Jenner. The Jenner was sporty, and it had all the basic design elements called for in the manifesto, but it wasn't macho. Instead, it looked like a half dozen other smoothed over, aero cars launched by Ford, Nissan, or Toyota in the late 1980s. The Mustang group's misgivings were confirmed when it took the Bruce Jenner out for a sneak preview with a group of Mustang enthusiasts in California. The Mustang nuts agreed that the "Jenner" reminded them a lot of the Mazda-built Probe. Bruce was a flop.

The skunks then launched a design contest. A second group of stylists was recruited from Ford's design staff to take the Jenner car and turn it into a no-holds-barred hot rod. The result was a rakish street racer with slanted headlights that gave the front end a decidedly snarly look. It was dubbed Rambo.

Meanwhile, the original Mustang design team took its design in for an overhaul. "Bruce was a little wimpy," Coletti would explain. "So we sent him back to the gym." The result was a more muscular look dubbed Arnold Schwarzenegger. The Arnold had scoops in the hood and sides, like the Rambo, but its front end wasn't as mean looking.

In early October 1990, the leaders of the Skunk Works team piled into a Ford jet and headed to San Jose for a six-day round of consumer tests. A total of some 300 people, most of them Mustang fans, looked at the Rambo, Bruce, and Arnold clay models. By the end of the week, it was clear that Arnold had done the trick. Coletti was ecstatic. Now they had a car.

As THE DESIGN DEBATE got settled, the Skunk Works team began the transformation from a guerrilla campaign to a legitimate new product program with a real budget. That brought a new player to the group, a forty-five-year-old junior executive named Will Boddie.

Boddie, a tall man with a mop of reddish brown hair, had joined Ford in 1972 just before the first oil shock, just like Coletti. He had a high-toned résumé for a fledgling Ford suspension engineer, having earned a BA and a Master's degree in engineering at Dartmouth, and then studied at the University of Paris on a Fulbright Scholarship. But behind the Ivy League sheepskin and the foreign study lurked a native New Yorker-turned-Texan who'd spent his teenage years in the Houston exurb of

Lake Jackson in a whirl of fast cars, big engines, and drag racing. At Dartmouth, Boddie found himself in a culture that viewed the big, brawny American automobiles of the time as barbaric contrivances. But he never lost his love of cars. In 1969, Boddie landed a job with Rockwell, and wound up in Pittsburgh as an engineer in a division that made snowmobile engines. His fascination with the complex mechanics of internal combustion reignited. Snowmobiles, however, weren't a high enough calling. In the spring of 1972, he applied for a job at Ford. Eight weeks later, at age twenty-seven, he was on his way to Dearborn.

Boddie's first job wasn't much of a step up, in terms of glamour, from the snowmobile business. He designed the spindles that held on the front wheels of cars. But steadily he jumped to bigger engineering jobs. In November 1985, Boddie even got a taste of manufacturing when he was assigned to manage Ford's big air-conditioner and heater factory in the Detroit suburb of Plymouth. His job boiled down to three imperatives: Ship goods to the assembly plants on time, improve quality, and cut labor and overhead costs. In the process of achieving these goals, Boddie got a fast immersion in the application of Toyota-style lean production methods. He emerged from the grueling experience humbler, wiser, and eager for the plum assignment he'd earned for his success at the factory: chief engineer for Alpha, Ford's answer to Roger Smith's Saturn. Like Saturn, Alpha was a laboratory for new ideas to design lower-cost, higher-quality small cars. Ford, however, never intended to spend billions on an Alpha factory or to sell an Alpha car. Boddie's experiences at Alpha reinforced his view that Ford had lots to learn. The company needed to be more disciplined, to do things right the first time, to accept change through continuous improvement—in short, to be more like its Japanese antagonists.

Boddie's chance to put his Alpha experiences into practice on a real car came on September 14, 1990, when he was offered the job of Mustang program manager. On paper, this was a big promotion. Boddie had never managed an entire car program. Success would steer his career into the passing lane. But he also pondered the consequences of failure. Red Poling's harsh treatment of Tony Kuchta and the Thunderbird team was by then legendary in Ford's engineering ranks. It didn't bolster Boddie's confidence that as word of his new job got around, friends began calling to offer condolences.

.   .   .

BODDIE SOON FOUND out why. Coletti's team had the basic framework of
a program, but not the kind of detailed plan required to pry hundreds of
millions of dollars out of Red Poling. Basic issues remained undecided.
The Skunk Works group, for example, hadn't nailed down whether to
contract outside engineering companies to do most of the design work,
or draft engineers from other Ford operations. As Boddie and the others
began wrestling with how to make the new Mustang a reality, they
decided to take a cue from Trotman. He had advised the skunks to act
as if they were running their own, independent car company. To that
end, the skunks had rented offices in a converted furniture warehouse in
the blue-collar Detroit suburb of Allen Park, a few miles south of Ford's
Dearborn headquarters and outside the orbit of Ford's product-development bosses. It was a thoroughly utilitarian location, with long, high-
ceilinged halls and open rooms cut into cubicles by partitions. The main
conference room was where a loading dock used to be. When the first
Mustang team members arrived, the toilets in the suite of offices hadn't
been finished. They used two portapotties that were set up in a space
that eventually became Will Boddie's office.

This was the headquarters for what Boddie and the others soon dubbed
the Mustang Car Company. Coletti remained on the team as its business
manager. He had recognized all along that a higher-ranking executive
like Boddie would be brought in to call the shots once the Skunk Works
phase was done. But at least he would still have a strong hand in shaping
the car. Boddie, however, quickly established himself as the chairman of
the board. One of his first acts was to convene a board meeting at the
warehouse conference room that ran for twenty hours across three
straight days. As the group brainstormed, members scrawled ideas about
organizational structure, scheduling, and finances on butcher paper
charts that eventually covered the walls of the conference room.

Above all, the Mustang team leaders realized, they needed to move
fast.

Ford executives had known before the Mustang project took shape
that the company took too long developing new models. That's why a
secret team had been formed to work on the problem of development
time. This group was called the 411 team, because it worked out of room
411 in the Ford Motor Credit building. The 411 group had created a
chart 48 feet long that mapped out every step in bringing a new car to
life. It labeled some steps "rods" and others "springs." The steps that
couldn't be avoided, and couldn't be significantly shortened, were

"rods." And the "springs," as the name suggested, were activities that could be compressed to cut days or weeks out of the engineering effort.

The 411 team's system became known as "world class timing." Coletti had heard about it in March 1990, when he got a call from a member of the 411 group. Coletti agreed to compare notes, and was stunned. The skunkers and the 411 team had come to virtually the same conclusions. Coletti and the Mustang team agreed to serve as guinea pigs for the new process, with one proviso: The Mustang would have to move even faster than "world class timing." Around the Allen Park warehouse, the project's three-year schedule was dubbed "Mustang timing." The term became a rallying cry, a slogan synonymous with superfast.

By November 1990, less than two months after joining the team, Boddie took his case to Red Poling and Ford's other top executives at a meeting in Ford's Design Center in Dearborn. On center stage was a clay model of the car, painted a striking color formulated specially for the occasion and dubbed "laser red." The color alone seemed to convince some members of Poling's inner circle. But Poling took a tough line. Told that the new Mustang might only break even, Poling balked. Ford had shareholders who deserved a return on their money, he lectured. Come back with a profitable proposition. The team went back to the drawing board.

In the end, the Mustang budget would total about $700 million for engineering the car and retooling the Dearborn Assembly plant to build as many as 200,000 Mustangs a year. That wasn't as efficient as the Japanese. But it was closer than Ford had managed to come in a long time. In return for meeting his financial demands, Poling gave Boddie and his Mustang team a valuable gift. Every six months, Boddie and his group would give him updates on their progress. Beyond that, however, they were on their own to decide how to meet the agreed-upon targets for the car's weight, fuel economy, and development costs. Senior management wouldn't meddle.

The race to save the Mustang was on.

STUDENTS OF AUTOMOTIVE history, and Coletti was one, knew that nothing could be so disastrous as launching a new car into a recession. And as the Mustang team began scrambling toward its deadline, the outlook was bleak. With the economy headed into a tailspin, Ford's automotive business began careening toward a huge loss that ultimately totaled $3.2 billion by the end of 1991. At Ford's North American Operations, cost-cutting pressure was so intense that four of every five lights in the hallways were turned off to shave the electric bill. Trotman was fighting to save his plan to spend billions developing modern engines and transmissions. To cover the huge investments, Ford had to raise $2.3 billion of new capital.

The Mustang was extremely vulnerable in this hostile environment. Boddie had to scuttle plans for a team picnic after the corporate accountants issued a policy forbidding the use of company money for such frivolity. But a picnic wasn't all the company could have canceled. The whole Mustang project depended on fulfilling the promise to make a quantum leap in engineering efficiency and speed.

The Mustang team leaders had one advantage. The time crunch meant no time for business as usual. Senior executives, following Poling and Trotman's lead, had vowed to remove roadblocks thrown in the Mustang's path. Now it was up to Boddie's team to overcome the pitfalls of the Ford system, and adapt the ideas that Japanese companies used to outrun Ford in product design.

The Mustang team leaders hit upon one idea early on to overcome the communication breakdowns that hobbled most Ford projects: putting engineers assigned to the Mustang in the same room.

This common-sense notion was so unusual that Ford had to invent special jargon to describe it: "colocation." In English, colocation meant that people responsible for designing parts of the new car would sit next to the engineers who tested the designs. It meant engineers could work together to solve problems without having to schedule a meeting on the other side of town. Boddie instituted regular weekly meetings at which engineers for parts that bolted together, so-called "mating parts," would lay their latest drawings on a table and check that their pieces really would fit. These simple decisions slashed weeks off the Mustang's engineering schedule.

As people began to fill up the Mustang's offices, Boddie started organizing groups of engineers to be responsible for large sections, or "chunks," of the car. There was a chassis chunk team, an engine-and-transmission chunk team, a suspension chunk team and so on. Each had a chunk team manager. The object was to force engineers to make decisions on the basis of what was good for the whole car, instead of just concentrating on a front-axle spindle, or a brake cable, or a shock absorber.

Boddie threw away the rule book in another key area: purchasing. Ford usually conducted what Boddie scornfully called a "rain dance" with parts makers. The company produced "final" drawings of parts late in the car's gestation period, sent them around to suppliers, and collected bids. The bids were sifted, and contracts were awarded largely on the basis of price. This process took a year or more, and often didn't conclude until a few months before the start of production. The Mustang team had no time for this. Moreover, Boddie needed engineers from supplier companies to do much of the design work on their pieces of the car. The Mustang team leaders decided to take a leap of faith.

Once again, they locked themselves away for a three-day series of marathon meetings. They evaluated lists of suppliers, debating which would likely offer the best price and the best engineering talent. Then the team's purchasing agents began calling up the suppliers at the top of the list to offer them on-the-spot contracts. In the process, the Mustang group narrowed the number of suppliers dramatically from the list that worked on the old car. The old Mustang had fifty-five suppliers for fenders, hoods, and other sheet metal parts. The new car would have only three. This was a very Japanese approach. But it meant substituting an intangible—trust—for the tangible insurance of having multiple suppliers available should one stumble.

The gamble worked. One supplier, National Electric, assigned three engineers to work with the Mustang team on the wiring system for the car. They accomplished the job in seven months. Coletti was amazed. On another program, Coletti had seen eleven engineers take three years to complete a wiring system.

IN AN ATMOSPHERE charged by the onrushing deadline, the team struggled to maintain both high morale and the necessary urgency. Among some foot soldiers, the Mustang project came to be known as the "team from hell." Boddie set a relentless pace. Coffee mug in hand, he'd roam around the warehouse offices, poking his head into cubicles to ask engineers how they were doing. One hour he'd review the schedules, the next he'd talk finances, then he'd race over to the test track, strap on a helmet, and fling himself around the course for a few laps. The least likely place to find him was his office. But wherever he was, Boddie kept the pressure on. Although he tried to nurture the notion of the Mustang "team," Boddie made it plain that staying on schedule was paramount.

Boddie didn't pound on tables. But he didn't always wait until a meeting was over to register his displeasure with a subordinate's performance.

The breathless pace had one welcome aspect. No one had time for the protocol of the plodding Ford management culture. Mustang team members learned to be comfortable making expensive decisions without much paperwork or ceremony. "Explain it to me on a napkin," became Boddie's way of encouraging subordinates to keep things simple. Among the engineers another slogan took hold: *JFDI*, short for "Just Fucking Do It."

Outside, however, the Ford bureaucracy carried on as before. The Mustang team leaders had won a major battle just getting engineers moved into their building and dedicated entirely to Mustang work. But they still had to deal with department managers outside the Mustang team, who ran their groups almost like separate companies. These "chimney" organizations—so called because of their vertical organization charts and narrow function—had their own policies on pay, promotions, and how workers were allocated to projects. The Mustang team didn't fit into these systems.

Some assigned to the Mustang worried that they would be orphaned within their home departments after the Mustang was done. To help ease those fears, Mustang team managers agreed to coauthor performance reviews with managers in the home departments. In time, Mustang managers learned to tell nervous team members to JFDI, and leave dealing with red tape for later.

The role of spiritual guide and ad hoc morale booster fell to Coletti. He was the team's most fanatical Mustang nut. And he liked to take time out once in a while to blow off steam. Coletti would collect several colleagues, round up cold cuts and sub buns, and head for a nearby park. Coletti and his buddies called these gatherings "Mafia picnics," a self-deprecating reference to the fact that most members of the group had Italian surnames.

But there wasn't much time for relaxing. By October 1991, the Mustang team was scheduled to deliver a progress report to Red Poling and the senior management, and by then the team was supposed to have running prototypes ready. To save time, the team dispensed with assembling a mechanical prototype using an old Mustang's chassis and sheet metal. Instead, they built test vehicles—a hardtop coupe and a convertible—that looked like the clay models of the new car. As engineers put the first two prototypes through their test drives, Coletti shot videotape of the cars on the track. When the day came to brief Poling, Boddie dispensed with the usual long dissertation, and instead, after a short introduction, he rolled a one-minute-and-forty-five-second video of the two prototype cars wheeling around the track.

"Any questions?" Boddie asked when the video was done.

"Congratulations," Poling answered. "And good luck."

THE MUSTANG TEAM would need good luck. They were cutting it close to the bone. How close was dramatized by the attractive convertible that had looked so inviting in the video shown to Poling. In fact, the first convertible prototype was a mess. The Mustang team leaders had agreed at the start that a critical measure of their success would be creating a new convertible that didn't shake, rattle, roll, or leak like the existing model. They wanted the new car to be 50 percent stiffer, 50 percent quieter, and 50 percent better at high-speed cornering. The convertible powered by the 5.0 liter V-8 would be the top of the line, setting the image for the rest of the models. Enthusiasts would pay top dollar for the convertible, and profits from convertible sales would be critical to the program's success.

To save time, the team's engineers had done much of the nuts-and-bolts design work for the convertible on a computer screen. They fed in data from the basic car, and then added steel braces and other reinforcements to the "virtual" car on the cathode ray tubes. On the basis of the computer design, they built a prototype that was ready for testing in July 1991.

But when the team's engineers took the first convertible out for a test drive, they got a shock. The new car shimmied, shook, and vibrated almost as badly as the old one. The computer modeling had failed. Coletti had his own test of stability. He'd drive with his elbow on the door and his hand on the upper edge of the windshield. If he could feel the windshield shake, it wasn't right. This car wasn't right.

Boddie and the team's engineers assembled a crisis crew. This SWAT team commandeered one of the big "shaker" devices that Ford used to simulate rough road conditions in the lab, and stuck the convertible on it. Within a week, they'd come up with a solution, in the form of several new metal braces to stiffen the car's frame. It was a piece of work that normally would have required months to get done. The speedy rescue transformed a potential setback into a morale booster. "Mustang timing" had won the day. The drill had been good practice, because the convertible wasn't quite finished.

While the Mustang engineers were scrambling to finish the car, Dia Hothi and his staff confronted the problem of the Dearborn factory. "You take care of the engineering," Hothi had told his boss. "I'll take care of the manufacturing."

Hothi's experience as the assistant plant manager gave him intimate knowledge of the shortcomings of the aging Dearborn assembly plant. There were many. Dearborn's hidebound mass production system, combined with an aged car designed before avoiding defects was a primary concern, made the Mustang one of Ford's worst quality cars. The Dearborn plant was more a museum than a modern manufacturing facility. Despite renovation over the years, at heart the plant remained the same factory the first Henry Ford had built in 1918 to anchor his massive Rouge works.

The Rouge was the archetype of automobile mass production—iron ore, sand, and coal went in one end, cars came out the other. At its peak in the 1920s, the Rouge had been a wonder of the modern world. But by the early 1990s, it was sputtering. The system the Rouge had pioneered was obsolete. Dearborn Assembly workers worried that they too would become obsolete. Their numbers had dwindled from a 1979 peak of 4,400 to just 2,400 people in 1990. United Auto Workers union laborers and their supervisors had clung to traditional work rules and job classifications. But by 1990, the threat to the plant forced union leaders and the plant's managers to take the first steps toward change. They agreed to adopt a "modern operating agreement" that would give Ford flexibility to streamline the production system. In return, Dearborn Assembly got an assurance that the old plant would get a shot at building the new Mustang.

The catch was that Ford wanted to spend only about $500 million to fix up the plant and outfit the Mustang manufacturing system—peanuts in a business where installing a new paint shop alone can cost $500 million.

Hothi had begun his quest to save money early on, by requisitioning a space in the Dearborn factory complex where he could set up the steel shell of a Mustang on a stand. With the help of a contract engineering company, Hothi and his small staff pored over the hundreds of steel pieces in the car's body, looking for parts they could continue to use in the new model. Those pieces they marked with yellow paint.

The most important pieces so marked were in the underbody—the "floor pan" in engineering jargon. Change the critical dimensions of a car's floor pan—width, length, certain attachment points for other body parts—and it meant spending $40 million to $50 million on new production tools. Hothi saw that the Mustang engineers could lop about $30 million off the tooling bill if they kept the floor pan's critical dimensions the same as the old Mustang. Preserving the old underbody really would save even more, because it would allow Dearborn Assembly to start rolling out new Mustangs without a long shutdown for overhauling the assembly line. This was a trick Honda used to bring off "rolling," one-weekend, model changes at its plant in Marysville, Ohio. Ford, like GM and Chrysler, still suffered through weeks-long "model changeover" breaks that cost millions in lost sales and payments to idled workers.

As the new car took shape in the Allen Park warehouse, Hothi and his manufacturing staff attacked other expensive manufacturing puzzles. Ford had specifications for building the dies that stamped out metal parts so they could pound out 250,000 parts a year for 10 years. Japanese companies, in contrast, designed lighter, less costly dies on the assumption that the model runs would be smaller and shorter. When it came time to decide what company was best suited to build the dies for the All-American car, the Mustang team settled on a company that understood the Japanese processes intimately: Ogihara Tool Works of Japan.

Hothi also took liberties with Ford's standard procedures when they conflicted with the project's goals. Mustang engineers had decided to hold down the cost of the convertible by designing the car so that a convertible could be built on the same assembly line as the hardtop, using the same body parts. In contrast, the old convertible had a different rear end, and was shipped out to a subcontractor who installed the convertible top.

Hothi's group decided the best way to keep the convertible in-house was to turn upside down Ford's normal system for building the rear flank of the car—known as the "quarter panel" to engineers. Ford usually built a rear fender by putting the exterior steel panel down first, and welding the inner reinforcement parts to it. But the Mustang team wanted first to lock in place the inner reinforcements—so the convertible attachments would be properly positioned in relationship to the rest of the car—and then drop the exterior skin of the rear fender on top of the metal bracing like the crust of a pie. Traditionalists fumed at the breach of convention. Hothi ignored them. "If we're responsible," he'd say, "we need power."

BY THE SUMMER of 1992, Team Mustang was heading into the final lap. August was the deadline to produce the final blueprints and begin making the dies and equipment to build the car. Outside the Allen Park warehouse, however, the world still looked bleak. Americans were still shying away from showrooms. The old Mustang was limping badly. Sales collapsed in 1991 to just 80,247 cars—half the sales of 1989, the year the "skunks" had started their crusade. Ford was skidding back into the red, after recording thin profits in the first half of the year. With $9 billion in the bank, Ford was in a lot better shape than GM. But Ford didn't have much room to brag. It was losing less than GM in North America, but in Europe, where GM was profitable, Ford was bleeding badly.

In early August, Boddie and a couple of the team's top engineers took a final prototype of the convertible for a spin around Dearborn. The car was supposed to be virtually identical to the cars that would roll off the Dearborn assembly line in a little more than a year. But as Boddie tooled down the Southfield Freeway near Ford world headquarters, he realized the car was still shaking and shimmying. The windshield wobbled when the wheels hit a bump, making images dance wildly in the rearview mirror.

Boddie had suspected that the convertible wasn't completely fixed. Now he had proof. And that left him with two options. Let the program slip behind schedule or find a real fix for the convertible in record time. For him, there was only one option.

Boddie mobilized another crisis team of about fifty engineers, augmented by technicians from supplier companies. "Mustang timing" went into overdrive. Boddie launched around-the-clock work sessions at Allen Park and in Ford's testing laboratories. Engineers worked through the night, catnapping on the floor by their desks. Boddie spent hours on weekends watching the car go through tests on the giant "shaker," and brainstorming with the engineers.

Finally, a real cure for the convertible's shakes took shape. A brace that ran under the front seats and up to the sides of the car needed to be bigger and beefier. More steel needed to be welded into the front end to make it stiffer. And to steady the dashboard, engineers devised an Xshaped brace that spanned the rearward end of the engine compartment. As the body engineers experimented with these new structural reinforcements, the engineers from the Mustang's wiring supplier worked to reroute cables around the new brace in the midsection. As a final touch, the rearview mirror was redesigned so it wouldn't wiggle as much.

Boddie still wasn't satisfied. He had read an article in an automotive magazine praising the solid feel of a new Mercedes convertible. One night, walking out of a restaurant in Phoenix with Coletti, Boddie saw a Mercedes convertible glistening in the parking lot. Admiring the car, Boddie declared: "We want to be that good."

Mustang engineers dug into the mystery of the Mercedes' ride, even tearing one of the cars apart. They discovered that Mercedes had bolted five large cylindrical weights at various spots on the frame. The weights dampened the car's natural vibration, like fingers on a vibrating tuning fork.

Mustang engineers started experimenting, and discovered that one 25-pound steel cylinder bolted to a spot behind the Mustang's front fender achieved the desired effect.

At last, the Mustang team had done it. The braces, the new mirror, and the damper produced a car that surpassed the old car's ride and quality—and without missing the deadline or overrunning the budget. It appeared the Mustang program would succeed where the Thunderbird team had failed.

THE MUSTANG SOON took on far more significance at Ford than just the rescue of a beloved name and a historic factory. In June 1993, as final work on the launch began at Dearborn, Will Boddie won a promotion to director of small and midsize car programs, overseeing development of some of Ford's most important cars—the Escort, the Taurus, the Tempo, and the Probe. Ford vice presidents drove home the message of Boddie's promotion by hailing the Mustang as the model for future product development at Ford. Soon every new vehicle program at Ford was collecting engineers and managers from various departments under one roof. Ford began a massive, $150 million renovation of its old engineering offices into a "program team facility" to house future Mustang-style teams.

The Mustang's success also put the spotlight on its patron, Alex Trotman. On paper, Trotman had seemed a longshot to succeed Red Poling as Ford's chief executive. He wasn't a native-born American, and he had spent most of his career outside the main U.S. operations. By 1990, however, Trotman had emerged as a leading candidate to resolve the succession puzzle Don Petersen left behind. Trotman had run Ford's vehicle operations in the three major world markets—Asia, Europe, and finally, North America. In November 1992, he became president of Ford's worldwide auto operations.

Trotman didn't lose his unaffected style as he gained rank. Ford vice presidents were privileged to use blue stationery, which was why their memos were reverently called "blue letters." But Trotman scorned this perk, and sent out his notes on plain white paper just like the company's plebes.[3] Trotman also shut down the executive dining room at Ford's North American Operations headquarters. Subordinates conditioned to making two or three presentations to a vice president before getting a decision found that Trotman wanted only one.

Trotman also had a way with plain English that made him stand out in a company saturated in technojargon. "I'll sell the bloody furniture before I cut out new product programs," he once told subordinates.[4] It was a remark that quickly found its way into company legend. But Trotman put his money where his mouth was. Consequently, Ford was able to brag as it entered 1993's recovery that it had sixteen completely new or updated models in the pipeline for introduction by 1995.

On the cool, bright fall morning of October 4, 1993, Trotman joined Red Poling and hundreds of Ford employees for the official Job One ceremony marking the official start of production of 1994 Mustangs. The atmosphere inside the seventy-five-year-old Dearborn factory was almost giddy as hundreds of workers, Ford dealers, and executives from Mustang subcontractors crowded around the end of the production line. The throng was dotted with bright red hats, which had been passed out to workers who'd been in the factory when the first Mustang was launched thirty years before.

In the first row of seats in front of the temporary stage sat William Clay Ford, grandson of the company's founder, and his son, William Clay, Jr. Billy, thirty-six years old, was running the Climate Control division where Boddie once had worked. His interest in the Mustang was more than casual. He had arranged to buy the Job One car for himself. On the stage, Poling, Trotman, and several union officials sat flanking a podium that was overshadowed by a large video screen.

As the sixty-seven-year-old Poling rose to speak, he got a rousing cheer. He reminisced about the original Mustang's debut in the same year that saw the first satellite pictures of the moon, Muhammad Ali's ascent to the world heavyweight boxing championship, and the advent of the Beatles. He saluted the Mustang team, the Dearborn Assembly workforce, and the dealers and suppliers in the audience. He led a round of applause for the two Fords, hailing "the family members who have lent their name and held this company especially close since its founding ninety years ago." Then, he paused and said:

"This new beginning for Mustang coincides with a new beginning for Ford's management. I have worked for this company for forty-two years, beginning here in the Rouge at the steel mill, a few steps away. So I thought it appropriate to return to this historic place—surrounded by warm memories and so many members of the family of Ford—to announce that I will retire at the end of this year.

"The work of building a great company is never finished," Poling continued. "From Henry Ford II, to Phil Caldwell, to Don Petersen, and to me, the role of chief executive has passed from one to the next. And now it passes to Alexander J. Trotman."

Trotman, the man whom Caldwell had once predicted would amount to nothing at Ford, beamed as he stepped to the podium. There were many reasons why he, at age sixty, had won the contest to succeed Poling. But saving the Mustang clearly was one. He now would become the first foreign-born chief executive of one of America's Big Three car makers. Even more than Jack Smith or Bob Eaton, both of whom had burnished their reputations in Europe with GM's turnaround there, Trotman represented Detroit's realization that the American auto industry was part of a globe-spanning enterprise. No longer could GM, Ford, or Chrysler be led solely by people whose world view was limited to the American Midwest. Now, all of the Big Three chief executives in Detroit would be men who understood that the Detroit way wasn't the only way, or even always the best way. For Alex Trotman, this was a moment to savor.

"It's a big day for the Mustang." He grinned. "It's a big day for me."

TROTMAN WAS RIGHT on both counts. The Mustang team had accomplished its mission. It had saved the car Trotman called "an American icon."[5] And it had proved that Ford could adapt ideas from Japan and Europe to produce the quintessential American car. The Mustang had demonstrated that a renaissance could take place in the very cradle of the old, outmoded American mass production system.

For Will Boddie, watching Alex Trotman and Red Poling clasp hands over the hood of a bright red Mustang was a moment of exhilarating pride. All the work wasn't done. The car still had to sell against strong competition, and Dearborn Assembly still had to prove it could meet the high quality standards of the new decade. But as he saw the drama of the car's launch and Trotman's ascension unfolding on the plant floor, Boddie had just one real regret. If only he hadn't allowed Ford's system to lock the October launch date in stone, the Job One ceremony could have happened in August, two months ahead of schedule. That's how fast Mustang timing had turned out to be.

As for John Coletti, his realization of victory had come earlier, on May 25, 1993, when the first new Mustang assembled at the Dearborn plant on production tools rolled off the line. There it was, he thought, the car so many people had doubted would ever exist. An old dog could learn new tricks, he would say later. Ford could fight back, and so could America.

"We've made the leap," Coletti said, recalling the sight of that wonderful red car. "We're in business."

CHAPTER 17

THE LÓPEZ FILES

On April 13, 1993, Tomas Andersson, a twenty-six-year-old Swede, returned from an Easter holiday to the house in Wiesbaden, Germany, where he lived. Parked outside on the street was a rented van containing several large bags filled with shredded papers. When he went inside, Andersson stumbled into two industrial-strength shredders, both about three feet tall, in the hallway. They were surrounded by scraps of paper. Nearby were two large suitcases.

Annoyed, Andersson went into his apartment and found two of his housemates, Jorge Alvarez and Rosario Piazza, hard at work.

"What the fuck are you doing?" Andersson asked the Spaniards.

"Destroying some GM papers," Alvarez replied.

Why, Andersson demanded to know, didn't Alvarez handle this messy chore down at his office.

"We didn't want to," Alvarez said matter-of-factly.

Andersson didn't realize it, but he had stumbled into a bizarre drama of international industrial espionage and personal betrayal that would symbolize the desperate struggle for survival by two of the world's largest and most troubled car companies: General Motors and Volkswagen. Battered by Japanese competition, GM and Volkswagen grappled for the soul of one man, José Ignacio López de Arriortúa, who seemed an almost magical catalyst for change. Entrusted by Jack Smith with leading a comeback at GM's American operations, López instead took GM and Volkswagen on a wild ride that Smith would later call "the biggest fiasco I've ever been involved with in my life."

WHEN JACK SMITH plucked José Ignacio López de Arriortúa from the obscurity of GM's European operations in May 1992 and made him GM's worldwide purchasing czar, it seemed like a bolt from the blue. In reality, however, it was a plan that had been brewing between López and Smith for nearly three years.

On Christmas Day, 1989, López, then head of purchasing for GM Europe, took some company stationery and neatly hand-printed a memo under the heading: "Personal and confidential notes to Mr. Jack F. Smith." What followed was a document that advocated a sweeping end run of GM's traditional system.

López wrote that he'd spent a week touring GM's U.S. purchasing operations in late 1989. GM had thirty-six quasi-independent purchasing managers in North America. This fragmented organization meant GM was dissipating its buying clout and missing a chance "to generate urgent cash" by negotiating lower prices from suppliers—including GM's own components subsidiaries. GM's North American purchasing managers had no "sense that we are fighting for our survival as first company in the world," López fretted.

"I will take the liberty," López continued, "to make some suggestions. . . ." First, he wrote, name a single purchasing vice president, reporting to the head of North American operations. "Give to purchasing the strategic role to generate urgent cash, via net price-cost reductions of purchased parts, in order to turn around the vicious circle that our Corporation could run, if our business is going down in U.S.A.," López added, as his pen outran his command of English. If GM started this immediately, López insisted, over the next three years it could generate an additional "cumulative figure of 5 BILLION DOLLARS . . ." (emphasis in original).

"You made it possible in Europe," López concluded. "You trusted us and now GM Europe is a recognized leader in the purchasing field." López signed with a flourish, and attached his suggested organizational chart.

Managers in a company as big as GM often don't get to see such radical ideas put into action. López might have been ignored, too, had GM's board of directors not made Jack Smith president and head of North American Operations on April 6, 1992. One of Smith's first moves was to give López the job he'd suggested, and an extraordinary mandate to smash the creaking bureaucracy that had changed little since the days of Alfred Sloan. Those who knew what the strange chemistry between Smith and López had produced in Europe fastened their seat belts.

SMITH AND LÓPEZ shared a deep conviction that GM could be great again if its leaders had the courage to change. Beyond that, they were as different as two people could be. Smith, an understated Irish-American from Worcester, Massachusetts, and López, a flamboyant, charismatic figure from Spain's Basque country, were the auto industry's Odd Couple.

Jack Smith's upbringing was solid middle-class American. His father ran Worcester's health department for some years, and the family also operated an ice cream business called Smithfield Famous Ice Cream. One of Smith's uncles became Worcester's mayor and later lieutenant governor. Born April 6, 1938, Jack Smith grew up in a time when Irish kids like him went to St. John's, French kids went to Assumption Prep, and the two groups battled for supremacy on the basketball courts.[1] Smith got a bachelor's degree in business administration from the University of Massachusetts, and then embarked on a career that would take him far from ice cream, Catholic school hoop rivalries, and Worcester politics. In 1960, he took a job in the accounting department at GM's big assembly factory in Framingham, Massachusetts.

Smith got his big break in 1966 when he was noticed by a fast-rising young GM finance executive who happened to share his last name, but no family tie: Roger B. Smith.

Roger Smith had interviewed Jack, then twenty-eight years old, for a job in GM's Treasurer's Office in New York. Roger concluded the hardworking young man from Massachusetts was just the type for the hotshot team he was building. But when Roger offered the transfer, Jack turned it down. New York, he informed his superiors, wasn't his kind of place. That made Roger want him all the more. "Knock that kid over the head and get him down here," he told Jack's boss. Soon, Jack was packing his bags.

Jack Smith began ascending the ladder in the finance staff, with Roger Smith as his guardian angel. Jack was Roger's can-do guy. One day, during the late 1960s, Roger Smith discovered that GM's director of research in Detroit had a computer that would allow the treasurer's office in New York to track the company's bond holdings. Roger was fascinated by the possibilities. GM had always kept records of its holdings by hand, and did little trading. He wanted to change that. So he had the terminal set up in a closet space in the New York office, and set Jack to work mastering the thing to step up trading in GM's bond portfolio. One day, GM's chairman, Frederic Donner, saw the Rube Goldberg system in the closet.

What's that guy doing? he asked. "That guy" was Jack Smith.

Over the years, Roger handed Jack many, far tougher tasks—selling GM's Frigidaire appliance business, hammering out the Nummi venture with Toyota, and saving GM Europe. But Jack Smith had never encountered anything like the mess he found in North America when he became GM's president in 1992. That Roger Smith, who had groomed him for so many years, bore so much of the blame added a final ironic twist.

Jack Smith realized fixing North America would require extraordinary action on a massive scale. He was the quintessential good cop; "everybody's big brother," one friend called him. He was a good listener, adept at drawing people out with firm but unthreatening questions. But saving GM would take another kind of person, too. Smith was accustomed to having someone close by who could play the tough enforcer once his gentle persuasion failed. Lou Hughes had played that role in Europe. In May 1992, it fell to López in North America.

López, who went by the disarming nickname Iñaki (ee-NYAA-kee), was Smith's secret weapon in the assault on the decadent GM system. López hailed from Amorebieta in the Basque province of northern Spain, where his father worked in a machining factory.[2] López would later recall his fascination as a ten-year-old boy watching the machinery. As a young engineer, López stayed close to his home, working in Spanish plants owned by Westinghouse and Firestone. Then, in 1980, he landed a job at GM's then-new assembly factory in Zaragoza in northern Spain.

At Zaragoza, López became a star. He launched a crusade to prove that Spaniards could surpass the productivity and quality of GM's German operations. He began developing a cost-cutting system built around relentless time-motion studies to eliminate unnecessary steps in the manufacturing process.[3] He zeroed in on suppliers, pushing them to cut prices and emulate his step-saving efficiency methods.

López's results got the attention of Jack Smith, then head of GM

Europe. In 1987, Smith persuaded López to leave Spain and try out his ideas at Opel, GM's main European car operation in the Frankfurt suburb of Rüsselsheim. López landed on Opel and its German parts suppliers like an incendiary bomb. Typical of his approach was his campaign to find a cheaper stabilizer bar for Opel cars. López told Opel's engineers about an English company that made a stabilizer bar 30 percent cheaper than Opel's incumbent German supplier. Opel's engineers grudgingly agreed to test López's substitute part, and were only too happy to report that the British component failed. López didn't give up. He insisted that Opel help the English metal-bender fix the part. The fix worked, and López got his 30 percent cost reduction.

Suppliers dubbed López the Rüsselsheim Strangler, López the Terrible, and the Inquisitor. But in the Basque region, López's business success made him a hero. There, people called him "Superlópez."

López was a hero to Jack Smith, as well. And López returned the admiration with interest. He got misty-eyed talking about "my leader, Yack Smith," whose picture he displayed on his office wall. When he arrived in Detroit, López defined his mission as helping Jack Smith save GM.

López came to Detroit itching to try on a grand scale the idiosyncratic theories he'd put together in Europe. López called his system PICOS, for Purchased Input Concept Optimization of Suppliers. PICOS was the center of a manufacturing cosmology, in which GM and its suppliers toiled like the pilgrim souls in Dante's *Purgatorio* up a great, terraced mountain toward the paradise of "customer satisfaction" and super-efficiency. López's mountain was divided into seven "plateaus," each representing a quantum-leap improvement in efficiency, achieved through teamwork, aggressive purchasing tactics, and his brand of lean production.

López began pushing GM's bureaucracy and its suppliers up the PICOS trail almost as soon as his plane landed in Detroit. He demanded complete control over GM's 2,000 North American buyers, and with Smith's support he steamrollered opposition to his power grab. By June 1, 1992, López was ready to reveal his revolutionary manifesto to GM's top 500 suppliers in a series of meetings that each lasted nearly four hours.

López began his stem-winders with his own history of Western industry, complete with slides of eighteenth century British weaving mills and old-style assembly lines. This culminated in slides showing the rise of Japan's auto industry, and López's declaration that GM and its suppliers now had to embrace immediately "the Third Industrial Revolution" in order to save Western Civilization. López's bigotry toward the Japanese was never far from the surface. "Not a single thing has been invented by the Japanese," he said on one occasion. "The Japanese, they copy." He had little patience for those who pointed out that PICOS owed a large debt to Toyota's lean production system.

The heart of López's message was far less esoteric, however. Bob Stempel's modest effort to cut GM's purchasing costs by 7 percent over three years was history, López declared. He would tear up GM's supplier contracts, and rebid them until he got price cuts of 10 percent or more. Stunned suppliers quickly learned López wasn't joking. One supplier was putting the finishing touches on a $20 million factory when López's troops yanked his contract.

López's purchasing agents, renamed "warriors," ran two, three, four, and sometimes six rounds of bidding in the quest for the lowest price on a part. López's warriors also besieged GM's own parts subsidiaries, forcing managers in those fiefdoms to scramble to defend contracts they'd once taken for granted.

Smith took an enormous risk by sanctioning this chaotic, instant revolution. But he saw no alternative. GM needed cash. And it needed a profound and immediate revolution in its corporate culture. Smith wasn't, by nature, a charismatic leader who could march people through walls. López was. Unlike many of the stunned holdovers from the Stempel era, López wasn't scared to push for radical reform. He was, in John Smale's phrase, a "change maker."

JACK SMITH, HOWEVER, wasn't the only one smitten by Lopez's charismatic energy, however. López had another powerful admirer: Ferdinand Piëch, the man anointed to do for Germany's largest car maker, Volkswagen, what Smith was doing for GM.

The grandson of Ferdinand Porsche, founder of the prestigious German sports-car maker of the same name, Piëch was a blue-blooded member of Europe's industrial nobility. Born in Austria, Piëch had followed in his grandfather's footsteps, training as an engineer and devoting himself to cars. By the mid-1980s, he was establishing a reputation as a tough cost cutter as head of VW's Audi luxury-car division. In March 1992, at fifty-four, Piëch emerged as the heir apparent to VW Chairman Carl Hahn, who led VW in a rapid expansion during the 1980s.

Hahn and Piëch were polar opposites. Hahn enjoyed the role of industrial statesman, and took pride in his commitments to invest billions of deutsche marks in redeveloping the auto industries of the former East Germany and Eastern Europe. Piëch was a pugnacious, impulsive man. He had twelve children by three women, including a distant cousin. His second wife had previously worked as his children's nanny.[4] Piëch's peppery personality made for heated moments in his professional relationships, as well. At an international conference of senior auto executives in Switzerland in early 1993, Piëch unleashed a tirade against Japanese trade policy. "How can you live with yourself?" Piëch snarled as he wagged his finger in the face of Shoichiro Toyoda, Toyota's dignified chief executive.

Piëch was taking over a company that, like GM, had sought salvation in automation and acquisitions, and failed. By 1992, VW's labor and fixed costs were so high that it had to run its German factories at full speed just to break even.[5] But with a recession, VW wouldn't sell enough cars to sustain profitable production rates.

The Japanese competition that had crippled GM had nearly routed VW out of the United States altogether. While the rest of the world went to smooth, aerodynamic styling, VW stayed with a boxy look. By 1992, VW, once the best-selling import brand in America, had less than 1 percent of the total U.S. market. VW was still No. 1 in Europe, but the European Community trade barriers that kept the Japanese at bay were crumbling as Japanese manufacturers opened plants in Britain and Spain. Other European producers, notably GM's Opel operations, were sprinting ahead of VW in quality, styling, and efficiency.

Europe wasn't the only battleground for VW and Opel. As the 1990s began, sluggish growth in Europe, North America, and Japan had launched a scramble among the world's car makers to exploit new markets in Latin America and Southeast Asia. Brazil, particularly, was a hot spot. There, GM was using new Opel models and López-style purchasing to undercut VW and Ford, which shared operations in the country.

Like Jack Smith, Piëch saw that his company was in crisis. Like Smith, Piëch wanted a fearless deputy to drive change, fast. And like Smith, Piëch concluded one man could make all the difference—Iñaki López.

In late 1992, Piëch began the chase. He arranged a secret meeting with López in late November at a hotel near the Frankfurt Airport. The two men hit it off. López, it turned out, had a complex personal agenda. Saving General Motors was only part of it.

Long before he arrived in Detroit, López had developed a grand vision. It was rooted in his Basque homeland, which had struggled for centuries to realize dreams of nationhood and economic independence. López wanted to combine patriotism and PICOS to strike a blow for Basque aspirations. His plan: build a car factory in his hometown of Amorebieta that would realize his ultraefficient manufacturing vision, which he called Plateau VI. Instead of twenty or thirty hours of assembly labor for each car, or even fifteen as at Toyota's high-tech Tahara plant, López envisioned his Amorebieta plant expending just ten hours of labor per car.

By the time Jack Smith brought him to North America, López seemed close to achieving his dream. He had marshaled a group of Basque business leaders and bankers who offered to form a joint venture with GM Europe to build and operate a plant according to López's methods. López's dream factory also had become linked to a top-secret new car Opel was developing, code-named the "O-car." This minicar was to be a super-low-cost model aimed at grabbing sales from Volkswagen in Eastern Europe, Latin America, and Asia.

López promoted the Amorebieta plant relentlessly, even contacting some GM directors to lobby for it. This began to annoy some of his colleagues, notably Lou Hughes. Hughes doubted that GM needed a new factory at a time when Europe was heading into an economic slump. GM had just started up the Eisenach plant, and keeping that on track would be challenge enough.

Hughes decided to clear the air. On January 8, 1993, he arrived at López's home in the Detroit suburb of West Bloomfield. Over dinner, Hughes got to the point. "Iñaki," he said. "We have a problem." GM simply couldn't risk money in Amorebieta at a time when GM was bleeding cash. How, Hughes asked, could GM gracefully postpone the Amorebieta deal?

López seemed to acquiesce. He offered to write a letter for Hughes's signature that would explain the situation and push the right buttons with the Basque officials. A week later, López delivered the letter telling the Basque consortium that the Amorebieta plant project would be "frozen" until economic conditions improved. Hughes considered the case closed.

But Hughes was wrong. On January 15, 1993, the day after he gave Hughes the letter shelving his dream factory, López went to Essen, not far from Opel's big factory in Bochum. There he met with Klaus Liesen, the head of VW's Supervisory Board, and Jens Neumann, a close aide to Ferdinand Piëch. Later that evening, he met Piëch himself. López had a message for the VW officials. He was open for offers to quit GM.[6]

IN THE WEEKS FOLLOWING López's secret meeting with Liesen and Neumann, rumors began to surface in the German business press that López was flirting with Volkswagen. López acknowledged to Smith, Hughes, and others that he had spoken to Piëch. But he insisted he would stay, particularly after he got a promotion to group vice president in early February 1993. On February 3, 1993, López arrived in Rüsselsheim for two days of meetings, including an update on the O-car. The meetings proceeded without incident, except that some GM staffers found it odd that López kept asking for copies of the presentation materials.

Then during the afternoon of Thursday, February 4, López left Opel headquarters. His destination was another rendezvous with Neumann. Piëch's emissary didn't mince words. He wanted to negotiate a contract under which López would join VW as its cost-cutter in chief. López didn't give a firm answer. But he assured Neumann that he didn't have a contract with GM. He could give notice to quit GM "from one day to another," López said. Neumann got the hint. In the following days, he spoke to López several times by phone, and began assembling an offer.

GM EXECUTIVES STILL discounted the rumors that López might leave. After some prodding from colleagues, López issued a public statement that he was "happy here at GM" and was "not leaving."

But others weren't so sure. In early March, Hughes flew from GM Europe headquarters in Zurich to Rüsselsheim for a meeting with two senior Opel executives: David Herman, the New York-born lawyer who'd replaced him as head of Opel, and Eddie Geysen, López's successor as Opel's purchasing boss. The conversation turned to the López rumors, and Geysen made a startling declaration.

"I think he'll go," Geysen said. "He's cleaned out his office."

ON MARCH 8, López showed up at Opel's proving ground near Rüsselsheim for a series of top-secret meetings on GM's international product strategy for the coming decade. The only hint of trouble came when López attended a presentation on future manufacturing plans that touched on the Amorebieta plant. Staffers who presented the plan suggested that Hungary would be a better site than Amorebieta for the facility. Hungary fit in with Hughes's strategy of building cars aimed at consumers in Eastern Europe. Locating in depressed Hungary also would qualify GM for European Community subsidies that might be denied for Amorebieta. López exploded. Hughes sought López out later and assured him his dream was still alive. "For Christ's sake, Iñaki," Hughes said. "It's just a feasibility study."

López appeared to settle down, and plunged back into the meetings, busily taking notes. At one point, López asked a GM planner named John Howell to give him a copy of a thick, 150-page summary of Opel's future product programs. Four other executives asked for copies, too. Howell tried to copy the thick folder during a break, but the copying machine broke down. It wasn't until after lunch that López and the others got their copies.[7]

LÓPEZ HAD LITTLE time to spare. At 7 P.M., March 9, shortly after the GM Europe meetings concluded, he had scheduled another meeting with Jens Neumann, this time at the Frankfurt airport.[8] Piëch's emissary brought with him a copy of a contract already signed on March 5— three days before the GM Europe strategy meetings began—by VW Supervisory Board Chairman Liesen. López would have at VW the power to realize the grand dream that had foundered at GM. He would have full power over both production and purchasing. López was also confident that Piëch would support his Amorebieta plant.

All that remained were details. López wanted assurances that schooling would be provided for his youngest daughter. He wanted VW to extend immediately an insurance policy that would cover him in case of his death. He wavered on when to announce his move. Neumann pressed him to make the switch immediately, so that it could be ratified at VW's scheduled March 16 supervisory board meeting. At 9:57 P.M., López signed the papers. Neumann called Piëch. López took the phone and assured the VW chairman that he was happy to be part of the Volkswagen family. López was now VW's man.

. . .

THE MORNING AFTER he signed the VW contract, López attended a personnel meeting at Opel and ordered his assistant to send a folder of material to Spain. At 1:40 P.M., he boarded the plane for the eight-hour flight back to Detroit.

López's decision to stick to his routine masked the reality that events were spinning out of control. López arrived back in his Warren, Michigan, office late in the afternoon. His staff was preparing a speech he was scheduled to deliver the next morning to GM's top 100 North American executives. But López curtly demanded that a video crew come to tape his talk that evening. Then around 6:15 P.M., López disappeared into Jack Smith's office. There, he handed Smith a letter of resignation.

Just hours before, Lou Hughes, tipped by a friend of López's, had called to warn Smith that his dynamic deputy might bolt. Still, López's letter was a shock. Smith pleaded with López to take his letter back, and allow Smith time to talk to Hughes and the three other members of GM's President's Council. The two men agreed to meet again early the next morning.

Smith worked late that night and before dawn the next day, March 11. When López arrived at 7:30 A.M., Smith hit him with a stunning offer. Stay, Smith said, and you'll be an executive vice president, a member of the President's Council, and president of North American Operations. In effect, Smith was offering to make López the second most important executive at GM. López asked to think about it until noon. At the appointed hour, Smith and López met again in a room at GM's North American headquarters. López said he'd made up his mind to go.

Smith accepted the letter of resignation, and López returned to his office and summoned about twenty members of his inner circle. As his shocked warriors wept, López confirmed that he really was quitting to join Volkswagen. GM, he said, had humiliated him by rejecting his "dream" factory in Amorebieta. He couldn't go on.

At around 1 P.M., López left his office for his West Bloomfield home. His meteoric career at GM was over.

Except that it wasn't, not yet. As evening fell, members of López's staff trooped to Smith's home, begging him to talk to López again. Smith was reluctant to reopen the matter. But his phone was ringing every few minutes with calls from other executives pleading with him to stop López's departure.

So began a soap opera more fitting for Hollywood than Detroit. The next morning, Friday, March 12, three of GM's five top executives—Jack Smith, Rick Wagoner, and Harry Pearce—dropped their plans for the day and headed for López's house. The mountains had come to Mohammed. A marathon soul-searching began. Smith pulled out the stops. He renewed his offer to let López lead North American operations, and insisted that López's dream plant would be built. Still, López was torn. He wanted to stay, he said, but he couldn't break his contract with Volkswagen. He asked to talk with his family, and Smith and the others left. As the day dragged by without a decision, Smith called López twice. The two men finally agreed to talk the next morning.

Hughes, separated by the Atlantic Ocean from the emotional riptides in López's living room, was appalled by what he heard from Detroit. It galled Hughes that Smith, GM's chief executive, had gone like a supplicant to López's house. But Hughes had to go along. He called López and assured him bygones were bygones. "When we get a concept for the car," Hughes said, "and when it's approved, we will build this car in Spain."

An emotional López told Hughes he had decided to stay. Hughes rang off satisfied he'd helped clinch the deal.

Saturday morning, March 13, López went to Smith's house. My head tells me to go to Volkswagen, López said. But my heart tells me to stay. And stay he would, López declared. But soap operas never end so neatly.

LÓPEZ HAD AGONIZED over his flip-flop, not just in his conversations with Smith, but in a flurry of transatlantic phone calls with Piëch's aide, Jens Neumann, and with Piëch himself. At 5:30 A.M. on Friday, March 12, before Smith arrived for his visit, López called Neumann to say that if he went to VW, Smith would be fired by John Smale. López insisted, though, that he still planned to come to Germany. At 5 A.M. the next day, Saturday, López called Neumann again to report that Smith and his wife had pleaded with him to stay, but that he wouldn't leave VW in the lurch. "The word of a Basque cannot be broken," López insisted.

Five hours later, around 10 A.M., Detroit time, Neumann called Piëch, who ordered his aide to keep in close touch with the wavering recruit. A half hour later, at around 10:30 A.M. Detroit time, Neumann called López back. López began pouring out a tale of woe. Smith and GM's board were begging him to stay, López declared, because otherwise GM "would go bankrupt and 400,000 families worldwide would go unemployed." López begged for Piëch's forgiveness, but he had decided to stay. He told Neumann: "I am a broken man."

Half an hour later, Piëch called López and offered a compromise. López could go back to GM any time he wanted to, but he should come to VW now. López agreed. But two hours later, López asked for a different deal. Now he wanted to stay at GM for one year, and then consider moving to VW.

López tried this idea on Pearce, and remarkably, GM's top lawyer didn't flinch. "There's no involuntary servitude," Pearce replied. "Judge it by your experience." Late Saturday, Smith met again with López and went to bed confident he had won the battle.

At 10:15 A.M. Sunday, (Detroit time/16:15 German), López called Neumann. He would spend one year straightening out GM, and then consider his options. López added that he hadn't slept in four days.

GM executives, meanwhile, were gleefully passing word of their coup to the press. López, brimming with emotion, bear-hugged colleagues who came to congratulate him. Then he and an aide put the finishing touches on a heart-tugging speech López would give the next day.

"I know what your first question will be—why did I change my mind?" began a draft, edited in López's hand. In the text that followed, López related the events of the previous days, and even thanked Piëch for agreeing to "release" him from his commitment to VW. The ending pulled out the stops: "I am very happy to be here, today at General Motors—the company I love, the people I love. My mission now is to channel this intensity, the sentiment of our people, into satisfying our customer. If we can do this, I am sure we will achieve our vision of having exciting products and enthusiastic customers, created by people working together to win."

LÓPEZ ARRIVED AT his office shortly after 7 A.M. on Monday, March 15. He rehearsed answers to likely questions from the press, such as "What makes you think you can run GM North America?" López smiled. "I will consult my mother and ask what she would do."

It was a remarkable show for a man who'd been up at 4 A.M. to make an edgy phone call to Neumann at VW. GM wants me to sign a five-year contract, López told Piëch's deputy. I will refuse, he said. And if they insist, I will fly to Germany tonight.[9]

López betrayed none of these misgivings to his delighted colleagues at

GM's North American headquarters. At about 10:30 A.M., Pearce called. He didn't mention a five-year employment contract, because there wasn't one. GM didn't have employment contracts with any senior executives, even Jack Smith. Pearce simply told López that GM's directors, in an emergency meeting via telephone conference call, had ratified his appointment as head of North American Operations.

"Congratulations on your new job!" Pearce said. "We're off and running."

Shortly after Pearce rang off, at 10:45 A.M., an agitated López reached Neumann at Volkswagen. GM had demanded that he sign a five-year contract, López told Neumann, but I refused. "My heart and mind are in Germany," he said, adding he had "a clear vision for Europe."[10]

At around 11 A.M., Piëch personally called López, urging him to fly to Germany that day. López agreed. A few minutes later, he slipped out of his office and headed for home.

HARRY PEARCE ARRIVED at GM headquarters a few minutes before 1 P.M. and quickly realized something was amiss. López hadn't shown up as scheduled. Instead, Pearce was confronted by one of López's Spanish confidants. The man had a note and was clearly distraught.

"This can only be read by Jack Smith," the man insisted.

"That's going to be a problem," Pearce snapped. "Jack Smith is on a plane coming back from Lansing. Give me the note." The man handed it over. Pearce retreated into Jack Smith's office and opened the letter. The words, scribbled in López's hand, rambled. But Pearce got the message instantly. He raised Smith on the phone.

"We've got a little problem, Jack," Pearce said. "Iñaki's gone."

Smith arrived at GM headquarters only a few minutes before the press conference was supposed to start. It was a nightmarish, humiliating moment. That very morning, Smith had assured his board that López could be trusted with the most critical job in the company next to his own. He had brushed aside those who argued that López was erratic and untrustworthy. Now, López had made Smith look gullible, naive, and downright foolish. Still, Smith chose to confront the disaster head-on. At about 3 P.M., Smith walked into GM's packed pressroom.

"Today, I had intended to announce that Iñaki López was staying with General Motors and would be given added responsibilities," Smith said. "Unfortunately, a short time ago, Dr. López sent me a letter saying he was not going to accept the position and is leaving General Motors. It's not clear to me what his intentions are, or where he is at this time."

At first, some of the reporters thought it was a joke. But Smith's ashen face plainly said this was for real.

Smith didn't know López's whereabouts, but VW did. At about 2:45 P.M., López called Neumann to inform him that he would arrive in Frankfurt at 8:20 A.M. the next day on American Airlines flight 084. Elated, Neumann passed a note to Piëch, who was meeting with VW's ruling presidium. "He is coming," Neumann wrote.[11]

AT 10 A.M., German time, on Tuesday, March 16, a Volkswagen plane bearing a weary Iñaki López landed at the Braunschweig airport near Volkswagen's Wolfsburg headquarters. The supervisory board soon was congratulating him on his appointment as VW's head of purchasing and production. That same day, two of López's former GM colleagues walked into his old office at North American headquarters. It was empty. None of the information he had amassed in his final weeks at GM could be found.

THE DAY LÓPEZ left Detroit, Harry Pearce brushed off the notion that GM would take legal action against him. "We're not in the litigation business," Pearce, a seasoned litigator, deadpanned. "We're in the car and truck business." But Pearce soon had second thoughts.

GM investigators discovered evidence that López and seven of his warriors who followed him to VW had received massive amounts of secret GM information in the weeks before they defected. GM records indicated López himself had received thousands of pages of data about GM's future products, its purchasing strategies, and the prices it paid for parts and production machinery. In the weeks after his first meeting with Piëch in November 1992, López, according to GM's records, obtained three copies of a supersecret list of costs for Opel and GM Europe vehicle parts. This 10,000-page document, a computer printout with several columns of figures on each page, was known as the European Purchasing Optimization System, or EPOS, list. It would be worth millions to a competitor trying to match GM Europe's purchasing costs. GM functionaries also logged requests from a top López aide, José Manuel Gutierrez, for information about a future diesel engine that GM Europe planned to introduce in the mid-1990s. In meetings from February 23 to 26, Gutierrez received reams of "benchmarking" data that compared GM's costs to rivals.

López, GM's gumshoes learned, had instructed an assistant to put papers from his Rüsselsheim office into cartons and ship them to his brother-in-law in Amorebieta. A GM driver recalled helping Gutierrez with a large, hard-shell suitcase so heavy that he could barely pick it up.

Information about GM Europe's future products and purchasing costs would be a road map to guide VW in attacking Opel and GM's Latin American operations. VW might take years to discover on its own that suppliers charged Opel less than they charged VW for robots or mufflers or brakes. But with GM's cost lists in hand, VW buyers could flush out such disparities within a few months. Viewed in the worst light, GM could suffer billions of dollars in lost sales and wasted product development.

The question was, Did López really take GM's most precious secrets to VW?

On March 22, 1993, a week after López's defection, Pearce decided to pursue the matter directly. He sent López a three-page letter, under the heading "PRIVILEGED AND CONFIDENTIAL."

"Dear Iñaki," Pearce began. "As you know, over the past couple of years, in recognition of the enormous competition that exists in the motor vehicle industry, General Motors has increased substantially its efforts to protect proprietary information. Your recent decision to leave General Motors and join Volkswagen's management team, one of our major European competitors, raises a concern on our part about the security of proprietary GM information. . . ."

Pearce summarized GM's corporate policies forbidding disclosure of confidential company information. He cited a *Business Week* article about the legal risks of using stolen secrets. Then, Pearce came to the point. He requested that López sign a statement that he hadn't taken any data or documents from GM. He further asked López to list and return any documents he had taken, along with all copies, "immediately."

The following day, March 23, Pearce sent a similar letter to Piëch. That letter added: "Thus far, we have not received the assurances we are seeking from each of our former employees. This of course heightens our concerns."

Nine days later, on April 2, 1993, López and Piëch responded.

"Dear Mr. Pearce," López wrote. "In response to your letter dated March 22, 1993, which I received by fax . . . in the afternoon of April 1, 1993, I herewith confirm that I have complied and will comply with my secrecy obligations with respect to proprietary GM information and documents not in the public domain."

Piëch's response came from Peter Frerk, Volkswagen's chief legal counsel. "In response to your March 23, 1993, letter to Dr. Piëch," Frerk wrote, "I would like to inform you that Volkswagen also has a longstanding policy with regard to proprietary information in line with generally accepted legal principles. Accordingly, we have not requested, and will not do so in the future, any employee joining us to reveal proprietary information of his prior employer."

Pearce considered both letters evasions, particularly López's exception for GM documents "in the public domain." As far as Pearce was concerned, there were no such things. On April 8, Pearce faxed another letter to Piëch, demanding the return of any GM documents. He sent a letter to López, bluntly declaring that his April 2 statement "does not provide the assurances we require . . ."

On April 15, López replied: "I did not take at the time of my resignation from GM nor do I possess today GM materials."

Pearce regarded that carefully crafted response as still another evasion. On April 21, Pearce's deputy, Michael Millikin, returned fire. "Data I have received from sources in GM and sources outside GM indicate you may have taken certain GM documents at or around the time of your departure for Volkswagen," Millikin wrote to López. He proposed that López meet with GM officials in Germany to discuss the matter.

On April 30, the skirmishing-by-fax reached its climax. "I reject the allegations I infer from Mr. Millikin's letter," López fumed to Pearce. "I will not even respond to such charges and stand by my previous statement. I consider the matter closed."

GM did not. The day López's letter arrived, GM lawyers marched off to the state prosecutor's office in Darmstadt, Germany, and filed a complaint accusing López and his associates of stealing GM trade secrets.

The largest car companies in America and Europe were now at war.

GM DIDN'T PUBLICIZE its sensational move immediately, and for good reason. GM had lots of circumstantial evidence, including tips that information taken from GM was entered into VW computers by a squad of interns working around the clock. GM investigators had even found documents indicating López reactivated two dormant Swiss bank accounts shortly before his departure. But none of this proved anything. Holding Swiss bank accounts was no crime. Lou Hughes, a wealthy resident of Zurich, had a Swiss bank account. Hughes was taking an enormous risk. But he was obsessed with bringing López down. "This is evil," he'd fume.

On May 21, GM executives gathered in Oklahoma City for the annual meeting with shareholders. It was the first time GM's shareholders had a chance to see and hear the new management installed six months earlier. During a press conference after the meeting, someone asked if GM was taking legal action against López. Hughes stood up.

"We have issued a criminal action against López and other individuals for taking confidential data," he said. The reporters turned to Jack Smith. Glumly, Smith pronounced judgment on his old friend: "It's a tragedy."

On Monday, May 24, the German magazine *Der Spiegel* laid out GM's case in riveting fashion. The cover story, titled "Der Skrupellose" or "The Unscrupulous One," read like the outline of a spy novel. The piece portrayed López as a calculating traitor.

López, however, seemed unfazed. In a lengthy June 14 press conference at VW headquarters that marked his public debut as the company's No. 2 man, López declared flat-out that GM's charges were baseless. "We have not taken anything," he said, displaying copies of two of the letters he'd sent to Pearce. "We don't have anything."

Four days after this command performance in Wolfsburg, López materialized in GM's backyard to attend the graduation of one of his daughters from the General Motors Institute in Flint, Michigan. Beaming with pride, López circulated at an outdoor reception for the graduates' families, chatting with well-wishers. When a reporter found him and asked about GM's accusations, López portrayed the controversy as merely a regrettable misunderstanding.

The problem, he said, was that "some people in GM . . . have gone too far."

Even some members of GM's board thought this might be true. Then, the case broke open.

. . .

IN THE DAYS after the *Spiegel* story, one of Opel's purchasing agents, who happened to be a Swede, approached Eddie Geysen, the Opel purchasing chief, with a bizarre story.

It was the story of Tomas Andersson, the young Swede who shared a house in Wiesbaden with Jorge Alvarez and Rosario Piazza. Alvarez and Piazza were two of López's "warriors" who'd defected with him to VW and who had spent the days after Easter conducting a shredding extravaganza in the house.

Andersson slowly became suspicious that he'd witnessed some kind of foul play. Finally, he mentioned the incident to a Swedish friend at Opel.

On May 25, during a meeting of senior GM Europe managers in Frankfurt, Geysen tracked down Hughes and told him what he'd learned. By June 3, a lawyer for GM had found Andersson and taken a deposition about the shredding party.

To Hughes and his aides, Andersson was a godsend. Here, at last, was a witness who could unlock the mystery of what happened to GM's missing papers. Andersson's detailed descriptions of the papers his housemates had shredded—computer printouts with columns of numbers—matched the description of the missing EPOS list.

On June 21, the case took another weird twist. Andersson returned home to find four cartons containing papers, plastic transparencies, and other materials in his room. Fearing he could be implicated in a crime and deported, Andersson the next day went to the Swedish consulate in Frankfurt. An official there called the Wiesbaden police. About 5 P.M., officers arrived and hauled away the cartons.

GM and the German authorities smelled blood. They persuaded Andersson to arrange a meeting on June 30 with Alvarez at the Frankfurt Airport. Andersson would wear a microphone and try to persuade Alvarez to retrieve the boxes, at which point he could be caught with the evidence in his hands. The airport sting fizzled when the listening device failed, and Alvarez didn't fall for the trap. Still, the boxes contained damaging evidence. When GM experts inspected the contents, in the presence of German authorities, they saw materials on the O-car and on the Amorebieta plant.

They also found a letter to López from Alvarez, dated before López's departure. In the note, Alvarez explained that he couldn't get a picture of the O-car as López had requested. It was a stunning find. Within days of the discovery, an official of the U.S. Justice Department contacted

GM's lawyers in Detroit. Justice, the official said, was getting into the case. Industrial espionage by foreign companies was a hot issue with the new Clinton administration, and the López affair had become too big to ignore. A few weeks later, a federal grand jury began hearing evidence in Detroit.

As PIËCH SCRAMBLED to contain the scandal that threatened to engulf his prized cost-cutter, he returned again and again to the argument that López was innocent until proven guilty. This, of course, was true. Lou Hughes tried to undermine Piëch's strategy by appealing directly to certain VW board members whom he knew. But he got nowhere. Nothing had been proved. No charges had been filed. Moreover, labor and the government of the German state of Lower Saxony, which owned a 20 percent stake in VW, were on the side of Piëch and López. López also appeared to be making great progress. VW, Piëch maintained, would break even for 1993 despite the worst slump in European auto sales since World War II.

ON AUGUST 6, VW's supervisory board held an emergency meeting on the López situation. Board members reviewed a report from VW's internal investigators, and late in the day, issued a remarkable statement, under the heading: "Unchanged Trust for Dr. López."

"No potentially secret documents belonging to the former GM/Opel employees got into the possession of Volkswagen AG," the statement said. "Both in Wiesbaden and in VW's guesthouse, Rothehof, those former GM employees ensured that documents which potentially could have been ascribed to GM and contained potentially sensitive information were destroyed in order to ensure that they were not distributed at Volkswagen."

After insisting for months that neither López nor the aides who had followed him had taken any GM documents, VW was abruptly reversing itself. The statement gave the lie to what López and Piëch had told both GM and the public. VW now took refuge in the argument of a child who pilfers a candy bar, but then professes innocence when caught because he threw it away uneaten.

. . .

AGAIN, VW DECLARED the case closed. But the machinery of the law didn't stop. In the early morning of August 26, a convoy of police vehicles rolled across the drab landscape of Lower Saxony toward VW's headquarters complex in Wolfsburg. At 9:30 A.M., the cars closed in on VW's central headquarters office and six other locations, including the Rothehof guesthouse and López's home. For the next eight and a half hours, some forty police officers combed through the buildings. They carted out reams of papers, dozens of computer data storage disks, and some twenty to thirty computers.[12] It would take months for the prosecutor's shorthanded staff to sift through the 2.5 million pages worth of data to find any matches between numbers on VW's price lists and numbers on the lists taken from Opel.

The German prosecutors, however, weren't the only investigators poking through VW's offices. As part of his effort to dispel suspicions about López's behavior, Piëch had earlier called in auditors from the German branch of the accounting firm KPMG Peat Marwick to conduct a probe of López's activities.

On November 26, 1993, the auditors delivered their findings to VW's supervisory board. In carefully hedged language, KPMG answered only the precise questions VW had asked. Was there any evidence VW had profited from secret GM information taken by López? KPMG said no. With a carefully edited nineteen-page summary of the report in hand, Liesen declared to reporters that evening that the KPMG findings exonerated the company.

In reality, the full KPMG report contained more startling disclosures. The events in Wiesbaden, it turned out, were just part of a paper-shredding orgy that López and his associates had undertaken in the days right after Harry Pearce sent his March 22 letter demanding the return of any GM papers. KPMG discovered that López and his associates had set up in Wolfsburg a busy document-sorting and -copying enterprise centered around some twenty cartons of papers that VW had flown from Spain to Wolfsburg on March 17, one day after López's arrival. López's team had commandeered space in VW's Rothehof guesthouse and a nearby office complex to sort the material. One of López's assistants oversaw the photocopying of some 10,000 pages. Others organized a group of eight VW employees and three trainees to transcribe into computers information from more than 1,800 slides, some having to do with the Basque factory plan and others related to PICOS. Some of the originals still bore the Opel logo.

The shredding began on March 23, the day after Pearce sent his letter, in three different places: At the Rothehof, in an apartment near VW's factory in Kassel, Germany, and at the Wiesbaden house, members of López's team spent hours shredding most, but not all, of what was inside the cartons. KPMG conceded there were some 5,000 pages of documents it couldn't trace. KPMG verified that at least three of the boxes found in Wiesbaden matched those used at the Rothehof. But the auditors reported that López's associates insisted those boxes were taken to Wiesbaden empty.

KPMG reconstructed previously deleted files in VW computers, and discovered information from 1,820 slides used in internal Opel presentations on purchasing strategy and on the Amorebieta plant proposal. López and his associates assured the KPMG investigators that none of the data was "secret," because it had been presented in public before.

KPMG, in short, had verified that much of GM's story was true. So it was that on Christmas 1993, four years after his fateful memo to Jack Smith, López was a hunted man. López had once said he took nothing from GM except what was in his head. That was false. Now, López was under criminal investigation by two German prosecutors and the U.S. Justice Department.

López pushed ahead with his work, professing to ignore the prosecutors. But by April 1994, the pressure on López was intensifying. GM even accused his second-oldest daughter, Begoña, of taking a cost-cutting plan for a new Chevrolet model from GM's Warren, Michigan, technical center when she left for Germany with her family. VW and López called GM's accusation absurd. But German investigators reported finding a computer disk with the data, which she accumulated during an internship, in her room.

There was a final twist. The revolutionary factory that López had hoped to build in Amorebieta—the dream for which he had abandoned his soaring GM career—was as far from realization as ever. Battered by financial losses, VW shelved the project shortly after López's arrival in Wolfsburg.

Ferdinand Piëch had his own troubles. He had staked his prestige and his job on the propositions that López was blameless and that he and López would lead VW to a break-even performance in 1993. In the fall, however, VW's Spanish subsidiary, Seat, had blindsided Piëch by disclosing it needed nearly $1 billion from the parent company to cover massive losses.[13] Audi and operations in North America and Asia were bleeding, too. Piëch conceded to his board that VW would lose more than $1 billion in 1993. By February 1994, Piëch had fired the heads of Seat and Audi, blaming them for the shortfalls. Volkswagen workers spent one day a week idle, for lack of sales.

López, it turned out, wasn't a miracle worker after all. Survival—at GM and Volkswagen—couldn't depend on just one person. Jack Smith had relearned that old lesson the hard way. He'd made a mistake that shook confidence among investors, employees, and others rooting for a GM turnaround. Fortunately for Smith, while VW writhed in the tangled web López and Piëch had spun, GM was showing signs that a turnaround could happen without a man on horseback.

CHAPTER 18

THE NEW GM

A sound man is good at salvage,
At seeing that nothing is lost.

—*The Way of Life*
According to Lao-tzu

JACK SMITH AND THE YOUNG reformers who clustered around him at GM had an unofficial motto: "Do the unexpected." This really was more a plea than a creed. With 750,000 employees worldwide, including 400,000 in the United States alone, spontaneity wasn't the General Motors way. Rather, GM had become a place for managers ready to devote their lives to learning the intricacies of the world's largest corporate bureaucracy, to mastering the arcane corporate patois (where "I'm doing my best under GM's crazy rules" became "I'm shooting for my BUGM target"), and to carefully dressing up failure so it would pass for success.

Jack Smith was an unlikely figure to tackle changing the GM mindset. Unlike Lee Iacocca, Smith wasn't much for ascending the bully pulpit or making the grand gesture. It seemed absurd even to imagine Smith appearing in commercials to rally Americans around the "New GM," as Iacocca had done in the early eighties to tout the "New Chrysler Corporation." Television lights made Smith curl into a slouch, his hands jammed in his pockets. He delivered most of his public addresses as if he were reading a dictionary.

Smith, nonetheless, had a daring streak. A few days after he'd taken over as GM's chief executive in November 1992, Smith publicly staked himself and his sick company to a single goal: breaking even in North American operations in 1993, before interest, taxes, and certain other charges. This seemed an unambitious target at first. After all, what household wouldn't come out ahead if it didn't pay taxes or interest on its mortgage?

But Smith was talking about reversing $4.5 billion of red ink in just one year. In terms of sheer dollars, such a turnaround would dwarf any previous corporate comeback. And as Smith himself made clear in surprisingly blunt terms, nothing less than GM's survival was at stake. "If we don't get efficient," he'd say, "we won't be around."

On October 19, 1992, Smith made a less publicized, but equally bold, move. Even as GM's board was preparing to oust Bob Stempel, Smith arranged to meet with the outgoing president of Toyota Motor, Shoichiro Toyoda, at GM headquarters in Detroit. A decade earlier, Smith had worked with Shoichiro Toyoda and his brother, Tatsuro, on the deal that had reincarnated GM's old Fremont, California, assembly plant as New United Motor Manufacturing Inc. Nummi had opened the door to other alliances between the two auto giants, and forged a personal bond between Smith and the Toyodas. Now, Smith and Toyoda wanted to deepen the ties some more. The October meeting led to another, in early December in Washington. This time, Toyota was represented by Tatsuro Toyoda, who was moving in as chief executive.

Soon afterward, Smith made a surprise call to Tom Davis, the vice president in charge of GM's effort to develop a competitive replacement for its bread-and-butter small car, the twelve-year-old Chevrolet Cavalier. Davis could hardly believe his ears as Smith outlined the idea he and the Toyodas had discussed. Toyota, Smith explained, would consider selling a U.S.-made GM car in Japan, if GM could supply a competitively priced, high-quality, small car with the steering wheel on the right, where Japanese drivers expected them to be. The kicker was that Toyota would sell as many as 20,000 of these cars a year—under its own name.

It was an audacious scheme. Toyota had spent the past fifteen years cleaning up in the United States because GM's cars—and particularly the Cavalier—were so bad. GM had sold just 8,300 American-made cars in Japan in 1992. Chevys and Cadillacs hovered in the Japanese consciousness somewhere between punk fashion statement and bad joke. But Smith wasn't kidding. Could you evaluate this? he asked Davis. Could you do it?

• • •

ONE OF THE UNUSUAL features of Jack Smith's office was a small, granite tablet upon which was affixed a brass placque engraved with an epigram from the Chinese mystic Lao-tzu.

> A leader is best
> When people barely know he exists.
> Not so good when people obey and acclaim him.
> Worse when they despise him.
> But of a good leader who talks little when his work is done, his aim fulfilled, they will say "We did it ourselves."[1]

The plaque was a gift from Smith's wife. The passage was one Lou Hughes had once sent to Smith as a tribute. The image of the leader who works in the background while others take credit was the epitome of Smith's style, Hughes would say. Smith would name a collection of Lao-tzu's wisdom as one of his favorite books, and even quote passages in speeches. Smith's interest in Lao-tzu pointed to a broader eclecticism that characterized his management style. For decades, GM's leaders had mostly looked inside their executive suite for ideas. Smith, however, seemed to borrow ideas from everywhere.

Confronted with the chaos in GM's financial system, Smith reached back for some of the rigorous discipline of the Sloan years, a time when GM could publish yearbooks showing the return on investment for each division next to a picture of the division manager. Smith directed his finance staff to junk the phony numbers GM managers had used in the past, and rebuild GM's books so that managers would know how much profit they'd returned on the assets invested in their operations, and how much each individual line of cars earned or lost. In monthly management meetings, Smith had his finance staff present simple cash flow statements—what the company took in and what it spent.

At the same time, Smith bemoaned the intramural turf fighting, divisional rivalries, and overlapping committees that were the legacy of the Sloan years. So he borrowed a remedy from GM Europe: Replace the committee system with a single strategy board made up of the top executives from each major functional group—car and truck engineering, manufacturing, finance, sales, and parts operations. With Smith as moderator, the functional barons met as often as four times a week. The meetings sometimes became virtual free-for-alls, but Smith encouraged the arguments. In another break from tradition, he saw to it that lower-level executives who'd be responsible for carrying out decisions were on hand to protest when the big shots assigned impossible tasks. Slowly the division chiefs overcame their distrust of each other, and began hashing out answers to long-avoided problems.

As Smith banged his turnaround program together, he sometimes seemed at odds with himself. He held up as models Saturn's drive for "customer enthusiasm," and the friendly, no-hassle sales approach Saturn used. But he delayed a decision on building a second factory for Saturn while he put heat on Saturn's managers to turn a profit.

But one message Smith broadcast consistently was that GM had to adapt the lessons of Nummi as quickly as possible.

Smith's embrace of the Nummi-Toyota system was evident to anyone who walked into his North American Operations headquarters, hidden behind a steam plant at GM's Technical Center campus in suburban Warren, Michigan. The offices were open from wall to wall, as they were at Nummi's front office. Many staff members strolled around in casual dress. Their offices were cubicles separated by waist-high partitions. Overhead signs informed visitors where finance or accounts payable could be found—"visual controls," in the Nummi style. Smith had a private office, but he spent most of his time in meetings with his strategy board or visiting plants to lead quality improvement meetings. For long-time GM operatives, it was all as joltingly foreign as their first sight of Tokyo.

Smith wanted GM to transform all its operations in the image of Nummi and Toyota. He set a goal that every factory in GM would convert itself to a Nummi-style operation by 1996. And he insisted that all GM cars should be so good that Toyota could sell them in Japan without anyone knowing the difference.

ANY BOOKMAKER PLACING odds on which GM factory would build cars for Toyota would likely have written off GM's big Lordstown, Ohio, complex as a 100–1 shot.

Once before GM had tried to make Lordstown a paradise of productivity. Annoyed by the popularity of the Volkswagen Beetle, GM's brass decided in the late 1960s that it was time for the General to remind the pipsqueaks who was boss. Using new automated factory machinery—

forerunners of the robots that would mesmerize GM a decade later—GM could speed dramatically its pace of production, thus cutting the labor cost for each car. Lordstown, built in 1966 and staffed with one of the youngest workforces in the company, became the launching pad for this great leap forward in 1970.

It was a debacle. The car, the Chevrolet Vega, was a quality disaster. Lordstown became a manufacturing hell. The plant's young workers represented the huge mass of Baby Boomers who didn't spend the late 1960s and early 1970s wearing flowers in their hair. Many were Vietnam veterans. Some were college graduates who settled for a factory job because it paid well. Most were natives of the area, which lay in the heart of the steel belt in eastern Ohio and Western Pennsylvania. They'd grown up steeped in the pugnacious traditions of the great steel and auto unions. That old fighting spirit and the rebellious attitude of the times created an explosive mixture. GM supplied a match in the form of managers from Detroit determined to crank up the Vega line from the normal speed of sixty to sixty-five cars per hour to a frantic pace of 100 cars an hour.

The Vega, however, wasn't designed for such rapid assembly. As the Lordstown line accelerated, each worker had just thirty-six seconds to attach his piece of the car. Even the *Wall Street Journal*, in a rare prolabor editorial, conceded that the "soul must panic" when confronted with the prospect of thirty years of working at such a pace.[2]

The more Lordstown workers complained, the less the GM managers seemed to listen. Instead, management accused union members of sabotaging cars. Union leaders retorted that GM had made working conditions intolerable by laying off 700 workers and demanding that the remaining 7,700 pick up the slack.[3] In March 1972, the workers rebelled. They stomped off the job for three weeks, crippling the Vega's launch and costing GM millions. Even after the workers returned, the feuding continued. Grievances piled up by the thousands. The disaffection of Lordstown's workforce briefly focused national attention on the "blue collar blues" felt by Baby Boomers stuck in the industrial grind.

When the spotlight turned away, Lordstown staggered on. GM dropped the 100-cars-per-hour plan, partly because the machinery couldn't take it any better than the people. As the 1980s began, Lordstown retooled to build a new line of small cars known inside GM as J-cars. Once again, GM set out to prove it could compete with the imports. Except this time the imports weren't gawky Volkswagen Beetles.

They were smart little cars from Japan loaded with nifty features and powered by engines and transmissions that never seemed to break. Once again, GM missed the mark. The J-cars—sold as the Chevrolet Cavalier, Pontiac J-2000 (later Sunbird), Oldsmobile Firenza, Buick Skyhawk, and Cadillac Cimarron—were underpowered, overweight, and overpriced. GM scrambled to fix the power and price problems, and eventually the J-car sales picked up in the Reagan recovery. The quality of the J-cars, however, remained shoddy compared to Toyota's standards. The slow-selling Olds, Buick, and Cadillac versions eventually had to be killed.

Lordstown and its J-car models, the Cavalier and Sunbird, soldiered on through the 1980s, emblems of GM mediocrity. The plant missed Roger Smith's automation craze. In Lordstown's welding shop, much of the work was still done the old-fashioned way—by people who muscled welding guns around to fasten metal pieces together amid showers of sparks.

While the daily grind of work at Lordstown seemed unchanged, however, attitudes among managers and workers at the factory began to shift. In the front office, GM replaced the arrogant taskmasters of the 1970s with younger people willing to concede that GM wasn't king anymore. "The Japanese are eating our lunch," these new managers moaned to their union counterparts.

The union leaders chuckled at this schoolboy phrase. Spit it out, Bill Bowers, the president of the local union, would reply: "They're kicking our ass!"

But it wasn't just the managers who seemed ready to change. The shop floor rebels of 1972 were turning inexorably into middle-aged men and women with kids, house payments, and no real choice amid the Mahoning Valley's dead steel mills but to stick it out at GM. During the mid-1980s, Lordstown's workers began trying to meet the bosses halfway. Managers and line workers began repairing to hotel conference rooms to talk about how to solve problems without fights.

But as the 1990s began, it became clear that Lordstown—like the rest of GM—would have to do a lot more than talk to survive.

RUNNING THE HUGE LORDSTOWN complex and preparing it for the launch of a redesigned J-car in fall 1994 was the biggest challenge Mike Cubbin had faced in his twenty-six-year GM career.

The new J-cars, one to replace the Chevrolet Cavalier and the other to replace the Pontiac Sunbird, would compete head-on with Japanese models like the Toyota Corolla and Honda Civic, as well as much improved small cars from Ford and Chrysler. But despite such strong competitors, GM expected the new Cavalier, and its Pontiac sister car, which had been renamed the Sunfire, to account for nearly 400,000 sales a year. Those were huge numbers, equivalent to about 4 percent of the total car market in a good year. All of Mazda's cars put together didn't account for that much. Even before GM's board swept out Lloyd Reuss and Bob Stempel, Cubbin's superiors understood they had to catch up to the Japanese competition to survive.

On paper, Mike Cubbin looked just like the plant managers who'd come before him. He'd worked for GM all his adult life, since the Fisher Body division sponsored him to be a nineteen-year-old student at the General Motors Institute in Flint in 1966. Armed with his GMI bachelor's degree in industrial engineering, Cubbin signed on full time with Fisher Body in 1971, joining one of the most tradition-bound organizations in the old GM.

Cubbin's career veered off the traditional track in 1980, when he took a trip to Japan and toured Toyota and Isuzu factories. As director of industrial engineering for Fisher Body at the time, Cubbin was mainly concerned with how to cut costs in Fisher Body's metal-stamping plants, which turned tons of steel into fenders, hoods, and doors. Cubbin was impressed by how Toyota stamping crews switched their huge metal presses from making a fender to a door in thirty minutes—a job that GM crews took six or eight hours to accomplish. Three years later, his education in the nature of Japan's challenge accelerated, when he was assigned to work under Jack Smith on the team that negotiated the formation of Nummi.

Cubbin spent hours poring over Toyota's proposals for building and staffing Nummi's steel-forming operations. At first, he couldn't believe the Toyota engineers were serious. They expected Nummi's stamping presses to run nearly all the time, changing parts every couple of hours, with less than thirty minutes of idle time between production of different parts. Slowly, Cubbin pieced together the puzzle of how the Toyota system worked—just as Steve Bera and the other members of the original Nummi commando squad would do in their stints at the factory.

Cubbin didn't get assigned to the first team of GM managers to go to Nummi itself. Instead, GM shipped him off to run a big metal-stamping plant in Lansing, Michigan. There, he began trying to apply what he'd learned in Japan, gradually training the workers in the plant to change the dies on their presses in less than six hours.

Cubbin continued his own reeducation as he moved up the ranks. In August 1987, he arrived in Lordstown as plant manager. Welcomed to town by a reporter for a local newspaper, Cubbin declared he had a new goal in life: building cars that would be sold in Japan.[4]

It sounded far-fetched, particularly in light of what GM wanted him to do first on his new assignment. As part of its retrenchment, GM had decided to close a van assembly line at Lordstown. The Lordstown car factory would continue as the only GM plant in the United States building the low-priced Cavalier and Sunbird. To meet GM's ambitious sales goals, however, Lordstown would have to pump out far more than the normal 240,000 cars per year. The question, given the plant's troubled past, was how?

In August 1990, Cubbin got his bosses' blessing to take a couple of his union counterparts on a ten-day excursion to Europe. There, the men from Lordstown would see firsthand the marvelous money machines of GM Europe: factories that ran around the clock.

First, Cubbin and his colleagues visited GM's plant in Zaragoza, Spain, where cars were built around the clock on three shifts a day. To do this, Zaragoza had lots of duplicate equipment—including an extra-large paint line—that Lordstown didn't have. If Lordstown ran around the clock, it couldn't maintain its welders or clean its paint machinery. Eventually the plant would grind to a halt.

Then, Cubbin's group went to Antwerp, Belgium, where GM once had operated two assembly plants. It had since closed one, and instituted an unusual work scheme in the other. Three crews of workers alternated shifts so that the plant produced cars twenty hours a day, six days a week. The financial advantages of this three-crew system were astounding. Using virtually the same equipment required to run the plant eighty hours a week—sixteen hours a day for five days—Antwerp was pumping out cars 120 hours a week. GM Europe's record profits were in no small measure the result of this system of spreading the costs for tools and equipment out over 40 percent to 50 percent more cars.

The icing on the cake was that adding the third crew absorbed most of the workers from the closed plant. This scheme seemed to suit Lordstown perfectly. Like Antwerp, the Lordstown complex had two assembly lines, one of which was soon to close, putting 1,700 workers on the street. Adding a third shift at the car plant would give those people someplace to go.

Negotiating the details with the union wasn't easy. Among other things, workers were wary about losing overtime pay, and shift-switching schedules that would keep them away from Friday night high school football games. But in July 1991, the Lordstown local agreed to begin a three-crew work system one year later. Lordstown's employees would put in four ten-hour days a week, banking two hours of overtime pay each day.

GM, meanwhile, would get almost as many cars out of Lordstown each week as it had tried to produce twenty years earlier using virtually the same size workforce and running the Vega line at 100 cars per hour. By April 1993, the three-crew system was working so well that GM was able to slash the prices of the aged Cavalier by as much as $1,200 and make it one of the best-selling cars in America.

THAT, HOWEVER, was only the start.

GM managers often tried to excuse their competitive shortcomings by arguing that they couldn't make dramatic improvements in quality or manufacturing cost until a new model and new production tools came along. GM's long product-development cycles meant Jack Smith would be stuck until 1996 or 1997 with cars, trucks, and factories designed under the old GM system. Smith and his aides realized that was too long to wait for a dramatic improvement in quality and efficiency. So as they dug through GM's North American morass, they began turning the screws on the managers running the programs that Stempel and Reuss had put in the pipeline before they left. One of these was the 1995 J-car.

Tom Davis had come to his job as the vice president in charge of GM's small-car operations by a well-traveled GM road. Born in 1946, he joined Pontiac as a trainee at age eighteen, and got his mechanical engineering degree from General Motors Institute in 1970. By 1989, he was chief engineer at the Lansing Auto division, one of the top 100 positions in GM's North American car-making empire. He also became directly responsible for the new J-car.

Well aware that the original 1982 J-cars were outclassed by their

Japanese rivals, GM's brass in late 1989 had ordered the Lansing division to overhaul the cars with Honda and Toyota as the targets. Davis had marched his team of engineers down the same trail as the enemy. J-car engineers began paying visits to the Mona Lisa–room facility Alex Mair had set up at GM's Technical Center, comparing parts from Toyotas and Hondas to the ones they planned. Davis forged an alliance with the technical center staff to short-circuit the customary GM engineering system, in which vehicle designers passed blueprints to engineers who laid out factories, who then passed them back after complaining that the car couldn't be assembled as designed. Davis recruited engineers and manufacturing managers who'd done stints at Nummi or in the liaison office GM maintained in Fremont, California, to study the venture. Then he and his engineering staff created thirty-five teams, each made up of mechanical engineers, assembly plant designers, and purchasing agents. Each team worked on a piece of the car. Every one of the teams also trooped to Fremont to visit the Toyota–GM plant. Later, some of the J-car teams went to Germany to see GM's new plant in Eisenach.

The more the J-car engineers learned, the harder they worked to eliminate extraneous parts and make the new model easier to build. The old Cavalier took nearly 50 percent more labor time to assemble than one of Nummi's Corollas. The new J-car would have nearly 20 percent fewer bolts and widgets than the old model.

In another cost-cutting move, Davis sent an expert in metal stamping to the styling studios in Detroit. His orders: play cop when the stylists pushed for curlicues that would require extra stamping dies to form. Davis had studied Honda's operations and concluded that Honda could produce fenders and hoods with an average of just three dies per part, compared to an average of more than five dies per part on the old J-car. Every die eliminated through simplified styling meant $250,000 or so in avoided costs for the new car. That freed up money to give the car better features or a lower price. If Honda could do that, Davis declared, then the J-car designers would do it, too. Unquestionably, the J-car was a better small car program than GM had run in the past.

Jack Smith's sudden installation as GM's president in April 1992 forced a radical rethinking among managers like Tom Davis and Mike Cubbin of whether better was good enough.

Smith declared his first priority was to "stop the bleeding." GM was gushing out some $11 million a day more cash than it was taking in. In the summer and fall of 1992, Smith and his team scrambled like doctors in an emergency room to apply tourniquets to this hemorrhage. One of Smith's key assistants in this process was Bob Hendry, the same man who'd led the first group of GM commandos to Nummi in 1984. His hair thinner and whiter than in the Nummi days, Hendry was named chief financial officer of Smith's North American Operations and given broad latitude. Hendry had dreamed at Nummi that he would someday help GM remake itself in Toyota's image. Now, however, his first task was to confront the holdovers from the Stempel era with the harsh truth. They'd been heading in the right direction, as the J-car team efforts showed. But they hadn't moved nearly fast enough or far enough. In July 1992, Hendry turned up the heat by demanding to review every capital spending proposal, including the budget for the J-car.

Davis had planned to spend between $1 billion and $1.5 billion developing the new J-car, compared to nearly $2 billion spent on Saturn's engineering. But Smith and Hendry's staffers, armed with detailed data on how much Toyota and Honda spent for new-product programs, pushed to slash the J-car's cost another 10 percent or more through tougher purchasing and leaner production methods. The new goal: spend about $900 million to engineer the new models, and retool Lordstown and a sister factory to build more than 500,000 of them a year.

At the plant, Cubbin heard the new message loud and clear. Despite the cash crisis of 1991, Cubbin had held on to a plan to build a football-field-sized addition to the massive, 2.5-million-square-foot Lordstown plant. He wanted the addition because he saw no room to install a new line of equipment to prepare car bodies for painting without shutting down the plant. Even one missed day of production cost some $10 million or more in lost sales, so the new bricks and mortar seemed worth the $1 million or more it would cost.

Cubbin didn't need a telegram to know this proposal wouldn't fly with the new management. So he decided to take the risk he'd tried to avoid.

In mid-October, one of the plant's engineers had come to Cubbin with an idea. Using Toyota methods to clear out more storage areas and rearranging some equipment could free up a 45-foot-wide alley in the plant—just barely enough space to fit the paint-preparation line without a new addition. The risk was that any glitch in installing the complicated machinery would cause the plant to fall behind schedule in converting to the new model. By rearranging the line, Cubbin also would forfeit a long conveyor full of bodies he'd counted on to keep production going should the new system fail.

On November 9, one week after GM's directors formally accepted Stempel's resignation, Cubbin decided to take the plunge. He jumped into a car and sped toward downtown Pittsburgh to a meeting he'd scheduled at the unlikely hour of 10 P.M. Cubbin presented his idea to his superiors, and when the meeting was over, the addition was history.

It was as if someone dropped a checkered flag. By the spring of 1993, Cubbin and his staff had used Nummi-style methods to free up 225,000 square feet of space that once had housed spare parts or assembly-line tools. That was the equivalent of five football fields—and seven times more space than the plant would have gained from the addition.

By June, contractors had installed a temporary wall in a cleared section of the plant. On one side, workers installed the new paint preparation machinery. On the other, production of Cavaliers and Sunbirds continued twenty hours a day.

Cubbin and his staff forged ahead with their campaign to transform their plant. They began installing lighted Nummi-style "andon" boards overhead to show at a glance the pace of work in each department. When a defective car caused trouble in a certain department, workers now could sound an alarm—which played the opening notes to the Beatles' hit "Hey, Jude." Most of the workers in the plant would remember the song's apropos opening line: "Hey, Jude, don't make it bad." They also realized that for the first time, management was trusting *them* to find and fix quality problems.

In the part of the plant where workers installed seats and decorative parts, the cars now had large labels, or manifests, attached to the hoods that displayed in large type the data that identified what parts belonged on each car. This, too, was a Nummi idea. In the welding shop, engineers began marking off space around the old line for tight circles of welding robots similar to those at Eisenach. By early December 1993, the new welding line started building cars. And at 2:01 A.M. on December 21, 1993, Cubbin's staff sent the first cars down the paint preparation line that had caused so much anxiety. The system worked. By February 1994, the first "pilot" test versions of the redesigned 1995 car had gone down the line.

As they overhauled their old plant, Cubbin and his staff also began trying to convert Lordstown's workers. Building on efforts by his predecessor to bury the plant's troubled past, Cubbin wooed union officials.

He convinced them of the difference between "work standards," meaning quotas, and "standardized work," meaning jobs designed to be done the same way on each shift. Cubbin and the engineers from Lansing began seeking advice from production workers about how to make jobs on the new J-car line easier to do.

An ambitious outgrowth of this effort was a $23 million program to teach workers their new jobs and the new assembly system before the new models started production. Much of the training occurred in the now-shuttered van factory where GM installed a miniassembly line similar to the system planned for the 1995 Cavalier. Lordstown's workers sometimes grumbled that the engineers still didn't listen. But they'd never seen anything like the prototype assembly line before. At least, this time, management was trying.

MEANWHILE, THE ENGINEERS designing the new J-car had to execute some somersaults of their own to meet Jack Smith's challenge to build a car for Japan.

When a car is designed to have the steering wheel on the left, overhauling it to put the wheel on the right is a multimillion dollar exercise. The dashboard has to be redesigned, new holes have to be punched into the body for the steering column and controls, wiring has to be rerouted, even the air-conditioner has to be relocated. Most of GM's American engineers hadn't bothered thinking about such problems for years. So what if GM's refusal to satisfy a Japanese customer's most basic requirement—a steering wheel on the right—made the company's protests about Japanese refusal to buy American cars seem silly? GM lost money on its *left*-hand drive cars. Certainly, there was no money in right-hand drive.

Jack Smith, however, had quietly fired a missile at the old excuses. So it was that in January 1993, John Cohoon, who'd taken over as the J-car's chief engineer after Davis became a vice president, prepared to fly to Japan to do the unthinkable. GM usually kept photos of forthcoming cars under lock and key. Now, Cohoon was about to show pictures of the clay models for the 1995 Chevrolet Cavalier and its Pontiac twin to Toyota. After all, Toyota couldn't be expected to buy a pig in a poke.

Toyota executives proved to be completely serious about selling GM's car. Tatsuro Toyoda himself joined the discussions. So did several other members of Toyota's managing board. First, they debated which of the two J-cars would sell best in Japan: the Chevy Cavalier, which had an understated look adapted from Opel's German styling, or the flashier Pontiac, designed to fit that division's boy-racer image. The Toyota executives opted for the Cavalier. In America, the 1995 Cavalier would sell as an economy car. But in Japan, Toyota saw the Cavalier fitting a niche similar to Buick or Oldsmobile in America—bigger than average, plush, but not ultra-expensive.

Toyota then sicced a team of engineers—some of them Americans based in the company's Ann Arbor, Michigan, office—to help the J-car engineers meet Japanese standards. Flipping the steering system and the dashboard over to a right-hand drive layout was the big job. There were dozens of other details. The windshield wiper and turn-signal levers had to be on the opposite side of the steering wheel from the American design. Even the relationship of the seat to the pedals was changed to match Japanese drivers' physiques.

By summer 1993, the Toyota engineers were driving prototypes of the right-hand drive Cavaliers around GM's test track. As the year rolled on, the biggest worry among Toyota's engineers wasn't whether GM could design a right-hand drive car. It was whether the cars would be built to Toyota's exacting quality standards.

QUALITY WAS A BIG concern for Jack Smith and GM's board, too. Japanese manufacturers and Detroit's Big Three all had reduced the average number of defects per car dramatically between 1986 and 1992. But an internal company study of GM's quality scores compared with the average Japanese car showed two parallel lines—both declining, but staying roughly the same distance apart. GM struggled to attain in 1992 the quality levels the Japanese left behind in 1986. GM's trucks were even worse. In 1992, GM trucks had the highest number of defects, on average, of any on the market.

This "quality gap" had grave consequences. GM had spent $3 billion in 1992 on warranty repairs, or about $829 a vehicle in the United States. Poor quality forced GM to accept less money for many of its cars. GM had lost millions of potential customers scared away by old quality horror stories.

Smith believed GM's quality would improve as it adapted Toyota's production methods. Shortly after he became president, Smith put his signature on thousands of brochures that looked like comic books, but actually were user-friendly primers for GM's version of the Toyota system. There, renamed and adapted to GM's uses, were nearly all the elements of the Nummi system—the "five whys" method of tracking down problems, producing small batches of parts instead of filling huge bins, taking continuous small steps to improve quality instead of waiting for a Big Bang, and so on.

But GM's quality problem couldn't wait for the plants to put all these ideas in place. So in the interim, Smith ordered a belt and suspenders approach to catching defective cars before they hit the road. In every factory, inspectors were assigned to stations in the middle of each assembly line, at the end of the line, and even at the depots where cars were shipped to dealers. In some plants, as many as twenty people would be arrayed along what was called a "finesse line" to check finished cars for scratched paint, electrical glitches, and other goofs. It wasn't efficient. But it was what GM had to do. These efforts, on top of earlier initiatives launched under Bob Stempel, improved quality dramatically. Between 1989 and 1993, GM's warranty payouts on Cavaliers during their first year on the road dropped by 42 percent, and the number of defects per car at the time of sale decreased by a third.

Still, at 1.26 defects per car,[5] Lordstown's 1993 Cavalier lagged well behind Nummi's Corollas, which averaged 0.65 defects per car. Lordstown had a long way to go to become the Nummi of Ohio, just as GM was a long way from becoming Toyota.

THE MOST PAINFUL PART of the transformation was its human cost.

Dissolving a generation's worth of distrust and bad habits wouldn't come easily for Lordstown's workers. Lordstown launched a program to get cost-cutting suggestions from workers, but management got just 1,200 ideas in 1992 from 7,700 employees. At Nummi, 4,250 workers generated more than 10,000 usable suggestions a year. Cubbin could walk around his plant and find a worker snoozing in a chair while colleagues fired off welding guns just a few feet away. At any given time, as many as 13 percent of Lordstown's workers were sitting down, drinking coffee, reading, or dozing. That was the system. One of every eight workers was a "relief" hand, kept aboard to step in when another worker wanted to take a break. That way the line could run ten hours a day without stopping. Such relief jobs wouldn't exist at a Toyota plant, or if they did, the spare workers would do something when they weren't on the line.

The leaders of the Lordstown UAW local were all for improving quality, and they appreciated management's efforts to consult workers about how to ease the strain of jobs on the line. But they weren't going to accept quietly the loss of more than 2,000 of the jobs in their plant when the new Cavalier came in. Bill Bowers, the local union president, had worked at Lordstown for twenty-seven years, and had been part of the 1972 strike. He didn't care what euphemism GM used for the new production system—"synchronous," or "lean production," or creating "value for the customer." Maybe the union couldn't save every position. But Bowers was determined to try.

"In those areas where technology is coming in, it's inevitable," Bowers would say. "But where you got Joe doing four parts, and Jane doing four parts, and someone else doing four, and you eliminate one of the jobs and give six parts to the other two, we say: Bullshit."

THE DETERMINATION AMONG Lordstown's labor leaders to fight the loss of jobs represented just a small part of a huge roadblock across Smith's path toward a New GM.

GM expended, on average, thirty-four hours of labor assembling each of its cars, compared to twenty-four for Ford. Closing this gap, without enormous increases in sales to support additional jobs, would mean unprecedented trauma. Stempel had stunned the country in February 1992 when he declared GM would need only 250,000 U.S. hourly workers in the mid-1990s, down from 304,000 in 1991. But Smith's lean production plans meant GM might need as few as 190,000 U.S. production workers —50,000 to 60,000 fewer production jobs than Stempel had targeted. Moreover, GM was accelerating the elimination of some 20,000 clerical and managerial positions. Once the country's greatest engine of opportunity, GM was becoming a job-destruction machine. GM's payroll had once accounted for nearly 600,000 jobs in America. By the mid-1990s, GM would employ half that many Americans. GM had vaporized more American jobs between 1990 and 1993 than existed on Chrysler's entire payroll. As 1993 drew to a close, GM had almost another Chrysler's worth of jobs still to cut just to reconcile its costs to the reality of lost sales.

The irony was that GM still couldn't shed workers fast enough because of the labor agreement Stempel had negotiated in 1990. Smith tried to break the Stempel pattern in contract talks during the summer of 1993, but United Auto Workers union President Owen Bieber wouldn't budge.

Smith, loath to risk a long strike just as the economy was recovering, backed down and renewed the provisions that had cost GM more than $3 billion in payments to idle workers during Stempel's brief term.

Smith could continue his lean production crusade at Lordstown, and every other GM plant. He just couldn't take full advantage of the cost savings, as Ford had done a decade before. Smith had to keep paying workers GM no longer needed. To offset the financial drain, Smith's staff scrambled to find work for displaced laborers to do. At Lordstown, Cubbin and local union leaders came up with a plan to employ nearly 300 people assembling seats in a joint venture with a supplier. About 200 more displaced assembly workers moved over to a nearby stamping plant. Time and an early retirement program would take care of the rest. More than 2,000 Lordstown's workers would have thirty years' service by 1996, and could retire with full pensions under GM's normal rules.

Still, GM's obligations to its workers had left the company a bizarre hybrid of a social welfare agency and a profit-seeking enterprise.

In early 1994, with sales booming, GM found itself in the absurd position of doling out layoff pay to 8,300 idled workers at certain U.S. plants, while at the same time hiring temporary workers at other factories to keep up with demand.[6]

ON OCTOBER 28, 1993, one year and two days after Bob Stempel's resignation, GM reported it lost $113 million in the third quarter, compared to a $1 billion loss the year before. Smith would have shown a profit, but for a $950 million before-tax write-off tied to the costs of the new labor contract. In all, GM had thrown more than $8 billion into the maw of "restructuring" since 1986. And for all that, GM's domestic vehicle operations in 1993 were still more than $1 billion in the red— even as Chrysler was raking in profits, and Ford's American operations were jumping back into the black.

But Smith was convinced his plan to steer GM away from the cliff was working. The problem was convincing the rest of the world, particularly investors whose money GM would need to finance the overhaul of virtually all its mainstream vehicles.

Five years earlier, when GM's leaders wanted to persuade Wall Street that a turnaround was at hand, Roger Smith rented the Grand Ballroom at the Waldorf-Astoria, commissioned the world's largest video display and feted the political and financial elite amid glitzy show cars. But as

Jack Smith's aides called around for a New York City venue where he could tell his comeback story, they found every major hotel conference room was booked. So the New GM's leaders had to repair to the rambling, middle-brow Rye Town Hilton in suburban Rye, New York. This was a hotel where the air conditioning was turned off after Labor Day, and even an unseasonably warm pre-Thanksgiving night couldn't persuade the management to turn the coolers back on. Jack Smith's New GM couldn't afford to be picky, however. That underscored the message Smith and his top lieutenants delivered on November 16, 1993, in a meeting that ran from breakfast to the cocktail hour: A humbler, wiser GM had really learned the hard lessons of the 1980s and was applying them as never before.

Smith's lieutenants went into remarkable detail to make their case. They offered a glimpse of their plan to replace the failed, midsized GM-10 cars brought out under Roger Smith. These cars had cost GM a whopping $7 billion. They had generated nothing but huge losses, steady market share erosion, and a belief among many consumers that GM didn't know how to design good cars.

Now, Smith's aides revealed, they had a plan to spend just $1.9 billion to design a single, simple-to-build chassis that could carry three new midsized sedans for Pontiac, Buick, and Olds, a new Pontiac coupe, and also a new minivan. GM's strategy board had forced the engineers in charge of the project to pass tests aimed at assuring they wouldn't repeat the sins of the past. They had asked customers what they wanted before the cars were designed, instead of after the styling and engineering were done. They had compared their new designs to the best in the field, and run their plans through Smith's new Vehicle Launch Center. This engineering clearing house, modeled on one at Opel in Germany, housed several hundred engineers whose main job was to impose discipline on GM's chaotic and costly product development process.

GM's American car engineers henceforth would have to choose components for a new model like someone ordering from an old-style Chinese restaurant menu—one brake system from among the four in Column A, shock absorbers from the five in Column B, gas caps from the two in Column C, and so on. The same would go for production tools.

One of Smith's aides described for the investors how a team of engineers—a "creativity team" such as those founded by López—had discovered how to save $100 per car by eliminating 80 percent of the different

brake systems the Old GM had built. Putting the lower-cost brakes in all
GM cars would take until 1997, but after that the savings would total
close to $500 million a year. "That's big money." Smith would grin
when he told the tale later.

Saving money, however, wasn't enough, Smith and his team declared.
GM needed to grow again. And to do that, it would start acting like the
global company it was. The plan to ship J-cars to Toyota for sale in
Japan was just the start. By the mid-1990s, Smith wanted GM to sell a
version of Opel's next generation Omega luxury car in both Europe and
America. Opel, meanwhile, would be transforming its Corsa sedan into
a sporty two-door and even a pickup truck. The Corsa would become a
true "world" car, sold from Rotterdam to Rio, Singapore to Sydney in a
variety of shapes suited to local tastes. Meanwhile, the new minivan
would be built in Georgia and sold in Europe by the mid-1990s.

The analysts and investors in the room understood that GM remained
vulnerable should the economy slump again before the late 1990s. They
recognized that the strong yen, and the resulting surge in Japanese car
prices, had given Jack Smith's turnaround effort a huge boost by easing
competitive pressure and allowing GM to raise its own prices. They
knew that the $24 billion gap between GM's pension obligations and its
pension fund assets would sap cash from the effort to overhaul new
products.

Still, Wall Street rejoiced that Smith and his team of reformers
seemed to have a realistic plan to exploit the good fortune they had.
Although 1993 wasn't over, it was clear Smith and his management
would produce the stunning one-year, $4.5 billion turnaround he had
promised a year earlier. The threat of disaster had lifted. America's
largest corporation hadn't died. Within days of the Rye meeting, exuberant investors bid GM's stock up to record high prices. And three months
later, in February 1994, GM would report that it had turned a full-year
profit for the first time since 1989. North American Operations would
turn a $427 million profit in the fourth quarter of 1993, marking the first
black ink in GM's domestic auto business since June 1989.

Amid the optimism created by the Rye meeting, Jack Smith flew west
to San Francisco for another meeting with Tatsuro Toyoda. The two
men and a small retinue of aides met at the Stanford Court Hotel on
November 18 to clinch the unprecedented deal they'd discussed nearly a

year before. The setting was appropriate. It was the same place they'd met a decade earlier to celebrate the signing of the Nummi agreement. Nummi had been GM's admission that it had lost its edge, that it needed to learn anew how to compete. Now, Toyota was symbolically putting a stamp of approval on GM's progress and on Smith's leadership. By 1996, Toyota agreed, it would indeed import 20,000 of GM's new J-cars for sale under its own name. Toyota's motives for this deal were, of course, not altruistic. Offering to sell American-made cars in Japan was good politics for a Japanese company that wanted to sell 1 million cars and trucks a year in America. Still, the agreement was a breakthrough. For the first time ever, a Japanese company would sell a Big Three model under its own name in Japan. Even two years earlier, it would have been unthinkable.

For Lordstown, the payoff came on December 10, 1993, when GM announced where the cars for Toyota would be built. At around 10 A.M., GM beamed the news over its closed-circuit television that Lordstown had been chosen. Amid the grins and the good feeling, Mike Cubbin remembered how he'd dreamed of this day. It was a moment that should have come years sooner. But now it was here, and it felt great. Lordstown, home of the Vega and the blue-collar blues, was beginning its comeback after all.

CHAPTER 19

NEON LIGHTS

Soft-spoken and short, with a pinched nose punctuating his homespun face, Chrysler engineer Bob Marcell was neither an imposing figure nor an inspiring speaker. If Lee Iacocca registered, say, a 12 on a 1–10 scale of rhetorical firepower, Marcell was a minus two. But now, on July 31, 1990, at a time when Chrysler was hemorrhaging cash, the fifty-year-old Marcell was trying to persuade Iacocca to bet hundreds of millions of dollars on a quest for the auto industry's Holy Grail: building a small car profitably in America.

Saturn hadn't even hit the streets yet, but already GM's great crusade clearly was a financial disaster. Ford, for its part, had tried to save money by enlisting Mazda to engineer the Escort, but was losing money on every one it sold. Iacocca knew Chrysler needed a new small car to replace the lackluster Plymouth Sundance and Dodge Shadow. But he was so sure Chrysler couldn't make the proposition pay off that he had scoured the world for potential partners: Fiat, Hyundai, and Mitsubishi.

Chrysler's president, Bob Lutz, wanted the company to develop a new small car on its own, and had lined up Chrysler's engineers behind him. But what Lutz and the engineers wanted meant nothing if they couldn't convince Iacocca. Now that was up to Bob Marcell.

The setting for his presentation was a conference room in Chrysler's aging brick headquarters complex. About a dozen senior executives were on hand, and all of them, including Iacocca, had seen the preliminary numbers for the proposed project beforehand. So Marcell ignored the financial data and started talking, improbably, about his northern Michigan boyhood.

"This is Iron River," Marcell declared, as a slide projector flashed a photo on the screen. "It's a little town in the western end of the Upper Peninsula, a hell of a good place to grow up, with a lot of blue skies and fresh air. Back in the forties and fifties, every day about three o'clock and eleven o'clock, the pictures all shook in the houses, the ground rumbled, the windows rattled, and everybody smiled. Because that meant the iron mines were blasting. There were jobs for everybody. There was no unemployment. And there was good pay. And snowmobiles, new cars, cottages, and boats. A lot of first- and second-generation Europeans had found a little bit of heaven."

Iacocca displayed a look of puzzlement. Another slide clicked into place, and Marcell continued.

"But there was trouble brewing. Iron ore was coming in from Brazil and from Canada. There was a lot of competition, foreign and domestic."

Marcell went on. "This happens to be the Hiawatha No. 2. My dad was the last person out of this mine. He pulled up the pumps and let the deepest iron mine in the world flood. And we shipped the pumps to Africa and South America, because we couldn't compete."

Now came a rapid series of images: more iron mines, Marcell's old school, the church Marcell was married in, the old Iron River train depot. All were abandoned. As each desolate image appeared, Marcell repeated the refrain: "Couldn't compete." Standing before a slide of an old mine shaft that had been turned into a melancholy museum of Iron River's better days, Marcell delivered his town's epitaph: "Chernobyl was a nuclear disaster, and you can't live there anymore. My home town had an economic disaster—every bit as devastating, a lot more insidious —and you can't live there anymore."

Marcell's presentation was, of course, an allegory. Iron River was Chrysler. The abandoned iron pits represented one more segment of the car market—small cars—given up as too difficult. The ghostly buildings stood for the future if America lost its industrial vigor and surrendered to decline.

"So," Marcell concluded, "what the hell are we going to do? Not come to work scared every day. We can roll in with a counterattack, and that's what this is all about. Because we can reestablish a beachhead in small cars. We can reverse the long downhill slide. And prove to the world that we're not soft, we're not lazy, we're not dumb, and, damn, we can compete." [1]

When Marcell finished, virtually every throat in the room had a lump in it. Lee Iacocca himself had never given a better speech. Eight months later, in April 1991, he gave the final go-ahead for Marcell's project to proceed.

MARCELL'S NEW CAR was given the code name PL. The car was supposed to combine the moderate size of Chrysler's P cars—the Plymouth Sundance and Dodge Shadow—with the low cost of the L cars, the defunct Dodge Omni and Plymouth Horizon. When the PL project was formally approved, Chrysler was already well along in developing another new car, actually a family of midsized sedans, code-named LH. Those initials, unlike PL, meant nothing in particular, but the gag around Detroit was that they stood for Last Hope. It wasn't entirely a joke.

Chrysler had survived between 1988 and 1991 thanks solely to the strength of its minivans and Jeeps. Both were technically trucks, although Chrysler had endowed them with so many carlike comforts that they had become suburban staples all across America. But in traditional passenger cars, the family sedans and compacts that accounted for half of all vehicle sales, Chrysler hadn't produced a hit since the K-cars a dozen years earlier. The succession of clunky and mediocre K-car derivatives that followed left the company reeling. Chrysler fell to fifth place behind Honda and Toyota in passenger-car sales, its bottom line plunged deeply into the red, and its debt ratings nosedived down to junk-bond status. Thus the LH cars—the Dodge Intrepid, Eagle Vision, and Chrysler Concorde—were virtually do-or-die products.

The LH cars were drastically different from Chryslers of the past. They sported sleek styling that Chrysler called "cab-forward," achieved by pushing the windshield out over the front wheels and pushing all four wheels out toward the edge of the vehicle. They had taut suspensions and powerful engines—up to 214 horsepower—in contrast to the wallowing, underpowered boxes that had long been Chrysler's specialty. And they had TV commercials that omitted Lee Iacocca, highlighting instead the cars themselves.

But the biggest differences between the LH cars and the Chryslers of the past, and the things that made these surprising cars possible, were items that customers would never notice. Chrysler had needed only thirty-nine months—barely over three years—to develop and launch the cars, compared with the four and a half years it took to bring the K-cars to market. The company had assigned just 740 engineers to work on the LH cars, compared to the 2,000 it needed to develop the K-cars. And the factory where the LH cars were made needed just 3,000 employees for full, two-shift production, whereas the K-car plants had needed 5,300. Chrysler had achieved these startling gains in efficiency even though the LH cars, with their dual air bags, independent rear suspensions, and other standard features, were far more complex and sophisticated than their K-car ancestors.[2]

The man most responsible for this leap was a veteran Chrysler engineer named Glenn Gardner, who had spent most of the late 1980s in virtual exile. In 1985 Chrysler had dispatched Gardner to Normal, Illinois, a town 120 miles southwest of Chicago that was home to a state university and also to Diamond-Star Motors, a joint venture between Chrysler and Mitsubishi. Diamond-Star drew its name from Mitsubishi's logo, which was three diamonds, and Chrysler's, a pentastar. Gardner was Diamond-Star's chairman.

The title sounded exalted, but the job wasn't. Gardner was there simply to look after Chrysler's interests while Mitsubishi handled the real work of developing and building a new car. But Gardner used his vantage point to learn and observe, and what he saw impressed him. Mitsubishi could develop new cars in less time and at lower cost than Chrysler had deemed remotely possible. The difference lay in how the companies went about it.

Mitsubishi organized itself for simultaneous decisions, instead of sequential ones, by using product-development teams that cut across departmental lines. Engineers, manufacturing men, and finance staffers sat around a single table and decided whether a body design was strong enough to use, feasible to build, and inexpensive to produce. At Chrysler, in contrast, the different departments worked independently and in sequence. The engineers often finished their designs only to have the manufacturing people raise objections weeks later, sending the engineers, quite literally, back to the drawing boards. When delays, cost overruns, and quality glitches appeared, each department pointed fingers at the others.

Gardner's initial efforts to pass his findings back to Chrysler headquarters, however, proved fruitless. The manufacturing people deemed the joint venture with Mitsubishi akin to sleeping with the enemy during wartime. Chrysler's engineering executives, meanwhile, simply ignored Diamond-Star. Until, that is, François Castaing came along.

Castaing was a Frenchman whose career had been shaped by automotive mergers. He had started with Renault in 1970, and been assigned to American Motors a decade later, after Renault bought into the struggling U.S. company. When Chrysler bought American Motors in 1987, Castaing stayed as head of Jeep and truck engineering. In late 1988, with an increasingly powerful Bob Lutz as his patron, Castaing was named vice president for engineering for all Chrysler products.

His promotion didn't sit well with Chrysler veterans, who were tired of seeing people from other companies—usually Ford—get the top jobs. Many of the veterans, including Gardner, wanted to be vice president of engineering themselves. But Castaing was just forty-three, and looked to have the job a long time.

At least, however, Castaing was enthusiastic about cars, and possessed of an exuberant personality that helped disarm his critics. "Zees weel knock zee clocks off zee competition!" he once declared in a planning meeting. No one reacted, but ten minutes later Castaing belatedly realized his idiomatic error. "Socks!" he announced, abruptly interrupting the meeting. "I meant eet weel knock zehr socks off." Everyone roared.

Right after his promotion, Castaing started looking for someone to give the LH program, which was foundering, a new direction. When Gardner's name popped up, Castaing decided to pay him a visit. To avoid raising hackles, he took a vacation day and flew down to Normal alone. There, he listened as Gardner described what he had learned and what Chrysler should do.

Castaing liked what he heard. At Renault, he had run a racing team that was a tiny version of what Gardner was describing. And American Motors had functioned like a single task force by default; it was too small for different departments to work separately.

Meanwhile, quite on their own, some of Chrysler's Young Turks were coming to the same conclusions as Gardner and Castaing. In 1988, when Chrysler could feel Honda's hot breath gaining on it, a group of junior managers suggested an in-depth study of Honda. They quickly ran across a system Honda called SED—for sales, engineering, and development. It wasn't exactly a secret; Shoichiro Irimajiri had provided a capsule description in a speech at Stanford University in April 1987. "S, or sales," he said, "comes up with the image of a new product through discussions with customers. Research and development—*D*—creates the specific design which realizes the sales image. Production and engineering—*E*—finds the way to build the design. None of these groups does its work alone."[3]

Gardner, Castaing, and the Honda study group were like three little creeks flowing together to make a river. Iacocca could have overlooked any one of them, but with all three suggesting the same thing, he had to take notice. Chrysler's late-eighties nosedive had proved the need to let younger men have their head. Standing back didn't come naturally to Iacocca, but now, despite his foibles and his ego, he started to do just that. After mulling it over, Iacocca agreed to let a Honda-like task force, dubbed a "platform team," take over the LH project. In February 1989, Castaing put Gardner in charge.

The LH team was an intriguing experiment, but one of just several around Detroit. Within months Ford was putting together a similar group in its scramble to save the Mustang. Chrysler's desperation, however, was running far deeper than just one car. So in the spring of 1990, encouraged by Gardner's rapid initial progress, Lutz and Castaing concluded Chrysler should break up its 7,000-member engineering organization and assign almost everyone to a platform team.

Iacocca, though, was skeptical, and understandably so. He sensed that assigning every new car to a team leader would threaten his own authority—which was exactly what Lutz and Castaing intended. And he knew full well that GM's wholesale engineering reorganization in 1984 had been a disaster, with bureaucratic confusion and infighting destroying what had seemed to be a good idea. In fact, Iacocca started getting a stream of anonymous letters, apparently from Chrysler engineers, claiming Castaing was destroying the LH and the company in a single stroke. For a while, the chairman didn't know what to believe. Then he hit on an idea.

Iacocca asked the vice presidents running major departments to pull double duty as the officer overseeing each platform team. Thus Castaing, while remaining head of engineering, would oversee the Jeep and truck development team. Tom Stallkamp, the vice president of purchasing, would take large cars, including the LH, with Gardner reporting to him. Tom Gale, Chrysler's young vice president for design, would get minivans. And Ron Boltz, VP for regulatory affairs, would take small cars.

The idea was to force all the functional bosses to work with the new structure by making them part of it. In a stroke, Iacocca had neutralized a minefield of potential turf battles.

When the LH cars debuted in September 1992, they proved an instant hit. They became for Chrysler a defining moment—what the CVCC engine had been for Honda and what the original Taurus had been for Ford. Iacocca's willingness to accept the judgment of Gardner, Castaing, Lutz, and the young people on the Honda study team was vindicated. At least in theory.

The problem was that, during the 1980s, Detroit had tried dozens of ideas, ranging from diversification to reorganization. But each fad du jour, after showing early success, had flamed out. The way to tell skill from luck was its duration. The real proof of platform teams would lie with Chrysler's next new car, and Bob Marcell.

MARCELL WOULD HAVE the advantage of assembling his PL team from the start of the project, instead of having to put it together in midstream as Gardner had done. And because Gardner had been the first to work with the new structure, Marcell could learn from his experience. Gardner wasn't shy about sharing it. "I think I'm a missionary," he would declare, "but others say I'm a zealot." The others included an appreciative Castaing, who followed Gardner to the podium after one presentation and announced, "Thank you, Reverend Gardner."

Chrysler, in Gardner's view, seemed to plan for failure. That is, it assumed delays and glitches were inevitable, so it provided for plenty of "slip time" in its product-development schedules. Mitsubishi, in contrast, planned for success. It assumed that all drawings and blueprints would be delivered on time. It crash-tested just one prototype car, taking pains to assure that the test—which cost $350,000 to conduct—would provide all the necessary safety data. But Chrysler conducted three separate crash tests, just in case the data from one or two might prove faulty.

Another Gardner revelation was that Mitsubishi delayed decisions on key specifications—such as whether to have air bags—until the last minute, but then allowed no changes once the decisions were made. Chrysler, in contrast, made major decisions early, but then changed them repeatedly along the way as different departments fought turf battles or executives ordered last-minute alterations. The repeated changes were costly, because some parts were designed and tooled several times. They also hurt quality, because Chrysler didn't have prototype cars ready for road testing until sixty-five weeks before the start of mass production. Mitsubishi had cars ready ninety-five weeks beforehand, providing extra time to work out the bugs. Following Gardner's example, Marcell extracted a pledge from senior management not to meddle after approving the PL's parameters.

But Marcell also had one disadvantage that Gardner didn't face: overwhelming pressure to control costs. The LH cars would sell for between $17,000 and $27,000 each, allowing Chrysler to recover its $1.6 billion investment and make a profit if the cars sold even moderately well. But the PL cars, being far smaller, would have to sell for between $9,000 and $13,000, with most about halfway in between. The investment couldn't be that high.

One "solution" would have been to forget about profits, and build the cars simply to satisfy federal gas-mileage standards. That's what GM was doing, albeit unintentionally, with Saturn. GM could never hope to recover its $3.5 billion investment in the cars. But selling high-gas-mileage Saturns allowed the company to sell Cadillacs and other big cars, and still satisfy the required average of 27.5 miles-a-gallon across its overall lineup. Likewise Ford had spent $2 billion to develop the Escort, but counted the losses there as the price to be paid for selling high-profit Lincolns.

Chrysler, though, couldn't afford a loss leader. As Marcell met with his bosses, they decided to limit the PL's development cost, including everything from salaries to machinery, to just $1.3 billion. That wouldn't permit building a new plant, as GM had for Saturn, or totally refurbishing an old one, as Ford had done for Escort. So Chrysler would use an existing factory—the one in Belvidere, Illinois, seventy-five miles northwest of Chicago, where the Dodge Dynasty and Chrysler New Yorker were being built. And it would have to use as much existing machinery as possible.

Reusing machinery had long been heresy at Chrysler. The manufacturing men always had seized on major model changes as a chance to get as many new presses, robots, and other machines as they could. But now Chrysler had a new vice president for manufacturing, Dennis Pawley.

Pawley was a big, burly man with the word "factory" written all over his face. He had started his career at GM in 1965 and wound up at the Pontiac Fiero factory, where he was made plant manager in 1984. At Fiero he had hired young Frank Faga and, like Faga, had convinced himself Detroit had much to learn from the Japanese. But GM didn't want to learn and had little use for people who did. So in 1986 Pawley quit to become the top American at Mazda's U.S. assembly plant in Flat Rock, Michigan.

At Mazda, Pawley was like a sponge, readily absorbing the principles of lean production. Manufacturing had been treated like a necessary evil at GM. At Mazda, in contrast, manufacturing got respect. Unfortunately, in Pawley's view, Americans didn't.

Mazda, because of its ties to Ford, had put its U.S. factory in the UAW's backyard—quite unlike any other Japanese company. Mazda and the union were a marriage of convenience, with predictable results. The two sides clashed bitterly over absenteeism and other issues. The Mazda men's resulting mistrust spilled over to American managers as well as workers. After two years at Flat Rock, Pawley quit to join Otis Elevator Company, leaving the auto industry entirely.

But a year later, in March 1989, Chrysler came calling, and Pawley jumped at the chance to get back in. Two years after that he succeeded the combative Dick Dauch as vice president for manufacturing. It was April 1991, right when the PL was getting formal approval to proceed.

"The hard part of the business is the soft part of the business," Pawley liked to say, referring to the process of motivating people to think beyond their narrow self-interest. Indeed, it was especially difficult in a company where different departments had viewed each other—often more than GM, Ford, or the Japanese—as the competition. But with Pawley in charge, manufacturing people were included in the PL's planning from the start, instead of being brought in later to build what the engineers and designers had cooked up on their own. The results were surprising.

The team members agreed early to make the distance between the PL's front and rear wheels 104 inches long, the same as on the Dynasty and New Yorker. The idea seemed impossible on its face, because the PL would be a much smaller car. But the Dynasty and New Yorker were stretched K-cars, with a long hood and trunk sticking out beyond the front and rear wheels. The PL, with cab forward design, would have smaller overhangs, and devote a much higher portion of the car's overall length to interior space. Thus, using the same wheelbase was feasible. So was reusing all sorts of equipment, notably the sledlike "skids" that carried cars through the assembly process, saving millions of dollars.

The designers, for their part, wanted to leave the PL's windows unframed. The windows would have to roll up and down unsupported, and fit snugly against the roof of the car when rolled up. The design would be strikingly distinctive, especially on a small car.

But it wouldn't be easy to build. The big risk was leaks, which was why manufacturing had resisted any such notion in the past. This time, however, engineering agreed to use a more expensive window-support mechanism in the car's doors. The engineers also tweaked the design of the doors' interior panels to make the glass fit more snugly. Manufacturing gave its approval.

As the give-and-take continued, the manufacturing people got a few new toys after all. For the Dynasty and New Yorker, fenders, hoods, and other stamped-metal parts had been shipped to Belvidere from a Chrysler stamping plant near Cleveland. For the PL cars, Marcell decided to build a small stamping facility adjacent to the Belvidere plant. It would cost $100 million, nearly 8 percent of his project's budget. But it would allow Chrysler to save millions in shipping costs and guarantee higher quality.

Besides, the PL was engineered to make stamping more efficient. Building Chrysler's previous compact cars, the Sundance and Shadow, required 597 dies, the huge steel cookie cutters that stamped out the parts. The PL, though, would need just 370 dies, because it was designed to be built more efficiently. Using fewer dies produced $42 million in savings.

Meanwhile, Pawley asked Belvidere's hourly workers a question many had never heard from management before: "What do you think?" It had taken years for Detroit to learn that asking blue-collar workers for ideas wasn't just a way to be nice to them, but—as the Japanese and then Ford had proved—could produce tangible benefits for the company. Nearly half of Belvidere's workers took trips to Detroit to spend time on a prototype PL assembly line, and offer their suggestions on tooling and manufacturing processes.

In addition, Belvidere workers were organized into such groups as the Rack and Container Team and the Fastener Commonization Task Force. The names sounded comical, but the savings were serious. The container group developed reusable racks, made of metal and plastic, to hold everything from brakes to radiators. Previously, the plant had received most parts in cardboard containers, which had to be shredded and hauled away. Now the need for expensive shredders was virtually eliminated.

The fastener folks suggested using the same size screws and bolts wherever possible, so line workers wouldn't have to constantly switch the drive heads on their tools. On the Dynasty and New Yorker, workers needed seven different drive heads to fasten the door windows into place. For the PL windows they would need just one. Overall, the number of screws and bolts was cut from 530 to 358, because more parts would arrive at the assembly line in one piece—improving quality and lowering production costs.

The PL team made dozens of other efficiency moves, but one in particular stood out. In the past, Chrysler had built slightly different versions of the same car for its Dodge and Plymouth divisions. That way the divisions could pretend to have something unique—just as Ford pretended with the Ford Tempo and Mercury Topaz, and GM did with a whole host of models—even though they really didn't.

Marcell, however, wanted to drop the pretense, and give Dodge and Plymouth the same car with the same name. "If it's really one car, let's don't give it two names," he argued. Eliminating minor differences, which buyers would barely notice anyway, would save millions. And more important, Chrysler could get more bang for its marketing bucks by promoting one model name instead of two. The top brass agreed. The Dodge and Plymouth PL would be the same car with the same name, taken from a bug-eyed futuristic "concept car" the company had unveiled at the Detroit Auto Show in 1991. The name was Neon.

CUTTING COSTS WAS just one challenge for Marcell's team. Hyundai and Yugo had gotten roaring starts with cheap cars in the mid-1980s, only to crash a few years later. It turned out that Americans didn't want just cheap cars. They wanted cheap *good* cars, like those the Japanese had once offered. The PL team's consumer research turned up some intriguing results.

Five years earlier, safety had ranked just sixth or seventh on the list of things that Americans wanted most in a small car. But the latest surveys showed safety—specifically defined as air bags—at or near the top. Fuel economy, while still important, now took a back seat to a term that Chrysler called "fun to drive." Clearly, consumer expectations had risen beyond spartan, sluggish econoboxes.

The trick, then, would be for Chrysler to take some of its savings from investment and manufacturing efficiency, and pass them on to buyers in the form of features—or "content" in car-guy jargon. "Anyone can decontent a car and make it cheap," Marcell would say. "We have to be different."

For starters, the Neon would have driver's- and passenger's-side air bags as standard equipment. The front shoulder belts would be mounted on an adjustable track to provide a comfortable but precise fit for tall and short people alike. The doors would be reinforced to meet the federal side-impact safety standards for 1997, even though the Neon would go on sale three years before that. Antilock brakes, more popular in the North than the South, would be optional instead of standard. But they would be available on even the least expensive versions of the car.

The safety features the Neon needed were fairly obvious, but making the car "fun to drive" was more art than science. Marcell ordered up a new five-speed manual transmission, synchronized for silky shifting so drivers wouldn't have to crunch the transmission into gear, as on Chrysler cars of the past. Likewise, the new steering and suspension would be far more taut than on prior models. Marcell also deemed the 2.2-liter, four-cylinder engine standard on Chrysler's previous small cars to be too sluggish for the Neon. But because developing a more powerful engine would be costly, the PL's power-train engineers mapped out a penny-pinching strategy.

They would develop a new engine based on the architecture of Chrysler's old one. The engineers would use a body, or block, derived from the existing engine, thus minimizing the need for new tooling. But they would give the engine a new top, or head, with four valves per cylinder instead of just two.

The Japanese had used powerful yet efficient multivalve engines on almost all their cars for years. Chrysler was coming late to the party, but better late than never. The new engine would come in two versions, but even the less expensive one would generate 132 horsepower, compared to the paltry 93 horsepower on the base engine in the Sundance and Shadow. Also, the Neon would be nearly 400 pounds lighter than those cars. The combination of less weight and more power meant the five-speed Neon could zip from a standing start to 60 miles an hour in just 8.8 seconds, virtually the same as a Toyota Celica GT coupe. Yet the Neon still would get twenty-eight miles a gallon in city driving, five miles a gallon more than the heavier Celica.

Another goal was giving the Neon a spacious feeling that belied its size. The solution: a "big glass" look that meant large windows all around. That required keeping the car's cowl, or dashboard height, lower than Chrysler had ever done before, to allow space for an oversized windshield. But that, in turn, posed an interior packaging problem. The height of the heating and air-conditioning system had to be compressed —which meant the wiring inside the dashboard had to be routed through precise and narrow channels.

Every decision produced a domino effect, as it did on all cars. The difference this time was that Chrysler could get team members from different departments to sit around the same table and promptly hammer out a solution, which often involved old-fashioned horse trading. When the engine and transmission wound up 10 pounds over their allotted weight limit, the power-train people got the manufacturing men to find weight savings elsewhere. In return, manufacturing was allowed to exceed its budget a bit, partly because the car's interior cost less than projected. Some of the savings came from using molded hard plastic, like that on desktop computers and printers, instead of the more expensive padded plastic found on most cars.

One of the PL team's biggest compromises, however, didn't work out so well. Because of the imperative to make the car both profitable to Chrysler and affordable to consumers, Marcell decided to use Chrysler's existing three-speed automatic transmission, instead of developing a four-speed like the ones on the Toyota Corolla and Honda Civic. Four-speed automatics provided both faster acceleration and better highway fuel economy than three-speeds. Customers who opted for an automatic transmission, as opposed to the Neon's new five-speed manual, would be getting inferior performance.

Nor would the Neon be nearly as quiet as the Corolla, which boasted the quietest interior among subcompact cars. But Toyota's achievement was costly in terms of both the engineering effort and structural components required. The PL team's research showed quietness wasn't crucial among the Neon's target buyers, twenty-six- to thirty-five-year-olds who were likely to be blaring their car radio. Even some Toyota officials deemed the Corolla to be overengineered. The Neon car wouldn't be as quiet. Nor would it carry anywhere near the $17,000 price tag of a top-of-the-line Corolla, even in the most expensive versions.

And the Neon stood at the head of its class in one feature other companies seemed to take lightly—cup holders. These were serious business to young people used to eating on the run, which often meant in their car. The cup holders in a $22,000 Ford Taurus had trouble holding anything bigger than a small Coke from McDonald's. But PL staffers tested 146 different cups at fast-food restaurants ranging from Arby's to White Castle, and virtually everything in between. They developed a design that would hold 80 percent of those cups, even including the Big Gulp soft drinks sold at 7–11 stores. "Now that," Marcell said with pride, "is attention to detail."

One reason the PL program progressed so quickly was that top management kept its pledge not to meddle. Over the years, men like Iacocca
and Lutz had gotten used to waltzing through a design studio and, with
a little wave of the hand, ordering a slight change in the curve of a
fender or a little tweak in the shape of a door handle—simply because it
looked better to them. It mattered not a whit that the engineering was
already completed or the tooling already built. Those things could be
done over and usually were, despite lengthy delays and hefty costs. The
PL, though, was different. Marcell kept top management abreast of his
team's plans, and sought approval for major decisions. But once decisions
got made, they stayed made.

Except for one.

In the spring of 1992, a year into the PL's development, Chrysler's
senior executives gathered at the company's design dome for a "walk-
around." It was a time-honored ritual in which the bosses would walk
around prototypes of the car while asking questions, making comments,
and offering ideas. Iacocca and Lutz were there, along with Castaing,
Pawley, Marcell, styling chief Tom Gale, and a few others.

The Neon, everyone agreed, looked great. The frameless windows
provided a subtle styling cue that gave it a distinctive side profile, even
though at first glance consumers might not know just why the car looked
so different. The tires had been placed out toward the sides of the car,
giving it a look of low-slung stability. The roof profile was properly
aerodynamic. And the headlights were narrow, rectangular slits that
made the Neon's front end look just like the latest small cars from Japan.

And that was just the problem.

Iacocca wanted the Neon to look unmistakably different—not only
from the subpar subcompacts that Chrysler had made in the past, but
also from the current crop of imported small cars he derided as "Japanese
generic." The Neon's face had lost its charm, he thought, in the transformation from a concept car to a real one. "You've lost the cuteness,"
Iacocca complained to his underlings.

It was a bizarre reversal of roles. For years, Gale and Lutz had fought
the chairman's edicts to keep Chrysler's styling stodgy and square. Now,
however, Iacocca was telling them they were being too conservative.
Stranger still, the more they looked at the Neon, the more they agreed
with Iacocca. He suggested using the same large, oval headlights that
had been on the concept car. Everybody quickly agreed. Except, that is,
for Marcell.

"If you say you're going to empower people," Marcell snapped to Lutz, "then you really have to do it." If the bosses insisted on ordering a change, Marcell added, they would be debasing all the new principles— working in teams, trusting subordinates, avoiding meddling from above —that they had been promoting for nearly three years. And besides, Marcell noted, the tooling for the slit headlights was already being built. Changing the design now would increase the cost, he said, and perhaps delay the car.

When Marcell told his own underlings what Iacocca wanted, they were even angrier than he was. The PL program, and perhaps even Chrysler's entire effort to reinvent itself, was facing a crisis.

At that point, Iacocca and his lieutenants did something nobody expected: They backed off. After giving Marcell and his team time to cool down, Lutz and Gale gingerly approached him again. Oval head-lights would evoke the goggle-eyed look of the Volkswagen Beetle, Gale explained to Marcell, and would give the Neon personality. "Can you trust us on this one?" Gale asked. "If you say no, we'll keep the head-lights the way they are, without any recrimination. But please, try to trust us."

Gale was just forty-eight years old, part of a generation that had grown up challenging its elders, and thus was more comfortable with leadership by persuasion than by edict. He was betting Marcell would find it harder to say no to a request than a demand. As for Marcell, he wanted to believe Gale's no-recrimination pledge. But he also knew Iacocca wanted this change badly. And besides, he was beginning to think Iacocca just might be right.

He took Gale's message back to the team, along with an offer from Lutz to meet with the group personally to explain top management's thinking. The team rejected Lutz's offer, but the fact that he had made it helped soften opposition. Marcell, the man in the middle, cajoled his troops to explore how much the change would cost. The final verdict was $7 million in extra tooling costs, instead of the $20 million that some PL staffers had feared.[4] And that extra expense was offset by the lower cost of each headlight, because the round ones were easier to make. The overall effect was a wash, and the executives got their way.

In October 1991, several months after the headlight fracas, Chrysler threw an elaborate dinner for employees to formally dedicate its new technology center thirty miles north of Detroit. Marcell was seated at Iacocca's table. And the chairman, at the risk of raising a sensitive subject, asked about the headlights.

"How did the team take it in the end?" Iacocca inquired. "Has everybody calmed down? Are things okay?"

Later, Marcell couldn't remember how he had responded, but only being impressed that Iacocca had asked. Maybe Iacocca really was serious about change, he thought. Maybe the headlight switch was the exception that proves the rule.

ON SEPTEMBER 5, 1993, Chrysler formally unveiled the Neon to the automotive press and the public. "We think the Neon will be one of the first small cars people will want to buy, instead of have to buy," Bob Lutz proclaimed to a crowded news conference. "There's an old saying in Detroit: 'Good, fast, or cheap. Pick any two.' We refuse to accept that."[5]

Lutz wasn't speaking in Detroit or Los Angeles or New York. Instead he was holding his press conference in Germany, at the biennial Frankfurt Auto Show. Chrysler wasn't simply unveiling a new car. It was making a statement.

In the early 1980s Chrysler had been forced to retreat from international markets. It had sold its operations in Europe as part of Iacocca's desperate effort to raise money to save the company. In 1987 Chrysler had returned to the Continent with a modest export program, shipping mostly minivans and Jeeps from the United States. And in 1992, Chrysler formed a joint venture, dubbed Eurostar, with an Austrian company to build up to 35,000 minivans a year in the city of Graz. All told, between Eurostar and exports from the United States, Chrysler sold 112,000 cars and trucks overseas in 1992, about 5 percent of its total sales. So by the time Iacocca handed Chrysler's helm to Bob Eaton on January 1, 1993, the company had regained the semblance of an international presence.

But Eaton and Lutz wanted more. One of the PL team's objectives was to export 20,000 to 30,000 Neons a year, or up to 10 percent of the Belvidere plant's maximum production capacity. That many cars would barely dent the annual $85 billion U.S. trade deficit in automobiles. But it was enough to make the difference between a car that made money and one that didn't. With the Neon, unlike other Big Three models, exports were a part of the business plan from the start. This was why Chrysler unveiled the car at Frankfurt. And it was a sign of a new mindset in Detroit.

Iacocca may have been famous around the world, but his entire career had been confined to the United States. Eaton and Lutz were different.

Bob Eaton, although not a household name in any country, had run GM Europe for four years. The Swiss-born Lutz, likewise, had been an executive of BMW, and later chairman of Ford of Europe. To them, selling cars outside the United States was more than just a sideshow. The same was true of GM's Jack Smith, who had made his mark running GM Europe and then all of GM's international operations. And of Ford's Alex Trotman, who was British by birth and had run Ford's automotive operations in Europe, the Far East, and North America. The auto industry had gone global with the first oil crisis in 1973. Finally, exactly twenty years later, Detroit was getting its first global CEOs.

Getting truly global products, however, would take longer. Six weeks after the Frankfurt show, Lutz traveled to Tokyo, for the auto show there. The Neon, however, didn't make the trip.

Chrysler, it turned out, didn't have any plans to export the Neon to Japan. Nor was the company planning to produce a right-hand-drive version of the car for Japan, England, or Australia—the three major markets where driving is done on the left side of the road. The company was studying the idea, Lutz said, but hadn't reached a decision.

So Chrysler displayed other vehicles in Tokyo—the Jeep Cherokee, which had recently added a right-drive version, and the LH sedans, which still came in left-drive only. Try as he might, however, Lutz couldn't escape from the Neon glow that Chrysler itself had created. Interest in the Neon among Japanese automotive reporters exceeded anything Chrysler had anticipated. After diplomatically deflecting dozens of questions about why the Neon wasn't being shown, Lutz finally got exasperated. The real reason, he conceded, was simple: "Somebody made a mistake."

Three weeks later, at the Job One ceremony to mark the start of Neon production at Belvidere, Eaton said Chrysler would indeed develop a right-hand-drive version of the car.

JOB ONE CEREMONIES are always full of hype and hoopla, and the Neon's was no exception. "It's really a big day, the right kind of day," a beaming Marcell declared as the ceremony got underway in Belvidere. "The sun is shining."

Indeed, November 10, 1993, was crisp and sunny in northern Illinois. Jim Edgar, the governor of Illinois, was on hand to apply the Neon nameplate to the rear end of the first car to roll off the line. Bob Eaton applied the same nameplate to the front. Then the two hopped into the front seat and drove the car onto a makeshift dais. There it was showered with confetti and streamers as the Belvidere High School marching band struck up the opening bars of Richard Strauss's "Also Sprach Zarathustra," aka the theme from *2001: A Space Odyssey.*

The Neon hadn't even hit the market yet, but already it was drawing rave reviews. The car looked "huggable," automotive reporters opined, thanks largely to the distinctive goggle-eyed headlights. Iacocca's instincts on that point had been right after all. And while the reviews couldn't guarantee sales success, Chrysler clearly had plenty to celebrate. The Neon wasn't the only thing.

In just over two years, between mid-1992 and the fall of 1994, the company was renewing and revitalizing virtually its entire product line. In the spring of 1992 it had launched the Grand Cherokee, a sleek new Jeep with far more creature comforts than the older Cherokee model. The two Jeeps bracketed the Ford Explorer in price—the Grand Cherokee taking the high road and the Cherokee the low—and reasserted Chrysler's leadership in off-road vehicles.

In late 1992 came the LH cars, which gave Chrysler its first modern midsized sedan in more than two decades. GM and Ford needed heavy rebates to sell their midsized sedans, but the LH cars sold without discounts.

In mid-1993, Chrysler launched the new Dodge Ram, its first new full-size pickup truck in twenty years. Full-size pickups, in contrast to their compact cousins, were vehicles that Japan hadn't yet mastered, and thus offered some of the highest profit margins in the industry. The Dodge Ram sported broad-shouldered, muscular front-end styling along with an optional 300-horsepower V-10 engine bigger than anything available from GM or Ford. Chrysler quickly started to cut into a market segment once dominated by its larger rivals.

The Neon went on sale in U.S. showrooms in January 1994 with a base price of just $8,975, far below the Corolla's $12,098. Even fully loaded, the Neon would cost just $12,500, some $4,500 below a comparably equipped Corolla. Chrysler's price advantage was enormous.

Also that January, Chrysler unveiled two more new cars that were nearing introduction. They were compact sedans, code-named JA, that would replace the adequate but uninspiring Dodge Spirit and Plymouth Acclaim, virtually the last two descendants of the K-car. Chrysler was revving up the JA cars for launch in the fall of 1994. The man in charge of their development was Glenn Gardner, whose journey from Mitsubishi to the LH cars had propelled Chrysler toward its latest comeback.

All these vehicles—Grand Cherokee, LH, Dodge Ram, Neon, and JA—provided evidence that Chrysler, at least for the moment, had achieved something beyond the reach of most other car companies: an efficient and repeatable system for turning out hits. Ford still was wrestling with learning the lessons of the Mustang, and GM was struggling to rationalize its engineering organization. The Japanese, for their part, were trying to adjust to the strong yen, in part by reining in engineers who had been reared on a cost-is-no-object mentality.

But Chrysler, which in late 1991 had seemed headed for the same fate as Iron River, had emerged just two years later as the leading symbol of an American renaissance in automobiles. By October 1993, the company's credit rating emerged from two and a half years in junk-bond purgatory and returned to investment grade. In December, Chrysler raised its quarterly dividend by 33 percent, its first such increase in five years. Chrysler shares, which sold for just $9.75 each in the fall of 1991, were fetching $57 apiece in the fall of 1993. It was a 485 percent increase in just two years—enough to turn a $10,000 investment into Chrysler stock worth more than $58,000. Chrysler executives, who had once despaired that their stock options were worthless, cashed in big.

As 1993 unfolded, these executives started worrying about a new problem: getting carried away with their own success. Bob Eaton punched the point home in July, when he assembled 500 top managers to announce that the company had just posted its best second-quarter earnings in a decade.

The chairman then proceeded to read a sampling of glowing press accounts describing Chrysler's turnaround. But just when everyone was feeling good, Eaton added an unexpected and unsettling twist. Every one of the articles he quoted had appeared in the distant past: 1956, 1965, 1976, and 1983. Chrysler had staged a death-defying comeback once a decade for the last forty years. "I've got a better idea," Eaton then declared. "Let's stop getting sick. My personal ambition is to be the first chairman never to lead a Chrysler comeback."[6]

Chrysler had a lot going for it, however, as it faced its newest challenge. It had emerged from its latest crisis as a company dominated by products and processes, not by personalities. It was no small irony that this transformation had occurred under the greatest automotive personality of the era, Lee Iacocca. In the early 1980s Iacocca had caused Chrysler's comeback to happen. But in the early 1990s he had stepped back and allowed it to happen. And that, for him, was far more difficult.

Iacocca continued to loom over Chrysler, but in ways that underscored how much the company had changed. On May 25, 1993, Chrysler joined GM, Ford, and the UAW in hosting a picnic in Washington, right in front of the Capitol, dubbed Drive American Quality. The companies trucked in dozens of new cars and trucks so government VIPs, from President Clinton to congressional staffers, could take test drives before grazing on catered food and chatting with industry and union officials. It was lobbying, Detroit style.

The guests drifted in and out all day. In the early evening Rep. Clifford Stearns, a Republican from Ocala, Florida, dropped by and ran into Bob Eaton.

"I'm Cliff Stearns, member of Congress," the visitor said. "Bob, are you an executive?"

"Yes," Eaton replied. "I'm the chairman of Chrysler."

"Oh," said Stearns, "does that mean you're the chief executive?"

"Yes," said Eaton matter-of-factly. "I am."

Stearns still looked puzzled, which prompted a man standing nearby to chime in with an explanation: "He succeeded Lee Iacocca."

"Ahh!" exclaimed Stearns, Eaton's identity snapping into focus. Then the congressman emitted a respectful echo: "He succeeded Lee Iacocca!"

CHAPTER 20

THE NEW LEADERS

NIGHTTIME DARKNESS and a foot of snow had fallen over Detroit. A cold winter wind sliced through tuxedos and evening gowns in the heart of the city, as sidewalk slush played havoc with high heels and patent-leather shoes. Nearly 10,000 resplendent members of the automotive elite and near-elite wheeled up to the glass front doors of the Cobo Hall Convention Center on January 7, 1994. Once again, it was time for Detroit's biggest gala of the year, the Charity Preview Night that officially opened the North American International Auto Show.

For the new leaders of America's auto industry, this was a moment to savor. Just over four years earlier, in October 1989, the world had gazed in awe at the displays of technological brilliance put on by Japan's auto giants at the Tokyo Motor Show. Americans had fretted then that soon the industry Henry Ford had pioneered would be taken over by Japan. Even a small Japanese company like Mazda could run circles around America's tottering dinosaurs.

How the tables had turned! Just days before the 1994 Charity Night, a floundering Mazda announced it would import three Ford executives into its senior management ranks in what amounted to a rescue mission. Mazda had spent itself out trying to become the next Honda. Now it faced a future as a de facto subsidiary of Ford instead of a fully independent player on the world industrial stage.

Japan's automakers had fallen victim to the age-old delusion that what goes up need not always come down. They'd slipped into the very sins Detroit had indulged—arrogance, pride, and complacency. Even mighty Toyota had overspent on engineering and technology, created too many models, and misjudged consumer tastes with models like the T-100 pickup truck. It offered American buyers less room and less power than a Chevy, but at a higher price.

Detroit was staging a stunning comeback, and America was ready to cheer. Three weeks before the auto show, the cover of *Time* magazine featured the chief executives of General Motors, Ford, and Chrysler standing together, shoulder to shoulder, in a first-ever photograph— gazing into the space ahead as if they were posing for a spot on Mount Rushmore. Now, as caterers poured Champagne for the Preview Night guests, Detroit's newest products gleamed under the perfectly modulated lighting of the display stands. They were cars and trucks America could be proud of.

One was a sleek new minivan from Ford, called Windstar. Nearby stood new Mustangs—the few Ford could spare in the crush of orders for the car. Just weeks earlier, Ford had announced it was gearing up the old Dearborn factory to build up to 200,000 new Mustangs a year, a third more than originally planned. Even GM, for all its turmoil and chaos, displayed a sporty new Monte Carlo coupe and an attractive replacement for its cramped, bumpy-riding, Jeep-fighting Jimmy.

The star of the show was a miraculously revived Chrysler. It had survived everything from the Japanese onslaught to executive-suite in-fighting to the debacle of diversification. At every corner of Chrysler's exhibit areas stood a hit: the Jeep Grand Cherokee, the Dodge Intrepid sedan, the Viper roadster, the burly new Ram pickup, and the Neon.

This party, however, wasn't just about new cars. It was the curtain call for a decade-long global drama complete with tragedy and comedy, hubris and humiliation, heroes and rogues. The auto industry had changed more between 1983 and 1993 than it had since the days of Billy Durant, Henry Ford, Ransom Olds, and the Dodge brothers. The honor of nations, not just the well-being of companies, had been at stake. For in automobiles, as in no other enterprise, Americans and Japanese and Europeans all saw reflections of their national egos. First-class industrial powers had vibrant, home-grown auto industries. Countries that didn't were second-class. Iñaki López, with his twisted hunger to build a car plant in the Basque country, knew that all too well.

There had been times since 1983 when America's car companies seemed headed for the ash heap. GM and Chrysler became all-purpose symbols of American economic decline. Cars were about to join television sets on the list of industries that couldn't compete. The Big Three were seen as bunglers and losers in Washington, on Wall Street, in business schools and universities, and in the entire state of California, where import brands grabbed more than half the market.

Detroit's leaders, for their part, seemed determined to live down to their image. They blamed their troubles on the government, on unfair trade, on brickheaded workers, on snooty American consumers, and —in Ben Bidwell's words—on the "congenital sickos" in the media. Everybody, in short, but themselves. It was the industrial version of the American Disease, in which nobody takes responsibility for any ill that befalls them. It's always somebody else's fault. "Hungry?" snarled one popular Detroit bumper sticker that played on this theme. "Eat your Japanese car."

A funny thing happened, though, on the way to becoming a nation of hamburger flippers. The great irony of the tumultuous decade that preceded the 1994 Detroit Auto Show was that the first to see that Detroit's whiners were wrong were a few enterprising Japanese. It took vision for men like Shoichiro Irimajiri to look at America in the mid-1980s and realize it could be a fabulous place to make cars. Detroit didn't think so. But Irimajiri—and his counterparts at Toyota, Nissan, Mitsubishi, Mazda, Subaru, and Isuzu—took the leap of faith. They transplanted to American soil not only Japanese capital, but a fresh approach to management.

On the eve of the auto show, *Automotive News* predicted that in 1994 America would build more cars and trucks than Japan for the first time in fourteen years. Thus the United States would once again become the leading car-producing nation in the world. But Japan's role in this was underscored by the fact that more than 2 million of the estimated 11.2 million vehicles to be built in the United States would be assembled by Japanese companies, or Japanese-American joint ventures.

Encouraged by Japan's success, the Germans were rejoining the party. Five years after Volkswagen had closed its plant in Pennsylvania, both BMW and Mercedes-Benz were building modern new assembly plants in the southeastern United States. BMW was tapping into Japan's expertise by hiring Al Kinzer and Ed Buker, two of the ablest American executives at Honda's Ohio factories, to run its new facility in South Carolina.

Throughout the 1980s, Detroit's protectionists had clamored for closing America to ideas and investment from abroad. But by 1994 America's openness was paying big dividends. One measure was a resurgence in automotive exports as the Big Three, the Japanese, and the German newcomers looked to America as a cost-effective place to build as many as a million cars and trucks a year for Mexico, Asia, and Europe.[1]

The Japanese, then, had created a new American auto industry, and it was a blessing that they did. Pushed almost to the breaking point by the success of the Japanese, Ford, Chrysler, and finally General Motors, woke up. Detroit decided to join the new American auto industry—led by anonymous men like Steve Bera, Fred Hubacker, Bob Marcell, John Coletti, and Frank Faga. They realized Detroit's old-line leaders were wrong about what ailed their companies and wrong about America.

The 1994 Preview Night found a tuxedo-clad Coletti standing proudly next to the new Mustang. He had just been promoted to head his company's specialty engineering group, responsible for developing high-performance versions of various Ford cars. Job One would be a hot-rod Mustang, with a 32-valve V-8 engine under the hood. Bob Marcell, meanwhile, hovered near the Neon like a proud new father. Nearby, Fred and Margie Hubacker cruised the auto-show floor greeting old friends from Chrysler—including Denny Pawley and Bob and Connie Eaton. Hubacker was doing well at Textron, but there were days when he was wistful to be back at Chrysler again.

Many other actors in this global industrial drama were playing new roles as well. Tom LaSorda, leader of the team that brought GM's Eisenach factory to life, was called back to America in late 1993 and promoted to oversee the three factories that built all the company's luxury cars, including the Hamtramck factory. Thus GM finally gave one of its leading lean-production experts a significant manufacturing role. Frank Faga, the man who trained Eisenach's workers by playing with Lego blocks, moved up, too. In the summer of 1993 he headed for Australia, as production manager at GM's Holden subsidiary there—which built cars for Toyota as well as GM.

Toyota's Bob McCurry, the redoubtable Captain Crunch, finally retired on January 1, 1994. Two years earlier his boss and friend, Yuki Togo, had called him in and declared, "Bob-san, it's time for us to go." At age sixty-eight, McCurry grudgingly gave in, but continued to work part-time in Toyota's Washington, D.C., office.

Steve Bera, who had bailed out of GM to become a management consultant, began 1994 back in the GM fold as a principal in GM/

Electronic Data System's fledgling Management Industry Consulting Practice. Bera's job: helping GM factory managers to make the switch to lean production.

Others left the automotive stage altogether. Jerry York, the West Point graduate who had felt Don Petersen's anger as a young man at Ford, later joined Chrysler, where he rose to become chief financial officer. Then in mid-1993, with Chrysler's comeback underway, the fifty-four-year-old York took the CFO's post at IBM, signing on to help with another corporate turnaround effort. A few months later York brought another former Chrysler finance man, Freddy Zuckerman, to IBM as well.

The high-tech highway of the future also lured Irimajiri, though his was not a rescue mission. In June 1993, fifteen months after quitting Honda, Irimajiri joined Japan's Sega Industries as executive vice president. Sega, maker of such video games as Sonic the Hedgehog and Mortal Kombat, was one of Japan's fastest growing companies, and an upstart challenger to industry-leader Nintendo. For Irimajiri, it was like Honda versus Toyota all over again, thirty years later.

He envisioned a series of "virtual reality" theme parks spanning the globe to provide entertainment experiences that Disney had never dreamed of. He saw an interactive video future in which new games would be delivered on television channels and personal computer networks. And many of those games would be aimed at adults—giving them the "virtual" experience of playing golf at Pebble Beach or driving in a Formula One race at Monaco. Irimajiri, just fifty-three when he joined Sega, was in pole position to become president one day.

Lee Iacocca, transplanted to Southern California, occasionally flew on ordinary commercial airlines. He nixed an offer to become a television talk-show host, and weighed writing another book. Detroit's archprotectionist, the man who spat venom at Japan for daring to exploit America's open markets, became a spokesman for the North American Free Trade Agreement. Just as when he had endorsed air bags, Iacocca sensed it was time to change, and executed the turnabout with style.

Ben Bidwell, Iacocca's long-time sidekick, built a handsome new home in Bloomfield Hills for his retirement years. So did Don Petersen, who divided his time between Bloomfield Hills and his condominium in Rancho Mirage, California, just twenty minutes' drive from Iacocca's place. Petersen remained a director of several major corporations, lectured occasionally at universities, and in 1991 published a book about his management philosophy. It was titled: *A Better Idea.*

Bob Stempel, once leader of the world's largest corporation, struggled against being perceived as a symbol of corporate failure. After his ouster, he set up a small office in suburban Southfield, on the same floor as WLTI radio, an easy-listening station that billed itself as "Detroit's Lite FM." In the days preceding the 1994 Auto Show, Stempel lurked in the back rows during GM press conferences, just as he had done the year before, awkwardly playing the spectator where he had once been the star. He consoled himself—and constantly reminded others—that pieces of his recovery plan for GM had survived under the new regime.

Where Stempel was pitied by the leaders of GM's boardroom revolt, Roger Smith was reviled. Without saying so outright, Jack Smith was tearing down virtually all the monuments to his former mentor's vision of the automated, diversified 21st-century corporation. But Roger Smith, dumped from GM's board, remained devoted to denial. Just weeks before the 1994 Auto Show he sat down to reflect on his record. He contended that GM had prospered mightily under his stewardship.

Smith's flight from reality didn't stop there. He had nothing to do, he maintained, with the accounting maneuvers that helped leave GM with a $24 billion deficit in pension funds that had been fully funded just a few years before. The changes occurred in late 1990, he said, after he had retired.

Except that they didn't. The accounting changes—including the assumption that all retirees would die two years earlier than previously assumed—were made in April 1990, three months before Smith stepped down. Though the changes inflated GM's earnings at the time, ultimately they couldn't hide the depths of GM's disastrous performance in the 1980s.

The aging cars on GM's auto show display stands gave silent testimony to how far GM had to go in its recovery crusade. But there were signs of hope, not least the willingness of GM's new leader, Jack Smith, to say aloud what his predecessors had denied for so long.

"All our difficulties were, in a sense, an overdue wakeup call," Smith acknowledged in a speech just two days after the gala auto show opening. "GM's unrivaled size and success made it easy for us to ignore the significance of change and the signs of potential future problems, as Alfred Sloan himself warned they could when he published his memoirs in 1963. The lesson we've learned is that, for unrivaled leaders, success itself breeds the roots of complacency, myopia, and ultimately, decline."

· · ·

THE CHIEF CHALLENGE for Detroit in 1994 was to keep its comeback in perspective. Reveling in success came all too easily. Even Jack Smith, for all his sober rhetoric, couldn't help exulting: "Detroit's in, Tokyo's out." He was right. The Big Three indeed had renewed themselves. But they also owed more than most Detroit executives would admit to a 20 percent increase in the value of the yen during 1993. This drastic currency shift forced Toyota to raise prices three times that year, boosting the price of the Camry more than $1,400. By the end of 1993, the average Japanese car was nearly $2,000 more expensive than a comparable Big Three model.

Even with that enormous price gap, Japanese brands still captured 23 percent of all car and truck sales in the United States in 1993. Adding in vehicles built by Japanese companies and sold by one of the Big Three, Japanese automakers actually owned more than 26 percent of total U.S. sales. Ten years before, that number had been 20 percent. Japanese companies accounted for 17 percent of all the cars and trucks built in America in 1993, up from just 2 percent a decade earlier.[2] Any doubts about Japan's continuing competitive viability could be swept aside by one look at the massive addition that Toyota completed during 1993 at its factory in Kentucky. The new assembly line would build the new Avalon, a full-sized sedan aimed straight at people who might otherwise buy Buicks. And Toyota had $35 billion in the bank to tide it over the hard times.[3]

Ultimately, the big winner in the global car wars wasn't Detroit or Japan. Instead, it was the American consumer. Anyone shopping for a car in America from 1994 onward would find a stunning array of high-quality choices. In the early 1980s, only the most expensive cars offered air bags or antilock brakes. By 1994, virtually every car, and many trucks, came with air bags as standard equipment, and antilock brakes either standard or readily available.

Instead of underpowered boxes on wheels, Americans could find cars like the Dodge/Plymouth Neon and Nissan Altima, with fluid, imaginative designs and peppy, efficient engines. And both were made in America. So were the Nissan Quest and Mercury Villager—slightly different versions of the same minivan, designed and engineered by Nissan and built by Ford in Avon Lake, Ohio. Was it American or was it Japanese? The question was ludicrous, and the answer impossible. It was proof that the auto industry in 1994 stood on the verge of a new form of global competition—one in which competitors would be defined not by their country of origin, but by the strength of their products. And by how they met a new set of challenges.

In smoggy Southern California, movie stars and displaced aerospace engineers zipped around in electric cars, and challenged car companies to put more nonpolluting vehicles on the market. In Europe, governments demanded cars that could be completely recycled with nothing left for the scrapyard. And all around the world, advances in computer and communications technology made it possible for millions of people to commute to work on highways made not of asphalt, but of fiberoptic cable. These were challenges for automakers of all nations. The companies could complain about demands for costly, "clean" vehicles, and they could ignore the impact of digital, interactive technology on the way people worked and played. But they would do so at risk of being left behind.

Which is exactly what happened to tens of thousands of American auto workers during the 1980s. They were flushed out of the industry, as low-skilled, high-wage jobs in ill-managed factories disappeared. The same went for thousands of salaried workers whose by-the-book existences were turned upside down as big corporations slashed away at their bureaucracies. Theirs were stories of broken dreams and often of broken families.

For those who survived, however, the road ahead pointed to a better future. Once, working in an American auto factory had meant signing up for a cruel bargain: Leave your brain at the door, spend thirty years doing mindless repetitive work, and you'll have the money to send your children to college so they don't have to live your life.

By 1994, millions of American factory workers—at the Big Three, at Japanese factories in the United States, and in thousands of tributary companies—were encountering the invigorating new system pioneered by Honda in Ohio and by Toyota at Nummi. Managers were, at long last, recognizing that the men and women on their assembly lines weren't machines or children who had to be ordered around. They had knowledge and ideas to be put to use.

Unchaining blue-collar workers from the stupefying grind of the old mass-production system—epitomized by Vega production at Lordstown —wouldn't promise them or their bosses easy lives. People who had chosen factory work precisely because it posed no intellectual challenges were finding the new ways disorienting and uncomfortable. So were many of their white-collar counterparts who had grown used to lives as corporate civil servants. For them, global competition meant jobs with less security, but with more opportunity to play meaningful roles at their companies.

The great paradox was that the foreign force that had almost destroyed Detroit ultimately helped save it. In 1993, for the first time ever, Detroit got new leaders who understood this. Jack Smith, Alex Trotman, and Bob Eaton had both international experience and horizons that extended beyond the Bloomfield Hills Country Club.

Detroit's awakening had come not a moment too soon. The global competition that would face GM, Ford, and Chrysler during the coming years would be unforgiving of relapses into the old ways. But America no longer seemed destined to walk the path taken by Britain, which had seen virtually all of its automakers pass into foreign ownership, culminating in February 1994 with the purchase of Rover by Germany's BMW.

Instead, Detroit had earned a second chance with cars such as the Dodge Stratus and Chrysler Cirrus. These hot-looking numbers, unveiled by Chrysler at the Detroit Auto Show, were just two of a wave of family sedans the Big Three planned to launch in 1994 to take on the Honda Accord and Toyota Camry. Once, it seemed that Chrysler had lost the ability to design good-looking cars. Now, here were two great-looking cars, ready for production. As crowds of people gathered to admire Chrysler's handiwork, a Toyota executive gave the new models a close inspection.

"Serious competition," the Toyota man muttered at last. "Serious competition."

CHAPTER 21

LIDO RIDES AGAIN

Lᴇᴇ Iᴀᴄᴏᴄᴄᴀ's second book, *Talking Straight,* was a rambling discourse on many things in American life, including the corporate raiders who made billions in the 1980s by buying and reselling companies. Iacocca heartily criticized financial buccaneers who would swoop in on a company afflicted with a low stock price, borrow heavily to buy control, and kill the company's future by cutting costs and selling assets to pay off their debt. "I see billions of dollars tied up in new corporate debt to keep the raiders at bay while research and development goes begging," Iacocca wrote in the book, published in 1988. "I see billions going for greenmail, dollars that ought to be building new high-tech factories. . . . But I don't see the raiders creating jobs. I don't see them boosting productivity. And worst of all, I don't see them doing anything to help America compete in the world."[1]

He went on: "You see, the typical takeover target isn't a company in trouble. It's a company with a solid asset base, low debt, consistent profits, and a few bucks in the bank to help it get through the next business downturn."[2]

That description precisely fit Chrysler in the spring of 1995. Except that Iacocca's old company had more than a few bucks in the bank. Its string of new-product hits, combined with improving factory efficiency, a booming American car market, and an ever-surging yen that kept Japan on the defensive, had produced a whopping $7.5 billion larder—even after the company had funded its employee-pension plan fully for the first time in decades. Chairman Bob Eaton said the cash hoard was intended to help Chrysler weather the next recession without almost going bankrupt again, as had happened in every recession since World War II. In short, Eaton was following Iacocca's own prescription. How ironic, then, that Iacocca in retirement would turn into a corporate raider in a bizarre effort to climb back into the driver's seat at Chrysler.

AFTER BEING EASED into a gilded but reluctant retirement at the end of 1992, Iacocca was a restless man. There simply had to be more to retirement, he would tell friends, than golf and gin rummy. So Iacocca went looking for ways to keep active in business. He invested in bringing a production of *Will Rogers' Follies*, with Pat Boone as the star, to a theater in Branson, Missouri, a town establishing itself as a country music mecca. The show was a box office flop, despite Iacocca's opening night cameo appearance, in which he sprang up from the audience and said, "Let's go flying, Will." Iacocca also joined the board of directors of MGM Grand at the behest of the man who controlled MGM, the billionaire investor Kirk Kerkorian. Kerkorian also happened to be the largest Chrysler shareholder.

In 1990, with Chrysler in crisis, Kerkorian had shelled out $272 million to buy nearly 10 percent of Chrysler's stock at an average price of just $12.37 a share—about one-fourth their value of just three years earlier. The move sent Iacocca into a mild state of panic. He quickly beefed up Chrysler's bylaws with a "poison pill" takeover defense that would dilute Kerkorian's holdings greatly if he continued to buy Chrysler stock.

From that rocky start, however, Kerkorian and Iacocca had grown to be good friends. Kerkorian assured Iacocca that his intentions weren't hostile, and proved good to his word. In fact, he was a fervent admirer of Iacocca. Like Iacocca, Kerkorian was a mercurial self-made man who liked to play by his own rules. A one-time pilot, Kerkorian had launched his fortune right after World War II by flying gamblers in and out of Las Vegas. In the 1960s, setting the pattern for his career as an opportunistic financier, Kerkorian sold his airline, bought it back, took it public, and sold it again for $104 million. In 1969 he acquired 30 percent of Western

Airlines in a hostile transaction, and then proceeeded to buy one hotel-casino in Las Vegas (the Flamingo) and build another one (the International, then the largest casino in the world). Then Kerkorian went Hollywood, buying major holdings in both MGM and Columbia Pictures, before selling both stakes a few years later for huge profits. His MGM deals alone—complex transactions carried out over several years—yielded him profits of about $1 billion.

In 1992, having won Iacocca's friendship, Kerkorian hosted the Chrysler chairman on his yacht off Barcelona during the summer Olympics in that city. A few weeks later, after having been egged on by Iacocca, Kerkorian lobbied the Chrysler board to give Iacocca a significant role in company affairs after his pending retirement. Kerkorian was politely but firmly rebuffed. After Iacocca retired, and then resigned from Chrysler's board of directors in September 1993, he and Kerkorian grew closer.

If Kerkorian was taken with Iacocca, Iacocca was smitten with Kerkorian's business: casino gambling. The early 1990s were a time of tremendous growth for Las Vegas and for gambling all around America. Liberal state laws allowed casinos on the Mississippi River in several states and on the Mississippi Gulf Coast. Indian tribes established casinos on tribal lands in the Upper Midwest and Pacific Northwest. Iacocca decided to get in on the action.

With a couple of rich associates, he hatched a plan to finance a casino for the Coquille Indian tribe on the site of an abandoned pulp mill on tribal land in North Bend, Oregon. So, in late 1994 he cruised into the down-and-out lumber town in a chauffeured limousine (a Cadillac, not a Chrysler) to promote the idea—promising a thousand jobs for the community and a rich take for the Coquilles. Alas, Iacocca ran into a coalition of opponents: local ministers, folks who had moved to North Bend to escape the seamier sides of civilization, and even rival Indians who claimed that the Coquilles weren't a true tribe.[3] Iacocca wound up mired in a backwoods controversy and looking slightly silly.

KERKORIAN, meanwhile, had hit the jackpot on a big gamble of his own: his 1990 investment in Chrysler stock. By early 1994 the shares he had purchased for $12.37 each had soared above $60, giving him a profit of 400 percent and adding another $1 billion to his fortune. But then the Federal Reserve board started raising U.S. interest rates to damp the threat of renewed inflation. The month-by-month rate hikes weren't enough to send car sales into an outright tailspin, but they made investors nervous enough to cast a pall over auto stocks. Afer hitting a year-long high of $63.50 a share in January, Chrysler's stock closed 1994 at just $49. By March of 1995 the stock was trading as low as $38.25. Kirk Kerkorian was not a happy man.

Neither was Iacocca, who was encountering problems that hit closer to home than the protests against his presence in the Northwest woods. In late 1994, he and his third wife, Darrien, sued each other for divorce. Darrien's suit accused Iacocca of hiring guards to spy on her in their mansion in Beverly Hills—a charge that Iacocca denied.[4] The bottom line, though, was that the breakup of his marriage left Iacocca more restless than ever, with plenty of time on his hands. He and Kerkorian, both septuagenarians, constituted a combustible duo.

ON APRIL 12, 1995, four days before Easter, Kerkorian and Iacocca issued a press release stating that they wanted "to provide Chrysler's shareholders with a substantial premium for their shares." To accomplish this, they proposed to buy the company by paying shareholders $55 a share, or a total of $20 billion.

It was a blockbuster announcement. The deal would be the second largest corporate buyout in U.S. history—trailing only the $30.6 billion acquisition of RJR Nabisco in 1988 that marked the height of the corporate takeover craze. Chrysler's shares surged on the news, ending a frantic day of trading at $48.75 a share, up 24 percent from the previous day's closing price of $39.25. Up and down Wall Street, investment bankers held marathon meetings to figure out how to get in on the action. Speculators immediately began guessing that the Kerkorian–Iacocca offer would attract even higher bids from foreign car companies—Renault, perhaps, or Volkswagen, Fiat, and maybe even Toyota. The Iacocca–Kerkorian announcement made front-page news, not just in the *New York Times* and the *Wall Street Journal,* but in newspapers across the country.

After the announcement, Iacocca told interviewers that he really wasn't interested in running Chrysler again, but instead would act as a "consultant"[5] to management under the new regime. That statement drew derision inside Chrysler, where executives and board members had been only too happy to see Iacocca depart peacefully two years earlier.

Chrysler soon issued a statement saying it was reconsidering plans to name its new corporate headquarters in Auburn Hills, Michigan, some thirty miles north of Detroit, the Lee Iacocca Center.

Iacocca's disclaimer also drew titters elsewhere around Detroit, where men who had known him for years had no doubt that Iacocca desperately missed the Four P's—power, podium, perks, and pay—that came with running a big car company. Iacocca's access to the Chrysler corporate jet, after all, had ended less than four months earlier.

Kerkorian's operatives quietly had signaled his intentions to Chrysler executives beforehand, but they nonetheless seemed taken by surprise. Bob Eaton canceled a speech at the New York Auto Show to fly back to Detroit, convened a hasty board meeting via telephone, and issued a staement saying the company was "not for sale." He added: "We don't want to put Chrysler at risk. We've worked hard to build this company's financial strength, to increase shareholder value, and to build the confidence of customers, employees, dealers, and suppliers. We have no desire to reverse the process."[6]

His desires notwithstanding, Eaton seemed to be in a tough spot. Kirk Kerkorian wasn't the only Chrysler shareholder frustrated with the stock's decline despite the company's record results. Inside Chrysler, executives privately assessed Kerkorian's odds of success at better than 50–50. Outsiders speculated that Eaton would have to do something: sharply raise Chrysler's dividend, spend at least $5 billion from its cash kitty on a massive share repurchase, look for an alternative buyer (such as Volkswagen or Renault), or line up the money for a management-led buyout that excluded Kerkorian. There was another, albeit decidedly risky, possibility as well: Just say no.

IN ALL THE HOOPLA surrounding the announcement of the Kerkorian–Iacocca move, one thing was largely overlooked: Kerkorian hadn't lined up the money in advance to complete what he had begun. That's standard practice in the takeover game, but Kerkorian and Iacocca didn't want word of their intentions to leak out in advance. Indeed, they succeeded in keeping a lid on their plans. But after the offer was announced, Kerkorian was like any other supplicant who has to go down to his bank and ask for a loan.

For it was he, not Iacocca, who was putting up the money. Iacocca willingly lent his name to the quest to buy Chrysler, but his only financial contribution was the $50 million of Chrysler stock that he already owned. Kerkorian's Chrysler shares, if valued at $55 each, would be worth nearly $2 billion. But he still needed $20 billion more.

To cover the shortfall, Kerkorian proposed to take $5 billion out of Chrysler's coffers. Then he would raise another $3 billion from a select group of private investors—players yet to be named. Finally, Kerkorian proposed to borrow $12 billion from banks, and pay the interest on the huge debt load by suspending dividends on Chrysler stock. It was a plan that depended on a lot of different things falling into place. And a plan that gave Chrysler's management lots of room to attack.

Chrysler had lines of credit and other business relationships with most major commercial banks in America, as well as with some of the biggest investment banks on Wall Street. Eaton's underlings began spreading the word that if the lenders and financiers wanted to keep their profitable business with Chrysler intact, they had better not help the Kerkorian takeover effort.

Besides, the Chrysler men noted, lending to Kerkorian could be risky if the banks wanted to get repaid. Chrysler always had led a boom-bust existence, and now its bulging bank account offered a chance to break that cycle. Chrysler needed $2–$2.5 billion to run its daily affairs, company executives offered, and the other $5 billion was the cushion that would let Chrysler get through a recession without cutting back the product-development programs that were the key to long-term prosperity. Bankers holding debt in a Chrysler stripped of financial staying power would be left holding an empty bag if the company couldn't survive a recession.

While Chrysler was deploying both muscle and logic, it was getting some unexpected assistance from the Kerkorian–Iacocca camp. Alex Yemenidjian, a spokesman for the reclusive Kerkorian, was hard-pressed to offer a coherent vision of how Kerkorian and Iacocca could improve on Chrysler's recent results. "I think they're excellent," Yemenidjian said of Bob Eaton's management team, "and I think there's a level above that called fabulous."[7] Yemenidjian got even mushier when he rhapsodized about how a new management team would seek global alliances with foreign car companies. To veteran auto analysts, it brought back memories of the days when Iacocca tried to negotiate alliances as a substitute for developing new cars.

Iacocca, meanwhile, seemed driven more by postretirement boredom than by any new vision for the company he once ran. "There's a whole third of your life, twenty to thirty years that God has given us," he told the *Wall Street Journal* the day the takeover offer was announced. "And what the hell do you do? You can't just read or play golf for twenty years."[8] It wasn't the sort of thing to persuade bankers to part with billions.

CHRYSLER'S "JUST SAY NO" defense worked. Kerkorian and Iacocca couldn't raise anywhere close to $20 billion. By the time Chrysler shareholders convened in St. Louis on May 18, 1995, for the company's annual meeting, the offer was a dead issue—at least for the time being. Chrysler's board raised the dividend 25 percent to an annual rate of $2 a share, but Kerkorian—who didn't attend the meeting—issued word that he was far from satisfied. Chrysler's stock dropped 1⅛ that day to close at $42.63—a few dollars above its price before the takeover offer was announced, but not much. Chairman Eaton, asked afterward by reporters about Iacocca's involvement, said he was "very disappointed."[9]

Kerkorian wasn't gone for good. In June he offered to buy another $700 million of Chrysler shares to raise his stake in the company to 13.6 percent. Meanwhile, the major damage from the affair was to Iacocca's reputation. His bald contradiction of the beliefs he had stated in *Talking Straight* came as little surprise to people who knew Iacocca well. Consistency had never been the strong suit for a man who had railed against Japanese imports whlie himself importing Japanese engines and steel to build Chrysler cars. But the takeover effort cast Iacocca as a greedy, self-serving man who simply couldn't let go. The Old Lion had tried to stalk back onto Detroit's stage, but had been firmly turned away.

AFTERWORD

THE 1994 DETROIT AUTO SHOW proved to be the kickoff to a banner year for the Big Three. General Motors, Ford, and Chrysler raked in a cumulative $13.92 billion in profits in 1994, an all-time record that may not be equaled again soon. Early 1995 brought a slowing of the U.S. economy that, while far short of a recession, prompted the Big Three to trim production and—mercifully for the consumers—ante up discounts to offset partly the big price hikes they had put through during the 1994 boom. It was yet the latest reminder that Detroit's fortunes always will swing with the cycles of the American economy.

The slowdown also raised a question that is central to the theme of this book: To what extent was the Big Three's remarkable comeback the product of simple good luck: a U.S. economy that boomed while Japan struggled to recover from its deepest postwar recession and the seemingly contradictory plunge of the dollar on the international currency markets? In early 1995 the dollar dropped to below eighty-five yen, barely more than one-third its value versus the Japanese currency a decade earlier. Much to Detroit's delight, the Japanese car companies were forced to keep raising prices to offset the dollar's decline. Yet the Japanese managed to hang on to their share of the U.S. market, if not to their once robust American profits.

Detroit's comeback, no doubt, was aided by good fortune, just as the bad luck of a strong dollar had accelerated its decline in the mid-1980s. But the events described in this book were propelled by forces far more fundamental than economic swings and currency fluctuations. It takes looking again at how bad Detroit was in 1983 to see that those external factors don't explain everything. The yen's rise didn't cause the huge productivity increases in American automobile factories, or the quantum leap in the quality of Big Three vehicles, or Chrysler's remarkable transformation from industrial basket case to the company with the highest profits per vehicle in the world. Those things happened because the American automobile industry, thanks to intense Japanese competition, took a painfully profound look at itself and began a far-reaching overhaul of nearly every aspect of its business.

The process isn't finished—or at least it shouldn't be. And things will not always, or even often, go smoothly. There will be lots of backsliding, particularly in times of prosperity, because old habits die hard. Certainly, Big Three executives still can't help yearning for relief from Japanese competition. When Washington threatened in May 1995 to slap huge tariffs on Japanese luxury cars as a penalty for Tokyo's refusal to "open" the Japanese market to American cars and parts, Detroit cheered the politicians on. Never mind that more than a decade of get-tough posturing toward Japan hadn't really protected the Big Three at home—or dramatically increased sales of their U.S.-made vehicles in Japan. The idea that a Lexus LS400 might suddenly cost more than $100,000 was a dream come true for Cadillac and Lincoln. Anyone with an understanding of the history of the 1980s, however, knew it was time to start planning for an American-made Lexus.

But Detroit's rivals can see the difference that a dozen years of upheaval and renewal has produced. "Now Detroit is the benchmark," Jurgen Hubbert, the head of Mercedes-Benz's automotive operations, declared to *New York Times* reporter James Bennet in March 1995.[1] It was a remarkable statement. But it was no more remarkable than the spectacle of once celebrated Japanese automakers Nissan and Mazda bleeding red ink and struggling to copy Detroit's cost-cutting success. Even Toyota and Honda, though healthy financially, groped to comprehend the new American idea of a "truck," as defined by Detroit's hugely popular minivans, four-wheel-drive vehicles, and pickups. Japan's versions of these new types of trucks kept missing the mark—and so boosting Detroit's revival.

But if Japan's car companies have had reason to regret their former hubris, Detroit's automakers have little room to gloat. For one thing, by 1995, the term "American auto industry" meant more than just Detroit.

Mercedes-Benz, at this writing, is preparing to open a new assembly plant in Alabama to build luxury four-wheel-drive vehicles. When the factory does open, twelve different companies will be building cars and trucks in the United States—more than at any time since the early years of this century. Of the twelve, three (GM, Ford, and Chrysler) are U.S.-based companies. Another seven (Toyota, Nissan, Honda, Mitsubishi, Mazda, Isuzu, and Subaru) have their headquarters in Japan. And two (BMW and Mercedes) are based in Germany. It's proof that America, despite its evolution toward a service economy, is once again a great place to make things—thanks to a broad and historic revival of American manufacturing that was led, in many respects, by the Japanese automakers. The men and women who worked in the American auto industry (whether their company was American, Japanese, or German) in the 1980s and early 1990s helped make industrial history. If they didn't know it at the time, perhaps they were too close to the action.

It doesn't diminish Detroit's achievement to note that a comeback is different from a victory. The Big Three must continue the kinds of efforts that produced the new Mustang and led General Motors in 1994 to its first profit from North American auto operations since 1989. But the road ahead won't be easy.

Ford will face a huge challenge in the late 1990s as it tries to follow Chairman Alex Trotman's bold plan to make the whole company work on "Mustang timing." Under a sweeping reorganization dubbed "Ford 2000," Trotman is merging Ford's once-distinct U.S. and European engineering operations into a global entity tied together with supercomputers and satellite communications. The idea is to eliminate duplication by developing "world cars" that can be sold from Oshkosh to Osaka.

But grand redesigns are fraught with risk, as Trotman knows from his study of the disastrous effects of Roger Smith's equally ambitious reorganization of General Motors in 1984. That effort to produce a "21st-century corporation" produced such mass confusion that, at the time, GM managers joked grimly about imploring their secretaries: "If my boss calls, please get his name." Ford 2000 must dodge myriad bureaucratic and technical obstacles, as well as the possibility that consumers might not want the same car as someone on the other side of the world.

At Chrysler, where Detroit's comeback has been most spectacular, the near term challenge is to kill the quality gremlins that have bedeviled its stylish new cars and trucks. Longer term, the company must stay nimble enough to see the next trend before the rest of the pack, particularly as the baby boomers who made its minivans and Jeeps so profitable begin to age—and to look for new kinds of transportation. And as the Detroit company with the smallest presence overseas, Chrysler must retain the financial staying power to survive the next U.S. recession and the likelihood that one day the dollar will regain some of its lost value.

Perhaps the toughest hurdles await General Motors. The United Auto Workers and GM seem fated to continue their costly warfare over layoffs and labor costs, slowing a restructuring effort that already is far too slow. Moreover, CEO Jack Smith's effort to create a new GM, following the lessons of Toyota, must confront the realities of too many redundant divisions, too many redundant models, and too many managers with little appetite for "doing the unexpected" after years of tumult, firings, and fear. Even as the rest of Detroit reveled in the comeback year of 1994, GM suffered again and again the punishments for having waited too long to attack its ills. Perhaps nowhere was the pain so public as at Lordstown.

There, in Ohio, in the fall of 1994, production of the long-awaited new Chevy Cavalier started. Then stopped. Then started. Then stopped again. Despite months of planning and preparation, the switch from GM's old mass production system to the Nummi methods championed by Jack Smith and his lieutenants taxed managers and workers to their limits—and beyond. By early 1995, the plant was still running well below capacity and well behind schedule. The cars that did get built were far better than any built before—with high enough quality to keep alive Smith's deal to ship some to Japan for sale under the Toyota nameplate. But only when GM can begin to get it all right—high quality at high production rates—will the company begin to realize its potential to become a global leader again.

In 1995 the ironic truth remained that the biggest danger to Detroit's success is its very success. If the 1980s taught anything, it is that arrogance and complacency, confusing comeback with victory, pave the road to ruin. It will not be easy for American car companies to follow the signposts toward growth opportunities: plunging into emerging economies in China, India, Thailand, Poland, or Russia. It won't be easy to pursue new technologies, such as natural gas or electric-powered vehicles, that will push engineers well outside their "comfort zones." And as the American companies try to become more aggressive global players, they will find old rivals from Europe and Japan striving to produce comebacks of their own.

But in a volatile global economy, the winners will be the players that adapt quickly when the world turns upside down. And there, the American car companies should have a big advantage. They know how that feels better than anyone else in the business.

—JBW and PI, May 1995

TIMELINE FOR *COMEBACK*

1981

- January—Roger Smith becomes chairman and CEO of General Motors.

1982

- November—Honda opens the first Japanese car assembly plant in America in Marysville, Ohio.

1983

- February—GM and Toyota form New United Motor Manufacturing Inc., a joint venture to build cars in California.
- June—Bennett E. Bidwell joins Chrysler as executive vice president, sales and marketing.
- August—Chrysler repays its government-guaranteed loans, seven years early.
- August—*Fortune* magazine cover shows GM's Chevy Celebrity, Pontiac 6000, Olds Cutlass Ciera, and Buick Century looking virtually identical.
- October—Chrysler introduces the first minivan.
- October—GM introduces the Pontiac Fiero.

1984

- January—Roger Smith announces sweeping reorganization of GM.
- February—Chrysler resumes dividends for the first time since 1979.
- May—GM purchasing manager Steve Bera starts work at NUMMI.
- June—GM agrees to buy Electronic Data Systems for $2.55 billion.
- June—Honda taps Shoichiro Irimajiri to head U.S. manufacturing.
- November—Bob McCurry becomes Toyota's U.S. sales chief.
- December—GM and Toyota build first cars at NUMMI.

1985

- February—Donald Petersen becomes chairman and CEO of Ford.
- June—GM agrees to buy Hughes Aircraft for $5.1 billion.
- June—Chrysler agrees to buy Gulfstream for $636 million.
- September—GM opens high-tech "Poletown" assembly plant in Detroit.
- October—Ford airs "Valet" television commercial, a parody of GM's lookalike cars.
- November—Lee Iacocca reorganizes Chrysler into holding company consisting of Chrysler Motors, Chrysler Aerospace, Chrysler Financial, and Chrysler Technologies.
- December—Steve Bera quits General Motors.
- December—Ford Taurus and Mercury Sable are introduced.

1986

- April—Honda launches Acura, first Japanese luxury nameplate.
- May—Bob Lutz leaves Ford to join Chrysler as executive vice president.
- June—GM holds gloomy "Techbrier" management conference in Detroit.
- November—GM says it will close nine factories and parts of two others, eliminating nearly 30,000 jobs.
- December—GM agrees to buy H. Ross Perot's shares in the company for $700 million in return for Perot's resignation from the GM board.

1987

- February—Ford reports 1986 earnings of $3.3 billion, exceeding GM's for the first time in sixty-two years.

- March—Chrysler agrees to buy American Motors (Jeep) for $1.1 billion.
- September—Bob Stempel becomes president and chief operating officer of GM.
- September—Henry Ford II dies.
- October—GM introduces Buick Regal, first of its $7 billion line of mid-sized cars code-named GM-10.

1988

- January—GM opens "Teamwork and Technology" exhibit in Waldorf-Astoria Hotel.
- January—Chrysler says it will close the American Motors factory in Kenosha, Wisconsin.
- March—GM announces it will kill the Pontiac Fiero.
- May—GM executive vice president Elmer Johnson resigns.
- October—GM's "people power" management conference in Traverse City, Mighigan.

1989

- February—Ford's 1988 earnings beat GM's for third straight year.
- May—Tony Kuchta, leader of Ford's Thunderbird team, takes early retirement. Edsel Ford II and William C. Ford Jr. get key board committee posts.
- October—Spectacular Tokyo Motor Show displays Japan's automotive dominance; Soicihiro Honda inducted to U.S. Automotive Hall of Fame.
- November—Ford acquires Jaguar for $2.5 billion.
- November—Don Petersen announces early retirement as chairman and CEO of Ford.
- November—Chrysler kills the ill-fated TC by Maserati, announces closing of its Jefferson Avenue plant in Detroit, and scraps its holding-company structure.

1990

- January—Honda Accord becomes top-selling car in United States, the first time for a foreign nameplate.
- February—Chrysler announces third assembly plant closing in fifteen months and posts largest quarterly loss ($664 million) in its history.
- March—GM signs pact to build cars in Eisenach, eastern Germany.
- May—Nobuhiko Kawamoto named president of Honda, beating Irimajiri for top job.
- May—Gerald Greenwald, Iacocca's heir apparent at Chrysler, quits.
- June—Hoot McInerney opens Toyota store in suburban Detroit UAW stronghold.
- July—Roger Smith drives first Saturn car off the assembly line.
- August—Bob Stempel succeeds Smith as chairman and CEO of GM.
- November—Stempel orders $2.1 billion write-off, largest in GM's history, to close seven assembly plants.

1991

- February—Honda cuts U.S. production plans for first time ever.
- March—Tom LaSorda becomes GM plant manager at Eisenach, Germany.
- May—Roger Penske declines chance to succeed Lee Iacocca at Chrysler.
- November—Fred Hubacker sends Iacocca a private letter, suggesting Robert Eaton as Iacocca's successor.
- November—Standard & Poor's announces that it may downgrade A-1 credit rating of General Motors finance unit.
- December—Bob Stempel announces GM will close twenty-one more factories, eliminating 74,000 more jobs by 1995.

1992

- January—GM board authorizes director John Smale to conduct independent review of company; board attorney Ira Millstein tells Stempel board wants decisive action.
- February—GM posts record $4.45 billion loss for 1991.
- February—R. S. Miller, Jr., a potential successor to Iacocca at Chrysler, quits.

- March—Chrysler board chooses Bob Eaten to succeed Iacocca.
- April—GM board demotes president Lloyd Reuss and installs Smale as chairman of the executive committee.
- May—J. Ignacio López becomes GM's global purchasing czar.
- May—Shoichiro Irimajiri resigns from Honda.
- September—GM launches production at Eisenach, Germany plant.
- October—Bob Stempel resigns as Chairman and CEO of GM.
- November—GM names Smale nonexecutive chairman, John F. Smith, Jr., president and CEO.
- December—Lee Iacocca retires.

1993

- January—Taurus ends Accord's three-year reign as top-selling U.S. car.
- February—Nissan announces first Japanese car-plant closing since World War II.
- March—Fred Hubacker leaves Chrysler to join Textron.
- March—J. Ignacio López quits GM, agrees to stay, then quits again to join Volkswagen, prompting GM probe of missing documents.
- April—Roger Smith resigns from GM board of directors.
- June—S. Irimajiri joins Sega Industries as executive vice president.
- September—Chrysler introduces Dodge/Plymouth Neon.
- October—Ford launches new Mustang; names Alex Trotman chairman and CEO.
- December—GM announces deal to build cars for Toyota in Lordstown, Ohio, plant.

1994

- January—Festive Detroit Auto Show highlights Big Three's comeback.
- December—Bit Three close year of record profits.

1995

- April—Kirk Kerkorian and Lee Iacocca announce $20 billion bid for Chrysler.
- May—Kerkorian-Iacocca bid for Chrysler collapses.

ACKNOWLEDGMENTS

WE OWE CONSIDERABLE DEBTS to colleagues at the *Wall Street Journal* and at Dow Jones & Co., in some cases for information and in other cases for encouragement and resources used during our two years researching and writing this book. Norman Pearlstine was instrumental in launching this project when he was managing editor of the *Journal*. His successor, Paul Steiger, was equally generous in allowing us time and resources to complete our work. A special thanks to Charles B. Camp. As a member of the *Journal*'s Detroit bureau from 1967 to 1981, and bureau chief from 1974 to 1981, Chuck established an approach to covering the auto industry that continues at the *Journal* to this day.

We want to thank past and present colleagues in the Detroit bureau of the *Journal*: John Bussey, Melinda Grenier, Doug Lavin, Krystal Miller, Jacqueline Mitchell, Amal Kumar Naj, Gregory Patterson, Linda Griswell, Andrea Puchalsky, Jacob Schlesinger, Bob Simison, Oscar Suris, Bradley Stertz, and Neal Templin. Reporting by Doron Levin and Dale Buss, who left the *Journal* in 1987, was valuable in reconstructing events in the period 1984–86.

Several colleagues in overseas bureaus of the *Wall Street Journal* generously acted acted as eyes, ears, and translators. In Germany, Audrey Choi was a tireless partner in researching the tale of J. Ignacio López's defection from General Motors to Volkswagen. Tim Aeppel, the *Journal*'s correspondent in Bonn until August 1993, provided valuable assistance in the López story's early stages. In Japan, Clay Chandler, John

Bussey, Michael Williams, and Jacob Schlesinger helped guide us through the thickets of Japanese language and business culture.

We also wish to acknowledge the fine work of automotive reporters at other publications. These include Alex Taylor III of *Fortune* magazine, Jerry Flint of *Forbes*, Kathleen Kerwin and David Woodruff of *Business Week*, Joseph Szczesny of the Oakland *Press* in Pontiac, Michigan, Greg Gardner of the Detroit *Free Press*, Jim Higgins of the Detroit *News*, John McElroy of *Automotive Industries*, Warren Brown and Frank Swoboda of the Washington *Post*, and Doron Levin of the New York *Times*.

Numerous auto industry experts contributed to our understanding and insights over the years, through numerous conversations or published works. Among them John Casesa, Christopher Cedergren, Stephen Girsky, James Harbour, David Healy, Maryann Keller, Wendy Needham, and James Womack.

Our editors at Simon & Schuster, Michael Korda and Alice Mayhew, saw the potential in our work long before it was obvious, and, with Chuck Adams, provided the guidance, editorial criticism, and moral support we needed to finish the job. We would be lost without our agent, Andrew Wylie, whose insight informed this work from its beginnings.

Our families endured many late nights and long absences in the months it took to complete this work. We're especially grateful to our wives, Susan Ingrassia and Laurie Mayers. They were our prime source of encouragement, editing, "reality checks," and overall support during the months of our work. Our children—Adam, Charles, and Daniel Ingrassia, and Katy and Annie White—often were more patient with us than we were with them. They have our abiding thanks.

NOTES

This book is based largely on the authors' reporting on the auto industry for the *Wall Street Journal* during the period 1985–94. During that time we conducted hundreds of interviews, on and off the record, visited dozens of factories, and had access to financial and product information assembled by the companies and by numerous independent analysts.

We interviewed nearly all of the participants in the events described, most specifically for this book, as well as in the course of preparing stories for the *Journal*. Many of the current and former industry executives who agreed to talk to us were surprisingly candid and generous with their knowledge. Many also agreed to contribute to this history on condition that they wouldn't be individually identified as sources.

In several instances, we have had to make judgments about which of two conflicting versions of key events or conversations to believe. In those instances, we have obtained corroboration from two or more sources for the version presented here.

The primary purpose of the following footnotes is to give credit for information obtained from the published works of others. We have not provided specific notes for most of the information obtained in our own interviews or reporting. In some cases, however, we have cited an interviewee as the source of certain information, where that seemed appropriate.

CHAPTER 1: Detroit's Lions in Winter

1. Amal Kumar Naj, "Tricky Technology: Auto Makers Discover Factory of the Future Is Headache Just Now," *Wall Street Journal*, May 13, 1986.

2. Mike Casey, "Pension May Double for Retiring GM Chief; Union Officials Objecting to Proposal," Dayton *Daily News,* May 1, 1990.
3. Paul Ingrassia, "Tire Makers Are Turning to Technology to Improve Gas Mileage, Wear, Traction," *Wall Street Journal,* March 27, 1982.

CHAPTER 2: The Nummi Commandos

The primary sources for this account of the Nummi joint venture are the authors' interviews with Steve Bera, Chuck Farley, Paul Thompson, Leonard Ricard, Susumu Uchikawa, Kan Higashi, and George Nano. Bob Hendry and Roger Smith, among others, also discussed Nummi and its significance for General Motors with the authors. Descriptions of Nummi, Toyota City, and GM's Technical Liaison Office at Nummi are based on the authors' visits there and interviews with managers and workers at those sites. Certain GM reports on Nummi's quality and operations provided statistics and data. Toyota's corporate history, *Toyota: A History of the First 50 Years,* was the source of certain historical background on Toyota. James P. Womack, Daniel T. Jones, and Daniel Roos's analysis of the Toyota Production System in *The Machine That Changed the World* guided the authors' reporting on and descriptions of the Nummi/Toyota manufacturing system and its differences from GM's methods.

1. Toyota Motor Corp., *Toyota: A History of the First 50 Years* (Toyota City: Toyota Motor Corp.: 1988).

CHAPTER 3: The Lions Roar

1. R. S. Miller, Jr., personal notes of recollections of the Chrysler Loan Guarantee Act of 1979, dictated in Bandon, Oregon, in July 1980 and provided to the authors.
2. Lee A. Iacocca with William Novak, *Iacocca: An Autobiography* (New York: Bantam Books, 1984), p. 53.
3. Ibid., p. 134.
4. Urban C. Lehner, "Lee Iacocca Wants You to Know: He Doesn't Do Free Bar Mitzvahs," *Wall Street Journal,* January 4, 1985.
5. Cary Reich, "The Innovator," *The New York Times Magazine,* April 21, 1985.
6. Amal Kumar Naj and Roy J. Harris, Jr., "High-Tech Drive: GM's Winning Offer for Hughes May Set Heavy-Industry Trend," *Wall Street Journal,* June 6, 1985.
7. Peggy Iacocca made these statements on the March 16, 1992, episode of *Geraldo.*
8. Jacob M. Schlesinger, "Plant Closings? Perot vs. Smith? Forget Them— THIS Is Big News," *Wall Street Journal,* January 8, 1987.

9. Donald Woutat, "Iacocca Criticizes Big Bonuses Paid to GM, Ford Brass," *Wall Street Journal*, May 16, 1984.

10. "Iacocca Says His Pay Role Is a High Principled Model," *Wall Street Journal*, April 28, 1987.

11. Cartoon by J. D. Crowl, Copley News Service, Detroit *News*, July 3, 1987.

12. John Bussey, "Lee Iacocca Calls Odometer Policy Dumb," *Wall Street Journal*, July 2, 1987.

13. Melinda Grenier Guiles and Paul Ingrassia, "Yellow Light: Chrysler Hits Brake, Starts Saving Money After Shopping Spree," *Wall Street Journal*, January 12, 1988.

CHAPTER 4: The General Loses Command

This account of GM's troubles in the mid-1980s is based largely on dozens of interviews with past and present GM executives, United Auto Workers officials, and others during that period and later, including Roger Smith, F. James Mc-Donald, Ross Perot, Alex Mair, Hulki Aldikacti, Jim Fitzpatrick, John Middlebrook, Ernest Schaefer, and Donald Ephlin. Certain details of the Pontiac Fiero's mechanical defects and GM's response to complaints about Fiero fires are based on documents on file with the National Highway Traffic Safety Administration. The tale of Ross Perot's break with Roger Smith and GM was extensively covered in the business press in 1986 and 1987. The most detailed account is found in Doron P. Levin, *Irreconcilable Differences: Ross Perot versus General Motors* (Boston: Little, Brown, 1989). In addition to our own interviews with Perot and others involved in the events of late 1986, the authors have drawn on testimony given in connection with litigation between Perot and GM's Electronic Data Systems Corp. in 1988 and 1989, and documents filed in connection with a shareholder's suit challenging the 1986 GM buyout of Perot's shares.

1. Description of Alex Mair's presentation is based on a videotape viewed by the authors.

2. Charles G. Burck, "Will Success Spoil General Motors?" *Fortune*, August 22, 1983, p. 94.

3. *Ward's Automotive Yearbook*, 1946 and 1978 vols. (Detroit: Ward's Communications).

4. The troubles arising from GM's 1984 reorganization are generally acknowledged by the past and present GM executives, including Roger Smith and F. James McDonald, who were interviewed by the authors. Maryann Keller's *Rude Awakening: The Rise, Fall and Struggle for Recovery of General Motors* (New York: William Morrow, 1989) also provides a detailed account of the backlash against the 1984 reorganization.

5. Information about stalling in 1986–87 GM models equipped with 3.8-liter

V-6 engines is based on documents filed with the National Highway Traffic Safety Administration, specifically case nos. EA 86–021, PE 86–034, DE 89–023, and EA-89-022.

6. NHTSA records.

7. Ibid.

8. *Ward's Automotive Reports.*

9. Description of the announcement to Fiero plant workers is based on videotape of the event.

10. Naj, "Tricky Technology"; author interviews with GM personnel.

11. GM Form 10-K Annual Report for the year ended December 31, 1985, filed with the Securities and Exchange Commission.

12. GM 1986 proxy statement; "GM Chairman Got $1.9 Million in '85 Salary, Bonuses," *Wall Street Journal,* April 21, 1986.

13. Doron P. Levin, "Groping Giant: In a High-Tech Drive, GM Falls Below Rivals in Auto Profit Margins," *Wall Street Journal,* July 22, 1986, p. 1.

14. Doron P. Levin, "GM Announces Drive to Trim Salaried Staff," *Wall Street Journal,* August 25, 1986.

15. GM financial statements; GM Form 10-K Annual Report for the year ended December 31, 1987, filed with the Securities and Exchange Commission; Doron P. Levin, "GM's Earnings Plummeted 49% in Third Period," *Wall Street Journal,* October 23, 1986.

16. Author interviews; Levin, *Irreconcilable Differences,* pp. 255–61.

17. The reporters were Paul Ingrassia and Doron Levin.

18. Todd Mason, Russell Mitchell, William J. Hampton, and Marc Frons, "Ross Perot's Crusade," *Business Week,* October 6, 1986.

19. Levin, *Irreconcilable Differences,* pp. 276–77; testimony of Elmer W. Johnson in *EDS* v. *Perot* in April 1989, Fairfax County, Virgina Circuit Court.

20. Doron P. Levin, Paul Ingrassia, and Janet Guyon, "General Motors' Move to Sell EDS Fails, Highlights Problem of Integrating Unit," *Wall Street Journal,* November 24, 1986.

21. Doron P. Levin and Dale D. Buss, "Titanic Battle: GM Plans Offer to Pay $700 Million to Buy Out Its Critic H. Ross Perot," *Wall Street Journal,* December 1, 1986.

22. Both GM and EDS officials involved in the buyout deal say Perot never established a formal escrow account, controlled by a third party, to hold the money from GM. Instead, as agreed, GM transferred the money into accounts controlled by Perot.

CHAPTER 5: Ford's Unlikely Hero

This account of Donald Petersen's rise to the top of Ford Motor Company and Ford's success in the mid-1980s is based on extensive interviews with Petersen himself as well as with more than two dozen other current and former

Ford executives. The others include Harold Poling, Alexander Trotman, Philip Caldwell, Allan Gilmour, Louis Ross, David Scott, Jack Hall, Kenneth Whipple, Dan Rivard, Robert Risk, Jack Telnack, Robert Rewey, and Jim Bakken. Ford Motor provided films and material from the 1984 Boca Raton management meeting. Young & Rubicam, the advertising agency for Ford's Lincoln–Mercury division, provided tapes of "The Valet" commercials. Robert Lutz provided his satiric memo on the "new Ford-speak." The text of Petersen's speech to Christ Church Cranbrook was obtained from an executive at General Motors, where the speech was widely circulated and highly praised. The authors also used their reporting on Ford during this period, as well as the work of *Wall Street Journal* colleagues, notably Melinda Grenier, Bradley Stertz, and Neal Templin.

1. *The Economist*, Vol. 300, No. 7457 (August 2, 1986), 57–58.
2. Neal Templin, "Team Spirit: A Decisive Response to Crisis Brought Ford Enhanced Productivity," *Wall Street Journal*, December 15, 1992.

CHAPTER 6: Dead in the Water

GM's decline in 1987 and 1988 was extensively covered in the *Wall Street Journal*. Much of the information in this chapter was collected by the authors at the time in the course of covering GM for the *Journal*. Reporting for the *Journal* by Doron P. Levin, Jacob M. Schlesinger, Amal Kumar Naj, John Bussey, Bradley A. Stertz, and Melinda Grenier was also influential in shaping this account. Roger B. Smith, Jack McNulty, Robert Stempel, Lloyd Reuss, Jim McDonald, Bob Rogers, Donald Ephlin, and others gave interviews to the authors either at the time of these events or subsequently. Other information was derived from GM sources who asked not to be identified, from company documents, such as Roger Smith's letter to shareholders, annual reports, and from certain internal studies made available to the authors.

1. Amal Kumar Naj and Doron P. Levin, "GM Buyback Set for Total of $5.18 Billion," *Wall Street Journal*, March 5, 1987.
2. Description of the Motoramas is based on information in *GM: The First 75 Years of Transportation Products*, by the editors of *Automobile Quarterly* magazine (Princeton, N.J.: Automobile Quarterly, 1983), pp. 140–45.
3. Jacob M. Schlesinger, "GM, with Hoopla, Seeks to Trade in Its Current Image," *Wall Street Journal*, January 4, 1988.
4. Jacob M. Schlesinger, "GM to Reduce Capacity to Match Its Sales," *Wall Street Journal*, April 25, 1988.
5. Donaldson Brown, "Pricing Policy in Relation to Financial Control," *Management and Administration*, Vol. 7, No. 2 (February–March–April 1924), p. 4. The standard volume concept is also discussed in Alfred Sloan's *My Years with General Motors* (New York: Doubleday, 1972), pp. 164–69.
6. Schlesinger, "GM to Reduce Capacity."

7. Jacob M. Schlesinger and Bradley A. Stertz, "GM-10 Cars Are Off to a Sluggish Start," *Wall Street Journal*, June 18, 1988.

8. The contrast between the labor costs of GM and Ford midsized cars is cited in Womack, Jones, and Roos, *The Machine That Changed the World*, pp. 96–98. GM's overall labor cost disadvantage to Ford and Toyota is detailed in a 1992 report by the consulting firm James Harbour and Associates. Numerous GM executives acknowledged the gap in interviews with the authors.

CHAPTER 7: People Power

The sources for material in this chapter are the authors' own reporting during the time and later, including dozens of interviews with GM executives and employees, plant tours, and videotapes and internal GM documents obtained by the authors. The biographical sketches of Bob Stempel and Lloyd Reuss drew on official GM biographies augmented by author interviews. The authors also drew on articles and reporting by *Wall Street Journal* colleagues Jacob M. Schlesinger, Gregory A. Patterson, Bradley Stertz, and Melinda Grenier.

1. GM Annual Reports; quarterly financial statements for 1987 and 1988.

2. Jacob M. Schlesinger, "Is Elmer Johnson Running for Something?" *Wall Street Journal*, November 3, 1987.

3. Ibid.

4. Ibid.

5. John Lippert, "Interview with GM Chairman Will Air with Erroneous Quote," Detroit *Free Press*, March 2, 1988.

6. Jacob M. Schlesinger and Paul Ingrassia, "People Power: GM Woos Employees by Listening to Them, Talking of Its 'Team,' " *Wall Street Journal*, January 12, 1989.

7. The description of the October 1988 Traverse City conference is based on two primary sources: Schlesinger and Ingrassia, "People Power," and a videotape of the proceedings obtained by the authors.

8. Paul Ingrassia and Gregory A. Patterson, "GM Posts Record 3rd-Quarter Earnings; Stock Surges on Evidence of Turnaround," *Wall Street Journal*, October 28, 1988.

9. Jacob M. Schlesinger, "GM's Smith Says He'd Endorse Raising Payout If Profits Stay at Current Levels," *Wall Street Journal*, November 23, 1988.

CHAPTER 8: Chrysler Crashes

For this chapter, the authors drew on their coverage of Chrysler between 1987 and 1992, as well as extensive interviews with current and former executives of the company. In general, the interviews were conducted on the condition that the sources would not be named. In addition, the authors benefited from the work of *Wall Street Journal* colleagues, notably John Bussey, Melinda Grenier, and Bradley A. Stertz.

1. Joseph B. White, "Chrysler to Stop Building K-Cars in U.S. Plants," *Wall Street Journal*, April 15, 1988.
2. Alex Taylor, "U.S. Cars Come Back," *Fortune*, Vol. 126, No. 11 (November 16, 1992).
3. Bradley A. Stertz, "Sperlich, Intense Chrysler Executive, Retires Unexpectedly; Lutz Is in Line," *Wall Street Journal*, January 22, 1988.
4. Notes from Lee Iacocca interview with Paul Ingrassia and Bradley A. Stertz at Chrysler headquarters, August 29, 1990.
5. Notes from Agnelli's press conference, held in New York, were provided by Amal Kumar Naj, who attended for the *Wall Street Journal*.
6. Ibid.

CHAPTER 9: Ford Falters

Most of the information for this chapter came from several dozen interviews with current and former executives and other officials of Ford Motor Company. Because of the sensitive nature of the material within Ford, those interviewed requested anonymity, and the authors acceded to these requests. The work of Alex Taylor III, *Fortune* magazine's automotive reporter, was influential in shaping the authors' thinking. Mr. Taylor was the first to report, in the pages of *Fortune*, about the feud between Donald Petersen and the young Fords, and also that Petersen's early retirement as chairman wasn't voluntary. In their research, the authors verified Mr. Taylor's accounts, and obtained more detailed descriptions of some of the events that he first reported.

1. *Ward's Automotive Yearbook*, 51st edition, 1989.
2. Paul Ingrassia and Neal Templin, "Cash Crunch: Hemorrhaging Money, Ford Cuts Spending and May Sell Assets," *Wall Street Journal*, January 24, 1991.
3. Ibid.
4. Speech by Donald Petersen to First Monday Forum, Christ Church Cranbrook, Bloomfield Hills, Michigan, October 2, 1989.
5. Collier and Horowitz, *The Fords: An American Epic*, p. 365.
6. Alex Taylor III, "The Young Fords: Struggling for Control of the Family Company," *Fortune*, Vol. 119, No. 2 (January 16, 1989).
7. Melinda Grenier Guiles, "Edsel Ford II Airs His Dissatisfaction, Worrying Officials," *Wall Street Journal*, January 5, 1989.
8. Paul Ingrassia and Neal Templin, "Running Strong: At Rebounding Ford, Picking a Chairman Is Next Big Challenge," *Wall Street Journal*, July 16, 1992.

9. Joann S. Lublin and Craig Forman, "Going Upscale: Ford Snares Jaguar, but $2.5 Billion Is High Price for Prestige," *Wall Street Journal*, November 3, 1989.

CHAPTER 10: The Japanese Juggernaut

The basis for this chapter was extensive interviews with Robert B. McCurry, Martin J. ("Hoot") McInerney, and the authors' coverage of the auto industry between 1985 and 1993. The description of the 1989 Tokyo Motor Show is based on the authors' coverage of the event.

1. *Ward's Automotive Yearbook*, 54th edition, 1992.
2. Doron P. Levin, "A Manager with a Feel for the Grass Roots," *New York Times*, October 27, 1991.
3. *Ward's Automotive Yearbook*, 55th edition, 1993.

CHAPTER 11: Lee Leaves

The information for this chapter was obtained in interviews with more than twenty current and former executives and independent directors of Chrysler. Most of those interviewed requested anonymity, and the authors agreed to this condition.

1. Joseph B. White, "Revved Up: How Detroit Diesel, Out from Under GM, Turned Around Fast," *Wall Street Journal*, August 16, 1991.
2. Ibid.
3. Ibid.
4. Ibid.
5. Doron P. Levin, "Iacocca Heir? A New Name Is Dropped," *New York Times*, March 12, 1992.
6. Author interview with Gerald Greenwald, October 29, 1992.
7. Chrysler says that its fees paid to Dewey Ballantine were "reasonable and appropriate."
8. Details of Lee Iacocca's retirement package are contained in Chrysler's 1993 and 1994 proxy statements.
9. Author interview with Lee Iacocca, January 31, 1994.
10. Douglas Lavin, "The Long Goodbye: The Party Isn't Over for Lee Iacocca," *Wall Street Journal*, December 22, 1992.
11. Lavin, "The Long Goodbye."
12. Author interview with Robert J. Eaton, Detroit, September 15, 1993.

CHAPTER 12: GM: The April Coup

The material in this chapter is based on numerous interviews with GM executives and other principals who figure in the events, some of whom spoke on condition that their remarks not be attributed directly to them. A primary source for the narrative in this and the following chapter on GM's October coup are contemporaneous memoranda and reports documenting deliberations in GM's boardroom, and made available to the authors. Some of the material in this chapter and the October coup chapter appeared in different form in *Wall Street Journal* articles written by the authors. Other documentary sources are noted. Where accounts from sources conflict in a significant aspect, we have noted those disagreements.

1. Figures from GM's 1992 Annual Report.
2. John F. Smith, Jr., speech and interview in Detroit, January 9, 1994.
3. GM 1992 annual report.
4. "S&P Puts GM On Watch Neg.; Ford Outlook Now Negative," Dow Jones News Wire, November 8, 1991.
5. Ira Millstein's emergence as a leading thinker in corporate governance was chronicled in Stephen Clark, "Ira Millstein Turns up the Heat," *Institutional Investor*, November 1989. This detailed article served as a guide for some of the authors' reporting on Millstein's activities in the 1980s.
6. Millstein's ideas on board responsibility are presented, among other places, in Winthrop Knowlton and Ira Millstein, "Can the Board of Directors Help the American Corporation Earn the Immortality It Holds So Dear?" in John R. Meyer and James M. Gustafson, eds., *The U.S. Business Corporation: An Institution in Transition* (Cambridge, Mass.: Ballinger Publishing Co., 1988).
7. Lloyd Reuss's interview with authors in Warren, Michigan, May 10, 1993.

CHAPTER 13: GM: The October Revolution

1. Joseph B. White and Neal Templin, "GM Net Fell 54 Percent, Ford's Plunged 69 Percent in First Quarter Because of Weak Sales," *Wall Street Journal*, May 4, 1990.
2. Joseph B. White, "Investors Hope for GM Move to Shed Units," *Wall Street Journal*, October 12, 1992.
3. Warren Brown and Frank Swoboda, "GM Board to Chairman: Stand up to the UAW," Washington *Post*, October 13, 1992.
4. Warren Brown and Frank Swoboda, "GM Chief Pressured to Resign; Outside Directors Reportedly Seeking to Replace Stempel," Washington *Post*, October 21, 1992.
5. Joan E. Rigdon, "Contrasting Images: The New Finance Chief at Kodak Has a Style Quite Unlike His Boss's," *Wall Street Journal*, April 28, 1993.

CHAPTER 14: The Bubble Bursts

This chapter draws from many sources, including the authors' coverage of Honda Motor Company, coverage by reporters from other publications where cited, and speeches by Honda executives, with the text provided by the company. The draft case study of Honda by Professor Jack McDonald of Stanford University, also provided by Honda's public-relations department, was a useful guide to Honda's history. The authors owe special thanks to Roger Lambert of the public relations department at Honda's manufacturing complex in Ohio, who provided films of Soichiro Honda's October 1989 emotional visit to the Ohio factories. Scott Whitlock and Susan Insley, Honda executives in Ohio, generously shared their memories and perspective on Honda's development in the United States.

1. Shoichiro Irimajiri, speech at Corporate Leadership Forum, Harvard Business School, November 14, 1985.
2. Ibid.
3. Lloyd Garrison, William J. Mitchell, and Edwin M. Reingold, "The Honda Way: Battling for Global Markets," *Time*, Vol. 128, No. 10 (September 8, 1986).
4. Jack McDonald, draft of Stanford University case study titled "Honda Motor Co. Ltd.," December 1987.
5. Ibid.
6. Shoichiro Irimajiri speech at Stanford University, April 7, 1987.
7. Irimajiri speech, November 14, 1985.
8. Ibid.
9. Ibid.
10. Garrison, Mitchell, and Reingold, "The Honda Way."
11. Clay Chandler and Paul Ingrassia, "Shifting Gears: Just as U.S. Firms Try Japanese Management, Honda Is Centralizing," *Wall Street Journal,* April 11, 1991.
12. Paul Ingrassia, "Welcome Mat: Japanese Firms Come to Detroit, and City Is Glad to Have Them," *Wall Street Journal,* May 7, 1991.
13. Ibid.
14. Ibid.
15. Ibid.
16. Chandler and Ingrassia, "Shifting Gears."
17. Japanese Automobile Manufacturers Association annual booklet, *The Motor Industry of Japan.*
18. Karen Lowry Miller, Larry Armstrong, and David Woodruff, "A Car Is Born," *Business Week,* September 13, 1993.
19. Author interview with Shoichiro Irimajiri, Tokyo, Japan, October 29, 1991.
20. Japanese Automobile Manufacturers Association annual booklet.
21. Author interview with Shoichiro Irimajiri, Tokyo, Japan, October 26, 1993.

CHAPTER 15: Tommy LaSorda's Team

The narrative in this chapter is based primarily on interviews and information gathered during two visits to the Opel Eisenach factory in 1992 and 1993, as well as interviews and tours at Opel's headquarters and factory in Rüsselsheim. Thomas LaSorda, Frank Faga, and Louis Hughes were generous with their recollections of the genesis and progress of the Eisenach project. Womack, Jones, and Roos's *The Machine That Changed the World* was a fundamental influence on Eisenach's leaders, and on our understanding of their efforts. Also valuable was a series of three cases written by Harvard Business School Professor Hugo Uyterhoeven, numbers N9-392-100, N9-392-101, and N9-392-127. Those papers were the source of certain details about Hughes's first trip to Eisenach, and to a general overview of the project's beginnings.

1. Horst Monnich, *The BMW Story—A Company in Its Time*, the authorized company history, trans. Anthony Bastow and William Henson (London: Sedgwick & Jackson, 1991).
2. "Volkswagen Plans Venture with Firm in East Germany," *Wall Street Journal*, December 5, 1989. Also, Hugo Uyterhoeven, Adam Opel AG, Case No. N9-392-100. Boston: Harvard Business School, 1992.
3. Lou Hughes, quoted in Uyterhoeven.

CHAPTER 16: The Mustang

The primary sources for this chapter are interviews with John Coletti, Will Boddie, Dia Hothi, and other members of the Mustang team. Some of the material in this chapter appeared in shorter form in the *Wall Street Journal* in a September 21, 1993, article, by Joseph B. White and Oscar Suris: "New Pony: How a Skunk Works Kept Mustang Alive—On a Tight Budget." Suris and Bob Simison of the *Wall Street Journal* contributed reporting to that story and to this account.

1. The term "skunk works" first gained currency in Al Capp's *Lil' Abner* comic strip, in which the "skonk works" was the place where kickapoo joy juice was brewed. Later, Lockheed Corp. used the phrase to describe its top-secret research operations and even registered the term as a service mark.
2. White and Suris, "New Pony," *Wall Street Journal*, September 21, 1993, p. 1.
3. Paul Ingrassia and Neal Templin, "At Rebounding Ford, Picking a Chairman Is Next Big Challenge," *Wall Street Journal*, July 16, 1992.
4. Ingrassia and Templin, "At Rebounding Ford"; also a biography of Alex Trotman written by Ford Motor Company and distributed October 4, 1993.
5. White and Suris, "New Pony."

CHAPTER 17: The López Files

The events described in this chapter were the focus of considerable media coverage in 1992, 1993, and 1994. This account is based on interviews with GM and VW executives, testimony in legal proceedings, and documents released publicly or obtained by the authors. The authors interviewed José Ignacio López de Arriortúa several times before his departure for Volkswagen, and once afterward during his appearance in Flint, Michigan. Ferdinand Piëch has discussed his attitudes and actions during a lengthy July 28, 1993, press conference and also in interviews with several European publications, including the *Financial Times*. We have drawn on those sources for general statements about Piëch's attitudes. Piëch's role is also described in chronologies of the events surrounding López's departure from GM released by VW Management Board member Jens Neumann. The authors also obtained a copy of the report on López's activities prepared by auditors from KPMG Deutsche Treuhandgesellschaft. In Germany, the groundbreaking reporting on the López case was done by *Der Spiegel* in a series of articles beginning in May 1993. *Der Spiegel's* May 24, 1993, article "Der Skrupellose" served as a guide to our own initial reporting on GM's accusations. Audrey Choi of the *Wall Street Journal Europe's* Bonn bureau provided valuable and tireless assistance gathering information from interviews and translating German documents. Timothy Aeppel of the *Wall Street Journal* also provided information from Germany, particularly on the discovery of GM documents in Wiesbaden and VW's competitive troubles.

1. Jack Smith speech at the commencement exercises for Quinsigamond Community College, May 22, 1993; Kathleen Kerwin, "The Man Who Would Be GM's Savior," *Business Week*, November 1, 1993.
2. "Automotive Industries 1993 Man of the Year: Ignacio López," *Automotive Industries*, February 1993.
3. Ibid.
4. Diana Fong, "A Family Affair," *Forbes*, April 27, 1992.
5. Timothy Aeppel, "VW Chief Declares a Crisis and Prescribes Bold Action," *Wall Street Journal*, April 1, 1993.
6. Chronology released by VW Management Board member Jens Neumann dated July 28, 1993. Also, GM chronology of May 28, 1994.
7. Testimony by John Howell in Hamburg court, July 15, 1993; author interviews.
8. Neumann chronology.
9. Ibid.
10. Ibid.
11. Ibid.
12. Timothy Aeppel, "Police Search Offices at VW in López Case," *Wall Street Journal*, August 27, 1993.

13. Audrey Choi, "Volkswagen Unit in Spain Requires $1 Billion Bailout," *Wall Street Journal*, September 15, 1993.

CHAPTER 18: The New GM

Information about the 1995 J-car program and the Lordstown plant is based primarily on a tour of the factory in June 1993 and interviews with Tom Davis, Michael Cubbin, James R. Wiemels, John Cohoon, and others associated with GM's Lansing (Small Car) Automotive Division in 1993 and 1994. President Bill Bowers and Shop Chairman Al Alli of United Auto Workers Local 1112 at the Lordstown assembly plant discussed the factory's turnaround in telephone interviews. While Jack Smith declined a formal interview for this book, he discussed aspects of his turnaround strategy in several interviews during 1992 and 1993 given to the authors in the course of covering GM for the *Wall Street Journal*. Several other members of Smith's senior management group discussed their experiences in 1992 and 1993, including Bob Hendry, Michael Grimaldi, Rick Wagoner, and Bill Hoglund. Other background information comes from plant tours and interviews with other GM executives and analysts during the 1992–93 period.

1. *The Way of Life According to Lao-tzu*, translation by Witter Bynner (New York: Putnam, 1972), p. 46.
2. Editorial, "The Soul Must Panic," *Wall Street Journal*, March 15, 1972.
3. Charles B. Camp, "Paradise Lost: Utopian GM Plant in Ohio Falls from Grace Under Strain of Balky Machinery, Workers," *Wall Street Journal*, January 31, 1972. This article is a primary source, along with author interviews, of the description of the labor strife surrounding the Vega program.
4. Neil Durbin, "New GM Manager Striving to Vie with Japan," *Youngstown Vindicator*, August 28, 1987.
5. General Motors survey.
6. Neal Templin and Joseph B. White, "GM Goes to Great Lengths to Match Workers and Work," *Wall Street Journal*, April 21, 1994.

CHAPTER 19: Neon Lights

1. Marcell is quoted at length from a videotape of the Iron River speech provided by Chrysler.
2. Bradley A. Stertz, "Importing Solutions: Detroit's New Strategy to Beat Back Japanese Is to Copy Their Ideas," *Wall Street Journal*, September 30, 1992.
3. Irimajiri speech, April 7, 1987.
4. David Woodruff and Karen Lowry Miller, "Chrysler's Neon: Is This the Small Car Detroit Couldn't Build?" *Business Week*, May 3, 1993.

5. Bryan Gruley, "Chrysler Unveils New Subcompact in Germany," Gannett News Service, September 8, 1993.
6. Douglas Lavin, "Straight Shooter: Robert Eaton Thinks 'Vision' Is Over-rated and He's Not Alone," *Wall Street Journal*, October 4, 1993.

CHAPTER 20: The New Leaders

1. Douglas Lavin and Audrey Choi, "Two-Way Traffic: A New Export Power in the Auto Industry? It's North America," *Wall Street Journal*, October 18, 1993.
2. *Automotive News Market Data Book* (Detroit: Crain Communications, 1984).
3. Interview with Scott Sprinzen, automotive analyst, Standard & Poor Corporation; Tim Andree, spokesman for Toyota.

CHAPTER 21: Lido Rides Again

1. Lee A. Iacocca with Sonny Kleinfield, *Talking Straight* (New York: Bantam Books, 1988), p.92.
2. Ibid., p. 97.
3. Jim Carlton, "Behind the Wheel," *Wall Street Journal*, Feb. 14, 1995.
4. Ibid.
5. James E. Bennett, "Detroit Anxiety Over Chrysler Appears on the Rise," *New York Times*, April 17, 1995.
6. Gabriella Stern, Steven Lipin, and Pauline Yoshihashi, "At the Factory Gate," *Wall Street Journal*, April 13, 1995.
7. Bennett, "Detroit Anxiety."
8. Jim Carlton, "Iacocca's Unexpected Role As Bid's Back-Seat Driver," *Wall Street Journal*, April 13, 1995.
9. Neal Templin and Robert L. Simison, "Chrysler Boosts Dividend 25%, but Firm Sees Earnings Falling from Year Ago," *Wall Street Journal*, May 19,1995.

BIBLIOGRAPHY

The following books and articles contributed to shaping our own reporting and interpretation of the events described in this book.

Automobile Quarterly Magazine, GM: *The First 75 Years of Transportation Products*. Princeton, N.J.: Automobile Quarterly, 1983. A GM-sponsored history that provided the basis for the description of the Motoramas.

Collier, Peter and David Horowitz. *The Fords: An American Epic*. New York: Simon & Schuster, 1987.

Halberstam, David. *The Reckoning*. New York: William Morrow, 1986. An inspiration to us for its scope and approach.

Hamper, Ben. *Rivethead: Tales from the Assembly Line*. New York: Warner, 1991. A firsthand account of the misery of mass production.

Iacocca, Lee, with William Novak. *Iacocca: An Autobiography*. New York: Bantam, 1984.

Keller, Maryann. *Rude Awakening: The Rise, Fall and Struggle for Recovery of General Motors*. New York: William Morrow, 1989. A chronicle of GM's problems in the mid-1980s that served as a guide for our own reporting of certain details of GM's 1984 reorganization.

Levin, Doron. *Irreconcilable Differences*. Boston: Little, Brown, 1989. A history of Ross Perot's battles with GM.

Sloan, Alfred P., Jr. *My Years with General Motors*. New York: Doubleday, 1972. Still the best guide to what made GM great in its heyday, and a source for this book's passages on Sloan's methods of financial management.

Toyota Motor Corp. *Toyota: A History of the First 50 Years*. Toyota City: Toyota Motor Corp., 1988. A detailed company history.

Womack, James P., Daniel T. Jones, and Daniel Roos. *The Machine That Changed the World*. New York: Macmillan, 1990. New York: HarperCollins, 1991. The work that best described for a nontechnical reader the development and impact of the Toyota Production System, or lean production.

Yates, Brock. *The Decline and Fall of the American Auto Industry*. New York: Empire Books, 1983. In particular, the chapter on "The Detroit Mind."

INDEX